T0324156

The Economic and Financial Impacts of the COVID-19 Crisis Around the World

Expect the Unexpected

The Economic and Financial Impacts of the COVID-19 Crisis Around the World

Expect the Unexpected

Allen N. Berger
Finance Department, Darla Moore School of Business, University of South Carolina, Columbia, SC, United States

Mustafa U. Karakaplan
Finance Department, Darla Moore School of Business, University of South Carolina, Columbia, SC, United States

Raluca A. Roman
Federal Reserve Bank of Philadelphia, Philadelphia, PA, United States

ACADEMIC PRESS
An imprint of Elsevier

Academic Press is an imprint of Elsevier
125 London Wall, London EC2Y 5AS, United Kingdom
525 B Street, Suite 1650, San Diego, CA 92101, United States
50 Hampshire Street, 5th Floor, Cambridge, MA 02139, United States
The Boulevard, Langford Lane, Kidlington, Oxford OX5 1GB, United Kingdom

Copyright © 2024 Elsevier Inc. All rights reserved.

Raluca A. Roman is an employee of United States Government, and that Raluca A. Roman's part of contributions to the Work are in Public Domain.

No part of this publication may be reproduced or transmitted in any form or by any means, electronic or mechanical, including photocopying, recording, or any information storage and retrieval system, without permission in writing from the publisher. Details on how to seek permission, further information about the Publisher's permissions policies and our arrangements with organizations such as the Copyright Clearance Center and the Copyright Licensing Agency, can be found at our website: www.elsevier.com/permissions.

This book and the individual contributions contained in it are protected under copyright by the Publisher (other than as may be noted herein).

Notices

Knowledge and best practice in this field are constantly changing. As new research and experience broaden our understanding, changes in research methods, professional practices, or medical treatment may become necessary.

Practitioners and researchers must always rely on their own experience and knowledge in evaluating and using any information, methods, compounds, or experiments described herein. In using such information or methods they should be mindful of their own safety and the safety of others, including parties for whom they have a professional responsibility.

To the fullest extent of the law, neither the Publisher nor the authors, contributors, or editors, assume any liability for any injury and/or damage to persons or property as a matter of products liability, negligence or otherwise, or from any use or operation of any methods, products, instructions, or ideas contained in the material herein.

ISBN 978-0-443-19162-6

For information on all Academic Press publications
visit our website at https://www.elsevier.com/books-and-journals

Publisher: Mica H. Haley
Acquisitions Editor: Kathryn Eryilmaz
Editorial Project Manager: Mason Malloy
Production Project Manager: Punithavathy Govindaradjane
Cover Designer: Greg Harris

Typeset by STRAIVE, India

Working together
to grow libraries in
developing countries

www.elsevier.com • www.bookaid.org

Dedication

To my wife Mindy Ring
Allen N. Berger

To my daughter Adora, my wife Işın, and my parents
Naime and Saim Karakaplan
Mustafa U. Karakaplan

To my son Oliver, my husband Catalin, and my parents
Rodica and Mihai
Raluca A. Roman

Contents

Part I
Focus of the book and other introductory materials

1. Introduction to the economic and financial impacts of the COVID-19 crisis and related topics

2. The COVID-19 pandemic vs past epidemics, pandemics, and other health crises

List of figures

List of tables

About the authors

Allen N. Berger is H. Montague Osteen, Jr., Professor of Banking and Finance in the finance department, Darla Moore School of Business, University of South Carolina, since 2008. He is also Carolina Distinguished professor, Cofounder and Codirector of the Center for Financial Institutions at the Darla Moore School of Business, and former PhD coordinator of the finance department. Professor Berger served as 2022 President and Conference Program Chair of the Financial Intermediation Research Society (FIRS), presiding over its annual conference in Budapest, Hungary. He is also a senior fellow at the Wharton Financial Institutions Center and has affiliations with other research centers around the world. He is on the editorial boards of eight research journals, former associate editor of others including the *Review of Financial Studies*, coeditor of eight special issues of four different research journals, coorganizer of numerous research conferences, and advisor for PhD students in multiple departments at the University of South Carolina and other universities in various countries, and editor of *Journal of Money, Credit, and Banking* from 1994 to 2001.

He has more than 130 publications in refereed research journals, at least one in 37 of the 38 years from 1987 to 2024, has several lead articles and best paper awards, and is the most prolific contributor to multiple journals and conference series. He has publications in top finance journals: *Journal of Finance, Journal of Financial Economics, Review of Financial Studies, Journal of Financial and Quantitative Analysis, Review of Finance, Journal of Financial Intermediation, Journal of Banking and Finance*, and *Journal of Corporate Finance*; top economics journals *Journal of Political Economy, American Economic Review, Review of Economics and Statistics, Journal of Monetary Economics*, and *Journal of Money, Credit and Banking*; and other top professional business journals *Management Science, Journal of Business*, and *European Journal of Operational Research*.

In addition to the current book, Professor Berger is the coauthor of other two research monographs, *TARP and Other Bank Bailouts and Bail-Ins around the World: Connecting Wall Street, Main Street, and the Financial System* (2020, Elsevier), and *Bank Liquidity Creation and Financial Crises* (2016, Elsevier). He is the coeditor of all four editions of the *Oxford Handbook of Banking*, 2010, 2015, 2019, and 2024, and has about 40 other research publications, such as book chapters and conference proceedings.

Professor Berger has over 100,000 Google Scholar citations, including 34 articles with over 1,000 citations each, and another 18 exceeding 500 each, and an H-Index of 108 (https://scholar.google.com/citations?user=uEKU998AAAAJ&hl=en).

He has given keynote addresses on five continents, been visiting scholar at Federal Reserve Banks and central banks of other nations, won many best paper awards from research journals and conferences, and received both research and teaching recognition at the University of South Carolina.

Professor Berger was an economist from 1982 to 2008 at the Federal Reserve Board of Governors. He earned, a BA in economics from Northwestern University in 1976 and a PhD in economics from the University of California, Berkeley, in 1983.

His most personally prized accomplishments are his parts in the successes of his students and coauthors, whose joint accomplishments greatly exceed his own. Some have earned their own endowed chairs and full professorships, a major journal editorship, Federal Reserve Bank President, chair of a major Finance department, head of a research department, and other major personal successes. Many more are on their way to such levels, including his two coauthors Mustafa and Raluca.

Mustafa U. Karakaplan is a professor in the finance department, Darla Moore School of Business at the University of South Carolina. He earned his PhD in economics from Texas A&M University, MA in economics from Bilkent University, and BS in economics from METU and Tilburg University, and he held appointments at the academia including Utah State University and Georgetown University.

He has a number of research papers in leading peer-reviewed journals in multiple fields, including finance papers in the *Journal of Financial Intermediation and Journal of Banking and Finance*, econometrics papers in the *Journal of Productivity Analysis*, and two solo-authored papers in the *Stata Journal* that has a higher impact factor than almost all finance journals. His research encompasses banking, financial intermediation, FinTech, international finance, financial markets, econometric programming, forecasting, and predictive analytics. He also specializes in the applications of Artificial Intelligence and Machine Learning in Finance at Stanford University, and is poised to make singular contributions to a number of the difficult but important topics of the future that require such a broad mix of skills. These include international management of climate issues, integration of legacy financial markets and institutions with new economy systems, and risk management of the transition to the more central role of artificial intelligence.

Professor Karakaplan has more than 10 years of post-PhD academic experience, presented his research at several meetings and conferences, and taught many entry-level, advanced, and graduate-level economics and finance courses including banking and financial markets, international finance, and corporate finance in a wide range of classroom settings. He has been awarded several teaching awards such as a senior thesis advisor award, a student-led award for teaching excellence, and an outstanding teaching award.

Professor Karakaplan has also been a coinvestigator of a $19 million policy randomized control trial research project funded by the US federal and state agencies and private organizations. He presented this project at the annual meeting of the Allied Social Science Association (ASSA) in 2015, and his team met with the US Secretary of Education and provided legislative testimony to the Senate in 2016.

Raluca A. Roman is a principal economist at the Federal Reserve Bank of Philadelphia, and she joined the bank in July 2018. From 2015 to 2018, she was a research economist at Federal Reserve Bank of Kansas City. She holds a PhD in finance from University of South Carolina. Raluca also holds an MBA with concentration in finance from University of Bridgeport, and a BA in economics from Alexandru Ioan Cuza University (Romania).

Raluca's research areas include a variety of topics related to banking and financial institutions (including bank government bailouts and bail-ins, bank stress tests, internationalization, corporate governance, and monetary policy), consumer finance (including retail credit, consumer behavior, and consumer market trends), corporate finance, and international finance. Raluca has presented her research and discussed the research of others at numerous finance and regulatory conferences and received six best research paper awards at conferences. She published a variety of research articles in academic journals including one in the *Journal of Political Economy*, three in the *Journal of Financial and Quantitative Analysis*, one in the *Management Science*, three in the *Journal of Financial Intermediation*, two in the *Journal of Money, Credit, and Banking*, two in *Financial Management*, one in *Journal of Corporate Finance*, one in the *Journal of International Money and Finance*, three in the *Journal of Banking and Finance*. She also published one book chapter in the *Handbook of Finance and Development*, one book chapter in the *Oxford Handbook of Banking*, and one book chapter in the *Oxford Research Encyclopaedia of Economics and Finance*, as well as several regulatory policy briefs. She also coauthored the book *TARP and other Bank Bailouts and Bail-Ins around the World: Connecting Wall Street, Main Street, and the Financial System* (2020, Elsevier). With just eight years of professional experience since her PhD, Raluca has about 1,500 Google Scholar citations and an H-Index of 15.

Raluca also has 7+ years of professional experience in banking, corporate finance, and anti-money laundering, and worked for top international organizations like UBS Investment Bank and MasterCard International, where she won various awards.

Foreword

Though the world has too much experience with crises originating in the financial sector, the COVID-19 crisis is unique in that it is a global crisis that originated through the emergence of a new contagious, lethal virus. This is a global crisis, affecting every country in the world, and is much more than an economic crisis. However, understanding the impacts of the COVID-19 crisis on the real economy, the banking sector, and financial markets is an essential task that has to be carried out globally. Allen N. Berger, Mustafa U. Karakaplan, and Raluca A. Roman do a splendid job of presenting a complete picture of the impacts of the COVID-19 crisis through reviews of the data and existing research. These authors, well-established researchers on their own, have considerable experience in working as a team and it shows. Their undertaking is no small task. The economics and finance professions have taken up the challenge of studying the COVID-19 crisis with considerable energy, as hundreds of studies were circulated within the first few months of the crisis.

Though understanding how the COVID-19 crisis affects the real economy, the banking sector, and financial markets is an important task, the authors go beyond that task. They draw lessons from the COVID-19 crisis for what I would call the risk management of the economy and the financial sector. The COVID-19 crisis shows that the whole world can be hit by a crisis that many countries were poorly prepared for and that had dramatic effects on businesses and individuals. For many of them, COVID-19 meant sudden interruptions or sharp curtailing of revenue. Governments stepped in aggressively to help. However, much can be learned from the COVID-19 crisis and the reaction of governments to devise policy approaches that can flexibly respond to unexpected crises of a new type. Given the evolution of the world economy since the emergence of COVID-19, there is much to think about. Most observers and economists were surprised at the rapidity and strength of the recovery that followed the initial economic collapse resulting from the emergence of the virus. However, this recovery eventually involved vertiginous valuations for stocks, a sharp bear market, and bouts of intense inflation that the developed countries had not seen for decades. This makes it very important to think through how to devise policy approaches that can deal well with the unexpected. Hence, the main focus of the authors is on "*Expect the Unexpected*," which is their way of putting forth an approach to deal with crises of unexpected origins. Irrespective of the origins, there are common aspects to the evolution of crises that help in devising strategies to cope with them.

This book is valuable for those who want to have an up-to-date and thorough understanding of the global impact of COVID-19 on the economy, the banking sector, and financial markets. It is first rate in providing a wealth of data and reporting on a considerable amount of research. It is also an important book for all those who are looking forward and want to be armed with a framework to deal with future crises. The book addresses these topics well. It takes the reader on a pleasant and rewarding journey. I am sure you will not regret joining me in taking this journey!

René M. Stulz
Everett D. Reese Chair of Banking and Monetary Economics, The Ohio State University

Preface

Allen and Raluca met in August 2010 when Raluca was a starting PhD student in finance at Darla Moore School of Business in the University of South Carolina and Allen was H. Montague Osteen, Jr., Professor of Banking and Finance in the same finance department. They had no idea at that time what lay ahead in terms of an extremely productive research relationship as well as a warm personal friendship. Mustafa and Allen met almost a decade later at Mustafa's job seminar in January 2020, and we began our research collaboration even before Mustafa joined the finance faculty in August 2020. However, due to COVID-19 restrictions, we never saw each other again in person until Mustafa's second year began in August 2021. Despite all the obstacles, the three of us now are a strong team with a number of COVID-19 articles, working papers, and a special issue of a research journal edited among our accomplishments, and much more to go! On September 7–8, 2022, the team presented a preliminary draft of the book as a keynote address to representatives of central banks of Latin America, the US, and other nations at the Center for Latin American Monetary Studies (CEMLA) in Mexico City, Mexico.

Allen earned his PhD in economics from the University of California, Berkeley, and his BA in economics from Northwestern University. He worked at the Federal Reserve Board in Washington prior to joining the finance faculty at the University of South Carolina in May 2008. Mustafa earned his PhD in economics from Texas A&M University, MA in economics from Bilkent University, and BS in economics from METU and Tilburg University, and he held academic appointments at Utah State University, Georgetown University, and other institutions. Raluca earned her MBA with concentration in finance from the University of Bridgeport, Bridgeport, Connecticut, and BA in economics from Alexandru Ioan Cuza University in her home nation of Romania. She worked several years in the banking industry before her PhD studies at the University of South Carolina. Both Mustafa and Raluca have joined Allen as proud US citizens in recent years.

Since his arrival in South Carolina, Allen has been promoted to Carolina Distinguished Professor at the University, cofounded and codirects the Center for Financial Institutions at the Darla Moore School of Business, and became the 2022 President and Conference Program Chair of the Financial Intermediation Research Society (FIRS), a global research organization, among other accomplishments. Mustafa started his professorship at the University of South Carolina remotely from his home near Chicago. Nonetheless, even remotely, Allen and Mustafa discovered their common interests, including playing music and poker, as well as their mutual love of research, and they became close friends quickly. Raluca served as research assistant, teaching assistant, and coauthor to Allen during her years of study before emerging with her PhD in May 2015. She earned several best paper awards at conferences even as a PhD student and continues to do so today. She will forever be Allen's first-ever PhD graduate student as a major advisor, but more importantly, she has gone on to many great accomplishments on her own since that time. Raluca worked at the Federal Reserve Bank of Kansas City and is now a senior economist at the Federal Reserve Bank of Philadelphia.

The research relationships among the three of us took time to bear fruit, but progress is now accelerating. Allen and Raluca's first joint project was "Did TARP Banks Get Competitive Advantages?" published in the *Journal of Financial and Quantitative Analysis* in 2015. Since then, we have published together several other TARP papers, and many other research papers in quality economics, finance, and management journals as well as other publications. The crown jewel of our TARP collection is our book *TARP and other Bank Bailouts and Bail-Ins around the World: Connecting Wall Street, Main Street, and the Financial System* (2020, Elsevier). That book also covers many other bank bailouts and bail-ins around the world and comprehensively reviews other banking research and makes informed suggestions regarding 14 other major policy approaches for handling bank distress and crises. The book includes more than 500 references.

Mustafa brought many talents and prior accomplishments to the research team, including research publications in banking, FinTech, international finance, and other economics and finance topics as well as technical skills and professional publications in programming, forecasting, and related topics. He is currently adding to his skill set, earning an additional graduate degree in the applications of artificial intelligence and machine learning in finance at Stanford University. He is also an outstanding teacher, gaining multiple awards at different universities.

The three of us have now recalibrated the focus of our research both together and separately in combination with others in studying COVID-19 issues, and we intend the current book to be a crown jewel of sorts on this new and important topic. Some of these efforts are now published or forthcoming in professional research journals, including the *Journal of Political Economy, Journal of Banking and Finance, and Journal of Financial Stability*; others are still in working paper form requiring additional attention, and still ideas are in process of production toward future book titles. We also have several COVID-19 related joint research projects as a full team of three, the first of which is titled "Whose Bailout is it Anyway? The Roles of Politics in PPP Bailouts of Small Businesses vs. Banks," and is now forthcoming in the *Journal of Financial Intermediation*. We believe that this body of research has paved the way nicely for this book, and we are delighted that Elsevier has agreed to publish it. We hope that the readers both enjoy and are informed by our contribution.

Finally, we once again thank the colleagues and students noted in the Acknowledgments as well as our family members to whom the book is dedicated. We could not have done it without you!

Acknowledgments

The views expressed herein are those of the authors and do not necessarily reflect the views of the Federal Reserve Bank of Philadelphia or the Federal Reserve System. The authors thank René M. Stulz for generously contributing the insightful Foreword; and Katy Eryilmaz, Mason Malloy, and Punithavathy Govindaradjane, and the publishing team at *Elsevier* for helpful support from start to finish.

Thank you also very much to Jin Cai, Onesime Epouhe, Zuzana Fungáčová, Iftekhar Hasan, Amanda Heitz, Scott Langford, Fabrizio López-Gallo Dey, Xiaonan (Flora) Ma, Tanakorn Makaew, Carola Müller, Steven Ongena, Matias Ossandon Busch, Manuel Ramos Francia, Koen Schoors, John Sedunov, Virginia Traweek, and Laurent Weill, who provided valuable comments. We also very much appreciate Xinming Li for crucial aid with a key dataset for the book.

We also greatly appreciate the organizers, donors, and conference participants for the keynote presentations of preliminary versions of the book at central banking organizations—The Workshop on Banking and Institutions at the Bank of Finland, Helsinki, organized by LaRGE Research Center (University of Strasbourg), Bank of Finland Institute for Emerging Economies (BOFIT), and Fordham University (New York), held on August 22–23, 2022, and The XII Meeting of Heads of Financial Stability for Latin American Central Banks, organized by the Center for Latin American Monetary Studies (CEMLA) and Banco de México, Mexico City, held on September 7–8, 2022.

Last but not in any way least, we appreciate Batraz Albegov, Hannah Boyajieff, Mary Grace Compton, Andrew Faille, Paul Freed, Jiarui (Jerry) Guo, Quentin Jacqueson, Alexander Lago, Cristina Ortega González, Jyoti Prasad, Giancarlo Valle, Alexander Weinberg, and Siwen Zhang for excellent research assistance without which the book could not have been completed.

Part I

Focus of the book and other introductory materials

COVID-19 is a global health crisis that became a global economic crisis as well. The World Health Organization (WHO) declared the disease a pandemic on March 11, 2020. The dictionary definition of a pandemic is a disease that is prevalent over a whole country or the world. The announcement came after at least 118,000 cases and 4291 deaths in 114 countries, and about 3 months after the first disease cluster in Wuhan, China was reported on December 12, 2019. The WHO has still not downgraded COVID-19 from a pandemic to an endemic as of this writing, suggesting that the disease is not yet considered to be spreading at normal or expected levels that are stable and manageable in communities. The health and death damages differ over time and continue to change across countries. The damages are now clearly much better managed overall with the available quality vaccines and ex post health treatments, but these are still not evenly applied around the world.

The economic crisis caused by COVID-19 was spreading similarly to the disease pandemic around the world in a fast and devastating fashion in early 2020. The economic and financial impacts of the COVID-19 crisis around the world—the main part of our book title—have also significantly abated and become more manageable. These problems also persist, resist control, and the policies to deal with them are unevenly applied. The continuing intertemporal and international twists and turns are demonstrated in this book.

COVID-19 continues to cause significant damage to all three key economic segments of society—the real economy, banking sector, and financial markets—in countries around the world. We define these segments in a broadly inclusive fashion to cover as many important corners of the economic and financial systems as feasible. The real economy we consider includes activities of households and nonfinancial firms and their demand- and supply-side actions. The banking sector includes commercial banks and other financial intermediaries that provide banking services, including Digital Technology Financial Firms (DTFFs) of financial technology (FinTech), big technology (BigTech), and Decentralized finance (DeFi) that use modern technologies to provide banking services online. The financial markets we contemplate are broad-based in terms of types of markets and financial claims studied. We include as financial markets standardized exchanges, over-the-counter markets, and online marketplaces. We also include capital market mixes with banks, such as securitization and syndication, and old and new conventional market methods such as initial public offerings (IPOs) and special purpose acquisition companies (SPACs), respectively, and newer nonconventional online exchange methods such as distributed ledgers. The financial claims considered cover stocks, bonds, structured products, and cryptocurrencies and other new online assets. Our coverage of these topics tilts toward the more traditional economic and financial agents, institutions, markets, and goods and services, given the much more accumulated and reliable data and research evidence on traditional items.[1]

The economic and financial data and research reveal how the COVID-19 virus shocks quickly brought about declines in real economic activity starting in 2020. These were often of unprecedented speed and magnitude and spread from country to country much as did the virus. For example, the US Centers for Disease Control (CDC) reported the first US case of the disease on January 19, 2021, the US economy was in recession by February, and the national unemployment rate had increased from 3.5% to 14.8% by April. Negative shocks to supply and demand for goods and services around the globe caused recessions and soaring unemployment as households and nonfinancial firms physically withdrew from economic activity, and governments took actions to reduce disease spread by restricting economic activity involving personal contact. These economic activity declines proceeded through financial channels to cause capital and liquidity shortfalls in the banking sector and deteriorations in asset values in financial markets, although these were mostly temporary.

Research also suggests that in many cases, subsequent damages during the crisis to the real economy, banking sector, and financial markets from COVID-19 were substantially less than were expected when the economic shocks began. The relatively modest spread of damages from the real economy to the other segments was remarkable. For example, banks set aside significant additional reserves for expected loan losses that largely did not materialize. Government policy responses to the economic and financial problems were also in some cases of unprecedented speed and magnitude. Research findings tie some of the crisis policy responses to the subsequent favorable economic and financial "surprises" of mitigated damages relative to expectations. The research also suggests how well private sector agents in the three economic segments behaved and the effects of their actions in dealing with the challenges brought on by the disease shocks.

In this book, we apply the conceptual framework of the boom, crisis, and aftermath cycle to economic and financial crises, including COVID-19. As discussed in the chapters below, this framework is not new and not a formal model, but is very helpful for analyzing crises and particularly useful in setting up our blueprint set of strategies for contending with future crises based on this assessment.

A key feature of the conceptual framework is the inclusion of a boom phase before the crisis, during which excessive risk-taking and other misbehavior may hasten the arrival and intensify the crisis that follows. While risk-taking excesses prior to COVID-19 did not cause this crisis and likely had relatively minor effects on its intensity, the framework is essential to our blueprint. This is because the type of crisis that is coming next is not known ex ante, so it is sensible to take actions to curb such excesses during the boom.

We refer to the period as of this writing as the COVID-19 crisis aftermath, and it is associated with very substantial additional economic and financial damages in many countries. These problems differ

---

[1] We recognize that some of this terminology about economic and financial terms may be somewhat confusing, but we try to be as clear and consistent as possible. Economics is a broad science and is inclusive of real human agents, firms, and goods and services traded in markets as well as financial agents, institutions, and claims traded in markets. Thus, the real economy, banking sector, and financial markets are all economic segments of society. However, some inconsistency arises when we use the terms economic and financial impacts. Economic impacts in this context refer to the real economy and financial impacts combine the effects on the banking sector and financial markets. This inconsistency is almost required to avoid keeping track of too many different terms and to be reflective of standard professional uses of these terms.

dramatically in types and causes from those experienced during the early stages of the COVID-19 crisis and appear to be triggered by very different origins than the virus shocks that precipitated the crisis.

The aftermath in the COVID-19 crisis context refers to the time period after which the real economy, banking sector, and financial markets had essentially achieved escape velocity from their early crisis nadirs. The aftermath roughly begins when recoveries in economic and financial markets are largely proceeding on their own without need of additional government monetary and fiscal stimuli or financial aid to distressed economic and financial sectors or industries. In addition, vaccines to reduce virus severity and spread are sufficient to quell much of the fear of additional widespread lockdowns, at least in nations with strong democratic traditions. Populations also have sufficient financial resources in many nations to return to confident spending in opening economies. The aftermath as we roughly describe it here arrived a significant time ago in some nations. For example, in the US, virtually all economic and financial indicators were pointing up by early 2021, vaccines were poised to be widely available, and the positive economic and financial "surprises" of recovery appeared to be accelerating.

The new and different damages to the real economy during the aftermath are in the form of high and variable inflation, domestic and international supply chain disruptions, insufficient labor force reengagements, and increased likelihoods and actualities in some nations of second COVID-19-related recessions. In the banking sector, traditional banks are again setting aside significant additional reserves for expected loan losses, reducing bank capital that might otherwise be available to support new lending as a cushion to absorb normal credit losses. In addition, nontraditional DTFFs dealing largely in cryptocurrencies in a number of cases have ceased functioning in relatively short order. Financial markets for traditional assets have in some cases entered bear market territory with losses of 20% or more, while some relatively new nontraditional assets such as cryptocurrencies have recorded much greater percentage losses.

The sources of these problems appear to differ substantially from the negative shocks to supply and demand to reduce disease spread in the early part of the COVID-19 crisis. In some cases, the sources are traditional misallocations of resources that occur during the exuberance that tend to occur when speculative bubbles are fed by human foibles during booms. In the case of COVID-19, the aftermath problems may have more origins in continuations into the aftermath of some of the public policy actions to respond to crisis conditions and other continuing factors and their interactions, some of which continue as of this writing. Thus, there may be cases of too much of what were initially good things. Additional policy stimulus after economic recovery escape velocity was achieved may have resulted in excess demand that exceeded supply chain capabilities as well as continued low labor force participation. There are additional key factors, such as deglobalization efforts to erect additional barriers to immigration and free trade across borders, and shocks, sanctions, and retaliations from the war in Ukraine, still ongoing as of this writing that also play important roles in creating or exacerbating these problems.

Because the aftermath damages remain ongoing as of this writing, it is too early to tote up the long-run costs, provide confident research-based assessments of the relative contributions of the different policies or events, or determine how such damages may have been significantly mitigated by better policy choices ex ante. Future economists and policy analysts will figure these out eventually, but we are not waiting with our book because there is plenty to report already.

The entire set of COVID-19 issues of economic and financial damages, the effects of policy actions on these, existing research findings, and unfinished research agenda on the aftermath call for current action in our view. What are needed now are compilations of the research and data on the economic and financial impacts of the COVID-19 crisis from around the globe, a comprehensive assessment of these findings, and a set of specific research and policy strategies or blueprint for contending with future crises based on this assessment. This book, *The Economic and Financial Impacts of the COVID-19 Crisis Around the World: Expect the Unexpected*, provides such compilations, assessments, and strategies. Our compilation of research is as complete as possible, drawing on theoretical contributions to the research literature and empirical papers and using data from many nations. We acknowledge overrepresentation of empirical research studies using US data, as often occurs in reviews of research in economics and finance. This reflects the supply of quality research available in the literature, as opposed to our intentions. This does not deter us from including research and data on other nations to the extent possible, and it does not impede us from drawing best-informed conclusions from the research.

The data we compile provides information over time from the years prior to the COVID-19 through the crisis and partially into the aftermath. In most cases, the real economy data shown are through 2022, the banking data continue through 2021 because of reporting lags, and differ by country and market for financial markets. The COVID-19 statistics for virus cases, deaths, and vaccination rates by country are cumulative as of December 2022. Additional statistics for the US and some other nations are available on a more ad hoc basis. The data are all publicly available, although not always free of charge. The data are drawn from a variety of sources, including central banks, other government agencies, educational institutions, news organizations, and international organizations such as the International Monetary Fund, and World Bank.

We display the data from a number of different views and grouping of countries in the various chapters and Appendix. Our data compilation does not significantly overrepresent US data as our research compilation does, although our examples often focus on US information. Such information is generally easier to find than information on other nations due to more intensive news coverage and greater public data availability.

To enhance the readability of the book, we avoid excessive footnotes with URLs of websites from which data or other information are drawn, many of which we access multiple times. We list the URLs that are not otherwise provided throughout the book in alphabetical order in a single footnote here for readers' reference.[2]

Given the ongoing economic and financial damages of the aftermath and inabilities to complete quality research concerning them, the chapters on the aftermath that appear later in the book are primarily focused on the compilation of data. Most of the compiling, assessing, and setting strategies based on the research are confined to the other parts of the COVID-19 crisis.

---

[2] www.aa.com.tr; www.adb.org; www.african-markets.com; www.aljazeera.com; www.bankofcanada.ca; www.bloomberg.com; www.bom.mu; www.bostonfed.org; www.boz.zm; www.businessreviewafrika.com; www.cbpp.org; www.cdc.gov; www.centralbank.go.ke; www.cepr.org; www.cnbc.com; www.cnn.com; www.comesa.int; www.congress.org; www.ec.europa.eu; www.ecb.europa.eu; www.economictimes.indiatimes.com; www.economist.com.na; www.evictionlab.org; www.federalreserve.gov; www.fhfa.gov; www.france24.com; https://fred.stlouisfed.org; www.goodwinlaw.com; www.gov.uk; www.gz.com; www.home.kpmg; www.ilo.org; www.imf.org; www.livemint.com; www.marketwatch.com; www.mfw4a.org; www.munichre.com; www.nasdaq.com; www.news.anz.com; https://news.sky.com; www.nytimes.com; www.oecd.org; www.pewresearch.org; www.politico.eu; www.reuters.com; www.scmp.com; www.statista.com; www.theatlantic.com; www.tralac.org; https://home.treasury.gov; www.un.org; www.washingtonpost.com; www.weforum.org; www.wikipedia.org; www.worldbank.org; www.wsj.com.

Our comprehensive approach assesses all three economic segments of the real economy, banking sector, and financial markets. We also take a holistic approach to economic and financial cycles by considering all three phases of the boom, crisis, and aftermath, with the limitation on aftermath coverage of the COVID-19 already noted.

Our blueprint for specific strategies for contending with future crises is summarized in the "*Expect the Unexpected*" catchphrase at the end of the book title. Deriving these strategies from all of the analyses beforehand is the ultimate focus and inspiration for the book. These strategies for dealing with future crises involve advanced planning over the boom, crisis, and aftermath phases of the cycle and keeping these plans flexible to absorb and utilize new information as it arrives. To borrow from our esteemed colleague René M. Stulz who generously contributed the Foreword to the book, our approach may be roughly thought of as a risk management plan for the economy and financial system. As we demonstrate at the end of the book, the "*Expect the Unexpected*" blueprint may also be adapted for contending with other types of crises.

As a guide to what follows, the chapters of Part I introduce the COVID-19 crisis and put it in context. Chapter 1 gives more details of the focus of the book, with background materials and two mostly pictorial views of the book, data, and research. We feature a tour of the book based on the artwork of the book cover, as well as supply colorful data maps and charts depicting the COVID-19 health, economic, and financial information at various geographic levels.

We recognize the unusual nature of asking readers to look at the many pictures near the start of a research book. However, we are confident that these pictures are indeed worth 1000 words each, and that the artwork and creativity will serve as an entertaining method of motivation, piquing readers' interest and encouraging them to proceed to the more conventionally communicated research and policy materials that follow. As noted below, the Appendix at the end of the book provides an even larger trove of colorful pictures that illustrate how the COVID-19 crisis evolved around the world.

Chapter 1 also briefly summarizes the other five parts of the book. Chapters 2 and 3 compare COVID-19 to other health crises and to natural disasters, respectively. Chapter 4 puts COVID-19 in the larger conceptual framework for economic and financial crises. Chapter 5 completes Part I with a comparison of COVID-19 with other global crises.

The remaining five parts of the book proceed with reviews of the COVID-19 economic and financial effects in Part II and government policy reactions and effects in Part III, integrating in all cases data and research compiled from around the world. Part IV reviews the extraordinarily positive economic and financial recoveries during the crisis, only to be somewhat offset by the aftermath disappointments covered in more limited fashion in Part V due to the constraints noted above. Part VI closes with lessons learned from the COVID-19 crisis—it shines the light directly on our inspiration of the "*Expect the Unexpected*" research and policy goals and tries to push these forward. The specifics await readers when they arrive. See you there!

The Appendix summarizes a wealth of additional data in various formats—summary statistics, bar charts, and graphs—from around the world by selected countries and by groups of countries. We include key performance indicators (KPIs) for the real economy, banking sector, and financial markets, as well as COVID-19 health statistics.

Chapter 1

Introduction to the economic and financial impacts of the COVID-19 crisis and related topics

Abstract

We introduce the COVID-19 economic crisis at a relatively high-level orientation and explain the *"Expect the Unexpected"* focus of the book. The main goal is to help researchers and policymakers continue to improve preparation for future economic and financial crises of unknown ex ante origin and intensity to mitigate the unfavorable economic and financial impacts of these future crises. This involves creating a blueprint set of strategies to pursue over the boom, crisis, and aftermath phases of economic and financial cycles based on the compilation and assessment of research and data from around the world. We cover all three key economic segments of society—the real economy, banking sector, and financial markets—defined in broadly inclusive fashions. Most of the chapter is visual in nature, telling the story of the book through our book cover artwork, and colorful maps and charts showing the COVID-19 crisis in multiple dimensions over time across the globe. The remainder of the book is described as well.

Keywords: COVID-19, Economic crisis, Financial crises, Boom, Aftermath, Real economy, Banking sector, Financial markets, Strategic preparation

We introduce the COVID-19 economic crisis at a relatively high-level orientation in this first motivating chapter. Section 1.1 provides more background and detail on the *"Expect the Unexpected"* focus of the book, and shows off our cover art and colorful maps and charts. Sections 1.2–1.6 briefly preview Parts II–VI, respectively, and how they contribute to the focus of the book. To further enable a smooth

The Economic and Financial Impacts of the COVID-19 Crisis Around the World
https://doi.org/10.1016/B978-0-443-19162-6.00003-7
Copyright © 2024 Elsevier Inc. All rights reserved.

and easy introduction to the book, we delay reporting details and specific references to individual research papers until later chapters.

1.1 The focus of the book—Be prepared by expecting the unexpected—and other introductory materials

The focus of the book—*"Expect the Unexpected"*—is to help researchers and policymakers continue to improve the preparation for future unknown economic and financial crises and act on it during all phases of the boom, crisis, and aftermath. All six parts and all 22 chapters of the book are trained on this focus in one way or another.

Our general focus on being prepared to contend with any type of future economic or financial crisis with advanced flexible strategies requires that we contend with specifics. The main specifics we use are data and research on the economic and financial impacts of the COVID-19 crisis around the world and comparisons to other economic and financial crises.

We evaluate private sector actions by economic and financial agents and government policies during COVID-19 and other crises and draw research and policy implications for prospective future crises. We do so in recognition of the fact that no one knows to any significant degree of certainty in advance the type or intensity of the next crisis. Economic and financial crises are when markets significantly malfunction, which largely defies finding a functional approach to predict them.

Our conceptual framework considers private sector actions of economic and financial agents and public policymakers before, during, and after crises—the **boom-crisis-aftermath** framework. Our set of *"Expect the Unexpected"* research and policy strategies require preparation for crises that originate in all three major economic segments—the real economy, banking sector, and financial markets—and requires attention during all three cycle phases of the boom, crisis, and aftermath. The real economy, banking sector, and financial markets segments are also interconnected, as are the effects of actions taken during the three cycle phases. It is not easy to be ready for anything, but that is exactly what we suggest that researchers and policymakers try to do, and we take our part seriously to try to facilitate this.

We use the terms economic crisis, banking crisis, and financial market crisis to differentiate among crises based on the economic segments of origin. As noted, the three segments are interconnected and impact each other, so keep the focus for this introductory chapter more on the general side of crises and the specifics of the COVID-19 crisis only. COVID-19 is not a purely economic crisis because it originated as a health crisis, but it did affect the real economy before the banking sector and financial markets, so the economic crisis is the correct term. As we show, the COVID-19 research is advantaged over the study of other economic, banking, and financial market crises because the crisis shock is most exogenous. To illustrate, studies of the effects of the Global Financial Crisis (GFC) on banks are disadvantaged by endogeneity, given that the banks helped cause that crisis, as are studies of the effects of the Crash of 1929, given the excesses of Wall Street participants that helped precipitate that event.

In setting our focus, we recognize that COVID-19 is also a public health tragedy at a large scale, not just an economic and financial event. We cover the health crisis issues in only a limited fashion. Our expertise does not allow us to help with these issues, so it is important to stick to our comparative advantages in research on economics and finance.

To facilitate the journey for the readers, we feature a tour of the book based on the artwork on the book cover, and we also supply colorful data maps and charts depicting COVID-19 health, economic, and financial information at various geographic levels that tell the story from different angles. We now begin the book tours.

1.1.1 The story of the book told by the book cover artwork

We tell the story of the book as much as possible in a single picture on the cover of the book, which we replicate for the reader's convenience in Fig. 1.1. The top of the picture, replicated in Fig. 1.2 for emphasis, shows how the COVID-19 virus rained down on the entire globe at the end of 2019 and the start of 2020, creating the pandemic, a global public health crisis of massive proportions. The virus, as represented by the spiky fuzz balls that have come to publicly represent it, is in the foreground and the map of the countries of the world is in the background, suggestive of the dominance of the virus over all other global influences at that time.

The middle section of the cover, shown in larger relief in Fig. 1.3, depicts the economic and financial impacts of the COVID-19 crisis. These impacts are what the book is primarily about—evaluating the economic and financial damages caused by COVID-19 and doing our part to help prevent or mitigate these types of impacts in future crises. The three buildings shown of the factory, bank, and stock exchange represent the key economic segments of society that are harmed—the real economy, banking sector, and financial markets, respectively. As a reminder, we define these segments in broadly inclusive fashion, so that the real economy has households and nonfinancial firms, the banking sector incorporates commercial banks and others that provide similar services, and the financial markets include many types of exchanges of financial claims. In some cases, the losses are caused by the reactions to the viruses of households, nonfinancial firms, banks, and financial market participants, while in others they are precipitated more by government policy reactions to curb the virus spread, such as required business lockdowns.

Importantly, the three economic segments are interdependent—problems in any one segment can drag down the other two segments. We illustrate their interconnectedness by intentionally drawing no lines of separation between the segments. The very nature of crises involves contagion or spread of damages within segments, between segments, and both in most cases. A unique feature of the COVID-19 crisis is the modest nature of the spread of damages from the real economy to the banking sector and financial markets.

We also show three boxes each underneath the buildings in Fig. 1.3. These boxes represent specific examples of challenges faced by the economic and financial agents in that economic segment resulting from the COVID-19 crisis. There are many more challenges—we just choose three examples for each segment for expositional purposes—and make no pretense of capturing here the enormity of the global economic and financial losses from the crisis.

The challenges we choose primarily represent those posed during the COVID-19 economic crisis itself, rather than those during the aftermath. We understand considerably less about the crisis aftermath ongoing as of this writing than the crisis period that is over in most countries. However, many of the COVID-19 economic and financial costs imposed during the crisis period are long-lasting, and so persist through the aftermath and perhaps long beyond.

To evaluate the real economy, Fig. 1.4 displays the factory and three boxes for the real economy in isolation. For this segment, the boxes illustrate different economic damages caused by the crisis. The

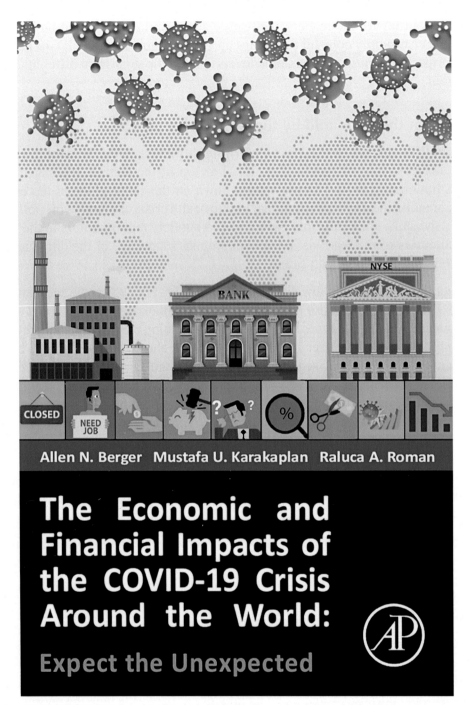

FIG. 1.1   Book cover explained.

boxes show a CLOSED sign hanging on a door, an unemployed worker advertising the need for a job, and a hand from above giving a coin of financial aid to a hand below. The first two are relatively straightforward to interpret—the damages accrued by stakeholders of nonfinancial firms that are closed, and the costs to unemployed workers struggling to find paid employment either after a lost job or upon entering the labor force. The third box directly illustrates financial aid handed down by the government to the first two groups and others through various government programs. The damages that this box represents are the taxes that will be required to be paid for the aid. Given that financial aid

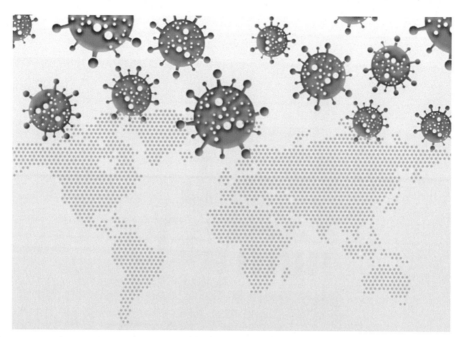

FIG. 1.2 Book cover explained (cont.).

FIG. 1.3 Book cover explained (cont.).

is typically deficit-financed, the burdens are mainly borne by future taxpayers who are required to pay for these programs.

Notably, the parties suffering the economic and financial damages are not necessarily cleanly separated. For example, unemployed workers in some cases also lost their wages and benefits as stakeholders in the closed firms. These workers may also be among the future taxpayers required to pay for financial aid handed down to them and to others by the programs plus accrued interest.

FIG. 1.4 Book cover explained (cont.).

Returning to the first box, the damages to stakeholders of closed nonfinancial firms include those caused by temporary closures related to government shutdown orders, other virus mitigation efforts, and economic and financial impacts of COVID-19, as well as those caused by permanent closures related to the pandemic and economic crisis. We note but do not discuss further that many of the same or similar economic and financial costs were also caused by closures during the pandemic of banks, financial markets, and government entities such as schools and government offices. Estimates suggest that about 200,000 additional US establishments with employees permanently closed in the first year of the pandemic relative to other years, with likely many more closures among the estimated 26 million US businesses without employees.

Short-term losses related to nonfinancial firm closures accrue for the business owners, managers, employees, contractors, customers, and other stakeholders that do not reap their normal benefits from business operations. The lost profits, wages and benefits, business opportunities, enjoyment from consumption, etc., are straightforward and need no elaboration. To the extent that the closed firms are individually or jointly highly significant to the real economy and/or financial system, the losses are multiplied by declines in economic activity and/or risks to the financial system.

The closures also involved longer-term damages in some cases extended through the crisis, aftermath, and perhaps well beyond, even from the temporary closures. These include economic scarring in which more persistent costs are imposed from lost productive capacity. This may occur because some workers do not improve their skills from on-the-job training, and others with high skills suffer atrophy while not working. Well-known cases of skills atrophy are airline pilots and medical surgeons who must continue to practice to maintain their skills.

Other scarring affecting productivity includes losses for the closed firms' stakeholders stemming from the absence of the firms' productive ideas that would normally arise from team members working and interacting together. Business closures also in some cases reduce or eliminate productivity-enhancing investments in updated plant and equipment and research and development (R&D) to build intellectual property.

Notably, in the crisis aftermath, some countries continue to have lower labor force participation rates than prior to the crisis. While there are many causes of these separations in addition to the pandemic, they raise labor costs and lessen productivity considerably on a continuing basis.

Turning to the unemployed worker box, the damages include costs from temporary and permanent closures of nonfinancial firms, banks, financial markets, and government entities. The lost compensation and skills atrophy discussed above are likely greater for the unemployed. The unemployed are subject to additional labor scarring costs by having to invest in some cases in additional skill development for different jobs and bear significant search costs in some cases. Those not rehired by the same firm may lose the value of their firm-specific human capital and have to reinvest in new work training or accept lower compensation from new employers. Labor market entrants who are delayed in gaining employment also lose compensation and skills that they would have acquired if they had obtained employment sooner.

For both former workers and new entrants, some had reduced attachment to the labor force and dropped out of it and have not returned thus far in the crisis aftermath, as noted above. A silver lining for the employed is higher wages from labor shortages, but these gains are limited to those who continue working or return to work.

Moving to the right in the figure, the damages caused by the nonfinancial firm closures in the first box and increased unemployment in the second box and the threats of these two types of damages and others result in much of the government financial aid depicted in the third box. During COVID-19, governments around the world open their wallets to ease the burdens and prevent further such damages.

Much of the government aid is targeted toward firms deemed to be in critical industries that are important parts of the economic and financial infrastructures of society to prevent additional widespread damages if these firms were to close. Similarly, unemployed workers, particularly those working for small businesses, often live paycheck-to-paycheck at the lower end of the wage scale. Many have few resources to keep food on the table and roof overhead, threatening much larger problems if not addressed. Not surprisingly, airlines and small businesses received subsidies in the 2020 CARES Act in the US to avoid closure and protect their workers. More generally, needs to mitigate labor and other economic scarring and prepare for recovery motivate further aid.

However, government financial aid is not limited to recipients damaged by the pandemic. Some are designed to stimulate macroeconomies in the form of transfer payments to broad categories for the purposes of encouraging them to spend. Although we are depicting the crisis period in the cover art, as already indicated, the stimulus continued into the aftermath and is included in the costs that future taxpayers are required to shoulder. The burdens faced by future taxpayers are very large in some countries and will absorb many economic and financial resources that have alternative productive uses.

FIG. 1.5 Book cover explained (cont.).

Importantly, all financial aid provided during and after COVID-19 and at any other time for any purpose is subject to unintended consequences. These include program waste, fraud, and abuse, as well as moral hazard incentives for additional risk-taking, diversion of funds, and other misuses. Many such consequences are already discovered and discussed later in the book.

Fig. 1.5 adds the bank building next to the factory to depict the dependence of the real economy on the banking sector in addition to the government aid. Households and small businesses are often financially constrained and bank dependent even in normal times for well-understood reasons. The health, economic, and financial consequences of COVID-19 raise their need for quality, prudently considered bank loans. Large firms that are less constrained and bank dependent also often need additional liquidity support from the banking sector during crises to keep their workers employed and play their roles in supply chains.

We move to Fig. 1.6 to focus on the banking sector. The three boxes shown underneath the bank building focus on impediments that the banks (broadly defined) face in supplying the needed credit to the real economy. These impediments to lending are also challenges to the banks themselves—the essence of banking is financial intermediation in which earnings from lending from the spread of loan rates over the costs of funds from deposits and other sources are the main way that banks support themselves. Banks need several key elements to extend credit, starting with equity capital and liquidity. Equity capital is needed to help absorb potential credit losses on the loans, and liquidity is needed to supply the funds to the borrowers. Both needs are reinforced by prudential regulation and supervision. We somewhat fancifully illustrate both access to capital and liquidity with the mallet breaking the child's piggy bank in the first box. The piggy bank represents equity capital as it has coins inside

FIG. 1.6   Book cover explained (cont.).

accumulated from past savings perhaps from restraint in purchasing candy or toys for real piggy banks. The use of the mallet to ferret out the coins for the emergency represents accessing liquidity. In reality, bank liquidity is primarily obtained by raising deposits and purchased funds rather than accessing equity, but we stretch our poetic license, in this case, to keep our illustration down to three boxes.

Bank access to both capital and liquidity is challenged in many ways by the tough economic and financial environments of the crisis. Bank capital is threatened by increased expectations of loan losses, primarily on previously existing loans extended without expectation of the COVID-19 crisis. Increases in expected credit losses reduce the market values of banks and their equity capital. On an accounting basis, banks increase their loan loss allowances, directly reducing the accounting capital that is needed for regulators and supervisors to allow lending. Bank liquidity is challenged in some cases by panic drawdowns of credit lines that reduce the liquid assets available.

The magnifying glass trained on the very small percent sign in the rightmost box is designed to call to mind the very low interest rate environment of the crisis. Central banks reduce rates to rock bottom lows for purposes of macroeconomic stimulation. While part of the intent is to increase bank credit through various channels of monetary policy, low rates also pose challenges that may deter banks from providing the quality, prudently extending bank credit needed. The low rates generally reduce margins of loan rates over costs of funds, squeezing the potential earnings on loans. These also create reach-for-yield moral hazard incentives that encourage extending riskier loans in place of more carefully considering loans to borrowers in need.

The middle box shows a banker with question marks surrounded by the challenges of the environment of capital, liquidity, and interest rate challenges. The question marks signify difficulties in acquiring and processing information that is also needed for bank lending. Banks are delegated screeners and monitors for their depositors and other stakeholders, and exercise comparative advantages in gathering and using the information in lending. COVID-19 provides unprecedented economic and financial conditions that would last for an unknown duration, making the screening and monitoring tasks quite difficult.

Banks employ various lending technologies to perform these tasks. Transactions-based technologies rely primarily on hard, quantitative information, while relationship lending is based more on soft, qualitative information acquired over the course of bank-borrower relationships. Hard information may be particularly unreliable during the COVID-19 crisis. The collateral value of a restaurant building that might not reopen is difficult to assess, as are credit scores that are based on prior payments made in more normal times. Relationship lending based on private information is also challenging. Financial markets might not supply capital and liquidity to banks to fund more bank-dependent and informationally opaque small businesses during a crisis in which these firms may not survive. Some theoretical and empirical research reviewed later in the book suggests that banks are able to overcome some of these obstacles to assist their bank-dependent relationship borrowers during COVID-19.

Fig. 1.7 shows the stock exchange next to the factory, illustrating interdependencies between the real economy and financial markets. Households and nonfinancial firms in the real economy need financial markets to help them to weather the crisis in addition to the government financial aid and bank credit already discussed. During normal times, households and nonfinancial firms invest much of their savings, personal wealth, and firm financial capital in financial market assets. Some investments are direct purchases of stocks, bonds, and other traditional and nontraditional securities, and others flow through mutual funds, pension funds, and other investment vehicles. The households and firms rely on being able to liquidate their own valuable assets built up from prior investments to help themselves cope with unforeseen financial difficulties such as the COVID-19 crisis.

The financial market crashes during the COVID-19 crisis hampered this process by reducing both the liquidity and value of the funds of the economic agents. In most cases, the financial markets did begin to recover relatively quickly, limiting the damages. For example, on March 23, 2020, shortly after US business shutdowns began, US stock markets hit rock bottom, with more than 30% drops for each of the three major stock market indices from their previous peaks. Nonetheless, they were near all-time highs 1 year later.

Fig. 1.8 similarly displays the stock exchange beside the bank building, demonstrating interdependencies between the two financial segments. Financial market difficulties also affect the banking sector as banks lose wealth from market crashes as do households and nonfinancial firms. Market crashes also inhibit the ability of banks to obtain equity and debt from financial markets that they need to fund loans and other banking operations. An additional problem for large money center institutions is that they normally derive significant earnings from supplying credit and other liquidity services to financial market participants and market activities—earnings that declined dramatically in the early days of the COVID-19 crisis.

Fig. 1.9 displays the financial markets block in isolation. We already discussed some of the losses, and the boxes underneath the picture of the stock exchange show three examples that help generate these losses. The scissors cutting the currency symbolize the slashed market values early in the crisis, and the remaining boxes show a COVID-19 spiky fuzz-ball bowling down future economic projections

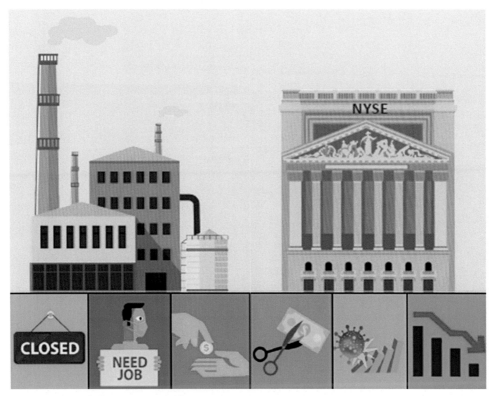

FIG. 1.7 Book cover explained (cont.).

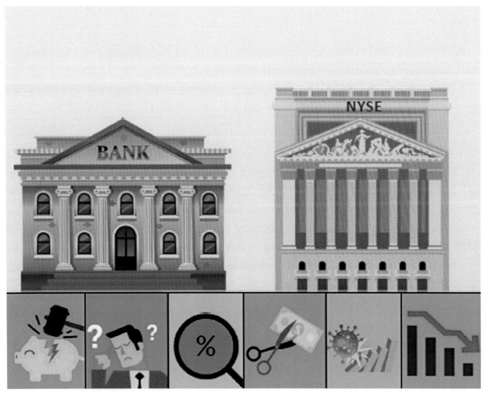

FIG. 1.8 Book cover explained (cont.).

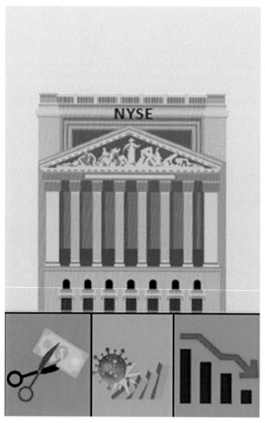

FIG. 1.9 Book cover explained (cont.).

in a bar chart and the expected continuing decline of financial indicators in a different bar chart. The values of financial assets are primarily determined by present discounted values of the net cash flows associated with the assets, so forecasts of future economic and financial declines should reduce financial market asset values quickly, and they did.

We conclude our storytelling for the middle of the cover artwork with returns to Figs. 1.7 and 1.8, but this time we flip the script on which economic segment harms the others due to COVID-19 difficulties. The factory and stock exchange together in Fig. 1.7 show the effects of households' and non-financial firms' losses on financial markets. As already alluded to, stock market values are based primarily on present discounted values of expected future corporate earnings, and bond market values are primarily determined by expected future interest and principal repayments. Additional value for financial markets and financial market participants comes from the flows of investment funds in securities, mutual funds, pension funds, and so forth that tend to prop up financial market values and provide fee income for market participants.

The bank and stock exchange together in Fig. 1.8 illustrate how banking problems harm financial markets. During normal times, banks provide the credit, liquidity, and payments services that allow the financial plumbing to work properly and the trains to run on time on the tracks of financial markets. Shortages of bank capital or liquidity, even when they are short-term in nature, can threaten financial markets, although no such large meltdowns occurred during the COVID-19 crisis.

Moving down the cover page, Fig. 1.10 shows the partial title of the book about the economic and financial impacts. These are primarily what we study, but the book title is not complete without our

The Economic and Financial Impacts of the COVID-19 Crisis Around the World:

FIG. 1.10 Book cover explained (cont.).

The Economic and Financial Impacts of the COVID-19 Crisis Around the World:
Expect the Unexpected

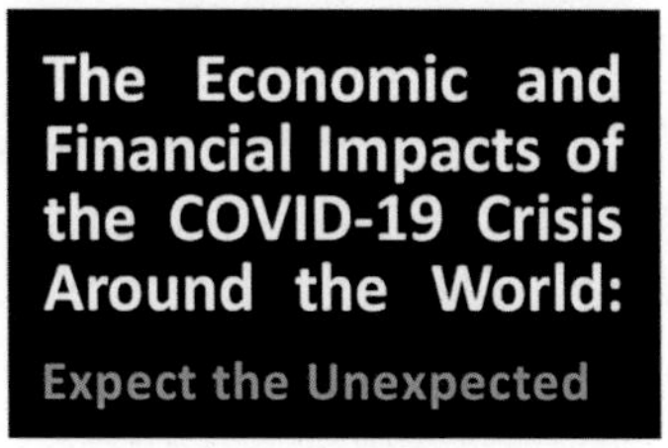

FIG. 1.11 Book cover explained (cont.).

Allen N. Berger   Mustafa U. Karakaplan   Raluca A. Roman

FIG. 1.12 Book cover explained (cont.).

"Expect the Unexpected" catchphrase added in Fig. 1.11, which is our research and policy prescription and the main value of the book. Preparing for the next crisis of unknown type, time, and intensity helps researchers and policymakers be ready for whatever comes. Importantly, policymakers must make these key future decisions with cool and collected mindsets, as indicated with the blue font for the catchphrase, and not in a panicked or frenzied fashion as would otherwise be indicated with red.

The cover artwork replicated in Fig. 1.12 also shows the name of authors in a plain small white font in alphabetical order. We de-emphasize these in favor of our goal for the book using research for positive purposes. Not shown, but consistent with this goal, is that much of the author proceeds from the book are directed to the Center for Financial Institutions at the Darla Moore School of Business to support consistent positive economic and financial research by others.

1.1.2   The story of COVID-19 as told by colorful data maps and charts

We next provide some different views of the COVID-19 crisis in a number of colorful maps and charts. They cover countries around the world in various ways over time, and often stretch from before the crisis and show the most recently available information as of this writing, varying by map or chart.

The maps and charts each summarize significant quantities of data, so we let the data do most of their own talking without significant editorializing. As discussed in the introduction to Part I, the data are all publicly available, but not always free of charge, and are drawn from a variety of sources noted in the figure captions. Discussions in later parts of the book are also based in part on these data, and in some cases rely on the URLs of helpful websites shown above in the Introduction to Part I.

Fig.1.13 shows the most recent available data from the latter half of 2022 on the health crisis across the world. There are more than 672 million COVID-19 cases in total around the world as of February 2023. There are more than 20 million total cases in a few countries, such as the US, India, France,

Cumulative confirmed COVID-19 cases per million people, Feb 28, 2023

Due to limited testing, the number of confirmed cases is lower than the true number of infections.

Our World in Data

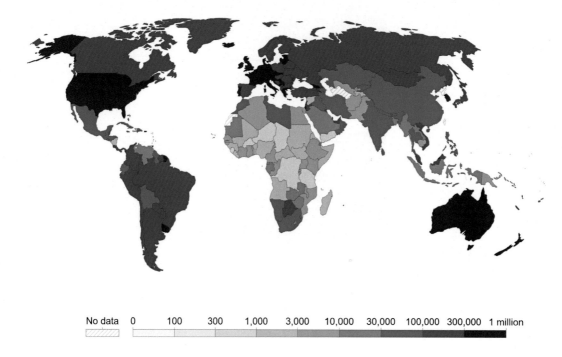

| No data | 0 | 100 | 300 | 1,000 | 3,000 | 10,000 | 30,000 | 100,000 | 300,000 | 1 million |

Source: WHO COVID-19 Dashboard

CC BY

Cumulative confirmed COVID-19 deaths per million people, Feb 28, 2023

Due to varying protocols and challenges in the attribution of the cause of death, the number of confirmed deaths may not accurately represent the true number of deaths caused by COVID-19.

Our World in Data

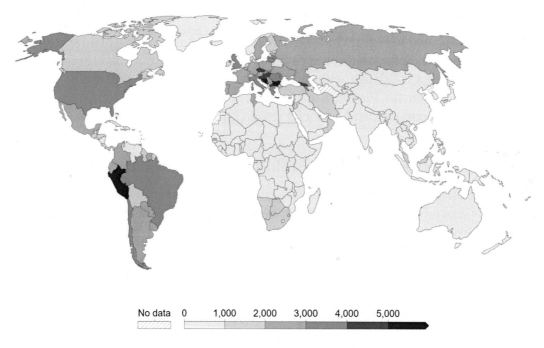

| No data | 0 | 1,000 | 2,000 | 3,000 | 4,000 | 5,000 |

Source: WHO COVID-19 Dashboard

CC BY

FIG. 1.13 (A) Health crisis: COVID-19 confirmed cases per million population in the World as of February 28, 2023; (B) Health crisis: COVID-19 confirmed deaths per million population in the World as of February 28, 2023. *(Sources: Our World in Data, https://ourworldindata.org.)*

Share of people who received at least one dose of COVID-19 vaccine, Feb 28, 2023

Total number of people who received at least one vaccine dose, divided by the total population of the country.

Our World in Data

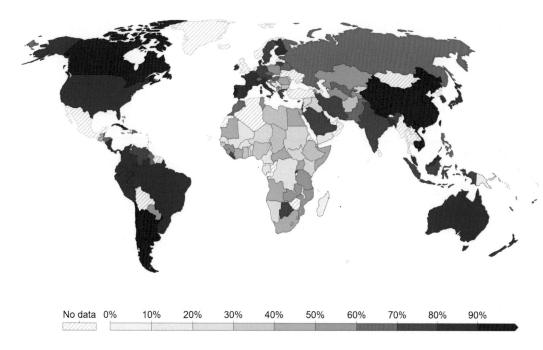

No data 0% 10% 20% 30% 40% 50% 60% 70% 80% 90%

Source: Official data collated by Our World in Data

CC BY

COVID-19 Containment and Health Index, Dec 31, 2022

Our World in Data

This is a composite measure based on thirteen policy response indicators including school closures, workplace closures, travel bans, testing policy, contact tracing, face coverings, and vaccine policy rescaled to a value from 0 to 100 (100 = strictest). If policies vary at the subnational level, the index is shown as the response level of the strictest sub-region.

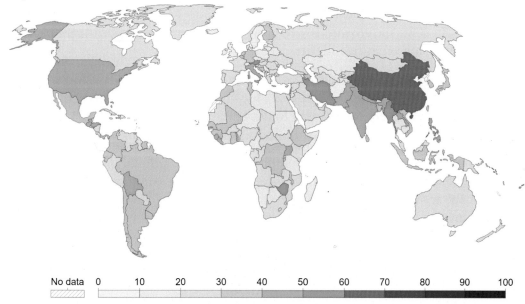

No data 0 10 20 30 40 50 60 70 80 90 100

Source: Oxford COVID-19 Government Response Tracker, Blavatnik School of Government, University of Oxford – Last updated 31 May 2023
OurWorldInData.org/coronavirus • CC BY

FIG. 1.13, CONT'D (C) Health crisis: Percent of vaccinated population in the World as of February 28, 2023; (D) Health crisis: COVID-19 containment and health index (government restrictions) in the World as of December 31, 2022. *(Sources: Our World in Data, https://ourworldindata.org.)*

Brazil, Germany, South Korea, the UK, Italy, Japan, and Russia, and there are more than 5 million total cases in many other countries, such as Turkey, Spain, Vietnam, Australia, Argentina, the Netherlands, Iran, Mexico, Taiwan, Indonesia, Poland, Columbia, Portugal, and Austria. Many other countries in America, Europe, and Asia have more than 500 thousand total cases. Countries in Africa, on the other hand, generally report the smallest numbers of total cases compared to the rest of the world, perhaps due to testing and reporting challenges in those countries.

The total number of COVID-19 deaths in the world is more than 6.86 million as of February 2023. The US, Brazil, and India have more than 500 thousand COVID-19 deaths, whereas many other countries, such as Russia, Mexico, Peru, the UK, Italy, Indonesia, France, Germany, Iran, Colombia, Argentina, Poland, Spain, South Africa, and Turkey, have more than 100 thousand COVID-19 deaths. Many other countries have at least 10 thousand COVID-19 deaths.

More than 13 billion total vaccine doses are administered around the world, and 63.6% of the world's population is fully vaccinated. Many countries, such as Turkmenistan, UAE, Qatar, Chile, Singapore, China, Hong Kong, Cuba, Nicaragua, Cambodia, Portugal, Vietnam, Taiwan, South Korea, Spain, Peru, Malaysia, Australia, Argentina, Uruguay, Canada, Costa Rica, Denmark, Japan, New Zealand, Ireland, Brazil, and Italy, have fully vaccinated population rates above 80%, while in some African countries the fully vaccinated population rates are less than 30%.

As of December 2022, government restrictions are extremely severe in Iran, Pakistan, India, China, Mauritania, Sudan, Columbia, Honduras, Panama, Ecuador, and Argentina. The least severe restrictions are in Kazakhstan, Uzbekistan, Poland, Belarus, Romania, Norway, Sweden, Finland, Iceland, and Paraguay.

Figs. 1.14–1.16 display data for the three key economic segments of the real economy, banking sector, and financial markets, respectively. Fig. 1.14 shows the size and duration of the impacts of the COVID-19 crisis on several key economic indicators: GDP growth, unemployment, and inflation. Starting with GDP, most countries had positive real GDP growth in 2019 with the average growth rate of around 3.5% globally. In 2020, the growth slowed down everywhere, but in 2021 it got back on track with many countries having a growth rate higher than that of 2019.

We observe a similar pattern for unemployment, except that the recovery is slower. The global unemployment rate was around 5.5% in 2019. In 2020, the unemployment rate was above 6.5%. After that year, the average unemployment rate begins to decline, but by the end of 2021, it has still not reached the prepandemic levels.

The effect of COVID-19 on inflation is more complex. The average global inflation rate was about 2.75% prior to the pandemic. In 2020, the inflation rate started increasing and in 2021, it was well above 4%. However, the inflationary dynamics are very different between developed and emerging market countries. In developed countries, the inflation rate was slightly above 2% in 2019, and then it *dropped to* below the 2% level through the pandemic as well as in 2021. In the emerging market countries, the inflation rate was around 6% in 2019. During the pandemic, the average inflation rate for these countries *increased* above 8%, and in 2021, it reached 9.5%.

Fig. 1.15 shows the impacts of the COVID-19 crisis on the banking sector. In particular, we examine the capital ratio and ROA as well as break down ROA by showing different items influencing bank profits and assets: costs-to-income ratio, NPL, risk-weighted asset-to-total asset ratio, and bank loan provisions ratio.

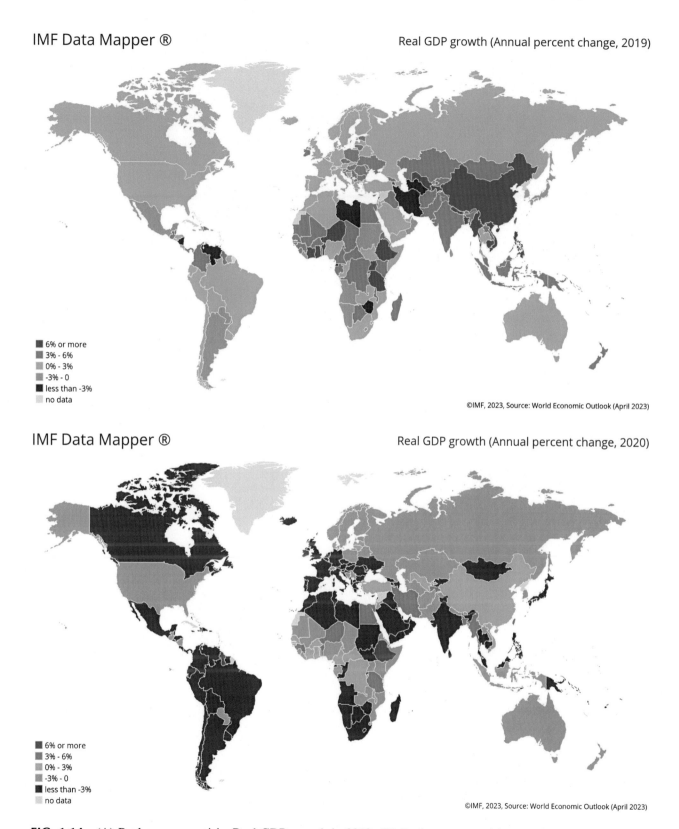

FIG. 1.14 (A) Real economy crisis: Real GDP growth in 2019; (B) Real economy crisis: Real GDP growth in 2020. *(Sources: International Monetary Fund (IMF), https://www.imf.org/external/datamapper.)*

(Continued)

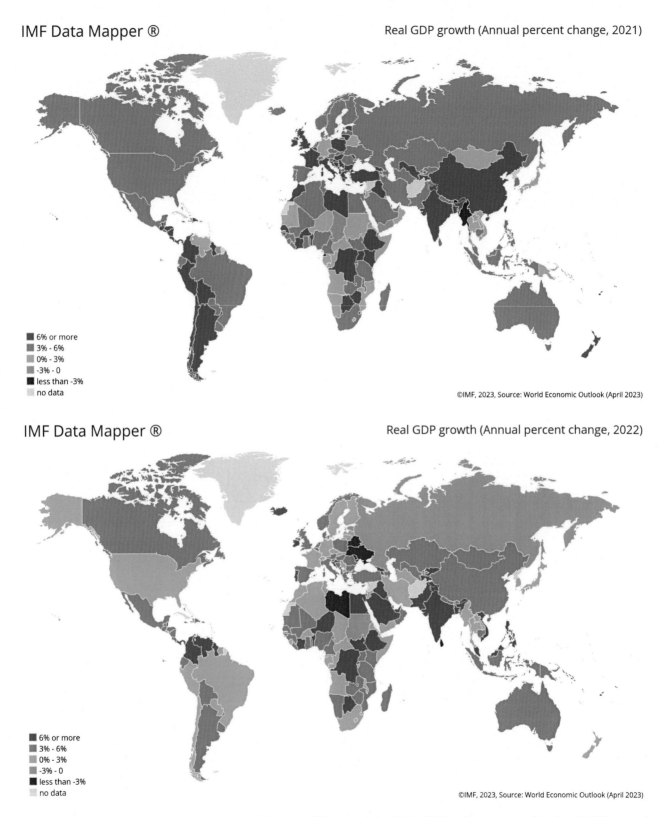

FIG. 1.14, CONT'D (C) Real economy crisis: Real GDP growth in 2021; (D) Real economy crisis: Real GDP growth in 2022. *(Sources: International Monetary Fund (IMF), https://www.imf.org/external/datamapper.)*

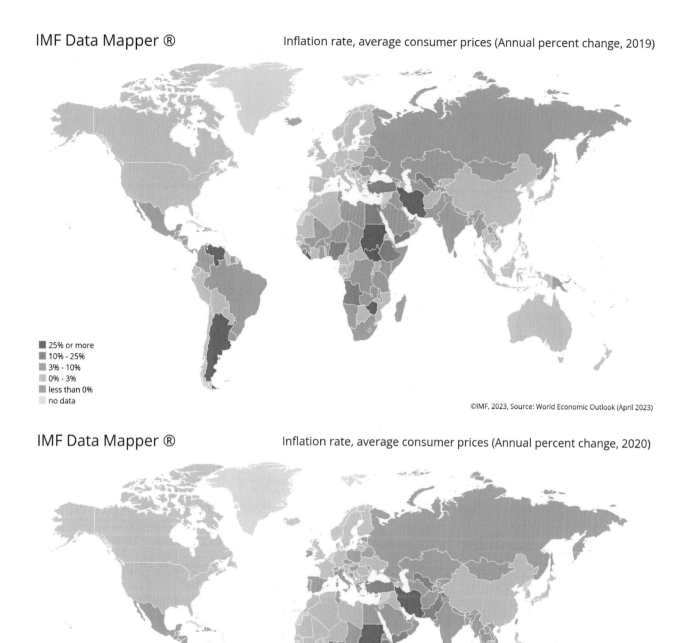

FIG. 1.14, CONT'D (E) Real economy crisis: Inflation rate in 2019; (F) Real economy crisis: Inflation rate in 2020. *(Sources: International Monetary Fund (IMF), https://www.imf.org/external/datamapper.)*

(Continued)

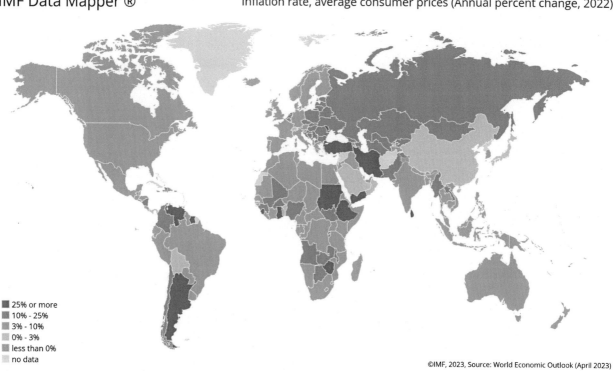

FIG. 1.14, CONT'D   (G) Real economy crisis: Inflation rate in 2021; (H) Real economy crisis: Inflation rate in 2022. *(Sources: International Monetary Fund (IMF), https://www.imf.org/external/datamapper.)*

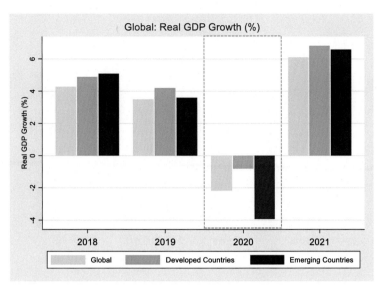

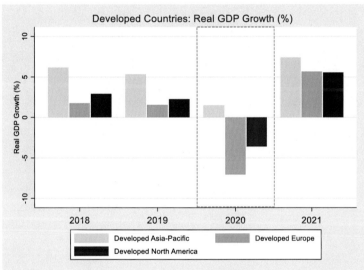

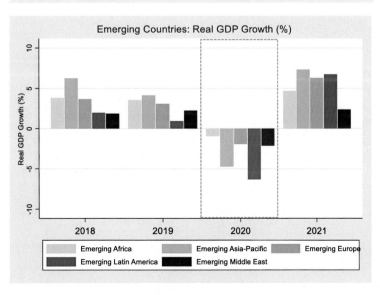

FIG. 1.14, CONT'D (I) Real GDP growth, for global, developed countries, and emerging countries over 2018–2021. *(Sources: Authors' figures based on raw data from International Monetary Fund (IMF).)*

(Continued)

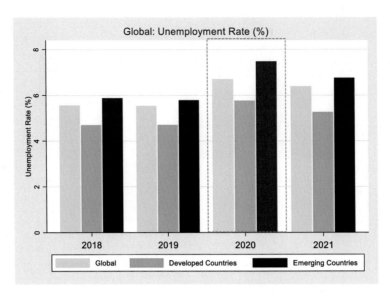

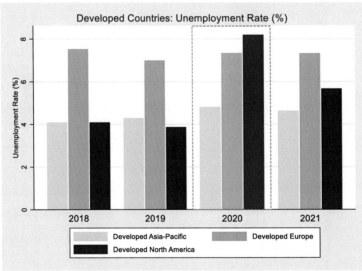

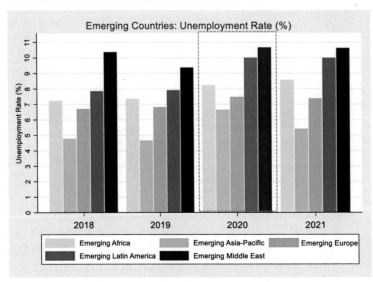

FIG. 1.14, CONT'D (J) Unemployment rate, for global, developed countries, and emerging countries over 2018–2021. *(Sources: Authors' figures based on raw data from International Monetary Fund (IMF).)*

(Continued)

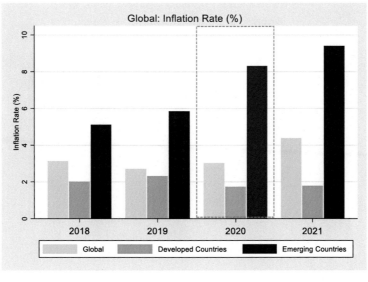

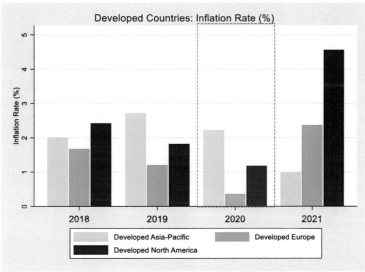

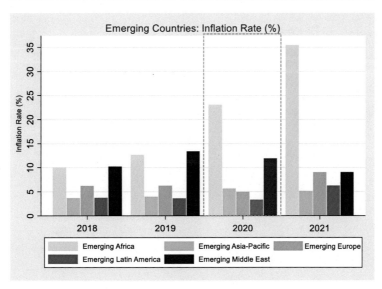

FIG. 1.14, CONT'D   (K) Inflation rate, for global, developed countries, and emerging countries over 2018–2021. *(Sources: Authors' figures based on raw data from International Monetary Fund (IMF).)*

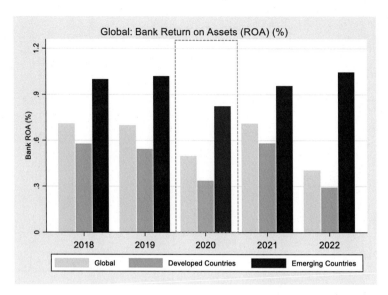

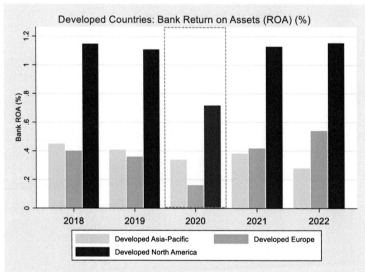

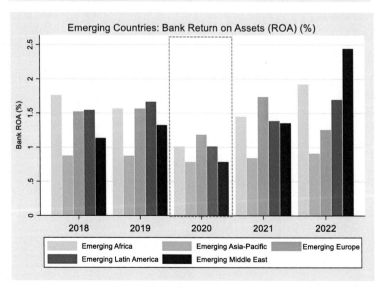

FIG. 1.15 (A) Bank return on assets (ROA), for global, developed countries, and emerging countries over 2018–2021. *(Sources: Authors' figures based on aggregated raw data from Bureau van Dijk (BvD) BankFocus and S&P Global Intelligence.)*

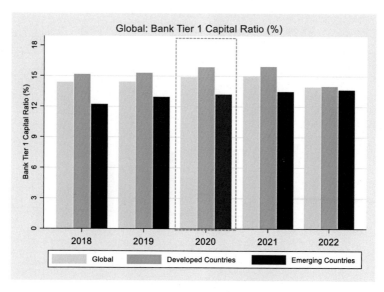

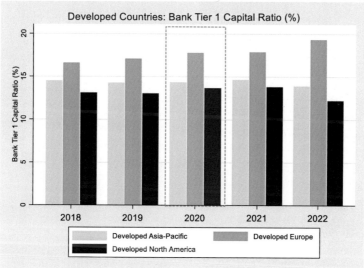

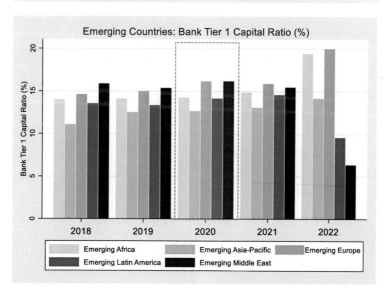

FIG. 1.15, CONT'D (B) Bank tier 1 capital ratio, for global, developed countries, and emerging countries over 2018–2021. *(Sources: Authors' figures based on aggregated raw data from Bureau van Dijk (BvD) BankFocus and S&P Global Intelligence.)*

(Continued)

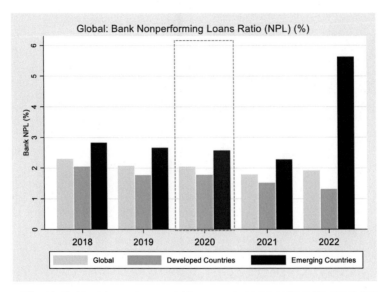

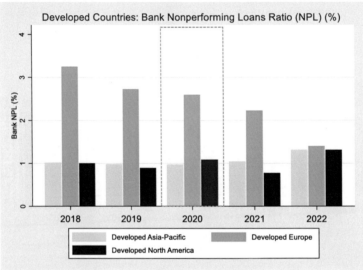

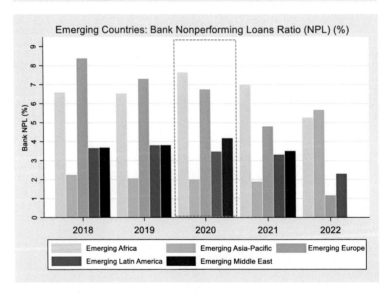

FIG. 1.15, CONT'D (C) Bank nonperforming loans ratio (NPL), for global, developed countries, and emerging countries over 2018–2021. *(Sources: Authors' figures based on aggregated raw data from Bureau van Dijk (BvD) BankFocus and S&P Global Intelligence.)*

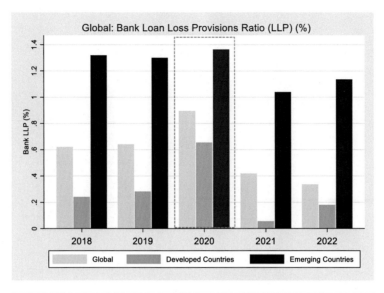

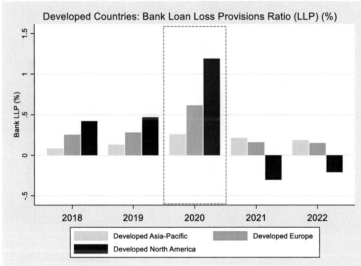

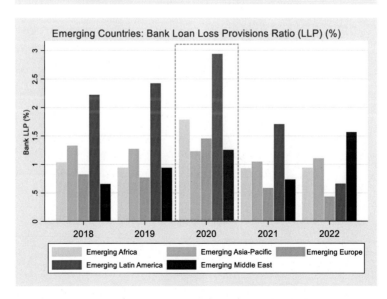

FIG. 1.15, CONT'D (D) Bank loan loss provisions ratio (LLP), for global, developed countries, and emerging countries over 2018–2021. *(Sources: Authors' figures based on aggregated raw data from Bureau van Dijk (BvD) BankFocus and S&P Global Intelligence.)*

(Continued)

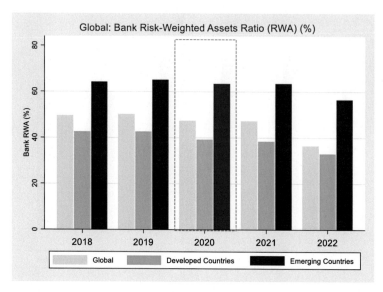

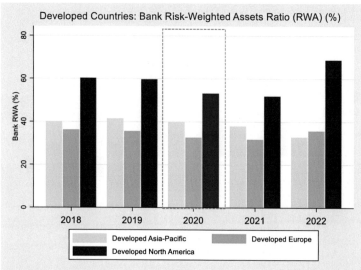

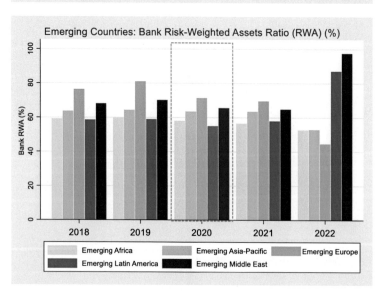

FIG. 1.15, CONT'D (E) Bank risk-weighted assets ratio (RWA), for global, developed countries, and emerging countries over 2018–2021. *(Sources: Authors' figures based on aggregated raw data from Bureau van Dijk (BvD) BankFocus and S&P Global Intelligence.)*

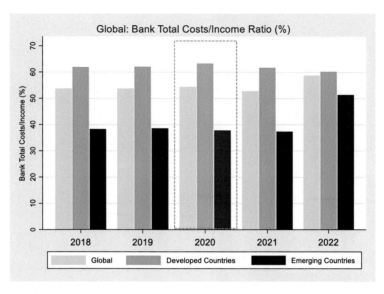

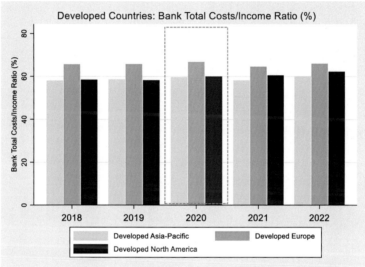

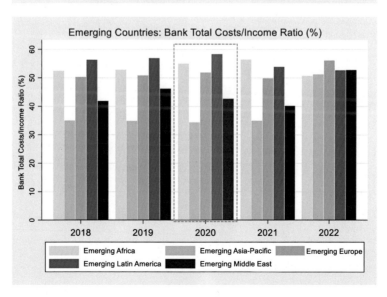

FIG. 1.15, CONT'D   (F) Bank total costs/income ratio, for global, developed countries, and emerging countries over 2018–2021. *(Sources: Authors' figures based on aggregated raw data from Bureau van Dijk (BvD) BankFocus and S&P Global Intelligence.)*

(A)

(B)

FIG. 1.16 (A) S&P 1200 Global Equity Index. (B) S&P Global BMI (USD) Index. *(Sources: Google Finance, https://www.google.com/finance/quote/SPG1200:INDEXSP.)*

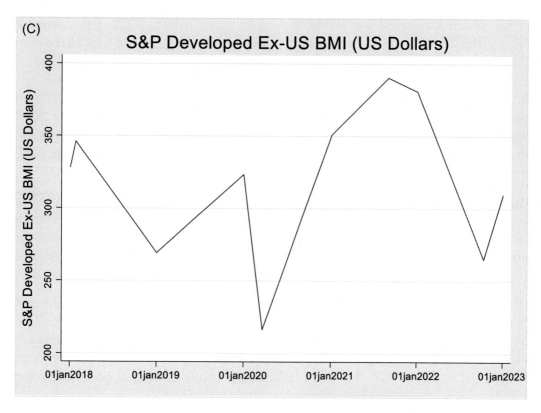

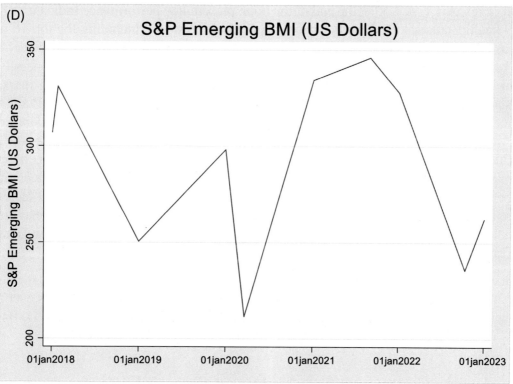

FIG. 1.16, CONT'D (C) S&P Developed Ex-US BMI (USD) Index. (D) S&P Emerging BMI (USD) Index. *(Sources: S&P Global public website.)*

The average bank tier-1 capital was stable above 14% from 2019 to 2021. The average ROA was around 0.7% in 2019. The ratio decreased to about 0.5% in 2020 but increased back to the prepandemic level in 2021. The average cost-to-income ratio was around 54% from 2019 to 2020. In 2021, however, the ratio decreased to 52.8%. The average bank nonperforming loan (NPL) ratio exhibited a similar pattern. The NPL ratio was 2% in 2019. In 2020, the ratio remained the same at 2%, and in 2021, it went down to 1.8%. The average global bank loan provisions ratio was 0.64% in 2019. During the pandemic in 2020, the ratio increased to 0.89%. The following year, it dropped to 0.42%. Turning to the average bank risk-weighted asset-to-total asset ratio, the average ratio was about 50% in 2019. During the pandemic, the ratio dropped to 47% and stayed at around that level in 2021.

Fig. 1.16 shows the impact of the COVID-19 crisis on major stock market indices. The S&P Global 1200 Index was below $2500 for the most of 2019. In November 2019, the index surpassed the $2500 level and kept going up until mid-February 2020. After reaching $2700 in February 2020, the index sharply plummeted in March 2020 to a level of around $1850. From that point forward, the index started increasing through 2020 and 2021. At the end of 2021, the index hit its all-time high point above $3500.

The S&P Global Broad Market Index (BMI) includes approximately 11,000 companies in more than 50 developed and emerging markets, and it follows a similar pattern to that of the S&P Global 1200 index. In 2019, the S&P Global BMI was within the $225–275 price band. In mid-February of 2020, the index peaked at around $285.78, and then dramatically dipped to $193.55 in the following month. For the rest of 2020 and through 2021, the index rallied until it hit the highest point at around $375 in November 2021.

Appendix Figs. A.1.1–A.1.39 at the end of the book present key performance indicators (KPIs) and COVID-19 health statistics for 39 major countries around the world, including the top 16 nations in GDP rank as of 2022. We include indicators for all three key economic segments of society—the real economy, banking sector, and financial markets. These stretch from 2018 onward, generally to 2022 for the real economy, to 2021 for the banking sector, and as available for financial markets. Real economy statistics include real GDP growth, unemployment rate, public debt to GDP and GDP per capita ratios, inflation rate, and indicators of whether government income and debt relief was extensive, limited, or none. Banking sector statistics cover various capital ratios, asset quality measures, profitability, and loan, deposit, and efficiency ratios. Financial market indicators include stock and bond market indices and CDS spreads when available. The COVID-19 statistics are cumulative as of December 2022 for virus cases, deaths, and vaccination rates of populations with at least one dose administered for each country. Data employed are from John Hopkins University Coronavirus Center, International Monetary Fund (IMF), Bureau van Dijk (BvD) BankFocus, Our World in Data, Google Finance, Trading Economics, and Wikipedia.

Appendix Figs. A.2.1–A.2.7 present real economy and banking sector key performance indicators (KPIs) for 2020 and 2021 compared for seven sets of selected groups of five countries each. Data are from International Monetary Fund (IMF), Our World in Data, and Bureau van Dijk (BvD) BankFocus.

1.2 Empirical evidence on economic and financial effects of the COVID-19 crisis around the world

Part II compiles and reviews empirical evidence on the worldwide COVID-19 economic and financial effects. This evidence is integral to devising research and policy strategies for the next crisis of unknown type—the main focus of the book. The findings reported in Part II are primarily from the early part of the crisis phase of the cycle, prior to the recovery and aftermath that are covered later in the book.

As discussed, COVID-19 is one of the three most significant global economic and financial crises of the last century, and the only one of the three that originated in the real economy instead of banking or financial markets. It is also one of these three crises driven by the most plausibly exogenous shocks. This helps improve the quality of inference for future research and policy input. We report research details and assessments for national and local economies, households, nonfinancial firms, banks, and financial markets—each of them defined in a broadly inclusive fashion—in Chapters 6–10, respectively.

The data sources for this and other parts of the book include the sources behind some of the data maps and charts shown and described there, and other sources include URLs of helpful websites shown in one place in the Introduction to Part I.

1.3 Government policy reactions to the COVID-19 crisis and their economic and financial effects around the world

Part III shifts to global policy reactions by governments to the COVID-19 crisis as well as their reactions to the economic crisis and financial consequences reviewed in Part II. We describe the policies and summarize the research and data to analyze them. Knowledge of research and data evidence on past policies is clearly necessary to plan and implement future crisis policies. This is particularly so for the strategic focus we advocate, which requires policy implementation during the boom phase prior to revelation of the type of crisis being treated.

The great numbers of the COVID-19 policy responses around the world limit our coverage in Part III to only a subset of the most consequential economic and financial policies tailored to our book focus on the best policy plans over the phases of economic and financial cycles. Chapter 11 provides the context for the COVID-19 crisis policies by comparing large policy responses for the US across crises—comparing the PPP financial aid to small businesses with the TARP financial aid to banks in the earlier GFC. Chapters 12 and 13 report details on other US and rest-of-the-world COVID-19 policies, respectively. The findings covered are again comprehensive across economic and financial agents as well as economic and financial cycles.

1.4 The extraordinary recoveries in real economies, banking sectors, and financial markets

Part IV is a relatively short, but important, two-chapter review of evidence on the extraordinary recoveries in the real economy, banking sector, and financial markets during the COVID-19 crisis. For the real economy, we refer to the historically unprecedented fast and steep gains in GDP, employment, and other economic measures. For the banking sector, the extraordinary recoveries more often meant that the expected credit and other losses that were provisioned for early in the crisis mostly never really occurred and the provisions for losses were reversed. The banks' reported profits and capital in effect had fast and steep gains. For financial markets, prices and returns are based largely on future economic prospects, and so also went on amplified rollercoaster rides.

Chapters 14 and 15 cover the US and the rest of the world, respectively, for the recoveries in the three segments. This type of evidence on cyclical turbulence associated with the COVID-19 crisis is important to our main book to focus on research and policy strategies for the next crisis of unknown type because mitigating such turbulence for the real economy, banking sector, and financial markets is the key objective of these strategies.

1.5   Economic and financial effects during the aftermath of the COVID-19 crisis around the world

Part V provides six chapters on the COVID-19 crisis aftermath policies and economic and financial effects. Chapter 16 discusses the policies, and Chapters 17–21 show the effects on the real economy, banking sector, and financial markets and the participants in the three economic segments around the world. As discussed above, the aftermath is very different, but the research is not complete, since the events of the aftermath are ongoing as of this writing.

Despite the incomplete report, it is important to take into consideration what we currently know about the aftermath policies and consequences in our book to focus on future research and policy strategies. The observations thus far during the aftermath period may be suggestive of strategies that pull back on stimulus more and faster during the aftermath of future crises to mitigate concerns about inflation, supply chain and labor force disruptions, asset market bubbles, and the second COVID-19 related recessions and financial market disruptions. We await confirmation or refutation of these ideas from future research.

1.6   Lessons learned from the COVID-19 crisis

Part VI has only a single chapter, Chapter 22, that takes lessons learned from COVID-19 plus all of the other materials in the book from other crises and events and redirects them toward our blueprint for preparation for future economic and financial crises of unknown type. We develop the plan and end with a surprise about how it may be adapted for other types of crises. We save the suspense for later!

Chapter 2

The COVID-19 pandemic vs past epidemics, pandemics, and other health crises

Chapter outline

Abstract

We focus in this chapter on COVID-19 as a global health crisis and compare it with other major health crises over the broad sweep of history. We find significant similarities and contrasts with previous epidemics, pandemics, and other health catastrophes. These experiences show that a significant segment of the population experiences shortened lifespans and physical health problems that also impact the real economy, banking industry, and financial systems. COVID-19 differs significantly from past health crises in terms of the magnitudes of the adverse impacts for long periods of time. A few favorable outcomes were the consequences of the swift steps taken by both policymakers and private-sector actors around the world to limit the damage with preventative measures such as masks, health-care resources to help those affected, vaccines, and other medical interventions to reduce long-term impacts.

Keywords: Epidemics, Pandemics, COVID-19, Justinian Plague, Black Death, Spanish Flu, Yellow Fever, AIDS, H1N1, Ebola Virus, Opioid Epidemic, Health crises, Vaccines

The Economic and Financial Impacts of the COVID-19 Crisis Around the World
https://doi.org/10.1016/B978-0-443-19162-6.00004-9
Copyright © 2024 Elsevier Inc. All rights reserved.

2.1 The effects of health crises on the populations of the world, their economies, banking sectors, and financial markets

In this chapter and those immediately following, we put the COVID-19 crisis in several different contexts to aid in our overall understanding of the crisis. Chapters 2–5 compare COVID-19 with other health crises, natural disasters, business cycle, and global crises, respectively. Thus, in this chapter, we treat COVID-19 as a health crisis that has important similarities with and differences from past epidemics, pandemics, and other health crises. We specifically compare COVID-19 with the Justinian Plague, Black Death, Spanish Flu, Yellow Fever, H1N1, Ebola Virus, the Acquired Immunodeficiency Syndrome (AIDS), and the Opioid Epidemic.

Major health crises generally share common characteristics—they not only damage the physical well-being and shorten the lives of significant portions of the population but also typically have significant impacts on the three sectors of society that are the primary focus of our book, the real economy, banking sector, and financial system. COVID-19 is neither the first nor likely the last health crisis with widespread and long-term consequences that are not confined to the health sphere. It is also not limited to any demographic group of the population or parts of the economic and financial systems, and not restricted geographically by region or international political borders.

Policymakers spend large sums of money supporting national and global healthcare systems. For example, in the US alone, health-care costs account for approximately 17%–20% of the country's GDP in recent years, exceeding $4 trillion in 2020 alone. Despite these large expenditures, health crises continue to occur. While outbreaks of new diseases cannot be controlled by policymakers, they can become crises and the magnitudes of these crises may be influenced by policymakers. From an economic viewpoint, health crises have large negative externalities that stretch beyond borders and may significantly disincentivize investment in prevention. Beyond these simple notes, further investigation of these larger issues is beyond the scope of this book, which is primarily about economic and financial implications.

In terms of key differences from other health crises, COVID-19 stands well above most of them in terms of the magnitude of the unfavorable effects. The virus caused an acute viral spread and resulted in large numbers of infections and deaths in many countries, whose populations and policymakers took preventative steps that created deep recessions and aftermaths with severe economic dislocations.

However, COVID-19 is also remarkable for some unusually favorable consequences. The immediate actions of policymakers and economic agents who cooperated on both domestic and international bases resulted in some positive outcomes. Effective and safe vaccines were developed and distributed in record times by pharmaceutical companies in collaboration with health departments. Several government actions also contributed to economic recoveries that caused unexpectedly limited damage to the banking sector and financial markets. Moreover, many private-sector actions greatly facilitated working and living through the crisis and economic agents were able to adapt quickly and apply new technologies that enabled food, medicine, and other essential services to be delivered to homes in response to online orders.

Section 2.2 discusses the COVID-19 pandemic in terms of the health consequences and policy reactions to contain them. To avoid repetition, most policy actions in the US and the world to address the economic and financial consequences of COVID-19 are excluded from Section 2.2—these are the main subjects of most of the remainder of the book.

Section 2.3 discusses research on other health crises and comparisons among them, in some cases including the COVID-19 crisis as well. We ordered these crises by date and noted that the quantity and quality of the research on the economic and financial consequences of these health crises increased substantially for the later crises, driven by better data collection, development of modern econometric techniques, and recognition of policy urgency. This is particularly the case for the last health crisis covered here, the Opioid Epidemic, which began before COVID-19 and continues some of its damages today.

2.2 The COVID-19 pandemic

As per the US Center for Disease Control (CDC) and World Health Organization (WHO), COVID-19 (coronavirus disease 2019) is a disease caused by a virus named SARS-CoV-2. It is a very contagious virus that has quickly spread around the world, as shown in Fig. 2.1A and B, resulting in many infections and great losses of lives. Most people with COVID-19 have had mild symptoms, but some people became severely ill and succumbed. Severe symptoms are more common in older adults and those with certain underlying medical conditions.

COVID-19 was first discovered in December 2019 in city of Wuhan, Hubei province, China. Then, on January 13, 2020, officials confirmed the first case of COVID-19 in Thailand, the first recorded case outside of China, and then it spread to other countries in Asia. Oceania confirmed its first case of COVID-19 on January 25 in Australia. Soon, subsequent cases were found on February 28, 2020, in New Zealand.

In North America, on January 20, 2020, the CDC confirms the first US laboratory-confirmed case of COVID-19 from samples taken on January 18 in Washington state. The Washington resident had returned from Wuhan, China, on January 15. Then, a second case was confirmed on January 24 in Illinois from another person who had traveled to Wuhan, China, in December 2019. Then, the CDC was also investigating another 61 potential cases from 22 states, and the disease began to spread in all states. A public declaration of crisis emergency was then issued by the governor of the state of Washington on February 27, 2020. The virus reached Canada on January 25, 2020, after an individual who had returned to Toronto from Wuhan, China, tested positive.

Looking at Europe, the first case of COVID-19 was recorded in France on January 24, 2020, also related to travel from East Asia. Then, another case was reported on February 19 in the region of Lombardy in Northern Italy. In the days that followed, Italy saw an exponential growth in cases, followed that by Spain, Belgium, France, the Netherlands, Switzerland, and the UK. In Africa, the first COVID-19 case was identified on February 14, 2020. On February 26, Brazil's government confirmed that a man who traveled to Italy got the South America's first confirmed case.

In the whole world, as of December 31, 2022, there have been 655,539,421 confirmed cases of COVID-19, including 6,683,993 deaths, reported to WHO. As of February 2023, at least 218 countries

(A1) COVID-19 Cases Per 100K Population (Dec 31, 2022)

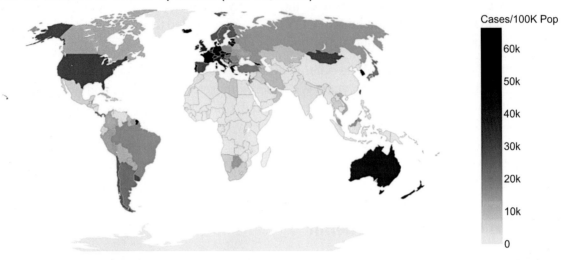

(A2) Daily new confirmed COVID-19 cases per million people

7-day rolling average. Due to limited testing, the number of confirmed cases is lower than the true number of infections.

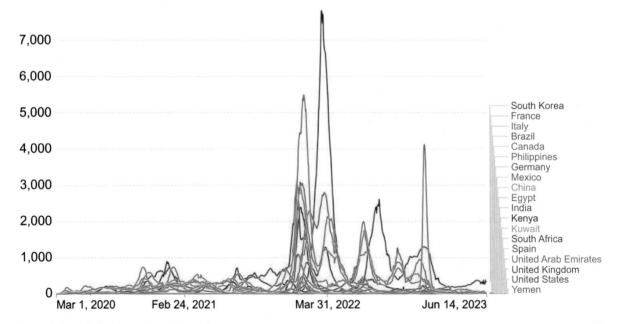

Source: WHO COVID-19 Dashboard

CC BY

FIG. 2.1 (A1) COVID-19 confirmed cases per 100K population in the World as of February 23, 2023; (A2) COVID-19 cases time series (daily 7-day rolling average new cases);

(Continued)

(B1) COVID-19 Deaths Per 100K Population (Dec 31, 2022)

(B2) Daily new confirmed COVID-19 deaths per million people

7-day rolling average. Due to varying protocols and challenges in the attribution of the cause of death, the number of confirmed deaths may accurately represent the true number of deaths caused by COVID-19.

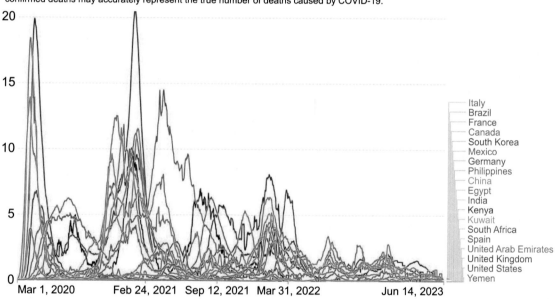

Source: WHO COVID-19 Dashboard

CC BY

FIG. 2.1, CONT'D (B1) COVID-19 confirmed deaths per 100K population in the World as of February 23, 2023; (B2) COVID-19 deaths time series (daily 7-day rolling average new cases). *(Sources: Authors' calculation based on data from Johns Hopkins University Center for Systems Science and Engineering and Our World in Data, https://ourworldindata.org for A2 and B2.)*

(Continued)

(C1) COVID-19 Government Restricitions Index (Dec 31, 2020)

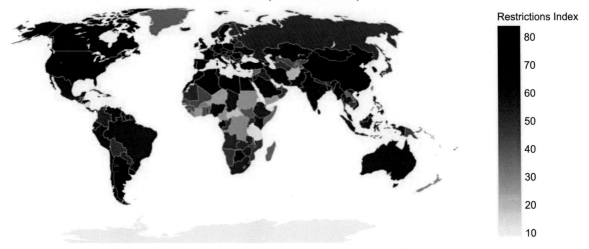

Restrictions Index

80

70

60

50

40

30

20

10

(C2) COVID-19 Containment and Health Index

This is a composite measure based on thirteen policy response indicators including school closures, workplace closures, travel bans, testing policy, contact tracing, face coverings, and vaccine policy rescaled to a value from 0 to 100 (100 = strictest). If policies vary at the subnational level, the index is shown as the response level of the strictest subregion.

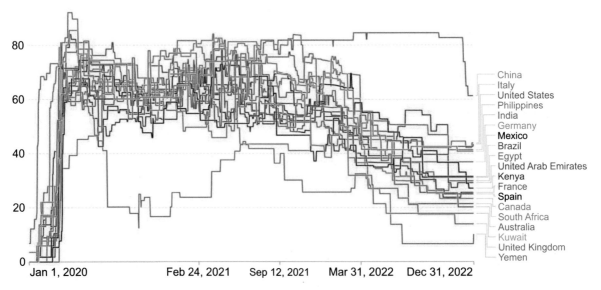

China
Italy
United States
Philippines
India
Germany
Mexico
Brazil
Egypt
United Arab Emirates
Kenya
France
Spain
Canada
South Africa
Australia
Kuwait
United Kingdom
Yemen

Source: Oxford COVID-19 Government Response Tracker, Blavatnik School of Government, University of Oxford — Last updated 14 June 2023
OurWorldInData.org/coronavirus • CC BY

FIG. 2.1, CONT'D (C1) COVID-19 restrictions in the World as of December 31, 2020, the most critical year of the crisis; (C2) Time series of the COVID-19 Restrictions Index for select countries;

(Continued)

(D1) COVID-19 Vaccination Rate (Feb 23, 2023)

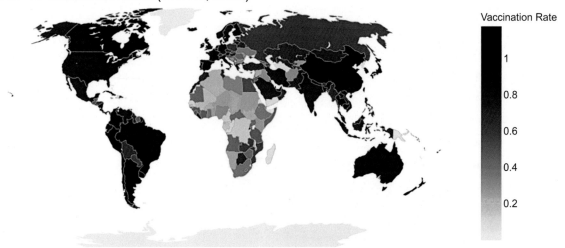

(D2) COVID-19 vaccine doses administered per 100 people, by income group
All doses, including boosters, are counted individually.

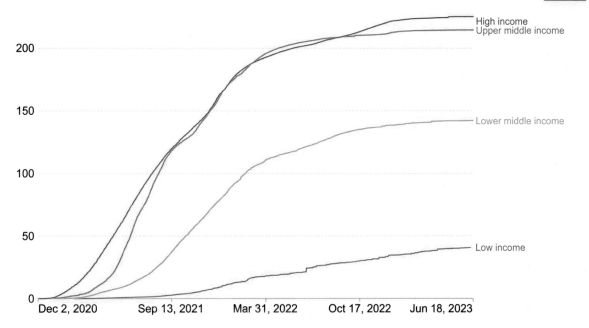

Source: Official data collated by Our World in Data, World Bank
Note: Country income groups are based on the World Bank classification.

OurWorldInData.org/covid-vaccinations • CC BY

FIG. 2.1, CONT'D (D1) COVID-19 vaccination rates in the World as of February 23, 2023; (D2) Vaccine doses per 100 population in the World by income group;

(Continued)

(D3) Total COVID-19 vaccine doses administered per 100 people, Feb 23, 2023

All doses, including boosters, are counted individually.

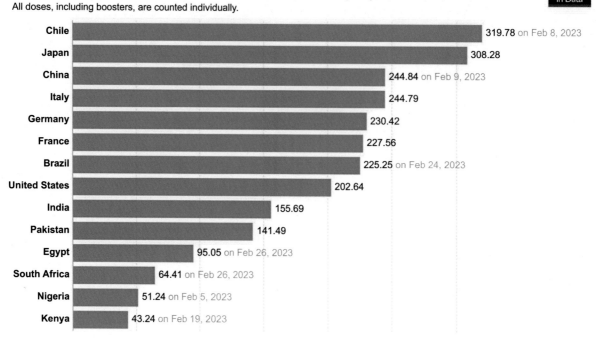

Source: Official data collated by Our World in Data – Last updated 19 June 2023

OurWorldInData.org/coronavirus • CC BY

(E1) Income support during the COVID-19 pandemic, Dec 31, 2020

Income support captures if the government is covering the salaries or providing direct cash payments, universal basic income, or similar, of people who lose their jobs or cannot work.

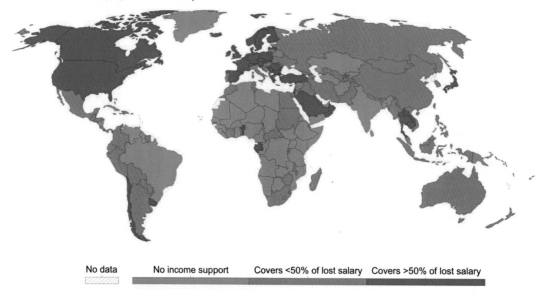

Source: Oxford COVID-19 Government Response Tracker, Blavetnik School of Government, University of Oxford – Last updated 14 June 2023
Note: This income support may not apply to workers in all sectors, and may vary at the subnational level.
OurWorldInData.org/Coronavirus • CC BY

FIG. 2.1, CONT'D (D3) Vaccine doses per 100 people for select countries in the World; (E1) Bailout income support intensity in the World;

(Continued)

(E2) Debt or contract relief during the COVID-19 pandemic, Dec 31, 2020

Debt or contract relief captures if the government is freezing financial obligations during the COVID-19 pandemic, such as stopping loan repayments, preventing services like water from stopping, or banning evictions.

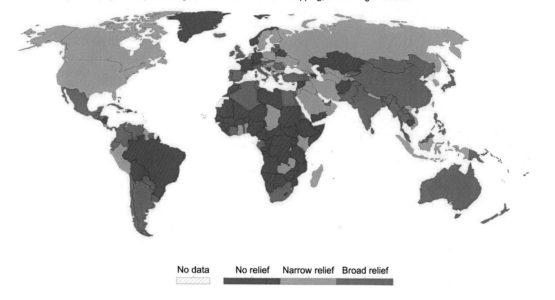

No data   No relief   Narrow relief   Broad relief

Source: Oxford COVID-19 Government Response Tracker, Blavetnik School of Government, University of Oxford – Last updated 14 June 2023
OurWorldInData.org/Coronavirus • CC BY

FIG. 2.1, CONT'D   (E2) Bailout debt relief support in the World. *(Sources: Authors' calculation based on data from Johns Hopkins University Center for Systems Science and Engineering, and Our World in Data, https:// ourworldindata.org.)*

and territories have administered more than 13 billion COVID-19 vaccine doses have been administered in the world to help fight the spread of the disease. Looking at US alone, as of December 31, 2022, there have been 99,892,513 confirmed cases of COVID-19, including 1,087,410 deaths as per the Johns Hopkins University Coronavirus Dashboard. In addition, a total of 671 million vaccine doses have been administered in the US (equivalent of 202 doses per 100 population) and 81.3% of the population received at least one vaccine dose. Other countries severely impacted in cases and loss of human lives are India with 44,677,310 cases and 530,674 deaths, France with 39,004,649 cases and 161,400 deaths, Germany with 36,980,883 cases and 159,884 deaths, followed by Brazil with 35,869,526 cases and 691,810 deaths, Japan with 27,138,615 cases and 53,327 deaths, Italy with 24,884,034 cases and 183,138, and the UK with 24,318,154 cases and 213,892 deaths, all as of December 31, 2022 (see details in Fig. 2.1 and Table 2.1).

Fig. 2.2 shows the time series evolution of 7-day rolling average new cases and deaths as well as cumulative cases and deaths all per 1 million population over time from January 2020 to March 2023 for different continents in the world, while Fig. 2.3 shows the evolution of the US alone. It shows that every continent in the world has had a significant impact, highlighting how contagious the COVID-19 disease has been.

TABLE 2.1 Select COVID-19 indicators for countries in the World, all health indicators as of December 31, 2022, population vaccination rate (at least one dose) as of February 2023, and government restrictions and income support and relief as of December 31, 2020 (for last three measures: 0 = no support or relief; 1 = limited; 2 = extensive).

Country	Code	Cases	Cases/100K pop	Deaths	Deaths/100K pop	Case fatality (%)	Vaccination rate (%)	Gov Restrictions Index	Gov income support	Gov debt relief
Afghanistan	AFG	207,037	532	7845	20.15	0.038	0.29	19.05	0	0
Albania	ALB	333,650	11,594	3594	124.89	0.011	0.47	62.5	1	1
Algeria	DZA	271,174	618	6881	15.69	0.025	0.18	64.88	0	2
Samoa	ASM	15,970	8145	29	14.79	0.002	1.18			
Andorra	AND	47,606	61,614	158	204.49	0.003	0.75	58.33	2	2
Angola	AGO	104,946	320	1928	5.87	0.018	0.45	52.38	0	0
Anguilla	AIA									
Antigua and Barbuda	ATG	9106	9299	146	149.09	0.016	0.66			
Argentina	ARG	9,766,975	21,611	130,041	287.73	0.013	0.92	71.96	1	2
Armenia	ARM	445,881	15,047	8712	294.00	0.02	0.38			
Aruba	ABW							38.69	1	0
Australia	AUS	10,975,374	43,107	16,692	65.56	0.002	0.87	63.69	1	2
Austria	AUT	5,648,626	62,719	21,317	236.69	0.004	0.77	82.62	2	2
Azerbaijan	AZE	825,409	8141	9993	98.56	0.012	0.53	79.17	1	0
Bahamas	BHM	37,491	9534	833	211.83	0.022	0.44			
Bahrain	BHR	697,810	41,012	1539	90.45	0.002	0.73	64.29	2	2
Bangladesh	BGD	2,036,928	1236	29,438	17.87	0.014	0.91	68.39	0	2
Barbados	BRB	104,944	36,518	568	197.65	0.005	0.57	51.19	1	1
Belarus	BLR	994,037	10,520	7118	75.33	0.007	0.69	49.94	0	0
Belgium	BEL	4,658,298	40,533	33,155	288.49	0.007	0.81	62.14	2	1
Belize	BLZ	69,376	17,448	688	173.03	0.01	0.63	66.07	1	2
Benin	BEN	27,982	230	163	1.34	0.006	0.26	39.29	2	1
Bermuda	BMU							61.9	1	0
Bhutan	BTN	62,521	8098	21	2.72	0	0.91	74.11	1	2

Continued

TABLE 2.1 Select COVID-19 indicators for countries in the World, all health indicators as of December 31, 2022, population vaccination rate (at least one dose) as of February 2023, and government restrictions and income support and relief as of December 31, 2020 (for last three measures: 0 = no support or relief; 1 = limited; 2 = extensive)—cont'd

Country	Code	Cases	Cases/100K pop	Deaths	Deaths/100K pop	Case fatality (%)	Vaccination rate (%)	Gov Restrictions Index	Gov income support	Gov debt relief
Bolivia	BOL	1,132,555	9702	22,269	190.77	0.02	0.64	49.4	1	0
Bosnia and Herzegovina	BIH	400,769	12,216	16,218	494.33	0.04	0.29	43.45	0	0
Botswana	BWA	327,511	13,927	2794	118.81	0.009	0.72	60.12	0	0
Brazil	BRA	35,869,526	16,875	691,810	325.47	0.019	0.89	60.42	0	0
British Virgin Islands	VGB									
Brunei	BRN	264,490	60,457	225	51.43	0.001	1.03	42.86	0	2
Bulgaria	BGR	1,290,186	18,568	38,082	548.07	0.03	0.3	50.83	2	1
Burkina Faso	BFA	21,631	103	387	1.85	0.018	0.21	31.55	0	0
Burma	MMR	633,555	1165	19,488	35.82	0.031	0.64	72.62	1	2
Burundi	BDI	51,481	434	38	0.32	0.001	0	17.26	1	1
Cabo Verde	CPV	63,164	11,360	412	74.10	0.007	0.64	63.69	1	2
Cambodia	KHM	138,387	828	3056	18.28	0.022	0.91	50	2	0
Cameroon	CMR	123,993	467	1965	7.40	0.016	0.12	25.6	0	0
Canada	CAN	4,477,829	11,708	48,807	127.61	0.011	0.9	68.33	2	1
Cayman Islands	CYM									
Central African Republic	CAF	15,311	317	113	2.34	0.007	0.41	16.67	1	0
Chad	TCD	7648	47	194	1.18	0.025	0.23	55.95	0	1
Chile	CHL	4,983,092	26,067	62,875	328.91	0.013	0.95	77.32	2	2
China	CHN	4,215,617	299	16,348	1.16	0.004	0.93	77.02	1	2
Colombia	COL	6,322,281	12,425	141,881	278.84	0.022	0.84	54.76	1	2
Comoros	COM	8979	1032	161	18.51	0.018	0.5			

Continued

TABLE 2.1 Select COVID-19 indicators for countries in the World, all health indicators as of December 31, 2022, population vaccination rate (at least one dose) as of February 2023, and government restrictions and income support and relief as of December 31, 2020 (for last three measures: 0 = no support or relief; 1 = limited; 2 = extensive)—cont'd

Country	Code	Cases	Cases/100K pop	Deaths	Deaths/100K pop	Case fatality (%)	Vaccination rate (%)	Gov Restrictions Index	Gov income support	Gov debt relief
Congo (Brazzaville)	COD	25,375	460	386	7.00	0.015	0.13	28.57	0	0
Congo (Kinshasa)	COG	94,970	106	1461	1.63	0.015	0.07	48.81	0	0
Cook Islands	COK									
Costa Rica	CRI	1,152,466	22,624	9051	177.68	0.008	0.9	63.21	1	1
Cote d'Ivoire	CIV	87,911	334	830	3.15	0.009	0.47	26.49	1	2
Croatia	HRV	1,259,369	30,677	17,452	425.11	0.014	0.57	73.1	1	1
Cuba	CUB	1,111,670	9815	8530	75.31	0.008	0.95	51.19	0	2
Curacao	CUW									
Cyprus	CYP	625,562	51,812	1250	103.53	0.002	0.55	77.62	2	2
Czechia	CZE	4,572,868	42,701	42,006	392.25	0.009	0.65	78.45	2	1
Denmark	DNK	3,418,420	58,563	7684	131.64	0.002	0.82	55.24	2	2
Djibouti	DJI	15,690	1588	189	19.13	0.012	0.32	43.45	1	0
Dominica	DMA	15,760	21,891	74	102.79	0.005	0.46	36.9	1	0
Dominican Republic	DOM	655,540	6043	4384	40.41	0.007	0.67	66.07	1	0
Ecuador	ECU	1,024,914	5809	35,940	203.71	0.035	0.87	65.48	1	2
Egypt	EGY	515,645	504	24,800	24.23	0.048	0.52	62.5	1	2
El Salvador	SLV	201,785	3111	4230	65.22	0.021	0.72	46.43	1	2
Equatorial Guinea	GNQ	17,186	1225	183	13.04	0.011	0.19			
Eritrea	ERI	10,189	287	103	2.90	0.01	–		0	2
Estonia	EST	610,473	46,020	2814	212.13	0.005	0.65	49.05	0	2
Ethiopia	ETH	496,160	432	7572	6.59	0.015	0.37	55.36	0	0
Falkland Islands (Islas Malvinas)	FLK									

Continued

TABLE 2.1 Select COVID-19 indicators for countries in the World, all health indicators as of December 31, 2022, population vaccination rate (at least one dose) as of February 2023, and government restrictions and income support and relief as of December 31, 2020 (for last three measures: 0 = no support or relief; 1 = limited; 2 = extensive)—cont'd

Country	Code	Cases	Cases/100K pop	Deaths	Deaths/100K pop	Case fatality (%)	Vaccination rate (%)	Gov Restrictions Index	Gov income support	Gov debt relief
Faroe Islands	FRO									
Fiji	FJI	68,553	7647	878	97.94	0.013	0.79	51.79	1	2
Finland	FIN	1,428,446	25,781	7783	140.47	0.005	0.82	49.94	2	1
France	FRA	39,004,649	59,778	161,400	247.36	0.004	0.84	62.8	2	0
French Polynesia	PYF									
Gabon	GAB	48,973	2201	306	13.75	0.006	0.14	61.9	2	2
Gambia	GMB	12,586	521	372	15.39	0.03	0.39	46.43	0	0
Georgia	GEO	1,808,085	45,325	16,895	423.52	0.009	0.41	73.81	1	1
Germany	DEU	36,980,883	44,472	159,884	192.27	0.004	0.78	73.69	2	0
Ghana	GHA	171,023	550	1461	4.70	0.009	0.39	41.67	0	1
Gibraltar	GIB									
Greece	GRC	5,500,737	52,775	34,614	332.09	0.006	0.76	83.21	2	2
Greenland	GRL							39.29	0	0
Grenada	GRD	19,644	17,458	238	211.52	0.012	0.39			
Guam	GUM								1	1
Guatemala	GTM	1,184,754	6613	19,983	111.54	0.017	0.49	47.32	1	2
Guernsey	GGY									
Guinea-Bissau	GNB	8848	449	176	8.94	0.02	0.39			0
Guinea	GIN	38,191	291	465	3.54	0.012	0.46	43.45	0	1
Guyana	GUY	71,757	9123	1285	163.37	0.018	0.63	60.12	0	1
Haiti	HTI	33,876	297	860	7.54	0.025	0.03	32.14	1	1
Honduras	HND	462,340	4668	11,060	111.67	0.024	0.65	70.24	1	2
Hong Kong	HKG							70.83	1	2

Continued

TABLE 2.1 Select COVID-19 indicators for countries in the World, all health indicators as of December 31, 2022, population vaccination rate (at least one dose) as of February 2023, and government restrictions and income support and relief as of December 31, 2020 (for last three measures: 0 = no support or relief; 1 = limited; 2 = extensive)—cont'd

Country	Code	Cases	Cases/100K pop	Deaths	Deaths/100K pop	Case fatality (%)	Vaccination rate (%)	Gov Restrictions Index	Gov income support	Gov debt relief
Hungary	HUN	2,176,249	22,528	48,380	500.81	0.022	0.66	66.9	1	1
Iceland	ISL	207,101	60,693	219	64.18	0.001	0.91	57.02	2	2
India	IND	44,677,310	3237	530,674	38.45	0.012	0.74	60.71	0	2
Indonesia	IDN	6,709,597	2453	160,398	58.64	0.024	0.74	60.42	1	1
Iran	IRN	7,560,444	9001	144,664	172.23	0.019	0.78	60.42	1	1
Iraq	IRQ	2,464,375	6126	25,366	63.06	0.01	0.28	52.38	1	1
Ireland	IRL	1,684,717	34,118	8270	167.48	0.005	0.83	76.79	2	2
Isle of Man	IMN									
Israel	ISR	4,747,992	54,856	11,954	138.11	0.003	0.82	84.05	2	1
Italy	ITA	24,884,034	41,157	183,138	302.90	0.007	0.84	78.75	1	2
Jamaica	JAM	152,669	5156	3447	116.41	0.023	0.28	70.24	1	1
Japan	JPN	27,138,615	21,456	53,327	42.16	0.002	0.83	50	2	2
Jersey	JEY									
Jordan	JOR	1,746,997	17,122	14,122	138.41	0.008	0.47	70.83	1	1
Kazakhstan	KAZ	1,488,306	7926	19,057	101.49	0.013	0.66	58.33	0	0
Kenya	KEN	342,336	637	5688	10.58	0.017	0.26	58.93	0	1
Kiribati	KIR	3430	2916	13	11.05	0.004	0.82	16.67	0	0
North Korea	PRK	1	0	6	0.02	6				
South Korea	KOR	28,214,915	55,031	31,434	61.31	0.001	0.88	66.37	1	1
Kosovo	KSV	272,232	15,037	3202	176.87	0.012	0.5			
Kuwait	KWT	662,747	15,519	2570	60.18	0.004	0.81	65	1	1
Kyrgyzstan	KGZ	206,553	3166	2991	45.84	0.014	0.25	42.26	0	2
Laos	LAO	217,458	2989	758	10.42	0.003	0.84	38.1	2	2
Latvia	LVA	970,286	51,441	6121	324.51	0.006	0.71	59.76	2	2
Lebanon	LBN	1,221,640	17,898	10,742	157.38	0.009	0.4	72.62	0	2

Continued

TABLE 2.1 Select COVID-19 indicators for countries in the World, all health indicators as of December 31, 2022, population vaccination rate (at least one dose) as of February 2023, and government restrictions and income support and relief as of December 31, 2020 (for last three measures: 0 = no support or relief; 1 = limited; 2 = extensive)—cont'd

Country	Code	Cases	Cases/100K pop	Deaths	Deaths/100K pop	Case fatality (%)	Vaccination rate (%)	Gov Restrictions Index	Gov income support	Gov debt relief
Lesotho	LSO	34,490	1610	706	32.96	0.02	0.47	38.69	0	0
Liberia	LBR	8043	159	294	5.81	0.037	0.76	33.93	0	0
Libya	LBY	507,112	7380	6437	93.68	0.013	0.34	65.48	0	0
Liechtenstein	LIE	21,170	55,511	88	230.75	0.004	0.7	56.55	0	0
Lithuania	LTU	1,283,384	47,144	9452	347.21	0.007	0.72	76.67	1	2
Luxembourg	LUX	310,066	49,534	1172	187.23	0.004	0.77	70.71	1	2
Macau	MAC							37.5	1	2
North Macedonia	MKD	345,197	16,569	9599	460.74	0.028	0.41			
Madagascar	MDG	67,684	244	1415	5.11	0.021	0.07	38.1	1	1
Malawi	MWI	88,220	461	2685	14.04	0.03	0.2	50	1	0
Malaysia	MYS	5,017,863	15,504	36,806	113.72	0.007	0.87	69.94	1	2
Maldives	MDV	185,651	34,342	311	57.53	0.002	0.74			
Mali	MLI	32,767	162	743	3.67	0.023	0.15	43.45	0	0
Malta	MLT	116,114	26,298	811	183.68	0.007	1.08	61.55	2	1
Marshall Islands	MHL	15,547	26,613	17	29.10	0.001	0.75			
Mauritania	MRT	63,425	1364	997	21.44	0.016	0.44	52.98	0	0
Mauritius	MUS	287,999	22,646	1038	81.62	0.004	0.88	29.17	2	0
Mexico	MEX	7,188,862	5625	330,795	258.85	0.046	0.78	62.14	1	2
Micronesia, Federated States of	FSM									
Moldova	MDA	595,745	14,791	11,922	296.00	0.02	0.27	61.31	1	1
Monaco	MCO	15,833	40,345	65	165.63	0.004	0.74	53.21	2	0
Mongolia	MNG	1,007,025	30,720	2135	65.13	0.002	0.7	69.35	1	2

Continued

TABLE 2.1 Select COVID-19 indicators for countries in the World, all health indicators as of December 31, 2022, population vaccination rate (at least one dose) as of February 2023, and government restrictions and income support and relief as of December 31, 2020 (for last three measures: 0 = no support or relief; 1 = limited; 2 = extensive)—cont'd

Country	Code	Cases	Cases/100K pop	Deaths	Deaths/100K pop	Case fatality (%)	Vaccination rate (%)	Gov Restrictions Index	Gov income support	Gov debt relief
Montenegro	MNE	284,352	45,274	2790	444.22	0.01	0.47		1	0
Morocco	MAR	1,270,820	3443	16,294	44.14	0.013	0.68	66.07	0	0
Mozambique	MOZ	230,816	738	2229	7.13	0.01	0.6	47.02	0	0
Namibia	NAM	169,946	6688	4080	160.57	0.024	0.24	47.02	0	1
Nepal	NPL	1,000,945	3435	12,019	41.25	0.012	0.94	55.6	1	1
Netherlands	NLD	8,668,302	50,588	23,648	138.01	0.003	0.75	67.26	2	1
New Caledonia	NCL									
New Zealand	NZL	2,068,999	42,908	2289	47.47	0.001	0.89	32.14	1	2
Nicaragua	NIC	15,308	231	245	3.70	0.016	0.93	12.5	0	0
Nigeria	NGA	266,381	129	3155	1.53	0.012	0.31	59.52	0	0
Niger	NER	9434	39	314	1.30	0.033	0.25	23.51	0	0
Niue	NIU									
Northern Mariana Islands	MNP									
Norway	NOR	1,472,301	27,159	4571	84.32	0.003	0.8	56.79	2	0
Oman	OMN	399,119	7816	4628	90.63	0.012	0.64	47.74	2	1
Pakistan	PAK	1,575,486	713	30,635	13.87	0.019	0.7	66.37	1	2
Palau	PLW	5955	33,070	9	49.98	0.002	1.12			
Panama	PAN	1,015,970	23,546	8543	197.99	0.008	0.81	75.6	1	2
Papua New Guinea	PNG	46,557	521	669	7.48	0.014	0.04	45.24	0	2
Paraguay	PRY	781,111	10,951	19,655	275.57	0.025	0.56	53.57	1	2
Peru	PER	4,412,141	13,382	217,855	660.73	0.049	0.92	63.69	1	1
Philippines	PHL	4,056,239	3702	65,064	59.38	0.016	0.71	63.39	1	2

Continued

TABLE 2.1 Select COVID-19 indicators for countries in the World, all health indicators as of December 31, 2022, population vaccination rate (at least one dose) as of February 2023, and government restrictions and income support and relief as of December 31, 2020 (for last three measures: 0 = no support or relief; 1 = limited; 2 = extensive)—cont'd

Country	Code	Cases	Cases/100K pop	Deaths	Deaths/100K pop	Case fatality (%)	Vaccination rate (%)	Gov Restrictions Index	Gov income support	Gov debt relief
Poland	POL	6,361,588	16,809	118,429	312.92	0.019	0.61	75.48	2	1
Portugal	PRT	5,551,364	54,442	25,643	251.48	0.005	0.96	73.1	1	2
Puerto Rico	PRI								1	2
Qatar	QAT	486,484	16,888	685	23.78	0.001	0.99	66.19	2	0
Romania	ROU	3,301,662	17,163	67,310	349.89	0.02	0.43	74.64	2	2
Russia	RUS	21,408,756	14,670	385,083	263.87	0.018	0.6	52.08	1	1
Rwanda	RWA	132,811	1026	1467	11.33	0.011	0.82	62.5	1	2
Saint Kitts and Nevis	KNA	6560	12,333	46	86.48	0.007	0.64			
Saint Lucia	LCA	29,736	16,193	409	222.73	0.014	0.33			
Saint Martin	MAF									
Saint Pierre and Miquelon	SPM									
Saint Vincent and the Grenadines	VCT	9500	8562	116	104.55	0.012	0.34			
Samoa	WSM	15,970	8145	29	14.79	0.002	1.18			
San Marino	SMR	22,615	66,637	120	353.59	0.005	0.78	69.64	1	2
Sao Tome and Principe	STP	6279	2865	77	35.13	0.012	0.58			
Saudi Arabia	SAU	826,516	2374	9496	27.28	0.011	0.77	62.62	2	1
Senegal	SEN	88,891	531	1968	11.75	0.022	0.12	45.24	0	0
Serbia	SRB	2,435,177	27,871	17,471	199.96	0.007	0.39	62.14	2	1
Seychelles	SYC	50,355	51,204	172	174.90	0.003	0.87	33.93	2	0
Sierra Leone	SLE	7760	97	126	1.58	0.016	0.48	43.45	0	0
Singapore	SGP	2,189,349	37,420	1709	29.21	0.001	0.88	60.36	2	2

Continued

TABLE 2.1 Select COVID-19 indicators for countries in the World, all health indicators as of December 31, 2022, population vaccination rate (at least one dose) as of February 2023, and government restrictions and income support and relief as of December 31, 2020 (for last three measures: 0 = no support or relief; 1 = limited; 2 = extensive)—cont'd

Country	Code	Cases	Cases/100K pop	Deaths	Deaths/100K pop	Case fatality (%)	Vaccination rate (%)	Gov Restrictions Index	Gov income support	Gov debt relief
Sint Maarten	SXM									
Slovakia	SVK	2,654,526	48,844	20,783	382.41	0.008	0.52	67.5	2	2
Slovenia	SVN	1,288,339	61,972	6970	335.27	0.005	0.61	75.48	2	1
Solomon Islands	SLB	24,575	3765	153	23.44	0.006	0.53	30.95	0	0
Somalia	SOM	27,300	172	1361	8.56	0.05	0.45	36.31	0	0
South Africa	ZAF	4,046,603	6823	102,568	172.94	0.025	0.4	55.95	1	2
South Sudan	SSD	18,368	164	138	1.23	0.008	0.19	39.29	0	0
Spain	ESP	13,651,239	29,197	116,658	249.51	0.009	0.88	71.31	2	2
Sri Lanka	LKA	671,813	3137	16,814	78.52	0.025	0.8	75.3	0	2
Sudan	SDN	63,663	145	4992	11.38	0.078	0.24	26.19	1	0
Suriname	SUR	81,581	13,907	1393	237.46	0.017	0.46	63.69	1	2
Swaziland	SWZ							53.57	1	1
Sweden	SWE	2,651,702	26,256	21,364	211.54	0.008	0.77	61.79	2	1
Switzerland	CHE	4,373,011	50,529	14,157	163.58	0.003	0.7	62.14	2	0
Syria	SYR	57,423	328	3163	18.07	0.055	0.17	34.82	0	0
Taiwan	TWN	8,498,195	35,679	14,722	61.81	0.002	0.92	35.12	1	1
Tajikistan	TJK	17,786	186	125	1.31	0.007	0.55	38.69	1	1
Tanzania	TZA	42,111	70	845	1.41	0.02	0.48	9.23	0	0
Thailand	THA	4,718,908	6760	33,505	48.00	0.007	0.82	57.44	2	2
Timor-Leste	TLS	23,379	1774	138	10.47	0.006	0.66			
Togo	TGO	39,339	475	290	3.50	0.007	0.27	61.9	1	2
Tonga	TON	16,182	15,305	12	11.35	0.001		36.31	0	0
Trinidad and Tobago	TTO	185,708	13,270	4271	305.18	0.023	0.54	63.1	1	0

Continued

TABLE 2.1 Select COVID-19 indicators for countries in the World, all health indicators as of December 31, 2022, population vaccination rate (at least one dose) as of February 2023, and government restrictions and income support and relief as of December 31, 2020 (for last three measures: 0 = no support or relief; 1 = limited; 2 = extensive)—cont'd

Country	Code	Cases	Cases/100K pop	Deaths	Deaths/100K pop	Case fatality (%)	Vaccination rate (%)	Gov Restrictions Index	Gov income support	Gov debt relief
Tunisia	TUN	1,147,282	9708	29,272	247.68	0.026	0.61	63.69	1	2
Turkey	TUR	16,919,638	20,062	101,203	120.00	0.006	0.69	77.68	2	2
Turkmenistan	TKM							47.02	0	1
Tuvalu	TUV									
Uganda	UGA	169,810	371	3630	7.94	0.021	0.41	49.7	0	0
Ukraine	UKR	5,657,698	12,937	118,613	271.22	0.021	0.36	57.74	1	1
United Arab Emirates	ARE	1,046,170	10,578	2348	23.74	0.002	1.01	52.62	0	2
United Kingdom	GBR	24,318,154	35,823	213,892	315.08	0.009	0.79	76.31	2	2
US	USA	99,892,513	30,319	1,087,410	330.05	0.011	0.81	69.29	2	1
Uruguay	URY	998,047	28,732	7548	217.29	0.008	0.86	64.29	2	2
Uzbekistan	UZB	248,625	743	1637	4.89	0.007	0.63	42.26	1	1
Vanuatu	VUT	11,981	4091	14	4.78	0.001	0.49	23.81	0	1
Venezuela	VEN	549,085	1931	5830	20.50	0.011	0.78	66.07	0	2
Vietnam	VNM	11,522,927	11,838	43,179	44.36	0.004	0.93	59.52	1	1
Virgin Islands	VGB									
West Bank and Gaza	WBG	703,228	13,785	5708	111.89	0.008	0.39			
Yemen	YEM	11,945	40	2159	7.24	0.181	0.03	25.6	0	0
Zambia	ZMB	333,746	1815	4019	21.86	0.012	0.59	52.38	0	1
Zimbabwe	ZWE	259,356	1745	5622	37.83	0.022	0.44	55.95	1	0

(Sources: Authors' table based on data from Johns Hopkins University Center for Systems Science and Engineering, and Our World in Data, https://ourworldindata.org.)

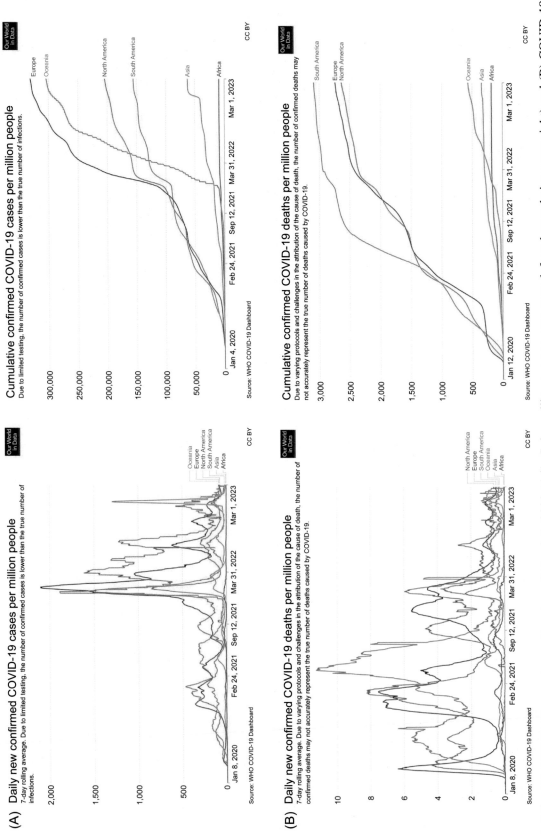

FIG. 2.2 (A) COVID-19 cases by continent as of March 1, 2023 (daily 7-day rolling average new cases left and cumulative cases right) and (B) COVID-19 deaths by continent as of March 1, 2023 (daily 7-day rolling average new cases left and cumulative cases right). (*Sources: Our World in Data, https:// ourworldindata.org/.*)

(A)

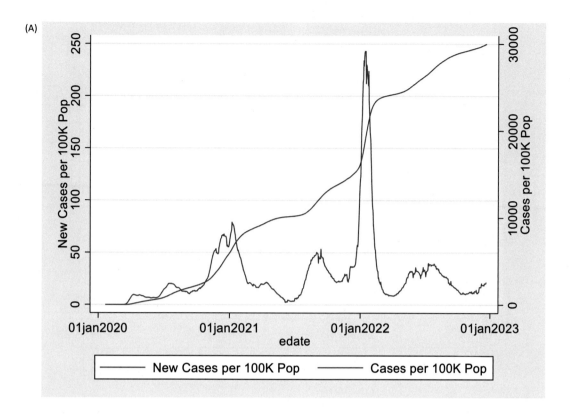

(B)

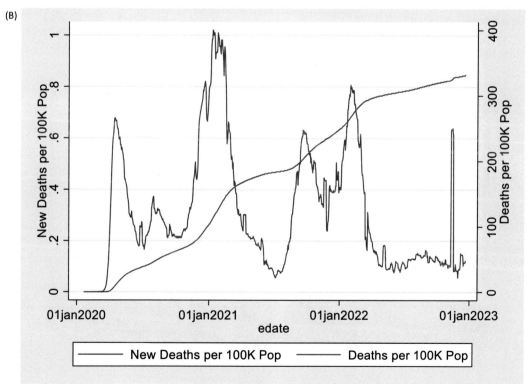

FIG. 2.3 (A) Confirmed COVID-19 new cases per 100K population in the US (in blue) and confirmed total cases per 100K population (in red) 7-day moving average, up to January 1, 2023; (B) Confirmed COVID-19 new deaths per 100K population in the US (in blue) and confirmed total deaths per 100K population (in red) 7-day moving average, up to January 1, 2023. *(Sources: Authors' calculations based on the Opportunity Insights data, https:// tracktherecovery.org/.)*

(Continued)

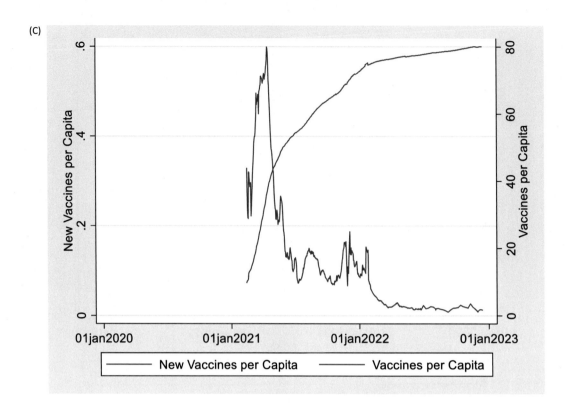

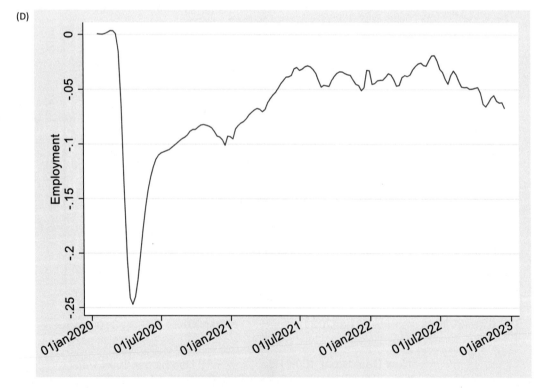

FIG. 2.3, CONT'D (C) New completed vaccinations per capita in the US (blue) and total vaccinations per capita (red) up to February 22, 2023; (D) Employment rate in the US indexed to January 4–31, 2020, data series goes up to February 22, 2023. *(Sources: Authors' calculations based on the Opportunity Insights data, https://tracktherecovery.org/.)*

(Continued)

(E)

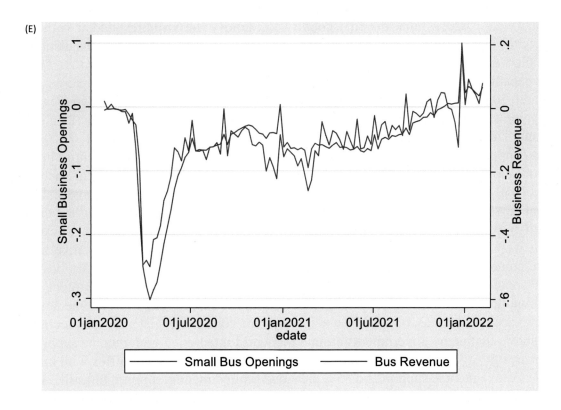

(F)

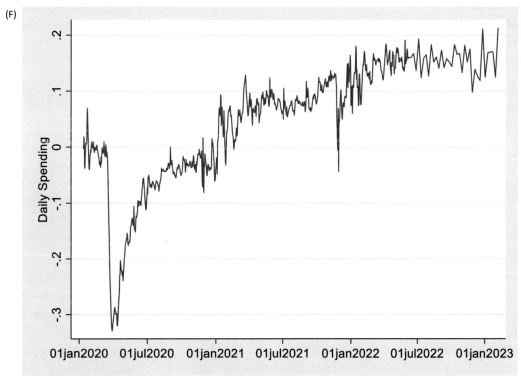

FIG. 2.3, CONT'D (E) The change in the number of open small businesses (blue) and change in net business revenue for small businesses in the US indexed to January 4–31, 2020, series goes up to January 1, 2022; and (F) Daily average consumer credit and debt credit card spending in the US indexed to January 4–31, 2020; series goes up to January 1, 2023. *(Sources: Authors' calculations based on the Opportunity Insights data, https://tracktherecovery.org/.)*

On January 23, 2020, China, the first country to identify the virus responded with very strict lockdown of the city of Wuhan and the surrounding Hubei province and strict social distancing measures, which were lifted only in staggered dates between March 13 and April 8. This type of lockdown became the standard adopted by most countries as COVID-19 spread across the world. By late March 2020, about one-fourth of the world's population was under lockdown measures given that no vaccine or treatment existed and this was the only way to contain the virus (Demirgüç-Kunt, Lokshin, and Torre, 2020; Hale, Angrist, Kira, Petherick, Phillips, and Webster, 2020). Together with lockdowns, governments imposed restrictions on social gatherings, nonessential business closures, school closures, and travel restrictions, resulting in a very large package of such measures, trying to keep people isolated as per Fig. 2.1C. Other countries introduced extensive testing, particularly Asian advanced nations, such as South Korea, Taiwan, and Singapore, that had the means to help identify potentially infected individuals and to control the further spread. Lockdowns and restrictions were relaxed only after record vaccine developments resulted in positive trial results, and people could get vaccinated, which happened late in 2020. Fig. 2.1D shows a heat map with percent of population that got at least one dose of the COVID-19 vaccine to protect against the disease around the world as of February 23, 2023. Most developed and high-income countries registered high vaccination rates, but middle and low-income countries registered low vaccination rates. Fig. 2.1E shows that many governments around the world intervened with income support and debt relief measures as of December 31, 2020. For example, about 27% of countries with known status provided extensive income support and 45% provided limited income support, but still 34% of countries had no support at all for the ailing households and businesses, while a significant percent had no status known and could be reasonably assumed to not have had any such support provided. For debt relief measures, 41% of countries with known status had extensive such relief or forbearances to households and businesses, while another 30% of countries had limited such relief, while all remaining provided no known relief programs to support the economy.

Importantly, the severe restrictions and social distancing measures have had a systemic impact on the economies around the globe. Government actions, such as requiring business closing and restricting travel as well as the reduced aggregate demand for goods and services by consumers and businesses in reaction to the spread of the disease, have plunged many economies into historic recessions. In the US alone, the measured unemployment rate increased to 16% in May, while estimated annualized GDP dropped by 33% by the end of Q2, marking the fastest descent of the US economy in history (see Fig. 2.4). Similar dramatic declines in GDP were recorded around the world in 2020, with countries in more fragile financial situations experiencing even greater declines. Thus, the COVID-19 crisis is different from other crises in many regards. It was a rare unanticipated black-swan event of historic proportions in many countries, causing great economic damage through no fault of participants in real economy, banking sector, or financial markets. The severe declines in the first parts of the crisis, however, were followed by fast recoveries, particularly in advanced economies, as news about the vaccines' development and relaxation about some restrictions stirred back economic activity and growth (see Figs. 2.4 and 2.5). The COVID-19 crisis still continues as of this writing with the virus experiencing different waves, evolving into different variants, and causing havoc more in some areas than in others, i.e., more localized outbreaks, but due to vaccines and treatments developed, the people became more resilient and less deaths were recorded worldwide. Economic effects remain uneven across countries to date, with developed countries having rebounded faster. The COVID-19 crisis has triggered a large amount of research work. In the later chapters of this book, we will review research literature on the COVID-19 crisis and its effects in the US and around the world.

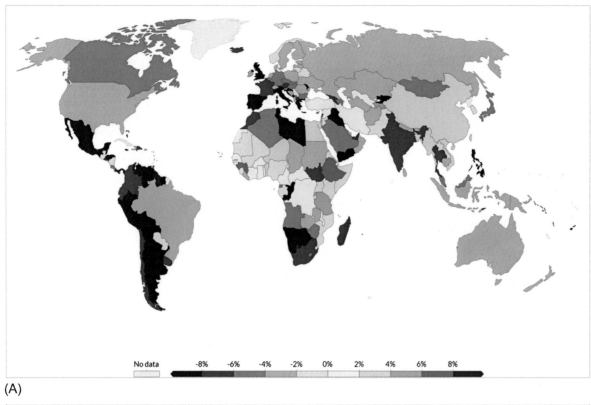

(A)

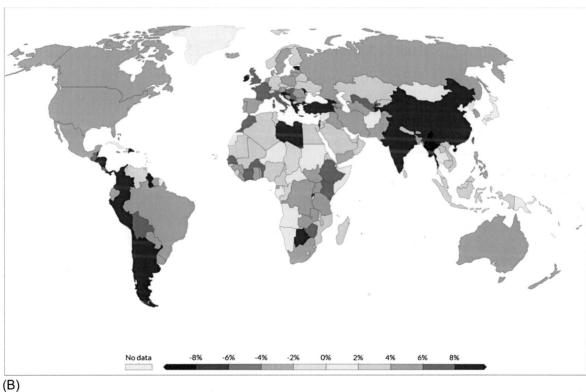

(B)

FIG. 2.4   (A) COVID-19 change in real GDP in the World in 2020 and (B) COVID-19 change in real GDP in the World in 2021. *(Source: IMF, https://www.imf.org/external/datamapper.)*

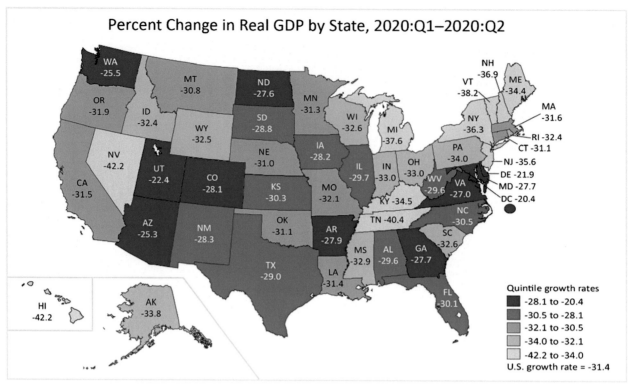

U.S. Bureau of Economic Analysis

(A)

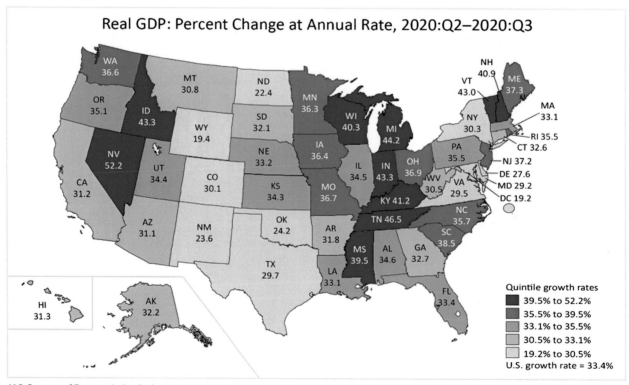

U.S. Bureau of Economic Analysis

(B)

FIG. 2.5 (A) COVID-19 change in real GDP in the US in 2020:Q2 and (B) COVID-19 change in real GDP in the US in 2020:Q3. *(Source: U.S. Bureau of Economic Analysis.)*

2.3 Other health crises: Justinian Plague, Black Death, Spanish Flu, Yellow Fever, Acquired Immunodeficiency Syndrome (AIDS), H1N1, Ebola Virus, and the Opioid Epidemic

When viewed in a broad historical context, the COVID-19 pandemic is but one of many health crises causing widespread damage over time. Two other major premodern pandemics, the Plague of Justinian and the Black Death, are also characterized by very high mortality rates and associated economic impacts on wages, prices, and growth. In these pandemics, there were also short-term market collapses (Jedwab, Johnson, and Koyama, 2022). These pandemics are also characterized by a lack of nearly any public health response, or any economic policy response.

In sharp contrast, more modern pandemics starting in the 20th century, such as the Spanish Flu of 1918, featured distinct and rapid policy responses designed to contain the devastation of the disease. These policies include the closure of schools and churches, banning of mass gatherings, mandating mask wearing, case isolation, and disinfection measures (e.g., Bootsma and Ferguson, 2007). The Spanish Flu is also associated with economic decline, with GDP declining 6% and consumption declining 8% as a result of it (e.g., Barro, Ursúa, and Weng, 2020). Several smaller pandemics in recent history are also associated with short-term economic declines. These include H1N1, SARS, and AIDS, which are discussed below.

2.3.1 Justinian Plague

"Justinian Plague" is a pandemic of bubonic plague, also known as "the Plague of Justinian" or "the Justinian's Plague." It is the world's first "plague" pandemic, and one of humanity's first major disease outbreak, with the first cases recorded in the summer of the year 541. Caused by the bacterium *Yersinia pestis*, the disease is named after the Byzantine Emperor Justinian I who, according to contemporary historical accounts, contracted the disease and eventually recovered (Stathakopoulos, 2018).

The disease was first reported in an Egyptian port town known as Pelusium. Like other pandemics, it quickly began to spread, and 1 year later in 542, the disease had spread through Syria, the Arabian Peninsula, Anatolia, Greece, Italy, and North Africa. By 543, it had spread to Gaul (modern-day France), and a year later, is recorded to have reached Ireland. It is also said to have reached nearly as far east as modern-day India, with the true extent of its range remaining unknown. The disease would continue to recur for about 200 more years into the middle of the 8th century (Eisenberg and Mordechai, 2020). The Justinian Plague is estimated to have killed 15 million to 100 million people during its two centuries of recurrence and about 25%–60% of Europe's population at the time of the outbreak (Mordechai, Eisenberg, Newfield, Izdebski, Kay, and Poinar, 2019). In the city of Constantinople, the hardest hit city of the pandemic, historical accounts record the death rate being as high as 5000 per day (Mordechai and Eisenberg, 2019).

Given such a high death toll, widespread economic devastation may also be assumed, but accounts are limited. Recently, economic historians pay increasing attention to the construction of GDP and wage estimates for premodern economies to understand better their structural characteristics as well as their standard of living. Recent evidence uses data to better understand the overall impact of the Justinian Plague. Pamuk and Shatzmiller (2014) analyzed price and wage data from medieval Arabian sources in order to estimate the true effect of the plague, collecting data from the period 700–1000 AD on the wages of day laborers throughout the Arab world. The wage and price data allows the authors to empirically examine the impact of the Justinian Plague on premodern Arabian economy. The data are consistent with a significant demographic decline and labor shortages. What occurred in the aftermath is predicted by economic theory: the purchasing power of wages increased to previously unseen high levels. As nominal wages rose, relative prices also moved against agricultural products, and, as such, the prices of wheat decreased. Overall, these factors led to higher levels of consumption and increased standard of living.

2.3.2 Black Death

The Black Death is the largest demographic shock in European history. In October of 1347, ships arrived in the port of Messina, Sicily, carrying Genoese merchants from the Crimean port of Kaffa. These merchants carry the first recorded cases of the Black Death. The bacterium that caused the Justinian Plague, *Y. pestis*, likely continued to evolve within animal populations in Europe, only to be reintroduced to Europe as the Black Death. Similar to the Justinian Plague, the Black Death likely also traveled along medieval trade routes.

The mortality rate of the Black Death was exceptionally high, around 40%–60% of the population died from it (Benedictow, 2004). The death rate was likely so high given the abundance of black rats, which acted as hosts, as well as generally poor hygiene. Jedwab, Johnson, and Koyama (2022) used data on wage, price, and GDP from England, northern Italy, and Spain at the time of the Black Death in order to analyze the economic effects of the pandemic. In the very short run, the pandemic caused a breakdown in markets and economic activity. Agricultural production stopped, and the demand for new buildings plummeted. Wages typically increased; for example, between 1348 and 1350, the wages of unskilled workers in Florence increased 87% and the wages of skilled workers increased by 27%. However, both England and France passed legislation limiting the rapidly rising wages of their workers (Jedwab, Johnson, and Koyama, 2022). Evidence suggests that prices around Europe also increased by 19%–27% (e.g., Álvarez-Nogal, Prados de la Escosura, and Santiago-Caballero, 2020).

As premodern pandemics, the Justinian Plague and Black Death preceded the rise of modern epidemiological practices, such as consistent quarantining measures and government containment policies, such as the banning of mass gatherings. These also existed before reliable medical treatment practices, which likely led to an inflated death rate. One clear difference between modern and premodern pandemics is that premodern pandemics have significantly higher death rates, about 40%–60% for the Black Death. This led to labor shortages and increased wages in the long run.

2.3.3 Spanish Flu

The Spanish Flu of 1918 is the most recent significant pandemic prior to COVID-19. Also called the "Great Influenza" pandemic, the health crisis lasted from 1918 to 1920, and coincided with the World War I. The war served to exacerbate the pandemic, given the large-scale movements across countries (Barro, Ursúa, and Weng, 2020). The pandemic occurred in waves. The first wave was in Spring 1918, with the deadliest in the winter of 1918, and a third for the rest of 1919. In 1918, Reuters reported "a strange form of disease of epidemic character has appeared in Madrid. The epidemic is of a mild nature; no deaths having been reported" (Trilla, Trilla, and Daer, 2008). The Spanish Flu would go on to kill so many that it was referred to as the single most deadly event in human history in terms of its body count (Shanks and Brundage, 2012). Estimates vary, but more conservative estimates suggest the pandemic killed around 40 million people, or about 2.1% of the global population at that time (Barro, Ursúa, and Weng, 2020). To put this in perspective, a death rate of 2.1% and the infection rate of the Spanish Flu pandemic would correspond to 150 million deaths worldwide, with 6.8 million in the US. Other estimates put the total deaths as a result of the Spanish Flu at around 50 million to 100 million around the world (Morens, Taubenberger, Harvey, and Memoli, 2010).

Recent research has attempted to measure the economic impacts of this crisis. Barro, Ursúa, and Weng (2020) examined the effects of the Spanish Flu on GDP, rates of return, and inflation rates. Using data on flu deaths and financials, the authors found that the flu likely accounted for declines in GDP and consumption in the average country by 6% and 8%, respectively. The evidence also suggests that higher flu death rates decreased returns on stocks and short-term government bills.

There are also several more subtle, long-term economic consequences of the Spanish Flu. Almond and Mazumder (2005) and Almond (2006) investigated the impact of the Spanish Flu on the lifetime health of cohorts in utero at the time of the Spanish Flu, when their mothers may have been subject to contracting the disease. Using data from the Survey of Income and Program Participation (SIPP), the authors found that the cohorts in utero have impaired health outcomes relative to cohorts born just before or just after the pandemic. The health crisis significantly reduced educational resources and increased the likelihood of physical disability, resulting in lower incomes and socioeconomic status. Beach, Ferrie, and Saavedra (2018) provided corroborating evidence for these findings and also found evidence that these unfavorable outcomes from the health crisis persist after controlling for parental characteristics. Fletcher (2014) adds evidence that the flu worsens the effects of cardiovascular health disease and educational outcomes. Parman (2015) further found that the Spanish Flu affected resource allocation among children. Families with at least one child born during the crisis allotted more resources to older children; as a result, older siblings had higher educational achievements.

Karlsson, Nilsson, and Pichler (2014) examined the economic effects of the pandemic in Sweden. Their evidence suggested that the pandemic led to significant increases in poor house rates, consistent with increases in poverty. They also found evidence that capital returns decrease, but no evidence that earnings changed as a result of the pandemic.

Basco, Domènech, and Rosés (2021) also examined the economic effects of the Spanish Flu and find a distinct, negative effect of the pandemic on wages. This effect was also greater in urban areas. Reminiscent of the COVID-19 pandemic, the authors also found the strongest declines in wages for "non-essential" services, such as shoemakers. In contrast to prior studies, the authors failed to find a relationship between the flu pandemic and returns to capital.

Correia, Luck, and Verner (1918) examined the effectiveness of nonpharmaceutical interventions (NPIs), such as social distancing, on economic activity in curtailing the effects of the Spanish Flu pandemic, with potential relevance to COVID-19. They found that the NPIs were associated with short-run economic disruptions, and that these disruptions were similar across cities with strict and lenient NPIs. Looking into the medium- and long term, the authors found that NPIs appear to be associated with better economic outcomes. The authors suggested that NPIs can curtail cases without disrupting economic activity.

Clay, Lewis, and Severnini (2018) examined the effect of air pollution on the pandemic mortality during the Spanish Flu. The authors measured the overall air pollution in US cities in 1918 based on the burning of coal. Their results suggest that air pollution contributed significantly to pandemic mortality. Cities with poorer air quality experienced tens of thousands of excess deaths than those with better air quality, also with potential relevance to the COVID-19 pandemic.

Velde (2022) explored the effect of government interventions to contain the contagion on economic factors, such as labor supply. Using cross-sectional, high-frequency data, the author found that the epidemic affected the labor supply briefly with no ensuing significant spillovers. At that time, most of the economic downturn was from the end of the World War I, rather than the pandemic itself. The author found that the government interventions designed to contain the spread of the influenza reduced mortality at very little economic cost. This was potentially due to the reduced infections mitigating the impact on the labor force.

Basco, Domenech, and Rosés (2021) examined two main economic questions—How did the Spanish Flu impact the returns on the factors of production? Are these effects persistent in the years that followed? The authors examined within-country variation in death rates from the pandemic in Spain. They found that the effect of the Spanish Flu on wages is large, but short-lived. The magnitude of the effect is as large as approximately a 30% decline. In addition, the effect on real estate prices driven by the economic recovery is positive.

Aassve, Alfani, Gandolfi, and Le Moglie (2021) explored the effect of the Spanish Flu on individual behavior, with implications for long-term economic development. The authors found that individual exposure to the Spanish Flu leads to a distinct decrease in an individual's social trust. In this case, the failure of government institutions and health services led civil societies to a level of generalized suspicion, which increased the damage to social trust, suggesting that poorly executed government intervention may lead to long-term damage to the social fabric.

Percoco (2016) examined the effect of the Spanish Flu on the accumulation of human capital in Italy. This is another example of how exposure to significant diseases in utero may have long-term implications for an individual's cognitive abilities. The author found that exposure to the disease led to a decrease in an individual's schooling by about 0.15–0.44 years, depending on the region. This study provides another example of how pandemics may have both short-term and long-term impacts, providing additional justification for government intervention.

Rao and Greve (2018) examined the impact of the Spanish Flu on community resilience in Norway, and found that communities exposed to the disease had difficulties in forming new retail cooperatives after the epidemic. Community members became labeled as threats, providing another example of how pandemics may foster distrust and lead to breakdowns in social norms.

2.3.4 Yellow Fever

Yellow Fever repeatedly appeared in the US in the 18th and 19th centuries, causing approximately 100,000–150,000 deaths in American port cities, according to the CDC. Although the vaccine has reduced its impact, there are still around 200,000 cases of Yellow Fever leading to 30,000 deaths worldwide every year (World Health Organization, 2014).

Saavedra (2017) found that Yellow Fever significantly affects the occupational choices of individuals whose parents were exposed to this disease at a young age. They are less likely to become professionals but tend to work as unskilled and earn a relatively lower income. The author also found that this effect dissipates after 3–4 years.

Pritchett and Tunali (1995) confirmed that Yellow Fever mortality significantly decreased the birth rate in New Orleans around 1853. They further showed that after controlling for economic measures, including local poverty rate, and community immunization featured by the length of being a resident, this negative effect disappeared.

2.3.5 AIDS

The human immunodeficiency virus infection (HIV), the virus that causes AIDS diseases, had jumped from chimpanzees to humans sometime early in the 20th century. The earliest known case of HIV infection in humans is from a sample taken in 1959 from a man who had died in Kinshasa in what was then the Belgian Congo in Africa. AIDS was first recognized as a new disease in 1981, when increasing numbers of young homosexual men incurred unusual opportunistic infections and rare malignancies (CDC, 1981; Sharp and Hahn, 2011). The virus, now known as immunodeficiency virus type 1 (HIV-1), was subsequently identified as the cause of what has since become one of the most devastating infectious diseases to have emerged in recent history. HIV-1 spreads by various routes, but is primarily a sexually transmitted disease. Since its first identification, approximately three decades ago, the pandemic form of HIV has infected at least 60 million people and caused more than 25 million deaths (Merson, O'Malley, Serwadda, and Apisuk, 2008). Developing countries have experienced the greatest HIV/AIDS morbidity and mortality, with the highest prevalence rates recorded in young adults in sub-Saharan Africa. Although antiretroviral treatment has reduced the toll of AIDS-related deaths, access to therapy is not universal, and the prospects of curative treatments and an effective vaccine are uncertain (Barouch, 2008). Thus, AIDS may continue to pose a significant public health threat for decades to come.

Bloom and Carliner (1988) ask the question: How large of an economic burden does AIDS place on American society? This study examined how this burden is shared among AIDS patients and their families, insurance companies, taxpayers, and hospitals. The authors calculate the overall lifetime cost of care for an AIDS victim and then scale this figure by the total number of AIDS victims, thus calculating the aggregate cost of AIDS care in the US over the lifetime of the patients. In addition to this, the authors calculate the indirect costs of AIDS, or the forgone earnings of each victim due to disability and premature death. The authors estimated the cost of AIDS to be about $22 billion between 1981 and 1991. The overall economic impact in the US is small relative to total healthcare spending. The authors estimated this cost is much higher for certain cities, such as San Francisco and New York. Finally, the authors highlighted that these costs are much greater for those without adequate insurance.

Rosen, Simon, Vincent, MacLeod, Fox, and Thea (2003) examined the AIDS pandemic in the broad context of globalization and supply chains. The authors argued that AIDS should be a major concern for the executives of public firms. AIDS has a particularly devastating impact on developing economies because it kills young and middle-aged people in their most productive years as employees and customers. In this way, AIDS erodes globalization by driving up health-care costs, decreasing productivity, increasing absenteeism, and increasing employee turnover. The authors also acknowledged the costs of lower morale in firms in developing countries impacted by AIDS. To provide evidence for the cost of AIDS for globalized firms, the authors examined six public firms with subsidiaries in countries severely impacted by AIDS. Given the total annual cost represented as a percentage of salaries and wages, authors estimated the AIDS "tax" to be about 0.4%–5.9%.

Thirumurthy, Zivin, and Goldstein (2008) examined the value of AIDS treatment programs on the labor supply in western Kenya. The authors studied the application of antiretroviral therapy, which is a staple in the policy response to fight the global impact of AIDS. They focused on the degree to which this particular medical intervention affects labor supply of treated patients and their household members. The authors found that within 6 months of treatment initiation, there is a 20% increase in the likelihood of participating in the labor force and a 35% increase in the weekly hours worked. This research highlighted the importance of widespread treatment in mitigating the economic and financial consequences of the AIDS pandemic.

2.3.6 H1N1

The H1N1 pandemic emerged at the end of 2009 and was declared by the WHO as the first flu pandemic in the recent half a century. According to CDC estimates, there were 60.8 million cases in the US and approximately 15,000–57,500 deaths globally during the first year the virus circulated. While some researchers document valuable lessons from this pandemic from the medical perspective (e.g., Condon and Sinha, 2010; Lai and Tan, 2012), there are also fruitful studies on the economic and financial outcomes for firms and countries.

Duarte, Kadiyala, Masters, and Powell (2017) studied how the H1N1 pandemic directly influences the labor system in the short term in Chile using sick-day leave data from the private health insurance system. They found that the spread of the virus significantly damages the productivity of the sector with an estimated loss of approximately $6.7 million in the private sector. An extrapolation analysis on the US estimated a loss of approximately $2 billion in labor productivity. Their findings suggested that a rapid vaccine program would have been cost-effective in saving work loss.

Adbi, Chatterjee, and Mishra (2022) studied the effect of H1N1 on firms' business environment, especially for multinational enterprises (MNEs). Compared to domestic firms, MNEs lost a relatively larger market share in areas with lower government health spending and poorer federal alignment. Furthermore, they showed that the decrease in market shares is due to the domestic firms' diversifying activities, and this firm reaction is not related to the preshock region coverage of MNEs and domestic firms.

2.3.7 Ebola Virus

The largest Ebola Virus epidemic identified by the WHO on March 23, 2014, marks a health crisis influential to not only West Africa but also to other geographically distant countries. The first case was reported in December 2013, in Guinea, and the virus later spread to seven more countries: Italy, Mali, Nigeria, Senegal, Spain, the UK, and the US, according to CDC. Guinea was declared Ebola-free in June 2016 after several other adjacent countries. In total, the outbreak ended with more than 28,600 cases and 11,325 deaths within 2 1/2 years after the first identified case.

Del Giudice and Paltrinieri (2017) studied the reactions of retail investors on mutual fund inflows and outflows using Ebola as a major event. They argued that mutual funds, which focus on African countries, were more likely to be affected by the Ebola outbreak in 2014 and found that retail investors overreact to the crisis by withdrawing their shares in these mutual funds after controlling for fund performance and market returns. This overreaction is exaggerated by media coverage as more articles reporting on Ebola are correlated with higher fund outflows. As a result, fund managers have to balance their portfolios and modify their equity positions although their judgments on the stocks do not change. These activities eventually decrease the investment inflow into African stock markets and affect economic development.

Christensen, Dube, Haushofer, Siddiqi, and Voors (2021) found a causal relationship between a resilient health system and epidemic outcomes. Before the outbreak of the 2014 Ebola crisis, they conducted a random field experiment on how individuals' perception of public health systems influences their behaviors, especially trust in the system during a health crisis. Even before the outbreak, there was a large decrease in new-born mortality under stronger community supervision and higher clinic visits and satisfaction. During the Ebola crisis, intervened groups also report more cases and significantly fewer deaths. Their findings suggested that improving the accountability of the health system provides benefits during both normal times and crises.

Kostova, Cassell, Redd, Williams, Singh, Martel, and Bunnell (2019) studied the spillover effect of a geographically remote health crisis on the US economy using the Ebola outbreak. They found that the peak negative effect in 2014 was an approximately $1.08 billion reduction in US exports to Ebola-affected areas and increased job losses related to these export products by 13,000 in 2 years.

Maphanga and Henama (2019) found that part of the negative economic influence of the Ebola outbreak is channeled through tourism, including fewer flights and other countries' travel warnings. These adverse impacts appeared to persist in the years immediately following Ebola.

Adegun (2014) studied another channel of the economic impacts of the Ebola outbreak and showed that the trade channel plays an important role for African countries, especially for those suffering the most from the disease. The noniron ore GDP of Sierra Leone is estimated to be 4.5% and total GDP goes up to 7.7%, compared to the precrisis estimated 8.9%; the total loss being about $142 million. For countries with a high number of Ebola cases, as much as $809 million is forecast to be lost due to the outbreak.

Finally, Omoleke, Mohammed, and Saidu (2016) reviewed over 50 articles published in around 2014 on the outbreak of the Ebola Virus. They concluded that this outbreak is driven by excessive human activities, which destroy the forest ecosystem and weaken sustainable local economies.

2.3.8 Opioid Epidemic

Drug overdose death is one of the leading causes of accidental death in the US. Two-thirds of them involved an opioid. As per the CDC, nearly 500,000 people died from an opioid overdose, including both prescription and illicit drugs over 1999–2019, and over 130 people die every day from an opioid overdose. There are three known distinct waves in the opioid crisis in the US. The first wave began with increased prescribing of opioids in the 1990s, with overdose deaths involving prescription opioids (natural and semisynthetic opioids and methadone) increasing since at least 1999. The second wave began in 2010, with rapid increases in overdose deaths involving heroin. The third wave began in 2013, with significant increases in overdose deaths involving synthetic opioids, particularly those involving illicitly manufactured fentanyl. The market for illicitly manufactured fentanyl continues to change, and it can be found in combination with heroin, counterfeit pills, and cocaine. In October 2019, the Trump administration and the Department for Health and Human Services officially declared the Opioid Epidemic a public emergency.

Empirical studies have investigated the impact of the Opioid Epidemic on socioeconomic and financial outcomes, such as labor market participation, firm values, municipal finance, and household finance. First, several papers documented that local opioid abuse also has a negative relationship with labor force participation (Krueger, 2017; Aliprantis, Fee, and Schweitzer, 2019). Ouimet, Simintzi, and Ye (2020) found that increased opioid prescriptions are associated with worse subsequent individual employment outcomes, which in turn, affect a firm's growth. Cornaggia, Hund, Nguyen, and Ye (2022) and Li and Zhu (2019) found negative impacts of the local opioid abuse on municipal bonds resulting in higher offering yield spreads for local municipal bond issuers, which impede municipalities' ability to provide the necessary public services and infrastructure. Custodio, Cvijanovic, and Wiedemann (2022) found declines in home prices in the areas more affected by the Opioid Epidemic. Agarwal, Li, Roman, and Sorokina (2022) examined the effects of the Opioid Epidemic on consumer finance such as delinquency, credit supply, and bank consumer portfolio risk. They found unfavorable credit consequences for consumers living in high-exposed areas and banks operating there. Namely, low-credit-score consumers in higher exposed areas were more likely to default on their credit card debt, auto loans, and first mortgages and banks suffered from higher nonperforming loans and net charge-offs across consumer loans. In reaction, banks contracted credit supply in more opioid-affected areas: they applied stricter credit card offer terms and were less likely to send credit offers to consumers. Riskier, minority, and younger consumers were more affected by this contraction. Jansen (2020) also found that the Opioid Epidemic leads to increased loan defaults for subprime auto loans.

Some epidemiological studies examined the causes of the Opioid Epidemic from socioeconomic factors, government policies, and financial forces. Ma (2021) studied the causes of the Opioid Epidemic from the finance perspective. Using the geographic variation on payday lending access, the author found that access to expensive credits affects the opioid pandemic from the finance perspective. From the policy perspective, prescription drug monitoring programs (PDMPs) were introduced, aiming to prevent the Opioid Epidemic. However, empirical research generally shows mixed findings about these laws in combating the Opioid Epidemic. Some studies found moderate or no effects on opioid initiation, use, or abuse, while some find sustained reductions in opioid prescriptions and abuse or significant declines in opioid-related deaths. For example, Kaestner and Ziedan (2019) and Bao, Pan, Taylor, Radakrishnan, Luo, and Pincus (2016) found that PDMPs reduced prescription rates, but did not help reduce deaths or improve socioeconomic outcomes. In contrast, Cornaggia, Hund, Nguyen, and Ye (2022) found that PDMPs reduced deaths and also partially reversed some negative effects on municipal finance. Agarwal, Li, Roman, and Sorokina (2022) ran a horse race considering several different opioid laws attempting to address prescription abuse and deaths from opioids and found that PDMPs, laws limiting opioid prescriptions directly and triplicate prescriptions (requirements to save the prescriptions in three copies that go to different parties) helped reduce prescriptions and prescription opioid deaths as well as reverse some unfavorable credit effects on credit supply to consumers in the credit card market.

2.3.9 Studies of multiple health crises

Finally, several research studies compared and contrasted multiple health crises in pursuit of more general lessons. Ma, Rogers, and Zhou (2020) studied the 1968 flu, SARS, H1N1, Ebola, and Zika and found that the economic output begins recovering quickly, but economic growth remains weak for long periods relative to precrisis levels. They also found that unemployment recovered but was uneven, as workers with less education and female workers tend to have more difficulties finding jobs. Health crises also create similar economic problems for the trading partners of the infected nations. The authors also found that stronger government aid programs, especially expenditures on healthcare, which started right after the outbreaks, are effective in mitigating these negative impacts of health crises.

Tut (2021) studied how companies react to various health crises by holding cash with a text-based firm risk exposure measure. Corporates might hold more cash due to return uncertainties. The author studied SARS, H1N1, Ebola, Zika, and COVID-19 and found evidence of such cash hoarding, and identified that the channel has negative sentiment around such health crises. Donadelli, Kizys, and Riedel (2017) investigated how investor mood from the WHO virus alerts is reflected in market equity prices and returns. They found that negative shocks from SARS, H1N1, polio, and Ebola increased returns on pharmaceutical stocks and yield higher abnormal returns for smaller firms.

Adda (2016) evaluated the implications of several policies on virus control, including school closures and public transportation system disclosure, using data from France about influenza, gastroenteritis, and chickenpox. The author found that developed transportation networks and close trading relations help explain the increasing rates of virus infections. Policies limiting interpersonal contact has different degrees of effectiveness in reducing the infection rates, depending on the characteristics of the diseases.

Hassan, Hollander, Van Lent, and Tahoun (2020) constructed a textual pattern measure to automatically capture and categorize firms' concerns regarding virus outbreaks globally, based on their quarterly earnings' conference calls. While SARS and H1N1 affected a large scale of firms, these firms are relatively limited in certain countries and industries. However, the COVID-19 pandemic is mentioned by virtually all the firms from most countries. Another difference between the COVID-19 pandemic and previous outbreaks is that COVID-19 shows a concurrent shock both in demand and in supply for most industries whereas other crises primarily influence demand. They also provided evidence on how these risk factors, which are perceived from managers' discussions, explain the decisions of firms on employment and capital expenditures.

Finally, Baker, Bloom, Davis, Kost, Sammon, and Viratyosin (2020) compared the stock market influence of COVID-19 with previous disease outbreaks, including the Spanish Flu, Ebola, H1N1, and SARS. They developed a measure of Equity Market Volatility (EMV) and found that COVID-19 has greater market volatility effects than the prior health crises. Consistent with this finding, Schell, Wang, and Huynh (2020) also found that COVID-19 has greater negative effects on market returns than Ebola did.

References

Aassve, A., Alfani, G., Gandolfi, F., and Le Moglie, M. (2021). Epidemics and trust: The case of the Spanish Flu. *Health Economics*, *30*, 840–857.

Adbi, A., Chatterjee, C., and Mishra, A. (2022). How do MNEs and domestic firms respond locally to a global demand shock? Evidence from a pandemic. *Management Science*.

Adda, J. (2016). Economic activity and the spread of viral diseases: Evidence from high frequency data. *Quarterly Journal of Economics*, *131*, 891–941.

Adegun, O. (2014). The effects of Ebola virus on the economy of West Africa through the trade channel. *IOSR Journal of Humanities and Social Science*, *19*, 48–56.

Agarwal, S., Li, W., Roman, R., and Sorokina, N. (2022). *Opioid epidemic and consumer finance: Quo vadis?* Working Paper.

Aliprantis, D., Fee, K., and Schweitzer, M. (2019). *Opioids and the labor market*. Working Paper.

Almond, D. (2006). Is the 1918 influenza pandemic over? Long-term effects of in utero influenza exposure in the post-1940 US population. *Journal of Political Economy*, *114*(4), 672–712.

Almond, D., and Mazumder, B. (2005). The 1918 influenza pandemic and subsequent health outcomes: An analysis of SIPP data. *The American Economic Review*, *95*, 258–262.

Álvarez-Nogal, C., Prados de la Escosura, L., and Santiago-Caballero, C. (2020). *Economic effects of the black death: Spain in European perspective*.

Baker, S. R., Bloom, N., Davis, S. J., Kost, K., Sammon, M., and Viratyosin, T. (2020). The unprecedented stock market reaction to COVID-19. *Review of Asset Pricing Studies*, *10*, 742–758.

Bao, Y., Pan, Y., Taylor, A., Radakrishnan, S., Luo, F., and Pincus, H. A. (2016). Prescription drug monitoring programs are associated with sustained reductions in opioid prescribing by physicians. *Health Affairs (Millwood)*, *35*, 1045–1051.

Barouch, D. H. (2008). Challenges in the development of an HIV-1 vaccine. *Nature*, *455*, 613–619.

Barro, R. J., Ursúa, J. F., and Weng, J. (2020). *The coronavirus and the great influenza pandemic: Lessons from the "Spanish Flu" for the coronavirus's potential effects on mortality and economic activity*. National Bureau of Economic Research.

Basco, S., Domenech, J., and Rosés, J. R. (2021). Unequal mortality during the Spanish Flu. In *Pandemics, economics and inequality* (pp. 33–50).

Basco, S., Domènech, J., and Rosés, J. R. (2021). The redistributive effects of pandemics: Evidence on the Spanish Flu. *World Development, 141*, 105389.

Beach, B., Ferrie, J. P., and Saavedra, M. H. (2018). *Fetal shock or selection? The 1918 influenza pandemic and human capital development*. National Bureau of Economic Research.

Benedictow, O. J. (2004). *The Black Death, 1346–1353: The complete history*. Boydell & Brewer.

Bloom, D. E., and Carliner, G. (1988). The economic impact of AIDS in the United States. *Science, 239*(4840), 604–610.

Bootsma, M. C., and Ferguson, N. M. (2007). The effect of public health measures on the 1918 influenza pandemic in US cities. *Proceedings of the National Academy of Sciences, 104*, 7588–7593.

CDC. (1981). Kaposi's sarcoma and pneumocystis pneumonia among homosexual men—New York City and California. *Morbidity and Mortality Weekly Report, 30*, 305–308.

Christensen, D., Dube, O., Haushofer, J., Siddiqi, B., and Voors, M. (2021). Building resilient health systems: Experimental evidence from Sierra Leone and the 2014 Ebola outbreak. *Quarterly Journal of Economics, 136*, 1145–1198.

Clay, K., Lewis, J., and Severnini, E. (2018). Pollution, infectious disease, and mortality: Evidence from the 1918 Spanish influenza pandemic. *The Journal of Economic History, 78*, 1179–1209.

Condon, B. J., and Sinha, T. (2010). Who is that masked person: The use of face masks on Mexico City public transportation during the influenza A (H1N1) outbreak. *Health Policy, 95*, 50–56.

Cornaggia, K., Hund, J., Nguyen, G., and Ye, Z. (2022). Opioid crisis effects on municipal finance. *Review of Financial Studies, 35*(4), 2019–2066.

Correia, S., Luck, S., and Verner, E. (1918). Pandemics depress the economy, public health interventions do not: Evidence from the 1918 flu. *The Journal of Economic History*.

Custodio, C., Cvijanovic, D., and Wiedemann, M. (2022). *Opioid crisis and real estate prices*. Available at SSRN 3712600.

Del Giudice, A., and Paltrinieri, A. (2017). The impact of the Arab spring and the Ebola outbreak on African equity mutual fund investor decisions. *Research in International Business and Finance, 41*, 600–612.

Demirgüç-Kunt, A., Lokshin, M., and Torre, I. (2020). *The sooner, the better: The early economic impact of non-pharmaceutical interventions during the COVID-19 pandemic*. World Bank Policy Research Working Paper (9257).

Donadelli, M., Kizys, R., and Riedel, M. (2017). Dangerous infectious diseases: Bad news for Main street, good news for wall street? *Journal of Financial Markets, 35*, 84–103.

Duarte, F., Kadiyala, S., Masters, S. H., and Powell, D. (2017). The effect of the 2009 influenza pandemic on absence from work. *Health Economics, 26*, 1682–1695.

Eisenberg, M., and Mordechai, L. (2020). The Justinian plague and global pandemics: The making of the plague concept. *The American Historical Review, 125*, 1632–1667.

Fletcher, J. (2014). *Examining the long-term mortality effects of early health shocks*. US Census Bureau Center for Economic Studies Paper No. (CES-WP-14-19).

Hale, T., Angrist, N., Kira, B., Petherick, A., Phillips, T., and Webster, S. (2020). *Variation in government responses to COVID-19*. Working Paper.

Hassan, T. A., Hollander, S., Van Lent, L., and Tahoun, A. (2020). *Firm-level exposure to epidemic diseases: COVID-19, SARS, and H1N1*. National Bureau of Economic Research.

Jansen, M. (2020). *Spillover effects of the opioid epidemic on consumer finance*. National Bureau of Economic Research.

Jedwab, R., Johnson, N. D., and Koyama, M. (2022). The economic impact of the black death. *Journal of Economic Literature, 60*, 132–178.

Kaestner, R., and Ziedan, E. (2019). *Mortality and socioeconomic consequences of prescription opioids: Evidence from state policies (no. w26135)*. National Bureau of Economic Research.

Karlsson, M., Nilsson, T., and Pichler, S. (2014). The impact of the 1918 Spanish Flu epidemic on economic performance in Sweden: An investigation into the consequences of an extraordinary mortality shock. *Journal of Health Economics, 36*, 1–19.

Kostova, D., Cassell, C. H., Redd, J. T., Williams, D. E., Singh, T., Martel, L. D., and Bunnell, R. E. (2019). Long-distance effects of epidemics: Assessing the link between the 2014 West Africa Ebola outbreak and US exports and employment. *Health Economics*, *28*, 1248–1261.

Krueger, A. B. (2017). Where have all the workers gone? An inquiry into the decline of the US labor force participation rate. *Brookings Papers on Economic Activity*, *2017*(2), 1.

Lai, A. Y., and Tan, T. B. (2012). Combating SARS and H1N1: Insights and lessons from Singapore's public health control measures. *ASEAS-Austrian Journal of South-East Asian Studies*, *5*(1), 74–101.

Li, W., and Zhu, Q. (2019). *The opioid epidemic and local public financing: Evidence from municipal bonds*. Available at SSRN 3454026.

Ma, X. F. (2021). *Payday lending and the opioid epidemic*. Working Paper.

Ma, C., Rogers, J. H., and Zhou, S. (2020). *Modern pandemics: Recession and recovery*. Available at SSRN 3565646.

Maphanga, P. M., and Henama, U. S. (2019). The tourism impact of Ebola in Africa: Lessons on crisis management. *African Journal of Hospitality, Tourism and Leisure*, *8*, 1–13.

Merson, M. H., O'Malley, J., Serwadda, D., and Apisuk, C. (2008). The history and challenge of HIV prevention. *Lancet*, *372*, 475–488.

Mordechai, L., and Eisenberg, M. (2019). Rejecting catastrophe: The case of the Justinian plague. *Past & Present*, *244*, 3–50.

Mordechai, L., Eisenberg, M., Newfield, T. P., Izdebski, A., Kay, J. E., and Poinar, H. (2019). The Justinian plague: An inconsequential pandemic? *Proceedings of the National Academy of Sciences*, *116*, 25546–25554.

Morens, D. M., Taubenberger, J. K., Harvey, H. A., and Memoli, M. J. (2010). The 1918 influenza pandemic: Lessons for 2009 and the future. *Critical Care Medicine*, *38*, e10.

Omoleke, S. A., Mohammed, I., and Saidu, Y. (2016). Ebola viral disease in West Africa: A threat to global health, economy and political stability. *Journal of Public Health in Africa*, *7*.

Ouimet, P., Simintzi, E., and Ye, K. (2020). *The impact of the opioid crisis on firm value and investment*. Available at SSRN 3338083.

Pamuk, Ş., and Shatzmiller, M. (2014). Plagues, wages, and economic change in the Islamic Middle East, 700–1500. *The Journal of Economic History*, *74*, 196–229.

Parman, J. (2015). Childhood health and sibling outcomes: Nurture reinforcing nature during the 1918 influenza pandemic. *Explorations in Economic History*, *58*, 22–43.

Percoco, M. (2016). Health shocks and human capital accumulation: The case of Spanish Flu in Italian regions. *Regional Studies*, *50*, 1496–1508.

Pritchett, J. B., and Tunali, I. (1995). Strangers' disease: Determinants of yellow fever mortality during the New Orleans epidemic of 1853. *Explorations in Economic History*, *32*, 517–539.

Rao, H., and Greve, H. R. (2018). Disasters and community resilience: Spanish Flu and the formation of retail cooperatives in Norway. *Academy of Management Journal*, *61*, 5–25.

Rosen, S., Simon, J., Vincent, J. R., MacLeod, W., Fox, M., and Thea, D. M. (2003). AIDS is your business. *Harvard Business Review*, *81*(2), 80–87.

Saavedra, M. (2017). Early-life disease exposure and occupational status: The impact of yellow fever during the 19th century. *Explorations in Economic History*, *64*, 62–81.

Schell, D., Wang, M., and Huynh, T. L. D. (2020). This time is indeed different: A study on global market reactions to public health crisis. *Journal of Behavioral and Experimental Finance*, *27*, 100349.

Shanks, G. D., and Brundage, J. F. (2012). Pathogenic responses among young adults during the 1918 influenza pandemic. *Emerging Infectious Diseases*, *18*, 201.

Sharp, P. M., and Hahn, B. H. (2011). Origins of HIV and the AIDS pandemic. *Cold Spring Harbor Perspectives in Medicine*, *1*(1), a006841.

Stathakopoulos, D. (2018). *Plague, justinian (early medieval pandemic)*. The Oxford Dictionary of Late Antiquity, Oxford University Press.

Thirumurthy, H., Zivin, J. G., and Goldstein, M. (2008). The economic impact of aids treatment labor supply in Western Kenya. *The Journal of Human Resources*, *43*(3), 511–552.

Trilla, A., Trilla, G., and Daer, C. (2008). The 1918 "Spanish Flu" in Spain. *Clinical Infectious Diseases*, *47*, 668–673.

Tut, D. (2021). *Cash holdings and firm-level exposure to epidemic diseases*. Working Paper.

Velde, F. R. (2022). What happened to the US economy during the 1918 influenza pandemic? A view through high-frequency data. *The Journal of Economic History*, *82*, 284–326.

World Health Organization. (2014). *Yellow fever fact sheet*. https://www.who.int/news-room/fact-sheets/detail/yellow-fever.

Chapter 3

The COVID-19 pandemic as a "black swan" event—Comparisons with natural disaster shocks

Chapter outline

Abstract

We discuss how COVID-19 and other health crises compare with natural disaster shocks around the world in terms of manifestation, temporal duration, geographic dispersion, and contagion. Natural disasters and pandemics can both be regarded as environmental disasters, but with different origins. Other similarities between the two types of crises are many, including the effects of government policy. For example, the effects of COVID-19 mortgage loan forbearances in which borrowers were temporarily relieved of repayment responsibilities appear to have similar moral hazard consequences as forbearances for natural catastrophes. The two types of crises also have many differences, such as the usually more short-lived nature and fewer contagion effects of natural disasters than health crises.

Keywords: COVID-19, Pandemics, Natural disasters, Environmental disasters, Forbearance, Contagion

3.1 How natural disaster shocks differ from health shocks in terms of manifestation, temporal duration, geographic dispersion, and contagion

Natural disasters and pandemics may be regarded as environmental disasters with different origins. While the natural disasters are thought to be consequence of imbalances in the natural habitat such as increased dioxide carbon pollution caused by human activities, pandemics are consequences of viruses escaped from the natural habitat that infect humans.

The Economic and Financial Impacts of the COVID-19 Crisis Around the World
https://doi.org/10.1016/B978-0-443-19162-6.00015-3
Copyright © 2024 Elsevier Inc. All rights reserved.

Natural disasters also differ from health shocks in terms of manifestation, shock duration, geographic coverage, and contagion. Natural disasters manifest as extreme weather events such as hurricanes, severe storms and floods, wildfires, sea-level rise, heat waves or extreme temperature events, earthquakes, volcanic eruptions, cyclones, and tsunamis. They tend to cause displacement, damage, or destruction of physical capital such as houses and other commercial buildings and properties, and sometimes also loss of human lives; but, unlike a health shock, their effects are generally short-lived, tend to be confined to the localities and economic agents affected, and may not directly cause much contagion to other unaffected localities. While most countries around the world tend to experience some form of natural disaster at various points in time, they generally do not happen at the same time and affect different locations, which most often prevents that from becoming an economic and/or financial crisis.

In contrast, health shocks or pandemics such as COVID-19 caused by virus or referred to as medical conditions directly affect human life and health. Health shocks can have a long duration if no particular treatment or vaccine is found to address the virus that caused it and to protect people's immunity. Health shocks can spread over large geographic areas, especially if contagious via contact among people, which allows the viruses to thrive. While not all health shocks are necessarily contagious, the COVID-19 virus has been highly contagious and has been rapidly spreading across the globe. Pandemics due to contagious viruses can quickly turn into economic crises due to the significant decline in economic activity and government restrictions imposed to avoid further spread of the disease.

McManus and Yannopoulos (2021) is the only paper we are aware of which compared the COVID-19 crisis and natural disaster conditions. They do so by focusing on effects on mortgage borrowers. Specifically, they examined forbearance accommodations for mortgage loans during the COVID-19 crisis and compared them to forbearances for natural disasters. They found that mortgage forbearance rates in the COVID-19 crisis are similar to historical rates in natural disaster areas. In both periods, they found that higher forbearance rates are associated with more financially constrained borrowers, i.e., lower credit scores, higher debt ratios, and higher loan-to-value ratios.

3.2 Natural disasters: Institutional details

The scientific community posits that climate change from increasing levels of dioxide carbon pollution and resulting natural disasters pose dangers to many economies and countries throughout the globe (e.g., Committee on Extreme Weather Events and Climate Change Attribution, NASA Earth Observatory, 2017; NOAA, 2017; Ackerman and Stanton, 2008, 2012; UN IPCC, 2021).[1] The number and/or frequency of natural disasters are expected to increase over time (e.g., Burke, Hsiang, and Miguel, 2015; NASA Earth Observatory, 2017).[2] In fact, various sources have revealed that economic losses of natural disasters did increase over time and this increase was driven not only by economic and population growth but also by climate change (Estrada, Botzen, and Tol, 2015; UN IPCC, 2021, 2022). The report for 2021 from the UN on the climate crisis came as a red warning code for humanity

---

[1]Evidence for climate change brought by scientists includes rising sea levels, rising global temperature, warming oceans, shrinking ice sheets, declining Arctic Sea ice, glacial retreat, extreme weather events, ocean acidification, and decreased snow cover.

[2]In contrast, some scientists are of a different opinion that dioxide carbon may not be a pollutant and could actually be beneficial, being an essential nutrient for most plants (Van Wijngaarden and Happer, 2020).

(UN Secretary-General António Guterres) as widespread and rapid changes have already taken place, impacting all regions on Earth, with many changes being already impossible to reverse.

Pricing the costs of these disasters is difficult and uncertain due their many ramifications on human lives and health, species, ecosystems, social interactions, and other consequences that extend far beyond monetary measures. While research on costs is still in progress, one Munich RE report found that natural disasters resulted in over $5.2 trillion in losses globally since 1980, while a report by 13 US federal agencies in 2018 predicted the damage would result in about 10% reduction in the US economy by the end of the century. Some researchers built catastrophe models that produce estimates of the direct impacts of natural disasters and argued that since the 1990s, a number of natural disasters have caused economic losses in tens of billions of US dollars (e.g., Botzen, Deschenes, and Sanders, 2020). Such major disaster examples include the 1994 Northridge earthquake in the US, the 1995 Kobe earthquake in Japan, the 2004 Indian Ocean earthquake that caused the Asian tsunami, the 2005 Hurricane Katrina in the US, the 2011 earthquake and tsunami in Japan, and the 2017 Hurricane Harvey in the US, among others. The economic losses of natural disasters have been increasing over the last few decades, with the number of disasters causing losses, which tripled since the 1980s (e.g., Hoeppe, 2016; Botzen, Deschenes, and Sanders, 2020). Taking a global approach, Burke, Hsiang, and Miguel (2015) found that changes in temperature have substantially shaped economic growth in both rich and poor countries over the last half century, and that future warming is likely to reduce global economic output by about 23% by 2100, relative to a world without climate change.

Despite the very different estimates discussed, the above sources suggest that natural disasters can pose large economic costs. Reducing the natural disasters and climate change effects may require a considerable investment, but not doing anything may lead to even greater costs in the near future (e.g., Ackerman and Stanton, 2008; Ackerman, Stanton, Hope, Alberth, Fisher, Biewald, and Economics, 2008). A more rigorous evaluation of the economic costs is discussed in the sections below.

In response to rising risks, governments around the world have formed alliances and debated extensively around ways to adapt and combat the effects of climate change. One notable action to adapt and combat the effects of climate change is the Paris Agreement on December 12, 2015, under which signing countries (191 countries plus the European Union) agreed to limit global temperature rise this century to 1.5°C above preindustrial levels and report regularly on emissions and implementation efforts.[3] Additionally, climate change is a pressing policy issue, with regulators mobilizing to determine banks' risk sensitivities and management strategies to climate change (e.g., Brainard, 2021).

While it is challenging to assess the costs of the climate change ex ante due to their many ramifications, valuable lessons can be learned by assessing the effects of past natural disaster events on the financial lives and wealth of economic agents. In addition to the direct effects, impacts also refer to mitigation efforts to prevent the future negative consequences of climate change-induced disasters as well as adaptation efforts, such as risk management, to adjust and better control risks once they emerge.

It is important to note that some research does find some mitigating factors for the direct impacts of natural disasters, particularly on deaths from such shocks. These factors may be considered in

---

[3]In April 2016 under President Obama, US became a signatory to the Paris Agreement, and accepted it by executive order in September 2016. However, US retreated from it on November 4, 2020, under President Trump, but decided to rejoin on February 19, 2021, under President Biden.

future policy design to help adapt to climate change. Kahn (2005) found that countries with higher income, more democratic, and with higher quality of institutions are associated with fewer disaster deaths. Kellenberg and Mobarak (2008) confirmed in general these findings but further showed that the fatality-country income relationship is nonlinear, so that the number of fatalities from natural disasters increases at lower levels of per capita income but at a certain point they start decreasing. Li, Xu, and Zhang (2021) highlighted level of urbanization as another mitigant of natural disasters. Taking the Pearl River Delta as a case study, they presented an index system for urbanization and natural disasters and established a coupling coordination model to explore the coupling relationship between them. The urbanization level was evaluated from their dimensions: population, space, society, and economy. The disaster-causing factors, disaster prevention and mitigation, and disaster loss were used to describe the disaster system. The coupling coordination model indicated that the development of urbanization to a certain level was beneficial for reducing disaster loss. The coupling degree between urbanization and the disaster system increased, which in the central cities was significantly higher than that in the eastern and western cities. Cities with high urbanization levels had higher coupling degrees, indicating that a high level of urbanization helped prevent natural disasters. Conevska (2021) identified trade liberalization as another mitigant. The author examined whether the impact of natural disasters on trade varied for trading partners with differing levels of market integration. That is, the author analyzes whether preferential liberalization serves to protect or buffer against the negative economic consequences of natural disasters. The author showed that deep preferential liberalization can not only protect countries against the negative macroeconomic impact of natural disasters but can also allow countries to increase exports during natural disaster events that otherwise induce trade decline. These findings suggested that by allowing countries to expand the quantity and the range of exports, preferential trade agreements lead to enhanced resilience against exogenous shocks. Still other mitigants highlighted in the literature to address borrower financial distress and improve credit performance after disasters are government assistance and insurance (e.g., Kousky, Palim, and Pan, 2020; Ratcliffe, Congdon, Teles, Stanczyk, and Martin, 2020; Billings, Gallagher, and Ricketts, 2022).

We focus next on the literature exploring the impact of natural disasters on economic outcomes, banking sectors, and financial markets in the US and other countries. We reviewed the effects of natural disasters not only on real estate prices, and household and business finance, but also on local and national economies impacted. We include a notable number of papers, but they caveat that it is impossible to keep up with all the relevant research that is continuously evolving on the topics of natural disasters and climate change covered here.

3.3 Natural disasters and economies around the world

3.3.1 Real estate prices

There is a vast literature on natural disasters and real estate markets, given that natural disasters tend to cause significant damage and destruction to properties in their path (see e.g., Canals-Cerda and Roman, 2021). We will next synthesize a select number of prominent research studies for brevity. First a number of academic papers looked at hurricanes and flooding as extreme weather natural disasters. The impact of hurricanes and ensuing floods on home prices can be difficult to forecast ex ante. Researchers often use hedonic valuation models to show that home sale prices can capitalize property risk factors, such as flood zones, with properties that have higher flood risk selling at a discount. Almost all extant research points toward flood risks driving home prices down and price differentials reflecting flood risk becoming much larger in the wake of large events. However, events like Hurricane Katrina can generate significant supply-and-demand disruptions in housing and labor markets that can make the impact of specific events difficult to predict beforehand.

Ortega and Taspınar (2018) analyzed the effects of Hurricane Sandy on the New York City housing market and documented a significant negative impact on home prices in the aftermath of this hurricane. They found a 17%–22% price decline instantly after the storm for damaged properties and a price penalty as high as 8% for nondamaged flood zone properties, consistent with increased perceived risk of large-scale flooding incidents in that area.

Fang, Li, and Yavas (2021) used residential transaction data from Miami, FL, and found that the impact of a property's flood risk exposure on its value changes over time, having a price penalty of 4% in the hurricane striking period. Conversely, during a tranquil hurricane period, properties in high-flood hazard zones demand a price premium ranging roughly from 4% to 6%, which may represent the price impact of water-related amenities. The premium declined significantly once Hurricane Sandy hit. The authors surmised that the occurrence of a hazardous hurricane, which impacted distant regions, also raised local home buyers' perception of flood risk, but only for a short period of time such as one quarter.

Atreya, Ferreira, and Kriesel (2013) used property sales data from a county in Georgia and found that, after the flood of the century in 1994, prices of properties in the 100-year floodplain fell significantly, but this effect was relatively short-lived. They found that flood risk discount vanished between 4 and 9 years after the flood. Bin and Landry (2013) used data for a county in North Carolina taking into account many storm events and found that prior to Hurricane Fran in 1996, there is no market risk premium for being in a flood zone. However, the authors found significant price differentials after major flooding events in the areas, leading to a 5.7% price decrease after Hurricane Fran and 8.8% price decrease after Hurricane Floyd. Results from a different model using more recent data without significant storm-related flood events show a significant risk premium ranging between 6.0% and 20.2% for homes sold in a flood zone, but this effect decreases over time, vanishing about 5 or 6 years after Hurricane Floyd.

Finally, Gibson and Mullins (2020) estimated the price effects of three flood risk signals: (1) the Biggert-Waters Flood Insurance Reform Act, which raised price premiums, (2) Hurricane Sandy, and (3) new floodplain maps reflecting three decades of climate change. Estimates are negative for all three signals, and some are large in magnitude. For example, properties included in the new floodplain after flooding by Hurricane Sandy experienced 18% price reductions. Harrison, Smersh, and Schwartz (2001) and Zhang (2016) also found that homes with comparable characteristics located in a flood zone sell, on average, for less than homes located outside flood zones, with the lower priced houses being most adversely affected.

Despite all these studies suggesting negative effects on house prices from flooding, there is a lack of a persistent effect. This may imply that buyers' and sellers' risk perceptions get altered with the frequency or novelty of events or their personal beliefs about climate change. Consistently, Baldauf, Garlappi, and Yannelis (2020) find that house prices reflect heterogeneity in beliefs about long-run climate change risks. It can also suggest that some homebuyers and sellers may not have a good understanding of flood risks and/or insurance requirements for houses (e.g., Chivers and Flores, 2002; Atreya and Ferreira, 2015; Hino and Burke, 2020). For example, Bakkensen and Barrage (2018) find that the

US market for coastal homes over 2007–16 exceeded fundamental values by 10% as the market did not fully control for flood risk.

In contrast to the other studies, one paper finds that flood risk can also lead to house price increases. Vigdor (2008) finds that Hurricane Katrina lead to a 50% decline in the number of housing units in New Orleans between 2000 and 2006, and the reduction in housing supply exceeded the reduction in housing demand, and consequently, home prices in New Orleans increased a lot in the aftermath of Hurricane Katrina.

In addition to hurricanes and floods, a number of studies analyzed the impact of sea-level rise (SLR) expectations on current home prices.[4] There are studies that look at the price effect of SLR directly, like the recent work by Bernstein, Gustafson, and Lewis (2020).[5] Other studies such as Ortega and Taspınar (2018) look at the impact of SLR on property values. Researchers often analyze both properties damaged by SLR and also those not damaged but exposed to SLR risk or flood zone considerations that may incur a price penalty as well.[6] The studies vary by data source, time horizon, and other design features but also share many similarities while effects of SLR estimates on home prices vary significantly.

The studies generally compare prices of SLR-exposed houses with non-SLR-exposed houses that are similar to each other in other features. Bernstein, Gustafson, and Lewis (2020) use data over 2007–16 and find that homes exposed to SLR incur a 7% increase in the average price. This increase is higher in later years and when the level of SLR exposure is higher. Thus, the increase reaches 14.7% for properties facing two to three feet of SLR and is higher for sophisticated buyers and communities that are more concerned than others about global warming. Relatedly, Baldauf, Garlappi, and Yannelis (2020) find that houses estimated to be underwater in neighborhoods with more believers in climate change sell at a discount relative to houses in neighborhoods where residents are less convinced of climate change impacts. In sharp contrast, Murfin and Spiegel (2020) use data from coastal home sales and only uncover limited price effects of SLR,[7] while Athreya and Czjkowski (2019) use data from a county on the coast in Texas and uncover that homes in the highest flood risk area require a price premium.

There is no yet consensus on the impact of SLR and natural disasters on home prices and more work is yet to be done. The lack of consensus is partly driven by differences in time periods, events, and locations analyzed among other factors. Further research may consider natural disaster effects on houses by encompassing also the continuous changes in climate risk estimate, communities' perceptions about climate change risks, as well as housing insurance for natural disasters and government aid policies.

---

[4]See UN IPCC (2013) for a widely publicized report on a broad range of timing and magnitude of SLR, available at https://www.ipcc.ch/site/assets/uploads/2018/03/WG1AR5_SummaryVolume_FINAL.pdf.

[5]Other prominent works are Baldauf, Garlappi, and Yannelis (2020); Keys and Mulder (2020); Murfin and Spiegel (2020); Atreya and Czjkowski (2019); and Hino and Burke (2020).

[6]See also Vigdor (2008), Dillon-Merrilly, Gez, and Getex (2018), and Cohen, Barr, and Kim (2021).

[7]Keys and Mulder (2020) find that communities most affected by SLR in coastal Florida appreciated at a slower rate in recent times, and home sale volumes declined. Hino and Burke (2020) measure the effect of information about flood risks in the universe of US homes and uncover limited evidence that housing market fully incorporates flood risk in prices on the aggregate.

3.3.2 Household finance

There exists more limited research on the effects of natural disasters (wildfires, hurricanes and floods, sea-level rise, etc.) on household finances. This is perhaps surprising given that natural disasters can lead to large property destruction, personal injury, and loss of human life. But particularly from a financial standpoint, natural disasters can inflict major negative shocks on household finances because of large, mostly unexpected expenses from damaged or destroyed homes, job and income interruptions, as well health and other related personal problems.[8]

Some notable studies explore the effects of natural disasters on household income and financial well-being. To start, Groen, Kutzbach, and Polivka (2020) analyze household employment and earnings changes after Hurricanes Katrina and Rita. These researchers find negative effects on household earnings in the first year after the hurricane, but surprisingly on average positive and higher earnings in the three years after the hurricanes relative to an observationally similar control group. The household earnings' recovery was heterogenous across work sectors, so that those sectors related to rebuilding were particularly highly benefited while other sectors such as tourism incurred significant net losses. Another paper by Deryugina, Kawano, and Levitt (2018) provides one of the first comprehensive analyses of the Katrina hurricane's long-term economic impact on households. They document large and persistent impacts on where people live, small and mostly transitory impacts on wage income, employment, total income, and marriage, and no impact on divorce or fertility. Similar to prior study, they also find that within just a few years, Katrina victims' incomes fully recover and even surpass that of controls from similar cities that were unaffected by the hurricane. Finally, a paper by Farrell and Greig (2018) analyzes the effects of Hurricanes Harvey and Irma on households' checking accounts and observe a reduction in inflows and outflows of funds after the hurricanes, but such effects only exist for a couple of weeks.

Some research studies how climate change risk affects household delinquency, foreclosure, and default. Some prominent work by Issler, Stanton, Vergara-Alert, and Wallace (2020) studies wildfires in California between 2000 and 2018 and documents significant increases in mortgage delinquency and foreclosures after wildfires. They show that effects on household financial outcomes are inversely related to the magnitude of the wildfire, which may be due to coordination externalities from large fires. Then, Billings, Gallagher, and Ricketts (2022) use the quasi-random flooding generated by Hurricane Harvey, which hit Houston in August 2017, to study the implications of flood losses for households with differing access to insurance and credit. They document that outside the floodplain, credit-constrained homeowners experience a 20% increase in bankruptcies and a 13% increase in the share of debt in severe delinquency in flooded blocks relative to nonflooded areas. Effects are insignificant inside the floodplain as flood insurance mitigates the financial impact of flooding. Disaster assistance however does not appear to help counteract inequalities on postdisaster credit outcomes. Authors find that SBA disaster loans and also FEMA grants tend to be regressive in allocation. Neighborhoods where residents qualified but had a more limited ability to repay experienced a 28% lower credit from Small Business Administration (SBA) loan dollars. In same areas, heavy flooding increased the delinquency and bankruptcy rate much more relative to similar areas that did not flood. They warn that average effects can mask important heterogeneity after natural disasters, which raises some concerns about how well Federal disaster programs mitigate the financial burden of households from natural disasters.

---

[8]See e.g., Canals-Cerda and Roman (2021) for a brief survey of the literature.

Consistent with Issler, Stanton, Vergara-Alert, and Wallace (2020) which show that disaster magnitude matters, another paper by Ratcliffe, Congdon, Teles, Stanczyk, and Martin (2020) find that natural disasters that are smaller are less likely to receive government recovery funds, and this leads to larger declines in household credit scores. Then, Kousky, Palim, and Pan (2020) use data on Hurricane Harvey and examine the relationships among property damage, flood insurance, and mortgage credit risk. They find mortgages on moderately to severely damaged homes are more likely to become delinquent shortly after Hurricane Harvey than similar homes with no damage.

Other research by JPMorgan Chase & Co. (2018) uses transaction-level data on household checking accounts to investigate effects of Hurricanes Harvey and Irma on household financial outcomes. This research documents checking account inflow declines by 20% and outflows declines by more than 30% after a natural disaster, with significant welfare losses for some families. Another study by Gallagher and Hartley (2017) looks at effects of Hurricane Katrina and find that increases in credit card borrowing and delinquency rates for the most disaster-struck residents, but that such effects are small and short lived. They also find larger reductions in total debt, driven by households using flood insurance to repay their mortgages rather than to rebuild. Roth Tran and Sheldon (2019) also find that households have higher credit card utilization after a disaster to smooth the shock, but delinquency and other outcomes for the average household residing in areas affected by natural disasters does not appear to be significantly impacted with some exceptions which we discuss below.

Then, a few studies have investigated effects on spending and saving behavior after disasters in an international context. Luo and Kinugasa (2020) used a synthetic control method to examine the short- and long-term effects of the 2008 Sichuan earthquake on saving behavior. The results indicated that, in the short run, the earthquake caused drastic declines in household saving rates—from 24% to 7% and from 23% to 21% for rural and urban populations, respectively. However, household saving rates recovered to the baseline shortly after the shock, and the outcome exactly matches the counterfactual counterparts in the following period. The estimates imply that, at the aggregate level, the earthquake has had no discernible long-run impact on the saving propensity of the affected population. Another study by Filipski, Jin, Zhang, and Chen (2015) contended that emotional shocks and increased risk awareness may trigger changes in the preferences and behavior of economic agents. Based on panel datasets from China's Sichuan province, which was struck by an earthquake in 2008, and using distance from the epicenter as a proxy for earthquake severity, they empirically showed that the saving and consumption behavior of households closer to the epicenter changed after the earthquake. They saved less, spent more lavishly on alcohol and cigarettes, and played majiang (a Chinese game) more often. The magnitude of the estimated impact on saving behavior, a drop of 6 percentage points for each degree of earthquake intensity, is economically significant. It appears that the earthquake has induced a shift in people's preferences characterized by a *carpe diem* attitude toward spending and greater preference for the present.

The economic literature surveyed here thus far implies that natural disasters can have negative effects on household credit scores, delinquency, default, personal income, and also can significantly impact their spending and saving behavior. However, the unfavorable effects of natural disasters are relatively short lived in some cases but not in all. Some studies also highlight the role of government aid and insurance against natural disasters which could ameliorate or not household finances after natural disasters.

It is also important to note that there could be heterogenous effects of climate change and natural disasters on households. Some studies demonstrate that consumers in a more precarious financial position prior to a natural disaster may be more likely to be more materially negatively affected by it.

For example, Roth Tran and Sheldon (2019) show that, although average consumer financial outcomes for households residing in disaster-struck areas are not significantly affected by the disasters, more disadvantaged consumers do incur worse outcomes. Thus, subprime and low-income households hit by disasters and without access to aid are more likely to experience credit card delinquency and also to declare bankruptcy after disasters. Complementary evidence is given by Sheldon, Gall, and Collins (2017) which finds that low-income households appear to incur larger declines in their earnings after natural disasters.

Also complementary, Ratcliffe, Congdon, Teles, Stanczyk, and Martin (2020) find reductions in credit scores of impacted residents and increases in mortgage delinquencies and foreclosures. Such declines are particularly large for low score households and for those living in minority communities. Billings, Gallagher, and Ricketts (2022) find that the negative financial impact of Hurricane Harvey is concentrated on households who entered the hurricane in a weaker financial position. On the other hand, Ratnadiwakara and Venugopal (2020) find that areas more hardly hit by major disasters tend to attract less wealthy and less creditworthy households which leads to de-gentrification of at-risk neighborhoods.

Thus, research reviewed highlights that there are different effects of natural disasters on more disadvantaged or less affluent households. It also suggests that appropriate financial aid may be needed to help such households weather natural disasters.

3.3.3 Corporate finance

A number of papers focused on the effects of high temperatures, environmental disasters, and pollution on firm real outcomes and whether various firm corporate governance mechanisms shape managerial decisions regarding compliance with climate change policies. First, a paper by Dessaint and Matray (2017) studies how managers respond to hurricane events when their firms are located in the neighborhood of the disaster area. They found that the sudden shock to the perceived liquidity risk leads managers to increase corporate cash holdings and to express more concerns about hurricane risk in their financial filings (10-Ks/10-Qs), even though the actual risk remains unchanged. However, both effects are temporary and over time, the perceived risk decreases while the bias disappears. Still, the distortion between perceived and actual risk is large, and the increase in cash decision seems suboptimal.

Some studies looked at effects on corporate sales, productivity, employment, and investment. Focusing on the US alone (a high-income economy), Addoum, Ng, and Ortiz-Bobea (2020) estimated how location-specific temperature shocks affect establishment-level sales and productivity. They combined granular daily data on temperatures across the continental US with detailed establishment data from 1990 to 2015. Using a large sample yielding precise estimates, they could not find evidence that temperature exposures significantly affect establishment-level sales or productivity, including among industries traditionally classified as heat sensitive. At the firm level, they found that temperature exposures aggregated across firm establishments are generally unrelated to sales, productivity, and profitability. However, their results support existing findings of a fragile relation between temperature and aggregate economic growth in rich countries, in that negative effects from natural disasters may be muted in high-income economies. Graff Zivin and Neidell (2012) evaluated the impact of pollution on worker productivity by relating exogenous daily variations in ozone with the productivity of agricultural workers as recorded under piece rate contracts. The authors found robust evidence that ozone levels well below federal air quality standards have a significant negative impact on productivity. These results suggest that, in contrast to common characterizations of environmental protection as a tax on producers, environmental protection can also be viewed as an investment in human capital, and thus a tool for promoting economic growth. Leiter, Oberhofer, and Raschky (2009) used a panel of European firms and investigate the effects of disasters (exposure to floods) on firm-level outcomes, namely employment, asset accumulation, and productivity. They found that floods led to significant increases rather than decreases in assets and employment growth, while productivity is not significantly impacted. This may imply that after a flood, damaged production capabilities are offset by increased investments in assets and increased labor, which contribute to the increased growth observed. Hosono, Miyakawa, Uchino, Hazama, Ono, Uchida, and Uesugi (2016) investigated the effect of credit availability after disasters on firms' investment. To identify exogenous shocks to loan supply, they utilized the natural experiment provided by Japan's Great Hanshin-Awaji earthquake in 1995. Using a unique dataset that allows them to identify firms and banks in the earthquake-affected areas, they found that the investment ratio of firms located outside the earthquake-affected areas but having a main bank inside the areas was significantly smaller than that of firms located outside the areas and having a main bank outside the areas. These findings suggest that loan supply shocks affect firm investment. Cevik and Miryugin (2022) addressed how climate change affects the performance of firms by empirically investigating the impact of climate change vulnerability on corporate performance using a large panel dataset of more than 3.3 million nonfinancial firms from 24 developing countries over the period 1997–2019. They found that nonfinancial firms operating in countries with greater vulnerability to climate change tend to have difficulty in accessing debt financing even at higher interest rates, while being less productive and profitable relative to firms in countries with lower vulnerability to climate change. They confirmed these findings with alternative measures of climate change vulnerability. Furthermore, partitioning the sample reveals that these effects are significantly greater for smaller firms, especially in high-risk sectors and countries and countries with weaker capacity to adapt to and mitigate the consequences of climate change.

One study looked at effects on innovation activities by firms. Chu, Liu, and Tian (2021) exploited evacuation spill information from the US Coast Guard's National Response Center database and examined how firms alter their green innovation activities and strategies in response to environmental spills occurring near their headquarters. They found that, in response to nearby environmental spills, firms increase both environmental innovation input and output. Investigating underlying economic channels through which environmental risk affects firm innovation activities, they showed that some plausible explanations for the observed effects are increases in managers' perceived risk and compliance cost, in part due to public outrage and reprobation, but also possible redeployment of human capital.

Berger, Chu, Roman, and Yoon (2023) use loan-level data to link banks to their borrowers and a within-firm estimation method and find that banks' climate risk exposure leads to more and better green innovation by their corporate borrowers. Moreover, banks more exposed to climate risk reward borrowers' green innovation efforts by lowering the loan spreads on subsequent loans. The effect of banks' climate risk exposure on green innovation is stronger when the bank and the firm share a past lending relationship and when the firm is more financially constrained.

Finally, two papers investigate how corporate governance mechanisms at the firm level can shape firms' actions toward climate change. Shive and Forster (2020) showed that firm ownership structure affects the pollution externalities of the firms. Using comprehensive data on greenhouse gas emissions from 2007 to 2016, they showed that independent private firms are less likely to pollute and incur EPA penalties than are public firms, and there are no differences between private sponsor-backed firms and public firms, controlling for industry, time, location, and a host of firm characteristics. Within public firms, they found a negative association between emissions and mutual fund ownership and board size, suggesting that increased oversight may decrease environmental externalities. Chu and Zhao (2019) found that firms targeted by hedge fund activist investors reduce emissions of toxic chemicals by approximately 20%. In particular, they closed 60% more heavy polluting plants and generated 15% green patents than control firms, suggesting that hedge fund activists induce positive environmental changes in the target firms. Linsenmeier, Mohommad, and Schwerhoff (2022) examined to what extent the adoption of carbon pricing in a given country can explain the subsequent adoption of the same policy in other countries. They combined a large international dataset on carbon pricing with several other datasets and estimated semiparametric Cox proportional hazard models for identification. They found robust and statistically significant evidence of international diffusion of carbon pricing policies. For two neighboring countries, policy adoption in one country increases the probability of subsequent adoption in the other country on average by several percentage points. The results suggest that, for most countries, indirect emission reductions of carbon pricing can exceed direct emission reductions.

3.3.4   Local and national economies

Scientific evidence shows that mean temperatures around the globe have been rising. Temperatures over each of the previous three decades have been higher than the last. Collectively, the 30-year period from 1983 to 2012 was likely the warmest in the Northern Hemisphere over the last 1400 years. On a global scale, the prevalence of cold and warm temperature extremes has increased, and in some locations, the frequency of heat waves has more than doubled and is expected to increase by a factor of almost five over the next 50 years (e.g., Lau and Nath, 2012).

On the other hand, it has long been observed that hot temperature is associated with poverty, a correlation noted as early as De Montesquieu (1750) and Huntington (1915); it was also reconfirmed in more recent data (e.g., Nordhaus, 2006). Jones and Olken (2010) noted that temperature alone can explain 23% of the variation in cross-country income today. Despite the strength of this correlation, substantial debate continues over whether there is also a causal relation, i.e., whether climatic factors can explain current economic activity, beyond other correlated country variables that could drive growth and prosperity, leaving no important role for geography (e.g., Acemoglu, Johnson, and Robinson, 2002; Sachs, 2003; Rodrik, Subramanian, and Trebbi, 2004). Addressing this issue is often challenging. A number of recent research papers using better data and stronger identification methodologies tried to understand how extreme heat shocks affect the economies around the world, using metrics such as income, inequality, employment, and GDP growth, among others.

Dell, Jones, and Olken (2009) used both country-level and subnational data at the municipal level from 12 countries in the Americas and documented a negative cross-sectional relationship between temperature and income both within countries and across countries. The within-country cross-sectional relationship is substantially weaker than the cross-country correlation, but it remains statistically significant and of an economically important magnitude, with a 1°C rise in temperature associated with a 1.2%–1.9% decline in municipal per capita income. The fact that the cross-sectional relationship holds within countries, as well as between countries, suggests that omitted country characteristics are not wholly driving the cross-sectional relationship between temperature and income. They also provided a theoretical framework for reconciling the substantial, negative association between temperature and income in cross section with the even stronger short-run effects of temperature shown in panel models. Their theoretical framework suggests that half of the negative short-term effects of temperature are offset in the long run though adaptation efforts.

Jones and Olken (2010) used data for all countries with international trade information to examine the effects of climate shocks on economic activity relating the annual growth rate of a country's exports in a particular product category to the country's weather in that year. They found that a poor country being 1°C warmer in a given year reduces the growth rate of that country's exports by between 2.0 and 5.7 percentage points, with no detectable effects in rich countries. They found negative effects of temperature on exports of both agricultural products and light manufacturing products, with little apparent effects on heavy industry or raw materials. The results confirmed the large negative effects of temperature on poor countries' economies and suggest that temperature affects a much wider range of economic activity than conventionally thought.

Dell, Jones, and Olken (2012) used historical fluctuations in temperature within countries to identify its effects on aggregate economic outcomes. They found three primary results. First, higher temperatures substantially reduce economic growth in poor countries. Second, higher temperatures may reduce growth rates, not just the level of output. Third, higher temperatures have wide-ranging effects, reducing agricultural output, industrial output, and political stability.

Both Jones and Olken (2010) and Dell, Jones, and Olken (2012) demonstrated the negative impact of temperature shocks on economies across a large sample of countries. They also highlighted that two channels through which climate shocks affect economic output are decreased labor supply amid extremely high temperatures, especially in sectors with high climate exposure (e.g., light manufacturing) and agriculture and food-related industries sensitive to temperature extremes.

Mu and Chen (2016) analyzed impacts of large natural disasters on county per capita income between 1990 and 2012 in the US. Using a difference-in-differences model with fixed effects and controlling for serial correlation, they found that the incidence of large disasters in a county significantly reduces its income as compared to its neighboring counties.

Arouri, Nguyen, and Youssef (2015) used commune fixed-effects regressions to estimate the effect of natural disasters on the welfare and poverty of rural households in Vietnam, and subsequently examined household and community characteristics that can strengthen the resilience of households to natural disasters. They found that all disaster types considered in this study including storms, floods and droughts, have negative effects on household income and expenditure. Households in communes with higher mean expenditure and more equal expenditure distribution are more resilient to natural disasters. Access to microcredit, internal remittances, and social allowances can help households strengthen the resilience to natural disasters.

Also related to income outcomes, two studies looked at effects on income inequality. Cevik and Jalles (2022) focused on the relationship between climate change shocks and income inequality. They provided new evidence on the association between climate change and income inequality, using a large panel of 158 countries during the period 1955–2019. They found that an increase in climate change vulnerability is positively associated with rising income inequality. More interestingly, splitting the sample into country groups reveals a considerable contrast in the impact of climate change on income inequality. While climate change vulnerability has no statistically significant effect on income distribution in advanced economies, the coefficient on climate change vulnerability is seven times greater and statistically highly significant in the case of developing countries due largely to weaker capacity for climate change adaptation and mitigation. Keerthiratne and Tol (2018) explored the relationship between natural disasters and income inequality in Sri Lanka as the first study of this nature for the country. The analysis uses a unique panel dataset constructed for the purpose of this paper. It contains district inequality measures based on household income reported in six waves of the Household Income and Expenditure Survey of Sri Lanka during the period between 1990 and 2013, data on disaster-affected population and other economic and social indicators. Employing a panel fixed effects estimator, they found that contemporaneous natural disasters and their immediate lags significantly and substantially decreased inequality in per adult equivalent household income as measured by the Theil index. Findings are robust across various inequality metrics, subsamples and alternative estimators such as ordinary least-squares and system GMM. However, natural disasters do not affect household expenditure inequality. Either households behave as if they have a permanent income or all households reduce their expenditure proportionately irrespective of their income level in responding to natural disasters. Natural disasters decrease nonseasonal agricultural and nonagricultural income inequality but increase seasonal agricultural income inequality. The income of richer households is mainly derived from nonagricultural sources such as manufacturing and business activities and non-seasonal agricultural activities. Poorer households have a higher share of agricultural income.

Theory suggests that natural disasters can both hamper and increase economic growth. The Solow growth model suggests that natural disasters adversely affect gross domestic product (GDP) since these disrupt the production of inputs. On the contrary, the Schumpeterian growth theory provides an explanation behind a possible positive effect of natural disasters on economic growth. A good number of studies have investigated this question empirically in various and many countries and for different shocks. Most studies suggest that natural disasters significantly tend to reduce economic growth, and this is especially pertinent to low-income or less developed countries.

Thus, Felbermayr and Groeschl (2014) evaluated the relation between natural disasters (covering many types of disasters) and GDP growth rate using a new database based on physical measures of disaster intensity and panel regression that includes country and year fixed effects. They found that natural disasters have a robustly negative effect on the GDP growth rate and this relation is highly nonlinear for disaster intensity. For example, a disaster in the top 1% of the disaster intensity distribution reduces the GDP growth rate by 7%, while a disaster in the top 5% of the distribution reduced it by only 0.5%. Hsiang (2010) used data for 1970–2006 to study the effect of cyclone intensity on economic activity (measured by GDP) in 28 Caribbean countries and employed a panel model with country fixed effects for identification. He found a small effect of cyclones on total economic output, but when this effect is decomposed by industrial sector, he uncovered both large negative and large positive output responses. Specifically, agriculture, wholesale, retail sales, and tourism sectors are all impacted negatively by cyclones, while the construction sector benefits from them. The same author also found evidence of a dynamic relationship between lagged cyclone intensity and current sectoral GDP, suggesting that the economic impact of cyclones may last beyond their year of occurrence. Anttila-Hughes and Hsiang (2013) examined tropical cyclones using household-level data for the Philippines (one of the most typhoon-exposed countries in the world). They showed that the average typhoon affects both richer and poorer households, reducing annual household income by 6.6% in the short run. These losses persist for a few years after a typhoon, especially for poorer households. They also found that the income losses caused by a typhoon lead to a nearly one-for-one reduction in household expenditures in the Philippines, most notably expenditures related to human capital investments.

Strobl (2011) focused on counties in the US and examined the economic effects of hurricanes using US county-level data over 1970–2005. He built a hurricane destruction index based on a monetary loss equation, local wind speed estimates derived from a physical wind field model, and local exposure characteristics. Using a county fixed effect panel data, he uncovered the fact that a hurricane landfall in a county reduces the growth rate of per capita income by 0.45 percentage points, which is large compared to the average growth rate of 1.68%. An important component of the reduction in per capita income comes from an endogenous mobility response to the hurricane, whereby richer individuals are more likely to migrate out of the affected county.

Hsiang and Jina (2014) studied the effect of cyclones on economic growth over the short and long term using a country-year panel covering almost every country over the period 1950–2008 and its exposure to cyclones. When allowing for past cyclones to affect current GDP growth, they found persistent and negative effects of disasters on GDP growth. That is, they showed that incomes do not fully recover, even 20 years after a cyclone strikes, and an additional meter per second of wind exposure lowers per capita income by 0.4% 20 years later. These effects are found for both rich and poor countries, with higher losses in countries where cyclones are not as frequent and smaller in countries that are frequently exposed to cyclones. Their results imply that countries with less adaptation (less investments in protective capital) and experience with cyclones are more at risk to the negative effects of cyclones. An important implication is that natural disasters, in particular cyclones, reduce economic growth for several years beyond the year of the disaster, so that long-term effects are very important to be considered in the evaluation.

Ghazouani (2022) looked at the impact of natural disasters on the economy of African countries. In many economically weak countries in Africa, destructive natural events threaten people's lives. Unpredictable disasters such as floods or earthquakes have devastating consequences on the populations and economies of these countries. Based on a Bayesian spatial model propensity score matching model they tried to determine the possible impacts of natural disasters on African countries. The results showed a negative and significant impact of natural disasters, which led to a decrease of 35% of GDP over the entire period for the affected countries. For countries that did not experience extreme weather conditions, GDP increased by 1.43%.

Studies clearly show differences between high- and low-income countries in how they are impacted by the natural disasters. Importantly, Hoeppe (2016) showed that higher-income countries suffer higher direct property losses from natural disasters, but Kahn (2005) showed that they experience lower deaths from disasters and smaller negative economic growth impacts. Botzen, Deschenes, and Sanders (2020) suggested that richer nations may have better developed health-care systems and more resilient economies, which may be better able to cope with the natural disasters. They pointed to the importance of a country having a developed, diversified, and open economy with sound institutions to help weather the natural disaster shocks. Other studies also found other factors that can make countries more resilient in front of natural disasters. Noy (2009) found that countries with higher literacy rates, better institutions, and a higher degree of trade openness incur much smaller losses from natural disasters. Similarly, Toya and Skidmore (2007) found that increases in average education and trade openness help reduce damages from natural disasters as a share of GDP. Felbermayr and Groeschl found that natural disasters have smaller negative impacts on country GDP growth in countries that are democratic, are more open to trade, and have better developed financial markets.

Henkel, Eunjee, and Magontier (2022) found that postdisaster aid aims to relieve affected communities, but excessive financial aid may encourage economic activity to remain in exposed areas. They provided new empirical and theoretical evidence on the spatial consequences of postdisaster policies related to political motives. Using the exogenous variation in the timing of natural disasters, the authors showed that hurricanes close to elections lead to increased postdisaster efforts at the local level and result in increased population sorting into the impacted areas. To quantify and comprehend the implications of this new sorting pattern for the aggregate economy, they introduced the relationship between electoral cycles and postdisaster policies as a new feature in a dynamic spatial general equilibrium model. They showed that households respond to current postdisaster policies by sorting in hazard-prone coastal areas. Under the assumption of no climate change, current postdisaster policies improve aggregate welfare at the expense of overall GDP and productivity losses.

Boustan, Kahn, Rhode, and Yanguas (2020) constructed the universe of US federally designated natural disasters from 1920 to 2010 and found that severe disasters increase out-migration rates at the county level by 1.5 percentage points and lower housing prices/rents by 2.5%–5.0%. The migration response to milder disasters is smaller but has been increasing over time. This economic response to disasters is most consistent with falling local productivity and labor demand. Finally, they showed that disasters that convey more information about future disaster risk increase the pace of out-migration.

Bayoumi, Quayyum, and Das (2021) analyzed the impact of natural disasters on per-capita GDP growth. Using a quantile regression and growth-at-risk approach, the paper examines the impact of disasters and policy choices on the distribution of growth rather than simply its average. They found that countries that have in place disaster preparedness mechanisms and lower public debt have lower probability of witnessing a significant drop in growth because of a natural disaster, but their innovative methodology in this paper finds that the two policies are complements since their effectiveness varies across different disaster scenarios. While both are helpful for small- to mid-size disasters, lower debt and hence more fiscal space is more beneficial in the face of very large disasters. The authors suggest that a balanced strategy would thus involve both policies.

Pakoksung, Suppasri, Matsubae, and Imamura (2019) estimated potential losses from tsunami damage on Okinawa Island. They combined a tsunami hazard map with their proposed economic loss model to estimate the potential losses that would be sustained by Okinawa Island in the event of a tsunami. Their results show that the maximum total damaged area under the six earthquake scenarios is approximately $30\,km^2$. Inundation depth ranging from 2.0 to 5.0 m covers the largest area of approximately $10\,km^2$ and is followed by areas with inundation depths of 1.0–2.0 m and >5.0 m. Their findings show that direct losses will occur, while indirect losses are only approximately 56% that of direct losses. This approach could be applied to other areas and tsunami scenarios, which will aid disaster management and adaptation policies.

Haddad and Teixeira (2015) looked at the economic impacts of natural disasters in megacities, taking the case of floods in São Paulo, Brazil, through the use of a Spatial Computable General Equilibrium (SCGE) model integrated to GIS information related to the location of points of floods and the firms within their influence. It estimated that floods contributed to reduced city growth and residents' welfare, as well as hampering local competitiveness in both domestic and international markets. An intracity total impact-damage ratio of 2.2 and an economy-wide total impact-damage ratio of 5.0 were found.

Panwar and Sen (2019) reexamined the relationship between natural disasters and economic growth. Based on panel data consisting of 102 (29 developed and 73 developing) countries over the period 1981–2015, it looked at the growth effects of their types of natural disasters, namely, floods, droughts, storms, and earthquakes that were explored using the system generalized method of moments (GMM) approach. The results indicate that natural disasters have diverse economic impacts across economic segments depending on disaster types and their intensity. The study confirms that the economic impacts of natural disasters are statistically stronger in developing countries. These findings may stimulate policymakers, especially in developing countries, to explore the efficacy of viable ex ante disaster risk financing tools (such as insurance, microinsurance, and catastrophic bonds). This would not only safeguard population and physical assets but also ensure adherence to sustainable development goals.

Dyason (2022) analyzed the effects of the 2011 earthquakes in Canterbury, New Zealand, where the regional economy outpaced national economic growth rates for several years during the rebuild. The repair work on the built environment created years of elevated building activity. The results reveal a strong growing underlying economy, and while convergence was expected as the stimulus slowed down, the results found that growth had already crossed over for some time. The results reveal that the investment stimulus provides an initial 1.5%–2% growth buffer from the underlying economy before the growth rates cross over. This supports short-term economic recovery and enables the underlying economy to transition away from a significant rebuild stimulus. Once the growth crosses over, 5 years after the disaster, economic growth in the underlying economy remains buoyant even if official regional economic data suggest otherwise.

Athukorala and Resosudarmo (2005) analyzed the immediate economic impact of the Indian Ocean tsunami generated by the Sumatra-Andaman earthquake of 2004 and the disaster management process in the immediate aftermath of the disaster with a focus on the two most severely affected countries—Indonesia (Aceh province) and Sri Lanka. This tsunami is unique among large disasters in recorded human history, not only because of the sheer number of casualities and massive displacement of people, but also because of the unprecedented international donor response and the logistic challenges faced by international organizations and aid agencies in organizing and coordinating relief efforts. Their preliminary findings point to the importance of educating the public about simple precautions in the event of a disaster and enforcement of coastal environmental regulations as disaster prevention policies. The findings also make a strong case for designing policies and programs, as an integral part of a national development strategy, for mitigating the impact of natural disasters on the poor and highlight the need for combining international aid commitments with innovative approaches to redressing problems of limited aid absorptive capacity in disaster-affected countries.

Lee, Zhang, and Nguyen (2018) discussed the economic impact of natural disasters in Pacific Island countries, which are highly at risk of various natural disasters, which are destructive, unpredictable, and occur frequently. They identified the intensity of natural disasters for each country in the Pacific based on the distribution of damage and population affected by disasters and estimated the impact of disasters on economic growth and international trade using a panel regression. The results showed that severe disasters have a significant and negative impact on economic growth and lead to a deterioration of the fiscal and trade balance. They also found that the negative impact on growth is stronger for more intense disasters.

Bringas, Bunyi, and Manapat (2022) analyzed the relationship among natural disasters (i.e., earthquake, flood, and storm), economic activities (i.e., foreign aid and foreign direct investment), and GDP per capita income in the Philippines from 1990 to 2019. This study employed a multivariate analysis, time series regression, and autoregressive distributed lag (ARDL) approach. The results revealed a complex relationship between GDP per capita and the regressors. In the short run, the independent variables have a negative and significant relationship with the country's per capita income. On the contrary, only FDI has a significant long-run relationship with the economy of the Philippines. The results highlight the Philippines' need for comprehensive disaster plans and to lessen its dependence on foreign and external factors.

Weerasekara, Wilson, Lee, Hoang, Managi, and Rajapaksa (2021) examined the economic impact of climate-induced disasters on Sri Lanka's agricultural, industrial, and services sectors and their subsectors. Using cross-provincial panel datasets for Sri Lanka for the period 1997–2018, they showed that the agricultural sector is the most affected by climate-induced disasters, although not all agricultural subsectors are equally at risk. Similarly, the industrial sector is shown to suffer a significant negative impact due to strong winds and landslide events. The textiles and garment subsectors are negatively impacted while the machinery subsector shows a positive impact. This indicates the effect of higher demand for new machinery and equipment employed in disaster reconstruction efforts. The study further reveals that the services sector derives a mostly positive impact following disasters, especially the public administration and health subsectors. The study also indicates that for Sri Lanka during the current decade, there has been a considerably greater negative impact from climate-induced disasters compared to the previous decade.

Huang, Malik, Lenzen, Jin, Wang, Faturay, and Zhu (2022) evaluated the postdisaster economic impacts due to the Sichuan earthquake in 2008 and its regional and industrial spillover effects based on a Chinese multiregional input–output table. The results show that the 2008 Sichuan earthquake caused approximately 1725 billion US dollars of value-added losses and 69.9 million people of employment losses. The chemical industry in Guangdong and Zhejiang suffered severe value-added losses due to indirect effects through supply chains. Furthermore, public administration in Henan, Sichuan, and Guangdong suffered large employment losses. In general, they found that the economically less-developed provinces are more susceptible to larger losses as compared to the economically developed provinces.

While most studies documented negative economic effects from natural disasters, few studies found positive effects mostly due to recovery efforts and/or government aid. Heger and Neumayer (2019) exploited the unexpected nature of the 2004 Indian Ocean tsunami for carrying out a quasi-experimental difference-in-differences analysis of flooded districts and subdistricts in Aceh. The Indonesian province saw the single largest aid and reconstruction effort of any developing world region ever afflicted by a natural disaster. The authors showed that this effort triggered higher long-term economic output than would have happened in the absence of the tsunami. Guo, Liu, Wu, Gu, Song, and Tang (2015) used a newly developed integrated indicator system with entropy weighting; they analyzed the panel data of 577 recorded disasters in 30 provinces of China from 1985 to 2011 to identify their links with the subsequent economic growth. They found that meteorological disasters promote economic growth through human capital instead of physical capital, geological disasters did not trigger local economic growth from 1999 to 2011, and generally, natural disasters overall had no significant impact on economic growth from 1985 to 1998. Thus, human capital reinvestment should be the aim in managing recoveries, and it should be used to regenerate the local economy based on long-term sustainable development. Yamamura (2016) analyzed the impact of the Great Hanshin-Awaji (Kobe) earthquake that struck Japan in 1995, which caused devastating damage to the economic landscape of South-central Japan. This study investigated how the earthquake enhanced participation in community activity. The key findings are: (i) people were more likely to participate in community activities in 1996 than in 1991, (ii) the effects of the earthquake on community participation decreased as the distance of one's place of residence increased from Kobe, and (iii) the earthquake significantly increased the community participation rate of Kobe residents, whereas it had no significant influence on the investment rate of residents of large cities close to Kobe.

A few studies found mixed effects from natural disasters. Strulik and Trimborn (2019) showed that GDP is driven above its preshock level when natural disasters destroy predominantly durable consumption goods (cars, furniture, etc.). Disasters destroying mainly productive capital, in contrast, are predicted to reduce GDP. Insignificant responses of GDP can be expected when disasters destroy both durable goods and productive capital. The authors extended the model by a residential housing sector and showed that disasters may also have an insignificant impact on GDP when they destroy residential houses and durable goods. They showed that disasters, irrespective of whether their impact on GDP is positive, negative, or insignificant, entail considerable losses of aggregate welfare. Atsalakis, Bouri, and Pasiouras (2021) proposed the use of a quantile-on-quantile (QQ) approach to shed more light on the relationship between natural disasters and economic growth. This approach combines standard quantile regression analysis with nonparametric estimations and allows us to examine how different quantiles of natural disasters affect different quantiles of GDP growth. Using data from over 100 countries over a 30-year period, the authors confirmed that the results of the QQ approach differ from the ones obtained by standard approaches like fixed effects regressions. They documented that the relationship between the intensity of natural disasters and economic growth is mostly negative. Nonetheless, there are some exceptions to this. Their findings revealed that the effect of natural disasters can be occasionally positive, depending on the quantiles that they examine. The magnitude of the effect also differs across different combinations of the quantile of economic growth and the quantile of natural disasters. Finally, they obtained somewhat different results when they estimated separate QQ regressions for groups of countries that differ in terms of climate, and economic and democratic development, and across different year lags of the natural disaster index. Sardar, Javed, and Amirud-Din (2016) estimated the impact of three flood-related hazards (mortality, damage to property, and nonfatal effect on the population) on GDP growth in Pakistan for the period 1972–2013. They argued that damages caused by floods are endogenous and the 2SLS technique is used to address the problem of endogeneity in the model. The evidence suggests that GDP per capita growth and disaster management mitigate the scale of flood-related hazards. Most importantly and counter to the evidence from many other countries, floods' frequency accentuates flood-related hazards in Pakistan suggesting lack of learning from the past experience with floods. Regarding the relationship between floods and economic growth, this study found that flood-related hazards have significant negative impact on the GDP growth of the economy. The damage to property leaves the strongest impact on economic growth.

3.4 Natural disasters and banking sectors around the world

In addition to governments, banking organizations tend to offer assistance that often includes payment relief and credit relief for customers affected by natural disasters.[9,10] A smaller body of literature investigates how banks and the banking sector more broadly are affected by climate risks, how they react to climate-change concerns such as extreme weather events, and whether they help the recovery efforts in communities affected by natural disasters.[11]

We start with risks that natural disasters could pose to the banking sector given that policymakers are keenly interested in understanding the risks that climate change and related natural disasters could pose to banks. Importantly, the extant literature discusses both physical and transition climate risks for banks. To detail, physical risks can refer to physical and operational losses and other related risks, erosion of collateral, or erosion of asset values of banking organizations due to increased extreme climate-related events such as hurricanes, floods, and wildfires. Transition risks are related to climate

---

[9]The Federal Emergency Management Administration (FEMA) offers government relief for consumers suffering from natural disasters; see https://www.fema.gov/assistance/individual. Using data on US hurricane landfalls from 1979 to 2002, Deryugina (2017) finds that government disaster aid averaged around $160 per capita, while nondisaster social insurance transfers increased around $1000 per capita in the disaster areas over the 10 years following the hurricane.

[10]Regulators often encourage banks to lend to disaster-struck areas. Credit relief can take the form of restructuring existing loans, extending repayment periods, or providing new credit at more favorable terms to the consumers.

[11]Governments and financial institutions tend to offer assistance that often includes payment relief and credit relief for customers affected by natural disasters.

policies, regulation, and economic agents and market sentiments and new preferences related to climate-related events and can lead to reevaluations of risks and asset values of banking organizations. At the microlevel, these climate risks can manifest via increased operational losses for both the bank and their customers due to business disruption but also increased regulatory and legal risks. It can increase market risks such as asset repricing and fire sales due to exposures to local markets with higher depreciation and damage from climate events. Both banks and their customers can suffer from reputational and political climate risk when having larger exposures and damage from carbon-intensive sectors and local markets. Finally, there could be increased bank portfolio credit and liquidity risk if economic agents that receive credit from the banks incur severe deterioration in their financial outlook from climate-related shocks which increases their likelihood of default on their loan obligations to the banks. The empirical research explores many of these climate shock risk dimensions and we review some of the most prominent papers below.

From a credit risk perspective, existing literature recognizes credit losses as a potential channel affecting banks but does not find that weather disasters had only small and often insignificant impact on US banks' performance over the last quarter thus far (e.g., Blickle, Hamerling, and Morgan, 2021). In addition, several papers suggest that banking organizations take measures to mitigate some of these risks via securitization of some of loans exposed to the risks, charging higher prices or providing less credit overall when risks are perceived as higher, or maintaining higher capital levels among others (e.g., Lambert, Noth, and Schüwer, 2019; Ouazad and Kahn, 2019; Correa, He, Herpfer, and Lel, 2022; Duanmu, Li, Lin, and Tahsin, 2022). For example, Ouazad and Kahn (2019) find a substantial increase in bank mortgage securitization activity in the years following natural disasters, with effects being larger in areas where the disaster was new news. This suggests that bank lenders have incentives to sell their worse flood risk to the agency securitizers to mitigate some of their credit risks in affected areas. Similarly as protective measure, Lambert, Noth, and Schüwer (2019) show that stand-alone banks (not owned by a bank holding company) based in the disaster areas increase their risk-based capital ratios after the Katrina hurricane, while those that are not part of a bank holding company on average do not.

In contrast to findings on bank credit risk, from an operational risk perspective, Berger, Curti, Lazaryan, Mihov, and Roman (2022) use supervisory operational data from large US bank holding companies (BHCs), and document that banks suffer more operational losses during episodes of extreme climate risk shocks, i.e., extreme storms. Among different operational loss types, losses due to external fraud, banks' failure to meet obligations to clients and faulty business practices, damage to physical assets, and business disruption are most important identified. Moreover, banks with past exposure to extreme storms reduce operational losses from future exposure to storms, consistent with experience sharping risk assessments of such future events and future risk management decision making for handling them. Also consistent with this, Cheney and Rhine (2006), analyze the US financial system's response to Hurricane Katrina and the safety nets in place for disaster-area residents. They emphasize the significant disruptions to local banking networks, and simple financial transactions, resulting from damage to physical infrastructure and the lack of electric power in the area. These papers highlight the importance of preparedness and contingency planning on the part of financial institutions and the government to serve the public around the time of a natural disaster.

A larger literature investigates how banks react in their credit provision when faced with natural disasters and/or how do they help the recovery efforts in communities affected by natural disasters. Thus, a paper by Cortés and Strahan (2017) uses disaster data over 2001–10, and test how increases in credit demand from natural disasters affect lending in other markets connected to banks exposed to the shocks. Using mortgage origination data, authors document that banks reallocate funds toward disaster-struck markets with high credit demand in which they own branches and away from other markets (connected markets) in which they lend. Thus, credit seems to flow toward high-demand markets and away from lower-demand ones. They find that this is driven by small banks, defined as those with assets below $2 billion. Also, credit supplied to connected markets declines by a little less than 50 cents per dollar of increased lending in their shocked areas. In contrast, larger banks do not reduce credit in connected markets, likely because of the lower costs of external finance for them. Moreover, small banks increase sales of more liquid, smaller mortgage loans and increase deposit rates in the connected markets to help lessen the impact of the demand shock on credit supply.[12] Gallagher and Hartley (2017) find that areas flooded by Katrina that had a larger presence of local banks had higher lending growth, consistent with local banks encouraging rebuilding. Cortés (2015) finds that areas with a greater relative presence of local lenders recover faster after disasters. The authors show that an increase in local finance offsets the negative effects of the disaster and leads to 1%–2% higher employment growth at young and small firms. Importantly, banks' increased lending in disaster areas does not lead to higher default rates which could jeopardize the banks' portfolio quality. Somewhat in contrast, Garmaise and Moskowitz (2009) find that earthquake risk decreased commercial real estate bank loan provision by 22% in California properties in the 1990s, and the most severe effects were in African American neighborhoods.

Chavaz (2016) finds that banks with higher concentration in markets hit by the 2005 hurricane season (specifically Hurricanes Katrina, Rita, Wilma, and Dennis) increased lending more than banks with a lower concentration in those areas. Compared with diversified banks, local banks originate a higher share of new mortgages and small business loans in affected areas but sell a higher share of the new mortgages into the secondary market. These results suggest a potential bank specialization, under which loans in affected areas are originated more by banks with incentives to take opportunities in a distressed market, but then get them transferred to agents that can better support the associated risk. Lambert, Noth, and Schüwer (2019) explore how banks reacted to Hurricane Katrina in 2005, and what the effects of banks' involvement were on local economic development. They find that disaster-affected counties with a relatively large share of stand-alone banks and relatively high-average bank capital ratios show higher economic growth than other affected counties following the catastrophic event. This suggests that local banks do help in the disaster recovery efforts.

Bos, Li, and Sanders (2022) analyzed how banks adjust their asset structure in response to changes in loan demand following natural disasters. Their theoretical model shows the banks' credit allocation behavior in a dynamic model with multiple assets and quantifies the potential impact of climate change on banks via the natural hazard channel. Their empirical analysis used a difference-in-differences method and found that US banks increase real estate lending after disasters and sell government bonds to finance this disaster-driven credit surge.

Dlugosz, Gam, Gopalan, and Skrastins (2022) used natural disasters as shocks to local economies, and documented that a bank branch's ability to set deposit rates locally has real effects. Following disasters, branches with rates set locally increase deposit rates more and experience higher deposit volumes in affected counties. Consistent with imperfect insurance from internal capital markets, banks with more

---

[12]Focusing on payday lenders rather than banks, Morse (2011) finds that poor residents fare better across a number of outcomes following natural disasters in areas served by payday lenders.

branches setting rates locally, expand mortgage lending more in affected counties. In addition, they showed that house prices recover faster in local areas where more such branches' rates are set locally.

Koetter, Noth, and Rehbein (2020) showed that local banks provide corporate recovery lending to firms affected by natural disasters. Banks that reside in counties unaffected by the natural disaster increase lending to firms inside affected counties by 3%. Firms domiciled in flooded counties, in turn, increase corporate borrowing by 16% if they are connected to banks in unaffected counties. They found no indication that recovery lending entails excessive risk-taking or rent-seeking. However, within the group of shock-exposed banks, those without access to geographically more diversified interbank markets exhibit more credit risk and less equity capital.

Berg and Schrader (2012) analyzed the effect of unpredictable aggregate shocks on loan demand and access to credit by combining client-level information from an Ecuadorian microfinance institution with geophysical data on volcanic eruptions. The results of this "natural experiment" show that while credit demand increases due to volcanic activity, access to credit is restricted. Yet, they also found that bank-borrower relationships—known to help overcome the problems of asymmetric information—can lower these lending restrictions and that clients who are known to the institution are about equally likely to receive loans after the volcanic eruptions occurred.

Bradley, Henriksson, and Valsalan (2021) used natural disasters as exogenous shocks to the peer-to-peer (P2P) loan market and documented a local increase in loan demand postdisaster. They showed that interest rates and delinquencies from loans approved during this demand shock are similar to preevent levels. Moreover, loans allocated prior to a disaster are more likely to suffer delinquency over the life of the loan, but loans granted a hardship accommodation delay of payment reduce the likelihood of future delinquency providing relief to borrowers and reduced delinquency costs to investors. Contrary to regulatory concerns that P2P lending is predatory, their results suggest that they provide positive social welfare benefits.

In contrast, a number of studies documented a decline in credit supply from banks and increase in the cost of credit for corporate borrowers, suggesting that banks may be cautious. When dealing with natural disaster risk, Duanmu, Li, Lin, and Tahsin (2022) studied how bank residential mortgage lending standards are affected by risks to the local economy from natural disasters. Namely, banks tighten lending standards in disaster-hit counties, suggesting that lenders are more cautious in these locations since environmental disasters can increase the long-term risks to the local economy. Tighter bank lending standards can lower access to mortgage credit and can have negative consequences for the housing sector. But, they do not find any statistically significant change in the lending standards of banks that specialize in subprime loans. Finally, they showed that banks tighten lending standards in those disaster-hit counties where there is a strong belief about the negative effects of climate change, suggesting that disasters impact lending standards through increasing existing disaster risk awareness among lenders, whereas lenders do not update their risk assessment in low-belief counties. Correa, He, Herpfer, and Lel (2022) investigated how corporate loan costs are affected by climate change-related natural disasters. They constructed granular measures of borrowers' exposure to natural disasters and then disentangled the direct effects of disasters from the effects of banks updating their beliefs about the impact of future disasters. Following a climate change-related disaster, spreads on bank loans of at-risk, yet unaffected borrowers, spike and are amplified when attention to climate change is high. Weaker borrowers with the most extreme exposure to these disasters suffer the highest increase in spreads. Importantly, authors found that there is no such effect from disasters that are not aggravated by climate change. Garmaise and Moskowitz (2009) provided a model of the effects of catastrophic risk on real estate financing and prices and demonstrate that insurance market imperfections can restrict the supply of credit for catastrophe-susceptible properties. Using unique microlevel data, they found that earthquake risk decreased commercial real estate bank loan provision by 22% in California properties in the 1990s, with more severe effects in African American neighborhoods. They showed that the 1994 Northridge earthquake had only a short-term disruptive effect. Their basic findings are confirmed for hurricane risk. Elsadek Mahmoudi (2020) found that the local credit shock, induced by Hurricane Katrina, propagated through banks' internal networks and led to real and credit markets' effects in distant regions. Driven by abnormal mortgage and housing demand in Katrina-hit areas, financially constrained multimarket banks reallocated resources toward the damaged areas leading to a credit tightening in the undamaged local markets. Depending on their housing supply elasticity, local housing markets in the undamaged regions responded to this credit disruption with a mix of housing prices and housing supply declines. These spillovers depended on undamaged markets' financial linkages to disaster areas. In the undamaged regions, community banks, being local and unexposed to disaster areas, partially helped insulate their markets from these spillovers.

Jiang, Li, and Qian (2020) examined whether climate-change risk affects firms' cost of capital when firms can adapt to the risk. They found that firms' cost of long-term bank loans increases with sea level rise (SLR) risk, but this effect mainly holds among firms with high adjustment costs to the risk, i.e., firms for whom it is hard to relocate or otherwise diversify SLR risk. Moreover, the spread-risk sensitivity is higher if the bank has more experience with the risk and in times of heightened media attention. This suggests banks pay limited attention to this unconventional risk. Ivanov, Kruttli, and Watugala (2021) estimated the effect of carbon pricing policy on bank credit to firms with greenhouse gas emissions. Their analyses exploit the geographic restrictions inherent in the California cap-and-trade bill and a discontinuity in the embedded free-permit threshold of the federal Waxman-Markey cap-and-trade bill. They documented that banks quickly mitigate their exposure to climate transition risks. Thus, the affected high-emission firms face shorter loan maturities, lower access to permanent forms of bank financing, higher interest rates, and higher participation of shadow banks in their lending syndicates. These effects are concentrated among private firms, suggesting banks are less concerned about the policy's impact on public firms.

Ivanov, Macchiavelli, and Santos (2020) studied how syndicated lending networks propagate natural disasters. They first showed that natural disasters lead to an increase in corporate credit demand in affected regions and banks meet the increase in credit demand in part by reducing credit to distant regions, unaffected by disasters. Capital constraints play a key role in this effect as lower-capital banks propagate disasters to unaffected regions to a greater extent. While shadow banks offset the reduction in bank credit supply on term loan syndicates, they do not offset the loss in credit line financing. Overall, they showed that corporate credit in unaffected regions falls by approximately 3%, a possible unintended consequence.

Finally, Blickle and Santos (2022) found that the quasi-mandatory US flood insurance program reduces mortgage lending along both the extensive and intensive margins and found unintended consequences of the well-intentioned regulation. The authors measure flood insurance mandates using FEMA flood maps, focusing on the discreet updates to these maps that can be made exogenous to true underlying flood risk. They found that reductions in lending are most pronounced for low-income and low-credit-score borrowers, implying that the effects are at least partially driven by the added financial burden of insurance. Their results are also stronger among nonlocal or more distant banks, which have a diminished ability to monitor local borrower adherence to complicated insurance mandates. The results suggest the importance of factoring in affordability and enforcement feasibility when introducing mandatory standards.

Thus, this economic research found mixed results on whether banks help mitigate the negative effects of natural disasters in highly impacted areas by increasing the provision of loans. Research also found that banks may be protecting themselves by securitization of high-risk loans and increasing their capital base. When increases in credit in impacted areas occur however, these contribute to higher employment growth at young and small firms.

Three papers looked at the direct impact of natural disasters on bank credit risk. Klomp (2014) explored the impact of large-scale natural disasters on the distance-to-default of banks using data for more than 160 countries over 1997–2010. The financial consequences of natural catastrophes may stress and threaten the existence of a bank by adversely affecting their liquidity and solvency position. They found strong evidence that natural disasters increase the likelihood of a banks' default. When looking at types of disasters, they uncovered that geophysical and meteorological disasters reduce the distance-to-default the most due to their widespread damage caused. In addition, the impact of a natural disaster depends on the size and scope of the catastrophe, the rigorousness of financial regulation and supervision, and the level of financial and economic development of a particular country. Erhemjamts, Huang, and Tehranian (2022) assessed the climate risk exposure of US commercial banks by combining branch-level deposit data with city-level climate risk scores. Their results revealed that climate risk exposure is (i) positively associated with the environmental, social, and governance (ESG) performance of banks and (ii) negatively associated with stakeholder ESG sentiment toward these banks. Bank financial performance is negatively affected by such exposure. However, a stronger ESG performance mitigates this adverse effect. Consistent with this observation, an ESG sentiment factor loads positively in factor models that predict bank stock returns. They also provided evidence that bank ESG performance spills over benefits to local economies: When matched on determinants of ESG performance, banks that exhibit stronger ESG performance are associated with greater city-level readiness for climate events compared to otherwise similar banks exhibiting weaker ESG performance. Kotsantonis and Bufalari (2019) showed that banks that consistently scored high on material ESG issues delivered higher risk-adjusted returns compared to those banks that performed poorly on the same issues, while the opposite was found for immaterial ESG issues.

More on ESG lending, Kim, Kumar, Lee, and Oh (2022) examined the environmental, social, and governance (ESG) loan market, which has grown from $6 billion in 2016 to $322 billion in 2021. This growth is driven primarily by ESG-linked loans where loan spreads are contingent on borrower ESG performance, as well as by use-of-proceeds-based green loans issued for specific green projects. ESG-linked loans are mostly issued by large and publicly traded firms with superior ESG profiles. These loans are often structured as revolving credit facilities and syndicated by dominant global banks with good ESG profiles and preexisting lending relationships with borrowers. Green loans, on the other hand, are mostly issued to privately held borrowers by nonrelationship lenders. ESG loan borrowers enjoy a net pricing advantage, suggesting improved ESG profiles reduce credit risk or that lenders' value is associated with ESG loans. The authors found that ESG-linked loans are opaque and vary widely in the extent of their contractual disclosures. Consistent with greenwashing, borrowers with low-quality disclosures about ESG contract features experience deterioration in ESG scores after loan issuance. Borrowers with high quality disclosures continue to maintain good ESG profiles and stock markets react positively to such loan announcements. Overall, the authors' results indicate market vigilance against potential greenwashing and suggest that as the market matures, the ESG loan market has the potential to make a positive impact on corporate ESG performance. Shin (2021) examined the impact of corporate Environmental, Social, and Governance (ESG) profiles on the matching between lenders and borrowers and loan pricing. High ESG firms are more likely to obtain loans, which come with lower interest rates. These effects are driven by low ESG banks that attempt to improve their ESG profiles by lending to high ESG firms at lower rates. The author found support for these findings using the FTSE4Good US Index rebalance events as shocks to borrowers' ESG reputation. Also, borrowers appear to improve ESG ratings while seeking a loan but reduce effort after obtaining it.

Two papers focus on climate change lending in an international context. Benincasa, Kabas, and Ongena (2021) provided evidence that banks increase cross-border lending in response to higher climate policy stringency in their home countries. Saturating with a granular set of fixed effects and including a rich set of control variables, they showed that the increase in cross-border lending is not driven by loan demand and/or other bank home country characteristics. In line with banks use cross-border lending as a regulatory arbitrage tool, the increase in cross-border lending occurs only if banks' home countries have more stringent climate policies compared to their borrowers' countries. The effect is stronger for large, lowly capitalized banks with high NPL ratios and for banks with more experience in cross-border lending. These results suggest that without global cooperation, cross-border lending can be a channel that reduces the effectiveness of climate policies. Degryse, Goncharenko, Theunisz, and Vadasz (2021) investigated whether and how the environmental consciousness (greenness for short) of firms and banks is reflected in the pricing of bank credit. Using a large international sample of syndicated loans over the period 2011–19, they found that firms are indeed rewarded for being green in the form of cheaper loans however, only when borrowing from a green consortium of lenders, and only after the ratification of the Paris Agreement in 2015. Thus, they found those environmental attitudes matter when green meets green. They further constructed a simple stylized theoretical model to show that the green-meets-green pattern emerges in equilibrium as the result of third-degree price discrimination about firms' greenness.

3.5 Natural disasters and financial markets around the world

A number of papers focus on how natural disasters in US and around the world affect financial markets. Two papers looked at effects on the municipal bond market. Starting with Garrett and Ivanov (2022), the authors studied how government regulation limiting the adoption of environmental, social, and governance (ESG) policies distorts financial market outcomes. The State of Texas enacted laws in 2021 that prohibit municipalities from contracting with banks that have certain ESG policies. This led to the exit of five of the largest municipal bond underwriters from the state. The authors found that municipal bond issuers with previous reliance on the exiting underwriters are more likely to negotiate pricing and incur higher borrowing costs after the implementation of the laws. Among the remaining competitive sales, issuers face significantly fewer bidding underwriters and higher bid variance, consistent with a decline in underwriter competition. Additionally, underpricing increases among issuers most reliant on the targeted banks and bonds are placed through a larger number of smaller trades. Overall, their estimates imply Texas entities will pay an additional $303–$532 million in interest on the $32 billion in borrowing during the first 8 months following Texas laws. Painter (2020) showed that counties more likely to be affected by climate change pay more in underwriting fees and initial yields to issue long-term municipal bonds compared to counties unlikely to be affected by climate change. This difference disappears when comparing short-term municipal bonds, implying the bond market prices climate change risks for long-term securities only. Higher issuance costs for climate risk counties are driven by bonds with lower credit ratings. The author found that investor attention is a driving factor, as the difference in issuance costs on bonds issued by climate- and nonclimate-affected counties increases after the release of the 2006 Stern Review on climate change.

One paper investigates effects on the corporate bond market. Huynh and Xia (2021) examined whether climate change news risk is priced in corporate bonds. They estimated bond covariance with a climate change news index and found that bonds with a higher climate change news beta earn lower future returns, consistent with the asset pricing implications of the demand for bonds with high potential to hedge against climate risk. Moreover, when investors are concerned about climate risk, they are willing to pay higher prices for bonds issued by firms with better environmental performance. Their findings suggest that corporate policies aimed at improving environmental performance pay off when the market is concerned about climate change risk.

Another paper discusses new bond instruments. Sakai, Roch, Wiriadinata, and Fu (2022) discussed the role that financial markets play in financing the adaptation and mitigation to climate change. Catastrophe and green bonds in the private sector have become the most prominent innovations in the field of sustainable finance in the last 15 years. Yet, the issuances at the sovereign level have been relatively recent and are not well documented in the literature. They discussed the benefits of issuing these instruments as well as practical implementation challenges impairing the scaling up of these markets. The issuance of these instruments could provide an additional source of stable financing with more favorable market access conditions, mitigate the stress of climate risks on public finances, and facilitate the transition to greener low-carbon economies. Emerging market and developing economies stand to benefit the most from these financial innovations.

Then, the vast majority of studies have focused mostly on the stock market or option market. A number of papers try to understand climate risk, relying on rational asset pricing vs deviations from purely rational pricing. Bansal, Kiku, and Ochoa (2019) argued that market prices accurately reflect long-run climate risks, as proxied by temperature fluctuations. Particularly, the authors used the forward-looking information from the US and global capital markets to estimate the economic impact of global warming, specifically, long-run temperature shifts. They found that global warming carries a positive risk premium that increases with the level of temperature and that has almost doubled over the last 80 years. Consistent with their model, virtually all US equity portfolios have negative exposure (beta) to long-run temperature fluctuations. The elasticity of equity prices to temperature risks across global markets is significantly negative and has been increasing in magnitude over time along with the rise in temperature. They found that the long-run impact of temperature on growth implies a significant social cost of carbon emissions.

Giglio, Maggiori, Rao, Stroebel, and Weber (2021) estimated the term structure of discount rates in real estate markets to help inform the appropriate discount rates to be used in valuing investments required for mitigating climate change. Specifically, they estimated the term structure of discount rates for an important risky asset class, real estate, up to the very long horizons relevant for investments in climate change abatement. They showed that this term structure is steeply downward sloping, reaching 2.6% at horizons beyond 100 years. The analysis demonstrates that applying average rates of return that are observed for traded assets to investments in climate change abatement is misleading. In addition, the discount rates for investments in climate change abatement that reduce aggregate risk, as in disaster-risk models, are bounded above by our estimated term structure for risky housing and should be below 2.6% for long-run benefits. This upper bound rules out many discount rates suggested in the literature and used by policymakers. Their framework also distinguishes between the various mechanisms the environmental literature has proposed for generating downward-sloping discount rates.

Along similar lines, Daniel, Litterman, and Wagner (2016) showed how asset pricing theories can help guide the optimal tax on carbon emissions. Pricing greenhouse gas emissions involves making trade-offs between consumption today and unknown damages in the (distant) future. This setup calls for an optimal control model to determine the carbon dioxide (CO_2) price. It also relies on society's willingness to substitute consumption across time and across uncertain states of nature, the forte of Epstein-Zin preference specifications. The authors developed the EZ-Climate model, a simple discrete-time optimization model in which uncertainty about the effect of CO_2 emissions on global temperature and on eventual damages is gradually resolved over time. They embedded a number of features including potential tail risk, exogenous and endogenous technological change, and backstop technologies. The EZ-Climate model suggests a high optimal carbon price today that is expected to decline over time as uncertainty about the damages is resolved. It also points to the importance of backstop technologies and to very large deadweight costs of delay. They decomposed the optimal carbon price into two components: expected discounted damages and the risk premium.

Considering deviations of asset prices or economic agents from pure rationality, Hong, Li, and Xu (2019) investigated whether stock markets efficiently price risks brought on or exacerbated by climate change. They focused on drought, the most damaging natural disaster for crops, and food-company cash flows and found that stock prices of firms in the food sector do not accurately reflect the underlying climate risks, at least in the context of natural disasters. Specifically, they showed that prolonged drought in a country, measured by the Palmer Drought Severity Index (PDSI) from climate studies, forecasts both declines in profitability ratios and poor stock returns for food companies in that country. A portfolio short food stocks of countries in drought and long those of countries not in drought generates a 9.2% annualized return from 1985 to 2015. This excess predictability is larger in countries having little history of droughts prior to the 1980s. Their findings support the regulatory concerns of markets inexperienced with climate change underreacting to such risks.

Engle, Giglio, Kelly, Lee, and Stroebel (2020) proposed and implemented a procedure to dynamically hedge climate change risk. To create their hedge target, they extracted innovations from climate news series that they constructed through textual analysis of high-dimensional data on newspaper coverage of climate change. They then used a mimicking portfolio approach based on a large panel of equity returns to build climate change hedge portfolios. They disciplined the exercise by using third-party ESG scores of firms to model their climate risk exposures. They showed that this approach yields parsimonious and industry-balanced portfolios that perform well in hedging innovations in climate news both in-sample and out-of-sample. The resulting hedge portfolios outperform alternative hedging strategies based primarily on industry tilts. They discussed multiple directions for future research on financial approaches to managing climate risk.

Bolton and Kacperczyk (2021) explored whether carbon emissions affect the cross-section of US stock returns. They found that stocks of firms with higher total CO_2 emissions (and changes in emissions) earn higher returns, after controlling for size, book-to-market, momentum, and other factors that predict returns. They cannot explain this carbon premium through differences in unexpected profitability or other known risk factors. They also found that institutional investors implement exclusionary screening based on direct emission intensity in a few salient industries. Overall, their results are consistent with an interpretation that investors are already demanding compensation for exposure to carbon emission risk.

Stroebel and Wurgler (2021) surveyed 861 finance academics, professionals, and public sector regulators and policy economists about climate finance topics. They identified regulatory risk as the top climate risk to businesses and investors over the next 5 years, but they viewed physical risk as the top risk over the next 30 years. By an overwhelming margin, respondents believed that asset prices underestimate climate risks rather than overestimate them. They also tabulated opinions about the expected correlation between growth and climate change, social discount rates appropriate for projects that mitigate the effects of climate change, most influential forces for reducing climate risks, and most important research topics.

Ilhan, Sautner, and Vilkov (2021) explored carbon tail risk looking at the options market. Strong regulatory actions are needed to combat climate change, but climate policy uncertainty makes it difficult for investors to quantify the impact of future climate regulation. They showed that such uncertainty is priced in the option market. The cost of option protection against downside tail risks is larger for firms with more carbon-intense business models. For carbon-intense firms, the cost of protection against downside tail risk is magnified at times when the public's attention to climate change spikes, and it decreased after the election of climate change skeptic President Trump.

Two papers looked at the foreign exchange and remittances markets, respectively. Asongu (2012) used unadjusted and adjusted correlation coefficients to test for contagion effects across 33 economies in the aftermath of the Japanese earthquake, the ensuing tsunami, and the worst nuclear crisis in recent history. The results indicate no international foreign exchange markets experienced significantly stronger correlations with the Japanese Yen 2 months after. However, for international stock markets, Taiwan, Bahrain, Saudi Arabia, and South Africa experience contagion, consistent with the widely held notion that contagion is mostly a concern for emerging countries. The effects of natural disasters on financial markets are important in investment decisions, as the benefits of portfolio diversification are severely limited during periods of high volatility and increased cross-market correlations. With financial globalization, investors can gain from diversification if returns from financial markets are stable and not correlated. However, with volatility spillovers, increase in cross-market correlations exist as a real effect and are not considered for asset allocation and portfolio composition. The results have two paramount implications. Firstly, they have confirmed the existing consensus that in the face of natural crises that could take an international scale, only emerging markets are contagiously affected for the most part. Secondly, they have also shown that international financial market transmissions not only occur during financial crises but also natural disaster effects should not be undermined.

Bettin and Zazzaro (2018) offered novel empirical evidence on the impact of natural disasters on remittance flows toward low- and middle-income countries. They considered a panel of 98 countries over the period 1990–2010. Their findings show that remittances increase after a disaster, thus contributing ex post to the reconstruction process. At the same time, they found that remittances play a key role in terms of ex ante risk preparedness for those countries that experienced more disruptive events in the past. Finally, when taking into account the interaction with the level of development of local financial markets, remittances seem to substitute for less efficient financial systems both in terms of ex post response to disasters and in terms of ex ante risk management strategy.

Some studies have examined the implications of climate risks for investor behavior. In the context of fund managers, Bernile, Bhagwat, Kecskés, and Nguyen (2021) showed that the risk attitudes of professional investors are affected by their catastrophic experiences even for catastrophes without any meaningful economic impact on these investors or their portfolio firms. They studied the portfolio risk of US-based mutual funds that invest outside the US before and after fund managers personally experience severe natural disasters. Using a difference-in-differences approach, they compared managers in disaster vs nondisaster counties matched on prior disaster probability and fund characteristics. They found that monthly fund return volatility decreases by roughly 60 basis points in year +1 and the effect disappears by year +3. Systematic risk drives the results. Additional analyses do not support wealth effects (using disasters with no property damage) or managerial agency, skill, and catering explanations. Goetzmann, Kim, Kumar, and Wang (2015) showed that weather-based indicators of mood impact perceptions of mispricing and trading decisions of institutional investors. Using survey and disaggregated trade data, they showed that relatively cloudier days increase perceived overpricing in individual stocks and the Dow Jones Industrial Index and increase selling propensities of institutions. They introduced stock-level measures of investor mood; investor optimism positively impacts stock returns among stocks with higher arbitrage costs, and stocks experiencing similar investor mood exhibit return comovement. These findings complement existing studies on how weather impacts stock index returns and identify another channel through which it can manifest. Krueger, Sautner, and Starks (2020) used a survey about climate risk perceptions and found that institutional investors believe climate risks have financial implications for their portfolio firms and that these risks, particularly regulatory risks, already have begun to materialize. Many of the investors, especially the long-term, larger, and ESG-oriented ones, consider risk management and engagement, rather than divestment, to be the better approach for addressing climate risks. Although surveyed investors believe that some equity valuations do not fully reflect climate risks, their perceived overvaluations are not large.

Finally, Alok, Kumar, and Wermers (2020) examined whether professional money managers misestimate climatic disaster risk. The risk associated with climatic disasters can enter a manager's portfolio if a disaster affects portfolio firms. Using a difference-in-differences strategy, they first showed that relative to the distant funds, funds closer to the disaster zone reduce their portfolio holdings of firms located in the disaster area. They do not observe such a differential underweighting by close funds relative to the distant funds with respect to the firms located in the neighboring counties. Consistent with the fund managers overestimating the adverse impact of disasters on stocks located in the disaster zone, they found that the bias in their trading response is transitory and vanishes with time and distance. Moreover, the response of close funds is not driven by any information advantage they may possess over the distant funds as they do not find any difference in the postdisaster profitability across firms in the disaster area and those in the neighboring counties. The greater underweighting of the disaster zone firms by close funds relative to distant funds is not driven by flow-driven trading pressure created by biased investors or due to the drop in stock price of the disaster zone firms. Finally, they found that climatic disaster risk misestimation is costly to the fund investors as it adversely affects portfolio returns. Specifically, a portfolio that goes long on the disaster zone stocks that experience the sharpest reduction in weights in portfolios of close funds and goes short on the stocks that experience the least reduction generates statistically and economically significant positive risk-adjusted returns after the disaster.

References

Acemoglu, D., Johnson, S., and Robinson, J. A. (2002). Reversal of fortune: Geography and institutions in the making of the modern world income distribution. *Quarterly Journal of Economics, 117*, 1231–1294.

Ackerman, F., and Stanton, E. A. (2008). *The cost of climate change: What we'll pay if global warming continues unchecked.* Natural Resources Defense Council.

Ackerman, F., and Stanton, E. A. (2012). Climate risks and carbon prices: Revising the social cost of carbon. *Economics, 6.*

Ackerman, F., Stanton, E. A., Hope, C., Alberth, S., Fisher, J., Biewald, B., and Economics, S. (2008). *Climate change and the US economy: The costs of inaction.* Tufts University Global Development and Environment Institute.

Addoum, J. M., Ng, D. T., and Ortiz-Bobea, A. (2020). Temperature shocks and establishment sales. *Review of Financial Studies, 33*, 1331–1366.

Alok, S., Kumar, N., and Wermers, R. (2020). Do fund managers misestimate climatic disaster risk. *Review of Financial Studies*, *33*, 1146–1183.

Anttila-Hughes, J. K., and Hsiang, S. M. (2013). *Destruction, disinvestment, and death: Economic and human losses following environmental disaster*. Working Paper. Available at: SSRN 2220501.

Arouri, M., Nguyen, C., and Youssef, A. B. (2015). Natural disasters, household welfare, and resilience: Evidence from rural Vietnam. *World Development*, *70*, 59–77.

Asongu, S. A. (2012). The 2011 Japanese earthquake, tsunami and nuclear crisis: Evidence of contagion from international financial markets. *Journal of Financial Economic Policy*, *4*, 340–353.

Athukorala, P. C., and Resosudarmo, B. P. (2005). The Indian Ocean tsunami: Economic impact, disaster management, and lessons. *Asian Economic Papers*, *4*, 1–39.

Atreya, A., and Czajkowski, J. (2019). Graduated flood risks and property prices in Galveston county. *Real Estate Economics*, *47*, 807–844.

Atreya, A., and Ferreira, S. (2015). Seeing is believing? Evidence from property prices in inundated areas. *Risk Analysis*, *35*, 828–848.

Atreya, A., Ferreira, S., and Kriesel, W. (2013). Forgetting the flood? An analysis of the flood risk discount over time. *Land Economics*, *89*, 577–596.

Atsalakis, G. S., Bouri, E., and Pasiouras, F. (2021). Natural disasters and economic growth: A quantile-on-quantile approach. *Annals of Operations Research*, *306*, 83–109.

Bakkensen, L. A., and Barrage, L. (2018). *Flood risk belief heterogeneity and coastal home price dynamics: Going under water?* National Bureau of Economic Research Technical Report.

Baldauf, M., Garlappi, L., and Yannelis, C. (2020). Does climate change affect real estate prices? Only if you believe in it. *Review of Financial Studies*, *33*, 1256–1295.

Bansal, R., Kiku, D., and Ochoa, M. (2019). *Climate Change Risk*. Federal Reserve Bank of San Francisco Working Paper.

Bayoumi, M. T., Quayyum, M. S. N., and Das, S. (2021). Growth at risk from natural disasters. *International Monetary Fund, 2021*(234). Available at: https://www.elibrary.imf.org/view/journals/001/2021/234/article-A001-en.xml.

Benincasa, E., Kabas, G., and Ongena, S. (2021). *There is no planet B, but for banks there are countries B to Z: Domestic climate policy and cross-border bank lending*. Centre for Economic Policy Research.

Berg, G., and Schrader, J. (2012). Access to credit, natural disasters, and relationship lending. *Journal of Financial Intermediation*, *21*, 549–568.

Berger, A., Chu, Y., Roman, R., and Yoon H. J. (2023). *Through the looking glass: How banks' climate risk exposure affects green innovation*. Working Paper.

Berger, A., Curti, F., Lazaryan, N., Mihov, A., and Roman, R. (2022). *Climate risks in the U.S. banking sector: Evidence from operational losses and extreme storms*. Working Paper. Available at: SSRN 4294026.

Bernile, G., Bhagwat, V., Kecskés, A., and Nguyen, P. A. (2021). Are the risk attitudes of professional investors affected by personal catastrophic experiences? *Financial Management*, *50*, 455–486.

Bernstein, A., Gustafson, M. T., and Lewis, R. (2020). Disaster on the horizon: The price effect of sea level rise. *Journal of Financial Economics*, *134*, 253–272.

Bettin, G., and Zazzaro, A. (2018). The impact of natural disasters on remittances to low- and middle-income countries. *Journal of Development Studies*, *54*, 481–500.

Billings, S. B., Gallagher, E., and Ricketts, L. (2022). Let the rich be flooded: The distribution of financial aid and distress after hurricane Harvey. *Journal of Financial Economics*, *146*(2), 797–819.

Bin, O., and Landry, C. (2013). Changes in implicit flood risk premiums: Empirical evidence from the housing market. *Journal of Environmental Economics and Management*, *65*, 361–376.

Blickle, K., and Santos, J. A. (2022). *Unintended consequences of "mandatory" flood insurance*. Staff Report, No. 1012, Federal Reserve Bank of New York.

Blickle, K., Hamerling, S. N., and Morgan, D. P. (2021). *How bad are weather disasters for banks?* FRB of New York Staff Report No. 990.

Bolton, P., and Kacperczyk, M. (2021). Do investors care about carbon risk? *Journal of Financial Economics*, *142*, 517–549.

Bos, J. W., Li, R., and Sanders, M. W. (2022). Hazardous lending: The impact of natural disasters on bank asset portfolio. *Economic Modelling*, *108*, 105760.

Botzen, W. W., Deschenes, O., and Sanders, M. (2020). The economic impacts of natural disasters: A review of models and empirical studies. *Review of Environmental Economics and Policy*.

Boustan, L. P., Kahn, M. E., Rhode, P. W., and Yanguas, M. L. (2020). The effect of natural disasters on economic activity in US counties: A century of data. *Journal of Urban Economics*, *118*, 103257.

Bradley, D., Henriksson, M., and Valsalan, S. (2021). *The social welfare of marketplace lending: Evidence from natural disasters*. Working Paper. Available at: SSRN 3940557.

Brainard, L. (2021). The role of financial institutions in tackling the challenges of climate change, at the 2021 IIF U.S. In *Climate finance summit: Financing a pro growth pro markets transition to a sustainable, low-carbon economy hosted by the Institute of International Finance*. Washington, DC. Available at: https://www.federalreserve.gov/newsevents/speech/brainard20210218a.htm.

Bringas, B., Bunyi, L. J., and Manapat, C. L. (2022). An analysis on the impact of natural disasters on the economy of the Philippines. *Journal of Economics, Finance and Accounting Studies*, *4*, 163–183.

Burke, M., Hsiang, S. M., and Miguel, E. (2015). Global non-linear effect of temperature on economic production. *Nature*, *527*, 235–239.

Cevik, S., and Jalles, J. T. (2022). For whom the bell tolls: Climate change and inequality. *International Monetary Fund*, *2022*(103).

Cevik, S., and Miryugin, F. (2022). Rogue waves: Climate change and firm performance. *Comparative Economic Studies*, 1–31.

Chavaz, M. (2016). *Dis-integrating credit markets: Diversification, securitization, and lending in a recovery*. Bank of England Working Paper No. 617.

Cheney, J. S. (2006). *The role of electronic payments in disaster recovery: Providing more than convenience*. Federal Reserve Bank of Philadelphia.

Cheney, J. S., and Rhine, S. L. W. (2006). *How Effective Were the Financial Safety Nets in the Aftermath of Katrina?* Discussion Paper Payment Cards Center, Federal Reserve Bank of Philadelphia.

Chivers, J., and Flores, N. E. (2002). Market failure in information: The National Flood Insurance Program. *Land Economics*, *78*, 515–521.

Chu, Y., Liu, A.Y., and Tian, X. (2021). *Environmental risk and green innovation: Evidence from evacuation spills*. Working Paper. Available at: SSRN 3740551.

Chu, Y., and Zhao, D. (2019). *Green hedge fund activists*. Working Paper. Available at: SSRN 3499373.

Cohen, J. P., Barr, J., and Kim, E. (2021). Storm surges, informational shocks, and the price of urban real estate: An application to the case of hurricane Sandy. *Regional Science and Urban Economics*, *90*.

Conevska, A. (2021). International cooperation and natural disasters: Evidence from trade agreements. *International Studies Quarterly*, *65*, 606–619.

Correa, R., He, A., Herpfer, C., and Lel, U. (2022). The rising tide lifts some interest rates: Climate change, natural disasters, and loan pricing. In *International Finance Discussion Paper 1345*.

Cortés, K. R. (2015). *Rebuilding after disaster strikes: How local lenders aid in the recovery*. FRB of Cleveland Working Paper No. 14–28.

Cortés, K. R., and Strahan, P. E. (2017). Tracing out capital flows: How financially integrated banks respond to natural disasters. *Journal of Financial Economics*, *125*, 182–199.

Daniel, K. D., Litterman, R. B., and Wagner, G. (2016). *Applying Asset Pricing Theory to Calibrate the Price of Climate Risk*. National Bureau of Economic Research.

De Montesquieu, C. (1750). *The spirit of laws*. Cambridge, UK: Cambridge University Press.

Degryse, H., Goncharenko, R., Theunisz, C., and Vadasz, T. (2021). *When green meets green*. Working Paper. Available at: SSRN 3724237.

Dell, M., Jones, B. F., and Olken, B. A. (2009). Temperature and income: Reconciling new cross-sectional and panel estimates. *The American Economic Review*, *99*, 198–204.

Dell, M., Jones, B. F., and Olken, B. A. (2012). Temperature shocks and economic growth: Evidence from the last half century. *American Economic Journal: Macroeconomics*, *4*, 66–95.

Deryugina, T. (2017). The fiscal cost of hurricanes: Disaster aid versus social insurance. *American Economic Journal: Economic Policy, 9*, 168–198.

Deryugina, T., Kawano, L., and Levitt, S. (2018). The economic impact of hurricane Katrina on its victims: Evidence from individual tax returns. *American Economic Journal: Applied Economics, 10*, 202–233.

Dessaint, O., and Matray, A. (2017). Do managers overreact to salient risks? Evidence from hurricane strikes. *Journal of Financial Economics, 126*, 97–121.

Dillon-Merrilly, R. L., Gez, L., and Getex, P. (2018). *Natural Disasters and Housing Markets. The Tenure Choice Channel.* Unpublished paper Washington, DC: McDonough School of Business, Georgetown University.

Dlugosz, J., Gam, Y. K., Gopalan, R., and Skrastins, J. (2022). *Decision-making delegation in banks.* Working Paper. Available at: SSRN 3155683.

Duanmu, J., Li, Y., Lin, M., and Tahsin, S. (2022). Natural disaster risk and residential mortgage lending standards. *Journal of Real Estate Research, 44*, 106–130.

Dyason, D. (2022). Disasters and investment: Assessing the performance of the underlying economy following a large-scale stimulus in the built environment. *Journal of Risk and Financial Management, 15*, 263.

Elsadek Mahmoudi, S. (2020). *The propagation of local credit shocks: Evidence from hurricane Katrina.* Working Paper. Available at: SSRN 3751526.

Engle, R. F., Giglio, S., Kelly, B., Lee, H., and Stroebel, J. (2020). Hedging climate change news. *Review of Financial Studies, 33*, 1184–1216.

Erhemjamts, O., Huang, K., and Tehranian, H. (2022). *Climate Risk, ESG Performance, and ESG Sentiment for US Commercial Banks.*

Estrada, F., Botzen, W. J. W., and Tol, R. (2015). Economic losses from US hurricanes consistent with an influence from climate change. *Nature Geoscience, 8*, 880–884.

Fang, L., Li, L., and Yavas, A. (2021). The impact of distant hurricane on local housing markets. *Journal of Real Estate Finance and Economics*, 1–46.

Farrell, D., and Greig, F. (2018). *Weathering the storm: The financial impacts of Hurricanes Harvey and irma on one million households.* JPMorgan Chase Institute.

Felbermayr, G., and Groeschl, J. (2014). Naturally negative: The growth effects of natural disasters. *Journal of Development Economics, 111*, 92–106.

Filipski, M. J., Jin, L., Zhang, X., and Chen, K. (2015). *Living like there's no tomorrow: Saving and spending following the Sichuan earthquake.* IFPRI Discussion Paper 1461.

Gallagher, J., and Hartley, D. (2017). Household finance after a natural disaster: The case of hurricane Katrina. *American Economic Journal: Economic Policy, 9*, 199–228.

Garmaise, M. J., and Moskowitz, T. J. (2009). Catastrophic risk and credit markets. *The Journal of Finance, 64*, 657–707.

Garrett, D., and Ivanov, I. (2022). *Gas, guns, and governments: Financial costs of anti-ESG policies.* Working Paper. Available at: SSRN 4123366.

Ghazouani, A. (2022). Impact of natural disasters on the economy of African countries. *International Journal of Innovation Scientific Research and Review, 4*, 2956–2960.

Gibson, M., and Mullins, J. T. (2020). Climate risk and beliefs in New York floodplains. *Journal of the Association of Environmental and Resource Economists, 7*, 1069–1111.

Giglio, S., Maggiori, M., Rao, K., Stroebel, J., and Weber, A. (2021). Climate change and long-run discount rates: Evidence from real estate. *Review of Financial Studies, 34*, 3527–3571.

Goetzmann, W. N., Kim, D., Kumar, A., and Wang, Q. (2014). Weather-induced mood, institutional investors, and stock returns. *Review of Financial Studies, 28*, 73–111.

Graff Zivin, J., and Neidell, M. (2012). The impact of pollution on worker productivity. *The American Economic Review, 102*, 3652–3673.

Groen, J. A., Kutzbach, M. J., and Polivka, A. E. (2020). Storms and jobs: The effect of hurricanes on individuals' employment and earnings over the long term. *Journal of Labor Economics, 38*, 653–685.

Guo, J., Liu, H., Wu, X., Gu, J., Song, S., and Tang, Y. (2015). Natural disasters, economic growth and sustainable development in China—An empirical study using provincial panel data. *Sustainability, 7*, 16783–16800.

Haddad, E. A., and Teixeira, E. (2015). Economic impacts of natural disasters in megacities: The case of floods in São Paulo, Brazil. *Habitat International, 45*, 106–113.

Harrison, D., Smersh, G., and Schwartz, A. (2001). Environmental determinates of housing prices: The impact of flood zone status. *The Journal of Real Estate Research, 21*, 3–20.

Heger, M. P., and Neumayer, E. (2019). The impact of the Indian Ocean tsunami on Aceh's long-term economic growth. *Journal of Development Economics, 141*, 102365.

Henkel, M., Eunjee, K., and Magontier, P. (2022). *The unintended consequences of post-disaster policies for spatial sorting.* MIT Center for Real Estate Research Paper 22/08.

Hino, M., and Burke, M. (2020). *Does Information About Climate Risk Affect Property Values.* National Bureau of Economic Research.

Hoeppe, P. (2016). Trends in weather related disasters—Consequences for insurers and society. *Weather and Climate Extremes, 11*, 70–79.

Hong, H., Li, F. W., and Xu, J. (2019). Climate risks and market efficiency. *Journal of Econometrics, 208*, 265–281.

Hosono, K., Miyakawa, D., Uchino, T., Hazama, M., Ono, A., Uchida, H., and Uesugi, I. (2016). Natural disasters, damage to banks, and firm investment. *International Economic Review, 57*, 1335–1370.

Hsiang, S. M. (2010). Temperatures and cyclones strongly associated with economic production in the Caribbean and Central America. *Proceedings of the National Academy of Sciences of the United States of America, 107*, 15367–15372.

Hsiang, S. M., and Jina, A. S. (2014). *The causal effect of environmental catastrophe on long-run economic growth: Evidence from 6,700 cyclones (No. w20352).* National Bureau of Economic Research.

Huang, R., Malik, A., Lenzen, M., Jin, Y., Wang, Y., Faturay, F., and Zhu, Z. (2022). Supply-chain impacts of Sichuan earthquake: A case study using disaster input–output analysis. *Natural Hazards, 110*, 2227–2248.

Huntington, E. (1915). *Civilization and Climate.* New Haven, CT: Yale University Press.

Huynh, T. D., and Xia, Y. (2021). Climate change news risk and corporate bond returns. *Journal of Financial and Quantitative Analysis, 56*, 1985–2009.

Ilhan, E., Sautner, Z., and Vilkov, G. (2021). Carbon tail risk. *Review of Financial Studies, 34*, 1540–1571.

Issler, P., Stanton, R., Vergara-Alert, C., and Wallace, N. (2020). *Mortgage markets with climate-change risk: Evidence from wildfires in California.* Working Paper. Available at: SSRN 3511843.

Ivanov, I., Kruttli, M. S., and Watugala, S. W. (2021). *Banking on carbon: Corporate lending and cap-and-trade policy.* Working Paper. Available at: SSRN 3650447.

Ivanov, I. T., Macchiavelli, M., and Santos, J. A. (2020). Bank lending networks and the propagation of natural disasters. *Financial Management, 51*, 903–927.

Jiang, F., Li, C. W., and Qian, Y. (2020). *Do costs of corporate loans rise with sea level?* Working Paper. Available at: SSRN 3477450.

Jones, B. F., and Olken, B. A. (2010). Climate shocks and exports. *The American Economic Review, 100*, 454–459.

JPMorgan Chase & Co. (2018). *Weathering the Storm. The Financial Impacts of Hurricanes Harvey and Irma on One Million Households.* Available at: https://www.jpmorganchase.com/institute/research/cities-local-communities/report-weathering-the-storm.

Kahn, M. E. (2005). The death toll from natural disasters: The role of income, geography and institutions. *The Review of Economics and Statistics, 87*, 271–284.

Keerthiratne, S., and Tol, R. S. (2018). Impact of natural disasters on income inequality in Sri Lanka. *World Development, 105*, 217–230.

Kellenberg, D. K., and Mobarak, A. M. (2008). Does rising income increase or decrease damage risk from natural disasters? *Journal of Urban Economics, 63*, 788–802.

Keys, B. J., and Mulder, P. (2020). *Neglected no more: Housing markets, mortgage lending, and sea level rise (No. w27930).* National Bureau of Economic Research.

Kim, S., Kumar, N., Lee, J., and Oh, J. (2022, March). ESG lending. In *Proceedings of Paris December 2021 Finance Meeting EUROFIDAI-ESSEC.*

Klomp, J. (2014). Financial fragility and natural disasters: An empirical analysis. *Journal of Financial Stability, 13*, 180–192.

Koetter, M., Noth, F., and Rehbein, O. (2020). Borrowers under water! Rare disasters, regional banks, and recovery lending. *Journal of Financial Intermediation, 43*, 100811.

Kotsantonis, S., and Bufalari, V. (2019). Do sustainable banks outperform? Driving value creation through ESG practices. In *Report of the Global Alliance for Banking on Values (GABV)*.

Kousky, C., Palim, M., and Pan, Y. (2020). Flood damage and mortgage credit risk: A case study of hurricane Harvey. *Journal of Housing Research, 29*, 86–120.

Krueger, P., Sautner, Z., and Starks, L. T. (2020). The importance of climate risks for institutional investors. *Review of Financial Studies, 33*, 1067–1111.

Lambert, F., Noth, F., and Schüwer, U. C. (2019). How do banks react to catastrophic events? Evidence from hurricane Katrina. *Review of Finance, 23*, 75–116.

Lau, N. C., and Nath, M. J. (2012). A model study of heat waves over North America: Meteorological aspects and projections for the twenty-first century. *Journal of Climate, 25*, 4761–4784.

Lee, D., Zhang, H., and Nguyen, C. (2018). *The economic impact of natural disasters in Pacific Island countries: Adaptation and preparedness.* International Monetary Fund.

Leiter, A. M., Oberhofer, H., and Raschky, P. A. (2009). Creative disasters? Flooding effects on capital, labor and productivity within European firms. *Environmental and Resource Economics, 43*, 333–350.

Li, H., Xu, E., and Zhang, H. (2021). Examining the coupling relationship between urbanization and natural disasters: A case study of the Pearl River Delta, China. *International Journal of Disaster Risk Reduction, 55*, 102057.

Linsenmeier, M., Mohommad, A., and Schwerhoff, G. (2022). *The international diffusion of policies for climate change mitigation.* Working Paper. Available at: https://papers.ssrn.com/sol3/papers.cfm?abstract_id=4137208.

Luo, K., and Kinugasa, T. (2020). Do natural disasters influence long-term savings?: Assessing the impact of the 2008 Sichuan earthquake on household saving rates using synthetic control. *China: An International Journal, 18*, 59–81.

McManus, D., and Yannopoulos, E. (2021). COVID-19 mortgage forbearances: Drivers and payment behavior. *The Journal of Structured Finance, 27*(2), 13–25.

Morse, A. (2011). Payday lenders: Heroes or villains? *Journal of Financial Economics, 102*, 28–44.

Mu, J. E., and Chen, Y. (2016). Impacts of large natural disasters on regional income. *Natural Hazards, 83*, 1485–1503.

Murfin, J., and Spiegel, M. (2020). Is the risk of sea level rise capitalized in residential real estate? *The Review of Financial Studies, 33*.

NASA Earth Observatory. (2017). *How is Today's Warming Different from the Past?* Available at: https://earthobservatory.nasa.gov/Features/GlobalWarming/page3.php.

NOAA. (2017). *Global Climate Change Indicators.* Available at: https://www.ncdc.noaa.gov/monitoring-references/faq/indicators.php.

Nordhaus, W. (2006). Geography and macroeconomics: New data and findings. *Proceedings of the National Academy of Sciences, 103*, 3510–3517.

Noy, I. (2009). The macroeconomic consequences of disasters. *Journal of Development Economics, 88*, 221–231.

Ortega, F., and Taspınar, S. (2018). Rising sea levels and sinking property values: Hurricane sandy and New York's housing market. *Journal of Urban Economics, 106*, 81–100.

Ouazad, A., and Kahn, M.E. (2019). *Mortgage finance in the face of rising climate risk.* National Bureau of Economic Research. Working Paper 26322. Available at: http://www.nber.org/papers/w26322.

Painter, M. (2020). An inconvenient cost: The effects of climate change on municipal bonds. *Journal of Financial Economics, 135*, 468–482.

Pakoksung, K., Suppasri, A., Matsubae, K., and Imamura, F. (2019). Estimating tsunami economic losses of Okinawa Island with multi-regional-input-output modeling. *Geosciences, 9*, 349.

Panwar, V., and Sen, S. (2019). Economic impact of natural disasters: An empirical re-examination. *Margin: The Journal of Applied Economic Research, 13*, 109–139.

Ratcliffe, C., Congdon, W., Teles, D., Stanczyk, A., and Martin, C. (2020). From bad to worse: Natural disasters and financial health. *Journal of Housing Research, 29*, 25–53.

Ratnadiwakara, D., and Venugopal, B. (2020). Do areas affected by flood disasters attract lower income and less creditworthy homeowners? *Journal of Housing Research, 29*, 121–143.

Rodrik, D., Subramanian, A., and Trebbi, F. (2004). Institutions rule: The primacy of institutions over geography and integration in economic development. *Journal of Economic Growth, 9*, 131–165.

Roth Tran, B., and Sheldon, T. L. (2019). *Same storm, different disasters: Consumer credit access, income inequality, and natural disaster recovery.* Working Paper. Available at: SSRN 3380649.

Sachs, J. D. (2003). *Institutions don't rule: Direct effects of geography on per capita income.* NBER Working Paper No. 9490.

Sakai, A., Roch, F., Wiriadinata, U., and Fu, C. (2022). Sovereign climate debt instruments: An overview of the green and catastrophe bond markets. *International Monetary Fund. Staff Climate Notes, 2022*(004).

Sardar, A., Javed, S. A., and Amirud-Din, R. (2016). *Natural disasters and economic growth in Pakistan: An enquiry into the floods related hazards' triad.* Department of Environmental Economics, Pakistan Institute of Development Economics. Islamabad, Pakistan, Working Paper 10.

Sheldon, T. L., Gall, M., and Collins, L. (2017). *Disaster response, public safety, and community: The hidden costs of school closures.* Working Paper.

Shin, D. (2021). *Corporate ESG Profiles, Matching, and the Cost of Bank Loans.* University of Washington.

Shive, S. A., and Forster, M. M. (2020). Corporate governance and pollution externalities of public and private firms. *Review of Financial Studies, 33*, 1296–1330.

Strobl, E. (2011). The economic growth impact of hurricanes: Evidence from US coastal counties. *The Review of Economics and Statistics, 93*, 575–589.

Stroebel, J., and Wurgler, J. (2021). What do you think about climate finance? *Journal of Financial Economics, 142*, 487–498.

Strulik, H., and Trimborn, T. (2019). Natural disasters and macroeconomic performance. *Environmental and Resource Economics, 72*, 1069–1098.

Toya, H., and Skidmore, M. (2007). Economic development and the impacts of natural disasters. *Economics Letters, 94*, 20–25.

UN IPCC. (2013). Summary for policymakers. In *Climate change 2013. The physical science basis. Assessment report of the intergovernmental panel on climate change.* Cambridge, UK: Cambridge University Press. Available at: chrome-extension://efaidnbmnnnibpcajpcglclefindmkaj/https://www.ipcc.ch/site/assets/uploads/2018/03/WG1AR5_SummaryVolume_FINAL.pdf.

UN IPCC. (2021). Summary for policymakers. In *Assessment report of the intergovernmental panel on climate change.* Cambridge, UK: Cambridge University Press. Available at https://www.ipcc.ch/report/ar6/wg1/.

UN IPCC. (2022). Mitigation of climate change. In *Summary for policymakers, assessment report of the intergovernmental panel on climate change.* Cambridge, UK: Cambridge University Press. Available at https://www.ipcc.ch/report/sixth-assessment-report-work.

Van Wijngaarden, W. A., and Happer, W. (2020). *Dependence of Earth's thermal radiation on five most abundant greenhouse gases.* arXiv preprint arXiv:2006.03098.

Vigdor, J. (2008). The economic aftermath of hurricane Katrina. *The Journal of Economic Perspectives, 22*, 135–154.

Weerasekara, S., Wilson, C., Lee, B., Hoang, V. N., Managi, S., and Rajapaksa, D. (2021). The impacts of climate induced disasters on the economy: Winners and losers in Sri Lanka. *Ecological Economics, 185*, 107043.

Yamamura, E. (2016). Natural disasters and social capital formation: The impact of the Great Hanshin-Awaji earthquake. *Papers in Regional Science, 95*, 143–164.

Zhang, L. (2016). Flood hazards impact on neighborhood house prices: A spatial quantile regression analysis. *Regional Science and Urban Economics, 60*, 12–19.

Chapter 4

Conceptual framework for economic, banking, and financial market cycles featuring crises

Chapter outline

Abstract

This chapter puts the COVID-19 economic crisis into context by providing a more general conceptual framework covering economic, banking, and financial market cycles. These cycles include booms that occur before crises and aftermaths that materialize subsequently and can each last long periods of time. We compare economic, banking, and financial market crises that originate in the three economic sectors. We also provide some illustrative examples. While the concepts do not arise in the context of a formal economic model, the framework serves as the basis for our blueprint set of strategies we employ later in the book to mitigate unfavorable economic and financial impacts of the future crises.

Keywords: COVID-19, Economic cycles, Financial cycles, Boom, Crisis, Aftermath

The goal of this chapter is to put the COVID-19 economic crisis into context by providing a more general conceptual framework covering economic, banking, and financial market cycles. Crises are phases of these cycles that last various lengths of time from months to years. These cycles also include booms that occur beforehand and aftermaths that materialize subsequently, each with own time period of variable length.

While this three-phase framework is simple and lacking in critical detail, it is quite sufficient for the job at hand of providing orientation for the COVID-19 crisis. A working understanding of this or any other crisis requires basic comprehension of the main phases in common of cycles, which we supply in this chapter.

It is also necessary to recognize differences among types of crises to see how COVID-19 compares with other major economic and financial crises. In Chapter 5, we directly compare economic and

The Economic and Financial Impacts of the COVID-19 Crisis Around the World
https://doi.org/10.1016/B978-0-443-19162-6.00020-7
Copyright © 2024 Elsevier Inc. All rights reserved.

financial characteristics of COVID-19 crisis with the two other most significant global crises of the last century. The Global Financial Crisis (GFC) and the Crash of 1929 originated in the banking sector and financial markets, respectively, but both had devastating impacts on the real economies, banking sectors, and financial markets of many nations around the world. COVID-19 is also a global crisis that largely harmed the real economy before affecting banks and financial markets, and has other significant differences from these other crises.

Our focus in this chapter is on concepts, rather than empirical regularities. We proceed with a relatively high-level orientation or 30,000-ft view that is inclusive of all these crisis types, although we do pause on occasion with some illustrative examples. We concentrate primarily on fundamental similarities among economic, banking, and financial market crises, and leave more of differentiating among them to the discussion of the three global crises in Chapter 5 and subsequent chapters.

4.1 Why economies, banking sectors, and financial markets are subject to significant cycles and crises

Explanations of concepts generally require formal or informal resort to models. What follows is decidedly informal in nature and does not closely adhere to any one model. Rather, our discussion is based primarily on our research experiences in toto, and roughly matches some of the findings in previous books and papers (e.g., Berger and Bouwman, 2013, 2016, 2017; Berger and Roman, 2020; Berger and Demirgüç-Kunt, 2021; Berger and Sedunov, 2022).

The key reasons behind economic, banking, and financial market cycles may be best understood by examining what typically occurs during each of the boom, crisis, and aftermath phases. Of these three phases, the most important one to consider is actually the boom, and we allocate the majority of the space in this discussion and in this chapter as a whole on this phase.

4.1.1 The boom

The boom is when the seeds of the crisis to follow are often sown and factors that intensify the crisis are almost always formed. Before visiting these unfavorable seeds and factors, we acknowledge that the boom is also when most of the favorable economic and financial outcomes also occur. These include strong economic growth, job creation, and expansions of firm profits. Such gains broadly raise standards of living, lift many out of poverty, and create opportunities for switching careers and starting businesses that change lives for the better.

Financial asset prices generally appreciate in booms as well. These gains in financial markets—as well as those in goods and services and labor markets—help drive wealth accumulations that benefit society in many ways. In some cases, these wealth increases turn into small and large fortunes that make for fundamental improvements that change lives for the better. The small fortunes may allow households and firms to make investments in alternative passions, such as charity work and higher education. Large fortunes can be employed to fund high-reward-high-risk "moon-shot" projects and other world-changing ventures to affect social change, such as efforts to reduce international tensions or help prevent or prepare for climate change.

Unfortunately, many of these economic and financial gains are lost and social and aspirational dreams are dashed in the crisis that follows, and only the remains continue to improve society. These losses require us to focus more intensely on the unfavorable seeds that tend to sew crises and the unfavorable factors that tend to intensify these crises to find ways to mitigate them.

During the boom, the unfavorable common denominator is widespread and seemingly irrational risk-taking and inattention to risk management. We delay our discussion about whether such behavior is irrational until Section 4.2. Significant laxity about risk-taking builds as the time since the prior crisis increases and memories fade of the associated problems and how to deal with them. The inattention to risk management is widespread and correlated over time, and characterizes behavior by large numbers of households, nonfinancial firms, banks, financial market participants, and even the policymakers charged with prudential supervision and regulation.

In many cases, economic and financial agents engage in lowering credit and asset quality standards. These efforts often actively made even as the high risks are publicly observable. This behavior has particularly strong negative social consequences when it occurs for banks, whose behavior has significant effects on the real economy (e.g., Berger, Molyneux, and Wilson, 2020).

As one of our pauses for an illustrative example, we discuss some evidence suggesting that banks expand into making riskier and riskier loans, even by their own reported standards. Bank credit standards are not always clearly defined, but may be roughly considered as the minimum requirements banks impose to consider lending or expending significant resources on evaluating loan applicants.[1] The data reviewed here also indicate that they are aware that they are lowering their lending standards and that other banks are also doing so in a correlated fashion, suggestive of poor risk management as well.

We use results from the Federal Reserve Board of Governors' Senior Loan Officer Opinion Survey (SLOOS). The survey queries up to 80 large domestic banks and 24 US branches and agencies of foreign banks quarterly about lending standards, although these change over time. Reporting banks can see the trends in the data that they submit, and all banks can easily access to the aggregate trends from the published summary results. Thus, any increases in bank risk-taking revealed in the survey should be considered as components of the information sets available to banks for their risk management activities.

In the survey, banks are asked about standards for bank loans to businesses over the past 3 months, generally corresponding to the prior calendar quarter. We focus on the numbers of respondent banks reporting their lending tightened, remained about the same, or eased for credit to small firms with annual sales of less than $50 million. Such small businesses are typically riskier and more informationally opaque than larger firms, so changes in standards in lending to them should well demonstrate changes in laxity about risk-taking. A limitation is that sometimes fewer respondent banks answer the small-bank questions. A more general limitation of the SLOOS data found by research is that banks are understandably reluctant to report easing to avoid supervisory scrutiny (e.g., Owens and Schreft, 1991).[2]

---

[1]The standards would include consideration of the likelihood of repayment, expected losses given default, projections about any performance issues in terms of repaying on time, and any forecasted difficulties in enforcing contract terms such as seizing and disposing of pledged collateral. They would also cover the quality and transparency of the information available from the documents provided by the loan applicant, the bank's existing information about the borrower, and any relevant public information.

[2]Other research points to difficulties in parsing credit supply from credit demand changes with the SLOOS data (e.g., Bassett, Chosak, Driscoll, and Zakrajšek, 2014).

The time of the October 2008 survey occurred shortly after the Lehman Brothers bankruptcy had intensified the magnitude of the GFC, and this bankruptcy was in third-quarter period covered. It was also clear to all that a significant crisis was underway, and so likely a time that any bias to underreport easing to avoid scrutiny would be in full force. Of course, this time period is part of the crisis, not the boom, but provides a useful counterpoint for comparison to the boom that lasted until the COVID-19 crisis hit the US in the early 2020.

In the October 2008 SLOOS, 41 respondents reported tightening their lending standards to small firms, while 14 kept these standards about the same, and 0 reported easing. These data are consistent with both an overall strong increase in lending standards with vast majoring tightening. There is no evidence at that time of easing or laxity, but as noted, the lack of easing could also reflect reporting bias.

Just 1 year later, these figures changed to 9, 47, and 0 in October 2009. Thus, as the boom was getting underway, the data reflect a strong shift away from tightening toward a more neutral credit standards stance. The data that no banks reported easing their standards in lending to small businesses that are often risky and opaque might reflect that actual increases in laxity had not yet begun, although again heighted reporting bias cannot be ruled out.

Data for subsequent Octobers through 2019 all show small positive numbers of respondents reporting easing, evidence of the increased laxity during booms we describe above, but likely still underreported to avoid supervisory scrutiny.

During booms, households, and financial market participants as well as banks also engage in reaching-for-yield investments in assets that are clearly publicly marked as risky. Reaching for yield is particularly strong when interest rates on relatively safe assets are low, such as occurred for almost the entire period between the Global Financial Crisis (GFC) and COVID-19 crisis due to extraordinarily aggressive central bank conventional and unconventional monetary policies. Examples include subinvestment grade bonds that have rates that are even sometimes referred to as "junk," which should give a clear message of risk. Other examples are sovereign debt of nations with evidence of prior default, as well as high-risk leveraged loans originated by banks and mostly syndicated to investors for which the "leveraged" in the name indicates risk.

During booms, many economic and financial agents also invest large amounts in relatively new asset classes and financial vehicles for which risks are poorly understood or some cases are misleadingly touted as risk reducing. For example, mortgage-backed securities and similar structured finance products were sold to many who did not understand either the underlying risks in mortgages or how the financial models employed to engineer the new secondary securities from them worked. The inventory of such securities and the opaque values of them were key drivers of the Lehman bankruptcy. In more recent times, many appeared to invest in new financial instruments, such as nonfungible tokens (NFTs), special purpose acquisition companies (SPACs), cryptocurrencies, and meme stocks, which in some cases do not even have clear logic behind why they might generate long-term returns.

For another illustrative pause, we consider the entire set of investments in decentralized finance or decentralized finance (DeFi) for short as a relatively new asset class for which risks are misunderstood or misled. DeFi generally refers to firms that apply blockchain, machine learning, and modern financial and information technologies. They offer their services primarily online using smartphones and other new devices, and often transact in cryptocurrencies. To the extent possible, they intend to supply a relatively complete alternative to conventional currencies, financial institutions, and government financial activities.

The case of DeFi firm Celsius provides examples of some of these features and their potential consequences. CEO Alex Mashinsky marketed Celsius as a safe alternative to banks paying much higher interest rates. Celsius claimed about 1.7 million customers and was paying up to 18.6% interest on cryptocurrency deposits, and higher interest rates for those accepting payment in Celsius' own token. In the widespread market crash in the first half of 2022, in which cryptocurrency values fell especially hard, Celsius paused all withdrawals, swaps, and transfers between accounts, and slightly later filed for bankruptcy, leaving investors with unknown fates for their billions of dollars in investments. The recent rapid bankruptcies of Futures Exchange (FTX) and Alameda Research, with billions of dollars of missing funds and the arrest of the founder and major owner of these and other DeFi firms such as Sam Bankman-Fried (SBF), may reduce the abilities of such firms to engage in such behaviors in the future because of the more widespread media and policymaker attention.

In addition to all the high-risk loans, bonds, sovereign debt, and misunderstood new assets, many also fail during booms to conform to basic risk management practices to limit these risks. For example, many US banks failed during and after the GFC and earlier crises due to concentrations in commercial real estate (e.g., Cole and White, 2012). Economic and financial agents of all types also typically take on additional leverage to fund their risky investments. Both of these risk management failures magnify the losses that are realized in the crises that follow and increase the spread of the losses to more banks and capital market participants that provide them with the extra credit.

As the boom continues, the risky investments, lack of diversification, and high leverage in most cases are profitable and may seem low risk on an individual or aggregate basis. After some time in which there are few risk-related losses, policymakers may ease prudential supervision, engage in financial deregulation, and reverse some of the other prudential safeguards instituted in the prior crisis and its aftermath. For example, most of the risk protections from the US Glass-Stegall Act of 1933 were undone in the 1980s and 1990s. Similarly, the 2018 Economic Growth Act scaled back some prudential requirements of the 2010 Dodd-Frank Act.

Even beyond the problems of risk-taking that are not adequately managed during the boom, there is another key factor often occurring near the end of booms that contributes to the likelihood of the subsequent crisis—a factor that has strong favorable effects on the real economy at other times, bank liquidity creation.

Banks create liquidity for their customers by lending, deposits, and in many other ways (see Berger and Bouwman, 2009 for more discussion), and research suggests positive effects on the real economy from this set of activities (e.g., Berger and Sedunov, 2017; Beck, Döttling, Lambert, and van Dijk, 2022). However, excessive bank liquidity creation on an aggregate basis may increase the risk of a future crisis by exposing the banks to additional liquidity risks, by fueling risk-taking by others, or by contributing to asset price bubbles that later burst (e.g., Rajan, 1994; Acharya and Naqvi, 2012). For illustration of these problems, we refer the reader to empirical research focused on the lending component of liquidity creation (e.g., Büyükkarabacak and Valev, 2010; Soedarmono, Sitorus, and Tarazi, 2017), and research on the aggregate bank liquidity creation as a whole (e.g., Berger and Bouwman, 2017; Chatterjee, 2018; Davydov, Vähämaa, and Yasar, 2021), both with mixed results.

4.1.2 The crisis

During the crisis, many of the consequences from the prior risk increases during the boom are realized, and the damages to all parts of the economic system are inflicted. At the beginning of the crisis, risks increase at both the individual and the systemic level as many agents and markets become distressed. Policymakers make crucial decisions about resolving this distress—including bailouts and other types of financial aid or bail-ins of financial institutions vs allowing them to fail—as well as potential rescues for private companies and sovereign governments. These decisions may significantly affect the intensity and duration of the crisis as well as create incentives such as moral hazard that may affect the likelihood of the future crises. However, very little intentional risk-taking takes place during the crisis, as private-sector agents act to restore their financial health and reduce their leverage, and policymakers try to mitigate risks in various ways.

4.1.3 The aftermath

In the aftermath, risks slowly decline as the reduced risk-taking and actions during the crisis take effect. Policymakers engage in longer-term policies to moderate cycles and lessen the likelihood and intensities of the future crises, as discussed in Section 4.3. If and when slow economic growth continues well into the aftermath and/or start of the next boom, policymakers may start to encourage bank lending and other risky activities to stimulate the real economy. This can include reduced prudential supervision and regulation and easier monetary policy, and the boom period with all of its contributions to the following crisis is soon underway.

4.2 Behaviors by households, nonfinancial firms, banks, and policymakers that exacerbate cycles and intensify crises

As discussed above, much of the increased risk-taking and failure to follow risk management principles during booms is widespread across economic and financial agents as well as government officials, and appears to be irrational. We suggest a few potential explanations from the research literature here. We also suggest why their behaviors might be considered either rational or irrational, but this question is likely more rhetorical than answerable.

Some candidates for explanation from the literature apply primarily to some groups of agents and may in combination help explain why risk-taking, concentrated risks, leverage, and prudential reversals all appear to increase with the temporal duration of the boom. These include the effects of corporate culture issues that may characterize large organizations of all types (e.g., Fahlenbrach, Prilmeier, and Stulz, 2012; Thakor, 2015a, 2015b, 2016), more specific career concerns of policymakers that are looking to other future positions (Kane, 1987; Boot and Thakor, 1993).

Another candidate for explanation may be the "institutional memory hypothesis," under which the abilities of individuals of all types to deal with risk-related issues decreases with the time since they last confronted similar problems. As more time elapses from the prior crisis, more individual members of households, nonfinancial firms, banks, financial market participants, and policymakers may have had their memories of how to deal with these issues atrophy, and additional others have entered their positions of influence since the last crisis and so have no closely related experience on which to rely. This institutional memory loss explanation was initially proposed and empirically tested for bank loan officers, but it likely applies more generally to human decision makers of all types (e.g., Berger and Udell, 2004).

It may be argued that the observations of seemingly irrational and repeated risk-taking and risk management behavior are either in fact rational or irrational. To the extent that they reflect conflicts of interest or limited information as the literature cited here suggests, they may be considered as rational constrained optimization. However, we cannot rule out other irrational explanations from outside our expertise and knowledge of the research literature.

4.3 Types of policies to moderate cycles and lessen the likelihood and impacts of crises

As briefly indicated above, policymakers have many options to moderate economic and financial cycles and reduce the likelihood and severity of the associated crises. These include the results of distress during crises, and first lines of defense and countercyclical policies in the subsequent aftermaths and booms. In the interest of brevity and to avoid unnecessary repetition, we only briefly note these policy options here and refer readers to Berger and Roman, (2020), that details 16 of these policies and their costs and benefits (see Table 27.1 p.411).

Policies to solve economic and financial distresses include bailouts and other financial aid, bail-ins, allowing for bankruptcy or failure, reorganization using living wills, supervisor and regulatory forbearance, and breaking up distressed entities to reduce their influence. All of these policies have both short run consequences for the distress at hand, and long-run consequences for the future risk-taking behavior.

First lines of defense aim to help agents refrain from excessive risk-taking during aftermaths and booms to help avoid or lessen distress during subsequent crises. These include capital requirements, liquidity requirements, stress tests, prudential regulatory activity restrictions, prudential supervision, deposit insurance, and direct government ownership. In contrast, countercyclical prudential and monetary policies lean in the opposite direction on risk-taking during all three phases of the cycles.

References

Acharya, V. V., and Naqvi, H. (2012). The seeds of a crisis: A theory of bank liquidity and risk-taking over the business cycle. *Journal of Financial Economics, 106*(2), 349–366. https://doi.org/10.1016/j.jfineco.2012.05.014.

Bassett, W. F., Chosak, M. B., Driscoll, J. C., and Zakrajšek, E. (2014). Changes in bank lending standards and the macroeconomy. *Journal of Monetary Economics, 62*, 23–40.

Beck, T., Döttling, R., Lambert, T., and van Dijk, M. (2022). Liquidity creation, investment, and growth. *Journal of Economic Growth*, 1–40.

Berger, A. N., and Bouwman, C. H. S. (2009). Bank liquidity creation. *Review of Financial Studies, 22*(9), 3779–3837. https://doi.org/10.1093/rfs/hhn104.

Berger, A. N., and Bouwman, C. H. S. (2013). How does capital affect bank performance during financial crises? *Journal of Financial Economics, 109*(1), 146–176. https://doi.org/10.1016/j.jfineco.2013.02.008.

Berger, A. N., and Bouwman, C. H. S. (2016). *Bank liquidity creation and financial crises*. Academic Press.

Berger, A. N., and Bouwman, C. H. S. (2017). Bank liquidity creation, monetary policy, and financial crises. *Journal of Financial Stability, 30*, 139–155.

Berger, A. N., and Demirgüç-Kunt, A. (2021). Banking research in the time of COVID-19. *Journal of Financial Stability, 57*, 100939.

Berger, A. N., Molyneux, P., and Wilson, J. O. (2020). Banks and the real economy: An assessment of the research. *Journal of Corporate Finance, 62*, 101513.

Berger, A. N., and Roman, R. A. (2020). *TARP and other bank bailouts and bail-ins around the world: Connecting wall street, main street, and the financial system* (1st ed.). Elsevier.

Berger, A. N., and Sedunov, J. (2017). Bank liquidity creation and real economic output. *Journal of Banking & Finance, 81*, 1–19. https://doi.org/10.1016/j.jbankfin.2017.04.005.

Berger, A. N., and Sedunov, J. (2022). *The life cycle of systemic risk*. Working paper.

Berger, A. N., and Udell, G. F. (2004). The institutional memory hypothesis and the procyclicality of bank lending behavior. *Journal of Financial Intermediation*, *13*(4), 458–495. https://doi.org/10.1016/j.jfi.2004.06.006.

Boot, A. W. A., and Thakor, A. V. (1993). Self-interested bank regulation. *The American Economic Review*, *83*(2), 206–212.

Büyükkarabacak, B., and Valev, N. T. (2010). The role of household and business credit in banking crises. *Journal of Banking & Finance*, 34(6), 1247–1256.

Chatterjee, U. K. (2018). Bank liquidity creation and recessions. *Journal of Banking & Finance*, *90*, 64–75. https://doi.org/10.1016/j.jbankfin.2018.03.002.

Cole, R. A., and White, L. J. (2012). Déjà vu all over again: The causes of U.S. commercial bank failures this time around. *Journal of Financial Services Research*, *42*(1–2), 5–29. https://doi.org/10.1007/s10693-011-0116-9.

Davydov, D., Vähämaa, S., and Yasar, S. (2021). Bank liquidity creation and systemic risk. *Journal of Banking & Finance*, *123*, 106031. https://doi.org/10.1016/j.jbankfin.2020.106031.

Fahlenbrach, R., Prilmeier, R., and Stulz, R. M. (2012). This time is the same: Using bank performance in 1998 to explain bank performance during the recent financial crisis. *The Journal of Finance*, *67*(6), 2139–2185. https://doi.org/10.1111/j.1540-6261.2012.01783.x.

Kane, E. J. (1987). Dangers of capital forbearance: The case of the FSLIC and "zombie" S&Ls. *Contemporary Economic Policy*, *5*(1), 77–83. https://doi.org/10.1111/j.1465-7287.1987.tb00247.x.

Owens, R. E., and Schreft, S. L. (1991). Survey evidence of tighter credit conditions: What does it mean? *FRB Richmond Economic Review*, *77*(2), 29–34.

Rajan, R. G. (1994). Why bank credit policies fluctuate: A theory and some evidence. *Quarterly Journal of Economics*, *109*(2), 399–441.

Soedarmono, W., Sitorus, D., and Tarazi, A. (2017). Abnormal loan growth, credit information sharing and systemic risk in Asian banks. *Research in International Business and Finance*, *42*, 1208–1218.

Thakor, A. V. (2015a). Lending booms, smart bankers, and financial crises. *The American Economic Review*, *105*(5), 305–309.

Thakor, A. V. (2015b). The financial crisis of 2007–2009: Why did it happen and what did we learn? *Review of Corporate Finance Studies*, *4*(2), 155–205.

Thakor, A. V. (2016). The highs and the lows: A theory of credit risk assessment and pricing through the business cycle. *Journal of Financial Intermediation*, *25*, 1–29.

Chapter 5

Putting the COVID-19 crisis into context—Comparison with earlier global crises

Chapter outline

Abstract

In this chapter, we provide additional insights into the COVID-19 global economic crisis by comparing it in more detail with the two most significant global financial crises of the past century of the Global Financial Crisis (GFC) and the Crash of 1929. COVID-19 entered the economic system through the real economy, while the GFC and Crash of 1929 began in the banking and financial market segments. All economic and financial crises spread to the other two segments, but a key feature of the COVID-19 economic crisis is how the spread to the other segments was markedly less during the crisis phase. Another key difference is the lesser effects of excesses during the preceding boom prior to the COVID-19 crisis.

Keywords: COVID-19, Global Financial Crisis, Crash of 1929, Economic crises, Banking crises, Financial market crises, Cycles, Financial cycles, Boom, Crisis, Aftermath

5.1 Similarities and differences among economic, banking, and financial market crises

This chapter puts the COVID-19 crisis in the larger context of economic and financial crises by differentiating among crises that originate in the real economy vs the banking sector vs financial markets. We focus on comparing the economic and financial characteristics of the COVID-19 crisis with those of the Global Financial Crisis (GFC) and the Crash of 1929, which were also global crises.

In terms of similarities, all economic and financial crises have in common is that markets significantly malfunction and precipitate substantial damages on at least one of the real economy, banking sector, or financial markets segments, but they most often significantly affect all three systems. Economic and financial crises also share that they are generally integral parts of recurring cycles that are exacerbated by numerous procyclical factors. These include increased risk-taking actions—such as

The Economic and Financial Impacts of the COVID-19 Crisis Around the World
https://doi.org/10.1016/B978-0-443-19162-6.00023-2
Copyright © 2024 Elsevier Inc. All rights reserved.

investing in riskier assets financed by increased leverage—during economic and financial booms. Such actions by private-sector economic and financial agents are often met by increased tolerance by public policymakers during these booms.

While the crisis-exacerbating effects of procyclical factors during booms may at first seem appropriate only for crises originating in the banking sector or financial markets, they may nonetheless apply as well to the COVID-19 economic crisis. While this crisis did not primarily emanate from economic and financial risk-taking, the high leverage of households, businesses, and governments leading to the crisis could have greatly exacerbated the economic and financial damages from the pandemic. As discussed, the very fast and very large government policy interventions early in the crisis appear to have effectively offset much of the effects of high leverage and risk-taking by flooding firms and households with liquid funds to keep them afloat and/or forbearance programs to forestall their credit profile deteriorations.

There are also many stark differences among crises in terms of their origin, spread, duration, policy responses, and other characteristics, some of which we highlight in our brief comparisons here. We emphasize the key distinction that COVID-19 affected the real economy first, while the GFC and Crash of 1929 originated in the banking and financial market sectors, respectively.

For expositional purposes, we use the term "real economy" to broadly represent the complete set of markets for nonfinancial goods and services. We often discuss the "banking sector" as meaning the entire complex of financial institutions that intermediate funds among economic agents. However, we also sometimes use the term "banks" as more narrowly meaning commercial banks that take deposits and make business loans. The term "financial markets" is inclusive of all domestic and international financial markets in which contingent and noncontingent financial claims are traded. It also encompasses the participants in these markets, including nonfinancial firms and households as well as financial institutions. Thus, we write as clearly as possible about the real economy, banking sector, and financial markets, but we rely on context in some cases to guide readers.

Crises typically originate as markets in one sector malfunction, followed by knock-on problems in the other two sectors due to the strong interconnections among them and other contagion mechanisms. For example, problems in the real economy frequently damage the banking sector because firms and households are less able to repay bank loans and other obligations to financial institutions. Real economy issues also impair financial markets, as the values of stock, bond, and other financial market claims depend on cash flows generated by firms to pay off these claims on the supply side, as well as financial flows from households employed by these firms and other investors to fund the investments in these claims on the demand side. Analogous chains of causation from the banking sector performance problems to the real economy and financial markets are relatively easy to construct for the reader without further explanation, as are how financial market malfunctions disrupt the real economy and banking sector.

There are also often significant contagion problems within these three systems. In the real economy, problems in one market for a nonfinancial good or service may hinder demands and supplies for other nonfinancial items. For example, a firm failure may reduce demands for products by the firm itself as well as its laid-off employees, and disrupt supply chains in which the firm plays roles. In the banking sector, the failure of one financial institution may injure others through financial interconnections such as loans or off-balance sheet claims between them, or through losses of market confidence that cause others to reevaluate additional institutions due to incomplete information about the failure causes. In financial markets, substantial value losses or volatility in one market may create panics in others due to incomplete information, or result in funds quickly shifting among markets for other financial claims, causing further disruptions.

In this chapter as well as in the rest of the book, we refer to economic, banking, and financial market crises based on the sector of origination or first major functional problems. Based on this classification, we consider the COVID-19, GFC, and Crash of 1929 crises as being economic, banking, and financial market crises. We again emphasize that the effects of crises are not confined to their sectors of origination. In some cases, the greatest crisis damages occur in a different sector, such as occurred when the economic losses from the Great Depression that followed the Crash of 1929 greatly exceeded the financial market losses from the Crash itself.

We acknowledge that our classification is not a universally accepted view of economic and financial crises. It is largely consistent with recent systemic analyses that incorporate COVID-19, such as Berger and Demirgüç-Kunt (2021) and Berger and Sedunov (2022). However, our approach differs in some significant ways from earlier survey articles, lists, and books about crises that largely preceded COVID-19, such as Demirgüç-Kunt and Detragiache (1998), Berger and Bouwman (2013, 2016), and Laeven and Valencia (2020). While no model for evaluating crises or any other topic is completely accurate, it is nonetheless important to choose a consistent framework for analysis.

To keep our focus sharp and avoid redundancy, we stick closely to big-picture concerns in this chapter. We exclude detailed discussions of the economic and financial effects of the COVID-19 crisis around the world and the policy reactions to them that are reported in depth in Parts II and III, respectively. We also avoid repeating intricate details of the extraordinary recoveries in Part IV and the aftermath in Part V. Here we simplify things and focus on differences from prior crises. To facilitate our comparisons, we also give only big-picture views of the other two global crises and keep their descriptions relatively short as well.

5.2   The COVID-19 crisis (economic crisis)

The COVID-19 economic crisis is in many ways unprecedented. It featured the most unanticipated, largest, and most widespread exogenous economic shock of all time. It was even more global than the GFC, affecting numerous developed and developing nations alike, and caused recessions around the world, including the US recession with the sharpest economic descent in recorded history.

It is not necessarily obvious why a health shock should be a significant economic shock, but COVID-19 was. The disease directly caused economic damages by increasing the costs of health care and other business and household expenses of dealing with health and safety issues. The indirect effects from households, workers, firms, and governments trying to thwart the spread of the disease and its health consequences created vastly greater damages to the real economy. Consumers reduced their purchases involving personal contact to avoid catching the virus (e.g., travel, entertainment, restaurants, and shops), reducing demand for nonfinancial goods and services in the real economy. Workers also avoided places of employment involving personal contact to avoid catching the virus (e.g., factories, offices, restaurants, and shops), reducing economic supply as well. Government restrictions and shutdowns of businesses, schools, travel, and other economic activities further crippled supplies of goods and services.[1] These real economic losses were also magnified in some cases as some of those

---

[1]For examples of public and government efforts to reduce the negative health consequences of COVID-19 and their potential use in research, see COVID-19 shocks constructed from raw data by Berger, Bouwman, Norden, Roman, Udell, and Wang (2022).

that lost jobs or business income also reduced their demands for goods and services due to lower incomes and increased economic and financial uncertainties.

The magnitude and speed of some of the economic declines were unprecedented and on such a scale as to defy forecasters' expectations or worst-case scenarios. For example, in the US, the unemployment rate rose from a historically low rate of 3.5% in February 2020 to 14.8% in April 2020, a rate not seen since the Great Depression. Real US GDP, which is measured in quarters, declined at an annualized rate of 5.0% in 2020:Q1 and a record rate of 31.4% in 2020:Q2, with every state having an annualized rate decline of real GDP in 2020:Q2 of at least 20%, with some over 40%. While annualized rates may be fairly considered as exaggerated since they did not last for a full year, they are well outside the bounds of historical experience. According to the International Monetary Fund (IMF), the median global GDP decreased by about 4% from 2019 to 2020. The United Nations (UN) reports that the global unemployment rate went up by about one percentage point to 6.5% at the beginning of the pandemic in 2020.

These types of damages significantly affected almost all countries around the world, quickly caused very steep recessions and financial losses in many of them, and considerably raised short-term risks in the global economic and financial systems. These effects are well documented in many of the broad reviews in the literature of the economic and financial effects of the first part of the COVID-19 crisis (e.g., Berger, Demirgüç-Kunt, Moshirian, and Saunders, 2021; Brodeur, Gray, Islam, and Bhuiyan, 2021; Colak and Öztekin, 2021; Duan, Ghoul, Guedhami, Li, and Li, 2021; Goldstein, Koijen, and Mueller, 2021; Hasan, Politsidis, and Sharma, 2021).

In addition to the essentially unprecedented short-term damages, the crisis had the potential and widespread expectation of inflicting even more severe long-term economic damages over an extended period of time and causing substantial financial problems as well. Consistent with the discussion of procyclical factors that amplify crises in Chapter 4 above, it seemed very likely early in the crisis that economic losses of a greater order of magnitude would bring down many banks and other financial institutions that had extended credit to nonfinancial firms and households under boom conditions in late 2019 and early 2020 (e.g., Zhang, Hu, and Ji, 2020; Albulescu, 2021). In addition, financial markets would likely experience significant crashes based on expectations of losses of cash flows to repay investors in stocks, bonds, and other financial markets and reductions in income flows to fund new investments in these markets, as discussed above.

Consistent with expectations of such considerable long-lasting financial damages, banks did increase their loan and lease losses allowances to reflect higher expected credit risk losses, major stock market indices did fall as well as indexes for bank stocks, and measures of systemic risk did increase in the short run. Banks also began reducing their lending in the short term, portending potentially significant feedback effects that may cause additional damages to the real economy (Berger and Demirgüç-Kunt, 2021).

However, most of these potentially expected long-term damages were largely unrealized, at least for some time until the aftermath period. In the medium term, some very favorable outcomes were realized. The US recession lasted only 2 months, the national unemployment rate was cut by more than half to 6.9% by October 2020, and real US GDP grew at an annualized rate of 33.4% in 2020:Q3 with increases across all the states. Liquid and well-capitalized banks are steady, and only four small banks failed in 2020 and no failures in 2021 (e.g., Li, Strahan, and Zhang, 2020). Major US stock market indices of Dow Jones, S&P 500, and Nasdaq had all dropped more than 30% from their prior peaks by March 23, 2020, but they all reached all-time highs later in the crisis (Richter, 2021). According to the UN, the global unemployment rate declined slightly by about 0.2% at the beginning of 2021, and the IMF finds that global GDP grew by more than 5% in 2021.

The economic and financial recoveries from the crisis were unexpectedly fast and steep in some cases, positive outcomes referred to as the "economic surprise" and "financial surprise" of the crisis, respectively (Berger and Demirgüç-Kunt, 2021). These "surprises" may be linked in part to favorable policy solutions to the crisis. These include some very quickly implemented massive government fiscal and monetary stimuli, such as the $2 trillion US Coronavirus Aid, Relief, and Economic Security (CARES) Act, which includes the Paycheck Protection Program (PPP), signed into law on March 27, 2020. These and other policy actions are described in more detail in subsequent chapters. The policies buoyed demand for nonfinancial goods and services and helped bolster the financial balance sheets of households and firms. For example, US households accumulated an estimated additional $2.5 trillion in excess savings (inflation-adjusted to 2020 dollars) between March 2020 and January 2022 (Barnes, Edelberg, Estep, and Macklin, 2022). Subprime US households in local markets in which banks distributed more Paycheck Protection Program (PPP) funds significantly reduced their debt burden, primarily driven by reductions in credit card and auto loan debt (Berger, Epouhe, and Roman, 2021). The Federal Reserve and other central banks around the world also engaged in very aggressive conventional monetary policies as well as quantitative easing.

The beneficial "surprises" likely were also caused in part by the strong prudential supervision and regulation of banks implemented in the wake of the GFC from a decade earlier that helped keep these institutions healthy and continue lending and providing other support for the real economy and financial markets. These prudential policies include enhanced capital and liquidity requirements, stress tests, and other "first lines of defense" improvements, as well as shifts from bailout to bail-in regimes (e.g., Acharya, Berger, and Roman, 2018; Berger and Roman, 2020; Cortés, Demyanyk, Li, Loutskina, and Strahan, 2020; Berger, Himmelberg, Roman, and Tsyplakov, 2022).

The private sector supply chain and the firms and workers in it also responded quite well to the crisis initially and eased the economic and financial pains caused by COVID-19 considerably. Technology companies allowed many employees and students to work, attend meetings, and go to class remotely, and gave households the opportunities to buy much of their groceries and other necessities and restaurant meals online. Some of the remote-working technologies performed so far above expectations that they appear to have created some more or less permanent changes to how some workers do their jobs. Delivery drivers, warehouse workers, restaurant employees, and others who brought the products of grocery stores, manufacturers, and restaurants, and other firms to households' doors also improved standards of living in ways that may also be enduring. The large pharmaceutical companies (Big Pharma) also reduced COVID-19 infections, hospitalizations, and deaths with their vaccines, treatment drugs, and other products. The vaccines were developed in record time with financial assistance from governments that paid for them (e.g., Operation Warp Speed). The reduced disease incidence and risks facilitated earlier and safer returns to work, school, travel, shopping, and other production, investment, and consumption, helping turn the economies around.

However, after a point in time that cannot be precisely pinpointed and varies across countries, the beneficial effects of government fiscal stimulus and central bank monetary stimulus became liabilities that resulted in reduced labor supplies, critical shortages, impediments to international trade, inflation, and other economic dislocations in what we call the aftermath of the COVID-19 crisis. We again here stick closely to big-picture concerns and keep details and redundancies of the aftermath to a minimum.

As the aftermath started, it became clear that the worst of the expectations of economic and financial doom and gloom would not occur, and the stimuli provided by governments, central banks, and the private sector were working well. Vaccines had arrived and were starting to be implemented that would free consumers and firms to engage in more normal economic activities, reducing the need for subsidies; employment opportunities were returning, lessening the need for extended unemployment insurance and other stimulus payments, and restrictions on enforcing households to honor their legal obligations to pay for their housing and student debt. Economic growth was proceeding apace and should have been expected to accelerate, and banks would obviously not be failing in large numbers. Housing prices and financial markets were turning frothy if not in bubble territory and needed no further conventional or unconventional monetary stimulus to encourage more housing price inflation or investments in risk-on securities sometimes known as "central bank puts."

To illustrate, market indices that value conventional stocks and bonds were at or near all-time record highs. Stocks had historically high P/E ratios and bonds were about 40 years into their bull market. More obvious signals of inflated asset values were apparent in some risk-on securities with questionable economic values. These were already in high demand and pushed way up in value by those with balance sheets swollen by stimulus and lack of opportunities to spend in what appeared to be gamified investing. For examples, Dogecoin, a cryptocurrency invented as a joke, went up in value, as did a Non-Fungible Token (NFT) of LeBron James dunking a basketball that was already viewed by millions with online ownership bragging rights as the key benefit. Special Purpose Acquisition Companies (SPACs) went up in number and values. These are shell companies that will merge with unknown real companies with unknown economic values that went public with much less due diligence afforded by the typical IPO process. In addition, market values soared for known firms such as GameStop and AMC and known commodities such as silver. These were bid up based on words posted on Reddit that referenced other reasons than economic value calculations.

Despite these warning signs, many policymakers continued their popular stimulus programs with additional stimulus payments, more business subsidies, continued suspension of legal obligations to pay, etc., in what might be considered examples of "policy traps" that are counterproductive but hard to reverse (e.g., Acharya, Lenzu, and Wang, 2021). These policies continued to stimulate demand for goods, reduce labor supplies, and result in destructive inflation and other disruptions. These disruptions later required additional government interventions to counter them, such as monetary tightening, that raise recession risks among other consequences.

To give a few brief examples, millions of job openings remained unfilled in the US despite rising wages and signing bonuses in part because savings from government stimulus, extended unemployment benefits that paid more than working and other factors led to early retirement and unwillingness to return to work. Tremendous backups of container ships at ports could not unload due to truck driver shortages and other difficulties, exacerbating supply chain difficulties. Such supply chain problems resulted in many stores having empty shelves and being unable to fill orders. Restaurants had to close or reduce hours because they could not find enough servers. Car and computer manufacturers could not get semiconductors, cutting back production. All of these demand increases and supply decreases helped stoke the inflation problems underway in several countries at the time of this writing.[2]

---

[2] Additional discussions of international supply chain disruptions are available in the literature. Consumers quickly shifted their demands among different goods and services as travel and work restrictions changed, making it difficult to meet their demands. In addition, some of the basic resource companies that would otherwise fulfill orders no longer existed due to earlier pandemic restrictions or were blocked by new restrictions. Other suppliers faced tighter controls on logistical systems for health reasons, and transportation difficulties were exacerbated by overwhelmed ports that could not find enough truck drivers (see Paul, Chowdhury, Moktadir, and Lau, 2021).

Notably, these problems are not all policy driven. Some unexpected COVID-19 outbreaks, including the Delta variant, also contributed to the supply chain problems. It was also difficult to predict the very strong antivaccine movement that would effectively prevent and significantly delay herd immunity and return-to-work conditions. Many companies failed to diversify their supply chains, so a problem in one microchip fabrication plant in Taiwan left many firms with no alternative sources, slowing up world economic growth. These issues are discussed in greater detail in Part V.

5.3 The Global Financial Crisis (banking crisis)

The Global Financial Crisis (GFC) differs very significantly from the COVID-19 crisis in causes, consequences, policies, and the aftermath that we highlight here. The GFC is widely recognized as a banking crisis because a key originating cause is the faulty subprime mortgages issued by US banks (e.g., Berger and Bouwman, 2013).

US banks, mortgage brokers, and other US lenders reduced their lending standards and made very risky mortgages, particularly to subprime borrowers. Some of these banks, as well as large investment banks and others, securitized large numbers of these loans in mortgage-backed securities (MBS) and other structured products (e.g., Brunnermeier, 2009). Many of these mortgages had additional features that increased their risks, such as low documentation (Lo Doc) or no income verification (liar loans), loan/value ratios exceeding 80% (sometimes above 100%), and repayment qualifications based on temporarily low "teaser" rates. Many of the securities received high ratings from rating agencies that may have been based on rosy forecasts of home price increases, and received implicit government support from investments by the government sponsored enterprises (GSEs) Fannie Mae and Freddie Mac. Thus, many parties played critical roles in exacerbating the crisis in addition to the banks.

The declines in credit standards by the banks and others are likely due to the institutional memory hypothesis and reasons why economies, banking sectors, and financial markets experience strong cycles emphasized in Chapter 4 above. They may also be due in part to some new motivations, such as relatively new private-label markets for MBS, faith in new risk management tools (e.g., VAR models), new structured investment vehicles (SIVs) with little capital backing. The new Basel II capital standards that had recently been adopted in Europe also encouraged investments in securities with high credit ratings.

Banks suffered capital shocks from real estate investment losses and reacted by hoarding liquidity from the public and financial markets, spreading problems to the real economy and financial system (e.g., Berger, Guedhami, Kim, and Li, 2022). The liquidity hoarding took the forms of reduced on-balance sheet loans (e.g., Cornett, McNutt, Strahan, and Tehranian, 2011; Acharya and Mora, 2015) and off-balance sheet loan commitments (e.g., Berger and Bouwman, 2017) that harmed the real economy and reduced interbank lending and other capital market freezes that damaged the financial system and created liquidity issues for other banks as well (e.g., Afonso, Kovner, and Schoar, 2011; Bech and Garratt, 2012; Acharya and Merrouche, 2013; Heider, Hoerova, and Holthausen, 2015). Investment banks that held MBS suffered even greater liquidity problems because of their lack of easy access to insured deposits and the central bank discount window, leading to the Bear Stearns and Lehman Brothers collapses that further reduced market confidence. The economic and financial damages of the crisis were very large—estimated to be about half or more of a year's GDP and about a quarter of the household net worth in the US alone (e.g., Luttrell, Atkinson, and Rosenblum, 2013).

The policy responses to the GFC were quite substantial and included many large financial aid packages for banks (e.g., the Troubled Asset Relief Program (TARP), discussed in detail in Chapter 12), other financial intermediaries (e.g., AIG insurance), nonfinancial companies (e.g., General Motors and Chrysler), and countries (e.g., Greece). However, the policy reactions were generally much more delayed and smaller than those for the COVID-19 crisis. For example, TARP was implemented in October 2008, well over a year into the crisis that was apparent in August 2007, and was much smaller than the PPP in the COVID-19 crisis; the bank stress tests and fiscal stimulus were not begun until 2009, the Dodd-Frank Act was signed into law in 2010, but took many more years to implement, and the Basel III capital and liquidity requirements were phased in over many years starting in 2013.

The aftermath of the GFC included a relatively slow return to full employment. For example, the US unemployment rate did not return to the pre-GFC May 2007 level of 4.4% until March 2016.

5.4 The crash of 1929 (financial market crisis)

The Crash of 1929 also has unique causes, consequences, policies, and an aftermath. We classify the Crash of 1929 as a financial market crisis because it began with dramatic drops in the US stock market on October 24, 1929 (Black Thursday) and October 29, 1929 (Black Tuesday). The financial losses of $30 billion exceeded the costs to the US of World War I, which would be substantial, even today at about $400 billion in current dollars. Following the Crash, almost 9000 US banks failed between 1930 and 1933, and the aftermath of the Crash includes the Great Depression, the worst economic disaster of all time with the US unemployment rate hitting almost 25% at the peak of the crisis in 1933.

The causes of the Crash include some of the procyclical factors described in Chapter 4, such as over-valued stock prices from market exuberance and large increases in debt over the prior decade that made the financial system fragile. Poor regulation and supervision, such as low margin requirements, little oversight, questionable financial market practices, also helped fuel panic selling.

At the time of the crash, there was no national deposit insurance in the US. The bank failures occurred in part because the absence of deposit insurance at a time of low confidence inspires bank runs that can destroy banks that are solvent, but illiquid (e.g., Diamond and Dybvig, 1983). The sequential service rule (first-come, first-served) means that all depositors should protect themselves by running on a bank on which others are already running or expected to run, whether or not the run is rational. Banks also failed because of limited liquidity due to low vault cash requirements and tightened monetary policy from the Federal Reserve to protect the gold standard (e.g., Friedman and Schwartz, 2008). Problems in the real economy resulted in borrowers not being able to repay their bank loans, further crippling the banks. The Great Depression was caused in part by the destruction of wealth from the stock market crash and reduced supply of credit from failed or impaired banks (e.g., Bernanke, 1983). The problems in the real economy further hurt financial markets and banks, amplifying losses in the real economy.

In terms of policy responses, their were very few for almost 4 years until Roosevelt took office in 1933. Many of the subsequent responses were substantial, such as the New Deal spending of $41.7 billion. There were also significant reforms to address bank stability, such as the Glass-Steagall Act of 1933 that created deposit insurance and separated investment and commercial banking activities, and to improve financial market stability, such as the creation of the Securities and Exchange Commission (SEC) in 1934. However, the delay to start these policies was clearly very costly and is likely the key factor in the disastrous aftermath of the Great Depression.

References

Acharya, V. V., Berger, A. N., and Roman, R. A. (2018). Lending implications of US bank stress tests: Costs or benefits? *Journal of Financial Intermediation, 34*, 58–90.

Acharya, V. V., Lenzu, S., and Wang, O. (2021). Zombie lending and policy traps. *SSRN Electronic Journal*.

Acharya, V. V., and Merrouche, O. (2013). Precautionary hoarding of liquidity and interbank markets: Evidence from the subprime crisis. *Review of Finance, 17*, 107–160.

Acharya, V. V., and Mora, N. (2015). A crisis of banks as liquidity providers. *The Journal of Finance, 70*, 1–43.

Afonso, G., Kovner, A., and Schoar, A. (2011). Stressed, not frozen: The Federal Funds Market in the financial crisis. *The Journal of Finance, 66*, 1109–1139.

Albulescu, C. T. (2021). COVID-19 and the United States financial markets' volatility. *Finance Research Letters, 38*, 101699.

Barnes, M., Edelberg, W., Estep, S., and Macklin, M. (2022). Bolstered balance sheets: Assessing household finances since 2019. *Economic Analysis*.

Bech, M. L., and Garratt, R. J. (2012). Illiquidity in the interbank payment system following wide-scale disruptions. *Journal of Money, Credit and Banking, 44*, 903–929.

Berger, A. N., and Bouwman, C. H. S. (2013). How does capital affect bank performance during financial crises? *Journal of Financial Economics, 109*, 146–176.

Berger, A. N., and Bouwman, C. H. S. (2016). *Bank liquidity creation and financial crises*. London, UK: Academic Press.

Berger, A. N., and Bouwman, C. H. S. (2017). Bank liquidity creation, monetary policy, and financial crises. *Journal of Financial Stability, 30*, 139–155.

Berger, A. N., Bouwman, C. H. S., Norden, L., Roman, R. A., Udell, G. F., and Wang, T. (2022). *Is a friend in need a friend indeed? How relationship borrowers fare during the COVID-19 crisis*. Available at SSRN 3755243.

Berger, A. N., and Demirgüç-Kunt, A. (2021). Banking research in the time of COVID-19. *Journal of Financial Stability, 57*, 100939.

Berger, A. N., Demirgüç-Kunt, A., Moshirian, F., and Saunders, A. (2021). *Banking research in the time of COVID-19 impacts of the crisis on banking research past, present, and future*. Working Paper.

Berger, A. N., Epouhe, O., and Roman, R. A. (2021). A tale of two bailouts: Effects of TARP and PPP on subprime consumer debt. *SSRN Electronic Journal*.

Berger, A. N., Guedhami, O., Kim, H. H., and Li, X. (2022). Economic policy uncertainty and bank liquidity hoarding. *Journal of Financial Intermediation, 100893*.

Berger, A. N., Himmelberg, C. P., Roman, R. A., and Tsyplakov, S. (2022). *Bank bailouts, bail-ins, or no regulatory intervention? A dynamic model and empirical tests of optimal regulation*. Financial Management.

Berger, A. N., and Roman, R. A. (2020). *TARP and other bank bailouts and bail-ins around the world: Connecting wall street, main street, and the financial system*. Academic Press.

Berger, A. N., and Sedunov, J. (2022). *The life cycle of systemic risk*.

Bernanke, B. S. (1983). Irreversibility, uncertainty, and cyclical investment. *Quarterly Journal of Economics, 98*, 85.

Brodeur, A., Gray, D., Islam, A., and Bhuiyan, S. (2021). A literature review of the economics of COVID-19. *Journal of Economic Surveys, 35*, 1007–1044.

Brunnermeier, M. K. (2009). Deciphering the liquidity and credit crunch 2007–2008. *The Journal of Economic Perspectives, 23*, 77–100.

Colak, G., and Öztekin, Ö. (2021). The impact of COVID-19 pandemic on bank lending around the world. *Journal of Banking & Finance, 133*, 106207.

Cornett, M. M., McNutt, J. J., Strahan, P. E., and Tehranian, H. (2011). Liquidity risk management and credit supply in the financial crisis. *Journal of Financial Economics, 101*, 297–312.

Cortés, K. R., Demyanyk, Y., Li, L., Loutskina, E., and Strahan, P. E. (2020). Stress tests and small business lending. *Journal of Financial Economics, 136*, 260–279.

Demirgüç-Kunt, A., and Detragiache, E. (1998). The determinants of banking crises in developing and developed countries. *Staff Papers, 45*, 81–109.

Diamond, D. W., Dybvig, P. H. (1983). Bank runs, deposit insurance, and liquidity. *Journal of Political Economy, 91*, 401–419.

Duan, Y., Ghoul, S. E., Guedhami, O., Li, H., and Li, X. (2021). Bank systemic risk around COVID-19: A cross-country analysis. *Journal of Banking & Finance*, 106299.

Friedman, M., and Schwartz, A. J. (2008). *A monetary history of the United States, 1867–1960*. Princeton University Press.

Goldstein, I., Koijen, R. S., and Mueller, H. M. (2021). *COVID-19 and its impact on financial markets and the real economy*. (Preprint).

Hasan, I., Politsidis, P. N., and Sharma, Z. (2020). Global syndicated lending during the COVID-19 pandemic. *Journal of Banking & Finance, 133*, 106121

Heider, F., Hoerova, M., and Holthausen, C. (2015). Liquidity hoarding and interbank market rates: The role of counterparty risk. *Journal of Financial Economics, 118*, 336–354.

Laeven, L., and Valencia, F. (2020). Systemic banking crises database II. *IMF Economic Review*, 1–55.

Li, L., Strahan, P. E., and Zhang, S. (2020). Banks as lenders of first resort: Evidence from the COVID-19 crisis. *Review of Corporate Finance Studies, 9*, 472–500.

Luttrell, D., Atkinson, T., and Rosenblum, H. (2013). Assessing the costs and consequences of the 2007-09 financial crisis and its aftermath. *Economics Letters, 8*, 1–4.

Paul, S. K., Chowdhury, P., Moktadir, M. A., and Lau, K. H. (2021). Supply chain recovery challenges in the wake of COVID-19 pandemic. *Journal of Business Research, 136*, 316–329.

Richter, F. (2021). *Stocks emerge from covid crash with historic 12-month run*. Statista.

Zhang, D., Hu, M., and Ji, Q. (2020). Financial markets under the global pandemic of COVID-19. *Finance Research Letters, 36*, 101528.

Empirical evidence on the economic and financial effects of the COVID-19 crisis around the world

The five chapters of Part II contribute to the mission of the book by compiling and providing assessments of the research and data on the effects of COVID-19 on the three economic segments of society, focusing primarily on the heart of the crisis before the recovery and aftermath that are covered in later parts of the book. We review findings for national and local real economies, households, nonfinancial firms, banks, and financial markets in different nations across the globe.

The pandemic caused widespread damage that primarily harmed the real economy by reducing the supplies of and demands for real economic goods and services, as demonstrated in Chapters 6–8, with less damage to banks and financial markets, as shown in Chapters 9 and 10. In fact, some of the findings in Chapter 9 are suggestive that banks were able to do quite a bit to soften the blows of the COVID-19 crisis on their relationship customers.

Chapter 6

Empirical evidence on the economic effects of the COVID-19 crisis on national and local economies

Abstract

This chapter reviews evidence on the effects of the COVID-19 crisis on national and local economies, focusing on the aspects of GDP, unemployment, and other economic vulnerabilities. We provide more detail on a global basis on these economic effects based on available research and data on the economic consequences of the virus and the reactions to it by policymakers and economic and financial agents. The reduced supplies of and demands for real economic goods and services caused swift and large reductions in economic activity and recessions during the early part of the crisis. Although the recoveries reviewed in later parts of the book were similarly jarring in terms of inflation and supply chain problems, many economic improvements, particularly in GDP and employment, were observed in this later period.

Keywords: COVID-19, GDP, Unemployment, Local economies, Recessions

Here we review the evidence on the effects of the COVID-19 crisis on the real economy—GDP, unemployment, and other economic vulnerabilities—at the national and local levels. Consistent with the common theme of Part II, we concentrated on the large economic changes that occurred quickly during the early part of the crisis.

As mentioned in the earlier chapters, the highly contagious COVID-19 virus was first detected in China in December 2019. Within just a few months after that, the world economy was disrupted by lockdowns and significant reduction in economic activities. Measures were taken in many countries around the world to protect people's health and save lives, but from an economic standpoint, they generated massive and sudden supply and demand shocks. They also "disrupted the global production value chain and trade" (e.g., Agarwal, He, and Yeung, 2020). They triggered *one* of the deepest global economic downturns in human history that we cover here.

The Economic and Financial Impacts of the COVID-19 Crisis Around the World
https://doi.org/10.1016/B978-0-443-19162-6.00028-1
Copyright © 2024 Elsevier Inc. All rights reserved.

6.1   Effects of COVID-19 crisis on GDP and unemployment outcomes

We focus on economic reactions in the early stages of the COVID-19 pandemic. According to the World Bank (2020), the global economy was expected to shrink by 5.2% in 2020, representing the deepest global recession since the World War II. Ellul, Erel, and Rajan (2020) in their *Review of Corporate Financial Studies* special issue and Financial Times (2020) reported that the gross domestic product (GDP) in the second quarter of 2020 fell by 9.5% in the US, compared to the previous quarter, a drop equaling an annualized pace of 32.9%, with the cumulative decline in the first two quarters of the 2020 recession being larger than the decline during the first two quarters of the Great Depression (e.g., Wheelock, 2020). Similar declines are reported by Ellul, Erel, and Rajan (2020) in Europe, where GDP shrank by 10.1% in Germany alone. Moreover, the social costs, of lost employment and the resultant negative impact on the well-being of individuals and communities, cannot be emphasized enough. The US job postings plummeted by 40% in April 2020 as compared to the same month in 2019, then slowly recovered, but still stood at −20% as of July 2020. In addition, job postings in July 2020 were at −40% in France, −35% in Italy, −50% in Spain, −55% in the UK, and −25% in Germany, compared to the same month in 2019.

Within the US states, the GDP decline was similarly widespread. Berger and Demirgüç-Kunt (2021) reported that "every state had an annualized rate decline of real GDP in 2020:Q2 of at least 20%.[8] The lowest rate occurred in Washington, DC (which we consider as a state for our purposes) with a 20.4% decline, likely due to steady federal employment. The greatest percentage declines were more than twice as high at 42.2% each for Nevada and Hawaii, likely due reliance on travel and tourism, which was effectively shut down."

Focusing on the economic situation in China, the first country to be hit by the COVID-19 pandemic, Agarwal, He, and Yeung (2020) and Chen, He, Hsieh, and Song (2020) found that China's industrial value added fell by about 4.3% and 25.9% in January and February 2020, respectively, on a year-by-year basis. Chen, He, Hsieh, and Song (2020) noted that "the economic impact of the lockdown on China is large, severe, and recovery is sluggish in economic activities involving face-to-face interactions. The deteriorating pandemic situation across the globe is bringing an almost complete halt to the export sector in China and Chinese firms have difficulty accessing critical inputs provided by firms outside of China." Nevertheless, Fang (2020) showed that the lockdown of Wuhan (China), the epicenter of the crisis, reduced infection rates in China by more than 50%. The author also discusses the successes in South Korea in restricting the virus spread using strict measures of quarantine and testing and how these actions actually lead to less severe economic disruptions than would have been if no lockdowns were in place. Importantly and similarly in thinking to Fang (2020), Hofman (2020) also pointed out that out of all parts of the world, East Asia has been most successful in containing COVID-19 and reducing its spread and has also experienced least economic damage, at least in the early stages of the pandemic in 2020. As per the World Bank, East Asia and Pacific were the only regions with some nonnegative growth in 2020. This is argued to be due to lower infection and death rates compared to the Western countries, people's strong inclination to wear masks from the beginning, acceptance of social distancing and strong lockdown measures. It is also likely that Asia's prior painful experience with another pandemic in 2003, the severe acute respiratory syndrome (SARS), also gave some lessons to better handle the COVID-19 pandemic (Agarwal, He, and Yeung, 2020).

Fernández-Villaverde and Jones (2020) combined data on GDP, unemployment, and Google's COVID-19 community mobility reports with data on deaths from COVID-19 to study the macroeconomic outcomes of the pandemic. They presented results from an international perspective using data at the country level as well as results for individual US states and key cities throughout the world. The data from these different levels of geographic aggregation offer a similar view of the pandemic despite the substantial heterogeneity. Countries such as South Korea, Japan, Germany, and Norway and cities such as Tokyo and Seoul have comparatively few deaths and low macroeconomic losses. At the other extreme, New York City, Lombardy, the UK, and Madrid had many deaths and large macroeconomic losses. There are fewer locations that seem to have succeeded on one dimension but suffered on the other, but these include California and Sweden. A look at states across the US alone shows that states such as New York, Massachusetts, and New Jersey had more than 1200 deaths per million residents as well as unemployment rates that even after several months of early recovery exceeded 10% in August. In contrast, states such as Utah, Idaho, Montana, and Wyoming have very few deaths and unemployment rates of between 4% and 7%. The variety of cases potentially offers useful policy lessons regarding how to use nonpharmaceutical interventions to support good economic and health outcomes.

Demirgüç-Kunt, Lokshin, and Torre (2020) estimated economic impacts of the nonpharmaceutical interventions implemented by countries in Europe and Central Asia over the initial stages of the COVID-19 pandemic. They documented that the nonpharmaceutical interventions led to a decline of about 10% in economic activity across the regions. On average, countries that implemented nonpharmaceutical interventions in the early stages of the pandemic appear to have better short-term economic outcomes and lower cumulative mortality, compared with countries that imposed nonpharmaceutical interventions during the later stages of the pandemic. Moreover, COVID-19 mortality at the peak of the local outbreak has been lower in countries that acted earlier. They concluded that the sooner nonpharmaceutical interventions were implemented, the better were the economic and health outcomes for the countries.

6.2 Effects of COVID-19 crisis on employment on the national and local levels

In terms of declines in employment and economic activity, the COVID-19 crisis proved to rival or exceed the Great Depression in the first two quarters, but overall, declines were short-lived (e.g., Wheelock, 2020). During the COVID-19 crisis, the unemployment rate increased sharply in the US in the initial months of the 2020 recession, from 3.5% in February 2020 to nearly 15% in April 2020, before falling back to 11.1% in June 2020. We compare this with the Great Depression that initially only increased about 2% in the late 1929 to about 4% in June 1930, albeit it did increase more later on (see Bureau of Labor Statistics, 2022).[1]

Chetty, Friedman, and Stepner (2023) suggest that the significant decline in the consumer spending at the heart of the pandemic previously discussed had chain reactions to other parts of the economy by significantly reducing the revenues of small businesses in wealthy areas, which further laid off many of their employees, leading to widespread job losses, especially among low-wage/low-income workers. They also contend that, while high-wage workers likely experienced a V-shaped recession that lasted a few weeks, low-wage/low-income workers experienced much larger job losses that persisted for several months.

This evidence is also supported by evidence from the COVID-19 Survey of Consumers from the Federal Reserve Bank of Philadelphia's Consumer Finance Institute. Akana (2020a, 2020b, 2020c, 2020d) used the surveys to assess how did the COVID-19 crisis affected consumer employment,

---

[1] https://www.bls.gov/cps/effects-of-the-coronavirus-covid-19-pandemic.htm

income, and financial security. Waves 2, 3, 4, and 6 report that lower-income, younger, and minority consumers (African American and Hispanics) experienced disparately higher rates of disruptions in employment and income and more financial insecurity. Fairlie, Couch, and Xu (2020) used the US Census Current Population Survey (CPS microdata) and also show the labor market disruptions have disproportionally affected more some of the minorities, raising concerns about long-term economic effects for them. The April 2020 upper-bound simple unemployment rates are an alarming 31.8% for African Americans and 31.4% for Hispanics. However, a more rigorous difference-in-difference analysis suggests that Hispanics have been more disproportionally impacted by the COVID-19 pandemic because of unfavorable occupational distribution and lower skills, leading to much higher unemployment rates than for Whites.

Alon, Doepke, Olmstead-Rumsey, and Tertilt (2020) further showed that the COVID-19 pandemic also has implications for gender inequality. The employment drop was larger in sectors with high female employment shares. The social distancing measures and closures of schools and daycare centers had a particularly large impact on working mothers, which are likely to be persistent, because of high returns to experience in the labor market. Furthermore, Clark, Lusardi, and Mitchell (2020) looked at financial fragility of individuals with different characteristics during the COVID-19 pandemic. They showed that one out of five older (45–75) consumers during April-May 2020 was financially fragile with difficulty facing a midsize emergency expense. Similar to other studies mentioned above, other subgroups at particular risk of facing financial difficulties were younger consumers, those with larger families, Hispanics, and those with low incomes. However, the more financially literate were better able to manage the shocks, indicating that knowledge may have added some protection.

On a more positive note, Levine, Lin, and Xie (2020) used high-frequency, US county-level data on employment, small business revenue, and COVID-19 cases, and found that employment, especially the employment of low-income workers, and the revenues of small firms fall by less in response to local COVID-19 cases in counties with a larger proportion of small banks. This was driven by small banks increasing lending to small businesses more than large banks in response to the pandemic. This may also reflect some of the government-sponsored programs like the CARES Act PPP bank lending to small businesses. Authors conclude that small banks provide countercyclical funding to small firms and communities following the COVID-19 adverse shock, and this is accompanied by positive ramifications on employment.

6.3 Effects of COVID-19 crisis on industrial exposure and other economic vulnerabilities/supply chain

The COVID-19 pandemic has had an unequal effect on industrial sectors across the globe, by hampering the operation of certain industries while enabling the operation of others, mostly driven by the nature of the crisis and/or vulnerabilities to shutdowns and social distancing measures. Thus, the air travel, hospitality, public entertainment, and most service industries were shut down almost entirely during the early stages of the pandemic, while pharmaceuticals, food and beverages, manufacturers of masks and other pandemic-related health goods like tests, and also online retailers did very well due to a sudden increase in demand for their services. Pagano and Zechner (2022) mentioned that due to such asymmetries, "which reshuffled both the demand for output and the supply of labor across industries and firms, COVID-19 can be seen as a reallocation shock." Similar views are expressed by Barrero, Bloom, and Davis (2020), Barrero, Bloom, Davis, and Meyer (2021), and Bloom, Han, and Liang (2022).

Papanikolaou and Schmidt (2022) analyzed the supply-side disruptions associated with COVID-19. They found that a one-standard deviation increase in the COVID-19 work exposure measure is associated with a 6.2%–23.0% greater decline in industrywide employment. Moreover, sectors in which a higher fraction of the workforce was not able to work remotely experienced greater declines in employment and expected revenue growth, and a higher likelihood of default. At the individual level, a one-standard deviation increase in the COVID-19 work exposure measure is associated with a 4.5 percentage point increase in the probability of a worker in a noncritical industry being without employment in April 2020, compared to a 1.0 percentage point increase for a worker in a critical industry. Moreover, relative to workers in noncritical industries with similar characteristics, employees in critical industries were 8 percentage points less likely to remain employed. Finally, authors also documented that lower-paid workers, especially female workers with young children, were significantly more affected by these disruptions.

We close with a brief discussion on some economic vulnerabilities related to international supply chain and trade. The asynchronous nature of the pandemic and the unexpected repeat outbreaks in some countries or even across regions in a country added uncertainty about the recovery of supply chain and trade. The pandemic disruption and also partly the previous trade frictions between China and the US made the US imports from China shrink by 40% during February and March 2020 and significantly dampened global trade (e.g., Agarwal, He, and Yeung, 2020; Charoenwong, 2020; Chor, 2020; Fang and Yeung, 2020). There are concerns that these COVID-19 crisis disruptions could have long-lasting consequences on the future global supply chain and global trade. Chor (2020) suggests that the pandemic made firm reevaluate their exposure to the global supply value-chain disruptions and possible try to scale back offshoring some of their activities. These trends may amplify future decisions for keeping production of essential goods at home and preserving manufacturing capabilities, while governments may push forward protectionist agendas that can contribute to deglobalization. The pandemic may have also affected to a certain extent international cooperation in trade and supply chain. This can affect future production resilience and efficiency that may ultimately harm economic agents in the global economy.

References

Agarwal, S., He, Z., and Yeung, B. (Eds.). (2020). *Impact of COVID-19 on Asian economies and policy responses.* World Scientific.

Akana, T. (2020a). *CFI COVID-19 survey of consumers—Wave 2 updates, impact by race/ethnicity, and early use of economic impact payments.* Federal Reserve Bank of Philadelphia Consumer Finance Institute Special Report (June 2020).

Akana, T. (2020b). *CFI COVID-19 survey of consumers—Wave 3 reveals improvements, but not for everyone.* Federal Reserve Bank of Philadelphia Consumer Finance Institute Special Report (August 2020).

Akana, T. (2020c). *CFI COVID-19 survey of consumers—Wave 4 tracks how the vulnerable are affected more by job interruptions and income disruptions.* Federal Reserve Bank of Philadelphia Consumer Finance Institute Special Report (September 2020).

Akana, T. (2020d). *CFI COVID-19 survey of consumers—Wave 5.* Federal Reserve Bank of Philadelphia Consumer Finance Institute Special Report (November 2020).

Alon, T. M., Doepke, M., Olmstead-Rumsey, J., and Tertilt, M. (2020). *The impact of COVID-19 on gender equality (w26947).* National Bureau of Economic Research.

Barrero, J. M., Bloom, N., and Davis, S. J. (2020). *COVID-19 is also a reallocation shock (no. w27137).* National Bureau of Economic Research.

Barrero, J. M., Bloom, N., Davis, S. J., and Meyer, B. H. (2021, May). COVID-19 is a persistent reallocation shock. In *AEA papers and proceedings* (Vol. 111, pp. 287–291).

Berger, A. N., and Demirgüç-Kunt, A. (2021). Banking research in the time of COVID-19. *Journal of Financial Stability*, *57*, 100939.

Bloom, N., Han, R., and Liang, J. (2022). *How hybrid working from home works out (no. w30292)*. National Bureau of Economic Research.

Bureau of Labor Statistics. (2022). *Effects of the coronavirus COVID-19 pandemic (CPS)*. Available at: https://www.bls.gov/cps/effects-of-the-coronavirus-covid-19-pandemic.htm.

Charoenwong, B. (2020). COVID-19 in the global production network. In *Impact of COVID-19 on Asian economies and policy responses* (pp. 147–149).

Chen, Q., He, Z., Hsieh, C. T., and Song, Z. (2020). Economic effects of lockdown in China. In *Impact of COVID-19 on Asian economies and policy responses* (pp. 3–10).

Chetty, R., Friedman, J., and Stepner, M. (2023). The economic impacts of COVID-19: Evidence from a new public database built using private sector data. *Quarterly Journal of Economics*. Forthcoming.

Chor, D. (2020). International trade has suffered a one-two punch: Can it recover after COVID-19? In *Impact of COVID-19 on Asian economies and policy responses* (pp. 141–145).

Clark, R. L., Lusardi, A., and Mitchell, O. S. (2020). *Financial fragility during the COVID-19 pandemic (w28207)*. National Bureau of Economic Research.

Demirgüç-Kunt, A., Lokshin, M., and Torre, I. (2020). *The sooner, the better: The early economic impact of non-pharmaceutical interventions during the COVID-19 pandemic*. World Bank Policy Research Working Paper (9257).

Ellul, A., Erel, I., and Rajan, U. (2020). The COVID-19 pandemic crisis and corporate finance. *Review of Corporate Finance Studies*, *9*(3), 421–429.

Fairlie, R. W., Couch, K., and Xu, H. (2020). The impacts of COVID-19 on minority unemployment. In *First evidence from April 2020 CPS microdata (no. w27246)*. National Bureau of Economic Research.

Fang, H. (2020). Public policy tools to address the COVID-19 pandemic: Health versus economy. In *Impact of COVID-19 on Asian economies and policy responses* (pp. 17–18).

Fang, H., and Yeung, B. (2020). Post-COVID-19 reconfiguration of the global value chains and China. In *Impact of COVID-19 on Asian economies and policy responses* (pp. 151–156).

Fernández-Villaverde, J., and Jones, C. I. (2020). *Macroeconomic outcomes and COVID-19: A progress report (no. w28004)*. National Bureau of Economic Research.

Financial Times. (2020). *Pandemic crisis: Global economic recovery tracker* (accessed 01.08.20) https://www.ft.com/content/272354f2-f970-4ae4-a8ae-848c4baf8f4a.

Hofman, B. (2020). The impact of COVID-19 on Asia and the future of global supply chains. In *Impact of COVID-19 on Asian economies and policy responses* (pp. 131–139).

Levine, R., Lin, C., and Xie, W. (2020). *Local financial structure and economic resilience*. Working Paper. Available at: SSRN 3755560.

Pagano, M., and Zechner, J. (2022). COVID-19 and corporate finance. *Review of Corporate Finance Studies*, *11*(4), 849–879.

Papanikolaou, D., and Schmidt, L. D. (2022). Working remotely and the supply-side impact of Covid-19. *Review of Asset Pricing Studies*, *12*(1), 53–111.

Wheelock, D. C. (2020). *Comparing the COVID-19 recession with the great depression* (p. 39). Economic Synopses: Federal Reserve Bank of St. Louis.

World Bank. (2020). *Pandemic, recession: The global economy in crisis*. Report, Washington, DC. https://www.worldbank.org/en/publication/global-economic-prospects.

Chapter 7

Empirical evidence on the economic effects of the COVID-19 crisis on households

Chapter outline

Abstract

This chapter narrows the focus of the economic effects of COVID-19 to households. The crisis inflicted economic harm to households around the world, with differences that varied with the disease spread and the reactions to it. Within nations, households that were more at financial risk—low income, minorities, younger—were more severely affected. We detail research and data on these effects through consumer demand and spending; health, mobility, income, and employment; and credit cards, mortgages, auto loans, and student loans. The effects were often devastating during the heart of the crisis, with historically sharp declines in consumer spending and credit card balances in some countries. Many households also experienced damages well after quality vaccines became available.

Keywords: COVID-19, Households, Minorities, Credit cards, Mortgages, Auto loans, Student loans

This chapter reviews the effects of the COVID-19 crisis on households in the US and other countries. The extant research suggests that the COVID-19 health shocks and economic shutdowns led to unprecedented changes in consumer behavior in spending and balances, employment, income, and housing and financial security. In many countries, we also saw some of the sharpest declines ever seen in consumer spending and credit card balances during the heart of the crisis, with spending remaining depressed relative to precrisis levels for long time even after vaccines became available. The crisis also affected both credit demand and supply in various ways. The more vulnerable consumers (low income, minority, younger) were more severely impacted. We focus first on the COVID-19 research related to consumer-spending behavior and consumption. Then, we discuss COVID-19 research on consumer income and employment conditions. We then study effects on credit supply for credit cards, and finally we review effects on mortgages, auto loans, and student loans.

The Economic and Financial Impacts of the COVID-19 Crisis Around the World
https://doi.org/10.1016/B978-0-443-19162-6.00007-4
Copyright © 2024 Elsevier Inc. All rights reserved.

7.1 Effects of COVID-19 crisis on consumer demand and spending

Consumer spending plays a critical role in any economy. For the US economy alone, it accounts for over 70% of the US GDP. Thus, depressed consumer spending can drive negative economic consequences. Most of the research we review here is about credit card spending, which is an important component.

A growing literature documents unprecedented changes in the typical consumer spending behavior in response to the COVID-19 pandemic and resulting government economic shutdowns (e.g., Adams and Bord, 2020; Baker, Farrokhnia, Meyer, Pagel, and Yannelis, 2020a; Coibion, Gorodnichenko, and Weber, 2020; Dong, Gozgor, Lu, and Yan, 2021; Horvath, Kay, and Wix, 2021; Chetty, Friedman, and Stepner, 2023). There is an increase in spending in the early March, particularly in retail and food items, followed by a dramatic fall in consumer spending from March to April (e.g., Baker, Farrokhnia, Meyer, Pagel, and Yannelis, 2020a). Stronger declines occurred in areas with a higher number of infections, shelter-in-place orders, and greater social distancing (e.g., Baker, Farrokhnia, Meyer, Pagel, and Yannelis, 2020a; Chetty, Friedman, and Stepner, 2023). Shapiro (2020) divided underlying price data according to the spending category and found that the decline in core consumption expenditures inflation comes from a large decline in consumer demand, which outweighs price pressure from COVID-19-related supply constraints.

Adams and Bord (2020) documented that outstanding revolving credit on credit cards in the G.19 Consumer Credit statistical release fell by an annualized rate of 32% by 2020:Q2. The 65% plummet in April is the largest since the Federal Reserve began collecting data on revolving credit in 1968. They further found that the most important factor in the decline is the consumer purchase volume falling by almost 25% from March to April, primarily in revolver credit card accounts. Spending fell most in restaurants, hotels, travel, entertainment, and oil and gas. Chetty, Friedman, and Stepner (2023) further suggested that the depressed spending was particularly acute in affluent areas with high rates of COVID-19 infection. This decline was also concentrated in sectors that require in-person interaction and was driven mainly by high-income/lower-risk consumers.

In May and June, when some of the economic restrictions were eased, the situation improved slightly as the credit card purchase volume picked up by about 10%, most of it driven by lower-income and riskier consumers. However, higher-income consumers or those expecting employment losses or benefit cuts did not see any significant changes in spending in this period (e.g., Adams and Bord, 2020; Baker, Farrokhnia, Meyer, Pagel, and Yannelis, 2020b; Cox, Ganong, Noel, Vavra, Wong, Farrell, and Greig, 2020; Horvath, Kay, and Wix, 2021).

Spending upticks were most prevalent in durables and food items. At the same time, revolving balances declined in part because of smaller previous months' spending, as well as an unusually high number of consumers paying down their balances (credit cards, mortgages, rents, etc.) partially or completely. This suggests that the set of government measures to help consumers during the COVID-19 crisis, including extended unemployment insurance benefits, stimulus checks, as well as other CARES Act policies, mitigated some of the effects of the economic disruptions on consumer spending. However, it also led some more wary consumers to pay down some of their debts, reducing the stimulative effect on consumer spending.

Despite these ups and downs, the US consumer spending overall remained depressed relative to precrisis levels. This experience is generally mirrored by other international studies using transactions-level data. However, there are differences related to the different times that the pandemic hit a particular country or different intensities within the crisis in different countries. The largest decline was recorded in Wuhan province in China, where the pandemic originated, which registered a 70% decline in total consumer spending in the late January.

Thus, in the UK, Hacioglu Hoke, Känzig, and Surico (2020) documented a decline of 40%–50% in consumer spending during the COVID-19 crisis, mainly for services such as retail, restaurants, and transportation. The initial rise in online shopping and grocery purchases has been subsequently reverted. Income reductions have become far more frequent, with a median decline around 30%. The share of borrowers facing financing issues has increased significantly for both secured and unsecured lending. In Spain, Carvalho, García, Hansen, Ortiz, Rodrigo, Rodríguez Mora, and Ruiz (2021) analyzed daily sales transactions from both credit cards and point-of-sales terminals in Spain. They found immediate, large, and sustained reductions in spending right after the national lockdown. In Denmark, Andersen, Hansen, Johannesen, and Sheridan (2020) examined transaction-level customer data from the largest bank in Denmark and showed that consumer spending decrease by 27% in the 7 weeks following the shutdown. The spending drop was mostly concentrated on goods and services affected by the shutdown and larger for consumers with higher ex ante risk of job loss, wealth destruction, severe disease and disrupted consumption patterns, and ex post unemployment.

In Poland, Waliszewski and Warchlewska (2021) conducted an analysis of the change in the financial behavior of households under the shock of the pandemic and documented a fall in expenditure compared to the period before the pandemic, which may explain the lack of opportunities to spend money, the fall in revenue, and the freezing of expenditures due to uncertainty. There has also been a change in the way payments are made. Payment cards and purchases made over the Internet became increasingly popular. In the face of the COVID-19 pandemic, consumers were trying to save more, but not everyone could afford to do so.

In China where the virus originated, Chen, Qian, and Wen (2020) used daily transaction data in 214 cities to study the impact of COVID-19 on consumption after China's outbreak in the late January 2020. Based on the difference-in-differences estimation, daily offline consumption, via bank card and mobile QR code transactions, fell by 32% during the 12-week period, with the largest decrease for dining and entertainment (64%) and travel (59%) and in Wuhan (70%). Consumption further decreased when the crisis unfolded although social distancing measures remained stable. Consumption came back to the baseline level by the end of March but decreased again by 20% in the early April due to the elevated risk of a second wave of infections.

Other studies also cover the aspects of the COVID-19 pandemic on credit card demand. A report by the Consumer Financial Protection Bureau (2020) investigates the volume of credit card inquiries in the last week of March 2020 with that in the first week, while adjusting for within-month trends in the earlier years from 2013 to 2019. They found a 40% decline in credit card inquiries, with effects being significantly more pronounced for high-quality than for low-quality consumers. The documented decline could be a reflection of decreased consumer demand, discouraged borrowing, or decreased credit card supply.[1]

---

[1]The Senior Loan Officer Opinion Survey on Bank Lending Practices also reported lower percentage of banks with strong credit demand and higher percentage of banks tightening lending standards across credit cards and other consumer products up until 2020Q3.

7.2 Effects of COVID-19 crisis on consumer health, mobility, income, and employment

The literature emphasizes also the effects on consumer health, income, and unemployment and their differential effects across different types of consumers, such as low income vs high income, minorities vs other races, or those of different gender and age groups. This literature shows that the COVID-19 pandemic may have exacerbated long-standing race and gender inequalities in some cases.

In terms of mobility, Bailey, Johnston, Koenen, Kuchler, Russel, and Stroebel (2020) found that social network exposure to COVID-19 cases shapes individuals' beliefs and behaviors concerning the coronavirus. Using de-identified data from Facebook, they saw that the consumers with friends in areas with worse COVID-19 outbreaks reduce their mobility more than otherwise similar individuals with friends in less-affected areas. Li and Su (2022) used individual-level microdata of location histories in the US and documented a sudden rise of net migration toward the suburban neighborhoods and less densely populated MSAs during the COVID-19 pandemic. This migration wave has been driven disproportionately by the movement of the high-income population. As a result, housing costs rose more in the locations receiving the influx than in the locations experiencing the exodus. Job losses were milder and unemployment rates increased by less during the height of the pandemic for low-skilled workers in the locations receiving the influx than they did in the locations experiencing the exodus. The equilibrium response in housing costs due to migration reduced the rent exposure faced by the average person, especially that faced by the average low-income person. Migration also led to a higher job growth in lower-income labor markets and mildly mitigated unemployment rates faced by the average low-income person during the pandemic peak.

In terms of declines in employment and economic activity, the COVID-19 crisis proved to rival or exceed the Great Depression in the first two quarters, but overall, declines were short-lived (e.g., Wheelock, 2020). During the COVID-19 crisis, the unemployment rate increased sharply in the initial months of the 2020 recession, from 3.5% in February 2020 to nearly 15% in April 2020, before falling back to 11.1% in June 2020. We compare this with the Great Depression that initially only increased about 2% in the late 1929 to about 4% in June 1930, albeit it did increase more later on. Regarding declines in economic activity during the COVID-19 pandemic, the US GDP shrank 9.5% by the end of 2020:Q2, a drop equaling an annualized pace of 32.9%, with the cumulative decline in the first two quarters of the 2020 recession being larger than the decline during the first two quarters of the Great Depression (e.g., Wheelock, 2020). Chetty, Friedman, and Stepner (2023) suggested that the significant decline in consumer spending at the heart of the pandemic previously discussed had chain reactions to other parts of the economy by significantly reducing the revenues of small businesses in affluent areas, which further laid off many of their employees, leading to widespread job losses, especially among low-wage/low-income workers. They also contend that, while high-wage workers likely experienced a V-shaped recession that lasted a few weeks, low-wage/low-income workers experienced much larger job losses that persisted for several months.

This is also supported by evidence from the COVID-19 Survey of Consumers from the Federal Reserve Bank of Philadelphia's Consumer Finance Institute. Akana (2020a, 2020b, 2020c, 2020d) used the surveys to assess how did the COVID-19 crisis affected consumer employment, income, and financial security. Waves 2, 3, 4, and 6 reported that lower-income, younger, and minority consumers (African American and Hispanics) experienced disparately higher rates of disruptions in employment and income and more financial insecurity. Fairlie, Couch, and Xu (2020) used the US

Census Current Population Survey (CPS microdata) and also showed the labor market disruptions have disproportionally affected more some of the minorities, raising concerns about long-term economic effects for them. The April 2020 upper-bound simple unemployment rates are an alarming 31.8% for African Americans and 31.4% for Hispanics. However, a more rigorous difference-in-difference analysis suggests that Hispanics have been more disproportionally impacted by the COVID-19 pandemic because of unfavorable occupational distribution and lower skills, leading to much higher unemployment rates than for Whites.

Alon, Doepke, Olmstead-Rumsey, and Tertilt (2020) further showed that the COVID-19 pandemic also has implications for gender inequality. The employment drop was larger in sectors with high female employment shares. The social distancing measures and closures of schools and daycare centers had a particularly large impact on working mothers, which are likely to be persistent, because of high returns to experience in the labor market. Furthermore, Clark, Lusardi, and Mitchell (2020) looked at financial fragility of consumers with different characteristics during the COVID-19 pandemic. They showed that one out of five older (45–75) consumers during April-May 2020 was financially fragile with difficulty facing a midsize emergency expense. Similar to other studies mentioned above, other subgroups at particular risk of facing financial difficulties were younger consumers, those with larger families, Hispanics, and those with low incomes. However, the more financially literate were better able to manage the shocks, indicating that knowledge may have added some protection.

Benfer, Vlahov, Long, Walker-Wells, Pottenger, Gonsalves, and Keene (2021) found that during the COVID-19 crisis, housing precariousness and the risk of eviction increased and worsened during the pandemic, especially among people of color and low-income populations, with implications on their health and inequity. They explained that eviction risks may have increased COVID-19 infection rates and deaths because evictions are commonly associated with overcrowded living environments, doubling up, transiency, limited access to health care, and a decreased ability to comply with the pandemic mitigation strategies, such as social distancing, self-quarantine, and hygiene practices. Eviction was also a driver of inequality as people of color were more likely to face eviction and associated comorbidities. In fact, they found that African Americans have been dying at 2.1 times the rate of non-Hispanic Whites, while Indigenous Americans and Hispanics faced an infection rate almost three times the rate of non-Hispanic Whites.

7.3 Effects of COVID-19 crisis on consumer credit cards

Examining Y-14M credit card data from the Federal Reserve for credit cards up to August 2020, Horvath, Kay, and Wix (2021) showed increases in the interest rates of new credit cards to less creditworthy consumers, consistent with a tightening of credit supply and a flight-to-safety response of banks to the COVID-19 shock. An Experian report by Lembo Stolba (2021) mentions that the average consumer credit scores increased significantly in 2020 likely due to government interventions. The author contends the credit score increases are mostly driven by a significant reduction in the number of consumers with subprime designation, who typically have most constraints to accessing credit. Improvements in credit scores for subprime consumers are regarded as opening more credit opportunities for them.

Berger, Bouwman, Norden, Roman, Udell, and Wang (2024) also used Y-14M credit card data to investigate the effects of the COVID-19 pandemic on credit card terms in the US for relationship consumers relative to nonrelationship consumers. They found that relationships matter for credit card consumers, despite the transactions-based nature of this lending. During the COVID-19 crisis, they found that consumers with relationships benefited from better credit card terms relative to normal times (lower annual percentage rate (APR) spreads), consistent with intertemporal smoothing.[2] The relationship benefits primarily derive from conventional banking relationships (deposits and other non-credit card loans), rather than from prior credit cards. Importantly, their findings also suggest that banks shifted their orientation somewhat from primarily seeking profitability toward more risk management during the crisis, consistent with classic procyclical bank lending behavior (e.g., Berger and Udell, 2004; Thakor, 2015, 2016). Finally, this paper also found that the 2020 CARES Act §4021 provision regarding impediments to reporting consumer delinquencies to credit bureaus during the crisis may have reduced the informational value of consumer credit scores. This may have also penalized apparently safer consumers with better credit scores with less favorable credit terms—resulting in higher APR spreads and lower credit limits for them.

7.4 Effects of COVID-19 crisis on consumer mortgages, auto loans, and student loans

Four papers touch on credit demand and supply effects in the mortgage market during the COVID-19 pandemic as well as some related aspects of government relief for homeowners. Gascon and Hass (2020) found negative effects on home sales in the US residential real estate market during the 2020 spring months of the pandemic, particularly in metro areas. These findings are likely due to health concerns, stay-at-home orders, and economic uncertainty. The drops in sales are lowest in April and May 2020, the worst levels since the housing and financial crisis started in 2007, but they improved in the summer of 2020. A report by the Consumer Financial Protection Bureau (2020) mentions decline in the volume of credit hard inquiries for mortgages (27%), with effects being stronger for high-quality borrowers than for low-quality borrowers. Fuster, Hizmo, Lambie-Hanson, Vickery, and Willen (2021) assessed whether the COVID-19 pandemic has led to a contraction in mortgage credit supply. They found that the mortgage interest rates increased significantly, proven by a 75–100 bp rise in the gap between mortgage primary rates and secondary market yields as well as higher gains-on-sale earned by lenders. They stated that mortgage demand shocks are historically associated with changes in markups, but this historical relationship accounts for only part of the recent increase in the mortgage interest rates. The authors also found that interest rate spreads increased relatively more for mortgages posing the greatest credit risk for lenders, consistent with a potential flight to safety. Despite the mortgage market undergoing a historic boom, the intermediation frictions may have restricted the pass-through of lower-interest rates to consumers.

One study investigates distributional effects of savings from mortgage refinancing across income groups during the COVID-19 crisis. Agarwal, Chomsisengphet, Kiefer, Kiefer, and Medina (2023) found that between February and June 2020, the gap in savings from refinancing between high- and low-income consumers—was 10 times higher than before, consistent with an increase in refinancing inequality. This amounted to a difference of $5 billion in savings from refinancing between the top income quintile and the rest of the market. Authors also found that the results were driven by consumers in the top income quintile increasing their refinancing activity more than comparable ones in the bottom quintile and capturing the largest improvements in interest rates. In addition, the

---

[2] The authors also found improvements in credit card terms during the COVID-19 crisis for small business credit card customers with relationships relative to other customers, again consistent with intertemporal smoothing.

refinancing inequality was higher in the areas most affected by the pandemic. Results have implications for the effectiveness of the monetary policy during the COVID-19 pandemic.[3]

Inequality is a key policy issue during the COVID-19 crisis in the mortgage markets. Benfer, Vlahov, Long, Walker-Wells, Pottenger, Gonsalves, and Keene (2021) found that during the COVID-19 pandemic, African Americans have had less confidence in their ability to pay rent, while a report by the Consumer Financial Protection Bureau (2021) found that 11 million renter and homeowner households were significantly overdue on their regular housing payments as of December 2020, being at heightened risk of losing their homes to foreclosure or eviction. Out of these, African American and Hispanic households were more than twice as likely to be behind on their payments as White households. Inequality consequences were also studied and highlighted by An, Cordell, Geng, and Lee (2022), who used mortgage forbearance and payment data from McDash Flash together with McDash mortgage servicing records, credit bureau data, and confidential Home Mortgage Disclosure Act (HMDA) loan application information. They showed that lower-income and minority borrowers had twice as high the nonpayment rates relative to *higher income* and Whites during the COVID-19 pandemic, even after controlling for conventional risk factors.

But stimulus payments, unemployment assistance, forbearances, and moratoria on eviction from the CARES Act may have helped mitigate some of these inequalities. For example, Bhutta, Blair, Dettling, and Moore (2020) used household data on savings, income, and expenses from the Federal Reserve's Survey of Consumer Finances and showed that cash assistance included in the CARES Act has been instrumental in allowing almost all families to cover their recurring, nondiscretionary expenses in the event of long-term unemployment. An, Cordell, Geng, and Lee (2022) found that government- and private-sector forbearance programs may have mitigated these inequalities in the near term, as lower-income and minority borrowers have taken up the short-term debt relief at higher rates. An, Gabriel, and Tzur-Ilan (2022) found that eviction moratoria reduced evictions and resulted in redirection of limited household financial resources to immediate consumption needs, such as food and grocery spending. They also found that this reduced household food insecurity and mental stress, with larger beneficial effects among African American households. See Chapter 12 on other policy reactions to the COVID-19 crisis in the US and their effects on local economies, households, nonfinancial firms, banks, and financial markets for more details on these programs of assistance for households.

Finally, three articles touch on the auto-loan market during the COVID-19 pandemic. The report by the Consumer Financial Protection Bureau (2020) previously mentioned for other products finds a decline in the volume of credit inquiries for auto loans by 52%. Foohey (2020) showed that throughout 2020, auto lenders granted more payment forbearances to consumers, while slashing interest rates on new loans. Auto manufacturers similarly made promises to buyers, such as the ability to return new cars for up to a year upon job loss. The author warns of the possibility of an auto-loan bubble burst. Canals-Cerdá and Lee (2021) used FRBNY Consumer Credit Panel (CCP)/Equifax data to investigate auto-loan origination trends during the pandemic. They found a significant decline in auto-loan originations from March to April 2020 that rebounded in May and June 2020, which flattened afterward. The initial decline is significant for both banks and nonbanks, but there is a stronger subsequent rebound for nonbanks. In addition, while the decline in

---

[3]For a review and findings about the monetary policy effects on households during the COVID-19 pandemic, please see An, Cordell, Roman, and Zhang (2023).

originations applies to all consumers, the weakest rebound is found among the subprime borrowers, consistent with lenders' potential flight to safety and potentially shying away from risky auto lending during the pandemic uncertain times.

References

Adams, R. M., and Bord, V. (2020). *The effects of the COVID-19 shutdown on the consumer credit card market: Revolvers versus transactors.* FEDS Notes 2020-10, 21-1.

Agarwal, S., Chomsisengphet, S., Kiefer, H., Kiefer, L. C., and Medina, P. C. (2023). *Refinancing inequality during the COVID-19 pandemic.* Available at: SSRN 3750133.

Akana, T. (2020a). *CFI COVID-19 survey of consumers—Wave 2 updates, impact by race/ethnicity, and early use of economic impact payments.* Federal Reserve Bank of Philadelphia Consumer Finance Institute special report.

Akana, T. (2020b). *CFI COVID-19 survey of consumers—Wave 3 reveals improvements, but not for everyone.* Federal Reserve Bank of Philadelphia Consumer Finance Institute special report.

Akana, T. (2020c). *CFI COVID-19 survey of consumers—Wave 4 tracks how the vulnerable are affected more by job interruptions and income disruptions.* Federal Reserve Bank of Philadelphia Consumer Finance Institute special report.

Akana, T. (2020d). *CFI COVID-19 survey of consumers—Wave 5.* Federal Reserve Bank of Philadelphia Consumer Finance Institute special report.

Alon, T. M., Doepke, M., Olmstead-Rumsey, J., and Tertilt, M. (2020). *The impact of COVID-19 on gender equality* (w26947). National Bureau of Economic Research.

An, X., Cordell, L., Geng, L., and Lee, K. (2022). *Inequality in the time of COVID-19: Evidence from mortgage delinquency and forbearance.* Available at: SSRN 3789349.

An, X., Cordell, L., Roman, R. A., and Zhang, C. (2023). Central Bank Monetary Policy and Consumer Credit Markets, In *Oxford Research Encyclopedia of Economics and Finance*, Forthcoming.

An, X., Gabriel, S.A., and Tzur-Ilan, N. (2022). More than shelter: The effect of rental eviction moratoria on household well-being. *AEA Papers and Proceedings, 112*, 308–312.

Andersen, A. L., Hansen, E. T., Johannesen, N., and Sheridan, A. (2020). *Consumer responses to the COVID-19 crisis: Evidence from bank account transaction data.* Available at: SSRN 3609814.

Bailey, M., Johnston, D. M., Koenen, M., Kuchler, T., Russel, D., and Stroebel, J. (2020). *Social networks shape beliefs and behavior: Evidence from social distancing during the COVID-19 pandemic.* Available at: https://www.nber.org/papers/w28234.

Baker, S. R., Farrokhnia, R. A., Meyer, S., Pagel, M., and Yannelis, C. (2020a). How does household spending respond to an epidemic? Consumption during the 2020 COVID-19 pandemic. *The Review of Asset Pricing Studies, 10*, 834–862.

Baker, S. R., Farrokhnia, R. A., Meyer, S., Pagel, M., and Yannelis, C. (2020b). *Income, liquidity, and the consumption response to the 2020 economic stimulus payments (No. w27097).* National Bureau of Economic Research.

Benfer, E. A., Vlahov, D., Long, M. Y., Walker-Wells, E., Pottenger, J. L., Gonsalves, G., and Keene, D. E. (2021). Eviction, health inequity, and the spread of COVID-19: Housing policy as a primary pandemic mitigation strategy. *Journal of Urban Health, 98*, 1–12.

Berger, A. N., Bouwman, C. H., Norden, L., Roman, R. A., Udell, G. F., and Wang, T. (2024). Piercing through opacity: Relationships and credit card lending to consumers and small businesses during normal times and the COVID-19 crisis. *Journal of Political Economy, 132*, forthcoming.

Berger, A. N., and Udell, G. F. (2004). The institutional memory hypothesis and the procyclicality of bank lending behavior. *Journal of Financial Intermediation, 13*, 458–495.

Bhutta, N., Blair, J., Dettling, L. J., and Moore, K. B. (2020). *COVID-19, the CARES Act, and families' financial security.* Available at: https://papers.ssrn.com/sol3/papers.cfm?abstract_id=3631903.

Canals-Cerdá, J. J., and Lee, B. J. (2021). *COVID-19 and auto loans origination trends.* Working paper Federal Reserve Bank of Philadelphia.

Canals-Cerda, J. J., and Roman, R. (2021). *Climate change and consumer finance: A very brief literature review.* FRB of Philadelphia Payment Cards Center Discussion Paper (21–4).

Carvalho, V. M., García, J. R., Hansen, S., Ortiz, Á., Rodrigo, T., Rodríguez Mora, J. V., and Ruiz, P. (2021). Tracking the COVID-19 crisis with high-resolution transaction data. *Royal Society Open Science*, 8, 210218.

Chen, H., Qian, W., and Wen, Q. (2020). *The impact of the COVID-19 pandemic on consumption: Learning from high frequency transaction data*. Available at: https://papers.ssrn.com/sol3/papers.cfm?abstract_id=3568574.

Chetty, R., Friedman, J., and Stepner, M. (2023). The economic impacts of COVID-19: Evidence from a new public database built using private sector data. *Quarterly Journal of Economics*. Forthcoming.

Clark, R. L., Lusardi, A., and Mitchell, O. S. (2020). *Financial fragility during the COVID-19 pandemic (w28207)*. National Bureau of Economic Research. Available at: https://www.nber.org/system/files/working_papers/w28207/w28207.pdf.

Coibion, O., Gorodnichenko, Y., and Weber, M. (2020). *The cost of the COVID-19 crisis: Lockdowns, macroeconomic expectations, and consumer spending (w27141)*. National Bureau of Economic Research. Available at: https://www.nber.org/papers/w27141.

Consumer Financial Protection Bureau. (2020). *The early effects of the COVID-19 pandemic on consumer credit*. Special issue brief. Available at: https://files.consumerfinance.gov/f/documents/cfpb_issue-brief_early-effects-covid-19credit-applications_2020-04.pdf.

Consumer Financial Protection Bureau. (2021). *Housing insecurity and the COVID-19 pandemic*. Staff Reports. Available at: https://www.consumerfinance.gov/data-research/researchreports/housing-insecurity-and-the-covid-19-pandemic/.

Cox, N., Ganong, P., Noel, P., Vavra, J., Wong, A., Farrell, D., Greig, F., and Deadman, E. (2020). Initial impacts of the pandemic on consumer behavior: Evidence from linked income, spending, and savings data. *Brookings Papers on Economic Activity*, 2020, 35–82.

Dong, D., Gozgor, G., Lu, Z., and Yan, C. (2021). Personal consumption in the United States during the COVID-19 crisis. *Applied Economics*, 53, 1311–1316.

Fairlie, R. W., Couch, K., and Xu, H. (2020). *The impacts of COVID-19 on minority unemployment: First evidence from April 2020 CPS microdata (No. w27246)*. National Bureau of Economic Research. Available at: https://www.nber.org/papers/w27246.

Foohey, P. (2020). Bursting the auto loan bubble in the wake of COVID-19. *Iowa Law Review*, 106, 2215.

Fuster, A., Hizmo, A., Lambie-Hanson, L., Vickery, J., and Willen, P. (2021). *Mortgage credit supply during the COVID-19 pandemic*. Working paper Federal Reserve Bank of Philadelphia.

Gascon, C. S., and Hass, J. (2020). The impact of COVID-19 on the residential real estate market. *The Regional Economist*, 28, 4. Available at: https://www.stlouisfed.org/publications/regional-economist/fourth-quarter2020/impact-covid-residential-real-estate-market.

Hacioglu Hoke, S., Känzig, D.R., and Surico, P. (2020). *Consumption in the time of Covid-19: Evidence from UK transaction data*. CEPR Discussion Paper No. DP14733.

Horvath, A., Kay, B. S., and Wix, C. (2021). *The COVID-19 shock and consumer credit: Evidence from credit card data*. Available at: SSRN 3613408.

Lembo Stolba, S. (2021). *Experian 2020 consumer credit review*. Available at: https://www.experian.com/blogs/ask-experian/consumer-credit-review/.

Li, W., and Su, Y. (2022). *The great reshuffle: Residential sorting during the COVID-19 pandemic and its welfare implications*. Available at: https://doi.org/10.2139/ssrn.3997810. https://ssrn.com/abstract=3997810.

Shapiro, A. H. (2020). Monitoring the inflationary effects of COVID-19. *FRBSF Economic Letter*, 2020, 01–06.

Thakor, A. V. (2015). Lending booms, smart bankers, and financial crises. *The American Economic Review*, 105, 305–309.

Thakor, A. V. (2016). The highs and the lows: A theory of credit risk assessment and pricing through the business cycle. *Journal of Financial Intermediation*, 25, 1–29.

Waliszewski, K., and Warchlewska, A. (2021). Comparative analysis of Poland and selected countries in terms of household financial behaviour during the COVID-19 pandemic. *Equilibrium. Quarterly Journal of Economics and Economic Policy*, 16, 577–615.

Wheelock, D. C. (2020). *Comparing the COVID-19 recession with the great depression*. Federal Reserve Bank of St. Louis, Economic Synopses 39.

Chapter 8

Empirical evidence on the economic effects of the COVID-19 crisis on nonfinancial firms

Abstract

Similar to households, the nonfinancial firms that provide most of the employment income and collect most of the consumption spending also suffered significant economic damages from COVID-19 that we review in this chapter. We cover the effects of the COVID-19 crisis on their failures and performance; stockholders and other stakeholders; and their risks, dividends, and other outcomes based on research and data across the globe. The findings are consistent with our other findings about COVID-19 economic effects—very large losses for these firms in terms of business failures and decline in sales during the business shutdowns and other events during the heart of the crisis. Many firms never returned or recovered.

Keywords: COVID-19, Nonfinancial firms, Business shutdowns, Business failures, Stakeholder losses

In addition to the research on households, there is also COVID-19 crisis research focused on large and small nonfinancial businesses, which we describe below. These firms suffered from the same demand and supply shocks as households. We cover several consequences including firm failures and performance, firm stockholders and other stakeholders' responses, and other nonfinancial firm effects such as risk, financial needs, and dividend policy. Many firms, particularly the smallest, did not survive the crisis.

8.1 Effects of COVID-19 crisis on nonfinancial firm failures and performance

The COVID-19 pandemic combines the aspects of both supply and demand shocks (see e.g., Brinca, Duarte, and Faria-e-Castro, 2020). Lockdown measures prevented workers from doing their jobs and reduced the economy's capacity to produce goods and services, which can be seen as a supply shock.

The Economic and Financial Impacts of the COVID-19 Crisis Around the World
https://doi.org/10.1016/B978-0-443-19162-6.00031-1
Copyright © 2024 Elsevier Inc. All rights reserved.

People avoiding business establishments for fear of contagion and reducing their ability or willingness to purchase goods and services are demand shocks. In addition, as service sector workers lose jobs and income, they stop purchasing goods, such as cars and appliances, which is a sectoral demand shock. Due to these shocks, studies report that the COVID-19 crisis and social distancing restrictions led to dramatic reductions in the number of active small businesses, high failure risk, drops in their sales, revenues, and consumption with much stronger declines being reported in areas affected by mandatory lockdowns up through 2002:Q2 (Fairlie, 2020; Gourinchas, Kalemli-Özcan, Penciakova, and Sander, 2020; Kim, Parker, and Schoar, 2020; Bloom, Fletcher, and Yeh, 2021; Fairlie and Fossen, 2021).

To detail, Fairlie (2020) found that the number of active business owners in the US plummeted by 3.3 million or 22% over the crucial 2-month window from February to April 2020. The drop in business owners was the largest on record, and losses were felt across nearly all industries and even for incorporated businesses. African American businesses were disproportionally hit hard experiencing a 41% drop. Latino business owners fell by 32%, and Asian business owners dropped by 26%. Industry compositions partly placed these groups at a higher risk of losses. Immigrant business owners experienced substantial losses of 36%. Female-owned businesses were also disproportionately hit by 25%. These findings have important policy implications and ramifications for job losses and economic inequality. Similarly, focusing on failure and survival, Bartlett III and Morse (2020) used some unique data from the City of Oakland during COVID-19, and documented that small business survival capabilities varied by firm size as a function of revenue resiliency, labor flexibility, and committed costs. Nonemployer businesses relied on low-cost structures to survive 73% declines in own-store foot traffic. Microbusinesses (1–5 employees) depended on 14% greater revenue resiliency. Enterprises (6–50 employees) had twice-as-much labor flexibility but faced 11%–22% higher residual closure risk from committed costs.

Fairlie and Fossen (2021) provided the first analysis of losses in sales and revenues among the universe of businesses in California using administrative data from the California Department of Tax and Fee Administration. The losses in sales average 17% in the second quarter of 2020 relative to the second quarter of 2019 even though year-over-year sales typically grow by 3%–4%. They found that sales losses were largest in businesses affected by mandatory lockdowns such as accommodations, which lost 91%, whereas online sales grew by 180%. Losses also differed substantially across counties with large losses in San Francisco (50%) and Los Angeles (24%), whereas some counties experienced small gains in sales. Placing business types into different categories based on whether they were essential or nonessential (and thus subject to the early lockdowns) and whether they have a moderate or high level of person-to-person contact, they found interesting correlations between sales losses and COVID-19 cases per capita across counties in California. The results suggest that local implementation and enforcement of lockdown restrictions and voluntary behavioral responses as reactions to the perceived local COVID-19 spread both played a role, but enforcement of mandatory restrictions may have had a larger impact on sales losses.

Gourinchas, Kalemli-Özcan, Penciakova, and Sander (2020) estimated the impact of the COVID-19 crisis on business failures among small- and medium-size enterprises (SMEs) in 17 countries using a large representative firm-level database. They used a simple model of firm cost minimization and measure each firm's liquidity shortfall during and after COVID-19. They estimated a large increase in the failure rate of SMEs under COVID-19 of nearly 9 percentage points, without government support. Accommodation and food services, arts, entertainment and recreation, education, and other services were among the most affected sectors. The jobs at risk due to COVID-19-related SME business failures represented 3.1% of private sector employment. They evaluated the cost and effectiveness of various policy interventions. The fiscal cost of an intervention that narrowly targeted at risk firms was found as modest (0.54% of GDP). However, at a similar level of effectiveness, nontargeted subsidies were substantially more expensive (1.82% of GDP).

Wang, Yang, Iverson, and Kluender (2020) examined the impact of the COVID-19 economic crisis on business bankruptcies in the US using real-time data on the universe of filings. Historically, bankruptcies have closely tracked the business cycle and contemporaneous unemployment rates. However, this relationship has reversed during the COVID-19 crisis. While aggregate filing rates were very similar to 2019 levels prior to the severe onset of the pandemic, filings by small businesses dropped dramatically starting in mid-March, contrary to media reports and many experts' expectations. The total number of bankruptcy filings was down by 27% year-over-year between January and August. Business Chapter 7 filings rebounded moderately starting in mid-April and stabilized around 20% below 2019 levels, but Chapter 13 filings remained at 55%–65% below 2019 levels through the end of August. In contrast to the 2007–09 recession, states with a larger increase in unemployment between April and July experienced greater drops in bankruptcies. Although they make up a small share of overall bankruptcies, Chapter 11 filings by large corporations have increased since 2019 and are up nearly 200% year-over-year from January through August. These patterns suggest that the financial experiences of small and large corporations deviated during the COVID-19 crisis. Large businesses have continued to receive relief from the bankruptcy system as they would during a normal recession. However, small businesses may have faced financial, physical, and technological barriers to accessing the bankruptcy system, especially in the areas hardest hit by unemployment.

Kim, Parker, and Schoar (2020) showed that the revenues of small businesses and the consumption spending of their owners both decline by roughly 40% following the declaration of the national emergency in March 2020 in the US. However, through May 2020, the vast majority of this average decline in revenues is due to national factors rather than to variation in local infection rates or policies. Furthermore, there is only a modest propensity for business owners to cut consumption in response to their individual business losses: comparing owners in the same county but whose businesses operate in industries differentially impacted by local infections and state-level policies, the authors showed that each dollar of revenue loss leads to a 1.6 cent decline in the consumption of the owner at this early stage of the pandemic. This partial pass-through appears to be explained by the liquidity of households and businesses entering the crisis—consumption is twice as responsive for small business owners who operate with low liquidity; government support programs—median account balances in both business and checking accounts decline in March but rebound in April and May; the crisis induced declines in the ability to spend on consumption—spending on travel, restaurants, or personal services dropped dramatically.

Bloom, Fletcher, and Yeh (2021) used survey data on around 2500 US small businesses to assess the impact of COVID-19 and documented a significant negative sales impact that peaked in 2020:Q2, with an average loss of 29% in sales. The large negative impact masks significant heterogeneity, with over 40% of firms reporting zero or a positive impact, while almost a quarter reporting losses of more than 50%. These impacts also appear to be persistent, with firms reporting the largest sales drops in mid-2020 still forecasting large sales losses a year later in the mid-2021. In terms of business types, they found that the smallest offline firms experienced sales drops of over 40% compared to less than 10% for the largest online firms. Finally, female and black owners reported significantly larger drops in sales than male-owned business and other races. Owners with a humanities degree also experienced far larger losses, while those with a STEM degree saw the least impact, suggesting that certain degrees provide some defense during crisis circumstances. Gascon and Hass (2020) also noted that the COVID-19 pandemic significantly affected the US residential real estate market and because of health concerns, stay-at-home orders, and economic uncertainty, many metro areas experienced a noticeable drop in home sales. In fact, in April and May 2020, nationwide home sales dropped to their lowest levels since the housing and financial crisis that began in 2007, but improved in the summer.

The private sector business total factor of productivity and productivity growth also declined during the COVID-19 crisis as firms had to spend time dealing with the pandemic. Bloom, Bunn, Mizen, Smietanka, and Thwaites (2020) analyzed the impact of COVID-19 on firm productivity in the UK. They estimated COVID-19 reduction in the total factor of productivity (TFP) in the private sector by up to 5% in 2020:Q4, falling back to a 1% reduction in the medium term. Firms' large reduction in "within-firm" productivity is led by measures to contain the crisis, which increase intermediate costs. The negative "within-firm" effect was partially offset by a positive "between-firm" effect as low-productivity sectors, and the least productive firms among them, were disproportionally affected by the crisis and consequently made a smaller contribution to the economy. In the longer run, productivity growth was reduced by diminished R&D expenditures and diverted senior management time spent on dealing with the pandemic.

On the bright side, one paper finds that the negative effects of the pandemic on firms are mitigated by corporate culture. Li, Liu, Mai, and Zhang (2021) fit a topic model to 40,927 COVID-19-related paragraphs in 3581 earnings calls over the period January to April 2020 and obtain firm-level measures of exposure and response related to COVID-19 for 2894 US firms. They showed that despite the large negative impact of COVID-19 on their operations, firms with a strong corporate culture outperform their peers without a strong culture. Moreover, these firms were more likely to support their community, embrace digital transformation, and develop new products than their peers. Thus, corporate culture may be regarded as an intangible asset designed to meet unexpected contingencies.

Another paper found that the presence of small banks may also be a key mitigant for firm's operations during the pandemic. Levine, Lin, and Xie (2020) used high-frequency, US county-level data on employment, small business revenue, and COVID-19 cases, and documented that employment, especially the employment of low-income workers, and the revenues of small firms fell by less in response to local COVID-19 cases in counties with a larger proportion of small banks. Their evidence suggests that small banks provide countercyclical funding to small firms following an adverse shock, with positive repercussions on employment.

8.2 Effects of COVID-19 crisis on firm stockholders and other stakeholders

Studies also report declines in public firms' stock returns. Wheelock (2020) discussed that the 2020 recession began with sharp declines in equity prices that rivaled or exceeded the initial declines of the Great Depression. Ding, Levine, Lin, and Xie (2021) evaluated the connection between corporate characteristics and the reaction of stock returns to COVID-19 cases using data on over 6700 firms across 61 economies. The pandemic-induced drop in stock returns was less severe among firms with stronger pre-2020 finances (more cash and undrawn credit, less total and short-term debt, and larger profits), less exposure to COVID-19 through global supply chains and customer locations, more CSR activities, and less entrenched executives. Furthermore, the stock returns of firms controlled by families (especially through direct holdings and with nonfamily managers), large corporations, and governments performed better, and those with greater ownership by hedge funds and other asset management companies performed worse. Stock markets positively price small amounts of managerial ownership but negatively price high levels of managerial ownership during the pandemic. Fahlenbrach, Rageth, and Stulz (2021) find that firms with high financial flexibility within an industry withstood better the

COVID-19 shock and experienced a smaller stock price drop that was 26%, or 9.7 percentage points, lower than those with low financial flexibility. This differential return persisted as stock prices rebounded. Moreover, firms more exposed to the COVID-19 shock also benefited more from having higher cash holdings. Ozik, Sadka, and Shen (2021) used the staggered implementation of stay-at-home advisory across the US states and investigate the impact of retail investors on stock liquidity during the pandemic lockdown in spring of 2020. They found that retail trading exhibited a sharp increase, especially among stocks with high COVID-19-related media coverage. Retail trading attenuated the rise in illiquidity by roughly 40%, but less so for high-media-attention stocks.

Gompers, Gornall, Kaplan, and Strebulaev (2020) surveyed over 1000 institutional and corporate venture capitalists (VCs) on how the COVID-19 pandemic affected their decisions and investments. Although individual funds and portfolio companies were dramatically impacted, VCs expected aggregate returns to be largely unchanged because winners offset losers. This suggests the primary impact of COVID-19 was an increase in volatility and uncertainty. Consistent with that, VCs report initially delaying investment due to a difficulty evaluating deals and an expectation that the future financings will offer investors more downside protections. They found only moderate evidence of disruption to VC capital flows, with investments expected to be down less than one-fifth, and only one-sixth of VCs reporting any pressure from limited partners to conserve capital. Despite the historical importance of in-person meetings, VCs do not report difficulty finding quality entrepreneurs. They also found little change in how VC allocated their time in the pandemic compared to before the pandemic.

8.3 Effects of COVID-19 crisis on other nonfinancial firm outcomes

As regards risk and financial needs for nonfinancial firms, the start of the crisis was characterized by extreme precaution, heightened aggregate firm risk, and a massive drawdown of existing bank credit lines by firms, dubbed "dash for cash" (e.g., Acharya and Steffen, 2020; Chodorow-Reich, Darmouni, Luck, and Plosser, 2020; Greenwald, Krainer, and Paul, 2020; Li, Strahan, and Zhang, 2020; Acharya, Engle, and Steffen, 2021). This effect was concentrated in large firms, but banks were able to accommodate this increase in demand for liquidity likely due to solid precrisis capitalization and liquidity levels. In the second phase after adoption of stabilization measures, only the highest rated firms switched to capital markets to raise cash, while lowest quality BB-rated firms behaved more similar to noninvestment grade firms, the observed corporate behavior revealing the significant impact of credit risk on corporate cash holdings (Acharya and Steffen, 2020).

The banks responded swiftly to the crisis with reduced credit supply to large firms generally, particularly those most affected by the drawdowns (e.g., Greenwald, Krainer, and Paul, 2020; Acharya, Engle, and Steffen, 2021; Kapan and Minoiu, 2021). Moreover, Berger, Bouwman, Norden, Roman, Udell, and Wang (2022) used Y-14Q supervisory loan-level data and investigated how large relationship business borrowers fared relative to others in loan contract terms (spread, maturity, collateral) during times of need. They found worse terms (dark-side dominance) for most relationship borrowers early in the crisis, which is reversed by better treatment during recovery. The channel behind dark-side effects is banks imposing costs on less-bank-dependent relationship borrowers to protect the value of long-term relationships with more-bank-dependent relationship borrowers. The financial situation of small businesses during the COVID-19 crisis is more complicated. Li and Strahan (2021) and Amiram and Rabetti (2020) found that small existing/relationship borrowers are more likely to receive

PPP loans, the approvals are faster, the loan amounts received are larger than those for nonrelationship borrowers. Using matched bank-firm data from the supervisory dataset Y-14Q, Chodorow-Reich, Darmouni, Luck, and Plosser (2020) found that small businesses that receive PPP loans reduce their non-PPP borrowings in 2020:Q2 dramatically.

Cejnek, Randl, and Zechner (2021) studied how dividends behave in extreme states of the world under the COVID-19 crisis. They found that, contrary to the folklore that near-future dividends are smoother than earnings or share prices, the opposite is true in disaster states. They showed that the proportion of index values attributable to the first 5 years of dividends dropped substantially in the first quarter of 2020 and that this drop has not been reversed by the end of the year. In the cross section, this breakdown of dividend smoothing due to COVID-19 was less severe for firms with higher operating cash flows and more positively skewed stock returns and more pronounced for those with higher leverage and in financial markets. Heavy dividend cutters also experienced a substantial increase in exposure to systematic risk. Results suggest that firms do not appear to fulfill their role as liquidity intermediaries for their shareholders in precisely those states, in which predictable cash payments would be valued most highly. This is consistent with the apparent puzzle that near-maturity dividend futures have provided investors with "anomalously" high returns in the past years. In light of the recent COVID-19 disaster, these risk premia are consistent with compensation for negative skewness and exposure to disaster risk. The findings imply that policy setters who consider banning dividends in a crisis should take into account the potential effect this is likely to have on firms' future cost of capital.

References

Acharya, V. V., Engle III, R. F., and Steffen, S. (2021). *Why did bank stocks crash during COVID-19?* National Bureau of Economic Research Working Paper No. w28559.

Acharya, V. V., and Steffen, S. (2020). The risk of being a fallen angel and the corporate dash for cash in the midst of COVID. *Review of Corporate Finance Studies*, 9(3), 430–471. Available at: https://academic.oup.com/rcfs/article-abstract/9/3/430/5879284.

Amiram, D., and Rabetti, D. (2020). *The relevance of relationship lending in times of crisis.* https://doi.org/10.2139/ssrn.3701587. Available at: SSRN 3701587.

Bartlett, R. P., III, and Morse, A. (2020). *Small business survival capabilities and policy effectiveness: Evidence from Oakland. vol. w27629.* National Bureau of Economic Research.

Berger, A. N., Bouwman, C. H., Norden, L., Roman, R. A., Udell, G. F., and Wang, T. (2022). *Is a friend in need a friend indeed? How relationship borrowers fare during the COVID-19 crisis. How relationship borrowers fare during the COVID-19 crisis.* Kelley School of Business Research Paper.

Bloom, N., Bunn, P., Mizen, P., Smietanka, P., and Thwaites, G. (2020). *The impact of COVID-19 on productivity (no. w28233).* National Bureau of Economic Research.

Bloom, N., Fletcher, R. S., and Yeh, E. (2021). *The impact of COVID-19 on US firms (no. w28314).* National Bureau of Economic Research.

Brinca, P., Duarte, J. B., and Faria-e-Castro, M. (2020). Is the COVID-19 pandemic a supply or a demand shock? *Economic Synopsis*, (31). https://doi.org/10.20955/es.2020.31. Available at: SSRN 3612307.

Cejnek, G., Randl, O., and Zechner, J. (2021). The COVID-19 pandemic and corporate dividend policy. *Journal of Financial and Quantitative Analysis*, 56(7), 2389–2410. https://doi.org/10.1017/S0022109021000533.

Chodorow-Reich, G., Darmouni, O., Luck, S., and Plosser, M. C. (2020). Bank liquidity provision across the firm size distribution (no. w27945). *Journal of Financial Economics.* https://doi.org/10.3386/w27945.

Ding, W., Levine, R., Lin, C., and Xie, W. (2021). Corporate immunity to the COVID-19 pandemic. *Journal of Financial Economics.*

Fahlenbrach, R., Rageth, K., and Stulz, R. M. (2021). How valuable is financial flexibility when revenue stops? Evidence from the COVID-19 crisis. *The Review of Financial Studies, 34*(11), 5474–5521.

Fairlie, R. (2020). The impact of COVID-19 on small business owners: Evidence from the first three months after widespread social-distancing restrictions. *Journal of Economics and Management Strategy, 29*(4), 727–740.

Fairlie, R. W., and Fossen, F. M. (2021). *Sales losses in the first quarter of the COVID-19 pandemic: Evidence from California administrative data (no. w28414).* National Bureau of Economic Research.

Gascon, C. S., and Hass, J. (2020). The impact of COVID-19 on the residential real estate market. *The Regional Economist, 28*(4).

Gompers, P., Gornall, W., Kaplan, S. N., and Strebulaev, I. A. (2020). *Venture capitalists and COVID-19 (no. w27824).* National Bureau of Economic Research.

Gourinchas, P. O., Kalemli-Özcan, S., Penciakova, V., and Sander, N. (2020). *COVID-19 and SME failures (no. w27877).* National Bureau of Economic Research.

Greenwald, D. L., Krainer, J., and Paul, P. (2020). *The credit line channel.* Working Paper Federal Reserve Bank of San Francisco.

Kapan, T., and Minoiu, C. (2021). *Liquidity insurance vs. credit provision: Evidence from the COVID-19 crisis.* Credit Provision. Available at: SSRN 3773328.

Kim, O. S., Parker, J. A., and Schoar, A. (2020). *Revenue collapses and the consumption of small business owners in the early stages of the COVID-19 pandemic (no. w28151).* National Bureau of Economic Research.

Levine, R., Lin, C., and Xie, W. (2020). *Local financial structure and economic resilience.* Available at: SSRN 3755560.

Li, L., and Strahan, P. E. (2021). Who supplies PPP loans (and does it matter)? Banks, relationships, and the COVID crisis. *Journal of Financial and Quantitative Analysis, 56*(7), 2411–2438.

Li, L., Strahan, P. E., and Zhang, S. (2020). Banks as lenders of first resort: Evidence from the COVID-19 crisis. *Review of Corporate Finance Studies, 9*(3), 472–500.

Li, K., Liu, X., Mai, F., and Zhang, T. (2021). The role of corporate culture in bad times: Evidence from the COVID-19 pandemic. *Journal of Financial and Quantitative Analysis.*

Ozik, G., Sadka, R., and Shen, S. (2021). Flattening the illiquidity curve: Retail trading during the COVID-19 lockdown. *Journal of Financial and Quantitative Analysis, 56*(7), 2356–2388.

Wang, J., Yang, J., Iverson, B. C., and Kluender, R. (2020). *Bankruptcy and the COVID-19 crisis.* Available at: SSRN 3690398.

Wheelock, D. C. (2020). *Comparing the COVID-19 recession with the great depression.* Available at: SSRN 3745250.

Chapter 9

Empirical evidence on the effects of the COVID-19 crisis on banks

Abstract

In this chapter, we review the evidence from research and data around the world on the effects of the COVID-19 crisis on banks, including their lending and relationships, profitability, and risk. The crisis severely threatened the banking sector around the world at the beginning of the crisis, primarily due to the expectation of credit losses and other earning problems. However, these problems did not significantly materialize in many cases. Some evidence suggests that banks were able to overcome some of the difficulties and engage in intertemporal and cross-sectional smoothing behavior to soften the blows of the COVID-19 crisis on their most vulnerable relationship customers.

Keywords: COVID-19, Banking sector, Bank lending, Banking relationships, Bank profitability, Bank risk

We review in this chapter research and data from around the world on the effects of the COVID-19 crisis on banks, broadly inclusive of commercial banks and other financial intermediaries that provide banking services. We cover their lending and relationships, profitability, and risk. The crisis severely threatened the banking sector at the beginning of the crisis, primarily due to the expectation of losses, but many of these losses did not significantly materialize, helping the banks to early recoveries. As discussed in Chapter 1, banks in some cases provided valuable credit when the crisis imposed capital, liquidity, and interest rate challenges on them and made it difficult to evaluate their borrowers. Research discussed in this chapter suggests that in some cases, banks were able to overcome these challenges and help their relationship borrowers with credit to survive the crisis.

9.1 Effects of the COVID-19 crisis on lending and relationships

We start by discussing evidence on bank lending covering many countries as well as individual-level country evidence. The overall main result is that the COVID-19 crisis, for the most part, significantly decreased bank lending, particularly during the peak period of the pandemic, but there are some

The Economic and Financial Impacts of the COVID-19 Crisis Around the World
https://doi.org/10.1016/B978-0-443-19162-6.00012-8
Copyright © 2024 Elsevier Inc. All rights reserved.

mitigating factors. An important one is relationship lending, which helped address increased information asymmetry problems for some liquidity-constrained borrowers during the crisis.

The early phase (first few weeks) of the pandemic saw extreme precaution and heightened aggregate risk, which was accompanied by a massive drawdown of existing bank credit lines by large businesses, dubbed "*dash for cash*," but large banks were able to accommodate the increase in liquidity demand, independent of their precrisis deposit or capital positions (e.g., Acharya and Steffen, 2020; Li, Strahan, and Zhang, 2020). Acharya and Steffen (2020) document that firms in all risk categories drew down their credit lines and raised their cash holdings, but BBB-rated and noninvestment-grade firms had the largest credit line drawdowns from banks and term loan issuances as a result of their limited access to public debt. Li, Strahan, and Zhang (2020) noted that it is the coincident inflows of funds to banks from both the Federal Reserve's liquidity injection programs and from depositors, along with strong preshock bank capital that enabled banks to accommodate these liquidity demands from the corporate sector.

Later in the crisis, banks responded swiftly with reduced credit supply and tighter credit terms for conventional credit to businesses (e.g., the Senior Loan Officer Opinion Survey (SLOOS); Li, Strahan, and Zhang, 2020; Acharya, Engle III, and Steffen, 2021; Greenwald, Krainer, and Paul, 2021; Kapan and Minoiu, 2021; Chodorow-Reich, Darmouni, Luck, and Plosser, 2022). The inferences from the extant studies largely depended on the type of bank credit and borrower heterogeneity. For example, Li, Strahan, and Zhang (2020), Greenwald, Krainer, and Paul (2021), and Chodorow-Reich, Darmouni, Luck, and Plosser (2022) used the Federal Reserve Y-14Q supervisory data for the US commercial and industrial loans to document important heterogeneities across loan types and corporate borrowers during the first two quarters of the pandemic in the US, with differences becoming stronger over time. Acharya and Steffen (2020) and Li, Strahan, and Zhang (2020) reported a decrease in total bank lending during the first quarter of the crisis in 2020, but their reported effects are relatively small.

Using matched bank-firm data from Y-14Q, Chodorow-Reich, Darmouni, Luck, and Plosser (2022) found that small firms (SMEs) obtain shorter maturity credit lines than large firms; have less active maturity management; post more collateral; have higher utilization rates; and pay higher spreads. They rationalized these facts as the equilibrium outcome of a trade-off between lender commitment and discretion. Using the COVID-19 recession, they tested the prediction that SMEs are subjected to greater lender discretion by examining credit line utilization. They found that SMEs do not draw down in contrast to large firms despite SME demand and SMEs that receive PPP loans reduce their non-PPP borrowings in 2020:Q2 dramatically, suggesting that government-sponsored liquidity can overcome private credit constraints.

Kapan and Minoiu (2021) used syndicated loan-level data from LPS Dealscan, confidential data from the Senior Loan Officer Opinion Survey on Bank Lending Practices (SLOOS), and loan-level data on small business lending (for loans smaller than $150,000) extended through the Payroll Protection Program (PPP) during April-June 2020. For identification, they used the unexpected credit line drawdowns as a shock that created unprecedented pressure for banks. They investigated how banks that were more affected by these shocks changed their credit supply during the COVID-19 crisis. They showed that banks with larger ex ante exposure to draw down risk due to credit lines tightened lending standards on new C&I loans and limited the supply of large syndicated loans since March 2020. They also showed that this loan supply reduction was more pronounced for smaller borrowers, which tend to be more opaque and more dependent on bank credit. Finally, borrower heterogeneity was an important determinant of banks' response to the credit line drawdown shock. In particular, banks with greater exposures to firms in sectors more affected by the COVID-19 outbreak (such as airlines, hotels, and oil and gas) and with higher ex ante cash buffers reduced the provision of new loans more than other banks.

Greenwald, Krainer, and Paul (2021), used Y-14Q supervisory data on C&I loans, and similarly showed that banks that experience larger drawdowns (from large firms) restricted term lending more—which is interpreted as a negative externality onto smaller firms. Using a structural model, they showed that credit lines are necessary to reproduce the flow of credit toward less constrained firms after adverse shocks. While credit lines increase total credit growth, their redistributive effects exacerbate the fall in investment.

There is also evidence of a generally reduced supply of credit and tighter lending standards to consumers (Consumer Financial Protection Bureau, 2020; Canals-Cerdá and Lee, 2021; Horvath, Kay, and Wix, 2021), but exceptions exist, and demand factors also played big roles in this crisis. Horvath, Kay, and Wix (2021) used credit card data from the Federal Reserve's Y-14M reports to study the impact of the COVID-19 shock on the use and availability of consumer credit across borrower types from March through August 2020. They reported, among other effects, also a large reduction in credit card originations and an increase in interest rates, especially for risky borrowers. This is consistent with a tightening of credit supply and a flight-to-safety response of banks during the COVID-19 crisis.

Çolak and Öztekin (2021) used quarterly bank balance sheet data from Orbis Bank Focus for 125 different countries from 2017:Q3 to 2020:Q3 to evaluate the influence of the pandemic on global bank lending (intensity of the bank credit activities from the rate of change in loans). They used a sample of banks from 125 different countries and applied a difference-in-difference methodology and controlled for various bank and country attributes as well as time-invariant, unobservable characteristics that can shape banks' lending behavior. To improve the identification, they also used the entropy-balanced matching technique of Hainmueller (2012). This method applies a reweighing scheme such that the distributional properties of the control variables for the treatment and control observations are similar, which eradicates biases due to observable control variables or other latent variables which can distort the distributions of control variables across samples. In other words, entropy-balanced matching can reduce endogeneity bias caused by simultaneity or latent variable problems. They documented that bank loan growth declined globally in response to the pandemic shock. This effect is economically significant: the post-COVID era is associated with 1.04%, 0.69%, and 5.50% lower quarterly loan growth in the overall, US, and non-US samples, respectively. The decline in bank credit growth largely depends on the country's pandemic intensity. A one-standard deviation increase in disease results in a 0.20% decline in quarterly bank loan growth in all countries, 0.21% in the US and 0.87% in the rest of the world. Compared to the corresponding sample averages, these percentages represent declines of 16%, 15%, and 90%, respectively. Qualitatively similar results are obtained using monthly frequency loan growth data, manually collected by authors for a subset of countries. The authors also found that effects apply to both consumer and corporate loans.

They also investigated the heterogeneous effects based on borrower and lender characteristics: bank financial conditions, market structure, regulatory and institutional environment, financial market development, ease of access of corporate firms to debt capital, and the response of the public health sector to the crisis. They found that lending is most adversely affected among small, foreign, and government-backed banks, and banks with lower returns on assets. Stronger negative effects on bank lending are seen present in countries with less developed financial intermediaries, credit markets, and bond markets, which impose more constraints on the supply of credit. In contrast, strong institutions alleviate the adverse effects of the pandemic on bank loan supply as measured by sufficient hospital capacity, contact tracing, and containment measures. Borrower heterogeneity also matters. In affected countries, where fewer firms have constraints on the supply of debt capital (especially bank capital) and where firms can exploit a variety of debt sources to raise capital, the deterioration in bank loan supply is less severe. Importantly, they found no evidence that regulatory restrictions (e.g., high capital requirements) hamper credit availability by lenders. Rather, the adverse impact of the shock on bank loan supply is alleviated by strict regulation and supervision. These results call for greater policy emphasis on appropriate bank monitoring in countries that are susceptible to macroeconomic and financial risks during periods of high uncertainty. Finally, they also found that the contraction in bank loan growth is less pronounced in countries that are better prepared to handle a sudden health crisis.

Hasan, Politsidis, and Sharma (2021) used LPS DealScan data to investigate the impact of the COVID-19 crisis on the pricing of more than 4000 global syndicated loans granted from 77 lead bank lenders in 11 countries to 820 borrowers in 28 countries. They provided evidence of a significant rise in the cost of global syndicated loans following an increase in the lending banks' and borrowing firms' exposure to COVID-19. They maintained that this increase is of a supply-side (primarily) and demand-side (secondarily) nature as loan spreads respond to both bank- and firm-level exposure. To detail, the authors constructed measures of the lenders' and borrowers' exposure to COVID-19 and quantified their effect on all-in spread drawn (AISD), the primary price measure in the syndicated loan market. Their sample is over the 2019–20 period, effectively contrasting the year of the pandemic with the year before. Each loan counterparty's exposure to COVID-19 is based on a text-based measurement from Hassan, Hollander, Van Lent, Schwedeler, and Tahoun (2020), reflecting the risks to each company associated with the spread of the COVID-19 based on the word combinations referring to COVID-19 in the transcripts of the quarterly conference calls held by the company. They used regressions with strong fixed effects and controls that account for borrower, lender, and country characteristics. The identification is later strengthened using a seemingly unrelated regression to account for the simultaneous setting of the price and nonprice loan terms at loan origination and a Heckman-type model to account for selection issues. Their main finding is that loan spreads rise by over 11 basis points in response to a one-standard deviation increase in the lender's exposure to COVID-19 and over 5 basis points for an equivalent increase in the borrower's exposure. This implies excess interest of about $5.16 million and $2.37 million, respectively, for a loan of average size and duration.

The aggravating effect of the pandemic is exacerbated by the level of government restrictions to tackle the COVID-19 disease spread, with firms' financial constraints and reliance on debt financing. Also, the increase in the cost of credit is larger when loans are granted by larger, better capitalized but less-profitable banks. But the increase in price is attenuated for borrowers that have had a prior relationship with their lender. This is important as prior bank-firm relationships can help minimize uncertainty regarding the firm's ability to repay the loan and convey information to banks that firms cannot credibly communicate to the capital markets (e.g., Kang and Stulz, 2000; Bharath, Dahiya, Saunders, and Srinivasan, 2011). This suggests that firms can capitalize on such relationships in bad times (Bolton, Freixas, Gambacorta, and Mistrulli, 2016). Other shielding effects from the COVID-19 crisis are for borrowers listed in multiple exchanges, and those headquartered in countries that can attract institutional investors, which may provide positive signals about the borrower quality.

Beck and Keil (2022) exploited geographic variation in the exposure of the US banks to COVID-19 and lockdown policies and documented an increase in corporate, especially small business, lending growth from government-guaranteed loans. They also found a reduction in the number and the average amount of syndicated loans for banks more affected by the pandemic as well as an increase in interest spreads and a decrease in maturities. These findings point to an overall negative impact of the pandemic and swift reactions by banks.

Temesvary and Wei (2021) investigated how the US banks' exposure to the economic fallout due to governments' response to COVID-19 in many foreign countries has affected their credit provision to borrowers in the US. For identification, they employed a rarely accessed dataset on the US banks' cross-border exposure to borrowers in foreign countries with the most detailed regulatory (credit registry) data that is available on their US-based lending and used the banks' exposure to COVID-19-related restrictions abroad—a balance sheet "shock" that affects only banks' credit supply, but not their US borrowers' demand for loans. They compared the change in the US lending of banks that are more vs less exposed to the pandemic abroad, during and after the onset of COVID-19 in 2020. They documented that the US banks with higher foreign COVID-19 exposure cut their lending to US firms, and tightened terms on such loans, significantly more. Effects are particularly strong for longer-maturity loans and term loans and are robust to controlling for firms' pandemic exposure. Banks became less risk tolerant, and foreign borrowers defaulting and drawing down on their cross-border credit lines were potent mechanisms through which foreign COVID-19 crisis exposure reduced banks' domestic lending. Their results suggest that global shocks have substantial consequences for domestic credit conditions, so regulators may consider accounting also for risks relevant to the bank's global operations.

Dursun-de Neef and Schandlbauer (2021) examined how European banks adjusted lending at the onset of the pandemic depending on their local exposure to the COVID-19 outbreak and capitalization and documented heterogeneous lending effects based on banks' capitalization level. Using European banks' COVID-19 exposure measure, they showed that higher exposure to COVID-19 led to worse-capitalized banks lending more whereas their better-capitalized peers lent less. Findings are in line with the zombie lending literature that banks with low capital have the incentive to issue more loans during contraction times to help their weaker borrowers to avoid loan loss recognition and write-offs on their capital.

Kara, Nanteza, Ozkan, and Yildiz (2022) investigated the role of board gender diversity and whether it matters for banks' initial responses to the COVID-19 pandemic to support their customers and communities. They constructed a unique and comprehensive COVID-19 Bank Response Measure (C19BRM) by compiling a novel hand-collected dataset on supportive measures announced by the US and European banks during the first wave of the pandemic. They found that banks with higher board representation of women directors supported their customers and communities much more via increased lending. Additionally, banks with more women on the boards increased their charity and donations. Results are robust to the potential self-selection bias of women choosing to join boards of more responsible banks, the omitted variables bias, and alternative measures of gender diversity.

In Chapter 1, we deferred reporting specific research literature details and references, promising to eventually provide theoretical and empirical evidence on how banks were able to overcome COVID-19 obstacles to assist their bank-dependent relationship borrowers during COVID-19. We now arrive at that point.

Relationship lending is an important lending technology primarily focused on private information produced over the course of a relationship with the borrower from the provision of past loans, deposits, and/or other services, and may include soft, qualitative information, such as the moral character of the borrower, the judgment of the loan officer, as well as hard information such as cash flows from deposit accounts (e.g., Boot and Thakor, 1994). Soft information may be at its most valuable relative to hard information underlying other lending technologies during crises when markets are less functional and prices are less informative (Liberti and Petersen, 2019). The theory also suggests that benefits for relationship borrowers may be the greatest during crises, as banks may engage in intertemporal smoothing—better treatment during crises compensated for by harsher treatment during other times (Bolton, Freixas, Gambacorta, and Mistrulli, 2016). Empirical research on the GFC and other crises supports this, but our empirical focus here is directed at COVID-19 results.

Berger, Bouwman, Norden, Roman, Udell, and Wang (2022) investigated bank lending to business relationship borrowers and whether these borrowers fared better or worse than others in their loan contract terms (spread, maturity, collateral) during times of need in the COVID-19 crisis over 2019–2021: Q1, i.e., test whether banks smooth intertemporally between normal times and the COVID-19 crisis. In other words, they explore whether banks are "friends indeed" to their relationship borrower "friends in need." Alternatively, banks may effectively "pull the umbrella away" from their relationship customers "the minute it starts to rain." They use COVID-19 as a quasi-natural experiment employing public health and borrower industry shocks that occurred during the crisis. They combine these with the Federal Reserve's Y-14Q supervisory dataset for C&I loans, covering large BHCs with significant US operations and covering over 60% of the C&I market. The Y-14Q dataset represents well both syndicated and nonsyndicated loans and both small and large firms, unlike other loan datasets. Their sample has over 80,000 loans issued from April 2018 to March 2021, covering the precrisis as well as both the COVID-19 shock and recovery periods.

The authors introduced a novel shock-and-recovery econometric approach that includes both the COVID-19 shock phase (initial part of the crisis) and the recovery (later part of the crisis), helping to identify the COVID-19 effects on relationship borrowers. If the COVID-19 shock drives the difference between those firms with a relationship vs those without, they should observe a reversal of the effects during the recovery. Indeed, the rapid and severe COVID-19 downturn in the US was brief by historical standards and was quickly followed by an economic recovery. This allowed them to study whether the effects of the COVID-19 shocks continued or were reversed during this recovery. They actuated their methodology employing a difference-in-difference (DID) framework, regressing loan contract terms on bank-borrower relationships; a COVID-19 public health or industry employment shock; and their double and triple interactions (the DID terms). They included interactions with a recovery dummy for the period starting in June 2020 to test whether COVID-19 effects on relationship borrowers persist or change after the economy turned around. They control for a rich menu of controls for the loan, borrower, and bank, including bank private credit ratings on the loans, stringent fixed effects of bank × time, state × time, and industry, and two-way clustering of standard errors to aid in identification.

Authors documented worse terms (dark-side dominance) for most relationship borrowers early in the COVID-19 crisis, however, the dark side of relationship lending that they observed during the COVID-19 shock period is reversed by better treatment and a bright side during the recovery period. The authors also investigated channels that might explain why banks temporarily penalize some relationship borrowers and benefit others during COVID-19. Their evidence supports a *protecting the value of long-term relationships to banks* channel. This poses that relationship lending creates value as the information gathered can be redeployed for future loans and/or services. Realization of this value requires that both borrowers and banks remain viable in the long term, and this viability may be uncertain during the first months of the COVID-19 crisis. Banks increase the likelihood of long-term viability of some customers and themselves through redistribution, easing terms for one set of borrowers while imposing harsher loan terms on others. Since they cannot impose harsher terms on nonrelationship borrowers, as they may have the lowest switching costs, they impose harsher terms on a subset of relationship borrowers. Specifically, under this channel, less-bank-dependent relationship borrowers bear the brunt of the harsh treatment in return for future benefits when normal conditions return, while more-bank-dependent relationship borrowers receive the subsidies that are needed for their long-term financial viability.

Other studies suggest that the Paycheck Protection Program (PPP) was effective in banks providing credit to business relationship borrowers during the COVID-19 crisis or that certain relationship borrowers, particularly larger ones, received priority access to funds (e.g., Amiram and Rabetti, 2020; Balyuk, Prabhala, and Puri, 2021; Li and Strahan, 2021; Glancy, 2023). For example, Glancy (2023) found that half of banks' PPP loans went to borrowers within 2 miles of a branch, mostly driven by relationship-oriented banks. Borrowers near more active PPP lenders received credit earlier, indicating a benefit to such relationships. His estimates imply that relationship borrowers receive credit 5–9 days before nonrelationship borrowers. This is valuable evidence that at least in the context of the PPP program, relationship lending worked and benefited business borrowers. However, the PPP findings for relationship borrowers may not be directly comparable to conventional bank lending decisions. This is because banks participating in PPP loans were distribution agents for government loans that were not intended to be repaid and posed zero risk to the banks, different from the conventional financial intermediation with risk management studied by Berger, Bouwman, Norden, Roman, Udell, and Wang (2022).

A second study on conventional financial intermediation and relationship lending is by Berger, Bouwman, Norden, Roman, Udell, and Wang (2024). The authors applied bank relationship lending (an extensive topic in conventional commercial lending) to a unique context, credit card lending, which is typically considered a transactions lending technology. They are the first to investigate the effects of relationships on credit card terms for customers as well as differential effects during normal times vs the COVID-19 crisis. The authors used monthly individual loan-level data from the Federal Reserve's supervisory Y-14M dataset (and other sources) from June 2013 through June 2020 to examine the effects of relationships on key credit card terms (APR spreads and credit limits). The Y-14M data contains detailed information on credit terms for consumer and business credit cards extended by large banking organizations with significant US credit card portfolios and includes relationship information as well as a rich set of customer and loan characteristics that they use as controls. To assess changes during the COVID-19 crisis, they employ a difference-in-difference (DID) regression model using an interaction term between the relationship and alternative COVID-19 proxies. Using over 1 million accounts, they found that during normal times, consumer relationship customers enjoy relatively favorable credit terms, consistent with the bright side of relationships, while the dark side dominates for small businesses. During the COVID-19 crisis, however, both groups benefit, reflecting intertemporal smoothing, with more benefits flowing to safer relationship customers. When splitting results among several different types of bank relationships, authors found that conventional banking relationships (deposit relationships in particular) benefit consumers more than credit card relationships, with mixed findings for small businesses.

Other research with supporting findings includes Berger, Feldman, Langford, and Roman (2022), who found that the shared identity mechanism—through which lenders may more efficiently collect and process information for borrowers with racial or ethnic similarities, may have augmented relationship lending during the COVID-19 crisis as well as the GFC.

Finally, Ben-David, Johnson, and Stulz (2021) find severe constraints and sharp decline in credit supply also from FinTech lenders (banks' direct competitors) to small businesses. Because FinTech lenders fund loans mostly through credit facilities and securitizations and may not be able to use relationship lending, their business model made them more financially fragile relative to banks during the COVID-19 shock which reduced the value of existing loans. Using detailed data from a platform that intermediates loans between dozens of FinTech lenders and small businesses, they show that during March 2020, the transacted loan volume of small business FinTech declined sharply from its precrisis levels. Specifically, the number of funded loans and the total amount funded declined by 80.3% and 81.0%, respectively, from February 2020 to the last week of March 2020. Authors show that the volume of FinTech loans to small businesses dropped precisely because of a decrease in the supply of loans.

9.2   Effects of the COVID-19 crisis on bank profitability

We next evaluate the evidence of how banks fared in terms of profitability during the COVID-19 crisis, considering both market as well as accounting performance. Acharya, Engle III, and Steffen (2021) used data from all publicly listed bank holding companies in the US and studied the crash of bank stock prices during the COVID-19 pandemic. They found evidence consistent with a "credit line drawdown channel." That is, stock prices of banks with large ex ante exposures to undrawn credit lines as well as large ex post gross drawdowns declined more. They found that this effect was attenuated for banks with higher capital buffers. These banks reduced term loan lending, even after policy measures were implemented. They demonstrated that the balance-sheet liquidity risk of banks helps understand the significant and persistent underperformance of bank stocks relative to other financial and nonfinancial firms during the COVID-19 pandemic, explaining both the cross section and the time-series of bank returns during the pandemic, and even after controlling for banks' on-balance-sheet portfolio exposure to the pandemic. They concluded that bank provision of credit lines appears akin to writing deep out-of-the-money put options on aggregate risk. In addition, they showed how the resulting contingent leverage and stock return exposure can be incorporated tractably into future bank capital stress tests.

Demirgüç-Kunt, Pedraza, and Ruiz-Ortega (2021) analyzed bank stock prices around the world to assess the impact of the COVID-19 pandemic on the banking sector. The authors used bank data including stock prices, balance sheets, and ownership, for 53 countries covering 896 commercial banks. They documented a systematic underperformance of bank stocks at the onset of the COVID-19 crisis, between March and April 2020. More precisely, for most countries, bank stocks underperformed relative to other publicly traded companies in their home country, and relative to nonfinancial institutions. The evidence highlights the nature of the COVID-19 shock and the expectations at that time of market participants that banks would experience deeper and more protracted profit losses than other firms.

Using a global database of policy responses during the crisis, Demirguc-Kunt, Pedraza, Ruiz-Ortega (2020) also examines the role of financial sector policy announcements on the performance of bank stocks. Precisely, they studied the stock market reaction to different policy measures, by identifying financial sector initiatives by government authorities from February 2 to April 17, 2020, made publicly available by the World Bank. Their final sample contains 429 financial sector policy announcements in 44 countries (16 developed and 28 developing). The effectiveness of policy interventions was found to be mixed. Measures of liquidity support, borrower assistance, and monetary easing moderated the adverse impact of the crisis, but this was not true for all banks or in all circumstances. For example, borrower assistance and prudential measures exacerbated the stress for banks that were already undercapitalized and/or operated in countries with little fiscal space.

In terms of accounting performance, two studies measured bank performance for banks that participated in the PPP program and found somewhat contrasting effects. Researchers found that banks played an outsized role in the distribution of PPP funds to small business borrowers, so it is natural to ask whether such involvement was profitable for banks or not, given that profitability may have been bottom-line goal of the banks. First, Marsh and Sharma (2021) focused on bank-level PPP participation data from 2019:Q3 to 2020:Q3 and found that bank PPP participation boosted community banks' balance sheets by supporting asset and interest income growth. However, they also found that it lowered their profitability, at least initially, because the low yields and deferred fee collection on PPP loans reduced banks' net interest margins—a measure of net interest income expressed as a share of interest-earning assets. They showed that low loan yields led net interest margins to decline by 69 basis points at banks with high PPP exposure compared with 48 basis points at banks with low PPP exposure.

In contrast, Berger, Karakaplan, and Roman (2023) investigated the role of political connections for the PPP program using bank data from 2019:Q1 to 2020:Q4. In addition to showing that banks exercised partisan political connections, influencing PPP funding through lobbying, they also investigated whether banks profited from their PPP involvement. They analyzed bank accounting performance proxies such as ROA and ROE as well as two main channels through which the profitability may be achieved—additional lending above and beyond the PPP loans and greater competitive advantages in terms of market shares and market power relative to other banks with less involvement. In all cases, they regressed measures of performance and channels of performance on bank PPP lending intensity. They showed results for all banks, smaller banks, and larger banks, and for both OLS and instrumental variables (IV) estimations, using political connections as instruments for PPP participation. Across both the OLS and IV specifications, and for both ROA and ROE, they found that banks with more intensive PPP participation increased their profitability. Moreover, the increases in profitability were much larger for smaller banks, consistent with prior findings in the PPP literature that smaller community banks played an outsized role in the program. Thus, the profitability findings are consistent in every case with banks' motives to use their political connections to increase their PPP involvement to improve profits. Economically, they showed that a bank with average PPP involvement would have higher predicted quarterly ROA and ROE by 25% and 39%, respectively, relative to a bank that did not participate in PPP. Moreover, the authors showed that banks with more intensive PPP participation increased non-PPP commercial lending such as C&I and CRE lending as well as their market shares and market power as measured by the Lerner Index, as channels through which they improved their profitability. Overall, the authors concluded that PPP appears to have effectively bailed out banks as much as it did small businesses.

9.3 Effects of COVID-19 crisis on bank risk

Evidence on the effects of the COVID-19 crisis in general suggests a significant increase in both systemic risk and bank portfolio risk in the early stages of the crisis with some exceptions, dependent on the crisis period under study and methodology. Importantly, Duan, El Ghoul, Guedhami, Li, and Li (2021) discussed that government measures related to lockdowns, business shutdowns, and social distancing could have resulted in adverse economic effects on firms and households. Firms may have faced significant revenue drops and increases in costs, and households suffered from potential job and income losses and/or declines. If the firms and households were no longer able to repay their debt, that could have increased their default probabilities. Such effects were likely to spread to banks, resulting in lost revenue and losses and a surge in nonperforming loans, negatively affecting banks' profits, solvency, and capital.

Two studies investigated the effects of the pandemic on banks' contributions to systemic risk. Duan, El Ghoul, Guedhami, Li, and Li (2021) used 1584 listed banks from 64 countries during the COVID-19 pandemic and conducted the first broad-based international study of the effect of the pandemic on bank contribution to systemic risk over February 6-December 10, 2020. They found that the pandemic increased banks' systemic risk across countries. The effect operated through both the government policy response as well as default risk channels. Additional analysis suggests that the adverse effect on systemic stability was more pronounced for large, highly leveraged, riskier, high loan-to-asset, undercapitalized, and low-network-centrality banks. However, this effect was moderated by formal bank regulation (e.g., deposit insurance), ownership structure (e.g., foreign and government ownership), and informal institutions (e.g., culture and trust). To the extent that informal institutions are harder to control, improving the regulatory environment may help reduce the adverse effects of pandemic shocks on banks' systemic stability.

Borri and Di Giorgio (2022) evaluated the systemic risk contribution of a set of large publicly traded European banks. Over a sample covering the last 20 years and three different crises, they found that all banks in their sample significantly contributed to systemic risk. Moreover, larger banks and banks with a business model that is more exposed to trading and financial market volatility contribute more. In the shorter sample characterized by the COVID-19 shock, sovereign default risks significantly affected the systemic risk contribution of all banks. However, the ECB announcement of the Pandemic Emergency Purchasing Program restored calm in the European banking sector.

Three papers reported increases in bank loan portfolio risk in the early stages of the pandemic based on data from different countries including the US, while one study reported no performance issues for the US banks. Beck and Keil (2022) combined US bank-, bank county-, and loan-level data from several sources and used a novel bank-level gauge of exposure to pandemic and lockdown policies to provide an assessment of the effect of COVID-19 and lockdown policies on the health of the banking system, exploiting variation in pandemic outbreaks and lockdown policies across the US counties and throughout 2020 and employing a variety of regression analyses. They found that banks more exposed to pandemic and lockdown policies in 2020 showed an increase in loss provisions and nonperforming loans. The effect of lockdown policies on nonperforming loans was observed both for C&I and household loans. Findings point to a potential negative impact of the pandemic on banks in the early stages. In contrast, Berger and Demirgüç-Kunt (2021) examined means and percentiles for several key measures of bank performance during the COVID-19 crisis including charge-offs and nonperforming loans from the Call Reports data. They discussed that mean charge-offs remained low throughout the time interval and were actually lower after the COVID-19 crisis began than their local peak of 0.14% in 2019:Q4. There was a minor upward movement in nonperforming loans from 0.61% in 2019:Q4 to 0.65% in 2020:Q1, but the ratio fell from there to 0.54% in 2020:Q4. Authors similarly concluded that no performance issued were observed from simple statistics for Globally Systemically Important Banks (GSIBs).

Dursun-de Neef and Schandlbauer (2021) examined the effects of the COVID-19 crisis on European banks at the onset of the pandemic depending on their local exposure to the COVID-19 outbreak and capitalization. They showed that higher exposure to COVID-19 led to a relative increase in worse-capitalized banks' loans whereas their better-capitalized peers decreased their lending more. Importantly, only better-capitalized banks experienced a significantly larger increase in their delinquent and restructured loans. The authors' findings suggest an increase in zombie lending as banks with low capital had the incentive to issue more loans during contraction times to help their weaker borrowers so that they can avoid loan loss recognition and write-offs on their capital. Kryzanowski,

Liu, and Zhang (2022) examined the resilience of Chinese banks during the COVID-19 pandemic by investigating the effects on their nonperforming loan ratios. They found that despite the reduction in the growth rate of total bank lending, bank nonperforming loan ratios significantly increased during the COVID-19 crisis. Banks with high-quality capital were more effective in controlling their nonperforming loan ratios during the crisis. They also found that the largest five Chinese banks, the state-owned banks, and domestic banks had lower nonperforming loan ratios than their counterparts during the crisis.

Two studies advocated for precautionary capital and other similar measures in the early pandemic stages. Schularick, Steffen, and Troeger (2020) focused on 79 Eurozone banks that took part in the 2019 transparency exercise by the European Banking Authority. They estimated the capital shortfall of these banks in response to the COVID-19 crisis and proposed that banks should recapitalize precautiously to provide insurance against further economic shocks coming from the pandemic. Bitar and Tarazi (2022) discussed the implications on banks and the economy of prudential regulatory intervention to soften the treatment of nonperforming exposures and ease bank capital buffers. They applied these easing measures to a sample of GSIBs and showed that these banks can play a constructive role in sustaining economic growth during the COVID-19 pandemic. Their analysis shows that prudential regulatory responses to COVID-19 along with high regulatory capital and low nonperforming loan ratios were positively associated with economic growth. They advocate that banks should maintain high capital ratios in the medium-term horizon to absorb future losses, as the effect of COVID-19 on the economy might take time to fully materialize.

Two studies suggested reduced funding risk for banks during the COVID-19 pandemic as massive deposits flowed into the banking sector. Levine, Lin, Tai, and Xie (2021) investigated why banks experienced massive deposit inflows during the first months of the pandemic. They used weekly branch-level data on interest rates and county-level data on COVID-19 cases, and documented that interest rates at bank branches in counties with higher COVID-19 infection rates fell by more than rates at other branches—even branches of the same bank in different counties. When differentiating weeks by the degree of stock market distress and counties by the likely impact of COVID-19 cases on economic anxiety, the evidence suggests that the deposit inflows were triggered by a surge in the supply of precautionary savings. Dursun-de Neef and Schandlbauer (2022) documented that the deposit inflows into the banks during the pandemic were driven by households having accumulated savings in their deposit accounts due to a reduction in their spending, triggered by restrictions on their mobility. Thus, a significant increase in bank deposits occurred for banks located in counties with a larger reduction in spending. Banks, in turn, used these additional funds to issue more real estate loans. This implies that policies that might affect household spending can lead to changes in the volume of deposits in the banking system, which have consequences on banks' loan supply.

References

Acharya, V. V., and Steffen, S. (2020). The risk of being a fallen angel and the corporate dash for cash in the midst of COVID. *Review of Corporate Finance Studies*, 9(3), 430–471.

Acharya, V. V., Engle, R. F., III, and Steffen, S. (2021). *Why did bank stocks crash during COVID-19? (No. w28559)*. National Bureau of Economic Research.

Amiram, D., and Rabetti, D. (2020). *The relevance of relationship lending in times of crisis*. Working Study.

Balyuk, T., Prabhala, N., and Puri, M. (2021). *Small bank financing and funding hesitancy in a crisis: Evidence from the paycheck protection program*. Working Paper.

Beck, T., and Keil, J. (2022). Have banks caught corona? Effects of COVID on lending in the US. *Journal of Corporate Finance*, *72*, 102160.

Ben-David, I., Johnson, M. J., and Stulz, R. M. (2021). *Why did small business Fintech lending dry up during March 2020?* National Bureau of Economic Research Working Paper No. w29205.

Berger, A. N., and Demirgüç-Kunt, A. (2021). Banking research in the time of COVID-19. *Journal of Financial Stability*, *57*, 100939.

Berger, A. N., Bouwman, C. H. S., Norden, L., Roman, R. A., Udell, G. F., and Wang, T. (2022). *Is a friend in need a friend indeed? How relationship borrowers fare during the COVID-19 crisis*. Available at SSRN 3755243.

Berger, A. N., Bouwman, C. H. S., Norden, L., Roman, R. A., Udell, G. F., and Wang, T. (2024). Piercing through opacity: Relationships and credit card lending to consumers and small businesses during normal times and the COVID-19 crisis. *Journal of Political Economy, 132*, forthcoming.

Berger, A. N., Feldman, M. P., Langford, W. S., and Roman, R. A. (2022). *Let us put our moneys together: Minority-owned banks, local economic development, and resilience to crises*. Working Paper.

Berger, A. N., Karakaplan, M., and Roman, R. A. (2023). Whose bailout is it anyway? The roles of politics in PPP bailouts of small businesses vs. banks. *Journal of Financial Intermediation*, Forthcoming.

Bharath, S., Dahiya, S., Saunders, A., and Srinivasan, A. (2011). Lending relationships and loan contract terms. *Review of Financial Studies*, 24, 1141–1203.

Bitar, M., and Tarazi, A. (2022). A note on regulatory responses to COVID-19 pandemic: Balancing banks' solvency and contribution to recovery. *Journal of Financial Stability*, *60*, 101009.

Bolton, P., Freixas, X., Gambacorta, L., and Mistrulli, P. E. (2016). Relationship and transaction lending in a crisis. *The Review of Financial Studies*, 29(10), 2643–2676.

Boot, A. W., and Thakor, A. V. (1994). Moral hazard and secured lending in an infinitely repeated credit market game. *International Economic Review*, 899–920.

Borri, N., and Di Giorgio, G. (2022). Systemic risk and the COVID challenge in the European banking sector. *Journal of Banking & Finance*, *140*, 106073.

Canals-Cerdá, J. J., and Lee, B. J. (2021). *COVID-19 and auto loans origination trends*. Working Paper.

Chodorow-Reich, G., Darmouni, O., Luck, S., and Plosser, M. (2022). Bank liquidity provision across the firm size distribution. *Journal of Financial Economics*, *144*, 908–932.

Çolak, G., and Öztekin, Ö. (2021). The impact of COVID-19 pandemic on bank lending around the world. *Journal of Banking & Finance*, *133*, 106207.

Consumer Financial Protection Bureau. (2020). *The early effects of the COVID-19 pandemic on consumer credit*. (Special Issue Brief).

Demirgüç-Kunt, A., Pedraza, A., and Ruiz-Ortega, C. (2021). Banking sector performance during the COVID-19 crisis. *Journal of Banking & Finance*, *133*, 106305.

Duan, Y., El Ghoul, S., Guedhami, O., Li, H., and Li, X. (2021). Bank systemic risk around COVID-19: A cross-country analysis. *Journal of Banking & Finance*, *133*, 106299.

Dursun-de Neef, H.Ö., and Schandlbauer, A. (2021). COVID-19 and lending responses of European banks. *Journal of Banking & Finance*, *133*, 106236.

Dursun-de Neef, H.Ö., and Schandlbauer, A. (2022). COVID-19, bank deposits, and lending. *Journal of Empirical Finance*.

Glancy, D. (2023). *Bank relationships and the geography of PPP lending*. Available at SSRN 3839671.

Greenwald, D., Krainer, J., and Paul, P. (2021). *The credit line channel*. Federal Reserve Bank of San Francisco Working Paper 2020-26.

Hainmueller, J. (2012). Entropy balancing for causal effects: A multivariate reweighting method to produce balanced samples in observational studies. *Political Analysis*, *20*(1), 25–46.

Hasan, I., Politsidis, P. N., and Sharma, Z. (2021). Global syndicated lending during the COVID-19 pandemic. *Journal of Banking & Finance*, *133*, 106121.

Hassan, T.A., Hollander, S., Van Lent, L., Schwedeler, M., and Tahoun, A. (2020). *Firm-level exposure to epidemic diseases: Covid-19, SARS, and H1N1 (No. w26971)*. National Bureau of Economic Research.

Horvath, A., Kay, B., and Wix, C. (2021). *The COVID-19 shock and consumer credit: Evidence from credit card data.* Working Paper.

Kang, J. K., and Stulz, R. M. (2000). Do banking shocks affect borrowing firm performance? An analysis of the Japanese experience. *The Journal of Business*, 73(1), 1–23.

Kapan, T., and Minoiu, C. (2021). Liquidity insurance vs. credit provision: Evidence from the COVID-19 crisis. In *Credit provision: Evidence from the COVID-19 crisis (September 30, 2021)*.

Kara, A., Nanteza, A., Ozkan, A., and Yildiz, Y. (2022). Board gender diversity and responsible banking during the Covid-19 pandemic. *Journal of Corporate Finance*, 102213.

Kryzanowski, L., Liu, J., and Zhang, J. (2022). Effect of COVID-19 on non-performing loans in China. *Finance Research Letters*, 103372.

Levine, R., Lin, C., Tai, M., and Xie, W. (2021). How did depositors respond to COVID-19? *Review of Financial Studies*, 34(11), 5438–5473.

Li, L., and Strahan, P. E. (2021). Who supplies PPP loans (and does it matter)? Banks, relationships, and the COVID crisis. *Journal of Financial and Quantitative Analysis*, 56(7), 2411–2438.

Li, L., Strahan, P. E., and Zhang, S. (2020). Banks as lenders of first resort: Evidence from the COVID-19 crisis. *Review of Corporate Finance Studies*, 9(3), 472–500.

Liberti, J. M., and Petersen, M. A. (2019). Information: Hard and soft. *Review of Corporate Finance Studies*, 8(1), 1–41.

Marsh, W. B., and Sharma, P. (2021). *Government loan guarantees during a crisis: The effect of the PPP on bank lending and profitability.* Federal Reserve Bank of Kansas City Working Paper (21-03).

Schularick, M., Steffen, S., and Troeger, T. H. (2020). *Bank capital and the European recovery from the COVID-19 crisis.*

Temesvary, J., and Wei, A. (2021). *Domestic lending and the pandemic: How does banks' exposure to Covid-19 abroad affect their lending in the United States?.*

Chapter 10

Empirical evidence on the economic effects of the COVID-19 crisis on financial markets

Chapter outline

Abstract

This chapter covers empirical research and data on the economic effects of the COVID-19 crisis on financial markets, with specific findings for the stock market, bond market, and CDS market. Not surprisingly, financial markets of all types around the world suffered high losses at the beginning of the crisis as economic losses and the prospects of their continuation devastated the financial market prices that depend on them. Even relatively safe US corporate bond yields rose sharply relative to Treasury yields during February and March 2020, reflecting severe stress. However, many markets, including those in the US, returned to precrisis averages later in 2020. The US recovery is likely due, in large part, to the fast and large policy responses in that country.

Keywords: COVID-19, Financial markets, Stock market, Bond market, Economic policy

In this chapter, we cover empirical research and data on the economic effects of the COVID-19 crisis on financial markets, with specific findings for the stock market, bond market, and CDS market. In some cases, the findings mimic those of the banking sector described in Chapter 9. As Goldstein, Koijen, and Mueller (2021) pointed out in their *Review of Financial Studies* special issue, the effects of the COVID-19 crisis on the economic sector, the unique combination of demand and supply shocks (Baqaee and Farhi, 2020), and the associated uncertainty about the path of the pandemic led to major disruptions in the financial markets. Even the US Treasury market showed signs of stress in March 2020, while corporate bond markets, money market funds, and stock markets experienced severe stress during the early stages of the crisis. For example, the US corporate bond yields (relative to 10-year Treasury yields) rose sharply during February and March 2020. Luckily, all these markets returned to precrisis averages later in the year 2020. This quick recovery of financial markets in the US can be, at least in part, attributed to the massive and quick monetary and fiscal interventions including the CARES Act, which helped avert an even more severe financial crisis. Still, the reactions in the

The Economic and Financial Impacts of the COVID-19 Crisis Around the World
https://doi.org/10.1016/B978-0-443-19162-6.00029-3
Copyright © 2024 Elsevier Inc. All rights reserved.

financial markets during the COVID-19 crisis reflect a possible disconnect between financial markets and the real economy, and we question here the relevance of financial market indicators for the crisis recovery.

10.1 Effects of the COVID-19 crisis on the stock market

Goldstein, Koijen, and Mueller (2021) demonstrated that stock markets showed severe stress during the COVID-19 crash of February and March 2020 as reflected by the S&P 500 index which lost one-third of its value during this critical period. Similarly, Haddad, Moreira, and Muir (2021) found that stocks as represented by the S&P500 index experienced a massive decline: a cumulative return of around -35% from peak to trough, with the minimum reached in the third week of March 2020. They subsequently rebounded, but the cumulative return was still as low as about 15% in late April 2020.

Other studies discuss cross-sectional differences in stock market reactions. Ramelli and Wagner (2020) found that companies with more export or supply chain exposure to China resulted in substantially lower stock returns in the incubation and outbreak periods of January 15 and early February, respectively. Furthermore, investors penalized not only firms trading with China but also those that were internationally oriented more generally. These results identified the disruption of global trade as an early effect of COVID-19 on the real economy. Importantly, toward the end of February, while the health situation in Europe and the US began worsening, the situation in China started improving, and stocks exposed to China did relatively better in anticipation of the reopening of the Chinese economy. However, they also showed that within the same industry and controlling for standard firm characteristics, firms with little cash holdings and high leverage suffered severely in the fever period, from February 24 to March 20, 2020. Their effects are economically sizeable: a one standard deviation in cash holdings explains approximately one-sixth of the standard deviation of returns in the fever period, net of the effects of other firm characteristics and market beta, with another one-sixth explained by a one standard deviation in leverage. What is interesting is that the effects of cash and leverage were more important in those industries that suffered stronger stock price declines, that is, those harder hit by the effects of the pandemic. Moreover, leverage was generally more problematic for investors in cash-poor firms, and in value firms.

On a somewhat similar topic, Fahlenbrach, Rageth, and Stulz (2021) investigated how a firm's financial flexibility affected its stock price reaction during the COVID-19-driven stock market collapse of February and March 2020. They defined financial flexibility as the ease with which a firm can fund a cash flow shortfall and, therefore, expected firms with greater financial flexibility to be less affected by the shock. Specifically, they considered firms to be more financially flexible if they had more cash, less short-term debt, and less long-term debt at the end of 2019. They contended that firms with greater financial flexibility should have been better able to fund a revenue shortfall resulting from the COVID-19 shock and benefited less from policy responses. They have strong results suggesting that firms with high financial flexibility within an industry experienced a stock price drop that was significantly lower than those with low financial flexibility by 26%%, or 9.7 percentage points. Importantly, this performance gap continued to persist during the subsequent rebound of the stock market, suggesting that the ability to fund cash shortfalls in times of crisis may have long-lasting value implications.

Then, Bretscher, Hsu, Simasek, and Tamoni (2020) used the first reported case of COVID-19 in each US county as the event day and reported that firms headquartered in an affected county experienced, on average, a 27-bps lower return in the 10-day postevent window. This negative effect nearly doubled in proportion for firms in counties with a higher COVID-19 infection rate (−50 bps). When testing for transmission channels, authors documented that those firms belonging to labor-intensive industries and those located in counties with a large mobility decline recorded worse stock performance. Furthermore, firms sensitive to COVID-19-induced uncertainty also had more negative returns. Finally, the authors also documented that more negative stock returns were further associated with downward revisions in their earnings forecasts.

Moving to the international arena, Ding, Levine, Lin, and Xie (2021) evaluated the connection between corporate characteristics and the reaction of stock returns to COVID-19 cases using data on more than 6700 firms across 61 countries. They documented that the pandemic-induced drop in stock returns was milder among firms with stronger pre-2020 finances (more cash and undrawn credit, less total and short-term debt, and larger profits), less exposure to COVID-19 through global supply chains and customer locations, more corporate social responsibility activities, and less entrenched executives. In addition, the stock returns of firms controlled by families (especially through direct holdings and with nonfamily managers), large corporations, and governments performed better, and those with greater ownership by hedge funds and other asset management companies performed worse. They argued that stock markets positively priced small amounts of managerial ownership but negatively priced high levels of managerial ownership during the pandemic.

Focusing on Italy, Carletti, Oliviero, Pagano, Pelizzon, and Subrahmanyam (2020) analyzed stock returns for 81,000 Italian firms. Importantly, Italy is the first country in the Group of Seven (G7) to be hit hard by the crisis and to enact government lockdowns. They documented huge negative impacts on firms in Italy during the pandemic. Firms in Italy faced an aggregate annual profit decrease of €170 billion (approximately 10% of the 2018 GDP) after a 3-month lockdown and, for loss-making firms, an aggregate equity erosion of around €117 billion. The shock forced about 13,500 firms to have negative net worth, putting at risk the employment of over 800,000 workers (almost 9% of employment of the firms). The equity shortfall of these distressed firms further required an equity injection of €31 billion in that country.

Gormsen and Koijen (2020) used data from aggregate stock and dividend futures markets from the US, Japan, and European Union to quantify how investors' expectations about economic growth evolved across horizons following the outbreak of COVID-19 and subsequent policy responses related to the crisis. Authors explained that dividend futures, which are claims to dividends on the aggregate stock market in a particular year, can be used to directly compute a lower bound on growth expectations across maturities or to estimate expected growth using a forecasting model, and authors showed how the actual forecast and the bound evolved over time. They found that as of July 20, 2020 in the crisis, the forecast of annual growth in dividends showed a decline of 8% in both the US and Japan and a 14% decline in the European Union relative to January 01, 2020. The economic forecast of GDP growth similarly reported declines of 2% in the US and Japan and 3% in the European Union. The lower bound on the change in expected dividends was −17% in the US and Japan and −28% in the European Union at the 2-year horizon. However, the authors showed that positive news about the US monetary policy and the fiscal stimulus bill around March 24, 2020, boosted the stock market and long-term growth but did not improve the short-term growth expectations. They also reported that the expected dividend growth improved since April 01, 2020 in various continents of the world.

Focused on dividend policy during the COVID-19 crisis, Cejnek, Randl, and Zechner (2021) showed that, for major equity markets, the proportion of stock index values attributable to the first 5 years of dividends dropped substantially in the first quarter of 2020, and this drop did not revert course by the end of the year. However, in the cross section, the breakdown of dividend smoothing due to COVID-19 was less severe for firms with higher operating cash flows and more positively skewed stock returns. However, the dividend drops were most acute for firms with higher leverage and firms in the financial sector. Perhaps surprisingly, the firms with heavy dividend cuts also experienced a substantial increase in their exposure to systematic risk.

Baker, Bloom, Davis, Kost, Sammon, and Viratyosin (2020) compared the COVID-19 crisis with prior pandemics. They found that no previous infectious disease outbreaks, including the Spanish Flu, affected the stock market as forcefully as COVID-19 did. What is impressive is their methodology: authors used text-based methods to develop points with respect to large daily stock market moves back to 1900 and with respect to overall stock market volatility back to 1985. They showed that in the period from February 24 to March 24, 2020, there were 22 trading days and 18 market jumps, more than any other period in history with the same number of trading days. Moreover, the jump frequency during this period was over 20 times the average pace since 1900, i.e., from February 24 through the end of April 2020, there were 27 such jumps. Next-day newspaper accounts attributed 23 or 24 of them to news about COVID-19 developments and policy responses related to the pandemic. However, it is notable that large daily stock market moves during this period were in both directions. On the one hand, the S&P 500 index plunged 33% from February 21 to its trough on March 23, 2020, but rose 30% back from its bottom by the last trading day in April 2020, the end of the authors' sample period. Looking for explanations for the reactions, the evidence indicates that government restrictions on businesses and social distancing were the main reasons that the US stock market reacted so much more forcefully to COVID-19 than to any previous pandemics in 1918–1919, 1957–1958, and 1968.

10.2 Effects of the COVID-19 crisis on the bond market

Goldstein, Koijen, and Mueller (2021) argued that the corporate bond market was, to a large extent, the epicenter of the financial turmoil during the COVID-19 crisis. Several papers investigated reactions in the bond market to the COVID-19 shocks. Falato, Goldstein, and Hortaçsu (2021) used daily microdata and documented major outflows in corporate-bond funds during the COVID-19 crisis that were unprecedented relative to what was seen over the decade in corporate bond markets. Between the months of February and March 2020, the average fund experienced cumulative outflows of about 10% of net asset value, far larger than the average cumulative outflows of about 2.2% at the peak of the Taper Tantrum in June-July of 2013, which was the other most stressful episode over the last decade. The large outflows were sustained over weeks and were most severe for funds with illiquid assets, those vulnerable to fire sales, and those exposed to sectors hardly hit by the crisis. By providing a liquidity backstop for their bond holdings, the Federal Reserve bond purchase program helped to reverse some of the outflows, especially for the most fragile funds. However, the latter program had spillover effects on primary market issuance and peer funds. Their evidence suggests that a "bond-fund fragility channel" was in operation through which the Federal Reserve's liquidity backstop transmitted to the real economy via bond funds.

Haddad, Moreira, and Muir (2021) studied the bond market during the height of the COVID-19 crisis in March and April of 2020. They reported on the returns of two large corporate bond ETFs of the iShares family, Investment Grade Corporate Bond ETF (LQD) and High Yield Corporate Bond ETF (HYG), capturing the universe of investment-grade and high-yield corporate bonds, respectively. These indices exhibited a similar pattern as stocks. While their decline started almost 2 weeks after that of the stock market, the magnitude was substantial: the two indices dropped by about 20% from the peak to trough of the COVID-19 crisis in March 2020. The stress in the bond markets was represented by an increase in spreads and a decrease in liquidity. Unique about this episode is that the greatest disruptions were most salient for assets on the safer end of the spectrum: investment-grade bonds in general (corporate, but also municipal bonds and Treasuries), and less of an effect in high-yield debt. Also, the increase in the spread of these corporate bonds was not accompanied by a similar increase in spreads of credit default swaps (CDS), so a large part of it must have been driven by sources other than an increase in credit risk that could have resulted from the real shock. The authors explained these patterns emerged as a result of liquidity shortages in the corporate bond market.

Kargar, Lester, Lindsay, Liu, Weill, and Zúñiga (2021) looked at the corporate bond market reactions during the COVID-19 crisis. To understand the changes in liquidity in this market, they distinguished between risky-principal trades, where dealers offer immediacy by purchasing the asset and holding it until finding a buyer, and agency trades, where the seller retains the asset until the dealer finds a buyer. They documented that the cost of risky principal trades in the bond market increased dramatically at the height of the crisis, forcing customers to switch to the less-preferred agency trade. The important takeaway from their paper is that the liquidity problems in the bond market manifested through both larger costs as well as a slower speed.

Finally, Bi and Marsh (2020) examined how the COVID-19 pandemic and subsequent policy actions impacted municipal bond pricing through liquidity and credit risk channels. They found that credit risks were an important component for short-term non-pre-refunded bonds at the onset of the pandemic. Specifically, the credit risk premia on non-pre-refunded bonds increased sharply, by 40 basis points, from early to late March 2020. This movement reflected the immediate impact, as well as the perceived temporary nature, of the pandemic on local budgets at the onset. On the other hand, credit risk premia for long-term non-pre-refunded bonds remained largely unchanged during the same period. The result reflected the expectation at the time that lockdown measures could contain the spread of the virus within a short period of time, even though financial conditions were rapidly deteriorating. However, later fiscal and monetary authority interventions successfully eased credit concerns for short-term bonds, as their credit risk premia against prerefunded bonds saw a steady decline of 20–30 basis points throughout April 2020 and remained at a relatively low level in May 2020. Between the end of March and May 2020, however, credit risk premia for long-term non-pre-refunded bonds increased by 30 basis points. This reflected that longer-term credit concerns became more relevant as the pandemic continued to drag on. Moreover, the shift in credit risk pricing from short-term to longer-term bonds over the course of the pandemic likely reflected policy intervention designs that primarily benefited short-term bonds, as well as investors' expectations of long-lasting recessional impacts on state and local government budgets.

10.3 Effects of the COVID-19 crisis on the CDS market

We also discuss briefly some results on the corporate credit default swaps (CDS) markets. CDSs are credit derivative contracts which allow investors to buy protection to swap/transfer credit risks on bonds or loans. The CDS buyer pays a premium to the seller to reimburse the buyer if a specific negative credit event occurs, i.e., a default of a third debtor. Similar to insurance, the buyer pays a periodic premium to a CDS seller to get compensated if a negative credit event occurs. Thus, the price or spread of CDS gauges the probability that a firm fails to repay in full, i.e., the firm's credit risk (Chiaramonte and Casu, 2013; Apergis, Danuletiu, and Xu, 2022). Given the severe shocks to economic operations and sudden declines in financial soundness at both macro- and firm-level, COVID-19 may have elevated the credit risks.

Liu, Qiu, and Wang (2021) studied how the COVID-19 shock affects the CDS spread changes and abnormal stock returns of the US firms with different levels of debt rollover risk. They used daily stock price data of all common stocks listed on NYSE, AMEX, and NASDAQ from CRSP and firms' CDS spread from Markit database for firms with CDS contracts of various maturities. Their sample includes 234 firms having CDS contracts followed over January 30, 2020 to March 26, 2020. They used the COVID-19 crisis as a quasi-natural experiment of adverse cashflow shock that increases the default risk of firms facing an immediate liquidity shortfall. They found that the COVID-19 shock significantly increased the CDS spreads and decreased the shareholder values for firms facing higher debt rollover risk. Their results indicate that the crisis led to a startling increase in CDS spread of 270–673 basis points across different CDS contract maturities for firms in the highest rollover-risk quartile relative to other firms. Moreover, the shorter the CDS maturity, the larger the increase in CDS spread, indicating that investors were more concerned about the short-term default risk for high rollover-risk firms than these firms' long-term default risk. The negative CDS effect was stronger for nonfinancial firms, for firms that are financially constrained, and for firms that were highly volatile. Moreover, they showed that firms with immediate refinancing needs suffered more than firms with distant refinancing needs during the COVID-19 shock, which further confirms that firms' debt rollover risk was indeed a key factor that drives the heterogeneous reactions to the shock.

Apergis, Danuletiu, and Xu (2022) used a large panel of US corporate CDS data collected from Bloomberg. The final dataset employed was comprised of 386 firms and 66,392 daily CDS spread observations followed over February 2020 to September 2020. They documented that US CDS spreads significantly increased since the beginning of the COVID-19 crisis. They showed that the pandemic severity, proxied by the number of COVID-19 cases and deaths both in the US and globally, were positively linked to the CDS spreads. However, there were significant heterogenous effects across sectors, in which banking, travel and leisure, transportation, airlines, and restaurants were the hardest hit sectors. Their analysis also documented that the COVID-19 pandemic increased corporate CDS spreads through increased firm financial distress.

References

Apergis, N., Danuletiu, D., and Xu, B. (2022). CDS spreads and COVID-19 pandemic. *Journal of International Financial Markets Institutions and Money*, 76, 101433.

Baker, S. R., Bloom, N., Davis, S. J., Kost, K., Sammon, M., and Viratyosin, T. (2020). The unprecedented stock market reaction to COVID-19. *Review of Asset Pricing Studies*, 10(4), 742–758.

Baqaee, D., and Farhi, E. (2020). *Supply and demand in disaggregated keynesian economies with an application to the Covid-19 crisis (no. w27152)*. National Bureau of Economic Research.

Bi, H., and Marsh, W. B. (2020). *Flight to liquidity or safety?: Recent evidence from the municipal bond market*. Federal Research Bank of Kansas City.

Bretscher, L., Hsu, A., Simasek, P., and Tamoni, A. (2020). COVID-19 and the cross-section of equity returns: Impact and transmission. *Review of Asset Pricing Studies*, 10(4), 705–741.

Carletti, E., Oliviero, T., Pagano, M., Pelizzon, L., and Subrahmanyam, M. G. (2020). The COVID-19 shock and equity shortfall: Firm-level evidence from Italy. *Review of Corporate Finance Studies*, 9(3), 534–568.

Cejnek, G., Randl, O., and Zechner, J. (2021). The COVID-19 pandemic and corporate dividend policy. *Journal of Financial and Quantitative Analysis*, 56(7), 2389–2410.

Chiaramonte, L., and Casu, B. (2013). The determinants of bank CDS spreads: Evidence from the financial crisis. *The European Journal of Finance*, 19, 861–887.

Ding, W., Levine, R., Lin, C., and Xie, W. (2021). Corporate immunity to the COVID-19 pandemic. *Journal of Financial Economics*, 141(2), 802–830.

Fahlenbrach, R., Rageth, K., and Stulz, R. M. (2021). How valuable is financial flexibility when revenue stops? Evidence from the COVID-19 crisis. *Review of Financial Studies*, *34*(11), 5474–5521.

Falato, A., Goldstein, I., and Hortaçsu, A. (2021). Financial fragility in the COVID-19 crisis: The case of investment funds in corporate bond markets. *Journal of Monetary Economics*, *123*, 35–52.

Goldstein, I., Koijen, R. S., and Mueller, H. M. (2021). COVID-19 and its impact on financial markets and the real economy. *Review of Financial Studies*, *34*(11), 5135–5148.

Gormsen, N. J., and Koijen, R. S. (2020). Coronavirus: Impact on stock prices and growth expectations. *Review of Asset Pricing Studies*, *10*(4), 574–597.

Haddad, V., Moreira, A., and Muir, T. (2021). When selling becomes viral: Disruptions in debt markets in the COVID-19 crisis and the Fed's response. *Review of Financial Studies*, *34*(11), 5309–5351.

Kargar, M., Lester, B., Lindsay, D., Liu, S., Weill, P. O., and Zúñiga, D. (2021). Corporate bond liquidity during the COVID-19 crisis. *Review of Financial Studies*, *34*(11), 5352–5401.

Liu, Y., Qiu, B., and Wang, T. (2021). Debt rollover risk, credit default swap spread and stock returns: Evidence from the COVID-19 crisis. *Journal of Financial Stability*, *53*, 100855.

Ramelli, S., and Wagner, A. F. (2020). Feverish stock price reactions to COVID-19. *Review of Corporate Finance Studies*, *9*(3), 622–655.

Part III

Government policy reactions to the COVID-19 crisis and their economic and financial effects around the world

Part III describes policy reactions to COVID-19 and analyzes research findings on their economic and financial effects around the world. We cover only some of the most consequential government policy actions, given the sheer numbers of such policy responses. We focus on policies to address the economic and financial stresses of the crisis, as opposed to the health problems, although some intermingling is unavoidable. We assimilate and integrate as much as possible the existing research literature, acknowledging that we undoubtedly miss current working papers, emerging publications at the time of this writing, and contributions produced afterward.

The evidence reviewed in this part of the book is quite consistent with a key overall theme of the book. The initial policy reactions to the crisis were very quickly designed and implemented. These measures were also very large in size relative to those in prior crises and the real economies and financial systems that they were designed to rescue. In normal times, such fast and large actions often lead to considerable waste, fraud, and misdirection of funds, and such unfavorable social consequences also occurred in the COVID-19 crisis.

However, it is possible that such costs may have been prices that needed to be paid during the COVID-19 crisis. The evidence suggests that these "throwing money at the problem" solutions may have helped spur the very fast economic and financial recoveries described earlier as the "economic surprise" and "financial surprise" of the crisis. However, as the recoveries gained steam and moved into the aftermath of the crisis, the large government stimulus policies may not have been curtailed fast enough. These continuing policies likely significantly contributed to the inflation, supply chain shortages, and other unfavorable economic and financial consequences the world experienced from 2021 onwards.

Chapter 11 provides context for the COVID-19 crisis policies by comparing the PPP financial aid to small businesses and their employees with the TARP aid to banks in the earlier GFC. We provide details of PPP as well as the nuances of the research, while the TARP review is much briefer, given that this program is from an earlier crisis that is not the main focus of our book. Chapters 12 and 13 provide specific information on COVID-19 policies other than PPP and research findings on their economic and financial effects in the US and in the rest of the world, respectively.

Some of the data for this part of the book are drawn the same sources as described in Chapter 1, the Appendix, and other parts of the book, the URLs of websites shown in the Introduction to Part I, other publicly available sources.

Chapter 11

Putting the COVID-19 crisis policies into context—The Paycheck Protection Program (PPP) vs the Troubled Asset Relief Program (TARP) during the Global Financial Crisis (GFC)

Abstract

In our first chapter on government policy reactions to COVID-19 and their economic and financial effects, we compare one very large COVID-19 policy program with one from the GFC—the Paycheck Protection Program (PPP) vs the Troubled Asset Relief Program (TARP) during the GFC. Both PPP and TARP are large financial aid programs and both were found by researchers to be largely successful in achieving their specific main goals— PPP helped small businesses and their employees, and TARP reduced systemic risk and improved the real economy. However, the programs differ significantly in the speed of implementation, size, and persistence of the financial aid, and these differences appear to matter in their effects. A key difference in results is that subprime consumer debt decreased with the presence of more PPP but increased with the presence of more local TARP banks.

Keywords: COVID-19, Policy, Financial aid, Paycheck Protection Program (PPP), Troubled Asset Relief Program (TARP), Small businesses, Banks, Subprime consumer debt

The Economic and Financial Impacts of the COVID-19 Crisis Around the World
https://doi.org/10.1016/B978-0-443-19162-6.00006-2
Copyright © 2024 Elsevier Inc. All rights reserved.

11.1 Comparisons of the programs

11.1.1 Key similarities between the two programs

There are strong similarities between the PPP and TARP policies. Both financial aid programs aimed at the origin of their crises—the real economy for PPP and the banking sector for TARP. Both were also very large by historical standards in the hundreds of billions of dollars and involved substantial misuse of funds, including the influence of political connections. However, the research also suggests that each of these policies was successful in achieving their specific main goals—PPP helped small businesses and their employees, and TARP reduced systemic risk and improved the real economy.

11.1.2 Key differences between the two programs

It is more important for our purposes to focus on the differences between the programs that exemplify some of the key policy lessons learned from the crises. These include the speed of implementation, size, and persistence of the financial aid as the crises unfolded into their aftermaths. However, as noted below, the TARP speed of implementation is comparable with that of PPP at the time when the public became widely aware of the crisis magnitudes.

Regarding speedy implementation, PPP began on March 27, 2020, with the passage of the CARES Act, only about a month into the crisis and recession in the US. Applications were issued about a week later, and most of the funds followed soon thereafter. In contrast, TARP was not passed and implemented until October 2008, well after the Federal Reserve and others had clearly taken notice that a crisis was underway in August 2007.

Part of this significant difference in response time by policymakers is very likely due to the nature of the crises themselves. The magnitude of the economic damage of the GFC was not apparent for some time after the crisis started. Market events such as the run on the ABCP market, the near bankruptcy of Countrywide in the US, and the Northern Rock run in the UK resulted in central bank responses in these nations in August 2007. The official National Bureau of Economic Research (NBER) date of the US recession was not until December 2007, and it was not announced until much later, as is NBER practice. Many observers and the general public then and even today view the crisis as beginning on September 15, 2008, when the GFC became much worse and commanded headlines with the Lehman bankruptcy. By this standard, the TARP implementation in October 2008 was quite prompt in the next month. In sharp contrast, the magnitude of the economic damage to come from COVID-19 became quickly apparent. The NBER dated the recession as starting in February 2020 before the disease was widespread in the US, although again this was not announced until later. Seasonally adjusted US unemployment went up almost a full percentage point in the month from February to March 2020, from 3.5% to 4.4%, and on its way to a jarring 14.8% the following month in April 2020. Viewed in terms of the public recognition of economic damages, the response times were about a comparable 1 month for both policies.

In terms of size, PPP distributed $525 billion to 5.2 million small businesses during the first round of PPP, primarily in the form of forgivable loans that need not be paid back in April and May 2020. These funds were much greater in magnitude and went to many more recipients than the TARP total of $204.9 billion to 709 banking organizations. Moreover, the TARP funds to banks were more than fully repaid with dividends, warrants, and principal repayments, while relatively few repayments may be expected from the PPP forgivable loans.

With regard to the persistence of new funding, PPP was reopened with additional funds on January 11, 2021, and included second financial aid payouts for some of those receiving money in the first round. This was after vaccines were being distributed, the unemployment rate had dropped, and the US economy was reopening. In contrast, most of the TARP funds to banks—$125 billion of the $204.9 billion—were given out on the very first day of distribution on October 28, 2008, to nine large institutions, and most of the remaining funds were distributed relatively quickly. During 2009, much of the funds were repaid, and no funds were distributed to banks after 2009.

Spatt (2020) examined differences between the GFC and COVID-19 and the TARP and PPP financial aid, including issues of moral hazard vs risk sharing. He highlighted the importance of postmortem analyses of the extent to which such financial aid programs achieved their purposes. In the case of PPP, the key question is: Did it facilitate the survival of firms—such as whether the recipients eventually liquidated or filed for bankruptcy, and the jobs saved. Berger and Roman (2020), which was written prior to COVID-19, asked whether TARP achieved its ultimate goals of reducing systemic risk and improving the real economy. This chapter addresses these key issues.

11.1.3 Description of PPP

PPP is part of the Coronavirus Aid, Relief, and Economic Security Act, or the CARES Act, passed by the 116th Congress on March 27, 2020, and signed into law by President Donald Trump a few days later. The US Department of Treasury and the US Small Business Administration (SBA) launched the PPP as a $659 billion loan project for small businesses to directly induce small businesses to retain their employees. PPP funding became available for loans generated between February 15, 2020, and June 30, 2020, after Title 15 of the US Code was amended for commerce and trade. The Senate extended the PPP application deadline till the end of August 8, 2020, just hours before the original deadline. The program then came to an end on that new deadline set by legislation, and lenders were no longer able to submit fresh applications.

Many small companies with fewer than 500 employees per physical site of the company, including those in NAICS code 72 (industries such as restaurants), were judged as acceptable borrowers. Importantly, the maximum amount of a PPP loan that a qualified small business may borrow to keep staff was set at $10 million, with salaries restricted at $100,000. The SBA declared that the loans will be erased provided that the debtors met the loan spending requirements. All current SBA-certified lenders were declared eligible to make PPP loans, and all federally insured banks and credit unions, along with farm credit systems and nonbank, noninsured depository organizations were invited to apply as PPP lenders. The SBA backed the whole sum, waived all guaranty fees, and reimbursed the lenders by giving them processing fees for PPP loans. Furthermore, the Federal Reserve Board allowed all Federal Reserve Banks to establish their PPP Liquidity Facilities (PPPLF) to provide money to financial institutions permitted to issue PPP loans, to improve the efficiency of the PPP. More than 5000 participating institutions granted over $5.2 million in approved loans, with an average loan amount of roughly $100,000, from the start of the PPP until the end of August, leaving $134 billion of the program's budget unclaimed. The PPPLF advanced a total of $67.5 billion in outstanding commitments.

In order to analyze the distribution of Paycheck Protection Program (PPP) loans and their effects, Joaquim and Wang (2022) used Dun and Bradstreet data on enterprises' financial situations. Three key conclusions are drawn: First, when allocating PPP loans, companies in stronger financial standing before the COVID epidemic were given an edge. Second, after receiving a loan, businesses' financial standing dramatically and consistently improved. This effect was more obvious for smaller, less financially stable businesses. Third, they empirically show that it is necessary to take into account company financial state heterogeneity in order to accurately identify and assess the PPP's overall effect.

According to surveys on the initial round of PPP, it has been effective in assisting borrowers. According to the National Federation of Independent Business's COVID-19 Small Business Survey (2020), 78% of respondents applied for a PPP loan, practically all their applications were granted, and 96% of PPP applicants were contented to some level with the initiative. Furthermore, according to the Federal Reserve System's Small Business Credit Survey (2021), businesses that received PPP money were more likely to keep their current personnel or hire back those who were laid off. Moreover, 71% of companies that did not obtain PPP money took steps to cut employment, whereas only 46% of firms that obtained all the PPP funds they sought for took efforts to curb jobs. Similarly, 77% of companies that obtained all the PPP money they applied for attempted to rehire personnel, compared to 44% of firms not receiving PPP funds.

Şahin and Tasci (2022) showed that companies whose headcount does not exceed 250 personnel played a disproportionally larger role in generating job cuts during the period of PPP. They further argued that the availability of Paycheck Protection Program funds might have prevented some "usual" reallocation from happening early on and thus subsequently created a pent-up demand for labor market reallocation later in the recovery.

A small business, sole proprietor, independent contractor, self-employed person, 501(c)(3) charitable organization, 501(c)(19) veterans' group, or tribal business was deemed as eligible for the PPP. Applicants should have been in business as a sole proprietorship, an independent contractor, or an eligible self-employed individual by February 15, 2020. The applicant and its affiliates should also have a global workforce of 500 or fewer people, including US and international affiliates; or meet the SBA's industry size guidelines, based on the average number of employees, or have a real net worth of no more than $15 million on March 27, 2020, and an average net income of no more than $5 million for the two fiscal years before the PPP application date. The applicant should be a citizen of the US or one of its territories. The applicant's major businesses must be based in the US or one of its territories, or the applicant's business must contribute significantly to the US economy.

The PPP amount was determined by the applicant's payroll expenditures. Salaries, commissions, tips, paid leave, severance pay, and other payments provided to workers were all included in payroll expenses. These expenses were capped at $100,000 per worker each year. Applicants analyzed their payroll expenses between January 1, 2019, and December 31, 2019 to determine the amount of the PPP loan. PPP loans were limited to $10 million. However, in certain situations, every affiliate of a firm was permitted to apply for and obtain its own PPP loan.

An applicant would file for a PPP loan directly with a qualified private lender, such as a federally insured bank, a federally insured credit union, a Farm Credit System institution, or an SBA-approved creditor. Neither the lending institution nor the federal government imposed an application fee on an applicant. Lenders were compensated by the SBA for executing PPP loans.

Some creditors only considered PPP applications from companies that already had a bank account with them.[1] Only until August 8, 2020, the loan applications were accepted, and loans were made. Falsifying information to acquire a PPP loan was a criminal activity punishable by imprisonment, penalties, or both.

Until the total sum appropriated by Congress was exhausted, applications for PPP loans were considered, confirmed, and paid on the order of first come, first served. On April 16, 2020, the first budget of $349 billion ran out, and the SBA ceased taking new loan applications as of that day. The Senate and House of Representatives enacted a bill to provide $320 billion in financing on April 21 and April 23, respectively. On April 24, President Trump signed it into law, and the SBA started accepting new loan requests on April 27. Creditors were required by the Equal Credit Opportunity Act to inform a PPP loan applicant about the outcome of the application within 30 days of receiving the loan or about the notification from the SBA on the availability of funding.

Furthermore, Bracht (2022) argued that congress approved PPP too quickly, not accounting for tax-exempt loan forgiveness, and the general guidance from the IRS was too confusing for most businesses and business owners. Bracht identifies tax issues caused by the Paycheck Protection Program and suggests a framework for future guidance regarding the sale of a partnership interest.

The interest rate on PPP loans was 1%. The SBA guaranteed each PPP loan. To apply for or be approved for a PPP loan, an applicant did not need to present any collateral or personal assurances. Unless the loan funds were utilized for unjustifiable uses, a PPP loan was a nonrecourse loan.

Under certain conditions, the principal of a PPP loan would be forgiven in part or in full. A company could petition for debt forgiveness at any point on or before the loan's maturity date, even before the covered term is up in the case of a firm that has used up all the PPP loan funds. PPP loan forgiveness was usually determined by what the loan funds were used on, whether or not the firm kept or hired back its employees, and whether or not the workers' pay and hours were sustained.

11.1.4 Description of TARP

TARP was authorized by the Emergency Economic Stabilization Act (EESA) enacted in October 2008. The original version of EESA was a plan to purchase large amounts of distressed assets such as mortgage-based securities (MBS). Similar to the successful Resolution Trust Corporation (RTC) in 1989, the market for "troubled assets" could become more stable, market values increased, and the institutions that hold them increased their capital and liquidity. The EESA was rejected by the House of Representatives on September 29, 2008, followed by the Dow Jones Industrial Average (DJIA) Index falling by 777 points. On October 3, 2008, an amended bill was passed and signed into law by President George W. Bush, authorizing $700 billion for TARP.

---

[1]For example, see: (1) Wells Fargo, "COVID-19 Update: Small Business Administration Paycheck Protection Program." "Who is eligible? … Have a Wells Fargo business checking account as of February 15, 2020." Source: Wells Fargo website, Retrieved April 14, 2020; (2) Bank of America: "We're here for our small business clients. To be eligible, you must have a Small Business lending and Small Business checking relationship with Bank of America as of February 15, 2020, or a Small Business checking account opened no later than February 15, 2020, and do not have a business credit or borrowing relationship with another bank." Source: Bank of America website, Retrieved April 14, 2020; (3) Capital One: "Business Customers: Paycheck Protection Program updates for business customers. Please note that business customers who apply for a Paycheck Protection Program Loan through Capital One must have an active business checking account as of February 15, 2020." Source: Capital One Bank website, Retrieved April 14, 2020.

No "troubled assets" purchases on the secondary market were made by the US Treasury, although trillions of dollars were purchased by the Federal Reserve as part of its multiple rounds of quantitative easing (QE). Instead, the US Treasury announced on October 13, 2008, that it would invest directly in the preferred equity of financial institutions to stabilize their capital ratios. On October 14, 2018, the Capital Purchase Program (CPP) was announced, allocating $250 billion for the US Treasury to purchase bank-preferred equity or debt securities and equity warrants from participating banking institutions, as well as other programs. The CPP, or bank financial aid portion of the program, is what is commonly referred to as "TARP."

On October 28, eight large bank holding companies (BHCs) plus Merrill Lynch which was soon to be purchased by one of the BHCs (Bank of America) received capital injections totaling $125 billion without a formal evaluation process. These institutions are considered to have been "forced" or strongly encouraged by the government to take the funds to restore public confidence and/or hide which institutions were having difficulties (e.g., Paletta, Hilsenrath, and Solomon, 2008; Solomon and Enrich, 2008; Duchin and Sosyura, 2012).

The remainder of the $204.9 billion in funds that were eventually distributed to 700 other BHCs and other bank and thrift firms required these institutions to apply for the program. The approval to receive TARP funds favored healthy and viable institutions, consistent with theoretical arguments that stronger banks are better able to reduce systemic risk (Choi, 2014).

The preferred equity injections, which raised the institutions' Tier 1 capital ratios, came with restrictions on dividends, repurchases, and executive compensation, which were further refined on February 17, 2009. However, there were no strings attached in terms of any compulsion to make additional loans.

The TARP injections ranged from 1% to 3% of a firm's risk-weighted assets or $25 billion, whichever was smaller. Many BHCs downstreamed some of the funds to their commercial banks (Mukherjee and Pana, 2018). The US Treasury purchased nonvoting preferred stock that paid quarterly dividends of 5% for the first 5 years and 9% afterward. The US Treasury also received warrants for an additional 5% of the banks' stock or subordinated debt.

It was initially expected that the US Treasury would lose money, but eventually, it recovered 112.7% of the total money invested. Most of the large banking organizations repaid the funds in 2009 (details in Berger and Roman, 2020, Table 3.8, p. 110). On an ex post facto basis, this was a relatively low rate of return to US taxpayers, given the risks (e.g., Flanagan and Purnanandam, 2023).

11.2 Empirical evidence on the economic and financial effects of PPP

11.2.1 Effects on households

The research on household impacts of PPP is primarily about the employment effects of the program. Many studies link PPP to low unemployment or job savings in the community but many times these appear to be modest relative to the program's grandiose size (e.g., Barraza, Rossi, and Yeager, 2020; Bartik, Cullen, Glaeser, Luca, Stanton, and Sunderam, 2020; Duchin and Hackney, 2021; Li and Strahan, 2021; Granja, Makridis, Yannelis, and Zwick, 2022). However, researchers have different estimates of the magnitudes of these effects. On the margin, Faulkender, Jackman, and Miran (2023) found that a 10% rise in PPP-eligible payroll resulted in a 1 to 2 percentage point lower increase in weekly first unemployment insurance (UI) claims as a proportion of total employment. With a lag, the same 10% increase in PPP coverage resulted in a 5-percentage point lower rise in insured unemployment. Early PPP coverage raises the insured unemployment rate from the 25th to the 75th percentile of counties, resulting in a gain of almost 12 percentage points, or 18.6 million jobs extrapolated nationally. Chetty, Friedman, and Stepner (2023) also found that PPP increased employment at PPP-eligible small businesses by 2%.

Hubbard and Strain (2020) found that PPP was associated with a modest 0.9% increase in employment for businesses that applied for PPP loans above $150,000. Granja, Makridis, Yannelis, and Zwick (2022) looked at sectors most affected by the pandemic and estimated that the PPP increased employment saving about 3.2–4.8 million jobs. Based on the estimated range of 1.3–4.8 million jobs saved between April and August 2020, the costs per job saved can go from $109,000 to $377,000 (Bi and Gulati, 2021; Granja, Makridis, Yannelis, and Zwick, 2022; Chetty, Friedman, and Stepner, 2023). Despite the estimated number of jobs saved by the PPP, this may not seem to be enough given the large job losses of 22.2 million between March and April 2020 (Bi and Gulati, 2021).

Other considerations are that the modest effects in early months may be due to firms taking PPP when they were not in need of it and were not planning to lay off any employees, also referred to as inframarginal firms (e.g., Bi and Gulati, 2021; Granja, Makridis, Yannelis, and Zwick, 2022; Chetty, Friedman, and Stepner, 2023) and that the effects of PPP continue beyond the early months of the pandemic.

Thus, Bartik, Cullen, Glaeser, Luca, Stanton, and Sunderam (2020) found a positive but statistically insignificant effect on employment at the end of April 2020. Hubbard and Strain (2020) found larger employment effects in August than in April or May, while Granja, Makridis, Yannelis, and Zwick (2022) found that the PPP did not raise employment but induced modest employment responses in the months following PPP loan receipt. Both Chetty, Friedman, and Stepner (2023) and Granja, Makridis, Yannelis, and Zwick (2022) cautioned that the employment effects could be larger in the longer run, as many firms used the loans to build up savings buffers and strengthen their balance sheets during stay-at-home orders. Joaquim and Netto (2021b) provided comprehensive evidence of heterogeneous allocations of PPP funds and how these allocations across different banks and regional economies affect our interpretation of the estimated effect of PPP on employment. They estimated that PPP resulted in a reduction in unemployment at eligible firms of 12.9 percentage points, which corresponds to roughly 7.5 million jobs at a cost of $70,000 per job.

Doniger and Kay (2023) provided findings suggesting the employment effects may have been limited due to limited initial financing under the CARES Act, and delays in the distribution of PPP loans. Between April and May, delayed loans fueled layoffs and labor force leave, while reducing recalls over the summer. The impacts are unequally spread, with the self-employed and very small businesses suffering the most. The extent and variability of the impacts imply that securing external finance is difficult, especially for small businesses. According to their calculations, the PPP saved millions of jobs, but greater early financing may have saved millions more, especially if it had been targeted at smaller businesses.

Faulkender, Jackman, and Miran (2023) identified the employment effects of PPP loans using the fact that different firms received loans at different times, based on which type of lender they used and reported an improvement in the unemployment rate of over 12 percentage points or job savings from PPP of about 18.6 million jobs. However, results from this latter study are not directly comparable to the others due to very different identification strategies.

Autor, Cho, Crane, Goldar, Lutz, Montes, Peterman, Ratner, Villar, and Yildirmaz (2022) analyzed administrative payroll data at the firm level and found that PPP increased employment at small businesses by about 3.25%. Autor, Cho, Crane, Goldar, Lutz, Montes, Peterman, Ratner, Vallenas, and

Yildirmaz (2022) found that PPP supported employment, but at a high cost to taxpayers. In the second quarter of 2020, PPP saved roughly 2.97 million jobs per week, and by the fourth quarter of 2020, it had saved about 1.75 million jobs per week. Overall, PPP rescued around 1.98 million job-years of employment at a cost of $258,000 per job-year saved, high compared to the average wages and benefits of $58,200 paid to small-business employees in 2020.

Berger, Epouhe, and Roman (2022) found that subprime consumer debt decreased in markets where more PPP loans were made, consistent with the role of PPP in alleviating financial constraints for consumers that are typically most constrained. Effects of a one-standard deviation increase are economically significant, suggesting an about 3 percentage point decline in the post-PPP period. Such decreases in debt are primarily driven by credit card and auto loan debt.

Most of the PPP employment research investigates income, gender, and racial disparities in how the funds were distributed. Autor, Cho, Crane, Goldar, Lutz, Montes, Peterman, Ratner, Vallenas, and Yildirmaz (2022) found that PPP loans were disproportionately distributed to high-income households. They estimated that just $13.2 billion of the $510 billion in PPP loans given in 2020 went to households in the poorest fifth of the income distribution, with $130.8 billion going to the second through fourth quintiles. The remaining $365.9 billion (72%) went to the top fifth of the income distribution. Despite the fact that the PPP only provided loans for up to $100,000 in yearly earnings, the wealthiest fifth of families account for around 35% of wage and salary earnings. Moreover, capital ownership is much more right-skewed than wage earnings, with the top fifth of families controlling 86.2% of capital income, implying that corporate subsidies are essentially subsidies to high-income households.

Fairlie and Fossen (2022) revealed that although PPP funding came to minority areas later than to places with lower minority shares, there exists a marginally positive association between PPP loan receipt per firm and the minority proportion of the population. However, the quantity of PPP loans per employee is inversely proportional to the population's minority representation.

Ong, González, Pech, Hernandez, and Domínguez-Villegas (2020) found that companies in California's communities of color are being left behind because they are receiving considerably less from the $600 billion in PPP loans, according to their report coauthored with the UCLA Latino Policy and Politics Initiative. This report explains how a lack of government funding would likely exacerbate economic disparity in minority communities, which already have fewer small businesses and employment than majority White areas.

According to research by Lederer and Oros (2020) at the National Community Reinvestment Coalition, there were considerable discrepancies in the amount of encouragement given to Black and White PPP loan applicants, as well as gender inequalities. In matched-test research, 32.1% of White males were informed they were qualified for a loan in some way, whereas just 8% of Black males were qualified. Compared to their White counterparts, several of the discrepancies in treatment went so far as to constitute a fair lending violation, and overall Black applicants were given less information and were discouraged from seeking the loan.

Based on the geographic examination and linear regressions, Sabasteanski, Brooks, and Chandler (2021) reported that districts with higher Black populations received lower PPP loan amounts. Republican-controlled congressional districts similarly had lower loan amounts than Democratic-controlled ones. One possible explanation that they discussed is that many Republican districts, particularly in the Southeast, are primarily Black, and hence the loans are often smaller. They also showed that PPP loan amounts were greater on average in White Republican districts in the Midwest and Northwest.

Similarly, Chernenko and Scharfstein (2022) identified significant racial inequalities in borrowing under the PPP and analyze the origins of these discrepancies using a large sample of Florida restaurants. They found that PPP loans are 25% less likely to be given to Black-owned restaurants. The location of the restaurant accounts for 5 percentage points of the difference. Restaurant features account for an extra 10% of the difference in PPP borrowing. They also presented that prior borrowing arrangements, on average, do not explain discrepancies. The remaining 10% difference is due to a 17% difference in PPP borrowing from banks, which is somewhat offset by higher borrowing from non-banks, mostly FinTechs. Minority-owned restaurants' lower demand for PPP loans and lesser awareness of PPP loans cannot explain the disparities in PPP borrowing. In regions with higher racial prejudice, Black-owned restaurants are much less likely to acquire bank PPP loans. Nonbank PPP loans are more likely to be substituted in these counties by Black-owned restaurants. However, this replacement is insufficient to remove racial inequalities in PPP borrowing. Finally, they showed that our findings apply more generally across industries.

Additionally, Chernenko, Kaplan, Sarkar, and Scharfstein (2022) studied racial disparities. They found that Sorting by Black-owned firms away from banks and toward FinTechs is significantly stronger in more racially biased counties, and the bank approval disparity is also larger in more racially biased counties. Thus, to the extent that automation at FinTechs reduces racial disparities in PPP take-up, it does so by mitigating disparities in loan application rates, not loan approval rates.

Atkins, Cook, and Seamans (2022) found that Black-owned firms obtained loans at a 50% lower rate than White-owned enterprises with identical characteristics. The effect is slightly less in places with more bank competition, and it fades over time when the PPP program was changed to allow FinTechs and other nontraditional lenders to participate.

In contrast, Calem and Freedman (2020) suggested that neighborhoods with a high percentage of racial and ethnic minorities received significantly more PPP dollars per small business than other areas. In particular, the nation's largest banks—those with more than $50 billion in assets—robustly channeled PPP credit into communities with a high percentage minority population. The pandemic relief program also directed a relatively large share of funds to neighborhoods encompassing opportunity zones as designated by the Treasury Department. The research shows a neighborhood made up entirely of opportunity zones that is in the top fifth of percent minority population would receive about 50% more PPP dollars per small business establishment than an area without those zones and with the bottom fifth percent minority population, according to BPI's estimates.

Finlay, Mueller-Smith, and Street (2020) found that some of the minority PPP's lack of success could also be attributable to some ineligibility criteria. They found that up to 2.6%–3.2% of sole proprietorships may have been ineligible for the PPP due to current or prior criminal justice involvement, based on data from seven states. Between 6.9% and 15.4% of former convicts relied on self-employment income, including over a quarter of Black and Hispanic women. All considered states showed Black and Hispanic men with sole proprietorship income being more likely to be PPP-disqualified due to criminal histories than White men. Ineligibility rates would at least triple if exclusion criteria were expanded to include older convictions and less serious crimes.

García and Darity Jr. (2021) used hand-collected race information about small business owners that concealed their race in PPP applications and found evidence that not disclosing race information in loan applications pays off significantly, particularly for minorities. Black-owned businesses that concealed their race obtained 52% more in funding than self-reported Black-owned businesses. Interestingly, White-owned businesses that also concealed their race information obtained approximately 10%

more in funding relative to self-reported White-owned businesses, but the latter effect is not statistically significant. Their findings are consistent with the expected equilibrium of the game-theoretic race-reporting prisoner's dilemma, in which all participants are better off by not self-reporting race.

Kickul, Griffiths, Robb, and Gundry (2021) discovered substantial discrepancies between women- and men-owned enterprises, with male-owned businesses receiving over 80% of PPP loans. Women-owned businesses, on the other hand, preserved more jobs on average in all but the largest loan category. There were also significant variations between minority- and White-owned firms, with minority-owned enterprises protecting more jobs on average across all loan types.

Howell, Kuchler, Snitkof, Stroebel, and Wong (2021) reported that FinTech lenders provided a disproportionate amount of PPP loans to Black-owned businesses, especially in areas with strong racial animosity. PPP financing to Black-owned firms improve once established banks streamline their loan application processes. Similarly, Battisto, Godin, Kramer, and Sarkar (2021) found that, while FinTech lenders disbursed only a small share of total loan amounts, they provided important support to minority business owners, who have in the past been underserved by the traditional banking industry. Applicants who approached FinTech lenders for PPP loans were more likely to lack banking relationships, be minority owned, and have fewer employees. Moreover, a higher share of applications by Black-owned businesses were approved by FinTech lenders as compared to firms with White, Asian, or Hispanic owners.

11.2.2 Effects on nonfinancial firms

A number of studies focus on the benefits to firms from PPP. Bartlett and Morse (2020), Hubbard and Strain (2020), and Berger, Freed, Scott, and Zhang (2021) presented evidence that the small businesses benefited from the PPP. For example, Bartlett and Morse (2020) showed that in the medium-run, PPP supported the survival of the smallest businesses, but for other small businesses, the evidence is not supported. Also, using the data from the Dun and Bradstreet Corporation, Hubbard and Strain (2020) found that PPP has greatly increased the survival of small businesses by boosting employment and improving financial health. Berger, Freed, Scott, and Zhang (2021) provided evidence that businesses in the industries that were impacted the most by the pandemic as well as businesses that are relatively smaller and in lower-income counties benefited the most. Bartik, Cullen, Glaeser, Luca, Stanton, and Sunderam (2020) showed that the expected survival rate of a business and employment increased with PPP loans, but the survival effects were heterogeneous. In contrast, Granja, Makridis, Yannelis, and Zwick (2022) analyzed whether the PPP accomplished its goals, and they showed that there is no evidence that PPP funds were allocated to the firms and locations more impacted by the pandemic. They presented that it is actually the opposite: PPP funds went to the less impacted firms and locations.

Others focus on issues regarding the distribution of the funds across firms. Chodorow-Reich, Darmouni, Luck, and Plosser (2022) examined the Federal Reserve Y-14 data and found some evidence that the businesses that received PPP funds in the Y-14 data decreased their non-PPP bank borrowings. Joaquim and Netto (2021b) explored the optimal allocation of funds across firms and the distortions caused by allocating these funds through banks. They developed a theoretical framework and showed that it can be optimal to allocate funds to the least or most affected firms depending on the underlying distribution of the shock that firms face, the firm's financial position, and the total budget available for the program. In an empirical application of the model, they estimated the PPP's effectiveness and compared it with alternative policies. They argued that a policy targeted at the smallest firms could have increased the program's effectiveness significantly.

A number of studies also investigate issues of distribution of funds to businesses in terms of political connections, banking connections, and business size. Duchin and Hackney (2021), Igan, Lambert, and Mishra (2021), and Berger, Karakaplan, and Roman (2023) found that political connections of firms helped boost the likelihood of firms receiving PPP loans, with some key differences in the types of political connections that mattered. Duchin and Hackney (2021) and Igan, Lambert, and Mishra (2021) found evidence that partisan political connections—i.e., those for which political party matters—worked for firms, while Berger, Karakaplan, and Roman (2023) found that nonpartisan political connections—i.e., those for which party does not matter—were important for firms in the distribution of PPP funds. As discussed below, these authors found that partisan political connections do matter, but for the banks rather than the firms.

In terms of firm connections to banks, Duchin, Martin, Michaely, and Wang (2022) found that firms with personal ties to banks are more likely to obtain PPP loans, but the role of personal ties weakens when firms are less opaque. Moreover, they found that connected firms are more likely to return their loans in response to public pressure or to avoid regulatory scrutiny/prosecution. Others also found that small businesses with prior banking relationships benefited relative to others and were more likely to be given PPP funds and to receive funds earlier than others (e.g., Amiram and Rabetti, 2020; Bartik, Cullen, Glaeser, Luca, Stanton, and Sunderam, 2020; Glancy, Gross, and Ionescu, 2020; Li and Strahan, 2021; Balyuk, Prabhala, and Puri, 2022), consistent with the discussion above.

In terms of firm size, Balyuk, Prabhala, and Puri (2022) showed that some small businesses were hesitant to borrow PPP funds, and larger businesses had an earlier access to the PPP funds in the first wave, which was also augmented by their banking with larger banks. Similarly, Humphries, Neilson, and Ulyssea (2020) presented evidence that since the smallest businesses had the least awareness of the PPP and they could not catch up with other small businesses. Joaquim and Netto (2021a) also provided empirical evidence of heterogeneity in the allocation of PPP funds. They also showed that firms that are larger and less affected by the COVID-19 crisis received loans earlier, even in a within-bank analysis.

Cole (2022) used administrative data from a private payroll processor having PPP application status to compare firms that did apply for PPP vs those that did not but are otherwise similar on observables for clients are primarily very small businesses (median 5 employees) to measure the effects of financial relief received through PPP. Firms that applied for PPP funds increased their average employment by 7.5% in the 5 months following the program's start relative to similar firms that did not apply. The positive effects on employment occur primarily in industries in which firms were less affected by government shutdowns or higher levels of COVID-19, namely industries with more employees that can work remotely, those that have fewer hourly workers and essential businesses. Their data on hiring also shows that the program worked as intended by preserving employment matches: positive employment effects occurred due to fewer layoffs, not through more hiring of new or former employees. The author's estimates imply a cost of approximately $270,000 per job per year at very small firms. Furthermore, Cole (2022) also showed that PPP had a much larger effect on employment for firms that are in industries with a lower number of hourly workers, a high number of workers with remote working capabilities, and essential businesses.

With regard to the effects of PPP on small business survival, some researchers found that PPP increased the survival probabilities and/or reduced bankruptcies of small businesses. Thus,

Hubbard and Strain (2020) found that the PPP has improved the PPP businesses' survival rate and financial health. Using survey data, Bartlett and Morse (2020) found similar results. Bartik, Cullen, Glaeser, Luca, Stanton, and Sunderam (2020) found that the first round of PPP loans led to about a 14–30 percentage point increase in the probability of surviving during December 2020, though the effects varied across firms given the often-debatable initial allocation. In contrast, Granja, Makridis, Yannelis, and Zwick (2022) did not find evidence that the PPP had large effects on local economic outcomes such as business closures during the first round of PPP.

In a theoretical framework, Elenev, Landvoigt, and Van Nieuwerburgh (2022) revealed that the government interventions, of which PPP is a big component, reduced corporate bankruptcies by about half, preventing a much deeper crisis and short-circuiting the doom loop between corporate and financial market fragility. The additional fiscal cost is zero since program spending replaces what would otherwise have been spent on intermediary financial aid. The model predicts rising interest rates on government debt and slow debt pay-down. Specifically, bridge loan programs such as PPP are successful at preventing many corporate bankruptcies. This prevents the pandemic from spilling over into a financial crisis. They concluded that absent policy intervention, a negative feedback loop between corporate default and financial intermediary weakness could have created a macroeconomic disaster, and the PPP was effective at breaking the vicious cycle.

11.2.3 Effects on banks

Berger, Karakaplan, and Roman (2023) compared and contrasted the political connections between the banks that distributed the PPP loans and those of the small businesses that received the loans. As discussed, the banks and other financial institutions were the ones that applied to the government for funds and had significant discretion over which small businesses that applied to them received funding. They found that partisan political connections for which political party matters were important for the banks and are positively associated with lobbying efforts, and that nonpartisan connections with congressional representatives on a key committee were influential for the firms. The measured effects are both statistically and economically significant—partisan political connections for banks yielded an estimated 5-percentage point greater likelihood of PPP funding, while nonpartisan connections for small businesses induced an estimated 6-percentage point higher likelihood of such funding.

Berger, Karakaplan, and Roman (2023) found that banks with more intensive PPP involvement enjoyed higher profitability, and provide additional evidence suggesting that this was likely due in part to the channels of increased lending beyond the PPP loans and competitive advantages relative to banks with less intensive PPP participation. Benefits from PPP to the banks are also shown in Lopez and Spiegel (2021) and Marsh and Sharma (2021) via increased conventional or non-PPP lending due to the bank PPP involvement.

James, Lu, and Sun (2021) presented distance-based evidence that community banks responded faster to the PPP loan applications than larger banks. Marsh and Sharma (2020) showed that community banks had a significant role in the allocation of PPP funds. Lee (2023) examined how regional variations in market concentration and community banks contribute to PPP loan disbursement using the US county-level data. The author found that greater market concentration reduces the number of PPP loans per business, but this negative effect is mitigated by a greater presence of community banks in highly concentrated markets.

An important question is whether PPP funds serve as substitutes for traditional bank loans rather than as complements to them. Karakaplan (2021) showed that especially for small banks, traditional small business loans of up to $1 million went up by an additional dollar of loans for each dollar of PPP loans. In a similar fashion, Berger, Karakaplan, and Roman (2023) found strong positive effects, especially for small banks and small businesses. According to Marsh and Sharma (2020), small banks also lent more money, while Lopez and Spiegel (2021) found that large banks lent more to small businesses and farmers in general. In contrast, Chodorow-Reich, Darmouni, Luck, and Plosser (2022) used Y-14 data from the Federal Reserve and reported that firms that received PPP loans obtained fewer conventional loans over $1 million from very large banks.

There is a growing body of evidence that shows small community banks played an important role in PPP, disbursing outsized amounts of loans (e.g., Levine, Lin, and Xie, 2020; James, Lu, and Sun, 2021). According to various research studies (e.g., Marsh and Sharma, 2020; Karakaplan, 2021; Lopez and Spiegel, 2021) conventional or non-PPP loans are increasing by bank PPP issuers, with the exception of large loans from large banks (Chodorow-Reich, Darmouni, Luck, and Plosser, 2022). A number of studies highlight the importance of community banks (e.g., Levine, Lin, and Xie, 2020; Marsh and Sharma, 2020; James, Lu, and Sun, 2021). Other studies found that banks often followed the policy suggestion of prioritizing small firms with existing bank relationships as opposed to new businesses (e.g., Amiram and Rabetti, 2020; Bartik, Cullen, Glaeser, Luca, Stanton, and Sunderam, 2020; Glancy, Gross, and Ionescu, 2020; Li and Strahan, 2021; Balyuk, Prabhala, and Puri, 2022) or with connections to bank officials, which suggests potential bias and favoritism (e.g., Duchin, Martin, Michaely, and Wang, 2022). Small businesses with prior banking relationships or deposit accounts with the banks were advertised as being prioritized or being offered PPP funds exclusively. There is some evidence in the press and research suggesting minority-owned small businesses without these relationships may have received less aid (e.g., Atkins, Cook, and Seamans, 2022).

Ballew, Nicoletti, and Stuber (2022) analyzed the effects of PPP on banks' risk aversion and if the shift to the current expected credit loss (CECL) model moderates this effect. They found that there was greater risk-taking outside of PPP and showed that this effect is more concentrated in banks not early adopting CECL and banks with timelier pre-PPP loan loss provisions, meaning that timelier loan recognition constrains risk-taking incentives. Their findings provide insight into the indirect effects of PPP and other stimulus programs of government administered through banks and the role of accounting in constraining bank risk-taking.

Two papers look at the role that the Federal Reserve's Paycheck Protection Program Liquidity Facility (PPPLF) played in helping banks actively participate in PPP. Kowalik and Schueller (2022) showed that despite a huge increase in bank deposits after the outbreak of the pandemic, US banks financed 15% of all PPP loans using the PPPLF. An average bank that went to the PPPLF issued significantly more PPP loans. Banks using PPPLF to make PPP loans were often less profitable, riskier, with higher deposit funding costs, and less well-capitalized than an average bank that did not use the PPPLF. Finally, the profitability of the banks using the PPPLF improved significantly during the pandemic compared to other banks. Hence, weaker banks may have used the PPP and the PPPLF programs to shore up their financial health in addition to using the PPPLF as a sole source of liquidity to improve PPP participation.

Anbil, Carlson, and Styczynski (2021) used a measure of banks' familiarity with the operation of the Federal Reserve's discount window as an instrument for PPPLF participation and also found that PPPLF boosted bank PPP lending. On average, commercial banks that used the PPPLF extended over twice as many PPP loans, relative to their total assets, as banks that did not use the PPPLF. They also documented that the availability of the facility as a backstop source of funds may also have supported bank PPP lending, especially for larger banks.

11.2.4 Effects on financial markets

Erel and Liebersohn (2020) investigated FinTech's reaction to the financial services demand produced by the PPP's implementation. They documented that FinTech is disproportionately used in ZIP codes with fewer bank branches, lower incomes, and a greater minority population, as well as in industries with limited ex ante small-business loans, according to our findings. In areas where the economic effects of the COVID-19 epidemic were more severe, FinTech's role in PPP provision is likewise larger. They estimated that increased PPP provision by traditional banks produces statistically significant but economically little substitution away from FinTechs, showing that FinTech primarily extends rather than distributes the total supply of financial services.

Gompers, Kaplan, and Mukharlyamov (2022) found that smaller PE firms, which likely have smaller portfolio companies under management, were more likely to help their companies access the PPP. They indicated that accessing the PPP program is a nondilutive (from an equity perspective) way to raise cash for portfolio companies and thus preferable to outside equity. Outside equity appears to be an option in only the most severely affected companies. Griffin, Kruger, and Mahajan (2023) looked at criteria including nonregistered firms, numerous enterprises at home addresses, abnormally high implied remuneration per employee, and major anomalies with occupations recorded in another government program in the PPP. These indicators regularly focus on specific FinTech lenders and are cross-verified by seven other indicators. FinTech market share has grown dramatically over time, and questionable lending by FinTechs is four times higher in 2021 than it was at the outset of the program. They presented that the suspicious loans are forgiven at similar rates to other types of loans.

Agarwal, Ambrose, Lopez, and Xiao (2022) focused on the performance of securitized commercial mortgages during the coronavirus pandemic to investigate the larger economic implications of the US federal government's PPP. They presented new evidence on the spillover effects of government interventions during economic downturns. They estimated that the PPP will cut mortgage delinquencies by $28.97 billion in 2020, which is almost half of the average annual CMBS defaults witnessed during the Great Financial Crisis. PPP funding targeted companies in regions most hit by COVID-19, where banks outperformed in offering PPP loans, and mortgages on retail and accommodation buildings had the largest benefits. Small company PPP support thereby alleviated economic pain outside the labor market.

Cororaton and Rosen (2021) tracked the results of PPP borrowers and all PPP-eligible enterprises. In particular, they looked at stock market reactions to PPP borrowing and compared profitability, balance sheets, and employment in the second half of 2020. These findings give crucial information into investors' perspectives and business circumstances that may not have been visible ex ante. PPP investors began to regard the announcement of a PPP loan as a negative indicator of business value, according to data. This data shows that borrowing revealed some underlying weakness when larger and seemingly stronger enterprises repaid their PPP loans. They also found that borrowers were more likely than nonborrowers to have negative profits and to suffer slower asset and staff development. Differential outcomes do not suggest causal impacts of the PPP since such an analysis would need a valid counterfactual for borrowers, which they do not have. They also do not presume that the group of PPP-eligible nonborrowers is the best control group from which to derive causality. Rather, their data merely demonstrate that businesses who borrowed from the PPP were more badly affected by the epidemic, which is consistent with the negative announced return on a PPP loan.

Balyuk, Prabhala, and Puri (2022) investigated the implications of PPP on stock market value. They provided three estimates: one for all PPP applicants, another for those who declare PPP in 8-Ks, and a third that excludes penny companies. The PPP abnormal returns for the entire sample are about 1.1%. For companies that announce PPP through 8-Ks, the estimates rise to around 1.6%. This rise is unsurprising, given that 10-Qs and 10-Ks contain other data and are thus less accurate at detecting PPP data. When penny stocks are excluded, the coefficients are somewhat higher, but the standard errors are unaffected. For the subset of larger applications, the announcement impacts are slightly stronger. In general, there is minimal evidence that PPP is harmful to shareholders. In reality, it suggests that PPP adoption increases share prices.

Using PPP loans issued to about 3000 investment advice businesses registered with the US Securities and Exchange Commission, Beggs and Harvison (2022) explored the type and scope of misuse in the PPP. According to the statistics, PPP misuse was rather common, as around 25% of enterprises receiving PPP loans said in their loan application that they would keep more positions than they revealed in their most recent regulatory filing. This study shows that an existing model of investment adviser fraud accurately predicts the most severe PPP loans at a rate that is comparable to real fraud occurrences. Investment advisers who took advantage of the program were far more likely to reveal a history of prior fraud and other legal and/or regulatory violations. Beggs and Harvison estimated that more than 6% of the $590 million in PPP money received by SEC-registered investment advisors was overallocated to entities abusing the Program.

Aman-Rana, Gingerich, and Sukhtankar (2022) however, studied screenings during the PPP program. They analyzed 11.5 million cases and found that subsets who were under screening, applied for smaller PPP amounts, as opposed who were not screened. Researchers estimated that over $750 million was saved during the PPP, despite major criticisms of the program.

11.2.5 Effects on local economies

As discussed above, the extant evidence on the effects of PPP on households and nonfinancial firms suggests a number of positive effects in terms of funds allocated that benefited both groups, which would also clearly benefit local economies. However, as indicated, the research also strongly suggests a number of issues in which the funds may have been allocated in noneconomic ways that would not promote local economies in the most efficient fashion. Here, we highlight some other more direct effects on the local economy.

An additional result in Berger, Freed, Scott, and Zhang (2021) is that smaller businesses in the sectors and geographic regions most affected by COVID-19 benefited most from PPP loans, suggesting that local economies most in need were positively affected. They also found that the economic impacts were very short-lived and temporary, within a month or two only. This could be viewed as an unfavorable economic effect in that PPP funds were wasteful without long-term benefits. It may also be viewed as favorable, helping through the worst economic times and avoiding longer-term entanglements that might otherwise keep unproductive "zombie firms" alive.

Joaquim (2021) presented evidence that counties less affected by COVID-19 and with a larger presence of community banks, as well as larger firms, received loans earlier in the program. This differential timing observed in the data suggests that the various estimates of the effect of the PPP may not represent well the overall effect of the program. He used a stylized model in an attempt to provide a unifying explanation across different phases of PPP or an overall effect of the program. He explained that firms of different sizes that were affected differently by COVID-19 received PPP loans at different moments in time. Hence, depending on variation in PPP happens, this will also determine the set of compliers, which is different from the overall set of firms.

Studies that use early variation in PPP allocation tend to find lower treatment effects, while studies that use variation later will generally find higher treatment effects, but only analyzing variation in all phases can provide an estimate of the overall effect.

The effectiveness of the allocation of PPP funds across different local markets and economies is another critical question. Bi and Gulati (2021) indicated that the PPP was not well targeted, as funds did not flow to the markets, sectors, and firms in most need or at most risk, particularly in the early stages. However, this may be due to the trade-off between getting funds to where they are most needed and distributing funds at a rapid pace, the latter being the priority for policymakers in the early stages of the pandemic. In fact, the first two rounds of PPP funding did not require firms to demonstrate hardship or ability to repay the loan but only to certify in good faith that current economic conditions made the loan necessary and qualify by the number of employees. Hubbard and Strain (2020) mentioned that despite being desirable, targeting businesses based on need would not have been feasible in the very beginning. Later stages added requirements for firms to demonstrate the need to qualify for a second loan, likely to ensure funds go mostly to more vulnerable firms.

Liu and Volker (2020) looked at whether the geographical distribution of PPP loans approved per number of small businesses matches that of COVID-19 cases in each US state in the first wave of the PPP program. The number of PPP loans per state translated one-to-one to the number of small businesses receiving loans, since PPP loans are capped at one per business. They found that some of the hardest hit areas such as New York, New Jersey, Michigan, and Pennsylvania were getting fewer loans than some mountain and Midwest states on a per-small-business basis. In New York, the epicenter of the coronavirus in the US, less than 20% of small businesses have been approved to receive PPP loans. In contrast, more than 55% of small businesses in Nebraska were expecting PPP funding. They showed a negative relationship between COVID-19 cases per capita and the share of small firms getting PPP funding, suggesting credit may have been misallocated in the first stage of the program. Birdthistle and Silver (2021) also pointed to widespread public criticism as some loans may have been awarded to borrowers who needed them less such as wealthy celebrities such as Kanye West, politically connected donors such as the Kushner family, and large corporations such as Shake Shack and Ruth's Chris Steak House.

Schweitzer and Borawski (2021) investigated the degree to which PPP loans reached small businesses in low- and moderate-income (LMI) local communities, given that the SBA announced in October 2020 that "27% of the PPP loan dollars were made in low- and moderate-income communities which is in proportion to the percentage of the population in these areas." The authors assessed the program's reach in a few ways and focus on the number of loans, rather than the amount of funds, that went to different areas in order to capture the program's impact on businesses with fewer than 50 employees, the vast majority of small businesses. They found considerable unevenness in the reach of the PPP loan program. While PPP loans were unevenly provided by income level, they found that PPP loans had higher coverage rates in LMI communities than conventional loans to small businesses.

11.3 Empirical evidence on the economic and financial effects of TARP

As discussed, we limit our review of the empirical TARP research to mitigate distraction from the focus on the COVID-19 crisis. We specifically cover research findings on the effects of TARP on households, nonfinancial firms, banks, financial markets, and local economies, but neglect the bulk of the indirect evidence, such as the many studies of whether TARP resulted in additional bank lending. Thus, we include direct evidence on the welfare of the borrowers, rather than the indirect evidence of whether they obtained more or less credit. For more complete reviews of empirical research on TARP, see surveys by Calomiris and Khan (2015), Berger (2018), Roman (2019), and Berger and Roman (2020).

The empirical research on TARP overall suggests that the program was successful in reaching both of its two main ultimate goals or outcomes of reducing systemic risk and boosting the real economy. In some cases, these benefits are limited to the short term during the heart of the GFC when the help was most needed. TARP also raises longer-term issues, such as the moral hazard effects of financial aid. During crises such as the GFC, excessive risk-taking due to moral hazard incentives or other causes is less problematic because most parties are trying to curtail their risks, but such problems reappear after time passes into the following boom period.

In fact, Del Viva, Kasanen, Saunders, and Trigeorgis (2021) studied how the US government's TARP program affected the risk tolerance and moral hazard behaviors of the US banks during the Global Financial Crisis. They found that TARP increases the probability of moral hazard occurring and was able to spot a pattern that was happening both before and after GFC in SIFI's, which allowed them to come up with certain important policy implications regarding government actions during the crisis, such as Global Financial Crisis of 2008.

Despite the short-term benefits of TARP, the research also suggests some significant social costs. The evidence shown below is consistent with the aggravation of moral hazard incentives, with banks shifting into riskier loans after receiving TARP funds and higher systemic risk contributions in the longer run. Although we do not allocate space for these below, many studies also found that political connections influenced funds distribution (e.g., Duchin and Sosyura, 2012, 2014; Blau, Brough, and Thomas, 2013; Li, 2013; Berger and Roman, 2015, 2017; Berger, Makaew, and Roman, 2019; Chavaz and Rose, 2019; Berger, Roman, and Sedunov, 2020). Thus, TARP funds may have given inefficient and unfair competitive advantages to some banks, consistent with some of the PPP results. Results on other important issues, such as whether TARP weakened or strengthened market discipline, are more mixed and not reviewed in detail here (e.g., Forssbæck and Nielsen, 2015; Berger, Lamers, Roman, and Schoors, 2023).

11.3.1 Effects on households

Most of the research suggests that households benefited from TARP. Berger and Roman (2017) found that TARP improved economic conditions for households by boosting net job creation, net hiring establishments, and reducing both business and personal bankruptcies. Although some of these are technically business outcomes, rather than household outcomes, it may be reasonably concluded that households are also better off when these variables show improvements. Household members are those with the jobs and being hired on the labor side and are also often significantly affected on the ownership side because many small businesses are proprietorships and partnerships in which personal and business finances are inexorably intertwined. Contreras, Delis, Ghosh, and Hasan (2022) and Contreras, Ghosh, and Kong (2021) also found reduced unfavorable real economic impacts of bank failures, such as on net business formation and net job creation that did occur.

However, Berger, Epouhe, and Roman (2022) found that subprime consumer debt increased in local markets with the presence of more TARP bank, essentially the opposite of the PPP finding noted above. This appears to be driven primarily by an increase in credit supply to these subprime borrowers, at odds with the fact that excessive provision of mortgage credit was at the heart of the GFC itself. Complementing the Berger, Epouhe, and Roman (2022) results, Duchin and Sosyura (2014) found that relative to banks that were denied federal assistance, approved banks increased their origination rates on riskier mortgage applications (measured by the loan-to-income ratio) by 5.4 percentage points.

The subprime household debt differences between TARP and PPP programs can be attributed to the difference in findings to structures of the programs as Berger, Epouhe, and Roman (2022) pointed out. PPP likely resulted in much bigger positive income shocks for subprime consumers that helped them repay their debts, given the strings attached to spending most of the funds on small business payrolls. TARP may have had more substitution effects, as banks were free to offer more high interest rate debt to subprime borrowers. The increased subprime debt is not unambiguously good or bad from a social view, given that it represents more opportunities for financial inclusion, but also is partially responsible for the GFC.

11.3.2 Effects on nonfinancial firms

The research just summarized suggests favorable effects for small businesses for which market measures of benefits are not easily available. However, the findings for the observable market values of publicly traded nonfinancial corporations with relationships with TARP banks are mixed. Norden, Roosenboom, and Wang's (2013) findings suggest positive abnormal stock returns for these firms, while Lin, Liu, and Srinivasan (2017) found significant stock market valuation losses.

11.3.3 Effects on banks

A number of research studies use stock market price data in various ways and consistently value increases associated with TARP announcements and funding. The results of these studies vary in terms of which banks benefited most or whether the value increases were primarily in common vs preferred stock (e.g., Veronesi and Zingales, 2010; Bayazitova and Shivdasani, 2012; Kim and Stock, 2012; Farruggio, Michalak, and Uhde, 2013; Zanzalari, 2014).

Others focus on the competitive advantages of TARP banks relative to others. Berger and Roman (2015) found such advantages both in terms of local market asset shares and higher market power measured by the Lerner Index. They also found that these benefits are concentrated in banks that repaid TARP funds early, which is not surprising, given that repayment early is only allowed for banks that were successful in rebuilding their capital ratios. Some of these results are corroborated by Cao-Alvira and Núñez-Torres (2019), but not the early repayment findings. Studies by Hakenes and Schnabel (2010) and Koetter and Noth (2016) also suggest some benefits for other banks.

The research literature additionally suggests the important effects of TARP on bank risks. Studies examine individual bank leverage risks and portfolio risks, and their contributions to systemic risk, the key to the ultimate success of the program.

Leverage risks may be measured on a market-based or accounting-based basis, and we review studies using both methodologies. However, we limit the accounting-based results to the effects of TARP on common equity ratios, as opposed to regulatory ratios such as Tier 1 capital ratios. Tier 1 and Total regulatory ratios of the Basel Accords are mechanically impacted by the preferred equity injections of TARP that are counted in these ratios. The leverage risk studies tend to all point in the same direction. Berger, Roman, and Sedunov (2020) found that banks that received TARP funds significantly reduced their market-based leverage risk, *LVG* (see Acharya, Pedersen, Philippon, and Richardson, 2017). Duchin and Sosyura (2014), Calabrese, Degl'Innocenti, and Osmetti (2017), and Berger, Roman, and Sedunov (2020) also found reduced leverage risks based on accounting equity capital ratios.

However, the research also suggests that TARP resulted in higher bank portfolio risks, although the evidence is not in complete agreement and sometimes varies by bank size. Most of the TARP studies on lending suggest increased credit supply, particularly for small banks (see Berger and Roman, 2020, Chapter 11, for more details). More on-balance sheet loans and more off-balance sheet loan commitments likely significantly increase the risks of TARP banks' portfolios unless they are very low risk and/or have returns that are negatively correlated with existing loans, which the next evidence presented suggests is not the case.

A number of studies control for the moral hazard effects of TARP by seeing whether TARP banks shifted their credit supplies toward riskier new loans at the extensive margin. Duchin and Sosyura (2014) found that TARP banks approved riskier residential mortgages and riskier large corporate loans, resulting in increased subsequent loan charge-offs. Black and Hazelwood (2013) found mixed results, with riskier new loans for large banks and safer additional credits for small banks, suggesting again that large banks tend to shift into riskier credits, but vice versa for small banks. Berger and Roman (2017) showed that TARP banks switch into commercial real estate lending on- and off-balance sheet, generally the riskiest commercial loans. Other studies found more ex post evidence of risk-shifting, with Chavaz and Rose (2019) finding more nonperforming loans and Agarwal and Zhang (2018) finding more modifications of residential mortgages for TARP banks. At the intensive margin, Berger, Makaew, and Roman (2019) found that TARP banks improved loan contract terms more for riskier borrowers than for safer borrowers, consistent with moral hazard effects.

Some researchers employ more complete measures of individual bank risks. Duchin and Sosyura (2014) found an increased overall risk of individual TARP banks compared to observably similar non-TARP banks using Z-Scores, earnings volatility, stock volatility, and stock market beta. Farruggio, Michalak, and Uhde (2013), Semaan and Drake (2016), and Del Viva, Kasanen, Saunders, and Trigeorgis (2017) also found higher bank risk from TARP using other measures. In contrast, Berger, Roman, and Sedunov (2020) found decreased bank risks based on Merton Expected Default Probability, Z-Score, and Sharpe Ratio.

Turning to the systemic risk issue, Berger, Roman, and Sedunov (2020) gave evidence that TARP banks reduced their contributions to several systemic risk measures relative to non-TARP banks. This finding holds during the heart of GFC, when systemic risk problems were at their peaks. However, these authors also showed that TARP banks likely increased their systemic risk contributions after the crisis, consistent with the other moral hazard evidence. Additional evidence mostly supporting the increased exploitation of moral hazard incentives may be found in the TARP review articles and books noted above.

11.3.4 Effects on financial markets

Many of the financial market effects of TARP are already covered by the findings above on the effects of the program on nonfinancial firm and bank stock market values, bank contributions to systemic risk, and the real economic outcomes that should be reflected in financial market values. Here, we simply add findings on other measures of market risks.

Coffey, Hrung, and Sarkar (2009) found declines in covered interest rate parity deviations after the TARP announcement, consistent with reduced risks. Nguyen and Enomoto (2009) and Huerta, Perez-Liston, and Jackson (2011) found consistent market calming effects using VIX and other measures.

11.3.5   Effects on local economies

The evidence discussed above suggests that TARP provided significant benefits to both households and nonfinancial firms in the vicinity of banks receiving TARP funds. These include more net job creation and net hiring establishments, and fewer business and personal bankruptcies (Berger and Roman, 2017), as well as milder consequences of bank failures in terms of net business formation and net job creation (Contreras, Ghosh, and Kong, 2021; Contreras, Delis, Ghosh, and Hasan, 2022). These findings strongly suggest positive local economic benefits from TARP in the short term.

However, other findings may be suggestive of the risks of long-term negative local economic consequences. Results suggest that local subprime borrowers significantly increased their debt (Berger, Epouhe, and Roman, 2022) and riskier mortgaged applications were approved (Duchin and Sosyura, 2014). Other findings consistent with long-term risk-taking consistent with moral hazard incentives in Duchin and Sosyura (2014), Berger and Roman (2017), Agarwal and Zhang (2018), Berger, Makaew, and Roman (2019), Chavaz and Rose (2019) and Berger, Roman, and Sedunov (2020) suggest that both local and national economies may have been endangered by TARP in the long term.

References

Acharya, V. V., Pedersen, L. H., Philippon, T., and Richardson, M. (2017). Measuring systemic risk. *Review of Financial Studies, 30*, 2–47.

Agarwal, S., Ambrose, B. W., Lopez, L. A., and Xiao, X. (2022). *Did the paycheck protection program help small businesses? Evidence from commercial mortgage-backed securities.* Available at: SSRN 3674960.

Agarwal, S., and Zhang, Y. (2018). Effects of government bailouts on mortgage modification. *Journal of Banking and Finance, 93*, 54–70.

Aman-Rana, S., Gingerich, D., and Sukhtankar, S. (2022). *Screen now, save later? The trade-off between administrative ordeals and fraud.* Available at: SSRN 4193659.

Amiram, D., and Rabetti, D. (2020). *The relevance of relationship lending in times of crisis.* Available at: SSRN 3701587.

Anbil, S., Carlson, M. A., and Styczynski, M.-F. (2021). *The effect of the PPPLF on PPP lending by commercial banks.* FEDS Working Paper No. 2021-030.

Atkins, R., Cook, L. D., and Seamans, R. (2022). Discrimination in lending? Evidence from the paycheck protection program. *Small Business Economics, 58*, 843–865.

Autor, D., Cho, D., Crane, L. D., Goldar, M., Lutz, B., Montes, J. K., Peterman, W. B., Ratner, D. D., Vallenas, D. V., and Yildirmaz, A. (2022). The $800 billion paycheck protection program: Where did the money go and why did it go there? *The Journal of Economic Perspectives, 36*(2), 55–80.

Autor, D., Cho, D., Crane, L. D., Goldar, M., Lutz, B., Montes, J., Peterman, W. B., Ratner, D., Villar, D., and Yildirmaz, A. (2022). An evaluation of the paycheck protection program using administrative payroll microdata. *Journal of Public Economics, 211*, 104664.

Ballew, H. B., Nicoletti, A., and Stuber, S. B. (2022). The effect of the paycheck protection program and financial reporting standards on bank risk-taking. *Management Science, 68*, 2363–2371.

Balyuk, T., Prabhala, N. R., and Puri, M. (2021). *Indirect costs of government aid and intermediary supply effects: Lessons from the paycheck protection program.* Available at: SSRN 3717259.

Barraza, S., Rossi, M., and Yeager, T. J. (2020). *The short-term effect of the paycheck protection program on unemployment.* Available at: SSRN 3667431.

Bartik, A. W., Cullen, Z. B., Glaeser, E. L., Luca, M., Stanton, C. T., and Sunderam, A. (2020). *The targeting and impact of paycheck protection program loans to small businesses.* National Bureau of Economic Research Working Paper No. w27623.

Bartlett, R. P., III, and Morse, A. (2020). *Small business survival capabilities and policy effectiveness: Evidence from Oakland.* National Bureau of Economic Research Working Paper No. w27629.

Battisto, J., Godin, N. Y., Kramer, C., and Sarkar, A. (2021). *Who benefited from PPP loans by fintech lenders?* Liberty Street Economics 20210527c. Federal Reserve Bank of New York.

Bayazitova, D., and Shivdasani, A. (2012). Assessing tarp. *Review of Financial Studies, 25,* 377–407.

Beggs, W., and Harvison, T. (2022). Fraud and abuse in the paycheck protection program? Evidence from investment advisory firms. *Journal of Banking & Finance.* 106444.

Berger, A. N. (2018). The benefits and costs of the TARP bailouts: A critical assessment. *Quarterly Journal of Finance, 8,* 1850011.

Berger, A. N., Epouhe, O., and Roman, R. A. (2022). A tale of two bailouts: Effects of TARP and PPP on subprime consumer debt. *SSRN Electronic Journal.*

Berger, A. N., Freed, P. G., Scott, J. A., and Zhang, S. (2021). *The paycheck protection program (PPP) from the small business perspective: Did the PPP help alleviate financial and economic constraints?* Available at: SSRN 3908707.

Berger, A. N., Karakaplan, M., and Roman, R. A. (2023). Whose bailout is it anyway? The roles of politics in PPP bailouts of small businesses vs. banks. *Journal of Financial Intermediation,* Forthcoming.

Berger, A. N., Lamers, M., Roman, R. A., and Schoors, K. J. (2023). Supply and demand effects of bank bailouts: Depositors need not apply and need not run. *Journal of Money, Credit and Banking* (Forthcoming).

Berger, A. N., Makaew, T., and Roman, R. A. (2019). Do business borrowers benefit from bank bailouts?: The effects of TARP on loan contract terms. *Financial Management, 48,* 575–639.

Berger, A. N., and Roman, R. A. (2015). Did TARP banks get competitive advantages? *Journal of Financial and Quantitative Analysis, 50,* 1199–1236.

Berger, A. N., and Roman, R. A. (2017). Did saving wall street really save main street? The real effects of TARP on local economic conditions. *Journal of Financial and Quantitative Analysis, 52,* 1827–1867.

Berger, A. N., and Roman, R. A. (2020). *TARP and other bank bailouts and bail-ins around the world: Connecting wall street, main street, and the financial system.* Academic Press.

Berger, A. N., Roman, R. A., and Sedunov, J. (2020). Did TARP reduce or increase systemic risk? The effects of government aid on financial system stability. *Journal of Financial Intermediation, 43,* 100810.

Bi, H., and Gulati, C. (2021). Fiscal relief during the COVID-19 pandemic. *Econometric Reviews, 106,* 5–24.

Birdthistle, W. A., and Silver, J. (2021). Funding crises: An empirical study of the paycheck protection program. *Buffalo Law Review, 69,* 1541.

Black, L. K., and Hazelwood, L. N. (2013). The effect of TARP on bank risk-taking. *Journal of Financial Stability, 9,* 790–803.

Blau, B. M., Brough, T. J., and Thomas, D. W. (2013). Corporate lobbying, political connections, and the bailout of banks. *Journal of Banking & Finance, 37,* 3007–3017.

Bracht, B. (2022). Partnership taxation and the paycheck protection program: Understanding existing guidance and how to resolve outstanding issues. *The Business, Entrepreneurship & Tax Law Review, 6*(1), 153.

Calabrese, R., Degl'Innocenti, M., and Osmetti, S. A. (2017). The effectiveness of TARP-CPP on the US banking industry: A new copula-based approach. *European Journal of Operational Research, 256,* 1029–1037.

Calem, P., and Freedman, A. (2020). *Neighborhood demographics and the allocation of paycheck protection program funds.* Available at: SSRN 3776794.

Calomiris, C. W., and Khan, U. (2015). An assessment of TARP assistance to financial institutions. *The Journal of Economic Perspectives, 29,* 53–80.

Cao-Alvira, J. J., and Núñez-Torres, A. (2019). On TARP and agency securitization. *International Finance, 22,* 186–200.

Chavaz, M., and Rose, A. K. (2019). Political borders and bank lending in post-crisis America. *Review of Finance, 23,* 935–959.

Chernenko, S., Kaplan, N., Sarkar, A., and Scharfstein, D. S. (2022). *Applications or approvals: What drives racial disparities in the paycheck protection program?* Available at: SSRN 4281960.

Chernenko, S., and Scharfstein, D. S. (2022). *Racial disparities in the paycheck protection program.* Available at: SSRN 3907575.

Chetty, R., Friedman, J., and Stepner, M. (2023). The economic impacts of COVID-19: Evidence from a new public database built using private sector data. *Quarterly Journal of Economics.* Forthcoming.

Chodorow-Reich, G., Darmouni, O., Luck, S., and Plosser, M. C. (2022). Bank liquidity provision across the firm size distribution. *Journal of Financial Economics, 144,* 908–932.

Choi, S. (2014). *Executive compensation in the banking industry and systemic risk.* (Thesis). Retrieved from: https://scholarcommons.sc.edu/etd/2635.

Coffey, N., Hrung, W. B., and Sarkar, A. (2009). *Capital constraints, counterparty risk, and deviations from covered interest rate parity.* FRB of New York staff report.

Cole, A. (2022). *The impact of the paycheck protection program on (really) small businesses.* Available at: SSRN 3730268.

Contreras, S., Delis, M. D., Ghosh, A., and Hasan, I. (2022). Bank failures, local business dynamics, and government policy. *Small Business Economics, 58,* 1823–1851.

Contreras, S., Ghosh, A., and Kong, J. H. (2021). Financial crisis, bank failures and corporate innovation. *Journal of Banking & Finance, 129,* 106161.

Cororaton, A., and Rosen, S. (2021). Public firm borrowers of the US paycheck protection program. *Review of Corporate Finance Studies, 10,* 641–693.

Del Viva, L., Kasanen, E., Saunders, A., and Trigeorgis, L. (2017). *Bank lottery behavior and regulatory bailouts.* Available at: SSRN 2944252.

Del Viva, L., Kasanen, E., Saunders, A., and Trigeorgis, L. (2021). US government TARP bailout and bank lottery behavior. *Journal of Corporate Finance, 66,* 101777.

Doniger, C., and Kay, B. S. (2021). *Ten days late and billions of dollars short: The employment effects of delays in paycheck protection program financing.* Available at: SSRN 3747223.

Duchin, R., and Hackney, J. (2021). Buying the vote? The economics of electoral politics and small-business loans. *Journal of Financial and Quantitative Analysis, 56,* 2439–2473.

Duchin, R., Martin, X., Michaely, R., and Wang, H. (2022). Concierge treatment from banks: Evidence from the paycheck protection program. *Journal of Corporate Finance, 72,* 102124.

Duchin, R., and Sosyura, D. (2012). The politics of government investment. *Journal of Financial Economics, 106,* 24–48.

Duchin, R., and Sosyura, D. (2014). Safer ratios, riskier portfolios: Banks' response to government aid. *Journal of Financial Economics, 113,* 1–28.

Elenev, V., Landvoigt, T., and Van Nieuwerburgh, S. (2022). Can the COVID bailouts save the economy? *Economic Policy, 37,* 277–330

Erel, I., and Liebersohn, J. (2020). *Does FinTech substitute for banks? Evidence from the paycheck protection program.* National Bureau of Economic Research.

Fairlie, R., and Fossen, F. M. (2022). Did the paycheck protection program and economic injury disaster loan program get disbursed to minority communities in the early stages of COVID-19? *Small Business Economics, 58,* 829–842.

Farruggio, C., Michalak, T. C., and Uhde, A. (2013). The light and dark side of TARP. *Journal of Banking & Finance, 37,* 2586–2604.

Faulkender, M. W., Jackman, R., and Miran, S. (2023). *The job preservation effects of paycheck protection program loans.* Available at: SSRN 3767509.

Federal Reserve System. (2021). *Small business credit survey. 2021 Report on employer firms.* Available at: https://www.fedsmallbusiness.org/survey/2021/report-on-employer-firms.

Finlay, K., Mueller-Smith, M., and Street, B. (2020). *Criminal disqualifications in the paycheck protection program.* Ann Arbor 1001, 48106-1248.

Flanagan, T., and Purnanandam, A. (2023). *Did banks pay 'fair' returns to taxpayers on TARP?* Available at: SSRN 3595763.

Forssbæck, J., and Nielsen, C. Y. (2015). *TARP and market discipline: Evidence on the moral hazard effects of bank recapitalizations.* Available at: SSRN 2674544.

García, R. E., and Darity, W. A., Jr. (2021). Self-reporting race in small business loans: A game-theoretic analysis of evidence from PPP loans in Durham, NC. In *AEA papers and proceedings*.

Glancy, D., Gross, M., and Ionescu, A. F. (2020). *How did banks fund C&I drawdowns at the onset of the COVID-19 crisis?* FEDS Notes 2020-07-31-1.

Gompers, P. A., Kaplan, S. N., and Mukharlyamov, V. (2022). Private equity and COVID-19. *Journal of Financial Intermediation, 51*, 100968.

Granja, J., Makridis, C., Yannelis, C., and Zwick, E. (2022). *Did the paycheck protection program hit the target?*. National Bureau of Economic Research.

Griffin, J. M., Kruger, S., and Mahajan, P. (2023). Did FinTech lenders facilitate PPP fraud? *Journal of Finance, 78*, 1777–1827.

Hakenes, H., and Schnabel, I. (2010). Banks without parachutes: Competitive effects of government bail-out policies. *Journal of Financial Stability, 6*, 156–168.

Howell, S., Kuchler, T., Snitkof, D., Stroebel, J., and Wong, J. (2021). *Racial disparities in access to small business credit: Evidence from the paycheck protection program*. CEPR Discussion Paper No. DP16623.

Hubbard, R. G., and Strain, M. R. (2020). *Has the paycheck protection program succeeded? (No. w28032)*. National Bureau of Economic Research.

Huerta, D., Perez-Liston, D., and Jackson, D. (2011). The impact of TARP bailouts on stock market volatility and investor fear. *Banking and Finance Review, 3*(1). Retrieved from chrome-extension://efaidnbmnnnibpcajpcglclefindmkaj/http://ccsu.financect.net/.

Humphries, J. E., Neilson, C., and Ulyssea, G. (2020). The evolving impacts of COVID-19 on small businesses since the CARES Act. *SSRN Electronic Journal*.

Igan, D., Lambert, T., and Mishra, P. (2021). *The politics of the paycheck protection program*. Available at: SSRN.

James, C., Lu, J., and Sun, Y. (2021). Time is money: Real effects of relationship lending in a crisis. *Journal of Banking & Finance, 133*, 106283.

Joaquim, G. (2021). *Allocation and employment effect of the paycheck protection program*. Federal Reserve Bank of Boston Research Paper Series Current Policy Perspectives Paper No. 93541.

Joaquim, G., and Netto, F. (2021a). *Bank incentives and the impact of the paycheck protection program*. Available at: SSRN 3704518.

Joaquim, G., and Netto, F. (2021b). *Optimal allocation of relief funds: The case of the paycheck protection program*. Available at: SSRN 3939109.

Joaquim, G., and Wang, J. C. (2022). *What do 25 million records of small businesses say about the effects of the PPP?* FRB of Boston Working Paper No. 22–23.

Karakaplan, M. U. (2021). This time is really different: The multiplier effect of the paycheck protection program (PPP) on small business bank loans. *Journal of Banking & Finance, 133*, 106223.

Kickul, J., Griffiths, M. D., Robb, C. C., and Gundry, L. (2021). All for one? The paycheck protection program distribution disparity. *Journal of Entrepreneurship and Public Policy, 10*, 323–335.

Kim, D. H., and Stock, D. (2012). Impact of the TARP financing choice on existing preferred stock. *Journal of Corporate Finance, 18*, 1121–1142.

Koetter, M., and Noth, F. (2016). Did TARP distort competition among sound unsupported banks? *Economic Inquiry, 54*, 994–1020.

Kowalik, M., and Schueller, S. (2022). *How did the banks finance PPP loans in 2020?* Federal Reserve Bank of Boston Working Paper.

Lederer, A., and Oros, S. (2020). *Lending discrimination within the paycheck protection program*. National Community Reinvestment Coalition.

Lee, S. (2023). Banking infrastructure and the Paycheck Protection Program during the Covid-19 pandemic. *Regional Studies, 57*(1), 84–96.

Levine, R., Lin, C., and Xie, W. (2020). *Local financial structure and economic resilience*. Available at: SSRN 3755560.

Li, L. (2013). TARP funds distribution and bank loan supply. *Journal of Banking & Finance, 37*, 4777–4792.

Li, L., and Strahan, P. E. (2021). Who supplies PPP loans (and does it matter)? Banks, relationships, and the COVID crisis. *Journal of Financial and Quantitative Analysis, 56,* 2411–2438.

Lin, Y., Liu, X., and Srinivasan, A. (2017). *Unintended consequences of government bailouts: Evidence from bank-dependent borrowers of large banks.* Available at: SSRN 3062484.

Liu, H., and Volker, D. (2020). *Where have the paycheck protection loans gone so far? (No. 20200506).* Federal Reserve Bank of New York.

Lopez, J. A., and Spiegel, M. M. (2021). *Small business lending under the PPP and PPPLF programs.* Federal Reserve Bank of San Francisco.

Marsh, W. B., and Sharma, P. (2020). *PPP raised community bank revenue but lowered profitability.* Federal Reserve Bank of Kansas City, Economic Bulletin. December.

Marsh, W. B., and Sharma, P. (2021). *Government loan guarantees during a crisis: The effect of the PPP on bank lending and profitability.* Federal Reserve Bank of Kansas City working paper.

Mukherjee, T., and Pana, E. (2018). The distribution of the Capital Purchase Program funds: Evidence from bank internal capital markets. *Financial Markets, Institutions & Instruments, 27*(4), 125–143.

National Federation of Independent Business. (2020). *COVID-19 small business survey* (accessed August 17–18, 2020). Available at: chrome-extension://efaidnbmnnnibpcajpcglclefindmkaj/https://assets.nfib.com/nfibcom/Covid-19-11-Questionnaire-and-Write-up-FINAL.pdf.

Nguyen, A. P., and Enomoto, C. E. (2009). The troubled asset relief program (TARP) and the financial crisis of 2007–2008. *Journal of Business and Economics Research (JBER), 7*(12). Retrieved from: https://www.clutejournals.com/index.php/JBER/article/view/2369.

Norden, L., Roosenboom, P., and Wang, T. (2013). The impact of government intervention in banks on corporate borrowers' stock returns. *Journal of Financial and Quantitative Analysis, 48,* 1635–1662.

Ong, P., González, S., Domínguez-Villegas, R., Ong, J., and Pech, C. (2021). *Disparities in the distribution of Paycheck Protection Program funds in California's congressional districts.* UCLA Center for Neighborhood Knowledge. Retrieved from: https://escholarship.org/uc/item/2wg7c3b6.

Paletta, D., Hilsenrath, J., and Solomon, D. (2008). At moment of truth, US forced big bankers to blink. *Wall Street Journal,* October 15, 2008. Retrieved from: https://www.wsj.com/articles/SB122402486344034247.

Roman, R. A. (2019). Bank bailouts and bail-ins. In *The Oxford handbook of banking* (3rd ed., pp. 630–684). Retrieved from: https://academic.oup.com/edited-volume/34288/chapter-abstract/290682789?redirectedFrom=fulltext (Chapter 20).

Sabasteanski, N., Brooks, J., and Chandler, T. (2021). Saving lives and livelihoods: The paycheck protection program and its efficacy. *Economia, 22,* 278–290.

Şahin, A., and Tasci, M. (2022). *The great resignation and the paycheck protection program.* Economic Commentary (2022-15).

Schweitzer, M. E., and Borawski, G. (2021). *How well did PPP loans reach low-and moderate-income communities?* Economic Commentary.

Semaan, E., and Drake, P. P. (2016). TARP and the long-term perception of risk. *Journal of Banking & Finance, 68,* 216–235.

Solomon, D., and Enrich, D. (2008). Devil is in bailout's details. *The Wall Street Journal,* October 15, 2008. Retrieved from: https://www.wsj.com/articles/SB122398468353632299.

Spatt, C. S. (2020). A tale of two crises: The 2008 mortgage meltdown and the 2020 COVID-19 crisis. *Review of Asset Pricing Studies, 10,* 759–790.

Veronesi, P., and Zingales, L. (2010). Paulson's gift. *Journal of Financial Economics, 97,* 339–368.

Zanzalari, D. (2014). *Does bank size matter? Investor reactions to TARP,* Working Paper, Clemson University.

Chapter 12

Other policy reactions to the COVID-19 crisis in the US and their effects on local economies, households, nonfinancial firms, banks, and financial markets

Chapter outline

Abstract

This chapter assesses research and data on other US COVID-19 policies, including CARES Act provisions other than PPP and their effects on the real economy, banking sector, and financial markets. We provide significant details about the different programs and the research studies evaluating their economic effects. These programs cost trillions of dollars with many provisions to help consumers, employees, and businesses cope with the economic effects of the crisis. Some were temporary and confined to the heart of the crisis, and other continued into the recovery and aftermath. While the research coverage is largely limited to the main part of the crisis, the findings are largely consistent with the main conclusions of our book that policies have the best effects if they are large in magnitude and near the start of a crisis.

Keywords: COVID-19, CARES Act, Federal Reserve, Debt purchase program, Households, Nonfinancial firms, Banks, Financial markets

The Economic and Financial Impacts of the COVID-19 Crisis Around the World
https://doi.org/10.1016/B978-0-443-19162-6.00027-X
Copyright © 2024 Elsevier Inc. All rights reserved.

This chapter assesses research and data on policy reactions to the COVID-19 crisis in the US other than the Paycheck Protection Program (PPP) covered in Chapter 11. We discuss their effects on the real economy, banking sector, and financial markets, and provide details about the different programs and the research studies evaluating their economic effects.

To clarify, the PPP was part of the government actions taken through relief bills such as the 335-page Coronavirus Aid, Relief, and Economic Security (CARES) Act, which authorized roughly $2.2 trillion of relief spending on March 27, 2020, containing provisions to help consumers, employees, and businesses cope with the economic effects of the crisis. We cover CARES Act provisions other than PPP here, as well as many other US policies including Federal Reserve actions.

Many of the policy measures were temporary, having various expiration dates for different programs written into the statutes. Nonetheless, these programs were often renewed and replaced all the way into the aftermath, and some are still underway. For example, due to fear that expiration of the CARES Act could adversely affect a large number of economic agents, its provisions were often extended through other subsequent programs, such as the Coronavirus Response and Relief Supplemental Appropriations (CRRSA) Act of 2021, which allocated $935 billion in December 2020; and the American Rescue Plan (ARP), which authorized $1.9 trillion in March 2021. Together, these relief programs are fiscal policy responses to a recession which are way larger than anything we have seen before in terms of size, design, and speed of implementation.

12.1 CARES Act provisions other than PPP

12.1.1 CARES Act forbearance programs and forbearance moratorium

Crises, whether originated in the banking sector such as the GFC or the health and real sector such as the COVID-19 crisis, often result in significant household financial distress, which when severe, can further endanger other parts of the economy (e.g., Mian and Sufi, 2009; Keys, Piskorski, Seru, and Vig, 2013; Duca, Popoyan, and Wachter, 2019; Cherry, Jiang, Matvos, Piskorski, and Seru, 2022). Another related issue is that of a possible increase in inequality during crises as more vulnerable (low-income and low-credit score) consumers and minorities are more affected, and creditors may not treat the same similarly situated borrowers, resulting in increased fair lending risk. One typical remedy for household distress for all consumers is providing forbearance assistance on various loans that the household owes. Forbearance was widely available to households via the CARES Act. Below we discuss some of the most important consequences of this and other related policies.

The CARES Act Section 4022 concerns the rights of consumers to forbearance and foreclosure moratorium. A forbearance agreement can take various forms but most often consists of a temporary relief or reduction in a borrower's loan payments for a fixed period of time. However, it is not equivalent to loan forgiveness or even loan modification. The interest still accrues over the forbearance period and the borrower still owes the lender the missed payments after the forbearance period ends. After the period ends, the borrower may have to pay a higher periodic amount or can obtain a loan modification that may make up for some of the missed payments or can turn into a further deferral of payment. To enter forbearance a borrower must typically provide the lender a proof that he/she is experiencing temporary hardship, and the lender must agree to provide this benefit to him/her. Forbearance is routinely used when borrowers are affected by some unexpected mishap such as a natural disaster or were used in other prior crises to address borrower financial distress, but it never reached the magnitudes observed during the COVID-19 crisis.

For mortgage forbearance, the CARES Act Section 4022 instructed lenders to allow borrowers to postpone mortgage payments for up to a year originally (March 27, 2020 to December 31, 2020, plus an extension of another 3 months upon request), which was later extended to 18 months, without borrowers incurring any penalty (forbearance). Borrowers who had mortgages could enroll in forbearance by simple affirmation that they suffered financial hardship caused by COVID-19 and no documentation was required to document this. Such forbearance benefits applied to 1–4 family federally backed mortgage loans which comprised nearly two-thirds of all borrowers and many servicers of mortgages not backed by the federal government also voluntarily provided the same benefits. To alleviate borrower hesitancy to participate in the program, "no fees, penalties, or interest beyond the amounts scheduled or calculated as if the borrower made all contractual payments on time and in full under the terms of the mortgage contract, shall accrue on the borrower's account."

Federally backed mortgage loans are loans purchased by the Government Sponsored Enterprises (GSEs) Fannie Mae and Freddie Mac and loans guaranteed by the Federal Housing Administration (FHA), the Veterans Administration (VA), and the US Department of Agriculture (USDA). The law applies to individual units in both cooperatives and condominiums. As for the terms under which the borrower is expected to repay the forbearance, this varied across agencies. For example, the Federal Home Financing Agency (FHFA, the federal regulator of the GSEs) announced that the GSEs will not seek forbearance repayment in one lump sum and will work with borrowers to find suitable repayment terms. FHA, VA, and USDA also announced that the entire forbearance will not be due at end of the forbearance period, and they will work with borrowers on repayment terms. For mortgages originated by lenders not covered by the CARES Act, each lender or investor will determine the forbearance repayment terms on its own.

The CARES Act also included a moratorium on foreclosures. Initially, the moratorium only went through May 17, 2020, for all cases, but it was extended twice and finally expired on July 31, 2021. Thus, mortgage servicers were prohibited from foreclosing on federally backed mortgage loans. The federal agencies whose mortgages were subject to this provision have individually extended the moratorium. FHFA extended the moratorium on foreclosures for borrowers with mortgages backed by Fannie Mae and Freddie Mac and the FHA, VA, and USDA extended their moratoriums on foreclosure of their respective guaranteed loans. For borrowers already covered by the CARES Act forbearance provisions, the moratorium was largely irrelevant because the forbearance prevented any action by the lender against a past due borrower. However, the moratorium was helpful for borrowers who had payment problems even before the pandemic as it allowed them to continue to stay in their homes.

The CARES Act Section 4023 concerns the right to forbearance for owners of multifamily properties with federally backed mortgage loans. From March 27, 2020 to December 31, 2020, the owner of a multifamily property (landlord) secured by a federally backed mortgage loan that was current as per the beginning of the pandemic could also apply for payment forbearance due to COVID-19 hardship for 30 days by submitting a request to the servicer, which could be extended for two additional 30-days, for a total of 3 months. Unlike regular borrowers, for landlords, financial hardship had to be documented before granting the forbearance.

The CARES Act Section 3513 concerns forbearance relief for federal student loans. It applies to Direct and Federal Family Education Loan (FFEL) student loans owned by the Department of Education (DOE) and does not affect private education loans and FFEL loans by private lenders. From March 13, 2020, to September 30, 2020, the Act automatically suspended interest and payment on these loans, prohibited collection of defaulted loans, and provided the ability to obtain refunds for payments made after March 12, 2020. This benefit was further extended to December 31, 2020, via an executive order by President Trump, and then further to January 31, 2021, by Education Secretary DeVos. Through various other changes, federal student loans are still under forbearance as of this writing.

Unlike the mortgage and student loan markets, the CARES Act did not include any explicit forbearance mandates for auto, credit cards, or personal loans for households. Thus, households had to contact their lenders for information about forbearance for these types of debt, and as a result, policies and eligibility may differ by lender. Despite addressing household distress, some potential concerns were raised if creditors may not offer equal opportunities to forbearance and foreclosure moratoria to all consumers. We next review the research to understand the effectiveness of these programs and whether they met their goals.

Research to date suggests that the CARES Act forbearance and foreclosure moratoria provisions may have helped mitigate household financial distress as well as reduce some consumer inequality effects during the crisis.

A very comprehensive study on consumer forbearances by Cherry, Jiang, Matvos, Piskorski, and Seru (2021) followed a representative panel of US consumers during the COVID-19 pandemic using the Equifax Analytic Dataset (monthly borrower-level data). They reported that between March 2020 and May 2021, more than 70 million consumers with loans worth $2.3 trillion entered forbearance, and missed about $86 billion of their payments, the vast majority being recorded in mortgages and auto loans. Precisely, over their period of study, 6.3 million mortgages ($1.4 trillion), 11 million auto loans ($198 billion), 68 million student loans ($655 billion), and 62 million revolving loans ($125 billion) were in forbearance. And while much of it was mandated by the CARES Act, substantial debt forbearance (about 20% of debt relief) in auto debt, revolving debt, and jumbo mortgages, all outside of the explicit government mandates and CARES Act rules were provided also by private intermediaries.

Implementation of forbearance policies is important. Student loans were automatically placed in administrative forbearance, providing relief that was not necessarily correlated with borrower need. For mortgages, authors found that borrowers' self-selection into forbearance is an important determinant of how debt relief is allocated in the population, and forbearance relief serves as a temporary bridge for liquidity shocks. To obtain mortgage forbearance, borrowers must request it from the lender, and in the case of private forbearance, lenders must approve such requests. Among the largest consumer debt category, residential mortgages, more than 90% of borrowers eligible for forbearance through the CARES Act decided not to take up the option of debt relief, clear evidence that self-selection was a powerful force in determining forbearance rates. Authors argue that allowing borrowers a choice of whether to request debt relief might have resulted in a potentially better-targeted and more cost-effective policy.

The private sector also played an important role in the provision of forbearance, both as an alternative to government forbearance and as a conduit given that government relief was provided through private intermediaries, more than half of whom are shadow banks in the mortgage market (Buchak, Matvos, Piskorski, and Seru, 2018; Jiang, Matvos, Piskorski, and Seru, 2020; Jiang, 2023). Private debt forbearance for debts which were not covered by the CARES Act provided more than a quarter of total debt relief. However, exploiting a discontinuity in mortgage eligibility under the CARES Act, authors found that government-provided debt relief was about 25% more generous than that provided by the private sector. Then given that the forbearance was mandated by the CARES Act, the expectation would be to see no differences between suppliers. Interestingly, the authors documented that, even accounting for borrower characteristics, traditional banks were more likely to offer forbearance assistance than shadow intermediaries. In a similar vein, Kim, Lee, Scharlemann, and Vickery (2022) found that servicer policies and practices played an important role in the implementation of the CARES Act mortgage forbearance program. Despite eligibility, about one-fourth of the past due federally backed loans in their sample failed to ever enter into forbearance. They found that these "missing" forbearances as well as associated forbearance-related complaints by borrowers vary significantly across servicers for similar loans. Forbearance outcomes are systematically related to servicer characteristics including size, liquidity, and organizational form. Thus, small servicers and nonbanks, and especially nonbanks with small liquidity buffers, had a lower propensity to provide forbearance to eligible borrowers. Using servicer-level variation, they also showed that assignment to a "high-forbearance" servicer translates to a significant increase in the probability of nonpayment, without any negative effect on borrowers' credit scores, which moves essentially 1:1 with the forbearance probability. They concluded that it does not appear that assignment to a high-forbearance servicer prevented negative housing outcomes like nonpayment outside of forbearance, default, or forced sales. To servicers, forbearance take-up that does not prevent delinquency or foreclosure is costly and the servicer does not internalize nonhousing program benefits, and unless the servicer is very large, it does not internalize general equilibrium benefits. Thus, servicers with fewer resources preserved liquidity by restricting access to forbearance for borrowers.

Finally, Bandyopadhyay (2022) exploited servicer comments that are proprietary and hardly accessible to shed light on borrower responses to the mortgage forbearance program contained in the CARES Act. The author found a higher incidence of forbearances for government-backed mortgages in response to communications initiated by the servicer, consistent with CARES Act requiring servicers to proactively reach out to borrowers with details about the forbearance program. In contrast, they did not find a higher incidence of forbearances in the private-label mortgages, consistent with different conditions for these. The CARES Act did not ask that servicers proactively contact private-label loan consumers, and the servicer could demand proof of financial hardship before granting forbearance, making it harder to get forbearances on these.

Cherry, Jiang, Matvos, Piskorski, and Seru (2021) argued that the massive debt relief programs during the COVID-19 crisis reduced financial distress and led to very low consumer delinquency rates relative to the crisis economic severity, different from prior crises when delinquencies increased along with unemployment. Authors estimated that the actual default rate average was below 2% instead of a predicted 6.8% at its peak, amounting to about 1.5–2.5 million missing defaults in the aggregate. While other policies also played roles in reducing consumer distress, the level of forbearance was large enough to account for averted potential delinquencies in the consumer markets. The surprising low-delinquency puzzle during the COVID-19 pandemic is also discussed by Dettling and Lambie-Hanson (2021). This latter study similarly suggests that the availability of forbearance programs and fiscal support from the government kept many consumers from entering into delinquency. A related reported effect also attributed at least partly to forbearances is an increase in the average credit score particularly for those in the lower part of the distribution. Gerardi, Lambie-Hanson, and Willen (2021) showed that borrowers who missed payments had significantly higher credit scores than those who were distressed in the GFC, which they attribute to the widespread availability of forbearance. A similar study by Kowalik, Liu, and Wang (2021) found that a decrease in credit card utilization and forbearance programs shielded individual households' credit scores from significant credit score penalties. Furthermore, Wang, Yang, Iverson, and Kluender (2020) found evidence that policies such as mortgage forbearance and foreclosure moratoria were associated with the decline in personal bankruptcies during the pandemic. Indeed, bankruptcy filing rates declined considerably more for homeowners than for nonhomeowners, and the share of consumer filings that included real property fell by 8 percentage points (13% relative to the pre-COVID average of 61%), a decline that corresponded with the start of the CARES Act effective date. On the other hand, they suggest that state shutdowns and eviction moratoria had no impact on bankruptcy filings.

Cherry, Jiang, Matvos, Piskorski, and Seru (2021) also found that the forbearance programs reached their intended target, given that the forbearance take-up was higher in regions with the highest COVID-19 infection rates and the worst local economic deterioration. In addition, they found that consumers in most need, those with lower credit scores, lower incomes, and higher debt balances as well as areas with higher shares of minorities did receive higher rates of forbearance. However, they also reported that over 50% of total forbearance dollar amounts and the highest dollar forbearances per individual went to borrowers with above median prepandemic income and higher debt balances whose credit situation may have deteriorated during the pandemic, that is consumers normally excluded from CARES Act income-based policies, such as the stimulus check program. This latter finding suggests that forbearances may have complemented other policy measures to help consumers of various backgrounds and situations. In contrast to this view, An, Kowalik, Liu, and Zhang (2022) found that wealthier individuals were more likely to enroll in mortgage forbearance, even after controlling for income, leverage, and other borrower and loan characteristics, which they consider to be an anomaly in forbearance take-up and suggests some wealth inequalities in debt relief. Investigating channels behind the results, they ruled out the possibilities that wealthier borrowers were more likely to take forbearance due to precaution or out of greater need. Their results suggest that instead financial sophistication and strategic behavior contribute to this anomaly. Possibly related to wealth as well, Cherry, Jiang, Matvos, Piskorski, and Seru (2021) suggested that a fifth of borrowers in forbearance continued making full payments, suggesting that forbearance acted as a credit line for them allowing them to draw on payment deferral if they needed it. The latter finding suggests that some consumers may not have needed the forbearance.

McManus and Yannopoulos (2021) examined mortgage forbearance in Freddie Mac loans during the COVID-19 crisis and compared them to those during two previous episodes: a baseline period (covering the months just prior to the crisis) and a natural disaster sample. They found that mortgage forbearance rates in the COVID-19 crisis are similar to historic rates in natural disaster areas but are much higher than in the months just prior to the crisis. In all three periods, they find that higher forbearance rates are associated with lower FICO scores, higher DTI ratios, higher LTV ratios, and larger mortgage payments. Forbearances are also more prevalent among two- to four-unit and investor properties, single borrowers, and refinances. Same as the previous studies, they found that higher number of the cumulative cases of COVID-19 are associated with higher forbearance rates. However, examining the payment behavior of borrowers who entered forbearance during the COVID-19 crisis, it was found that most mortgages in forbearance missed at least one payment within the first 3 months or were delinquent when entering forbearance but by the 7th month after entry into forbearance, about half of the mortgages transitioned to current status, but a similar share of loans remained delinquent.

As regards to whether the forbearance met the targets, a study on forbearances by Akana, Lambie-Hanson, and Vickery (2021) focused on mortgage forbearances using responses to the January 2021 COVID-19 Survey of Consumers. This survey was conducted by the Federal Reserve Bank of Philadelphia's Consumer Finance Institute, following a national sample of 1172 homeowners with mortgages, who reported the current and past forbearance status of their mortgage and other household credit accounts. They found that more than 10% of the respondents entered into a mortgage forbearance plan at some point during the COVID-19 pandemic, with consumers living in urban areas and those working in hardly affected industries having greater rates of forbearance use. Out of those using forbearances, about three-quarters experienced a job disruption or income loss during the pandemic. As for consumers not using forbearances, most did not need it or lacked a good understanding of available accommodations, as two out of three were unsure or pessimistic about whether they would qualify. Finally, homeowners using mortgage forbearances were also more likely to have payments deferred on credit cards or auto loans.

Targeting effects on inequality, An, Cordell, Geng, and Lee (2022) studied mortgage payments and forbearances using data from McDash Flash together with McDash mortgage servicing records, credit bureau data, and confidential Home Mortgage Disclosure Act (HMDA) loan application information. They showed that lower-income and minority borrowers had twice as high nonpayment rates relative to higher-income and white borrowers during the COVID-19 pandemic, even after controlling for conventional risk factors. But they also found that government- and private-sector forbearance programs may have mitigated these inequalities in the near term, as lower-income and minority borrowers have taken up the short-term debt relief at higher rates. In contrast, Bandyopadhyay (2022) used proprietary servicer call transcripts and found selective verification of unemployment status by the servicer processing these forbearance applications for nongovernment borrowers with a racial undertone, i.e., African Americans apply at a 22.2% lower rate than White Americans as evidenced by communications initiated by them due to lack of financial sophistication. Among the borrowers who are informed about the CARES Act via communications initiated by the servicer, African Americans are also dissuaded more from forbearance (apply by 10.8% less than White Americans) and are offered loan modification or no relief. This evidence of potential taste-based discrimination appears in both forbearance applications and the actual take-up rate of approved forbearance. Gerardi, Lambie-Hanson, and Willen (2021) also focused on pandemic-induced racial disparities in US mortgage markets. They showed that Black, Hispanic, and Asian borrowers were significantly more likely than white borrowers to miss payments due to financial distress, and significantly less likely to refinance to take advantage of the large decline in interest rates spurred by the Federal Reserve's large-scale mortgage-backed security (MBS) purchase program. However, the forbearance program provided approximately equal payment relief to all distressed borrowers, as forbearance rates conditional on nonpayment status were roughly equal across racial/ethnic groups. However, Black and Hispanic borrowers were significantly less likely to exit forbearance and resume making payments relative to their Asian and White counterparts. Persistent differences in the ability to catch up on missed payments may have unfavorable effects on the already large disparity in home ownership rates across racial and ethnic groups. While the pandemic caused widespread distress in mortgage markets, strong house price appreciation in 2020 suggests that foreclosure risk is lower for past due borrowers as compared with the GFC. Han, Meyer, and Sullivan (2020) indicated that government policies including forbearances during the pandemic also led poverty rates to fall and low percentiles of income to rise across a range of demographic groups and geographies.

Another issue discussed in extant research is that postponed repayments can bear implications for the future. Cherry, Jiang, Matvos, Piskorski, and Seru (2021) found that by May 2021, about 60% of borrowers had already exited forbearance while more financially vulnerable and lower income borrowers were still in forbearance with an accumulated debt overhang of about $60 billion in accumulated needed repayments, or about $3900 per individual, which is about 1.5 times their average monthly income, and more than 2.2 times for lower income borrowers. For mortgage borrowers alone, the estimated forbearance debt overhang was about $15 billion, amounting to about $14,200 per individual (about 3.4 times their average monthly income). The extent of forbearance overhang suggests that the unraveling of forbearance, depending on the way done, could have significant consequences for household distress and the larger economy. Kim, Lee, Scharlemann, and Vickery (2022) discussed that the CARES Act is silent about what should occur at the end of the forbearance period. But regulators and mortgage agencies stated a range of options that would be available, and borrowers would not be required to repay missed payments in a lump sum (e.g., Freddie Mac, 2020). For example, in April 2020, the Federal Housing Administration (FHA) announced a program (National Emergency Partial Claim) under which most borrowers that perform well after exiting forbearance can transfer accumulated missed payments into a subordinate interest-free note not due until the termination of the mortgage through a property sale, refinancing, or payoff, and Fannie Mae and Freddie Mac announced a similar payment deferral option in May (Department of Housing and Urban Development, 2020a, 2020b; Federal Housing Finance Agency, 2020).

Still another policy issue considered in the extant research regards whether borrowers should have been asked to demonstrate proof of COVID-19 hardship, either currently or retrospectively, before being grated forbearance, given that forbearance cost billions of taxpayers' dollars. Anderson, Harrison, and Seiler (2022) explored the economic implications of this policy using an experimental design to first identify strategic forbearance incidence, and then to quantify where the forborne mortgage payment dollars were spent. Their results suggest strategic mortgage forbearance could have been significantly reduced, saving taxpayers billions of dollars in potential losses, simply by requiring a one-page attestation with lender recourse for borrowers wishing to engage in COVID-19-related mortgage payment cessation programs. Additionally, they showed that the use of these forborne mortgage payments ranged from enhancing the financial safety net for distressed borrowers by increasing precautionary savings to buying necessities, and to equity investing and debt consolidation.

Studying the macroeconomic and real economic implications of mortgage forbearances, Annenberg and Scharlemann (2021) found a strong positive relationship between the availability of mortgage forbearance and house price growth at the county level during the COVID-19 pandemic. They found a 0.6 percentage point increase between April and August 2020, relative to the same 4-month period in 2019, controlling for the unemployment rate and other factors. They also showed that the prevalence of forbearance was positively correlated with unemployment and negatively correlated with new home listings, suggesting that forbearances supported house prices partly by restricting new listings by borrowers experiencing negative labor market shocks. Their results also suggest that forbearance relief in the mortgage market may have prevented a negative feedback loop since falling house prices could have further increased mortgage delinquencies.

Capponi, Jia, and Rios (2021) investigated the impact of mortgage forbearance on the real economy through the housing market but focusing on the refinancing channel. They showed that mortgage forbearance embedded in the CARES Act not only prevents a large wave of foreclosures that might otherwise have occurred but also supports refinancing activities by stabilizing house prices. Their analysis implies that the foreclosure moratorium has prevented approximately 900,000 foreclosures in the first 7 months of its enactment and a house price decline of up to 8% in the period from April to October 2020. They argued that forbearance supports household borrowing through refinancing by relaxing the eligibility constraints of mortgagors, increasing their equity extraction, and lowering their refinancing costs. During the first 7 months, the foreclosure moratorium allowed more than 60,000 mortgagors (about 3.3% of noncashout refinancing) to become eligible for refinancing, increased home equity cashed out for around 145,000 households (about 22% of cash-out refinancing) by around $15,000 on average and lowered the refinancing cost for at least 900,000 households (about 37% of total refinancing lenders) by around $5600 per loan in terms of interest payments. This suggests that forbearance helped increase aggregate consumption by $6.4 billion and greatly helped households who were subject to stricter credit standards and declining home equity. Households with low credit score benefited from saving in terms of refinancing costs by roughly $3700 as an up-front fee, or equivalently, $15,500 in the form of interest payment. Results imply that forbearance to households facing foreclosures had positive externalities on a broad range of households intending to refinance, amplifying the stimulative effect of monetary policy in this period.

This extant research suggests that the CARES Act forbearance and foreclosure moratoria provisions may have mitigated some financial distress effects and consumer inequality. These government reactions may have prevented a rise in consumer delinquencies and bankruptcies, supported house prices and refinancing activities for households, and overall averted a negative feedback loop.

12.1.2 CARES Act eviction moratoria

Over 3.5 million households face house instability and evictions every year in the US, and most low-income families spend over half of their income on housing costs. Understanding the eviction crisis is critical to effectively addressing these problems and reducing inequality.

Much of the issue comes from an insufficient supply of affordable housing predominantly in bigger cities and incomes that typically do not keep up with the increase in rent and other housing costs. Until recently, no national database tracking evictions existed. Studying causes and consequences on a national level was impossible, and most knowledge was only from local-based information in various cities. The Eviction Lab at Princeton University started to track this information from 2017 onward, giving researchers the tools to better understand the eviction crisis. The Eviction Lab shows that in some cities, as many as one in eight families faces eviction every year, and that low-income families and individuals, females, minorities, and victims of domestic violence as well as families with children are at a higher risk of eviction. In New York City alone, approximately 230,000 households faced eviction in housing court in 2017 (NYC Office of Civil Justice, 2017). Emergent literature shows that eviction is associated with severe economic hardship (e.g., Bäckman, Brännström, and Kahlmeter, 2018), worse health outcomes (e.g., Desmond and Kimbro, 2015), and prolonged residential and financial instability (e.g., Desmond, 2016). Recent papers by Collinson and Reed (2018) and Humphries, Mader, Tannenbaum, and van Dijk (2019) used quasi-experimental designs to show the effects of evictions on households' welfare. They found that evictions often lead to homelessness, increased hospitalizations for mental health, and reduced credit scores and access to credit. These outcomes are significantly magnified during economic downturns such as the COVID-19 pandemic. Renters of color and low income have disproportionally been impacted by income loss during the pandemic, representing a higher percentage of cost-burdened renters. Addressing evictions has been the subject of heightened debates among policymakers.

To increase affordability, previous research shows that typically a mix of several measures such as rent regulation, upzoning, inclusionary zoning, housing vouchers, and developer tax credits have been discussed (e.g., Favilukis, Mabille, and Van Nieuwerburgh, 2019). Abramson (2022) discusses policies that address evictions which can be classified into tenant protections, which make it harder to evict renters who have already defaulted on their rent, such as "Right-to-Counsel" and policies that prevent tenants from missing rent in the first place, such as rental assistance and affordable housing programs. He found that tenant protections against evictions can result in increased screening and homelessness as landlords might be less willing to rent to risky tenants if evictions become more burdensome to them.

However, government assistance programs such as cash transfers to tenants can prevent both homelessness and eviction. The author showed that a monthly subsidy of $400 to households with less than $1000 of cash can reduce homelessness by 45% and evictions by 75%. The difference relative to "Right-to-Counsel" is that rental assistance lowers the likelihood that tenants default on rent in the first place, as opposed to making it harder to evict them once they have already missed rent payments. Overall, rental assistance improves welfare and may also be cost-effective given that savings in terms of reduced expenses on homelessness services outweigh the cost of subsidizing rents.

The COVID-19 pandemic increased the urgency of the eviction crisis as about 10 million American renters were estimated to be behind on $60 billion in rent as of February 2021 alone (Favilukis, Mabille, and Van Nieuwerburgh, 2019). To address immediate eviction hardships on households during the COVID-19 crisis and the virus spread, the CARES Act Section 4023 provides eviction relief for certain tenants. During the period March 27, 2020, to December 30, 2020, the owner of a multi-family building secured by a Federally backed mortgage loan that applied for and received a CARES Act forbearance cannot evict tenants in the building for nonpayment and cannot charge late fees or penalties for nonpayment. A landlord of a building secured by a Federally backed mortgage loan not seeking forbearance must still provide a 30-day notice before evicting Some state and local laws provided additional eviction protections. The CARES Act Section 4024 covers eviction relief which prohibits landlords of "covered dwellings" from initiating eviction proceedings or charging fees, penalties, or other charges against a tenant for the nonpayment of rent during the period of March 27, 2020, to August 24, 2020. "Covered dwellings" include properties with a federally backed mortgage loan or a federally backed multinational mortgage loan as well as housing under certain federal programs.

The CDC issued an extraordinary order under Section 361 of the Public Health Service Act initially effective from September 4, 2020, to December 31, 2020, which temporarily suspended all residential evictions in the US to prevent the further spread of COVID-19. This order is much broader than the CARES Act provisions described above. As a result of these provisions and orders, many state and local governments in the US enacted rental eviction moratoria in order to assure shelter of households affected by the pandemic and reduce the spread of the COVID-19 disease.

The eviction moratorium has been extended several times and the last update indicated an extension through June 30, 2022, to tenants earning less than 80% of the area median income if they submitted a completed application for rental relief before March 31, 2022. Otherwise, since April 01, 2022, all renters were required to pay their rent and utilities. Evictions have been on a rising trend since then, suggesting that a looming eviction crisis affecting millions is possibly unavoidable as per the Princeton Eviction Lab.

Several papers show that the COVID-19 pandemic exposed many US households to increased eviction risk (Benfer, Greene, and Hagan, 2020; Benfer, Vlahov, Long, Walker-Wells, Pottenger, Gonsalves, and Keene, 2021). Other papers investigated the effects of the CARES Act eviction moratoria on households' welfare measured in several ways. First, focusing on the impacts of eviction policies during the pandemic on COVID-19 infections and deaths, Jowers, Timmins, Bhavsar, Hu, and Marshall (2021) found that policies that limit evictions helped reduce COVID-19 infections by 3.8% and reduce deaths by 11%, while moratoria on utility disconnections reduced COVID-19 infections by 4.4% and mortality rates by 7.4%. These effects are very strong as pandemic housing precarity, which includes both the risk of eviction and utility disconnections or shut-offs, reduces a person's ability to abide by social distancing orders and comply with hygiene recommendations. Authors argue that if such federal policies would have been in place much earlier from March 2020, they could have reduced COVID-19 infections by 14.2% and deaths by 40.7%. For moratoria on utility disconnections, COVID-19 infection rates could have been reduced by 8.7% and deaths by 14.8%. Overall, the authors concluded that eviction policies were effective mechanisms for decreasing both COVID-19 infections and deaths.

An, Gabriel, and Tzur-Ilan (2022) investigated the effects of the rental eviction moratoria on household spending, food security, and mental health. They used novel data on COVID-19 rental eviction policy interventions at state-level from governor, court, and legislation websites (43 states that enacted eviction moratoria) plus county-level information on evictions from the Eviction Lab at Princeton University which they merge with the Y-14M credit card data and US Census COVID-19 Household Pulse Survey among others from March to August 2020. They found that eviction moratoria significantly reduced evictions and resulted in the redirection of limited household financial resources to immediate consumption needs, such as food and grocery spending. They also found that eviction moratoria reduced household food insecurity and mental stress, and that larger beneficial effects were seen among African American households, suggesting eviction moratoria also beneficially helped address inequality concerns.

Ambrose, An, and Lopez (2021) investigated how the financing choice of landlords (GSE financing) impacts eviction decisions in rental markets during the COVID-19 crisis. Since multifamily loans rely on timely rental payments, strict underwriting factors can increase the chances that landlords withstand income shocks. Lender-provided relief may further create flexibility for landlords to work with tenants who default on rent. A stylized model reveals the linkage between credit supply and eviction risk is given that having a GSE loan could lead to a lower likelihood for the landlord to pursue evictions. In the empirical analysis, using a sample of nationwide multifamily loans that were securitized, authors found lower eviction rates in counties with a larger share of multifamily loans that are insured by Fannie Mae, Freddie Mac, or Ginnie Mae than in counties with a smaller share of multifamily loans insured by the three GSEs. Thus, GSE financing appears to have helped shield households or get better eviction treatment during severe economic shocks such as the COVID-19 pandemic.

Finally, an earlier study by Spatt (2020) discusses some benefits and costs of eviction moratoria. It mentions that some arguments for eviction bans are a recognition of substantial deadweight losses and a desire to avoid those as well as adverse neighborhood spillovers. However, he also revealed that such a policy may leave open the possibility that it can lead to high incremental delayed payments, moral hazard, and once the calendar restriction ends, the potential for a spurt of evictions. Such a spurt is already visible in the Eviction Lab data as of the time of this writing, however, the mitigation of household distress during the pandemic time may outweigh the perceived costs.

12.1.3 CARES Act restrictions on delinquency reporting to credit bureaus

The CARES Act Section 4021 concerns restrictions on credit bureau reporting to protect consumer credit scores during the pandemic. It amends the Fair Credit Reporting Act to protect a consumer's credit report when a lender provides a forbearance accommodation for an account related to COVID-19, such as to defer one or more payments, make a partial payment, forbear any delinquent amounts, modify a loan or contract, or any other assistance or relief to a consumer affected by COVID-19. This provision was set to expire 120 days after the national emergency ended. Under the National Emergencies Act, the national emergency declaration will automatically terminate on the 1-year anniversary of the declaration (i.e., March 12, 2021) if the President does not extend it during the 90-day period before the anniversary or can also be terminated if Congress enacts a joint resolution or the President issues a proclamation. Thus, if a lender makes forbearance accommodation for a consumer on any loan, the lender must report the account as current unless the account was delinquent before the accommodation was made. This reporting requirement does not apply to charged-off accounts. This provision effectively prohibits lenders and servicers from reporting to credit bureaus those payments skipped through a forbearance plan and may likely encourage borrowers to take up forbearance. Some media outlet articles expressed concern that this provision impairs lenders' ability to evaluate accurately consumer credit applications because some credit histories may be distorted (e.g., Andriotis, 2020).

Several studies found distortions resulting from this provision restricting delinquency reporting to credit bureaus for consumers. Berger, Bouwman, Norden, Roman, Udell, and Wang (2024) used Y-14M credit card data to investigate the effects of the COVID-19 pandemic on credit card customers in the US. Among the results, authors found that the 2020 CARES Act §4021 provision during the crisis reduced the informational value of consumer credit scores. This may have distorted the usual relations between credit scores and delinquencies as lower-score rather than higher-score consumers appear to have lower delinquency rates. In addition, the provision may have penalized apparently safer consumers with better credit scores who were charged less favorable credit terms during the pandemic, i.e., higher APR spreads and lower credit limits or may have subsidized the lower credit score consumers, resulting in more favorable terms for them.

Relatedly, Elul and Newton (2021) discussed that this provision likely resulted in credit bureau scores rising during the pandemic, which is in sharp contrast to the Great Recession when borrowers who defaulted on their mortgages saw their scores drop and also experienced difficulty in using credit to finance consumption. Several studies have corroborated this conjecture. Thus, an Experian report by Lembo Stolba (2021) mentions that the average consumer credit scores increased significantly in 2020 likely due to both the 2020 CARES Act and other government interventions. The author contends that credit score increases are mostly driven by a significant reduction in the number of consumers with subprime designation, who typically have the most constraints to accessing credit. Improvements in credit scores for subprime consumers are regarded as opening more credit opportunities for them. Gerardi, Lambie-Hanson, and Willen (2021) showed that borrowers who missed payments have significantly higher credit scores, which they attribute to the widespread availability of forbearance for federally backed mortgages. Similarly, Kowalik, Liu, and Wang (2021) studied the drivers behind the increasing households' credit scores since the onset of the pandemic which is most visible for households with the lowest credit scores. They demonstrated that the decrease in credit card utilization and forbearance programs shielded individual households' credit scores from significant credit score penalties. The other unstated reason is the forbearance-related provision which stalls reporting of delinquencies if consumers have at least one forbearance accommodation in place during the pandemic, which protects their credit score.

12.1.4 CARES Act extended unemployment insurance (UI)

In the wake of the COVID-19 pandemic, many Americans suffered job losses as the unemployment rate reached close to 15% in April 2020, and, as a result, many people needed unemployment benefits. Three policy tools, the Federal Pandemic Unemployment Compensation (FPUC), the Pandemic Unemployment Assistance (PUA), and the Pandemic Emergency Unemployment Compensation (PEUC), were put in place to supplement regular unemployment insurance (UI) benefits from the states.

CARES Act Section 2105 temporarily provided $600 per week in extra unemployment benefits in Federal Pandemic Unemployment Compensation (FPUC) for all unemployment recipients, a provision which started on April 4, 2020, and was set to expire originally on July 31, 2020. This FPUC benefit was further extended several times at a reduced benefit of $300 per week on August 1, 2020, via the Lost Wages Assistance Program (LWA) and then again on December 27, 2020, via the Coronavirus Response and Relief Supplemental Appropriations (CRRSA) Act, and further on March 11, 2021, via the American Rescue Plan (ARP). The latter ARP further waived some federal income taxes on the first $10,200 of unemployment benefits received in 2020 by individuals with adjusted gross incomes less than $150,000 to further assist those who lost work due to COVID-19 to help cover life essentials. The tax relief applied to both workers who received benefits through federal unemployment programs as well as those who received traditional benefits through their state unemployment insurance fund.

The PUA assistance provided UI benefits to much broader unemployed population groups than were normally eligible. The CARES Act Section 2102 concerns PUA and provided up to 39 weeks of UI payment benefits for people ineligible for regular unemployment benefits starting March 27, 2020, through December 26, 2020. These benefits were also twice extended via the CRRSA and ARP Acts on December 27, 2020, and then on March 11, 2021, going through September 2021. People covered were the self-employed, independent contractors, part-time workers, and people unable to work because of a COVID-19-related issue such as providing care for a family or household member with COVID-19. Similar coverage extends to people who have exhausted all rights to regular unemployment benefits or extended unemployment benefits, and such provision went through December 31, 2020. Another similar benefit went through the CARES Act Section 2103 dealing with unemployment insurance benefits for nonprofits and governmental entities that do make regular contributions to state unemployment funds because they are self-insured. When workers for these entities file unemployment claims in regular unemployment programs, the entity must reimburse the state for the benefits (i.e., self-insured). The CARES Act helped these entities by paying 50% of their reimbursements.

Finally, CARES Act Sections 2107 and 2104 concern additional Pandemic Emergency Unemployment Compensation (PEUC) and additional Federal Pandemic Unemployment Compensation. Such provisions as PEUC provide extended benefits for up to 13 weeks for individuals who have exhausted their regular benefits, which were typically for 26 weeks. The 13 weeks under the PEUC is in addition to the "extended benefits" most states offered during periods of high unemployment. These provisions were set to expire on December 31, 2020, but were further extended through September 2021 via the CRRSA and ARP Acts.

The UI benefits to mitigate the effects on the unemployed during the pandemic have been generous, but they raise questions as to whether they indeed helped people in need weather a hard economic period or instead disincentivized working due to moral hazard with possible unfavorable economic outcomes. Existing research investigates a number of outcomes, including effects on restoring the income of unemployed people, but also impacts on the labor market and other economic outcomes such as consumption.

Looking at income effects, Ganong, Noel, and Vavra (2020) and Bi and Gulati (2021) documented that the UI benefits helped offset income losses of unemployed workers and were highly progressive in that relief, but that relief was disproportionally higher for lower-income, less educated, women, and minority workers. The FPUC program of the CARES Act is intended to replace 100% of the lost wages. Ganong, Noel, and Vavra (2020) found that 76% of the unemployed had a replacement rate while the ratio of an unemployed worker's UI benefit to their previous wages was often above 100%. However, the authors also showed that the $600 weekly supplement helped income for low-wage earners more than that for high-wage earners, which was an intention of the program. This is also shown by Carey, Groen, Jensen, Krolik, and Polivka (2021) who used the Household Pulse Survey from August to December 2020 and concluded that about 20% of low-income workers (<$35,000 income) received UI benefits as compared to only about 15% for the higher income works (≥$35,000 income). Greig, Zhao, and Lefevre (2021) documented that renters were more likely to receive UI benefits than homeowners. Bell, Hedin, Schnorr, and Von Wachter (2021) and Bell, Hedin, Moghadam, Schnorr, and Von Wachter (2021) further showed that the extended UI benefits up to 53 weeks (PEUC program) disproportionally helped women, less educated, younger, and people of color as these were seen to be at higher unemployment risk in California. They highlighted that more than half of the beneficiaries had no more than a high school degree, but they accounted for about one-third of the labor force. Moreover, beneficiaries after the additional extension after December 2020 disproportionally helped industrial sectors with low wages such as accommodation, food services, and retail. Chen and Shrider (2021) showed that UI benefits helped reduce the poverty rate in 2020 by 1.4 percentage points overall and by 2.5 percentage points for Black households helping address inequality.

To further quantitatively assess the unemployment insurance's ability to help recipients meet their basic needs during the first round, Karpman and Acs (2020) compared material hardship and worrying about basic needs between March and early April and mid/late July, between two groups of adults: those of households who received unemployment insurance in the 30 days before the May study and those who applied for the UI benefits since March 1 but did not receive them before the May study. Findings revealed that among those who received UI benefits, there was a 3.7% reduction in problems paying utility bills and a 7.3% reduction in the inability to pay for medical needs. Furthermore, for those who received UI benefits, there was a 12.4% reduction in worrying about having enough to eat between March/April and May, while this reduction was only 1.5% for those who applied for the benefits but did not receive UI. For those who received UI, there was a 17.1% reduction in worrying about paying rent or mortgage, while this reduction was only 1.5% for those who applied for UI benefits but did not receive them.

Looking at the effects on the labor market, a variety of studies found only limited labor market effects from UI benefits in the short term (up to July 2020) and little evidence that UI benefits may have reduced motivation of people to go back to work. Moral hazard incentives from UI benefits are shown to have been very low by historical standards. Thus, Dube (2021a, 2021b) found minimal effects on job gains from the reduction of benefits in July 2020, concluding that the cost of income replacement may be small in general, and even smaller for low-income and low-education households. Altonji, Contractor, Finamor, Haygood, Lindenlaub, Meghir, O'Dea, Scott, Wang, and Washington (2020) used small business Homebase data found no evidence that generous UI benefits disincentivized work following the introduction of the FPUC in the summer of 2020. Bartik, Bertrand, Lin, Rothstein, and Unrath (2020) documented that high UI replacement rates did not drive job losses or slow rehiring up to July 2020. Petrosky-Nadeau and Valletta (2021) found that the UI did not deter workers between April and June 2020 from accepting a job offer, and that disincentive effects were present for only a very small fraction of UI recipients, primarily those with less than a high school education. Marinescu, Skandalis, and Zhao (2021) suggested that employers did not have greater difficulty finding applicants for vacancies up to June 2020 despite the provision of large UI benefits over this period. Ganong, Greig, Noel, Sullivan, and Vavra (2022) showed that UI benefits exits were lower than in the prepandemic period and the exit rate from unemployment showed only a very brief but not sustained increase when the $600 UI benefit expired in July 2020, while Ganong, Greig, Noel, Sullivan, and Vavra (2022) showed that about 53% of unemployed workers that received the $600 UI benefit returned to work before the benefit expired suggesting that they chose to go back to work, and the majority of these workers were paid less than the $600 UI benefit, and 70% of those returning went back to work at their prior employers (e.g., Bell, Hedin, Schnorr, and Von Wachter, 2021). Finally, Ganong, Greig, Noel, Sullivan, and Vavra (2021) showed that the $600 UI benefit reduced employment by less than 0.8% while the $300 UI benefit reduced employment by less than 0.5%, which they regard as small relative to overall pandemic fluctuations in employment as well as relative to predictions of the labor supply disincentives from the prepandemic period. Boar and Mongey (2020) suggested that some workers had been receiving unemployment insurance benefits from the CARES Act that exceeded the wages of their previous jobs; however, in considering whether they would reject an offer from their previous employer to return to work for the same wage, it is unlikely. This is due to reasons such as the fact that the CARES Act is only temporary, there is uncertainty that the offer might expire, search frictions, and recession and wage losses.

Studies on longer-term effects and duration of the UI benefits also found only small effects on labor outcomes. Coombs, Dube, Jahnke, Kluender, Naidu, and Stepner (2022) used administrative data from Earnin on a sample of low-income workers found only small impacts of the early termination on job finding: ending pandemic UI increased employment by only 4.4 percentage points compared to the 35 percentage points decline in UI recipiency among workers who were unemployed, with most of the impact on employment coming from the workers who lost their benefits entirely instead of those who simply lost the $300 weekly supplement. The small work disincentive effects among lower-income workers suggest that these were generally more responsive to UI policy changes. Holzer, Hubbard, and Strain (2021) using Current Population Survey (CPS) data estimated that the flow of unemployed workers into employment increased by 14 percentage points following the early termination of benefits in June and July of 2021, and that the unemployment rate in July and August 2021 would have been 0.3 percentage points lower had all states opted to terminate benefits in June, also consistent with findings of Coombs, Dube, Jahnke, Kluender, Naidu, and Stepner (2022). Bi and Gulati (2021) argued that public health risk concerns may have played a greater role in discouraging people from returning to work than the size or duration of the UI programs. In support of this view, Fang, Nie, and Xie (2020) showed that UI benefits indeed reduced COVID-19 infections at the workplace and saved lives.[1]

Another goal of the UI benefits was to stir consumer spending and a number of studies documented positive effects on this (e.g., Bi and Gulati, 2021). Casado, Glennon, Lane, McQuown, Rich, and Weinberg (2021) showed that the higher replacement rates of UI benefits led to significantly more consumer spending despite the increases in the unemployment rate. They argued that eliminating the UI benefits program would lead to a 44% decline in local spending. Similarly positive, Bachas, Ganong, Noel, Vavra, Wong, Farrell, and Greig (2020) showed that UI policies likely helped mitigate the effects of labor market disruptions during the pandemic on spending for lower-income and more vulnerable households. Comparing results from Ganong, Greig, Noel, Sullivan, and Vavra (2022) and Ganong and Noel (2019), which essentially compares spending among jobless workers who received UI benefits during the pandemic vs workers who received UI benefits in prepandemic times, it is clear

---

[1] Studies on effects of UI benefits during the GFC find small or some mixed effects (e.g., Farber and Valletta, 2015; Hagedorn, Manovskii, and Mitman, 2016; Chodorow-Reich, Coglianese, and Karabarbounis, 2019).

that spending dropped significantly when workers lost their UI benefits entirely, highlighting the important role these benefits played for spending. Finally, Coombs, Dube, Jahnke, Kluender, Naidu, and Stepner (2022) found a 20% drop in spending among jobless workers in the 26 states that turned off expanded benefits before the federal expiration in the summer of 2021. This suggests a relatively high marginal propensity to consume out of UI benefits. Thus, the UI benefits extended generally helped households that needed the income help the most and boosted economic activity, making it an attractive policy for addressing household financial distress and stimulating aggregate demand.

12.1.5 CARES Act stimulus checks

To reduce the income loss and financial distress from the pandemic and stir consumption, the US Treasury Department, the Bureau of the Fiscal Service, and the Internal Revenue Service (IRS) sent out three individual rounds of direct relief income payments to individuals during the COVID-19 crisis. The first round, effective on March 27, 2020, via the CARES Act Section 2201 on 2020 recovery rebates for individuals, provided Economic Impact Payments (EIP) of up to $1200 per adult for eligible individuals and $500 per qualifying child under age 17. The payments were reduced for individuals with adjusted gross income (AGI) greater than $75,000 ($150,000 for married couples filing a joint return). For a family of four, these Economic Impact Payments (EIP) provided up to $3400 of direct financial relief.

These benefits were further extended via CRRSA and ARP Acts, enacted in late December 2020 and March 2021, which authorized additional payments. These were up to $600 per adult for eligible individuals and up to $600 for each qualifying child under age 17 under CRRSA. The AGI thresholds at which the payments began to be reduced were identical to those under the CARES Act. Under ARP, the payments were of up to $1400 for eligible individuals or $2800 for married couples filing jointly, plus $1400 for each qualifying dependent, including adult dependents. For this third round of Economic Impact Payments, the American Rescue Plan requires an additional "plus-up" payment, which is based on information (such as a recently filed 2020 tax return) that the IRS receives after making the initial payment to the eligible individual. In addition, the American Rescue Plan increases direct financial relief to American families by providing $1400 payments for all qualifying dependents of a family, rather than just qualifying children under age 17. Normally, a taxpayer will qualify for the full amount of payment if they have AGI of up to $75,000 for singles and married persons filing a separate return, up to $112,500 for heads of household, and up to $150,000 for married couples filing joint returns and surviving spouses. Payment amounts are reduced for eligible individuals with AGI above those levels.

The payments were also coordinated to reach out to millions of homeless, rural poor, and other disadvantaged Americans without a bank account or who do not file for taxes with IRS via new and continued relationships with homeless shelters, legal aid clinics, and other methods and provided assistance services in many languages for recipients.

Stimulus checks or economic impact payments (EIP) are other tools used to address household financial distress, maintain the ability to buy necessities, and stimulate consumption during the COVID-19 pandemic. The idea was to particularly help lower-income households and those that were sick to stay home without spreading the virus and without losing their hourly income. By 2020:Q2, stimulus checks raised household personal income by over 1 trillion US dollars

(Bi and Gulati, 2021). Several studies have assessed the impact of the EIP on households' welfare and the broader economy.

Extant research found that households did spend a large amount, roughly 35%–50% of the stimulus checks received, for necessities such as food, other nondurable categories, and recurring payments such as rent and they responded almost immediately to the EIPs. Baker, Farrokhnia, Meyer, Pagel, and Yannelis (2020) found that households spent about 35 cents of each dollar received from the stimulus check in the month following disbursal. The largest increases in expenditures are for food, nondurable goods, and recurring payments such as rent, mortgages, and student loans. Coibion, Gorodnichenko, and Weber (2020a, 2020b, 2020c) found spending of about 40% of the checks on goods and services, with about 30% being saved and the remaining 30% being used to pay down debt. They observed that consumers favored food, health and beauty aids, and other nondurable goods rather than large durables. Finally, Karger and Rajan (2020) found that households spent 50% of the checks upon receival, focusing on similar products as noted in the previous studies. Somewhat similar findings are reported by Sahm, Shapiro, and Slemrod (2020), Boutros (2020), and Parker, Schild, Erhard, and Johnson (2022). Boutros (2020) used the Household Pulse Survey and found that almost 75% of households receiving an EIP reported using it to mostly pay for expenses. Parker, Schild, Erhard, and Johnson (2022) used questions from the June and July 2020 Consumer Expenditure Survey (CE) and found figures of 56%, 26%, and 18% for individuals reporting they used the EIP to mostly spend on expenses, savings, and paying off debts, respectively.

Other research investigates the speed of spending after stimulus payments. Karger and Rajan (2020) found that households spent half of their stimulus payments within 2 weeks of receipt, while Baker, Farrokhnia, Meyer, Pagel, and Yannelis (2020) found that households spent more than one-fifth of the checks within the first 10 days of receipt. Cooper and Olivei (2021) who examined the longest period after EIPs using transaction-level data documented that two-thirds of the spending response was within the first 2 weeks. Bi and Gulati (2021) further showed that personal savings also increased substantially throughout 2020 and into 2021 after the EIPs as some households preferred to keep the EIP rather than spend it, some of which is due to limited ability to spend on services due to pandemic restrictions and fear of virus spread.

Other studies suggest there was unbalanced spending across different population groups due to different liquidity needs or situations. Karger and Rajan (2020) found that in the 2 weeks following the EIP disbursement, 11% of recipients decreased spending, 12% did not change spending, and 17% spent the entire stimulus payment. The remaining 60% spent some portion of the EIP. Coibion, Gorodnichenko, and Weber (2020a, 2020b, 2020c) reported that 40% of households did not spend anything after the EIP, while 30% spent almost all the EIP. Indeed, this is explained by differences in liquidity constraints among households. Baker, Farrokhnia, Meyer, Pagel, and Yannelis (2020) showed that households with less than $100 in their checking accounts spent over 40% of the EIP within the first month, or about $680 for the median stimulus payment amount, while households with more than $4000 in their checking accounts spent only 11 cents from the EIP. Chetty, Friedman, and Stepner (2023) showed that spending increased discontinuously upon receipt of the EIP, with low-income areas increasing spending the most. Coibion, Gorodnichenko, and Weber (2020a, 2020b, 2020c) found that liquidity-constrained households across different income groups spent the stimulus check. Furthermore, Misra, Singh, and Zhang (2022) showed that spending from EIPs was higher in more densely populated urban areas where the costs of living are higher and there is a greater need for liquidity.

Other research also finds that EIPs helped address the needs of liquidity-constrained and lower-income households and both increased income and reduced poverty. Cox, Ganong, Noel, Vavra, Wong, Farrell, Greig, and Deadman (2020) used US anonymized household-level bank account data of Chase customers which links income, savings, and spending to investigate the heterogeneous effects on spending and savings. They found that while households across the income distribution cut spending from March to early April, starting with mid-April, spending has rebounded most rapidly for low-income households. They also found large increases in liquid asset balances for households throughout the income distribution, but lower-income households again contribute disproportionately to the aggregate increase in balances, relative to their prepandemic shares. Effects in the initial months of the recession were primarily caused by direct effects of the pandemic, rather than resulting from labor market disruptions. But the substantial growth in liquid assets for low-income households suggests that EIP and UI benefit programs during this period likely played an important role in limiting the effects of labor market disruptions on the spending of these households. There are at least two arguments for why this may be the case. First, the timing of the more rapid rebound in spending for low-income households coincides closely with the timing of EIP stimulus and UI benefits stabilizing spending, especially for low-income workers and households at the bottom end of the income distribution who see the largest stimulus relative to prepandemic income and also have the largest growth in liquid savings during this period. This also suggests a temporary decline in liquid wealth inequality. Second, although labor income fell the most for lower-income households, total income increased the most for those at the bottom of the income distribution given that EIPs were a flat payment and constituted a larger share of income for low-income households.

Han, Meyer, and Sullivan (2020) also found that family incomes in the bottom quartile rose more than 10% between the start of the year and the few months following the onset of the pandemic, boosted by the EIPs. As household income increased, authors found that the poverty rate declined, from an average of 10.9% in January and February to an average of 9.4% in the 3 months following CARES Act implementation in March 2020. Thus, EIPs not only helped constrained households' spending on necessities and recurring payments but also significantly increased personal savings during the pandemic as a wide variety of households received EIPs.

12.1.6 CARES Act additional small business support other than PPP

Several additional programs also helped businesses through the COVID-19 pandemic, other than the PPP program covered in Chapter 11. Three additional programs directly helped small businesses, both sponsored by the Small Business Administration (SBA).

The first assistance is a forbearance program of $17 billion as per Section 1112 of the CARES Act in March 2020. It stipulated that SBA pay, for a 6-month period, 100% of the principal, interest, and associated fees that small business borrowers owed on covered 7(a) loans, 504 loans, and microloans (but not PPP loans).[2] Such payment relief was provided automatically to all SBA loans that were fully distributed prior to September 27, 2020, and were in good status. By the end of 2020, not all $17 billion allocated were used, and thus, $11.5 billion of this amount was rescinded, reducing the total assistance from the CARES Act to $3.6 billion. An additional provision Section 325 of the Economic Aid to Hard-Hit Small Businesses, Nonprofits, and Venues Act (Economic Aid Act), enacted in December 27, 2020, also provided an additional $3.5 billion in available funds for automatic loan relief, available

---

[2]Prior to the pandemic, SBA guaranteed only about 50%–85% of an SBA loan.

for all 7(a), 504, and microloans approved before September 27, 2020, and fully distributed after this date. Any additional funds were used to pay the first 3 months of payments for loans approved after September 27, 2020, based on availability.

The second assistance from SBA is in the form of subsidized loans to businesses with less than 500 employees that suffered from COVID-19, the COVID-19 Economic Injury Disaster Loan (EIDL) which provides funding to help small businesses recover from the economic impacts of the COVID-19 pandemic.[3] This type of COVID EIDL funding is nonforgivable loan in which the funds can be used for working capital and other normal operating expenses at very low rates and must be paid back. The businesses could request funds up to $150,000, although this amount was increased to $500,000 in March 2021 and further to $2 million in September 2021, and enjoy a flat rate of 3.75% interest rate and 30-year maturity, while not having to make payments for 2 years after the loan is issued. Also, business owners applying must have a credit score above 570 and must provide collateral for amounts borrowed above $25,000 and personal guarantee for those above $200,000. As of December 2021, this program disbursed $317 billion and 3.9 million loans, helping many small businesses fill their funding gap until their revenues were stable again.

A last type of assistance is the Targeted EIDL Advance program, featuring forgivable grants of up to $15,000 that can be given to existing EIDL applicants and do not have to be repaid. Only those applicants that qualify can use these. Criteria include that a business must operate in a low-income area, have fewer than 300 employees, and demonstrate that it has lost at least 30% of its revenue over an 8-week period in the COVID-19 crisis. These amounted to about $20 billion and 5.8 million advances disbursed. Overall, the SBA provided about $344 billion in additional support to small businesses apart from PPP loans, covering forbearances, subsidized loans, and forgivable grants or advances.

The non-PPP small business programs received very little coverage to date in academic research. Li (2021) used the Census Bureau's Small Business Pulse Survey and found that the local COVID-19 pandemic severity was unrelated to the likelihood that a small business applied for or received an EIDL loan or SBA loan forgiveness, suggesting possible poor targeting. On the positive side, firms that received SBA support were less likely to report revenue and employee hour decreases in subsequent weeks, suggesting that they may have weathered the COVID-19 pandemic better than other firms. Fairlie and Fossen (2022) studied the allocation of SBA assistance with a focus on whether the PPP and EIDL programs effectively reached minority communities. They found that the take-up of the PPP program was slow in many minority communities and that loan amounts were negatively correlated with the minority share across communities. However, they found that the EIDL program was more effective in its reach, with both loan numbers and amounts being positively correlated with minority communities.

Another issue raised on these programs was fraud. The Government Accountability Office (2021) found that at least $156 million in EIDL loans had been approved for ineligible businesses, such as real estate developers and multilevel marketers. Also, lenders filed more than 20,000 reports of suspicious activity for the EIDL program. The SBA's Office of Inspector General released a report in October 2020 finding that about 46% of total EIDL funding through July 2020 went to potentially fraudulent borrowers, many of whom submitted duplicate applications from the same IP address or email address (Small Business Administration, 2020).

---

[3]The EIDL loans are not new to SBA but the program was significantly expanded when COVID-19 hit.

Finally, no empirical studies exist on the effects of EIDL or SBA loan forgiveness programs on small business performance. However, Chodorow-Reich, Iverson, and Sunderam (2022) provided some conjectures on this. They argued that demand for EIDL loans was very strong, showing that the program's subsidized terms and 30-year maturity were attractive to many small-business owners and many small businesses were willing to take on additional debt despite the pandemic uncertainty. This suggests some expectation on the part of the businesses to be able to repay after the 2-year grace period. Plus, unlike PPP, EIDL loans had the benefit of providing liquidity now but at a lower cost to the government after repayment of the loans. They also argued that subsidized lending programs that force business owners to consider their ability to repay (e.g., the EIDL) can provide needed liquidity while still attempting to provide capital to firms with better prospects. But the downside of providing loans to struggling businesses instead of grants is that it leaves them with more debt, which could slow economic recovery due to debt overhang given to such firms which would use cash flows to repay debt instead of other potential investments during the recovery phase. Overall, more research is needed to evaluate the effectiveness of non-PPP SBA small-business lending and whether it achieved its intended goals.

12.1.7 CARES Act large business support: Employee retention credit and financial aid for the airspace industry and national security companies

A number of CARES Act provisions targeted help to large as well as small businesses. First, in March 2020, Section 2301 of the CARES Act provided refundable tax credit of 50% of up to $10,000 in wages paid by an eligible employer whose business has been financially impacted by COVID-19 with the goal to encourage businesses to keep employees on their payroll even in periods of reduced operations during the pandemic. Such credit was available to all businesses regardless of size, including tax-exempt organizations. The only exceptions were state and local governments and their instrumentalities and small businesses that take small business loans. To be eligible, businesses had to demonstrate a significant decline in gross receipts due to full or partial suspension of operations due to a government order in response to COVID-19. Also, the credit was calculated based on qualifying wages on the average number of a business's employees in 2019. Over $70 billion was claimed for wages paid through the end of the first quarter of 2021 and a further $31 billion after that date.

Due to industry-specific challenges created by the pandemic, Section 4003 of the CARES Act in March 2020 provided $32 billion in financial grants to passenger air carriers, cargo air carriers, and aviation contractors, with the vast majority of $25 billion going to passenger airlines. Another $17 billion in grants went to other businesses critical to maintaining national security. The CARES Act required borrowers to agree to maintain employment levels as of March 24, 2020, to the extent practicable, and in any case not reduce their employment levels by more than 10% from the levels on such date, until September 30, 2020. Under the statute, borrowers had to also agree to certain restrictions on employee compensation, agree not to repurchase stock, except to the extent required under a contractual obligation in effect as of March 27, 2020, and agree not to pay dividends or make other capital distributions with respect to the borrower's common stock until 12 months after the loan has been repaid. The grants to air carriers were based on their total payroll expenses from April 2019 through September 2019, subject to proration, and required that the funds be used exclusively for the continuation of employee compensation and other benefits.

The CARES Act also required that the US Treasury receives a warrant or equity instrument from the borrower if the borrower is a public company, or a warrant, equity instrument, or senior debt instrument if the borrower is a private company, to compensate taxpayers. Those passenger airlines receiving over $100 million ($50 million for cargo carriers) were required to issue a loan and warrants to the US Treasury, while airline contractors receiving over $37.5 million had to issue a loan only to the US Treasury. All funds were required to be used for "employee wages, salaries, and benefits."

Meier and Smith (2021) hand-collect individual data and discuss that the face value of the loans was up to 30% of the total funds received for passenger airlines, and 49% for Atlas Air, the only cargo airline that received more than $50 million in payroll support. In addition, the warrants were issued at-the-money, having a 5-year term while their amount is such that the strike price times the number of warrants is approximately equal to 10% of the face value of the loan (less than 3% of the total funds received for the passenger airlines).

In total, 611 passenger carriers, cargo carriers, and support contractors received grants between April and October 2020 alone. The vast majority of the money, $22 billion of the initial total, went to just six large airlines: American ($6.0 billion), Delta ($5.6 billion), United ($5.1 billion), Southwest ($3.4 billion), Alaska ($1.0 billion), and Jetp ($1.0 billion). The initial generous grants from the CARES Act were complemented by even additional grants of up to $16 billion provided via the Consolidated Appropriations Act, 2021, enacted on December 27, 2020, which created the Payroll Support Program Extension (PSP2) for passenger air carriers and certain contractors, and by another round of assistance of up to $15 billion from the ARP enacted on March 11, 2021. The airline industry also benefited from the excise tax holiday, which suspended certain aviation excise taxes, from March 28, 2020, until 2021.

Despite intended goals to link grant disbursements to payroll, some researchers and public press raise the possibility that they may instead have benefited shareholders especially for large, publicly traded firms, rather than employees alone, given such firms have access to a variety of capital market financing alternatives or could have undergone successful bankruptcy restructuring if needed, which some of them have already incurred on several occasions in the past.

Surprisingly, despite the large dollar amounts, there is virtually almost no research on these additional financial aid programs for large businesses. One exception is the research by Meier and Smith (2021). The authors used hand-collected data to investigate the COVID-19 aid for all publicly listed US firms during the COVID-19 crisis, a large part of which was aid for the aerospace industry. Their data covers 755 payouts worth $17.9 billion, with the mean and median airline financial aid per employee being $34.39 thousand and $31.76 thousand, respectively. The authors computed the number of years a recipient has to pay corporate income tax to generate as much tax revenue as it received in these payouts and determine that they were expensive when compared to past corporate income tax payments. They found that the mean and median number of years, respectively, are 267.9 and 138.3 years for the airline recipients. These values are driven by low effective tax rates and the size of the financial aid, where the median tax rate is 4% for aided firms and 16% for others, while the current statutory corporate income tax rate is 21%, and a small number of aided firms in the sample are resident in tax havens such as Bermuda and Ireland.

Authors suggest that numerous financial aid recipients made risky financial decisions, so bailing them out induced an increase in moral hazard incentives on the part of the firms. Thus, 66 of the 579 aided firms with nonmissing financials paid out more in dividends and net repurchases from

2015 to 2019 than they received in aid, potentially inducing future moral hazard problems. 437 firms had more cash and cash equivalents at the end of 2019 than they received in financial aid, suggesting that the aid might constitute an excessive subsidy for these firms. A substantial percentage of the aided firms can be considered start-up-like firms, for which the aid is likely also excessive subsidization. Finally, many recipients are quite large, implying that they might have been able to raise additional financing on their own absent this aid.

Investigating what factors were most important and predicted the likelihood and magnitude of financial aid, authors found that greater assets, greater cash/assets and higher Tobin's Q were all associated with a lower financial aid likelihood and amount. However, firm age and sales both had a positive effect on aid probability and amount. In addition, a dummy for firms with a persistent negative EBITDA significantly predicted the financial aid probability and amount, supporting the idea that some were start-up-like firms. Finally, lobbying expenditures also had a sizable effect on financial aid likelihood and amount. Authors caution that they are unable to establish causality and thus their results should be interpreted with caution.

Regarding policy implications, the authors mentioned that financial aid should have been conditioned on whether a firm has been impacted by the pandemic. Other concerns are that the airline aid was overly generous on a payout-per-employee basis, and expensive when compared to recent corporate income tax payments by the airlines. Moreover, the large publicly listed airlines paid out more to their shareholders in the last couple of years than they received in financial aid, suggesting that these payments might be inducing moral hazard. Authors exemplify that the four largest airlines went bankrupt 4.25 times since the 1980s, raising the question of why bankruptcy could not have been used instead of financial aid to restructure the airlines. Similar thoughts about using a Chapter 11 bankruptcy solution if needed were expressed by Chodorow-Reich, Iverson, and Sunderam (2022).

12.2 Federal Reserve actions

12.2.1 Main Street Lending Program (MSLP) and other credit and liquidity facilities for larger businesses

The Main Street Lending Program (MSLP) is a Federal Reserve policy program that intended to support lending to small and medium-sized businesses (below 15,000 employees or with 2019 revenues of $5 billion or less) that were affected by the pandemic and generally did not have access to the corporate bond market but that was financially healthy before the pandemic started.[4] Specifically, Minoiu, Zarutskie, and Zlate (2021) explained that MSLP wanted to reach bank-dependent firms that were likely too large to qualify for PPP loans but not large enough to issue bonds or syndicated loans, and thus could not access the Federal Reserve's Corporate Credit Facilities. These targeted firms account for a sizeable part of the economy, employing more than 50 million people or 30% of the labor force (English and Liang, 2020).

The program comprised three facilities for US businesses (Main Street New Loan Facility (MSNLF), the Main Street Priority Loan Facility (MSPLF), and the Main Street Expanded Loan Facility (MSELF)) and two facilities for nonprofit organizations (Nonprofit Organization New Loan Facility (NONLF) and the Nonprofit Organization Expanded Loan Facility (NOELF)). The business

---

[4]Details on the program are at: https://www.federalreserve.gov/monetarypolicy/mainstreetlending.htm and https://www.bostonfed.org/supervision-and-regulation/credit/special-facilities/main-street-lending-program.aspx.

facilities differed in some details of the loan features such as the eligible loan size, borrower leverage allowed, and other conditions for loan security and seniority relative to a borrower's other debts or shares retained by the bank.[5] The program also placed restrictions on the firms' uses of funds, executive compensation, dividends, and share repurchases. The facilities intended for US businesses accounted for most of the take-up. Firms may only participate in one of the three programs and only if they have not also participated in the PMCCF and have not received other direct support under the CARES Act.

What is unique is that MSLP relied on banks to screen and originate loans and the banks and government shared the loan risk. Banks originate the loans and sell 95% to a special purpose vehicle (SPV) maintained by the Federal Reserve while retaining 5% of the loans with the same risk on their balance sheets. This implies that loans made under the MSLP had to offer similar returns as those on other loans, discouraging subsidized lending. Though banks only had to retain a fraction of the loans, they had "skin in the game," incentivizing them to earn a satisfactory return on the retained portions. In addition, similar to PPP, the banks in MSLP received origination and servicing fees for their participation in the program. Principal and interest on the 4-year MSLP loans were deferred for 1 year. All loans carry an interest rate of LIBOR plus 300 bps. The facility's size was $600 billion in loans, backed by $75 billion in equity from the Treasury. The MSLP opened on June 15, 2020, and began accepting loan applications on July 6, 2020, and expired on December 31, 2020, with the deadline for processing submitted loans being January 8, 2021. Despite the large capacity put in place, the take-up of the MSLP program was very low, it only used just over $18 billion of its $600 billion total allocated, with about 11.7% (614) of the banks in the US participating in the program (see, e.g., Minoiu, Zarutskie, and Zlate, 2021).

There is very little research on MSLP—focused on supporting the flow of credit to small and mid-sized businesses during the pandemic—to date. One exception is Minoiu, Zarutskie, and Zlate (2021) who studied the effects of the MSLP on bank lending to businesses and used instrumental variables for identification and multiple loan-level and survey data sources for the analyses. Authors documented that the MSLP boosted banks' confidence that they would be able to continue lending through the MSLP to a large set of borrowers in the event of a worsening economic environment, motivating them to make more loans ex ante. Following the introduction of the program, bank participation in the MSLP is strongly and robustly associated with relatively less tightening of C&I lending standards and terms. MSLP banks were more likely to renew and originate new large corporate loans and made more small business loans after the program's implementation compared to non-MSLP banks. The estimates are larger for banks with stronger internal risk controls and MSLP banks were less likely to mention an increase in risk aversion as a reason for tightening standards.

Bräuning, Fillat, Lin, and Wang (2021) found that the MSLP extended more than $17.5 billion in loans to nearly 2500 companies across 49 states, the District of Columbia, and two US territories. Moreover, the MSLP directed more credit to places with more dire needs and likely also at times when credit was needed more. Thus, borrowers located in states that were more affected by declines in economic activity obtained more funding support from MSLP. In addition, businesses located in states where the economy was more adversely affected by COVID-19 increased their borrowing more when a state experienced a higher infection incidence. These findings suggest that MSLP was able to achieve one of its key objectives: providing liquidity support for firms in areas where the pandemic's impact

---

[5]MSPLF is the only facility where the banks retain 15% rather than 5% as in the other two facilities.

was more severe in terms of both the public health situation and the restraints on economic activity due to government imposed as well as voluntary restrictions on mobility.

Another question raised was why MLSP had low take-up. Minoiu, Zarutskie, and Zlate (2021) used detailed survey data on banks' experiences with the MSLP and documented that overly restrictive terms reduced bank interest and borrower demand. Most surveyed banks were able to meet credit demand outside the program, and the few firms that obtained MSLP loans were at the riskier end of the eligible population. Findings suggest that the program mainly served as a backstop and that banks viewed it as a safety net that they could activate if economic conditions deteriorated.

Bräuning and Paligorova (2021) also provided insights into the uptake of MSLP. They found that a wide range of borrowers used the program, with disproportionate uptake by firms that faced pandemic-related business disruptions. Loans made under MSLP totaled about 60% of comparable loans originated by the largest banks while the program was operational. Nevertheless, the terms of the MSLP were considered tight along several dimensions and in particular, the requirement of a leverage ratio lower than six prevented many potential borrowers from using it. Otherwise, they found that MSLP added substantially to the supply of credit to medium-sized borrowers, especially those with less than $50 million EBITDA that likely had limited access to large banks.

Morgan and Clampitt (2021) found that 90% of the MSLP loans were made by smaller banks with less than $31 billion in assets and 90% of the loans were small, less than $25 million. While weak demand was arguably the biggest roadblock, some program features also sidetracked participants. Authors mentioned that banks eschewing the program cited their uncertainty about how loss-sharing with the Federal Reserve and the US Treasury would play out. Some borrowers were deterred (according to loan officers) by restrictions on salaries or dividends. The lack of risk-based pricing may have deterred some safer borrowers though it did simplify matters.

Analyzing the characteristics of MSLP borrowers, Wang, Ballance, and Qing (2021) found that these borrowers tend to be larger than their peer firms (that is, firms in the same industry and state) and within the same size group, MSLP borrowers are on average younger than their peers. In addition, borrowers tended to have a slightly higher predicted risk of failure than their peers in March 2020 but their failure risk grew more than their peers' risk from March to the month when their MSLP loan request was submitted. These firms' relative performance in 2020 appears to be little correlated with their relative performance over the corresponding months in 2019. MSLP borrowers had worse actual delinquency records in March 2020, as well as more deterioration than their peers from March to the month of the MSLP loan submission. For borrowers with business spending data available from D&B, spending was on average higher in March 2020 than their peer companies' spending, and it fell somewhat less from March to the MSLP loan submission month. Taken together, these findings suggest that firms borrowed from the MSLP because of their greater growth or survival potential, and hence relationship value, which made lenders willing to lend to them, and also because of their higher credit risk which made the MSLP attractive, as it enabled the borrowers to pay a lower price or obtain more credit than they would have otherwise.

Finally, Elenev, Landvoigt, and Van Nieuwerburgh (2022) discussed that MSLP in addition to PPP were successful at preventing many corporate bankruptcies and prevented the pandemic from spilling over into a financial crisis. A program that combines MSLF, PPP, and the Corporate Credit Facility (CCF, discussed below) increases societal welfare by 6.5% in consumption equivalent units compared to a do-nothing scenario.

12.2.2 Conventional and unconventional monetary policy

The Federal Reserve also took unprecedented actions to address the COVID-19 crisis. In March 2020, in addition to cutting the federal funds rate to a range of 0%–0.25% and starting large-scale asset purchases, or quantitative easing (QE), in US Treasury securities and agency mortgage-backed securities. The QE program alone entailed $700 billion worth of asset purchases entailing Treasuries and mortgage-backed securities. On August 27, 2020, the Federal Reserve changed its language on inflation. It replaced its 2% inflation target commitment, and instead said it will "seek to achieve inflation that averages 2% over time." Essentially, this means allowing inflation to go over 2% to balance out time under 2% in order to raise inflation expectations to about 2%. In addition, the Federal Reserve also announced several measures for market liquidity, including putting in place facilities previously used in the GFC such as the Primary Dealer Credit Facility, the Commercial Paper Funding Facility, and the Money Market Mutual Fund Liquidity Facility, which all indirectly supported economic agents. Bordo and Duca (2021) provided an overview of these policy tools employed by the Federal Reserve during this crisis.

There is little to no direct evidence about individual monetary policy actions in the US and economic outcomes, mostly because disentangling effects of these from the many other programs happening at the same time during the COVID-19 crisis is difficult. We cover a few studies that discuss some effects of these but caution that despite expectations that actions positively affected agents, we cannot entirely attribute effects to one specific policy only.

Woodford (2022) showed that the challenge for stabilization policy presented by the COVID-19 pandemic stems above all from the disruption of the circular flow of payments, resulting in a failure of what Keynes (1936) calls "effective demand." Hence, economic activity in many sectors can be inefficiently low, and interest-rate policy cannot eliminate the distortions, not because of a limit on the extent to which interest rates can be reduced, but because interest-rate reductions fail to stimulate demand of the right sorts. He argues that fiscal transfers are instead well-suited to addressing the problem and can under certain circumstances achieve a first-best allocation of resources. Coibion, Gorodnichenko, and Weber (2020c) used a large-scale survey of US households during the COVID-19 pandemic to study how new information about policy responses affects the expectations and decisions of respondents. Specifically, they provided random subsets of participants with different combinations of information about the severity of the pandemic, recent actions by the Federal Reserve, stimulus measures, as well as recommendations from health officials. Then they characterize how their economic expectations and spending plans respond to these information treatments to assess to what extent these policy announcements alter the beliefs and plans of economic agents. By and large, authors found very little effect of these information treatments on the economic expectations of agents for income, mortgage rates, inflation or the unemployment rate nor do we find an effect on their planned decisions, contrary to the powerful effects they have in standard macroeconomic models.

Sims and Wu (2020) suggested that the Federal Reserve shifted during the COVID-19 crisis from a "Wall Street QE" which lends to financial firms to a "Main Street QE" in which it lends directly to, and purchases debt directly from, nonfinancial firms. They argued that when financial intermediary balance sheets are impaired, such as in the GFC, Main Street, and Wall Street QE are perfect substitutes, both helping stimulate aggregate demand. But during COVID-19, when the real sector is facing difficulties, Wall Street QE becomes almost completely ineffective, whereas Main Street QE can be highly stimulative.

Bergant and Forbes (2021) showed that countries that tightened macroprudential policy more aggressively before COVID, as well as those that eased more during the pandemic, experienced less financial and economic stress. Countries' ability to use macroprudential policy, however, was significantly constrained by the extent of existing "policy space," i.e., by how aggressively policy was tightened before COVID-19. The use of macroprudential tools was not significantly affected by the space available to use other policy tools (such as fiscal policy, monetary policy, FX intervention, and capital flow management measures), and the use of other tools was not significantly affected by the space available to use macroprudential policy. Elenev, Landvoigt, Shultz, and Van Nieuwerburgh (2021) showed that quantitative easing (QE), forward guidance, and an expansion in government discretionary spending all contribute to lowering the debt/GDP ratio and reducing the fiscal risk and that a transitory QE policy deployed during a crisis stimulates aggregate demand.

12.3   Corporate bond and loan purchase programs

The Federal Reserve also took unprecedented actions to address the COVID-19 crisis and to reduce financial frictions in corporate bond markets, providing direct liquidity support to large businesses with access to these markets. The Primary Market Corporate Credit Facility (PMCCF) is a program in which the facility could buy up to $100 billion of newly issued corporate bonds and loans with maturities of up to 4 years, from investment-grade US large businesses. Interest rates are informed by market conditions, in addition to a 100-bps facility fee. Loans could be syndicated, in which case the PMCCF would participate under the same conditions as other syndicate members. Then, the Secondary Market Corporate Credit Facility (SMCCF) is another program which would buy up to $100 billion of outstanding (mostly) investment-grade corporate bonds and loans and exchange-traded funds (ETFs) that held such bonds. Bonds were bought at fair market value. The ETF purchases allowed also for noninvestment-grade bond purchases, for example, through a high-yield credit index. In April 2020, the Federal Reserve and the US Treasury significantly expanded the scale of both programs, increasing their total capacity to $750 billion. It also expanded their scope, allowing the facilities to buy the bonds and loans of firms that had been investment grade at the beginning of the pandemic but were downgraded during the pandemic. However, the take-up of these facilities was very low, using only about $15 billion of the $750-billion allocated capacity.

Finally, the Term Asset-Backed Securities Loan Facility (TALF) program enabled the issuance of a variety of asset-backed securities backed by student loans, auto loans, credit card loans, loans guaranteed by the Small Business Administration (SBA), existing commercial mortgage-backed securities (CMBS), and collateralized loan obligations (CLO). The program is directed toward purchases of AAA-rated tranches.

Amid the early part of the COVID-19 crisis, the corporate bond markets experienced severe distress and liquidity problems accompanied by significant price declines, primarily driven by fire sale dynamics. Several papers show that the corporate credit facilities helped mitigate fire sale problems and bond market liquidity by reducing financial frictions in these markets (e.g., Falato, Goldstein, and Hortaçsu, 2021; Kargar, Lester, Lindsay, Liu, Weill, and Zúñiga, 2021; Ma, Xiao, and Zeng, 2021; O'Hara and Zhou, 2021; Boyarchenko, Kovner, and Shachar, 2022; Chodorow-Reich, Iverson, and Sunderam, 2022).

Chodorow-Reich, Iverson, and Sunderam (2022) showed that the take-up in the corporate credit facilities (CCFs) was very low, as they used only approximately $15 billion of their $750-billion capacity. Despite this, authors found that they had meaningful announcement effects on bond prices.

Investment-grade credit spreads fell sharply after the initial program announcement on March 23, while high-yield credit spreads were more significantly impacted when the programs were significantly expanded on April 9. Spreads fell further after Federal Reserve chairman's remarks on May 29: "The Fed is strongly committed to using our tools to do whatever we can for as long as it takes to provide some relief and some stability now. We crossed a lot of red lines, that had not been crossed before. This is that situation in which you do that, and then you figure it out afterward." Halling, Yu, and Zechner (2020) showed that these price movements were complemented by significant bond issuance by firms, which took advantage of improving market conditions to build liquidity.

Boyarchenko, Kovner, and Shachar (2022), Gilchrist, Wei, Yue, and Zakrajšek (2020), and Haddad, Moreira, and Muir (2021) used event study methodology and found that the announcement of corporate credit facilities generates significant declines in credit spreads. A second methodology using differences-in-differences that compares spreads on bonds that were eligible for corporate credit facility purchases and bonds that were not, before and after the key program announcements, finds that credit facilities lowered credit spreads, but generally yield smaller magnitudes than the event study approach.

However, Boyarchenko, Kovner, and Shachar (2022) also argued that purchases themselves had important effects on bond prices, over and above the simple announcements of the programs. They evaluated the impact of the Federal Reserve corporate credit facilities (PMCCF and SMCCF) on corporate bond markets and documented that conditions in primary markets improve once the facilities are announced. This improvement is higher for issuers that need to refinance before 2022 and that issuance accelerated before spreads normalized. The secondary market points to a causal role for the facilities, with a differential impact on eligible issues and a significant effect of direct bond purchases, but less so for purchases through ETFs.

Gilchrist, Wei, Yue, and Zakrajšek (2020) studied the impact of the Federal Reserve's announcements and the impact of its actual purchases of corporate bonds via SMCCF and found that the two announcements reduced credit and bid-ask spreads, and this appears to have had little to do with whether a particular bond was eligible for purchase by the corporate credit facility. The narrowing of credit spreads was due almost entirely to a reduction in credit risk premia, not a reduction in default risk.

Haddad, Moreira, and Muir (2021) argued that the market did indeed anticipate significant expansions of corporate credit facilities if the markets got deteriorated. They documented extreme disruption in debt markets during the COVID-19 crisis: a severe price crash accompanied by significant dislocations at the safer end of the credit spectrum. Investment-grade corporate bonds traded at a discount to credit default swaps and ETFs traded at a discount to net asset value, more so for safer bonds. However, they found that the Federal Reserve's announcement of corporate bond purchases via the CCFs caused these dislocations to disappear and prices to recover.

Other papers also documented the positive effects of corporate credit facilities on bond markets. Falato, Goldstein, and Hortaçsu (2021) documented major outflows in corporate-bond funds during the COVID-19 crisis. Effects were most severe for funds with illiquid assets, vulnerable to fire sales, and exposed to sectors hurt by the crisis. However, the Federal Reserve bond purchase program helped reduce fragility and reversed outflows, especially for the most fragile funds. In turn, the bond purchase program had spillover effects, stimulating primary market bond issuance by firms whose outstanding bonds were held by the impacted funds and stabilizing peer funds whose bond holdings overlapped with those of the impacted funds. This suggests a novel transmission channel of unconventional monetary policy via nonbank financial institutions. Similarly, O'Hara and Zhou (2021) found that during the 2 weeks leading up to Federal Reserve System interventions, volume shifted to liquid securities, transaction costs soared, trade-size pricing inverted, and dealers, particularly nonprimary dealers, shifted from buying to selling, causing dealers' inventories to plummet. By improving dealer funding conditions and providing a liquidity backstop, the corporate credit facilities stabilized trading conditions and most of the impact on bond liquidity seems to have materialized following its announcement. Kargar, Lester, Lindsay, Liu, Weill, and Zuniga (2021) found that during the COVID-19 pandemic, the cost of bond trading immediately via risky principal trades dramatically increased at the height of the sell-off, forcing customers to shift toward slower agency trades. But they showed that the Federal Reserve's corporate credit facilities had a positive effect on corporate market liquidity. They estimated that customers' willingness to pay for immediacy increased by about 200 bps per dollar of the transaction, but quickly subsided after Federal Reserve's actions. D'Amico, Kurakula, and Lee (2020) looked at returns on ETFs invested in bonds that were eligible vs others that were not eligible for purchase by credit facilities. They found improved functioning in the secondary market due to reduced disaster or tail risk of eligible issuers induced by the program. In contrast, Nozawa and Qiu (2021) found mixed evidence and few conclusive effects of the corporate programs on liquidity spreads for eligible and ineligible bonds.

One study found more mixed results. Elenev, Landvoigt, and Van Nieuwerburgh (2022) suggested that when compared to PPP and MSLP, the corporate credit facilities program was much less effective. It did help lower credit spreads as intended and boost investment compared to the do-nothing situation. However, the program had only minor effects on firm defaults, while it still had fiscal implications since the government had to issue US Treasury debt to buy the corporate debt. The issuance increased safe rates, which increased the cost of debt funding for intermediaries, increasing fragility. However, authors found that a program that combines all three of the PPP, MSLF, and CCF increases societal welfare by 6.5% in consumption equivalent units compared to a do-nothing scenario.

In general, most extant research reviewed implies that the corporate credit facilities interventions played a positive role in stabilizing and providing liquidity to the US corporate bond markets during the COVID-19 crisis, with benefits for many large businesses, but the program does come with fiscal costs just as all of the interventions and its effects could have been larger.

References

Abramson, B. (2022). *The welfare effects of eviction and homelessness policies*. Available at: SSRN 4112426.

Akana, T., Lambie-Hanson, L., and Vickery, J. (2021). *Recent data on mortgage forbearance: Borrower uptake and understanding of lender accommodations*. Federal Reserve Bank of Philadelphia CFI Brief, March 2021.

Altonji, J., Contractor, Z., Finamor, L., Haygood, R., Lindenlaub, I., Meghir, C., O'Dea, C., Scott, D., Wang, L., and Washington, E. (2020). *Employment effects of unemployment insurance generosity during the pandemic*. Yale University Manuscript.

Ambrose, B. W., An, X., and Lopez, L. A. (2021). *Eviction risk of rental housing: Does it matter how your landlord finances the property?*. Available from: SSRN 3745974.

An, X., Cordell, L., Geng, L., and Lee, K. (2022). *Inequality in the time of COVID-19: Evidence from mortgage delinquency and forbearance*. Available from: SSRN 3789349.

An, X., Gabriel, S., and Tzur-Ilan, N. (2022). More than shelter: The effects of rental eviction moratoria on household well-being. *AEA Papers and Proceedings*, *vol. 112*, 308–312.

An, X., Kowalik, M., Liu, L., and Zhang, A. (2022). *Wealth and COVID-19 consumer debt relief: Evidence from mortgage forberance*. Working Paper.

Anderson, J. T., Harrison, D. M., and Seiler, M. J. (2022). Reducing strategic forbearance under the CARES act: An experimental approach utilizing recourse attestation. *Journal of Real Estate Finance and Economics, 65*(2), 230–260.

Andriotis, A. (2020). Flying blind into a credit storm: Widespread deferrals mean banks can't tell who's creditworthy. *Wall Street Journal*.

Annenberg, E., and Scharlemann, T. (2021). *The effect of mortgage forbearance on house prices during COVID-19*. FEDS Notes.

Bachas, N., Ganong, P., Noel, P. J., Vavra, J. S., Wong, A., Farrell, D., and Greig, F. E. (2020). *Initial impacts of the pandemic on consumer behavior: Evidence from linked income, spending, and savings data (no. w27617)*. National Bureau of Economic Research.

Bäckman, O., Brännström, L., and Kahlmeter, A. (2018). Housing evictions and economic hardship. A prospective study. *European Sociological Review, 34*(1), 106–119.

Baker, S. R., Farrokhnia, R. A., Meyer, S., Pagel, M., and Yannelis, C. (2020). *Income, liquidity, and the consumption response to the 2020 economic stimulus payments (w27097)*. National Bureau of Economic Research.

Bandyopadhyay, A. P. (2022). Communications between borrowers and servicers: Evidence from COVID-19 mortgage forbearance program. *Quarterly Journal of Finance, 12*(1), 2240004.

Bartik, A. W., Bertrand, M., Lin, F., Rothstein, J., and Unrath, M. (2020). *Measuring the labor market at the onset of the COVID-19 crisis (no. w27613)*. National Bureau of Economic Research.

Bell, A., Hedin, T. J., Moghadam, R., Schnorr, G., and Von Wachter, T. (2021). *10 key trends from the unemployment crisis in California and their implications for policy reform* (eScholarship). University of California.

Bell, A., Hedin, T. J., Schnorr, G., and Von Wachter, T. (2021). *March 18th analysis of unemployment insurance claims in california during the COVID-19 pandemic*. California Policy Lab.

Benfer, E. A., Greene, S. J., and Hagan, M. (2020). *Approaches to eviction prevention*. Available from: SSRN 3662736.

Benfer, E. A., Vlahov, D., Long, M. Y., Walker-Wells, E., Pottenger, J. L., Gonsalves, G., and Keene, D. E. (2021). Eviction, health inequity, and the spread of COVID-19: Housing policy as a primary pandemic mitigation strategy. *Journal of Urban Health, 98*(1), 1–12.

Bergant, K., and Forbes, K. (2021). *Macroprudential policy during COVID-19: The role of policy space (no. w29346)*. National Bureau of Economic Research.

Berger, A. N., Bouwman, C. H., Norden, L., Roman, R. A., Udell, G. F., and Wang, T. (2024). Piercing through opacity: Relationships and credit card lending to consumers and small businesses during normal times and the COVID-19 crisis. *Journal of Political Economy, 132*, forthcoming.

Bi, H., and Gulati, C. (2021). Fiscal relief during the COVID-19 pandemic. *Econometric Reviews, 106*(2), 5–24.

Boar, C., and Mongey, S. (2020). *Dynamic trade-offs and labor supply under the CARES act (no. w27727)*. National Bureau of Economic Research.

Bordo, M. D., and Duca, J. V. (2021). An overview of the Fed's new credit policy tools and their cushioning effect on the COVID-19 recession. *Journal of Governance and Economics, 3*, 100013.

Boutros, M. (2020). *Evaluating the impact of economic impact payments*. Available from: SSRN 3742448.

Boyarchenko, N., Kovner, A., and Shachar, O. (2022). It's what you say and what you buy: A holistic evaluation of the corporate credit facilities. *Journal of Financial Economics, 144*(3), 695–731.

Bräuning, F., Fillat, J. L., Lin, F., and Wang, J. C. (2021). A helping hand to main street where and when it was needed. In *FRB of Boston current policy perspectives paper* (92116).

Bräuning, F., and Paligorova, T. (2021). Uptake of the main street lending program. In *Federal Reserve Bank of Boston research paper series current policy perspectives paper* (90326).

Buchak, G., Matvos, G., Piskorski, T., and Seru, A. (2018). Fintech, regulatory arbitrage, and the rise of shadow banks. *Journal of Financial Economics, 130*(3), 453–483.

Capponi, A., Jia, R., and Rios, D. A. (2021). *The effect of mortgage forbearance on refinancing: Evidence from the CARES act*. Available from: SSRN 3618776.

Carey, P., Groen, J. A., Jensen, B. A., Krolik, T. J., and Polivka, A. E. (2021). Applying for and receiving unemployment insurance benefits during the coronavirus pandemic. *Monthly Labor Review, September 2012*, 1–38.

Casado, M. G., Glennon, B., Lane, J., McQuown, D., Rich, D., and Weinberg, B. A. (2021). *The aggregate effects of fiscal stimulus: Evidence from the COVID-19 unemployment (no. w27576)*. National Bureau of Economic Research.

Chen, F., and Shrider, E. M. (2021). *Expanded unemployment insurance benefits during pandemic lowered poverty rates across all racial groups*. U.S. Census Bureau.

Cherry, S., Jiang, E., Matvos, G., Piskorski, T., and Seru, A. (2021). Government and private household debt relief during COVID-19. *Brookings Papers on Economic Activity, Fall 2021*.

Cherry, S., Jiang, E., Matvos, G., Piskorski, T., and Seru, A. (2022). Shadow Bank distress and household debt relief: Evidence from the CARES act. *AEA Papers and Proceedings*, *112*, 509–515.

Chetty, R., Friedman, J., and Stepner, M. (2023). The economic impacts of COVID-19: Evidence from a new public database built using private sector data. *Quarterly Journal of Economics*. Forthcoming.

Chodorow-Reich, G., Coglianese, J., and Karabarbounis, L. (2019). The macro effects of unemployment benefit extensions: A measurement error approach. *Quarterly Journal of Economics*, *134*(1), 227–279.

Chodorow-Reich, G., Iverson, B., and Sunderam, A. (2022). *Lessons learned from support to business during COVID-19*. *Recession remedies*.

Coibion, O., Gorodnichenko, Y., and Weber, M. (2020a). *The cost of the COVID-19 crisis: Lockdowns, macroeconomic expectations, and consumer spending (w27141)*. National Bureau of Economic Research.

Coibion, O., Gorodnichenko, Y., and Weber, M. (2020b). *How did US consumers use their stimulus payments? (No. w27693)*. National Bureau of Economic Research.

Coibion, O., Gorodnichenko, Y., and Weber, M. (2020c). *Does policy communication during COVID work? (No. w27384)*. National Bureau of Economic Research.

Collinson, R., and Reed, D. (2018). *The effects of evictions on low-income households* (Unpublished Manuscript) (pp. 1–82).

Coombs, K., Dube, A., Jahnke, C., Kluender, R., Naidu, S., and Stepner, M. (2022). Early withdrawal of pandemic unemployment insurance: Effects on employment and earnings. *AEA Papers and Proceedings*, *112*, 85–90.

Cooper, D., and Olivei, G. (2021). *High-frequency spending responses to government transfer payments*.

Cox, N., Ganong, P., Noel, P., Vavra, J., Wong, A., Farrell, D., Greig, F., and Deadman, E. (2020). Initial impacts of the pandemic on consumer behavior: Evidence from linked income, spending, and savings data. *Brookings Papers on Economic Activity*, *2020*(2), 35–82.

D'Amico, S., Kurakula, V., and Lee, S. (2020). *Impacts of the fed corporate credit facilities through the lenses of ETFs and CDX*. Available from: SSRN 3604744.

Department of Housing and Urban Development. (2020a). *FHA's COVID-19 loss mitigation options, mortgagee letter 2020–22, July 8*.

Department of Housing and Urban Development. (2020b). *HUD issues new CARES act mortgage payment relief for FHA single family homeowners, Press Release, April 1*.

Desmond, M. E. (2016). *Poverty and profit in the American city*. Lake Arbor: Crown Books.

Desmond, M., and Kimbro, R. T. (2015). Eviction's fallout: Housing, hardship, and health. *Social Forces*, *94*(1), 295–324.

Dettling, L. J., and Lambie-Hanson, L. (2021). *Why is the default rate so low? How economic conditions and public policies have shaped mortgage and auto delinquencies during the COVID-19 pandemic*. FEDS Notes (2021-03), 04-2.

Dube, A. (2021a). *A plan to reform the unemployment insurance system in the United States*. Hamilton Project Policy Proposal (p. 3).

Dube, A. (2021b). *Aggregate employment effects of unemployment benefits during deep downturns: Evidence from the expiration of the federal pandemic unemployment compensation (no. w28470)*. National Bureau of Economic Research.

Duca, J. V., Popoyan, L., and Wachter, S. M. (2019). Real estate and the great crisis: Lessons for macroprudential policy. *Contemporary Economic Policy*, *37*(1), 121–137.

Elenev, V., Landvoigt, T., Shultz, P. J., and Van Nieuwerburgh, S. (2021). *Can monetary policy create fiscal capacity? (No. w29129)*. National Bureau of Economic Research.

Elenev, V., Landvoigt, T., and Van Nieuwerburgh, S. (2022). Can the COVID bailouts save the economy? *Economic Policy*, *37*(110), 277–330.

Elul, R., and Newton, N. (2021). Helping struggling homeowners during two crises. *Economic Insights*, *6*(4), 2–8.

English, W. B., and Liang, J. N. (2020). Designing the main street lending program: Challenges and options. *The Journal of Financial Crises*, *2*(3), 1–40.

Fairlie, R., and Fossen, F. M. (2022). Did the paycheck protection program and economic injury disaster loan program get disbursed to minority communities in the early stages of COVID-19? *Small Business Economics*, *58*(2), 829–842.

Falato, A., Goldstein, I., and Hortaçsu, A. (2021). Financial fragility in the COVID-19 crisis: The case of investment funds in corporate bond markets. *Journal of Monetary Economics*, *123*, 35–52.

Fang, L., Nie, J., and Xie, Z. (2020). *Unemployment insurance during a pandemic*. Working Paper. FRB Atlanta Working Paper No. 2020-13.

Farber, H. S., and Valletta, R. G. (2015). Do extended unemployment benefits lengthen unemployment spells? Evidence from recent cycles in the US labor market. *The Journal of Human Resources*, *50*(4), 873–909.

Favilukis, J., Mabille, P., and Van Nieuwerburgh, S. (2019). *Affordable housing and city welfare (no. w25906)*. National Bureau of Economic Research.

Federal Housing Finance Agency. (2020). *FHFA announces payment deferral as new repayment option for homeowners in COVID-19 forbearance plans, News Release, May 13*.

Freddie Mac. (2020). *Freddie Mac: Lump Sum Repayment Is Not Required in Forbearance*. Homeownership Blog. April 16.

Ganong, P., Greig, F., Noel, P., Sullivan, D. M., and Vavra, J. (2021). *Micro and macro disincentive effects of expanded unemployment benefits*. Working Paper.

Ganong, P., Greig, F. E., Noel, P. J., Sullivan, D. M., and Vavra, J. S. (2022). *Spending and job-finding impacts of expanded unemployment benefits: Evidence from administrative micro data (no. w30315)*. National Bureau of Economic Research.

Ganong, P., and Noel, P. (2019). Consumer spending during unemployment: Positive and normative implications. *The American Economic Review*, *109*(7), 2383–2424.

Ganong, P., Noel, P., and Vavra, J. (2020). US unemployment insurance replacement rates during the pandemic. *Journal of Public Economics*, *191*, 104273.

Gerardi, K., Lambie-Hanson, L., and Willen, P. (2021). Racial differences in mortgage refinancing, distress, and housing wealth accumulation during COVID-19. In *2021 Series on current policy perspectives*. Federal Reserve Bank of Boston.

Gilchrist, S., Wei, B., Yue, V. Z., and Zakrajšek, E. (2020). *The fed takes on corporate credit risk: An analysis of the efficacy of the SMCCF (no. w27809)*. National Bureau of Economic Research.

Government Accountability Office. (2021). *Economic injury disaster loan program: Additional actions needed to improve communication with applicants and address fraud risks*. GAO Publication No. 21-589, Washington, DC.

Greig, F., Zhao, C., and Lefevre, A. (2021). *Renters vs. homeowners: Income and liquid asset trends during COVID-19. Homeowners: Income and liquid asset trends during COVID-19*.

Haddad, V., Moreira, A., and Muir, T. (2021). When selling becomes viral: Disruptions in debt markets in the COVID-19 crisis and the fed's response. *Review of Financial Studies*, *34*(11), 5309–5351.

Hagedorn, M., Manovskii, I., and Mitman, K. (2016). *The impact of unemployment benefit extensions on employment: The 2014 employment miracle? (No. w20884)*. National Bureau of Economic Research.

Halling, M., Yu, J., and Zechner, J. (2020). How did COVID-19 affect firms' access to public capital markets? *Review of Corporate Finance Studies*, *9*(3), 501–533.

Han, J., Meyer, B. D., and Sullivan, J. X. (2020). *Income and poverty in the COVID-19 pandemic (no. w27729)*. National Bureau of Economic Research.

Holzer, H. J., Hubbard, R. G., and Strain, M. R. (2021). *Did pandemic unemployment benefits reduce employment? Evidence from early state-level expirations in June 2021 (no. w29575)*. National Bureau of Economic Research.

Humphries, J. E., Mader, N. S., Tannenbaum, D. I., and van Dijk, W. L. (2019). Does eviction cause poverty? In *Quasi-experimental evidence from cook county, IL (no. w26139)*. National Bureau of Economic Research.

Jiang, E. X. (2023). Financing competitors: Shadow banks' funding and mortgage market competition. *Review of Financial Studies*. Forthcoming.

Jiang, E., Matvos, G., Piskorski, T., and Seru, A. (2020). *Banking without deposits: Evidence from shadow bank call reports (no. w26903)*. National Bureau of Economic Research.

Jowers, K., Timmins, C., Bhavsar, N., Hu, Q., and Marshall, J. (2021). *Housing precarity & the COVID-19 pandemic: Impacts of utility disconnection and eviction moratoria on infections and deaths across US counties (no. w28394)*. National Bureau of Economic Research.

Kargar, M., Lester, B., Lindsay, D., Liu, S., Weill, P. O., and Zúñiga, D. (2021). Corporate bond liquidity during the COVID-19 crisis. *Review of Financial Studies*, 34(11), 5352–5401.

Karger, E., and Rajan, A. (2020). *Heterogeneity in the marginal propensity to consume: Evidence from COVID-19 stimulus payments*.

Karpman, M., and Acs, G. (2020). *Unemployment insurance and economic impact payments associated with reduced hardship following CARES act*. Washington, DC: Urban Institute.

Keynes, J. M. (1936). *The general theory of employment, interest and money*. London: MacMillan.

Keys, B. J., Piskorski, T., Seru, A., and Vig, V. (2013). Mortgage financing in the housing boom and bust. In *Housing and the financial crisis*. University of Chicago Press. Chapter in housing and the financial crisis.

Kim, Y. S., Lee, D., Scharlemann, T. C., and Vickery, J. I. (2022). *Intermediation frictions in debt relief: Evidence from CARES act forbearance*. FRB of New York Staff Report (1035).

Kowalik, M., Liu, L., and Wang, X. (2021). *Credit scores since the COVID-19 outbreak*. Federal Reserve Bank of Boston Supervisory Research and Analysis Working Papers 21-04.

Lembo Stolba, S. (2021). *Experian 2020 consumer credit review. Staff report*. Available from: https://www.experian.com/blogs/ask-experian/consumer-credit-review/.

Li, M. (2021). Did the small business administration's COVID-19 assistance go to the hard hit firms and bring the desired relief? *Journal of Economics and Business*, 115, 105969.

Ma, Y., Xiao, K., and Zeng, Y. (2021). *Mutual fund liquidity transformation and reverse flight to liquidity*. Working Paper.

Marinescu, I., Skandalis, D., and Zhao, D. (2021). The impact of the federal pandemic unemployment compensation on job search and vacancy creation. *Journal of Public Economics*, 200, 104471.

McManus, D., and Yannopoulos, E. (2021). COVID-19 mortgage forbearances: Drivers and payment behavior. *Journal of Structured Finance*, 27(2), 13–25.

Meier, J. M., and Smith, J. (2020). *The COVID-19 bailouts*. Available at: SSRN 358551.

Mian, A., and Sufi, A. (2009). The consequences of mortgage credit expansion: Evidence from the US mortgage default crisis. *Quarterly Journal of Economics*, 124(4), 1449–1496.

Minoiu, C., Zarutskie, R., and Zlate, A. (2021). *Motivating banks to lend? Credit spillover effects of the main street lending program*.

Misra, K., Singh, V., and Zhang, Q. (2022). Frontiers: Impact of stay-at-home-orders and cost-of-living on stimulus response: Evidence from the CARES act. *Marketing Science*, 41(2), 211–229.

Morgan, D. P., and Clampitt, S. (2021). *Up on main street, Federal Reserve Bank of New York Liberty street economics, February 5, 2021*. https://libertystreeteconomics.newyorkfed.org/2021/02/up-on-main-street.html.

Nozawa, Y., and Qiu, Y. (2021). Corporate bond market reactions to quantitative easing during the COVID-19 pandemic. *Journal of Banking & Finance*, 133, 106153.

NYC Office of Civil Justice. (2017). *Annual report and strategic plan*. New York, NY: NYC Office of Civil Justice. Retrieved from: https://www1.nyc.gov/assets/hra/downloads/pdf/services/civiljustice/OCJ_Annual_Report_2017.pdf.

O'Hara, M., and Zhou, X. A. (2021). Anatomy of a liquidity crisis: Corporate bonds in the COVID-19 crisis. *Journal of Financial Economics*, 142(1), 46–68.

Parker, J. A., Schild, J., Erhard, L., and Johnson, D. (2022). *Household spending responses to the economic impact payments of 2020: Evidence from the consumer expenditure survey (no. w29648)*. National Bureau of Economic Research.

Petrosky-Nadeau, N., and Valletta, R. G. (2021). *UI generosity and job acceptance: Effects of the 2020 CARES act*.

Sahm, C., Shapiro, M., and Slemrod, J. (2020). *Consumer response to the coronavirus stimulus programs. Presentation November, 11* (p. 2020).

Sims, E. R., and Wu, J. C. (2020). *Wall street vs. main street QE (no. w27295)*. National Bureau of Economic Research.

Small Business Administration. (2020). *Inspection of small business administration's initial disaster assistance response to the coronavirus pandemic. Office of the Inspector General, U.S. Small Business Administration, Report Number 21-02, October 28, 2020.*

Spatt, C. S. (2020). A tale of two crises: The 2008 mortgage meltdown and the 2020 COVID-19 crisis. *Review of Asset Pricing Studies, 10*(4), 759–790.

Wang, J. C., Ballance, J., and Qing, M. (2021). *How did the MSLP borrowers fare before and during COVID-19?.*

Wang, J., Yang, J., Iverson, B. C., and Kluender, R. (2020). *Bankruptcy and the COVID-19 crisis.* Available at: SSRN 3690398.

Woodford, M. (2022). Effective demand failures and the limits of monetary stabilization policy. *The American Economic Review, 112*(5), 1475–1521.

Chapter 13

Policy reactions to the COVID-19 crisis in the rest of the world and their effects on economies, households, nonfinancial firms, banks, and financial markets

Abstract

We focus in this chapter on research and data on the effects of non-US COVID-19 policies. These include a wide variety of financial aid programs, forbearance policies, conventional and unconventional monetary policies, credit and liquidity facilities, asset and securities purchases, and fiscal and labor market support policies. As in the US, the total magnitudes are very large. We also assess research on the effects of these policies on the real economy, banking sector, and financial markets of the relevant countries in different parts of the globe. The research results are too varied to summarize briefly.

Keywords: COVID-19, Non-US policies, Financial aid, Forbearance, Monetary policies, Credit and liquidity facilities, Asset and securities purchases, Fiscal and labor market support policies

This chapter shifts attention to research, data, and descriptions of policies outside the US in reactions to the COVID-19 crisis and their consequences. The fiscal and monetary policies that we discuss take six different forms such as COVID-19 financial aid programs, forbearance programs and other related policies, conventional and unconventional monetary policies, credit and liquidity facilities, asset and security purchases, and fiscal and labor market support policies. We briefly review the research on the implications of each type to the real economy, banking sector, and financial markets of countries across the globe and consider the context of the country in a global setting. Some countries acted with more speed than others, and some were far more efficient with the use of these policies. Some countries were more vulnerable to the pandemic for reasons of preexisting poverty and inequalities, heavy dependence on trade, preexisting high government debt, poor infrastructure, lack of access to capital,

The Economic and Financial Impacts of the COVID-19 Crisis Around the World
https://doi.org/10.1016/B978-0-443-19162-6.00002-5
Copyright © 2024 Elsevier Inc. All rights reserved.

high dependence on tourism revenue, and a large portion of their economies being supported by micro-, small, and medium-sized enterprises that have smaller cash reserves to help survive a crisis.

13.1 COVID-19 financial aid programs

In reaction to the rapid spread of the novel coronavirus, the world's governments are racing to support people and businesses until the virus is contained. With businesses being shut down across the globe, millions of people are unable to work indefinitely, consumer spending and sentiment are plummeting, and the markets are collapsing. The need for a major expansionary policy is urgent. Governments across the globe must protect their economies from the possibility of a fast, deepening, and unprecedented recession. The primary questions being considered are how much money to shovel into the economy, what forms of stimulus will be the most effective and efficient, and whether the scale of the stimulus will be enough... or too much.

The first order on the agenda is to contain the spread of the deadly virus. Officials from around the world are using the original playbook that was used to contain the 1918 flu pandemic: they are restricting travel and cracking down on public gatherings. While those measures have the potential to reduce deaths and infections, they will also damage business prospects for many companies and cause a synchronized worldwide disruption.

When it comes to a complete shutting down of the economy, governments must act swiftly and aggressively in order to protect their economies from a deep and lasting recession. The initial response to most was anything but conservative. According to the Harvard economist Kenneth Rogoff, "The policy response needs to be massive... Fiscal policy response in the health sector needs to treat this like a war, and nothing less, converting facilities to temporary hospitals, factories to making respirators and face masks."

Countries around the world stepped in line to introduce the initial wave of the stimulus. Germany introduced a $800 billion stimulus plan, which accounts for 20.5% of its gross domestic product, while its Debt to GDP ratio was around 61%. The UK's stimulus package was $481 billion and accounted for 16.6% of GDP, with a government debt to GDP ratio of 84%. Spain has spent $219 billion on its stimulus package, which accounted for 15.6% of GDP with its government debt to GDP totaling 98%. Australia spent $196 billion, which accounted for 13.7% of GDP, and its debt to GDP ratio was 30%. Canada and China spent $57 and $394 billion on their stimulus packages to fight COVID-19, respectively, making the stimulus equal to 3.4% and 2.9% of GDP, with debt to GDP ratios of 85% and 61%. The European Union and the European Commission spent $480 billion, and while having a debt to GDP percentage of 90%, its stimulus package only accounted for 2.6%. Italy and France both spent $49 billion on stimulus packages. However, their debt to GDP ratios are 137% and 100%, respectively, while the stimulus as a percentage of GDP accounted for 2.3% and 1.8%, respectively. Japan spent the least amount on its stimulus package compared to its G20 peers, dedicating only $4B for stimulus packages, ultimately accounting for 0.1% of GDP, perhaps due to their staggering debt to GDP ratio of 237%.

Governments and other institutions around the world are looking to buy time for their countries until the crisis is curtailed. It is not enough to rely solely on the stimulus paid to individuals of the economy, but governments must look to more creative ways to survive the crisis. In China, where the COVID-19 outbreak originated, the government is reportedly planning around $394 billion of infrastructure spending, backed by local government bonds. Banks reportedly have approval from the government to roll over loans, relax guidelines on overdue debt, avoid reporting delinquencies, and for borrowers to skip making payments. The People's Bank of China cut bank reserve requirements to free up $79 billion for lending to crisis-hit companies and says it will reduce interest rates for borrowers. The Australian government is planning A$320 billion ($197 billion) of spending and available borrowing. The package includes wage subsidies of A$1500 every 2 weeks for each employee. Parliament had previously agreed to more than A$80 billion in fiscal stimulus. The Danish government is paying 75% of employees' salaries, up to $3288 per month, at private companies that have been impacted by the pandemic. The government has announced a spending package of about $4 billion that is focused on small and midsize companies. A government-affiliated lender will offer funds charging (effectively) no interest to small firms whose revenues have dropped because of the virus. The Bank of Japan will buy more than $100 billion worth of exchange-traded funds, twice its earlier pledge, while setting aside money to keep corporate funding markets operating. In Germany, the government in Berlin has signed off on a €750 billion ($800 billion) package as well as plans for loans, guarantees, government stakes in companies, and credit to keep businesses afloat. The German Economy Minister Peter Altmaier declared, "We promised that we will not fail because of a lack of money and political will… We will reload our weapons if necessary."

While the nations of the Eurozone are confined by the monetary policy set forth by the European Central Bank, it is interesting to see what individual decisions they made regarding their fiscal policy measures. In Spain, officials are prepared to make as much as $219 billion of aid available, including €100 billion of guarantees for company loans and €17 billion of direct support for enterprises. Prime Minister Pedro Sanchez reportedly stated that private investment will provide €83 billion of support.

Within the UK, integration between fiscal and monetary policy is theoretically more feasible. The British government said on March 20 that it will write a blank check for workers, and government grants will cover 80% of the salary of retained workers up to a total of £2500 ($3084) a month; no business will pay VAT until June, which is worth £30 billion. On March 26, Chancellor Rishi Sunak unveiled a similar initiative for the self-employed who earn up to £50,000, offering them 80% of their average earnings for the past 3 years. The spending measures will cost around £60 billion (paywall), according to Financial Times estimates. For closed or affected businesses that cannot make payroll, the government strives to provide relief to prevent layoffs. Officials said on March 17 that they are assembling an aid fund of £330 billion—roughly 15% of the gross domestic product—to offer state-backed loans to support UK businesses. Small operators in retail, hospitality, and leisure will be eligible for cash grants of up to £25,000. The March 17 package also includes 3-month mortgage holidays for homeowners in financial difficulty because of the pandemic. Officials in London pledged £30 billion of emergency spending on March 11. That includes a £5 billion emergency response fund for the National Health Service, statutory sick pay for people who have been told to self-isolate, and sick-pay refunds for companies with fewer than 250 employees. Fiscal policy was accompanied by synchronous monetary policy as well. The Bank of England cut its target rate to a record low 0.1% and boosted its bond-buying program by $230 billion on March 19. The central bank had previously rolled out a cheap credit program and gave banks more scope to lend. Its Term Funding Scheme is aimed at smaller companies.

Overall, Burni, Erforth, Friesen, Hackenesch, Hoegl, and Keijzer (2022) found that the European Union generally showed good cooperation. The COVID-19 epidemic comes at a crucial time in the history of the world. Under the banner of "Team Europe," the EU has worked to mobilize swift development aid to support partners in tackling the crisis effects while encouraging coordinated action among European players to stake out its position in a dynamic and cutthroat geopolitical environment.

This paper evaluates how the Union's worldwide COVID-19 reaction reflects the substantive and process-oriented EU development policy principles. The article demonstrates how the EU responded to this unusual catastrophe by furthering EU integration, focusing on the EU's actions during the first wave of the COVID-19 pandemic in the first half of 2020. As a result, the EU's development strategy placed more emphasis on process-oriented standards than substantive ones.

Aid to small businesses is a common theme across policy types and countries. In France, officials will spend €45 billion to help small businesses and employees, and President Emmanuel Macron said this aid will be "unlimited." The Italian government approved €25 billion ($49 billion) of support for companies and workers, including extra money for the health system, increased unemployment benefits, the freezing of tax and loan payments, and suspension of mortgage payments. The effort will also make use of €340 billion of financing, and more efforts are expected to follow.

The Indian government is reportedly pushing its banks to approve as much as 600 billion rupees ($8.1 billion) of loans by the end of March. The Reserve Bank of India announced long-term repo operations (LTRO) to reduce interest rates and boost lending. The Canadian government is planning a package totaling C$82 billion ($56.7 billion), which includes C$27 billion of support for individuals and companies and C$55 billion in temporary tax deferrals for businesses and households. This stimulus effort is accompanied by an expansionary monetary policy by the Bank of Canada, which will cut its overnight interest rate by 50 basis points to 0.75% on March 13.

International organizations took similar approaches as individual governments. The International Monetary Fund, an international organization with 189 member countries, says it is prepared to mobilize $1 trillion in lending, while as much as $10 billion is available for low-income countries using facilities that have zero interest rates. Authorities from the European Union are considering repurposing their fund, originally designed to combat the euro zone's sovereign debt crisis, to cushion the impact of a recession. The so-called European Stability Mechanism has more than €400 billion of unused capacity. The European Commission is assessing a €37 billion Coronavirus Response Investment Initiative to be used for healthcare, supporting workers, and small and medium-sized businesses. The European Central Bank (ECB) started a €750 billion Pandemic Emergency Purchase Program on March 18. The program is planned to last through the end of 2020, and is authorized to purchase a portion of Greece's debt. The ECB also began purchasing commercial paper, a form of short-term borrowing. The European Central Bank kept its overnight lending rate steady at −0.5% on March 12 while boosting asset purchases by €120 billion. Policymakers said they will offer cheap loans to the region's banks, while ECB president Christine Lagarde said governments need to spend money to contain the economic fallout.

However, not all the countries need billions in Spending. Uruguay's package, unlike the total packages of many countries with a high GDP, was not a large percentage of its GDP. Taylor (2020) explained how simple measures and following the science have put it above richer countries in fighting the novel coronavirus. The very swift action of the government to lock down public places and events and pool testing, as opposed to individual testing, all led to Uruguay's very quick recovery and stabilizing the pandemic.

13.2 COVID-19 forbearance programs and other related policies

The dramatic spread of COVID-19 has threatened human lives, disrupted livelihoods, and affected trade, economies, and businesses across the globe. The global economy has begun to show major disruptions and is heading toward a severe recession with an unprecedented economic crisis. As the global economy is highly integrated and interdependent through the global supply chains, it has been profoundly affected by the COVID-19 pandemic. Although all countries have faced difficulties due to COVID-19, South Asian countries in particular have had to deal with a more challenging situation due to their large population, weak health facilities, high poverty rates, low socio-economic conditions, poor social protection systems, limited access to water and sanitation, and inadequate living space necessary to maintain physical distancing and take other required measures to contain this pandemic. To contain the spread of the virus, South Asian countries have imposed stringent lockdowns, which have consequently affected the lives and livelihoods of millions of people in the region, where a third of the world's poor live. Against this backdrop, this paper examines the existing and prospective impacts, risks, and challenges of the COVID-19 pandemic on key sectors including migration, tourism, informal sector, agriculture, and social and economic consequences such as the rural livelihoods of South Asian countries (Rasul, Nepal, Hussain, Maharjan, Joshi, Lama, Gurung, Ahmad, Mishra, and Sharma, 2021). The analysis revealed that COVID-19 is likely to affect economic growth, increase both the fiscal deficit and monetary burden, increase the risks of macroeconomic instability, decrease migration and remittance, reduce income from travel and tourism, and result in a dwindling of micro-, small, and medium-sized industries and informal businesses. The likely result is an increase in unemployment and a deepening of the existing poverty and food insecurity. If not addressed properly, this may reinforce the existing inequalities, break social harmony, and increase tension and turbulence across the globe, disproportionately affecting rural and impoverished areas like South Asia with significant and long-lasting consequences. The future of these economies seems to appear more like an uncertainty rather than a risk, given that it is hard to estimate the effect of confounding variables on various parts of these already struggling economies, and overcoming this crisis will be that much more complicated.

With the possibility of transmission rates dwindling, thanks to robust vaccination rates across South Asia and the adaptation to new modes of behavior, inflation has become the biggest short-term risk for South Asian economies. Preexisting inflationary pressures exacerbate the global supply chain shocks from the war in Ukraine. Even before the war, consumer prices of edible oils rose by 20% in many South Asian countries, with the price of fuel for transportation reaching double digits in some. Higher commodity prices fueled by the war have further added to inflationary pressures. The global price of wheat rose by 20%, and Brent crude oil price increased by 15% as of early April. With Ukraine supplying nearly half of the world's sunflower oil, cooking oil prices have spiraled: India's average retail price of sunflower oil increased by 12% in the first 3 weeks after the war started.

Although global oil prices place relatively weak pressure on consumer prices, they yield a strong influence on producer prices. In India, Pakistan, and Sri Lanka, the wholesale price of crude petroleum and petroleum products is historically highly correlated with global oil prices. Higher global energy prices can raise the prices of fertilizers, which will in turn push up food prices, and increase the operating and transportation costs for the manufacturing sector, thus squeezing the profit margins of producers. Governments in the region use fuel subsidies to reduce the burden of global energy prices on consumers. However, as argued in Reshaping Norms, a better alternative may lie in policies that discourage the use of dirty fossil fuels and enhance green transition.

Seventy-three percent of SAEPN experts believe that stresses in financial markets will increase over the next 6 months, and close to half believe that asset quality will deteriorate. Loan forbearance programs during the COVID-19 pandemic supported businesses and allowed financial markets to continue lending while low lending rates also encouraged borrowing. However, as the latest World Development Report highlights, the programs may have created a lack of transparency about the health of the balance sheets of banks. As the support measures unwind and advanced economies hike policy rates, vulnerabilities in financial markets can resurface. Our findings in reshaping norms show that asset quality fell immediately following the ending of support programs in some countries, which suggests that the programs indeed masked some prior deterioration of asset quality.

To make matters worse, micro-, small, and medium-sized enterprises (MSMEs), which account for 99.6% of all enterprises, 76.6% of the workforce, and 33.9% of South Asia's gross domestic product (GDP) on average, were hard hit during COVID-19. The absence of credit record and audited financial statements made the credit risks of MSMEs difficult to assess and made it harder for these businesses to get access to financing. Even with the lending support programs, the financing conditions of the MSMEs are worrying. Among the surveyed experts, 47% believe that financing conditions have worsened for microenterprises over the past year, compared to only 18% who believe that conditions have deteriorated for large firms. The ending of support programs can hit these businesses particularly hard. In Pakistan, for example, nonperforming loans among microfinance borrowers were up 42.7% after the support programs ended, compared to a year ago.

As South Asia charts a new way forward to address the rising inequality, accommodate energy transition, and unleash new growth potential, an essential part of the economic recovery lies in reshaping norms to make the economies more conducive to growth and progress. Two notable approaches in this area are discussed below with the war in Russia and Ukraine and the situation in South Asia.

The war and its impact on fuel prices can provide the region with the much-needed impetus to reduce reliance on fuel imports and transition to a green, resilient, and inclusive growth trajectory. A quarter of the SAEPN experts surveyed believe that a carbon tax should have been implemented a long time ago, while 37% are in favor of a gradual phase-in of a carbon tax.

The situation in South Asia introduces a threat to the deepening of economic and social inequality. Economic development is intrinsically related to gender outcomes. A challenge facing South Asian countries is the disproportionate economic impact the pandemic has had on women. Reshaping norms includes in-depth analysis of gender disparities in the region and recommends policies that support gender outcomes for inclusive growth. Creative rethinking of policies will help South Asia counter external shocks, protect the vulnerable, and keep headwinds at bay during its economic recovery, while also laying the foundation for a green, inclusive, and resilient growth.

13.3   COVID-19 conventional and unconventional monetary policies

Monetary policies have the most immediate effect on financial markets. In order to examine the interaction between health crises, monetary policy, and financial markets, Wei and Han (2021) examined a case study of 37 countries with severe epidemics between January 1, 2011, and April 30, 2020. This study used event-study methodology to estimate the impact of the COVID-19 pandemic on the transmission of monetary policy to financial markets. The countries that they examine are Argentina, Australia, Austria, Belgium, Brazil, Canada, Chile, China, France, Germany, India, Indonesia, Ireland, Israel, Italy, Japan, Mexico, Netherlands, Pakistan, Peru, Poland, Portugal, Qatar, Romania, Russia, Saudi Arabia, Singapore, South Africa, South Korea, Spain, Sweden, Switzerland, Turkey, Ukraine, United Arab Emirates, UK, and US. Of the countries in this sample, 34 have severe COVID-19 pandemics, which is defined as having more than 10,000 confirmed cases as of April 30, 2020. Three G20 countries, Argentina, Australia, and South Africa, have confirmed cases of 4428, 6766, and 5647, respectively, but given the importance of the G20 countries and their influence on the world economy, they include these three countries in their sample. The goal of this study is to examine the emergence of the pandemic effect on the transmission of monetary policy to financial markets. Has the crisis strengthened the transmission of monetary policy to financial markets, or weakened it?

Their results suggest that the emergence of the pandemic has weakened the transmission of monetary policy to financial markets to a more significant degree. During their sample period following the outbreak of the pandemic, neither conventional nor unconventional monetary policies have significant effects on all four of the financial markets. The unconventional monetary policies are slightly more effective as they can affect the stock and exchange rate markets to some extent. Therefore, in the post-pandemic period, if monetary policy is used to stimulate financial markets, stronger policy adjustments, or other macroeconomic policies such as fiscal policies, may be needed to achieve the desired effect.

In deciding the methodology of the study, among the daily financial market indicators that measure dependent variables, they choose representative indicators that respond freely to changes in monetary policy and may be influenced by monetary policy. To test the transmission of monetary policy to yield curves, they include 10-year zero-coupon government bond yields. To estimate the transmission of monetary policy to equity markets, they include stock index returns. The data also include changes to each country's currency exchange rate against the dollar to estimate the transmission of monetary policy to exchange rate markets. Finally, they include the growth rates of credit default swap (CDS) spreads to represent the credit market. A CDS seller provides credit protection against the risk of default for CDS buyers. In return, CDS buyers pay periodic fees to sellers, and these are called CDS spreads. CDS spreads are therefore used as a direct measure of credit risk in economies and financial markets.

Their findings suggest that the emergence of the pandemic has weakened the transmission of monetary policy to financial markets to a more significant degree. What does this mean for design policy in practice? Questions that should be asked are whether this pandemic provides evidence for past and future crises. It is also important to consider the specific monetary policy that was in place at the beginning of the pandemic. Lastly, the study does not represent the developed world or smaller economies, and we will discuss the monetary policies, often radical, that are implemented in other parts of the globe further in this chapter.

Since the beginning of 2020, policymakers have been busy designing measures to contain the spread of COVID-19. Lockdowns resulted in an immediate decline in economic activities and surge in unemployment. In restricting the spread of the pandemic and the resulting economic downturn, many developed economies faced short-term interest rates nearing zero, or even slipping to negative in order to incentivize spending. Several central banks around the world engaged in unconventional monetary policy interventions in the form of long-term asset purchase programs, commonly referred to as quantitative easing (QE). Since March 2020, eight Central Banks of the developed economies have made QE announcements. Notably, the US initially announced a $700 billion purchase on March 16, 2020, followed by an announcement of "unlimited" purchase on March 23, 2020. The UK announced a purchase of $200 billion on March 19, 2020.

Amid an unprecedented economic shock and in the wake of decisive action from policymakers in the US and other developed countries, authorities across many regions in the world have effectively combined the fiscal and monetary tools at their disposal to protect the incomes and livelihoods of their citizens. They have combined increased transfers and healthcare spending with monetary expansion, carefully without provoking financial instability. As their economies went into lockdown, many central banks in the Asia Pacific region took similar steps. It was the region's first leap into QE. For example, the Reserve Bank of India, the Bank Indonesia, and the Bangko Sentral ng Pilipinas, the Bank of Korea, and the Bank of Thailand started purchasing government bonds. However, the size of asset purchases in some emerging Asian economies has been on a much smaller scale than in many advanced economies.

In Africa, emerging economies also tried to keep up as much as they could. The following are monetary policy measures which were introduced by some African countries to combat the economic impact of COVID-19. The Bank of Algeria decided to reduce the rate of compulsory reserve from 10% to 8% and to lower interest rates by 25 basis points. The Cote d'Ivoire government announced $200 million as a COVID-19 response under the establishment of a fund to boost the economic activity and assist affected businesses in order to mitigate jobs cuts by supporting payroll expenses. The Ethiopian government has announced that it has allocated $10 million to the fight against the pandemic and put forward the following three-point proposal on how G20 countries can help African countries cope with the coronavirus pandemic, which includes calls for a $150 billion aid package, known as the Africa Global COVID-19 Emergency Financing Package, debt reduction and restructuring plans, and support to international health organizations such as the World Health Organization (WHO) and Africa Centers for Disease Control and Prevention (CDC) as a means of strengthening public health delivery and emergency preparedness throughout the continent. This international fund was funded not only by G20 countries, but by those who would benefit from it as well. The Equatorial Guinean government committed to contribute $10 million to the special emergency fund.

African countries with notably high interest rates each reduced their respective interest rates within a common scale in an expansionary effort. The Central Bank of Eswatini announced it would reduce interest rates from 6.5% to 5.5%. The Central Bank of The Gambia decided to reduce the policy rate by 0.5 percentage point to 12%. The Committee also decided to increase the interest rate on the standing deposit facility by 0.5 percentage point to 3% and the standing lending facility from 13.5% to 13%. The government of Ghana announced a $100 million package to enhance Ghana's COVID-19 preparedness and the response plan. The Bank of Ghana's MPC has decided to lower the Monetary Policy Rate by 150 basis points to 14.5%. The Primary Reserve Requirement has been reduced from 10% to 8% to provide more liquidity to banks to support critical sectors of the economy. The capital conservation buffer (CCB) for banks of 3.0% was reduced to 1.5% in order to enable banks to provide the needed financial support to the economy, which effectively reduces the capital adequacy requirement from 13% to 11.5%. Loan repayments that are past due for microfinance institutions for up to 30 days shall be considered as "Current" as in the case for all other SDIs. All mobile phone subscribers are now permitted to use their already existing mobile phone registration details to be onboarded for a Minimum KYC Account.

The Central Bank of Kenya, to help alleviate the adverse effects of the pandemic, implemented the following emergency measures that will apply for borrowers whose loan repayments were up to date as of March 2, 2020. Firstly, banks will seek to provide relief to borrowers on their personal loans based on their individual circumstances arising from the pandemic. Secondly, in order to provide relief on personal loans, banks will review requests from borrowers for extension of their loan for a period of up to 1 year. To initiate this process, borrowers should contact their respective banks. Thirdly, small and medium-sized enterprises (SMEs) and corporate borrowers can contact their banks for assessment and restructuring of their loans based on their respective circumstances arising from the pandemic. Banks will meet all the costs related to the extension and restructuring of loans. Lastly, to facilitate the increased use of mobile digital platforms, banks will waive all charges for balance inquiry, and as earlier announced, all charges for transfers between mobile money wallets and bank accounts will be eliminated.

On March 20, 2020, the Bank of Namibia decided to cut the Repo rate by 100 basis points to 5.25%. The government of Niger announced $1.63 m to support the COVID-19 response. In Madagascar, Banky Foiben'I Madagasikara (BFM) announced the following plans: Firstly, to support economic activities by providing banks with the necessary liquidity to finance the economy. Secondly, after the initial injection of $111 million at the beginning of March, there will be a reinjection of $53 million at the end of the month. Thirdly, the bank will strive to maintain the availability of foreign currencies on the interbank market. Lastly, BFM made an announcement to discuss with banks and financial institutions the impact of the crisis and provide the necessary responses, which include five responses to keep credit flowing to the economy. First, it announced a decrease in the key repo rate (KRR) by 50 basis points to 2.85% per annum. Second, it announced a special relief amount of Rs. 5.0 billion through commercial banks to meet the cash flow and working capital requirements. Additionally, the central bank cut its cash reserve ratio by a percentage point to 8% and released $130 million to fund businesses struggling with the impact of the virus. Lastly, the central bank instructed banks to suspend capital repayments on loans for affected businesses and eased supervisory guidelines on handling credit impairments while issuing a savings bond.

In Morocco, the Bank Al-Maghrib announced the following: the implementation of the integrated business support and financing program, the fluctuation of the dirham from ±2.5% to ±5%, a reduction of the interest rate by 25 percentage basis points to 2%, an exemption for some enterprises to contribute to the national pension fund (CNSS), a debt moratorium as part of the measures to offset the economic impact of COVID-19, $1 billion to upgrade the health infrastructure and assist the affected sectors, and lastly the Hassan II Fund and regions to allocate $261 million to address the impact.

The Central Bank of Rwanda announced the following: A lending facility of around $52 million to commercial banks, a lowering of its reserve requirement ratio effective April 1 from 5% to 4% to allow banks more liquidity to support affected businesses, and lastly it will allow commercial banks to restructure outstanding loans of borrowers facing temporary cash flow challenges arising from the pandemic.

The Central Bank of Seychelles (CBS) has announced the following. Firstly, foreign exchange reserves will only be used to procure three items—fuel, basic food commodities, and medicines. Secondly, it will cut the monetary policy rate (MPR) from 5% to 4%. Lastly, it will set up a credit facility of approximately $36 million to assist commercial banks with emergency relief measures.

The Central Bank of Sierra Leone took the following actions. First, to lower the monetary policy rate by 150 basis points from 16.5% to 15% and to create a Le500 billion special credit facility to finance the production, procurement, and distribution of essential goods and services. Second, it announced that it would provide foreign exchange resources to ensure the importation of essential commodities. The list of commodities that qualify for this support will be published in due course. One last key measure of Sierra Leone's monetary policy is the injection of liquidity support to the banking sector.

The South African Reserve Bank announced a change to reduce interest rates from 6.25% to 5.25% and the South African government announced a $56.27 m plan to support small businesses during the outbreak. The Central Bank of Tunisia decided the following. First, to provide banks with the necessary liquidity to enable them to continue their normal operations and to carryover credits (principal and interest) due during the period from the March 1 until the end of September 2020. Additionally, the government announced a grant of new funding to beneficiaries of the deferral of deadlines and lastly, to make the calculation and requirements of the credit/deposit more flexible. The Bank of Uganda (BoU) took the following actions, according to a study by Zeidy (2020). First, to intervene in the foreign exchange market to smoothen out the excess volatility arising from the global financial markets. Additionally, to put in place a mechanism to minimize the likelihood of a sound business going into insolvency due to lack of credit. Lastly, it announced the provision of exceptional liquidity assistance for a period of up to 1 year to financial institutions supervised by BoU that may require it to waive limitations on restructuring of credit facilities at financial institutions that may be at risk of going into distress.

The Bank of Zambia decided to increase the limit on agents and corporate wallets: Individuals Tier 1 from 10,000 to 20,000 per day (K) and a maximum of 100,000. Individuals Tier 2 from 20,000 to 100,000 per day (K) and a maximum of 500,000. SMEs and farmers from 250,000 to 1,000,000 per day (K) and a maximum of 1,000,000; and additionally, to reduce the interbank payment and settlement system (ZIPSS) processing fees.

13.4   COVID-19 credit and liquidity facilities

Several studies aim to calculate the expected liquidity shortage of SMEs due to the pandemic and lockdown. These calculations vary widely according to the underlying assumptions, for instance, on the expected duration of the lockdown measures and the types of costs expected to be covered by governments. To calculate the liquidity gap, the studies in various ways try to assess: (i) the size of the drop in revenues, (ii) the ongoing costs, (iii) the access to resources to address this, and (iv) the government support offered. Some of these studies explicitly focus on SMEs, while others do not.

A presentation by Schivardi (2020) at an OECD webinar evaluates the risk of a widespread liquidity crisis using a cross-sector sample of almost one million firms in 16 European countries, covering all manufacturing and nonfinancial service sectors. The note focuses on the first-round effects of the containment measures induced by the crisis, abstracting from the potential cascading effects via supply chains (including global value chains), financial interconnections between firms and financial distress in the banking system—other than those implicitly assumed in the size of the sectoral shocks—as well as from the structural adjustments that will be needed in a second phase of the response to the crisis.

Comparing the share of firms that would turn illiquid under a no-policy change scenario and under policy intervention, results emphasize the key role of policies to avoid massive unnecessary bankruptcies. The note shows that without any policy intervention, 20% of the firms in the sample would run out of liquidity after 1 month, 30% after 2 months, and 38% after 3 months. If the confinement measures lasted 7 months, more than 50% of firms would face a shortfall of cash. This result is mainly driven by the impact of the confinement in the most hit sectors. The note underlines that these estimates on liquidity shortages should be seen as a lower bound, since the dataset excludes very small firms and, on average, includes mostly larger, older, and more productive firms, whereas liquidity shortages for smaller, younger, and less productive firms could be higher. Considering the sum of different policy measures (tax deferral, debt moratorium, and wage subsidies at 80% of the wage bill), the note suggests that, after 2 months, government interventions could decrease the share of firms running out of liquidity from 30% to 10% compared to the nonpolicy scenario.

Gourinchas, Kalemli-Özcan, Penciakova, and Sander (2020) estimated the impact of the COVID-19 crisis on business failures among SMEs for 17 countries and measured each firm's liquidity shortfall during and after COVID-19. For each country and sector, the paper estimates the fraction of SME businesses that would fail by year end, absent fresh liquidity injections or public support. Across the 17 countries, the authors estimated an average SME bankruptcy rate of 12.1% in the absence of any policy intervention compared to a baseline of 4.5% without COVID-19.

The paper also evaluates the impact of various policy interventions. Interest payment suspensions have only a very modest effect on business failures. Narrowly targeted interventions can have much larger effects for a relatively modest fiscal cost. The paper suggests that through such policies, at a cost of 1.1% of GDP, the bankruptcy rate could be brought back to its pre-COVID-19 level, a decline of 8.75%. This would save about 1.5% of GDP in wages and about 5% of employment. However, blanket interventions can be quite wasteful. As an illustration, a subsidy equivalent to the entire 2017 payroll for the duration of an 8-week lockdown would decrease SME's bankruptcy rates by 4% at a cost of 2.38% of GDP, saving 3% of employment. 2% of the fiscal cost, however, would be wasted on firms that do not need it.

Bircan, De Haas, Schweiger, and Stepanov (2020) provided a firm level analysis on 19 countries to assess not only the need of SMEs for cash and liquidity but also where these firms still have room on their balance sheets to take on more debt. They found wide variations between countries, indicating that the liquidity challenge for SMEs differs by country.

Revoltella, Maurin, and Pal (2020) presented that the European Union's cumulative net revenue losses for companies in a 3-month lockdown scenario amount to 13%–24% of GDP, with over half of the firms facing liquidity shortfalls even after substantial policy intervention. SMEs face larger revenue losses than larger firms as a percentage of total assets (6%–11% for SMEs, 2%–4% for larger firms).

McGeever, McQuinn, and Myers (2020) conducted a study at the Central Bank of Ireland on the size of the liquidity gap for Irish SMEs and assumed that the cause for liquidity challenges stems primarily from nonpersonnel costs, since wage costs are assumed to be largely compensated by the government. Distinguishing between various shares of SMEs in highly and moderately affected sectors that would seek external finance, and various proportions of nonpersonnel costs that would need to be covered over a period of 3 months, the study estimated the potential liquidity gap for SMEs to be between €2.4 and €5.7 billion. Although Irish SMEs in June 2019 had €2.7 billion in undrawn credit available from Irish retail banks, this is very unevenly spread across borrowers, with a relatively small set of borrowers accounting for a large majority of outstanding and undrawn balances. 80% of undrawn balances were committed to just 10% of borrowers. The authors therefore concluded that given this distribution across firms, the existing bank credit lines are unlikely to be sufficient to cover the €2.4–5.7 billion financing needs of all affected firms over a 3-month period.

Schivardi and Romano (2020) calculated the number of companies (all sizes) that run into liquidity problems and the size of the liquidity challenge in Italy. Under a mild scenario (i.e., the pandemic crisis ends in September), they estimated that 50,000 companies would need liquidity support. Under a more pessimistic scenario, with the crisis continuing into 2021, these estimates rise to 100,000 companies. The liquidity gap would amount to between €30 and 80 billion. Also, they considered the equity shortfall of Italian firms due to COVID-19. For a 3-month lockdown, they estimated an aggregate annual drop in profits of €170 billion, with an implied equity erosion of €117 billion. The share of SMEs that face distress because of liquidity challenges in the lockdown is higher than the share of large firms (17.2% compared to 6.4%).

A stress test on SMEs in the Netherlands shows that during the first 3 months of the crisis, 30% of SMEs ran into a liquidity shortage, amounting to €12 billion. After 6 months, 48% of SMEs were facing liquidity problems of a total of €30 billion. Even with the support policy measures in place, in 6 months' time, 25% of SMEs will have a negative liquidity position, which would reduce to 17% in a 3-month scenario.

The COVID-19 pandemic represents a serious health threat to people around the world and a significant disruption to daily life. The crisis is having a major impact on global economies. Like in many countries, in Canada, every sector of the economy is affected. Some sectors, such as the energy, travel and hospitality, and service industries, are particularly hard hit. The public health actions needed to contain the spread of the virus, such as school closures, states of emergency, and physical distancing measures, while necessary, are themselves significantly impacting economic activity. However, it is important to note that while the impact is large, it will be temporary. Authorities around the world have taken bold and necessary measures to contain the spread of the virus and to support people and businesses through a very challenging time.

Given that the size and duration of the impact of COVID-19 are highly uncertain, credit markets may become impaired. This is because financial institutions face difficulties in obtaining funding for their lending, and also because they may become reluctant to lend in fear that many borrowers may be unable to pay. This problem in funding is partly system-wide and partly specific to individual institutions: in the context of market turmoil, there is a generalized desire for safer assets, but even if that demand is satisfied in aggregate, some financial institutions may have difficulty obtaining funding.

13.5 COVID-19 asset and security purchases

Many central banks in emerging markets and developing economies have used asset purchases to reduce financial stresses during the COVID-19 crisis, and some are doing so to provide the macroeconomic stimulus. While such programs may be beneficial, they also raise concerns about the heightened risks of fiscal dominance and debt monetization. Central Banks must consider whether these programs are appropriate for EMDEs and, if so, how should they be designed to minimize risks to central bank independence and price stability (Adrian, Erceg, Gray, and Sahay, 2021).

Drawing on lessons from past episodes of fiscal dominance, asset purchase programs should be based on several key principles. First, the central bank must have operational independence to adjust its policy rate as needed to achieve its objectives. Second, it should make asset purchases on its own initiative, and at market prices. Lastly, it must be able to adjust the scale of purchases (or sales) as warranted for achieving its objectives. There should also be a strong preference toward purchases in the secondary market to avoid the many risks associated with direct financing.

EMDEs may benefit from using temporary and small-scale asset purchases (SSAPs) to improve market functioning, as proved instrumental during the COVID-19 crisis. EMDE asset purchases in the early months of COVID lowered domestic bond yields considerably without weakening exchange rates (Adrian, Erceg, Gray, and Sahay, 2021). Keeping the duration of these actions limited and the scale modest reduces risk to central bank balance sheets and price stability. Even so, EMDE experience with asset purchase programs remains limited, and exit from these programs may pose challenges.

The pandemic has shown that asset purchases are an indispensable monetary policy instrument during times of market stress and economic downturns, when the room for interest rate cuts has largely been exhausted. After having calmed financial markets, our asset purchases have helped to bolster confidence and shore up the economy and the inflation outlook (Schnabel, 2021).

As economic conditions begin to stabilize and the inflation outlook improves, there is a gradual shift in the way asset purchases benefit the economy as the portfolio rebalancing channel makes way for the signaling channel. Asset purchases can increasingly serve as a powerful commitment device, reinforcing forward guidance and reducing uncertainty around the future course of monetary policy. Given the remaining uncertainty regarding the pandemic and the economic and inflation outlook, asset purchases—both under the PEPP and the APP—will remain crucial in the time to come, paving the way out of the pandemic and toward reaching our inflation target.

For the purchases of public sector securities under the PEPP, the benchmark allocation across jurisdictions will be the Euro system capital key of the national central banks. At the same time, purchases will be conducted in a flexible manner on the basis of market conditions and with a view to preventing a tightening of financing conditions that is inconsistent with countering the downward impact of the pandemic on the projected path of inflation. The flexibility of purchases over time, across asset classes and among jurisdictions, will continue to support the smooth transmission of monetary policy.

On December 16, 2021, the Governing Council decided to discontinue net asset purchases under the PEPP at the end of March 2022. The maturing principal payments from securities purchased under the PEPP will be reinvested until at least the end of 2024. In any case, the future roll-off of the PEPP portfolio will be managed to avoid interference with the appropriate monetary stance.

13.6   COVID-19 fiscal and labor market support policies

The pandemic has brought large parts of the world economy to a standstill, with dire social and economic consequences, and has triggered what is likely to be the largest global recession since the Great Depression. Most countries and workers in the world will be affected. Furthermore, recent ILO estimates show that working hours have shrunk globally by the equivalent of 305 million full-time jobs as a result of COVID-19 and related measures.

During the early stages of the COVID-19 crisis, governments implemented broad measures to extend support to firms and workers to preserve solvency and prevent unemployment.

Job search requirements for social assistance were eased, as measures to prevent virus transmission shut down wide swathes of the economy. Public employment services (PES) faced the twin shocks of increased customer numbers and constraints on normal face-to-face operations. Many countries scaled up the resources for labor market services and active labor market measures in 2020 and 2021, and made significant changes to the use of resources and operating models.

A policy brief by the OECD reviews how countries have adapted the mix of their ALMPs to cope with the increased and changing needs of jobseekers, workers, and employers. It draws on the responses of 46 OECD and EU countries and regions to an OECD/European Commission (EC) Questionnaire on "Active labour market policy measures to mitigate the rise in (long-term) unemployment," conducted at the end of 2020. It reviews what set of ALMPs should be retained to ensure that the assimilation of jobseekers back into the labor market is quick and effective in matching them to the right jobs. In addition, it discusses the types of ALMPs that were necessary during the different phases of the crisis and those that will be necessary during the recovery and after.

To address the growing insolvency concerns, the OECD brief highlights several approaches that the fiscal authorities could take. In most cases, economies will need a combination of multiple if not all of these approaches to best support businesses via fiscal support measures. Their recommendation is to implement much greater targeted spending toward affected businesses and employees, to strengthen market and business confidence immediately. Another recommendation is to channel a combination of equity, debt, and credit guarantees to affected businesses. It is important to note that the program's design and terms of conditionality will be central to effectiveness while addressing the moral hazard. Within this recommendation, the OECD provides design approaches to help the channel be most effective. Their approach is to deliver the programs through existing banks, development banks, and SME loan agencies that are already well equipped to evaluate those solvent entities that would benefit from interim financing until economic conditions improve. The focus should be on getting cash to businesses on a timely basis, particularly by reducing bureaucratic obstacles to cash transfers. Additionally, there must be incentives to repay as the business recovers, for example, restrictions on dividends, and the use of equity warrants could help ensure taxpayer funds are amply compensated during business recovery. Another approach to implementing this recommendation is to include a clear path to exit this extraordinary support, so as not to raise sovereign debt sustainability concerns.

Another recommendation brought forth by the OECD is to include further support to improve near-term cash flows, which could include permitted delays in tax filings and support for particular operating expenses. Where fiscal initiatives include new forms of temporary to medium-term state ownership, adherence to the OECD Guidelines on Corporate Governance of State-Owned Enterprises is important to ensure that governments are effectively managing their responsibilities as company owners. This will help to make state-owned enterprises more competitive, efficient, and transparent. It is also important to emphasize commitments to internationally recognized instruments of responsible business conduct, such as the OECD Guidelines for Multinational Enterprises and the OECD Due Diligence Guidance for Responsible Business Conduct, which can help ensure that businesses benefiting from fiscal support are appropriately managing the broader environmental, social, or governance risks. Lastly, the OECD recommends assessing the need to temporarily share fiscal burdens from businesses affected by the pandemic where individual states are unable to shoulder the burden of the health and economic consequences of the pandemic. In this respect, extending lending facilities may serve to alleviate temporary pressures of countries undergoing a major upsurge in fiscal deficits to address the economic and health challenges from the virus.

Such measures could give financial markets confidence to make use of increased balance sheet availability from reduced capital buffers, and credit—through government loans, guarantees, or central bank facilities—could effectively address solvency concerns of viable businesses to overcome the economic effects of COVID-19. Furthermore, if implemented effectively, such programs can mitigate the moral hazard and even generate gains that can offset the costs of containing the growing health crisis.

Economies and governments across the globe must consider trade-offs when navigating the lasting effects of the COVID-19 pandemic's shock to their real economies, banking sectors, and financial markets. The initial policies focused on the trade-offs between mitigating the spread of the deadly disease and keeping economies afloat, while the policies during the easing of the pandemic must focus on the trade-offs between the long-lasting effects revolving around factors such as interest rates, inflation, fears of recession, unemployment, damaged sectors, highly volatile financial markets, and long-lasting social and economic consequences. Coordinated global integration will be needed in order to best and most efficiently navigate these trade-offs. Lessons from these policies and their contexts from the economies in which they were implemented can provide useful evidence for future crises.

References

Adrian, M. T., Erceg, C. J., Gray, M. S. T., and Sahay, M. R. (2021). *Asset purchases and direct financing: Guiding principles for emerging markets and developing economies during COVID-19 and beyond*. International Monetary Fund.

Bircan, C., De Haas, R., Schweiger, H., and Stepanov, A. (2020). *Coronavirus credit support: Don't let liquidity lifelines become a golden noose*. VOX CEPR.

Burni, A., Erforth, B., Friesen, I., Hackenesch, C., Hoegl, M., and Keijzer, N. (2022). Who called team Europe? The European Union's development policy response during the first wave of COVID-19. *The European Journal of Development Research*, 34(1), 524–539.

Gourinchas, P. O., Kalemli-Özcan, S., Penciakova, V., and Sander, N. (2020). *COVID-19 and SME failures. Vol. 27877* (pp. 1–9). Cambridge, MA: National Bureau of Economic Research. No. 1.

McGeever, N., McQuinn, J., and Myers, S. (2020). *SME liquidity needs during the COVID-19 shock (No. 2/FS/20)*. Central Bank of Ireland.

Rasul, G., Nepal, A. K., Hussain, A., Maharjan, A., Joshi, S., Lama, A., Gurung, P., Ahmad, F., Mishra, A., and Sharma, E. (2021). Socio-economic implications of COVID-19 pandemic in South Asia: Emerging risks and growing challenges. *Frontiers in Sociology*, 6, 629693.

Revoltella, D., Maurin, L., and Pal, R. (2021). *The economy post-COVID-19: How to support investment without too much debt?*. European Investment Bank.

Schivardi, F., and Romano, G. (2021). A simple method to estimate firms liquidity needs during the COVID-19 crisis with an application to Italy. *Economia Italiana*, 1, 17–50.

Schivardi, F., and Romano, G. (2020). *Liquidity crisis: Keeping firms afloat during COVID-19*. VoxEU.

Schnabel, I. (2021). Lessons from an unusual crisis. In *Speech at the FRB of New York* (p. 1).

Taylor, L. (2020). Uruguay is winning against COVID-19. This is how. *BMJ*, 370, 1–2.

Wei, X., and Han, L. (2021). The impact of COVID-19 pandemic on transmission of monetary policy to financial markets. *International Review of Financial Analysis*, 74, 101705.

Zeidy, I. A. (2020). *Economic impact of COVID-19 on micro, small and medium enterprises (MSMEs) in Africa and policy options for mitigation*. Nairobi: Common Mark. East. South. Africa.

Part IV

The extraordinary recoveries in real economies, banking sectors, and financial markets during the COVID-19 crisis around the world

In this part, we assess evidence on the extraordinary recoveries during COVID-19 in the three economic segments. The real economy in some cases had historically unprecedented fast and steep gains in GDP, employment, and other economic measures. Banks suffered relatively few losses after expectations of the worst were erased, and financial markets perhaps overrecovered after their initial declines. Chapter 14 covers the US, while Chapter 15 is based on the rest of the world. This evidence on recoveries is key to the goals of the book, which include strategies to use existing knowledge to enable future strong and steady recoveries in the three segments. Data in this part of the book are in some cases are also employed and described in other parts of the book and Appendix, are drawn from a variety of publicly available sources, including central banks, other government agencies, educational institutions, news organizations, and international organizations such as the International Monetary Fund, and World Bank.

Chapter 14

Recovery evidence from the US

Chapter outline

Abstract

This is the first of the two chapters on the extraordinary economic recoveries from COVID-19 recessions, focusing here on the US. We cover information on the recoveries in all three economic segments of the real economy, banking sectors, and financial markets. Consistent with the main themes of the book, the US recession in 2020 was only 2 months long, and a steep recovery followed starting in April. Banking and financial markets also recovered quite quickly. The data suggest that fast and large-in-magnitude COVID-19 policies along with prudential protections of the US banking industry from policies in the aftermath of the earlier GFC were helpful.

Keywords: COVID-19, US crisis policies, Economic recovery, Real economy, Banking sector, Financial markets

We focus in this chapter on the information about the recovery of US economy from COVID-19, and evidence suggests that this recovery from COVID-19 was quite extraordinary, consistent with the title of Part IV. The US recession in 2020 was only 2 months long, and a steep recovery followed starting in April. Banking and financial markets also recovered quite quickly.

The data suggest that fast and large-in-magnitude COVID-19 policies, along with prudential protections of the US banking industry from policies in the aftermath of the earlier GFC were helpful. Essentially, the fast and large policies of fiscal and monetary stimulus worked well prior to the aftermath, and strong bank balance sheets due to prior policies worked well. Fast vaccine rollouts and other policies were also helpful.

14.1   Real economy recovery in the US

The real economy of the US followed a relatively conventional pattern through crisis and recovery stages. With the world's largest economy, the real sector and GDP activity in the US will prove to be very predictive of real economy performance of countries around the globe. In the US, real GDP plummeted to negative growth in 2020, followed by a strong recovery in 2021 following President Biden's continuation of fiscal stimulus. Real GDP growth rose from about −3% in 2020 to almost 6% in 2021. However, real GDP growth in 2022 has since fallen to just over 1%. Interestingly, public

The Economic and Financial Impacts of the COVID-19 Crisis Around the World
https://doi.org/10.1016/B978-0-443-19162-6.00009-8
Copyright © 2024 Elsevier Inc. All rights reserved.

debt as a percentage of GDP has stayed relatively constant through 2020–22. After public debt as a percentage of GDP rose from approximately 80% in 2019 to about 100% in 2020, it has since stayed near 100%.

Alongside GDP activity, unemployment rates in the US have recovered well since the pandemic. After rising from a rate of just under 4% in 2019, unemployment rose to approximately 8% in 2020, but has since fallen relatively steadily back down to 2019 levels. While very low unemployment levels and period of labor shortages may be making it difficult to curb high inflation, the low unemployment levels that we see in 2022 certainly confuse recession predictions and give confidence to individuals in the US. In addition, not only have unemployment rates fallen during the recovery stage, but the US population has risen steadily from just over 334 million people in 2019 to just over 338 million people in 2022. The pool of human capital remains large in the US, and this combined with low unemployment levels is promising for the real economy.

In the near future, it will be interesting to see how policymakers' efforts to curb inflation affect unemployment levels. Inflation, while somewhat lower than in countries less agriculturally and energy independent, has risen from just over 1% in 2020 to approximately 8% in 2022 in the US. Consumer sentiment and household income growth remain strong in the US, and high demand, labor shortages, and supply-chain disruptions, along with the war in Ukraine have fed inflation. Median household income has risen steadily over the past few years, from approximately $89,000 in 2019, to just under $92,000 in 2020, and eventually to about $96,000 in 2022. Lastly, in discussing the real economy in the US, we note that the country's business confidence index has not once fallen to negative indices during or after the pandemic. However, they have fallen from a peak of 64 in the early 2021 to just over 50 in Q3 of 2022.

14.2 Banking sector recovery in the US

To promote recovery during the COVID-19 pandemic, banks and other depository institutions were encouraged by federal banking supervisors to use their capital and liquidity buffers to lend as a way to help borrowers affected by COVID-19. The Federal Reserve also introduced several facilities to support the flow of credit and access to capital among borrowers under the CARES Act, which include a commercial paper funding facility to facilitate the issuance of commercial paper, a primary dealer credit facility to help provide financing to the central bank's primary dealers collateralized by a wider range of investment grade securities, a money market mutual fund liquidity facility to provide loans to depository institutions to purchase assets from prime money market funds, and the Paycheck Protection Program Liquidity Facility to provide liquidity to financial institutions.

In the banking sector, capital ratios in the US rose significantly in 2020 and stayed relatively constant in the year thereafter. Total capital ratio rose from approximately 14.5% in 2019 to approximately 15.3% in 2020, and stayed at around 15.3% in 2021. Meanwhile, bank capital also changed during the pandemic in terms of banks' risk weighted assets as a percentage of total assets, falling from approximately 70% in 2018 and 2019 to just under 60% in 2020 and 2021.

In measuring asset quality, we note that the US has had relatively small numbers of problems loans as a percentage of cross customer loans and loan loss reserves as a percentage of gross loans. Problem loans as a percentage of gross customer loans were about 1.2% in 2020 and fell to just under 1% in 2021. Meanwhile loan loss reserves as a percentage of total loans jumped from just over 1% in 2019 and nearly doubled in 2020 but fell to approximately 1.6% in 2021. Nonperforming loans as a percentage of total loans rose slightly during the pandemic from approximately 1% in 2019 to approximately 1.2% in 2022, but fell back down to 2019 numbers in 2021. In 2021, the US banking sector has about $100,000 M in nonperforming loans, down over $20,000 M from 2020.

However, the US banking sector suffered in terms of profitability during the pandemic, with ROAA falling from approximately 1.3% in 2019 to approximately 0.7% in 2020. ROAA recovered to approximately 1.2% in 2021. Because policymakers strived to provide capital to financial institutions during the pandemic to help provide lending to borrowers, total assets in the banking sector rose steadily throughout the pandemic from approximately $17,000,000 M in 2019 to just over $20,000,000 M in 2020 to approximately $22,000,000 M in 2021. Alongside the growth in total assets, deposits grew at an even fast rate. Total deposits as a percentage of assets grew from just over 70% in 2019 to just over 74% in 2020 to just over 76% in 2021. However, total loans as a percentage of assets fell steadily throughout the pandemic, from approximately 55% in 2019 to approximately 48% in 2020 to approximately 45% in 2021. Monetary policy during 2020 included lowering the community bank leverage ratio to 8%, despite encouraging depository institutions to use their capital and liquidity buffers to lend. The US has relatively low loan ratios compared to other major economies.

14.3 Financial markets recovery in the US

Thanks to stimulus efforts in the US, combined with positive investor sentiment and buying opportunities provided by the stock market crash in the first quarter of 2020, the financial markets rallied strongly in the recovery period of the pandemic. After a short crash at the onset of the pandemic, the US stock market index experienced strong gains from the initial stimulus period until Q4 of 2021. Growth stocks, especially those in big tech and health care, experienced highs that they had never seen before. Many firms such as Netflix, Amazon, Tesla, Johnson & Johnson, Apple, Pfizer, Microsoft, Alphabet, and others inevitably experienced extreme overvaluation in their share prices. The S&P 500 and the NASDAQ rallied extremely well in 2021, but inevitably reached their peaks in November. Growth stocks heavily underperformed in 2022 as the Federal Reserve raised interest rates and the cost of raising capital increased. Investors were aware of the inevitable interest rate hikes, and the financial markets began to lock in this prediction in Q4 of 2021. The NASDAQ index, heavily comprised of growth shares, fell nearly 33% during the first three quarters of 2022. The NYSE fared slightly better, with a decline of approximately 23% during the first three quarters of 2022. As investors alter their portfolios to take some refuge in value shares and safer investments during volatile markets, it is unclear whether Q4 of 2022 provides an excellent buying opportunity for beaten up large cap growth shares or if the worst has yet to come. Inflation expectations, the dollar's exchange rate to other major currencies, Federal Reserve actions, consumer sentiment, supply-chain disruptions, and the war in Ukraine will each prove to be telling factors of financial market activity post pandemic.

While equity markets were providing excellent gains during the pandemic, the bond market was far less lucrative. In an expansionary effort, the Federal Reserve lowered the Fed funds rate to 0%–0.25% in March of 2020, and the yield on the US 10Y Treasury bond fell below 1%. Yields rose modestly in 2021, and eventually to nearly 4% in 2022. However, the first half of 2022 experienced a particularly usually phenomena, where both stocks and bonds experienced negative gains. The value of bonds began to fall as the Federal Reserve made it clear that it would take all actions necessary to ease inflation. In 2022, the US experienced an inverted yield curve, where the yield of a 3Y Treasury exceeds the yield of a 10Y treasury (since the first time since before the pandemic), rushing in recession fears. However, the US capital markets still appear to be a better investment opportunity than in other nations.

Chapter 15

Recovery evidence from the rest of the world

Chapter outline

Abstract

This chapter concerns economic recoveries from COVID-19 in the rest of the world other than the US. We cover the recoveries in the real economies, banking sectors, and financial markets of the different nations. The findings suggest important differences across countries and continents, as well as differences from the US experience in the various economic segments. With so many nations, so many disease paths, so many policies, and so many outcomes, general conclusions are difficult to draw, but we do not see any significant evidence to dissuade us from our general conclusion in the book that crisis policies that are large and implemented quickly tend to have the most impacts.

Keywords: COVID-19, Non-US crisis policies, Economic recovery, Real economy, Banking sector, Financial markets

This chapter concerns economic recoveries from COVID-19 outside the US except for some incidental comparisons with the US when discussing English-speaking nations. We cover recoveries in the real economies, banking sectors, and financial markets of the different nations.

We examine several major economies of Asia, Africa, the Middle East, Latin America, Western Europe, Eastern Europe, and English-speaking nations (New Zealand, Australia, Canada, the UK, and the US). The UK is not included in the Western Europe sample, given its independence from the European Union's regulatory framework and liberal market economy. Most of the data in this chapter are collected from International Monetary Fund (IMF), Bureau van Dijk (BvD) BankFocus, Our World in Data, Google Finance, and Trading Economics.

15.1 Real economy recovery in the rest of the world

Within the English-speaking nations that we include in our sample (the US, the UK, Canada, Australia, and New Zealand), we first examine the real economies during the COVID-19 pandemic. With economic shutdowns and supply chain disruptions, GDP, employment, income, inflation, and business

The Economic and Financial Impacts of the COVID-19 Crisis Around the World
https://doi.org/10.1016/B978-0-443-19162-6.00032-3
Copyright © 2024 Elsevier Inc. All rights reserved.

confidence were all affected. Looking at the real GDP growth in years 2018–22, we see large dips in 2020 in all five countries. Some recovered more efficiently than others. The five countries experienced significant rallies in real GDP growth in 2021, but the US is experiencing a larger dip in real GDP growth between 2021 and 2022 than the rest of the nations. All the five nations experienced negative real GDP growth in 2020, but positive growth in the years before and after.

Slow GDP growth is both a symptom and cause of rising unemployment. All five English-speaking nations experienced a rise in unemployment in 2020; however, Australia and New Zealand were more modest than their counterparts. In New Zealand, unemployment rose from just under 4.5% in 2019 to just over 4.5% in 2020 and dipped to just over 3% in 2022. Canada suffered from the highest rate of unemployment in this sample, with unemployment nearing 10% in 2020. However, even with rising unemployment in 2020, these countries did not experience dips in their median household income, likely due to the aggressive fiscal stimulus. Canada's median household income rose from approximately 52,000USD in 2019 to around 55,000USD in 2020, and then to close to 61,000USD in 2022. However, consumer price growth (CPI) was over 7% in 2022. The UK suffered the most from inflation in 2022, with CPI exceeding 8%, but being a European nation, the UK is experiencing confounding variables such as the war in Ukraine. Business confidence indices in 2022 were negative in the UK, and reached a staggering −60 in New Zealand, while they were positive in the other nations.

We next study the real economies of the selected Western European countries (Finland, Portugal, Italy, Spain, France, Switzerland, and Germany). Each country experienced a sharp decline in real GDP growth to negative territory in 2020, followed by positive growth in 2021 and 2022. Each country's public debt as a percentage of GDP rose in 2020, some more dramatically than others, but some (those with high public debt) recovered faster than others. Germany's public debt rose from just above 70% in 2020 to just below 70% in 2022, while Portugal's dropped from 135% in 2020 to just above 120% in 2022.

Interestingly, the unemployment activity varies widely across the selected countries. Staggeringly, Italy's unemployment rate dropped slightly from just under 10% in 2019 to just over 8% in 2020. It then rose slightly in 2021 but remained at 8% in 2022. Even more staggeringly, France experienced a steady, although modest, decline in unemployment rate, from just over 8% in 2018 to just over 7% in 2022. Spain's unemployment rate jumped most dramatically in 2020, from a staggering 14% to over 15.5%, but dropped to just over 13% in 2022.

The countries in the Eurozone all were found to suffer from heavy inflation in 2022, but as we stated earlier, this was also due to confounding variables like oil dependency and the war in Ukraine. Spain suffers from the worst inflation, with CPI reaching approximately 9% in 2022; meanwhile median household income fell from just under $39,000USD in 2021 to just above $38,000 in 2022. In Switzerland, inflation metrics are more attractive, as CPI in 2022 sits below 3.5%. Median household income fell by about $3000USD; however, it still remains at just over $110,000, which is significantly higher than before the pandemic. Lastly, in studying the real economies of the select countries, we found that the business confidence indices vary significantly. Spain currently experiences a negative business confidence index in 2022; however, its index reached a positive 10 earlier in the year. The business confidence index was negative in 2019 and fell dramatically at the onset of the pandemic. Italy, France, Switzerland, and Germany's business confidence indices remained consistently positive throughout the pandemic, and Switzerland's reached a healthy 140 in 2021, far higher than before than the pandemic.

The sample of countries studied from the Latin American region include Argentina, Chile, Peru, Brazil, and Mexico. The real economies of each of the countries in this sample all follow a similar trend. Each economy experienced negative real GDP growth in 2020 and positive real GDP growth in 2021 and 2022. Peru's real GDP growth variation between 2020 and 2021 was the most dramatic, with the real GDP growth sitting at −10% in 2020 and approximately 13% in 2021. The real GDP growth in all five countries was below 5% in 2022. We also highlight that public debt as a percentage of GDP varies significantly in each of the sampled economies. In 2020, public debt exceeded 100% in Argentina, but was approximately just 32% in Chile. Overall, public debt is lower in the Latin American sample than the Western European or English-speaking regions.

While the unemployment rates vary significantly among the countries of this sample, they all followed a similar trend, with a hike in 2020 and a gradual decline in 2021 and 2022. The pandemic affected Peru's employment the most heavily, with unemployment rising from approximately 7% in 2019 to over 14% in 2020. However, the figure fell back to its original 7% in 2022. All the five countries experienced high inflation in 2022; however, Argentina is an outlier, with its CPI exceeding 70% in 2022. Argentina's median household income rose from just over $15,000 in 2020 to over $25,000 in 2022, but this is nowhere near a large enough rise in income to compensate for inflation of 70%. To control inflation, the interest rates in Argentina are very high. The yield of a 7-year bond is close to 50%. Lastly, in studying the real economies of the Latin American sample, we found that the business confidence indices in each country are consistently positive in 2021 and 2022. Argentina was the only country to experience negative business confidence indices in 2020. However, although consistently positive, the indices never exceed 65.

The countries of the African region that we include in our analysis are South Africa, Morocco, Ghana, Nigeria, and Kenya. When analyzing the real economies of this region using real GDP growth, all five countries showed very similar behavior, with a sharp dip in real GDP growth in 2020, a quick recovery in 2021, and then a dip in 2022. The impact that the COVID-19 crisis had on GDP in 2020 varies between countries. Ghana, for example, never saw negative real GDP growth. The country's real GDP growth dipped from approximately 6.5% in 2019 to just under 1% in 2020, which is highly unusual. Kenya and Nigeria saw negative GDP growth in 2020, with their real GDP growth being approximately −0.5% and −2% respectively. Morocco and South Africa's real economies reacted in a more usual manner in 2020, with their real GDP dipping to approximately −7% and −6% respectively. Morocco's public debt as a percentage of GDP rose dramatically in the initial phase of the pandemic, jumping from just over 80% in 2019 to over 92% in 2020. It then dipped to about 5% in 2022. South Africa's public debt as a percentage of GDP is more consistent, jumping from just under 60% in 2019 to approximately 70% in 2020 and staying at around 70% in the following years. This region as a whole, especially Nigeria, has very low public debt.

We next examine unemployment activity in Morocco and South Africa to better understand their real economies. Unemployment data was not available for Ghana, Kenya, or Nigeria. Morocco had been experiencing a decline in unemployment between 2018 and 2019, while South Africa suffers from very high unemployment and experienced a slight rise between 2018 and 2019. Morocco's unemployment rose from approximately 10% in 2019 to just over 12% in 2020 and stayed at around 12% in 2021 and 2022. South Africa experienced hardly any effect on unemployment between 2019 and 2020 but rose in a delayed manner from approximately 28% in 2020 to just under 35% in 2021 and 2022.

This region as a whole has been suffering from high inflation, especially in Ghana and Nigeria. Unlike many countries, none of these countries experienced much of a dip in inflation during the first phase of the pandemic. Meanwhile, 2021 and 2022 have brought upon a rise in consumer price growth. Of the most affected countries in this region, Ghana's consumer price growth has risen from just above 10% in 2020 and 2021 to approximately 27% in 2022. Nigeria's consumer price growth rose from about 10% in 2019, to approximately 12% in 2020, to just under 20% in 2022. Morocco enjoyed low inflation of close to 0% in 2019, but consumer price growth rose to 1% in 2020 and eventually to approximately 6% in 2022. Of the five countries analyzed in this region, we note that Morocco experienced the biggest shock in the business confidence index during the pandemic, with the business confidence index dropping from 0.9 in early 2020 to −21.4 at the onset of the pandemic. However, the country's business confidence index recovered back to 1.8 in the second half of 2022.

The countries included in the Middle East region are Jordan, Egypt, the United Arab Emirates, Saudi Arabia, and Israel. In examining the real economies of the sampled countries in this region, we see some variation in activity when analyzing GDP growth and public debt. Egypt showed abnormal behavior during the crisis phase of the pandemic. Egypt's real GDP never experienced negative growth during the pandemic, but rather dropped from approximately 5% in 2019, to just under 4% in 2020, to just over 3% in 2021, and then eventually to approximately 6% in 2022. However, the country's public debt as a percentage of GDP rose consistently from 84% in 2019 to just over 94% in 2022. The remaining countries showed more conventional GDP behavior during the pandemic with negative real GDP growth in 2020 and a strong rally after stimulus. Jordan and Israel's real GDP growth slowed modestly in 2022 like most economies have. However, in the UAE and Saudi Arabia, real GDP has grown faster in 2022 than in 2021. Saudi Arabia's real GDP has shown very fast recovery, with growth jumping from −4% in 2020 to just under 8% in 2022. Additionally, the country's public debt as a percentage of GDP never exceeded 40%.

Jordan, Egypt, and Saudi Arabia have all suffered from relatively high unemployment over recent years. Data on unemployment was not available for the UAE, and Israel's unemployment behavior is more conventional. In Egypt, unemployment has been relatively stable between 2019 and 2022, but currently sits at about 7%. In Saudi Arabia, unemployment rose from about 12% in 2019 to about 13% in 2022 but is down to about 10% in 2022. Meanwhile, Jordan suffers from the highest levels of unemployment in this sample. Here, where unemployment sat at about 20% before the pandemic, figures rose to about 23% in 2021, and have only recovered very slightly in 2022.

Excluding Saudi Arabia, this region showed very similar inflationary behavior, with extremely low inflation or moderate disinflation during the first phase of the pandemic, and rising inflation in 2021 and 2022. Inflation cycles in Saudi Arabia are abnormal. The country had been experiencing *disinflation* of 2% in 2019 before the pandemic. Inflation rose from −2% in 2019, to just over 3% in 2020, and then leveled down to about 2% in 2022. Meanwhile, the country experienced a rise in median household income of about $10,000USD in each year between 2020 and 2022. Lastly, in analyzing the real economies of this region, we noted that the business confidence indices show great variation between countries in this sample. Jordan showed a unique situation, with business confidence varying moderately positive and negative indices throughout 2019, 2020, and Q1 of 2021, followed by a staggering rise to about 700 in Q2 of 2021, but then immediately back down to close to zero in each quarter after that. Egypt and the UAE showed consistently positive business confidence indices. In Israel, indices have been consistently positive except for the behavior of −20 during the onset of the pandemic. In Saudi Arabia, business confidence indices were almost consistently negative until Q4 of 2021, but have been positive since then.

The countries in our sample of the Eastern European region include Ukraine, Russia, Greece, Poland, Romania, and Turkey. Shifting focus to their real economy sector, Russia, Greece, Poland, and Romania all experience very typical COVID-19 trends in their real GDP growth during the crisis, recovery, and aftermath of the pandemic. Each of these countries experienced negative real GDP growth in 2020, a healthy recovery in 2021, and then an economic slowing in 2022. However, likely exacerbated by the war and its global trade implications, Russia's real GDP growth fell from a healthy 5% in 2021 to below −7% in 2022, which is below its 2020 figure of −2%. Russia has also experienced a rise in public debt as a percentage of its GDP from just 15% in 2021 to over 20% in 2022. We note that the public debt burdens vary greatly in this region. For example, Greece's public debt accounted for about 205% of its GDP in 2020, and although this figure has fallen, it still sits at about 185% in 2022.

As alluded to earlier, Ukraine and Turkey have not experienced normal GDP behavior in recent years. In Ukraine, real GDP growth only fell from just under 5% in 2019 to just over −5% in 2020. The country's real GDP recovered in 2021, but because of the war, it has fallen to a staggering −35% in 2022. Public debt has also risen from just under 50% of the country's GDP in 2021 to almost 90% of GDP in 2022. In Turkey, GDP behavior has been more conventional in the past year but was abnormal during the pandemic. Turkey experienced real GDP growth of just 1% before the pandemic, and then amazingly experienced real GDP growth of approximately 2% in 2020. This figure then rose to 12% in 2021 but was down to 5% in 2022.

Alongside GDP growth, other metrics such as unemployment also show varying behavior in the real economies of this region. In Greece, for example, unemployment levels had been very high before the pandemic, sitting at around 20% in 2018 with just a modest recovery in 2019. This figure was relatively unaffected during the first phase of the pandemic and has since dropped from approximately 17% in 2020 to about 13% in 2022. Meanwhile, in Ukraine, where unemployment was also moderately unaffected during the initial phase of the pandemic, unemployment has risen from around 10% in in both 2020 and 2021 to 20% in 2022, given the nation's current situation. Russia's employment has fared far better, with its unemployment rising from just under 5% in 2019 to about 5.5% in 2020 and has since dropped to about 4.5% in 2020. Poland, Romania, and Turkey each showed a more normal pandemic and unemployment behavior in its aftermath.

These countries have each experienced very high inflation levels in the aftermath of the pandemic, but in Turkey the situation is far worse than in the others. In Turkey, Inflation dipped slightly from just under 20% before the pandemic to just over 10% in 2020. This figure then rose back to 20% in 2021, and eventually to over a staggering 70% in 2022. To make matters incredibly worse, the country's median household income has fallen from approximately $14,500USD in 2021 to under $12,500USD in 2022.

We finally highlight that in reaction to the varying macroeconomic indicators discussed thus far in the real economy sector, the business confidence indices in these countries showed different activity in recent years. In Ukraine, Greece, and Turkey, business confidence indices have been consistently positive since 2019. Meanwhile, in Russia, Poland, and Romania, almost the opposite is true. These countries showed mostly negative indices except for a short period before the pandemic in Poland, Q2 of 2022 in Romania, and Q4 of 2021 and Q1 of 2022 in Russia. Romania's business confidence index reacted the most to the onset of the pandemic, dropping to approximately −32 in Q2 of 2020.

The countries in our sample of the Asian region include China, Japan, India, South Korea, the Philippines, and Indonesia. In examining the real economies of this region, we note that each country in this sample shared very similar trends in GDP behavior, with a strong dip in real GDP growth in 2020, followed by a strong rally in 2021 following stimulus, and finally a slowing of growth in 2022. The degrees to which these countries' GDP growth figures were affected by the stages of the crisis vary between countries. The Philippines, a country highly dependent on exports, saw the largest hit to its real economy when considering GDP growth. The country's real GDP growth fell from approximately 7% in 2019 to a staggering −10% in 2020, however recovered to over 6% in 2021 and eventually to close to 7% in 2022. Additionally, in 2020, the country's public debt rose from 40% in 2019 of its GDP to approximately 55%. India also experienced similar activity with its real GDP growth falling from just over 4% in 2019 to −7% in 2020, alongside a rise in public debt as a percentage of GDP. However, while the Philippines' real GDP growth grew continuously to 2022, India's real GDP growth fell from approximately 9% in 2021 to approximately 7% in 2022. The GDP behaviors of Indonesia, South Korea, and Japan showed a trend very similar to that of the Philippines, but with a more modest negative and positive growth in 2020 and the following years. We finally note that China never experienced negative real GDP growth in 2020, but rather its growth fell from just over 6% in 2019 to just over 2% in 2020. However, the country's growth has slowed from about 8% in 2021 to about 4% in 2022.

China has also experienced a rise in unemployment levels in 2022, unlike its counterparts in this sample. The country's unemployment rose to 5.25% in 2020, then fell to approximately 4.9% in 2021, but has since risen to 5.3%, higher than during the pandemic in 2020. The rest of these countries have shared a common trend of a rise in unemployment in 2020, followed by a lessening of unemployment levels through 2022.

We highlighted earlier that the Philippines' real sector was heavily affected by the pandemic when analyzing GDP, and the same can be said in terms of unemployment. The country's unemployment levels rose from 5% in 2019 to approximately 10% in 2020 but have since fallen to just over 7% in 2022. India also experienced unemployment of over 10% in 2020; however, its unemployment levels were close to 8% preceding the pandemic. India's unemployment has since fallen to its original numbers.

Inflationary behavior varies within the countries in this sample; however, all six countries are experiencing a rise in inflation in 2022. India is suffering the worst, with inflation of approximately 7% in 2022. The country's inflation also rose from just under 4% in 2019 to close to 7% in 2020, which is unusual. Inflation in India then fell slightly in 2021 but has since risen. In the rest of the countries, inflation is very modest compared to the rest of the world. In China, inflation in 2022 is under 2.5%, which is very low. The country was experiencing inflation of close to 3% before the pandemic, which fell to 2.5% in 2020, then to under 1% in 2021. Also, we highlight that China's median household income was largely unaffected by the pandemic, and has been consistently between $10,000USD and $13,000USD in recent years, with just slight fluctuation depending on stages of the crisis and recovery. China also retained solely positive business confidence indices throughout the pandemic and through 2022. The same can be said for South Korea and India. Indonesia, the Philippines, and Japan each saw a period of negative business confidence during the pandemic, with confidence in Indonesia being the most affected.

15.2 Banking sector recovery in the rest of the world

Comparing the banking sector from 2020 to 2021 in the English-speaking nations, the UK sees higher capital ratio than any of its English-speaking counterparts, with the total capital ratio exceeding 20% in 2020 and 2021. Excluding New Zealand where the capital ratio data was not available in 2021, the values stay relatively constant for all four countries between the 2 years. New Zealand and the US experienced the lowest capital ratios, with each totaling approximately 15% in 2020. The banking sectors in these economies showed more variability in asset quality, measured by problem loans as a ratio of gross customer loans and loan loss reserves as a ratio of gross loans. The US experienced the highest percentage of loan loss reserves in 2020 and 2021 (over 2% in 2020 and falling to approximately 1.5% in 2021), while the UK ranked the highest for problem loans as a percentage of gross customer loans (around 1.6% in both years). In terms of profitability, measured by both net interest margin and ROAA, the US exceeded all four of its counterparts. However, in the US, the net interest margin slipped slightly in 2021 from approximately 2.75% to just under 2.5%, and ROAA jumped from just over 0.5% to approximately 1.2%. Finally, we compare the five countries' banking sectors by examining loans as a percentage of assets and loans as a percentage of deposits. In 2020, New Zealand had the highest loan ratios, but data for 2021 was not available. For the rest of the countries, loan ratios stayed relatively constant between the 2 years.

The sample of countries that we study from Western Europe include Finland, Portugal, Italy, Spain, France, Switzerland, and Germany. Finland, Italy, Spain, France, and Germany are all member countries of the Eurozone and therefore are subject to the same regulatory framework of the European Union, the monetary policy of the European Central bank, and the same inflation of their currency. The capital ratios in this region were slightly higher on average than those of the English-speaking countries, excluding the UK. Finland experienced the highest capital ratios out of the seven countries studied, with its total capital ratio exceeding 20% in both 2020 and 2021. Germany's capital ratios were significantly lower than those of its counterparts, resting at approximately 12% in both years. In terms of asset quality, Finland's problem loans and loan loss reserves, both as a percentage of total loans, were significantly lower than those of its counterparts. Italy ranked highest, with its problem loans totaling nearly 4% of its total loans, although data for Portugal was not available. Italy, Spain, and France experienced much more problems with asset quality compared to Finland, Germany, and the English-speaking countries studied. We next examined bank profitability, and found that when measuring net interest margin, Spain's profitability far outperformed its Western European counterparts, with a net interest margin of approximately 2%. However, Spain experienced negative ROAA in 2020 and a ROAA of about a half of a percentage in 2021. Lastly, when discussing banking sector metrics, we notice that when measuring loans ratios, Finland's loans as a percentage of deposits were far higher than those of the other countries, with the ratio sitting at approximately 160% in 2020 and falling just slightly in 2021. When measuring loans as a percentage of assets, the countries' ratios were each between 40% and 60% in both years.

The sample of countries studied from the Latin American region include Argentina, Chile, Peru, Brazil, and Mexico. We use the same metrics for studying the banking sectors, real economies, and financial markets of these countries. In analyzing the capital ratios of the select Latin American countries, we found that total capital ratio stays relatively constant between 2020 and 2021. In 2020, Chile's total capital ratio was just below 15%, while Argentina's was just above 20%, but the other countries' total capital ratios are between 15% and 20% in both years. In examining asset quality, we found that Peru ranks the highest in both years for loan loss reserves as a percentage of its gross loans; however, the figure fell from just over 7% in 2020 to just under 6% in 2021. Chile ranks the lowest in loan loss reserves, while Mexico ranks the lowest in problem loans. Overall, Latin America seems to struggle with asset quality more than the English-speaking sample or the more successful countries of the Western European sample. When measuring bank profitability, Argentina far outperformed the rest of its counterparts, especially in terms of net interest margin. In 2020, Argentina's net interest margin was just under 12%, while that for the rest of the countries in the sample was under 6%. However, Argentina's net interest margin fell to approximately 9% in 2021, and its ROAA fell from about 2% to about 1%. We finally measure loan ratios as a banking sector metric. We found that in both years, Chile has the highest amount of loans as a percentage of deposits (120% in both years), and the highest amount of loans as a percentage of assets (60% in both years). We found that on average, the Latin American countries studied have lower loan ratios than the Western European countries.

The countries of the African region that we include in our analysis are South Africa, Morocco, Ghana, Nigeria, and Kenya. This sample showed variety in banking sector metrics. Ghana, for example, showed high capital ratios, with its total capital ratio sitting at approximately 25% in 2020 and just over 25% in 2021. Morocco has the lowest capital ratios out of the five countries, as its total capital ratio in both years is approximately 13%. In problem loans as a percentage of each country's gross customer loans, as a metric of asset quality, the region as a whole ranks very high but some rank higher than others. Kenya's problem loans total 13% of its gross customer loans in 2020, and this figure modestly drops to around 12% in 2021. South Africa ranks the lowest, although still high, with problem loans totaling 6% of its gross customer loans in 2020. Data for asset quality in 2021 was not available for South Africa. When measuring bank profitability, this sample showed very high variation. Ghana and Kenya showed very high bank profitability when using net interest margin as the metric to measure profitability. Ghana and Nigeria rank very high when using ROAA as a profitability metric. Ghana ranked the highest in both metrics, with its net interest margin exceeding 8% in both years and its ROAA exceeding 3% in both years. South Africa and Morocco showed more typical bank profitability with net interest margins of around 3% in 2020 and ROAAs under 1%. Lastly, in analyzing the loan ratios of each country, we see that Morocco has the most loans as both a percentage of deposits and as a percentage of assets in both years. Morocco's loans as a percentage of deposits were slightly over 80% in 2020 and 2021, and the country's loans as a percentage of assets was slightly over 50% in both years. Ghana ranked the lowest in loan ratios, with its loans as a percentage of deposits being at around 40% in both years and its loans as a percentage of assets just below 30%.

The countries included in the Middle East region are Jordan, Egypt, the United Arab Emirates, Saudi Arabia, and Israel. In examining banking sector metrics, we see little variation in capital ratios. Saudi Arabia had the highest total capital ratios of approximately 20% in 2020 and 2021, and Israel had the lowest total capital ratios of just under 15% in both years. More variation is seen in the banking sector when analyzing asset quality. Israel and Saudi Arabia had very little problem loans and loan loss reserves as a percentage of gross loans. Israel, ranking the lowest, had under 1% in problem loans as a percentage of gross customer loans and about 1.5% loan loss reserves as a percentage of gross loans in 2020, with a slight drop in 2021. Usually, these figures are relatively stable between 2020 and 2021. We see a unique situation in Egypt, which saw a large rise in these asset quality measures between the 2 years. The country's problem loans and loan loss reserves as a percentage of gross loans were just over 2% and just over 4%, respectively, in 2020 and jumped to 6% and 7% in 2021. The UAE ranked the highest for problem loans, totaling approximately 6.5% in both years. Meanwhile, Jordan ranked the highest for loan loss reserves, exceeding 7% in 2021.

The profitability of banks in this region is relatively similar across countries, and relatively similar to the metrics of bank profitability in the sample of English-speaking countries. In 2020, Egypt's bank profitability was the highest when using net interest margin as a metric, with a net interest margin of approximately 3.25%. However, this figure slipped to 2.5% in 2021. Saudi Arabia ranked the highest for bank profitability when using ROAA as a metric, with ROAAs of approximately 1.25% and 1.7% in 2020 and 2021, respectively. Israel ranked the lowest in both metrics, but saw modest improvement of ROAA in 2021. We finally analyze the loan ratios to better understand the banking sectors of these economies. As a whole, this region showed relatively average loan ratios. Saudi Arabia has the highest loan ratios in both years, with loans over total deposits and loans over total assets of 90% and 60%, respectively, in 2020 and a modest increase in loans over deposits in 2021. Egypt has the lowest loan ratios in both years, with loans as a percentage of deposits and loans as a percentage of assets of just under 50% and just under 40%, respectively, in 2020 and a slight decrease in 2021.

The countries in our sample of the Eastern European region include Ukraine, Russia, Greece, Poland, Romania, and Turkey. In first examining the banking sector of this region, we see that the members of our sample share relatively similar and typical capital ratios. Romania has the highest capital ratios, with a total capital ratio of approximately 23% in 2020. Turkey, Ukraine, and Greece all share the lowest capital ratios in this region, with total capital ratios of approximately 17% in 2020. Meanwhile, the countries showed much greater differences in their banking sector between one another when examining their asset quality. Compared to the rest, Ukraine has very high problem loans and loan loss reserves, both as a percentage of gross loans, of just under 40% in 2020. Greece's problem loans and loan loss reserves as a percentage of gross loans were approximately 25% and 15%, respectively, in 2020, but fell to 9% and just over 5% in 2021. Meanwhile, Poland, Romania, and Turkey have very low quantities of problem loans and loan loss reserves. Data for Russia was not available.

In measuring banking profitability, we see fairly low profitability in this region. In fact, Greece experienced negative profitability in both years when measuring with ROAA. However, Greece's net interest margins were approximately 2% in both 2020 and 2021. Ukraine experienced the highest bank profitability in the region, with a net interest margin and ROAA of just over 5% and approximately 2%, respectively, in 2020.

Lastly, in examining the banking sector, we notice that loan ratios in this region were fairly typical. Turkey had the most loans as a percentage of deposits in both years, with this ratio being around 100% in 2020 and dropping to 90% in 2021. Loans measured as a percentage of assets was approximately 60% in both Poland and Turkey in 2020, but in 2021, Turkey's fell slightly.

The countries in our sample of the Asian region include China, Japan, India, South Korea, the Philippines, and Indonesia. In analyzing the banking sector, we first note that each of these countries shares relatively similar capital ratios. Each country's total capital ratio was between 16% and 14% in both 2020 and 2021. However, the countries' banking sector vary more in their asset qualities. India had far more problem loans and loan loss reserves as a percentage of gross loans than its counterparts, with problem loans as a percentage of gross customer loans and loan loss reserves as a percentage of gross loans of just over 7% and 5%, respectively, in 2020, with a modest dip in 2021. The Philippines' problem loans as a percentage of gross customer loans and loan loss reserves as a percentage of gross loans were approximately 4% and 3.5% in both years. China, Japan, and South Korea had very small figures in this category, with South Korea having the fewest problem loans and loan loss reserves. Data for Indonesia was not available. As a whole, this region scores low in terms of problem loans and loan loss reserves.

In measuring bank profitability, we also see much variation. The Philippines and Japan showed higher bank profitability than do their counterparts, with net interest margins of close to 3.5% in both

2020 and 2021. Both countries' ROAAs were approximately 0.75% in 2020 and grew to approximately 1% in 2021. Meanwhile, Japan's profitability was very low with a net interest margin and ROAA of approximately 0.6% and 0.2% in 2020 and very slight growth in 2021. Japan also scored lower than the rest of the Asian countries sampled when measuring loan ratios. The country's total loans as a percentage of deposits and as a percentage of assets were approximately 50% and 35%, respectively, in both 2020 and 2021. South Korea showed the highest loan ratios, with loans as a percentage of deposits and as a percentage of assets of approximately 120% and just over 60% in both years.

15.3 Financial markets recovery in the rest of the world

We examine the financial markets in the English-speaking nations by measuring the markets for equity, bonds, and CDs to see where they fit in this crisis. The stock markets in all five countries plummeted far below the bear market territory at the onset of the pandemic but rallied following stimulus. In the US, the stock market's index more than doubled between the onset of the pandemic to Q3 of 2021, reaching its peak in November 2021 and eventually hitting bear market territory in June 2022. The bond markets in all five countries suffered in 2021, with investor fears of eventual interest rate hikes in 2022. We finally highlight a unique financial situation in Canada, with growth in the CD market in 2020, while each of the other countries' CD markets suffered at the onset of the pandemic.

Examining the financial markets of the selected countries in Western Europe (Finland, Portugal, Italy, Spain, France, Switzerland, and Germany), all these countries' stock markets plummeted in the onset of the pandemic, similar to all countries sampled in the English-speaking region, and all seven stock markets rallied in 2020 and 2021 following the stimulus period. However, Spain and Portugal's stock markets did not suffer as dramatically in Q4 of 2021 and the beginning of 2022 as did their counterparts. Portugal's stock market did not suffer until 2022, while Spain experienced an overall decline in stock market capitalization in 2021, but it was gradual. In studying the bond market, we see that among the Eurozone countries, the 10Y bond yield rose from close to 0% during the onset of the pandemic between 2% and 4% in Q1 of 2022 depending on the country. Switzerland's bond market is unique, because the 10Y bond yield was below negative 1% in 2019 but rose to 1.5% in Q1 of 2022. Lastly, among the Eurozone countries, the CD markets experienced a quick rise in the onset of the pandemic, followed by a decline in the second half of the year and a gradual decline in 2021.

The sample of countries studied from the Latin American region include Argentina, Chile, Peru, Brazil, and Mexico. Excluding Argentina, the financial markets in Latin America follow relatively similar trends to the markets of the Western European and English-speaking regions. Each stock market plummeted at the onset of the pandemic, rallied following stimulus, and peaked in Q4 of 2021. Argentina's stock market's behavior during the pandemic is extremely unique. It has experienced an upward trend from the end of 2019 until the beginning of 2022, with an extremely sharp rally in Q4 of 2021. Argentina's bond markets are unique as well, with interest rates rising from approximately 45% in September 2021 to over 50% in Q4 of 2021. The rest of the Latin American countries experienced a drop in bond yield during the beginning of the pandemic and a hike in 2021 and 2022. However, the yields are far more conservative than those of Argentina.

The countries of the African region that we include in our analysis are South Africa, Morocco, Ghana, Nigeria, and Kenya. We noted that the financial markets in each of the five countries in this sample, excluding Kenya, show similar pandemic trends, with a large and fast dip in the stock market during the onset of the pandemic, a fast and then slower recovery following stimulus, and finally a dip in Q4 of 2021 and 2022. Kenya's stock market behavior is extremely abnormal, as its stock market has been continuously suffering since before the pandemic. In recent years, it suffered the worst in 2019 and early 2020, but its behavior has been more horizontal in 2021 and 2022. We also note that Kenya's bond market is extremely volatile, but follows an inversely related pattern to the stock market. The yield of Kenya's 10Y bond has been rallying in the past year. Ghana also showed unusual bond market behavior. The yield of its 3 M bond sat at around 4% in 2019 and 2020, fell to just over 12% in early 2021, and has risen to over 28% in 2022.

The countries included in the Middle East region are Jordan, Egypt, the United Arab Emirates, Saudi Arabia, and Israel. Shifting the focus to the financial markets of this region, Jordan, Saudi Arabia, and Israel each showed very typical COVID-19 trends in their stock markets during the crisis, recovery, and aftermath. In Egypt, after the country's stock market plummeted during the onset of the pandemic, recovery was extremely modest, and the country's stock market in 2021 never recovered to levels from before the pandemic. The country's bond market was relatively stable during 2021, followed by a hike in the 10Y bond yield from just over 15% in January 2022 to over a staggering 18% in October 2022. The financial markets of UAE showed interesting behavior as well but followed a different trend. The country's stock market fell during the initial phase of the pandemic but rallied very strongly and consistently throughout the rest of the pandemic, and continuous to rally past 2022, reaching levels significantly higher than before the pandemic.

The countries in our sample of the Eastern European region include Ukraine, Russia, Greece, Poland, Romania, and Turkey. We highlight unusual situations in the financial markets of this sample. In Ukraine, for example, the stock market was not heavily affected from the initial phase of the pandemic, which is highly unusual. The stock market had rallied greatly throughout the entirety of 2019, fell very slightly at the onset of the pandemic, but remained much higher than a year prior. From early 2020 on, the stock market behavior has been mostly horizontal in Ukraine. In the country's bond market, we see a slight rise in yields at the onset of the pandemic, followed by little movement until early 2022, where the price of a 3Y bond jumped from a staggering yield, of approximately 20% to about 80% soon after. High yields on government bonds are expected in Ukraine given its current geopolitical and economic situation. Russia also experienced a spike in its 10Y bond during the start of the war to about 14%, but this figure has since dropped to 9.8% in October 2022.

We also highlight a unique situation in Turkey, where the stock market saw very little reaction to the initial crisis of the pandemic, after relatively horizontal behavior for the entirety of 2019 and into 2020, followed by a strong rally through 2021 and 2022 to current levels that are way above prepandemic figures. Turkey's bond market has been much more volatile, with many ups and downs before the pandemic and during the pandemic, followed by a rise in the yield of the Turkish 10Y from around 17% in early 2021 to over 26% toward the end of the year, but back down to around 12% in 2022.

The countries in our sample of the Asian region include China, Japan, India, South Korea, the Philippines, and Indonesia. We examine the financial markets of this region to better understand its crisis, recovery, and aftermath behavior. Excluding China and the Philippines, these countries each shared a common trend in their stock markets, including a large plummeting during the onset of the pandemic, followed by a strong rally post stimulus and a slowing of growth in 2022. Stock market behavior in the Philippines is slightly unusual, because the markets only rallied until Q4 of 2020, and in 2021, they moved more horizontally with heavy volatility. The Philippines' stock market has seen bearish behavior in 2022. In China, the stock market behavior has been highly unusual throughout the pandemic, with a very quick and strong rally in Q1 of 2020, followed by volatile but overall growth until 2021. The stock market has since fallen but remains at higher levels than it was for most of 2019. The bond market in China showed unusual behavior as well. Overall, the yield on a Chinese 10Y bond has fallen from 4% in early 2018 to 2.8% in early 2022. Overall, activity in the bond market has been mostly negative, with a hike in yields during the onset of the pandemic.

We finally highlight a unique situation in Japan, where the country has struggled with a long period of horizontal movement in the stock market before the pandemic, and bond yields were negative. After bearish activity in Japan's stock market during the onset of the pandemic, Japan showed a very strong rally with strong bullish activity for the first time in a while, but in 2021, the stock market reverted back to relatively horizontal activity. In the bond market, the yield on a Japanese 10Y bond rose from a low of −0.3% in 2019 to 0.1% at the onset of the pandemic, and eventually rose to 0.24% in 2022.

Part V

Empirical evidence on COVID-19 economic and financial effects during the aftermath around the world

As discussed above, we are mostly limited to reporting on the policies in the aftermath of the COVID-19 crisis and data on some of their empirical results. The story is incomplete as of this writing, with an unknown remaining time to go.

In addition to the data sources also employed and described in other parts of the book and Appendix, we supplement our conclusions here with recent press coverage of rapidly changing current conditions not currently easily collected as of the book deadline. Economic problems such as high and variable inflation and domestic and international supply chain disruptions appear around the globe and continue to add to the story.

We cannot draw definitive, science-based conclusions without more complete research agenda on the COVID-19 crisis aftermath in the future. Nonetheless, the findings to date are sufficient to help us conclude that the blueprint for strategies to improve future crisis outcomes in Part VI will require considerable attention on the aftermath phase.

In the chapters of Part V, we include the US with the other countries in the discussions of aftermath policies in Chapter 16, but we focus on these other nations only in Chapters 17–21 in our reviews of evidence on the real economy, banking sector, and financial markets during the COVID-19 aftermath. We do so to avoid excessive repetition of US evidence that is well-known and largely covered elsewhere in the book.

We discuss in Part I above that the aftermath essentially arrived in the US by early 2021. The real economy, banking sector, and financial markets had essentially achieved escape velocity and needed little to no additional stimulus. Indicators were positive, vaccines were poised to be widely available to allow return to work and in-person consumption, and pent-up consumer demand was ready with plentiful unspent stimulus funds. As shown in Chapter 16, monetary stimulus continued to March 2022, and fiscal stimulus has largely tapered, but not entirely eliminated entering 2023.

We add here that by mid-year 2021, inflation was exceeding 5%, and as 2021 progressed into 2022, supply chain problems were abundantly clear. Stores had empty shelves, restaurants could not find enough servers, workers had not returned to the labor force, and containers ships were backed up at ports and car manufacturers could not get semiconductors. Suppliers could not contend with consumer spending volumes and shifts among goods and services demanded. After the Federal Reserve began tightening monetary policy in March 2022, financial market losses were widespread, as even greater drops occurred in nontraditional investments. Bubbles burst in cryptocurrencies and high-profile exchanges and affiliated trading firms failed. Additional aftermath consequences in the US are yet to come as of this writing, including potential for a long-predicted but still uncertain COVID-19 aftermath recession.

Chapter 16

Continuations vs scale backs of COVID-19 crisis policies in the crisis aftermath

Abstract

This is the first of five chapters covering economic and financial effects around the world during the aftermath of the COVID-19 crisis. In all of these chapters, we focus on the policies and empirical results. Research findings on the aftermath would be incomplete. The fact that the aftermath remains ongoing suggests that well-informed conclusions based on research to date is not possible. In this particular chapter, the focus is almost exclusively on COVID-19 crisis policies around the world and the extent to which they might be continued vs scaled back. Some recent economic and financial problems such as inflation, which is historically linked to stimulative government fiscal and monetary policies is at least suggestive of support for the scale-back arguments.

Keywords: COVID-19, Policy, Aftermath, Real economy, Banking sector, Financial markets

In this first chapter of Part V on the aftermath, we cover COVID-19 crisis policies around the world and the extent to which they might be continued vs scaled back in the aftermath still ongoing as of this writing. We keep our scientific detachment and objective neutrality to the extent possible and recognize that research on the aftermath cannot be concluded for some time yet. We simply note here that inflation and other recent economic and financial problems that are linked in past research to highly stimulative government fiscal and monetary policies are at least suggestive of support for scaling back.

16.1   When and how should crisis policies be continued vs scaled back in crisis aftermaths to avoid policy traps

The first of Sir Isaac Newton's Laws of Motion is that of inertia—every object will remain at rest or in uniform motion in a straight line unless compelled to change its state by the action of an external force.

The Economic and Financial Impacts of the COVID-19 Crisis Around the World
https://doi.org/10.1016/B978-0-443-19162-6.00016-5
Copyright © 2024 Elsevier Inc. All rights reserved.

This law applies to human policymakers as well as to physical objects. Policymakers who engage in policies that have strong popular support and appear to have favorable economic consequences in the short run may be likely as humans to continue such policies.

In the case of COVID-19, providing additional stimulus checks for millions of voters, engaging in expansionary monetary policy that boosts stock market values and lowers unemployment without much inflation in the short run can be difficult to quit until the long-run consequences come due. Thus, policymakers often fall into such policy traps of continuing no-longer-needed policies during COVID-19. We discuss examples in this chapter and offer some potential solutions in our *"Expect the Unexpected"* plan in Chapter 22.

16.2 Policy continuations vs scale backs during the COVID-19 aftermath in the US

In response to the tremendous dread and misery from the economic damage of COVID-19, federal policymakers passed five relief acts in 2020, totaling an estimated $3.3 trillion in aid, and the American Rescue Plan in 2021, totaling an additional $1.8 trillion. As part of the Consolidated Appropriations Act of 2021, President Trump signed an $868 billion (approximately 4.1% of GDP) COVID-19 relief and government funding package on December 28, 2020. The Act included increased unemployment benefits of $300 per week through March 14, 2021, direct stimulus payments of $600 to citizens, an additional round of PPP loans, money for immunizations, testing and tracking, and K-12 education spending.

Following the COVID-19 disaster, the federal government in the US introduced The American Jobs Plan in March 2021, a $2 trillion investment plan to repair infrastructure and increase employment opportunities. The following investments in the American Jobs Plan included: $111 billion for water infrastructure, $100 billion for digital infrastructure, $100 billion for power infrastructure, and $213 billion for affordable housing.

President Biden signed the American Rescue Plan into effect on March 11, 2021, providing another phase of COVID-19 relief at a cost of $1844 billion (about 8.8% of GDP reported in 2020). The American Rescue Plan prioritized investing in public health response and delivering timely support to families, communities, and businesses. It extended unemployment benefits (including supplemental unemployment benefits), offered direct stimulus checks of $1400, provided direct help to state and local governments, improved financing for school reopening, and added resources to the immunization program.

By 2021, the US returned to prepandemic levels of economic activity which was faster than other international economies, thanks to a greater proportion of the US's GDP going to federal relief measures According to the Congressional Budget Office, GDP would have been 12% lower in 2020 and 9% lower in 2021 without the relief policies passed in March and April of 2020. The real gaps were significantly smaller after relief measures and laws were enacted: 5.8% in 2020 and 1.1% in 2021, respectively. Additionally, jobs were recovered faster than expected; in January 2022, the unemployment rate was 4%, which almost touches the 3.5% unemployment rate recorded before the pandemic.

Regarding unemployment, from February 2020 through April 2020, the COVID-19 pandemic triggered a temporary recession that dramatically reduced employment and GDP. The pandemic extended through 2021, which caused a continuation of significant impacts on the economy and the labor force. Workers were deterred or discouraged to return to the labor market. Even though the economy restored over 4.6 million jobs in 2021, the average annual unemployment rate during that period was still significantly lower than it was before the pandemic. In fact, the jobs lost between 2019 and 2020 doubled the amount of employment that was recovered in 2021. As a result, the Bureau of Labor Statistics' employment predictions for the years 2021 through 2031 are based on the average unemployment rate from 2021. The employment rate upswing has continued throughout the first half of 2022.

From roughly 15% during the crisis to just 4% as of March 2022, the US unemployment rate dramatically decreased. Although this decline is partially attributable to the retirement of baby boomers and an increase in early retirements (which may be temporary), a higher-than-average proportion of younger individuals are currently not in the labor force. To fully understand the "Great Resignation" phenomena, in which workers appear to be staying unemployed despite a surplus of employment possibilities, more research is required.

Compared to a 1.4% inflation rate in 2021, the US inflation rate has drastically increased to a high of 9.1% as of 2022. Inflation is putting pressure on US households. According to the Center on Budget and Policy Priorities, the majority of analysts anticipate a decline throughout the remainder of 2022, but the rate and magnitude of the decline are still unknown. With fluctuating supply and demand for goods, services, and labor, the postpandemic economy has been unlike anything ever seen before. Although the demand generated by pandemic relief policies contributed heavily to the emergence of inflation, other factors contributed as well, such as shortages and rising prices that resulted from supply chain limitations.

The Federal Open Market Committee announced in April 2021 that it would wait until inflation was "moderately above 2%" prior to adjusting rates to reach their desired long-term inflation average. According to the Center on Budget and Policy Priorities, the Federal Reserve has explicitly stated that it intends to fight inflation, and it has the resources to do so while adhering to its dual mission from Congress to promote both price stability and employment increases in the economy.

According to a statement released by the Board of Directors of the Federal Reserve System on September 21, 2022, long-term goals for the Federal Open Market Committee aim to attain a maximum unemployment rate and inflation of 2% in the long term. In furtherance of these objectives, the Committee decided to increase the target range of the federal funds rate from 3% to 3.25%, with the expectation that further increases will be appropriate. Furthermore, the Federal Open Market Committee will continue to reduce its holdings of Treasury securities, agency debt, and agency mortgage-backed securities, as stated in May 2022 Plans for Reducing the Size of the Federal Reserve's Balance Sheet. The Committee is adamant about restoring inflation to its target of 2%.

Another change made by the Federal Reserve Board of Governors was the unanimous approval of a 3/4 percentage point increase in the primary credit rate to 3.25%, beginning September 22, 2022. In executing this decision, the Board of Directors of the Federal Reserve Banks of Boston, Philadelphia, Cleveland, Richmond, Atlanta, Chicago, St. Louis, Kansas City, and Dallas authorized petitions to create that rate.

According to the World Economic Forum, after inflation reached a 40-year high in January 2022, consumer prices in the US continued to increase through February, making it abundantly clear that the most recent increase in consumer prices was not a statistical outlier and must be treated seriously. The Consumer Price Index for All Urban Consumers (CPI-U) climbed 7.9% from 2021 to 2022, while the core index increased 6.4%. These evaluations for January and February of 2022 were the highest seen since January and February of 1982, which has raised concern about an uncontrollable inflation rate.

Consumer prices during COVID-19 and the immediate aftermath exhibited a dynamic trend. Inflation increased in the spring and summer of 2021 resulting from efforts to stabilize consumer prices. In 2020, prices drastically reduced due to a dramatic decline in consumer expenditure caused by a decrease in demand and a change in consumer behavior. Generous stimulus checks strongly increased consumer spending over the course of the pandemic; however, prices trended upward resulting from low interest rates, supply issues, and dynamic consumer spending trends.

Recent discoveries of the Consumer Price Index for All Urban Consumers (CPI-U), which was stable in July 2022, showed an increase of 0.1% in August 2022 on a seasonally adjusted basis, according to a report released September 13th, 2022 by the US Bureau of Labor Statistics. Before seasonal adjustment, the all-items index rose 8.3% during the past 12 months.

According to the Pew Research Center, Americans stated that their top priority over all other concerns was to strengthen the economy in 2022. The US efforts to revitalize the economy after COVID-19 have been hindered by issues such as the Great Resignation phenomena and salary increases being countered by the highest inflation rate in 40 years. Since inflation has been growing faster than nominal wage growth, Americans no longer have as much buying power as they held in the past. Even if salaries appear to be improving, recent findings have discovered a general decrease in actual hourly earnings due to the quick rise in consumer prices. Official data showing significant price increases for consumer goods and services supported these evaluations. According to Statista's analysis of the change in real and nominal earnings and the Consumer Price Index for All Urban Consumers (CPI-U), between 2021 and 2022, consumer prices increased by 8.5% while average hourly wages increased by 5.2%, resulting in a 3% fall in real hourly earnings. Despite government attempts for economic stability, in 2021, the US economy expanded at its quickest annual rate since 1984.

Despite the Federal Reserve's most aggressive interest rate hikes since 2000, consumer prices surged in May 2022, raising concerns about out-of-control inflation. The Consumer Price Index for All Urban Consumers (CPI-U) climbed 8.6% over the previous 12 months prior to seasonal adjustment, the highest pace since December 1981, according to the US Bureau of Labor Statistics.

In a perhaps somewhat ironic twist, as the US economy presents challenging economic and financial conditions, the Small Business Administration's (SBA's) COVID-Disaster Loan Program from 2020 has recently started requiring repayments with interest of about $390 billion in loans to nearly 4 million small businesses and nonprofits.

16.3 Policy continuations vs scale backs during the COVID-19 aftermath in the rest of the world

Most of the evaluation in this chapter relies on the data that we collected from IMF's Policy Responses to COVID-19. All Canadian provinces began implementing thorough, data-driven plans to reopen in May 2020 after the Prime Minister of Canada, Justin Trudeau, and premiers from across the country issued a joint statement on April 28, 2020, outlining their shared public health approach to support doing so. More limitations in various areas of the country persisted in response to the spike in new viral infections. The limitations have been gradually loosening since the end of February 2021, only for them to be strengthened in some areas because of the third wave. Canada has made great strides in immunizing the populace after initial supply limitations. Over 65% of Canadians had gotten at least one dose of the COVID-19 vaccination as of mid-June.

The Canadian government dedicated $60.3 billion (2.7% of GDP) to support increased testing, vaccine development, medical supplies, mitigation efforts, and greater support for Indigenous communities. Households and businesses will also receive about $290 billion (13.2% of GDP) in direct aid, which includes wage subsidies, payments to workers without sick leave, and access to employment insurance, an increase from the previous year.

The Bank of Canada has taken several significant actions, including the following: (i) lowering the overnight policy rate by 150 basis points in March 2020 (to 0.25%); (ii) extending the bond buyback program across all maturities; (iii) establishing the Bankers' Acceptance Purchase Facility; (iv) extending the list of eligible collateral for Term Repo operations to include all eligible collateral for the Standing Liquidity Facility (SLF), with the exception of the Nonmortgage Loan Portfolio (NMLP); (v) supporting the Canada Mortgage Bond (CMB) market by purchasing CMBs in the secondary market; (vii) announcing a temporary increase in the amount of NMLP a participant can pledge for the SLF and for those participants that do not use NMLP; (vii) declaring that the goal for settlement balances will rise from $250 million to $1000 million; (viii) declaring, along with central banks from Japan, the Euro Area, the UK, the US, and Switzerland, that the provision of liquidity via the standing US dollar liquidity swap line arrangements will be further enhanced; (ix) declaring the establishment of the Standing Term Liquidity Facility, under which loans could be given to qualified financial institutions in need of short-term liquidity; and (x) announcing the Provincial Money Market Acquisition (PMMP) program, the Provincial Bond Purchase Program (PBPP), the Corporate Bond Purchase Program (CBPP), and the secondary market purchase of Government of Canada securities. In its "forward guidance," the Bank of Canada stated that it would not raise the policy interest rate until the recovery was well underway and inflation was steadily approaching its target level.

The Office of Superintendent of Financial Institutions (OSFI) reduced the Domestic Stability Buffer for D-SIBs from 2.25% to 1% of risk-weighted assets; under the Insured Mortgage Purchase Program, the government will purchase up to $150 billion of insured mortgage pools through the Canada Mortgage and Housing Corporation (CMHC); and $95 billion in credit facilities were announced (including $13.8 billion in forgiven loans) to lend to firms under stress. Additionally, the federal government will find farm Credit Canada, giving it an additional $5.2 billion in lending capacity to producers, agribusinesses, and food processors.

The Bank of Canada eliminated some of the liquidity measures in October 2020; the Bankers' Acceptance Purchase Facility, the Canada Mortgage Bond Purchase Program, and the Provincial Money Market Purchase Program. The Bank of Canada announced on March 23, 2021, that the Commercial Paper Purchase Program (CPPP), the Provincial Bond Purchase Program (PBPP), and the Corporate Bond Purchase Program (CBPP) will all be discontinued, with the cancellations taking effect between April and late May 2021. Additionally, as of May 10, 2021, and April 06, 2021, respectively, the biweekly Term Repo operations and the Contingent Term Repo Facility (CTRF) were suspended.

In April 2021, in response to the faster-than-expected recovery speed, the Bank of Canada decided to reduce its purchases of Government of Canada bonds to a target of $3 billion weekly net, down from a minimum of $4 billion weekly. Canada's housing costs have been rising quickly in 2020 and 2021. A "mortgage stress test" was introduced by OSFI to ensure homeowners do not borrow more than they can afford to pay back. As of June 01, 2021, the higher mortgage contract rate +2% or 5.25% will serve as the minimum qualifying rate for uninsured mortgages.

The authorities announced several fiscal measures totaling 12% of GDP in 2020 to reduce the repercussions of COVID-19, of which the direct impact on the primary deficit was 7.2% of GDP. At the start of the pandemic, Congress proclaimed a state of "public catastrophe," which released the government from its duty to meet the 2020 primary balance target. To meet unusual spending needs, the administration has also used the constitutional expenditure ceiling's escape clause. A distinct (so-called "war") 2020 budget that was exempt from the fiscal responsibility law and the Brazilian constitution's golden rule featured emergency measures. The fiscal measures included increasing health spending, providing short-term income support to vulnerable households, providing cash transfers to low-income workers and unemployed people (Emergency Aid program), delaying the payment of retirees' 13th pension, expanding the Bolsa Familia program to include more beneficiaries—over 1 million—and providing low-income workers with salary bonuses in advance, lower taxes and import levies on necessary medical supplies, support for employment (partial compensation for furloughed workers as well as temporary tax breaks), and new transfers from the federal government to state governments to support higher health spending and as a buffer against the anticipated decline in revenues. The government has backed over 1% of GDP in credit lines to SMEs and microbusinesses to cover payroll costs, working capital, and investment.

From mid-February through August 2020, the central bank cut the policy rate (SELIC) by 225 basis points, bringing it to a record-low 2%. Measures to boost liquidity in the financial system include a temporary relaxation of provisioning regulations, a reduction in reserve requirements, and capital conservation buffers. In order to promote lending, the reserve requirement on savings accounts was cut from 25 to 17, on top of a drop of 6 basis points in early March 2020. The central bank also changed the capital requirements for small financial institutions, opened a facility to provide loans to financial institutions backed by private corporate bonds as collateral, and permitted banks to reduce provisions for contingent liabilities as long as the money is lent to SMEs. Additionally, the Federal Reserve has planned for a swap facility that is still active to give the central bank up to US$60 billion. The majority of liquidity support measures were discontinued in 2021, and by June, the SELIC rate soared to 4.25%.

On May 14, 2020, the Mexican government unveiled plans to start the normalization of economic activity. These included the addition of the manufacturing of construction, mining, and transportation equipment as essential activities as well as a green-yellow-orange-red color system for states to indicate the extent of activities permitted (for example, red denotes states with the most active cases, which would remain in a forced quarantine). Beginning in December 2020, restrictions increased; however, following the relaxation of second wavein February 2021, they have decreased.

In addition to an increased health-care spending of 0.4% of GDP, Mexico's fiscal response in 2020 included the following actions: old-age and disability pension payments should be made 8 months in advance. Procurement procedures and Value Added Tax (VAT) refunds should be expedited. Lending to formal and informal sector businesses and workers should be encouraged. Development banks should provide liquidity support and guarantees (257.1 billion pesos). Specifically, the Ministry of Economy gave loans worth 37.9 billion pesos to family enterprises that had previously been registered in the Welfare Census and to SMEs that maintain payroll-paying employees, self-employed workers, and domestic workers (26.6 billion pesos). For 3 months, the government offered subsidized unemployment insurance to workers with mortgages with the Housing Institute (5.9 billion pesos). Additionally, 4 billion pesos were given to housing projects.

The year 2020 saw the implementation of additional government initiatives, such as low-interest housing loans for government employees (ISSSTE loans totaling 34.3 billion pesos), low-interest personal loans (3 billion pesos), and a special program to revive the economy by the Housing Fund of the Institute for Social Security and Services (Fovissste, 2 billion pesos). A total of 0.7% of GDP was spent on above-the-line fiscal measures in 2020, while 1.2% of GDP was spent on below-the-line fiscal measures. The President also announced an austerity program for public spending during the week of April 19, 2020, which included reallocating nonpriority spending to essential goods and voluntary compensation reductions for senior government personnel.

Since the onset of the pandemic, from March through February 2021, the central bank has lowered interest rates by 300 basis points. Additionally, it has enacted the following steps to support the financial system's operation, amounting to up to 800 billion pesos, or 3.5% of 2019s GDP. In response to looming inflation, the central bank raised its policy rate for the first time by 25 basis points on June 24th, 2021. The central bank has decreased the required regulatory deposit in order to support the flow of credit (by 50 billion pesos, or about 15% of the current stock). Additionally, it is developing financing channels for commercial and development banks worth 350 billion pesos, enabling them to direct funds toward micro-, small-, and medium-sized businesses that were subjected to lockdown procedures following the outbreak of the virus. Institutions' corporate loans and traditional repo collateral are being exchanged for credit, freeing up liquidity on the banks' balance sheets.

The central bank has significantly increased the availability and affordability of its liquidity facilities, as well as the range of entities that are qualified to use them in order to boost liquidity in the financial markets. A particularly effective measure was shown when the Central Bank established a facility to repurchase government assets for up to 100 billion pesos at maturities that are longer than those of standard open market operations. The repos came at a considerably lower price. To encourage organized debt markets and provide liquidity for trading instruments, a temporary swap facility for debt securities has been implemented. In order to strengthen the corporate bond market, the central bank also launched a corporate securities repo facility.

The central bank has used the US$60 billion swap line with the Federal Reserve in order to guarantee the proper operation of financial markets, conducted roll-over auctions with decreasing demand, and held two auctions for commercial banks worth a combined $5 billion on two separate occasions. To avert surges in short-term interest rates, more liquidity is being made available during trading hours and sterilized after the market closes.

In order to decrease the maturities of government bonds held by private institutions and enhance their liquidity position, the Central Bank actively participated in government bond swaps. Financially, the National Banking and Securities Commission (CNBV) released temporary special accounting norms that permit lenders to postpone loans for up to 4 or 6 months and made steps to digitally onboard legal people in order to open banking accounts and offer loans. The CNBV and the National Insurance and Surety Commission (CNSF) also advised banking and insurance companies against paying dividends, conducting share buybacks, or engaging in any other shareholder compensation-related activity.

According to estimates by law enforcement officials, the announced measures will total 6.5% of 2020 GDP, with 4.5% allocated in the budget and 2% off-budget. They have been designed to (i) increase health spending, including for better virus diagnostics, purchases of vaccines and medical supplies, and construction of clinics and hospitals; (ii) support workers and disadvantaged populations, such as via increased transactions to low-income families and social security benefits (particularly to low-income recipients), UI assistance, and payouts to minimum-wage employees; (iii) assistance for industries that have been particularly hard hit, such as diminished social security contributions, subsidies to cover payroll costs, and subsidized loans for construction-related activities; (iv) demand support, such as expenditures on public works; (v) forbearance, such as continuing to provide public utilities to households that have fallen behind on their payments; and (vi) credit guarantees for bank lending to micro-, small, and medium-sized enterprises (SMEs) for the production of foods and basic necessities. Additional antiovercharging measures taken by the authorities include price regulations for food and medical supplies, ringfencing of vital goods, export restrictions on medical equipment and supplies, and centralized sales of key medical supplies.

Regulations that limit banks' holdings of central bank paper to free up capital for SME lending, lower reserve requirements for bank lending to households and SMEs, a temporary relaxation of bank provisioning requirements and bank loan classification rules (i.e., an extension of the 60-day nonperforming loan definition), and a moratorium on both bank account closures caused by bounced checks.

The Colombian government has implemented cautious policies for the reopening of industries. On April 27, the construction and manufacturing sectors were permitted to resume operations, and on May 11, a broader range of industrial and commercial services sectors did the same. Although municipal governments (including Bogota) have been slow to loosen restrictions, some services, including a few retail segments, were permitted to reopen on June 01.

Colombia's government issued an emergency declaration for the state, which established the National Emergency Mitigation Fund (FOME), which will receive 1.3% of GDP from domestic bond issuance and other budgetary resources in addition to a portion of its funding from regional and stabilization funds (approximately 1.5% of GDP). The government was given permission by the Fiscal Rule Consultative Committee to temporarily suspend the fiscal rule in 2020 and 2021. Presently, the government expects the overall deficit to be 7.8% of GDP in 2020 and 8.6% of GDP in 2021. Supplemental government budget support for health was confirmed, including partial payment for COVID-19 tests and vaccines, faster direct contracting for emergency response services, payments to providers for ICU accessibility and the formation of a National Tracking and Contact Center, a one-time bonus for health workers, and new lines of credit offering liquidity support to the coffee sector, the education sector, the public transportation sector, and the technology sector, health and public sector providers, and all tourism-related companies, new credit lines for SME payroll and loan payments, working capital for large corporations, and corporates in the sectors most affected by the pandemic through the National Guarantee Fund, a 2-month suspension of pension contributions by both employees and employers, delayed tax collection, an exemption of tariffs and VAT for certain food industries and services and strategic health imports, a delay in utility payments for low- and middle-income households, and exclusions from certain taxes are just some of the measures that have been put in place. In addition, the government announced a payroll subsidy for companies that saw a 3-month revenue decline of over 20% equal to 50% of the minimum wage per worker.

The Central Bank of Colombia has reduced the policy rate by 250 basis points and taken several other steps to increase liquidity in both local and foreign currencies. These include an increase in the amounts, applicable securities, and qualified counterparts for their liquidity overnight and term facilities as well as the acquisition of debt issued by credit institutions, and lastly TES purchases in the secondary market. The reserve requirement for savings and checking accounts was also decreased from 11% to 8%, as well as the requirement for fixed-term savings accounts (less than 18 months) from 4.5% to 3.5%. All loans that were less than 30 days past due on February 29 were able to be reprofiled by supervised businesses due to Superfinanciera. The PAD (Program to Support Debtors) to support sustainable borrowers, which was scheduled to conclude on June 30, 2021, has been extended until August 31, 2021. Banks are prohibited from raising loan interest rates, adding interest on interest, or adding businesses to credit registries in exchange for forbearance. The SFC has released the countercyclical requirements and approved specific related-party transactions for fund managers, such as the acquisition of Certificados de Deposito a Termino (term deposit certificates) issued by a connected firm.

Chile's governing administration has undertaken a highly progressive plan to reopen the economy and gradually lift the quarantine. Municipalities will move through the five steps—quarantine to advanced opening—in line with a number of factors, including the virus's rate of reproduction, the number of hospital beds available, and the anticipated number of regional active cases. Chile continues to be in a State of Emergency until September 2021, and there is a daily curfew in place from 10:00 p.m. to 5:00 a.m. statewide. To immunize its citizens, the government has purchased vaccine doses from Pfizer-BioNTech, Sinovac, AstraZeneca-Oxford, and CanSino. The second round of vaccinations began at the end of December, and by the end of June 2021, over 10 million people—or 60% of the target population—had received it.

The Chilean administration unveiled a package of fiscal initiatives on March 19, 2020, totaling up to US$11.75 billion (or around 4.7% of GDP), with an emphasis on bolstering employment and business liquidity. The package consists of the following: more generous healthcare spending, enhanced unemployment benefits and subsidies, many tax deferrals, liquidity provision to SMEs, including through the state-owned Banco del Estado, and finally, accelerated payments for public procurement contracts. The following announcements were made by the authorities on April 08, 2020: an increase in support for the most vulnerable and independent workers in the amount of about US$2 billion, a credit-guaranteed strategy (in the amount of US$3 billion) that may be used to cover credits up to US$24 billion to facilitate firm financing. They announced a scheme to provide 2.5 million food baskets to those in need on May 17; the campaign is anticipated to cost US$100 million. A new fiscal package totaling US$12 billion over the next 24 months was announced by law enforcement agencies on June 14. It includes proposed tax measures to stimulate the economy and increase the liquidity of SMEs, including a temporary reduction of the CIT rate and allowing for instantaneous investment depreciation (announced on July 02), as well as a program of about US$1.5 billion to support the middle class experiencing significant income losses, including through soft loans (announced on July 14). The first pension fund withdrawal was authorized by legislation passed by Congress on July 23. A second withdrawal was authorized on December 03 and a third was authorized by the end of April 2021.

The Central Bank of Chile has instated several critical measures related to increased funding and liquidity including two policy rate reductions totaling 125 basis points to 0.5%, the introduction of a new funding facility for banks contingent upon them expanding credit, the addition of corporate securities as collateral for the Central Bank's liquidity operations, the introduction of high-rated commercial loans as collateral for the funding facility operations, the start of a program for the purchase of bank shares (up to US$8 billion), the expansion of the program for providing liquidity in pesos and US dollars through repo operations and swaps and the broadening eligibility of currencies for meeting reserve requirements in foreign currencies. The Central Bank's regulations for bank liquidity are also being made more flexible, and the liquidity coverage ratio is being loosened. A special asset purchase program totaling US$8 billion over a 6-month term and an additional funding-for-lending facility totaling US$16 billion were two additional steps to strengthen liquidity and credit that the Central Bank announced on June 16.

During the national lockdown, the government sanctioned S$3 billion (0.5% of GDP) for the health emergency and S$7 billion (1.1% of GDP) in direct handouts to assist poor households. In late July, it was reported that needy households would receive an additional cash transfer of around S$6.4 billion

(0.9% of GDP). Additionally, the government allowed a 3-month extension for SMEs' income tax declarations and is giving people and businesses flexibility in how they repay their tax debt. The interim assistance offered by these tax reforms is predicted to be in the range of 2.0% of GDP. The government has also announced plans to expand the program to include around 0.5% of GDP and approved the development of an S$800 million (or 0.1% of GDP) fund to aid qualified SMEs in obtaining operating capital and/or debt refinancing. The government has announced a delay in family payments for water and electricity as well as an S$800 million subsidy for power bills (0.1% of GDP). The government began a program called the Programa de Garantas COVID-19 on October 07 to give guarantees supporting loan restructurings for households and SMEs. The program is expected to cost around S$7 billion (1% of GDP). In late October, a new pay subsidy scheme was introduced, covering 35%–55% of the wage bill for businesses that reported a sales decline of at least 30% in April or May 2020 and either recalled furloughed employees or added new positions.

The policy rate was decreased by 200 basis points, or 1/4%, and the central bank is continuing to examine inflation trends and factors in order to increase monetary stimulus if needed. The central bank also approved a package of S$60 billion (over 8.8% of GDP) in liquidity assistance (backed by government guarantees) to support lending and the payments chain, which was set to expire in October 2020. Additionally, it has lowered reserve requirements and provided liquidity to the financial system through repo operations (Reactiva Peru). Financial institutions may alter the terms of their loans to people and businesses impacted by the COVID-19 outbreaks without modifying the loans' classification. To help banks manage the risk of rising rates on long-term loans such as mortgages and business loans, the central bank announced in December 2020 that it will issue long-term interest rate swaps and repos. With maturities ranging from 3 to 7 years, the swaps will require the central bank to pay a variable rate in exchange for a fixed rate. Repos will mature in 1–3 years. The bank also developed a facility for repurchasing business invoices from SMEs for a period of 1–2 months. By permitting banks to temporarily sell bundles of high-quality loans in repo operations, the central bank increased liquidity and extended the temporary suspension of extra reserves on foreign currency loans until April 2021.

Congress approved three fiscal packages for COVID-19 prevention and mitigation in 2020, totaling about 3.4% of GDP from the previous year. This fiscal stimulus was mostly funded by treasury bond issuance and loans from IFIs. The two main programs of the fiscal reaction were increasing healthcare resources (0.2% of GDP) and supporting various industries with cash transfers (1.2% of GDP), salary subsidies (0.3% of GDP), and funding for SMEs (0.6% of GDP). More focused actions were implemented as part of the National Emergency and Economic Recovery Plan including expediting the process for tax refunds to exporters, delaying income tax payments and Social Security contributions for a quarter, eliminating taxes on medical goods, expanding the availability and scope of energy subsidies, and promoting low-cost housing.

In June 2020, Banco de Guatemala cut its policy rate to a record-low 1.75%. The Board reiterated its position to keep its rate at 1.75 a year later. In order to enable debt restructuring for borrowers experiencing temporary liquidity shortages, the Monetary Board loosened credit controls in April 2020. A gradual phase-out of those relaxation measures began in January, and as of May data, the banking system is still sound. With special consent from Congress, Banco de Guatemala paid GTQ 10.6 billion for GTM Treasury Bonds (about USD 1.5 billion, 96.8% of the total bond issuance authorized by Congress). The government utilized the money to pay for COVID-19 emergency initiatives last year.

Early containment strategies in Ecuador centered on preventing the virus from spreading by shutting down borders, public areas, and unimportant commercial activity, as well as enforcing a curfew across the country. These actions appear to have contained the pandemic epidemic, as the virus has recently spread slowly in this country compared to other nations in the region (chart). The distribution of food baskets, temporary easing of the requirements for unemployment insurance eligibility, exceptional cash transfers to low-income families ($250 million), and increased health spending ($550 million) were among the policy measures to protect lives and livelihoods totaling $1.2 billion in 2020. Along with interim price limitations for basic food items, further initiatives included deferring payroll contributions, tuition, health insurance, utilities, and housing support. The possibility of mutually agreed-upon adjustments to employment agreements as well as the temporary adoption of shorter workweeks and more flexible work arrangements were all measures taken to sustain employment.

The authorities cut the banks' contribution rate to the Liquidity Fund by three percentage points of deposits (to 5%) to resolve the liquidity crisis in the financial system, releasing around $950 million in liquid assets. This action assisted in rebalancing internal liquidity as the demand for cash eventually decreased. Additionally, they mandated the adjustment of interest rate caps, launched a working capital facility (Reactivate Ecuador) for businesses receiving World Bank financing and introduced an unusual voluntary deferral of private loan commitments. The deferral measures will strengthen the real economy, but if they are kept in place for a long time, they could weaken the financial institutions' balance sheets and pose hazards to the financial system.

The initial economic initiatives launched by the prior administration totaled RD$32 billion (or $576 million USD, or 1/4 of GDP), or 34 of GDP. Among these are increased social expenditures: The most vulnerable households, including those of undocumented immigrants, are supported by the Quédate en Casa program (RD$17 billion). The number of households covered by the current Comer es Primero program, which pays RD$5000 (roughly US$90) per month, has increased from 0.8 to 1.5 million households; 452,817 families will receive additional transfers of RD$2000 (roughly US$36) per month; (ii) the newly established Employee Solidarity Assistance Fund (FASE) (RD$15 billion), which benefits about 754,000 families of formal workers who were laid off with a monthly transfer up to up to 70% of final formal pay (minimum of RD$5000, average RD$8104); and (iii) a new initiative called Pa'ti was launched on May 17 to support independent workers. It offers each beneficiary RD$5000 (about US$90) per month, with an additional RD$2.4 billion made available for medical professionals, members of the armed forces, and police officers. All social assistance programs will now run through the end of 2020, according to newly elected President Luis Abinader.

In order to lessen the difficulties brought on by the epidemic, the government approved a 2020 budget increase of RD$202 billion (4.5% of GDP). The authorities gathered loans and commercial credit lines from the IMF, World Bank, Interamerican Development Bank, Latin American Development Bank, and the Central American Bank for Economic Integration; in addition, they obtained private donations for medical expenses to fill the funding shortages. A financial support grant from the European Union in the sum of RD$725 million (US$12.4 million) was given out on October 05. Additionally, the administration issued domestic debt worth US$0.7 billion (in four series), with maturities ranging from 10 to 20 years and an interest rate of 10%–11%. Despite the ongoing global unrest, the nation issued a record amount of US$3.8 billion in sovereign bonds in September.

On December 7, the government announced a new incentive of RD$1500 that will be given to 1 million recipients in time for Christmas. The traditional food boxes the government used to distribute to the poorest households over the holidays will be replaced with this incentive.

The FASE I program (for formal employees with suspended labor contracts) will now run through April 2021, the government announced in December. An alternative initiative, to be revealed in

January, would take the place of FASE II (for formal employees with active labor contracts). On January 04, 2021, the President announced the extension of the Quedate en Casa program until April 2021 and its possible replacement with a new program (Superate), which will double the support provided by the current Comer es Primero and cover an extra 200,000 needy households (thus reaching a total of 1 million households). The National Employment Commission, which supports economic recovery and the creation of full-time, legal, and productive employment with a special emphasis on women and young people, was reactivated by the government in May. The QEC and FASE I programs concluded at the end of April, but the government has already launched a new program that specifically target the workers in the tourism industry from May to July 2021.

The Monetary Council of the Central Bank of the Dominican Republic (BCRD) relaxed its position on policy and took action on March 16, 2020 to increase liquidity and support the economy. Monetary policy rate reductions (from 4.5% to 3.5% and then to 3.0% each year), a decrease in the 1-day REPO facility rate (from 6.0% to 4.5% and subsequently to 3.5%), and a decrease in the overnight deposit rate are all interest rate-related actions (from 3.0% to 2.5%). To release RD$30.13 billion (US$553.7 million; roughly 2% of GDP) to the economy, banks were permitted to cover reserve requirements with public and BCRD bonds up to RD$22.3 billion (roughly 12% of GDP), which is equivalent to a 2% reduction in the reserve requirement rate. With an interest rate maximum of 8.0%, these funds are utilized to provide credit to individuals and companies. The Monetary Board lowered the requirements for accessing these resources on April 16, 2020, allowing financial intermediaries to lend to any industry and extending the loan maturity from 1 to 4 years. Additionally, the BCRD has made money available for microcredits to individuals and loans to small businesses. The initial window, worth RD$15 billion, is reachable through Banco de Reservas. Loans would have an interest rate of up to 8% and be available for 3 years. At the same time, the BCRD exempted RD$5.7 billion from reserve requirements (about 0.5% of reserve requirements) for new loans, debt consolidation for small enterprises, debt refinancing, and personal microcredit. These loans have a term of 4 years and an interest rate of up to 8%. US$150 million from a contingent line of credit agreed in March for disasters and health-related events, and another loan approved on June 20 for US$100 million to support the COVID-19 emergency response. To provide funds to the financial system, liquidity measures include easing other REPO operations for RD$50 billion (about 1% of GDP), providing US$0.622 billion through REPO operations (roughly 3/5% of GDP), and allowing banks to use public bonds to satisfy reserve requirements on foreign currency deposits. These REPOs now have an interest rate of 0.9% instead of 1.8%. Additionally, the BCRD negotiated a short-term repos facility worth US$1–US$3 billion with the Federal Reserve. Other debt relief options include classifying past due debts for a 60-day period, giving debtors 90 days to amend loan guarantees, and temporarily freezing debtor ratings and provisioning. The Monetary Council of the Central Bank announced fresh expansionary measures on July 22, 2020, including a new Rapid Liquidity Facility (RLF) to provide funding for productive sectors, consumption loans, and small and medium-sized businesses up to RD$60,000 million. Loans with ratings of A and B, as well as private and public debt, are acceptable collateral for this facility. Additionally, the REPO's maximum size was raised from RD$50,000 to 60,000 million, giving financial institutions more resources and extending the maturity by up to 360 days. In addition, the interest rate for REPO operations lasting up to 90 days was reduced from 5.0% to 4.5%, while the rates for operations lasting up to 180 and 360 days were set at 5.0% and 5.5%, respectively. The BCRD announced on August 22 that the requirements to enter the RLF would be significantly relaxed to permit the refinancing of loans for homes and businesses of any size. The BCRD reduced its monetary policy rate by 50 basis points to 3.00% at the August 2020 monetary policy meeting, as well as its interest rate on the Repo standing facility by 100 basis points to 3.50% and left the rate on the deposit standing facility unchanged, narrowing the corridor to a maximum of 50 basis points. The BCRD maintained its MPR during the meetings in September and October, considering that both external and internal estimates indicate that inflation will continue within the target range of 4.0%–1.0% over the course of the monetary policy horizon. The Rapid Financing Line would receive RD$40 billion of the resources previously provided to financial markets in the form of REPOS, the CBDR said on October 23, 2020. These funds were not rolled over at maturity because they had already been used using the REPO mechanism. The total sum made accessible to date, which is currently R$190 billion, is unaffected by this choice. On November 25, 2020, the CBDR made the announcement that mortgage loans could be made using the funds made available through the RLF. The CBDR announced on March 01, 2021, that the RLF would be increased by RD$25 billion, with the additional funds to be earmarked for specific industries such as manufacturing, construction, mortgages for affordable housing, business, and SMEs. Five billion RD has been allotted to each sector.

In Germany, in March 2021, the federal government announced an additional budget of €60 billion (i.e., 1.7% of GDP) to aid in the recovery. Moreover, the government continued to increase the amount of public guarantees for companies, credit insurers, and nonprofit institutions, raising the total support by approximately €757 billion (24% of GDP). Resources for public equity injecting into companies strategically important were provided by the newly formed Economic Stabilization Fund (WSF) and the public development bank KfW. In addition, numerous local governments have proposed their own initiatives to help their economies besides the federal government's budgetary packages.

In response to new infection signals and the ensuing lockdowns, the German government extended already existing fiscal measures to assist companies in need and brought new ones to assist families and young workers. These initiatives also provide revenue compensation for November and December 2020 (of up to 75%), as well as expanded access to grants, traineeship subsidies, public loan guarantees, and tax loss carryback. Considering the situation, some of these measures have been expanded until long after 2021.

All regulatory and operational support from the ECB given by the authorities was enlarged to German banks under national guidance. A temporary deferral of the requirement for highly indebted or fragile companies to file for insolvency was approved by Parliament in March 2020. However, given the circumstances, the suspension date was extended to late April 2021. German banks that were subject to national regulation have been instructed to delay buying back shares and dividend payments until October 2020. Following an ECB recommendation, German banks were still subject to limitations on dividend payouts, share repurchases, and bonus payments starting in December 2020. The Financial Stability Council extended the release of the countercyclical capital buffer until the end of February 2021.

In France, from March to November 2020, the government implemented four adjusting budget laws, bringing the total amount of funds allocated to tackle the crisis to nearly €180 billion (around 8% of GDP, including liquidity measures). Additional governmental guarantees totaling €327 1/2 billion were also included (close to 15% of GDP). The emergency programs were given more funds in the 2021 budget, and they were later increased in conjunction with ongoing containment measures (about 3% of GDP, including measures in an amendment).

The fiscal package ("Plan de Relance") released in September 2020 to aid in the recovery of the French economy was also partially incorporated into the 2021 budget. The reconstruction plan focuses on the ecological transformation of the economy, boosting the competitiveness of French companies, and promoting social and territorial cohesion. It comprises initiatives totaling around 100 billion euros over 2 years. The EU Recovery Fund was planned to provide grants for about 40 billion of the plan. Concerning the monetary policy, France has included some additional measures (in early 2020) to those decided at the level of the Euro Area's currency union.

In Italy, the government approved a €5.4 billion (0.3% of GDP) package in October 2020, including grants to SMEs and the self-employed and increased family income assistance, with the intention of bringing immediate help to the industries impacted by the most recent round of COVID-19 preventative measures. Additionally, the government has increased the impacted enterprises' social contribution waivers and agreed on additional support packages in March and May 2021 totaling €72 billion, including compensation for companies and the self-employed, an extension of the restriction on firing employees, and short-term employment programs.

Policies were made in the Italian government's Cura Italia and Liquidity Decree emergency programs in addition to monetary policy at the level of the currency union. To the end of 2021, the current liquidity support programs have been renewed. Loan moratoria would only be prolonged to cover principal payments. After the end of June, new guaranteed loans would be offered at slightly reduced guarantee rates. Additionally, the term of new and continuing guaranteed loans has been increased from 6 to 10 years. The SME Capital Strengthening Scheme ("Fondo Patrimonio PMI"), the Relaunch Fund ("Patrimonio Rilancio") with a total budget of €44 billion, the Fund for Start-ups and Innovative SMEs ("Fondo Rilancio") with a total budget of €200 million, and the National Tourism Fund ("Fondo Nazionale del Turismo") to deploy up to €2 billion are some of the capital injection programs that Italy has launched. The "Rilancio" regulation established a fund for company reorganization, targeting companies with brands that are crucial for the nation strategically, and companies that control key relationships or resources.

In line with the ECB and EBA's plans, the Bank of Italy has announced a number of initiatives to assist the banks and nonbank intermediaries that fall under its supervision. These possibilities include expanding some reporting requirements, operating temporarily below certain capital and liquidity standards, and delaying on-site inspections. Moreover, insurance companies were required to submit current Solvency II ratios on a weekly basis. IVASS (Insurance Supervisory Authority) followed the EIOPA advice and urged insurance companies to be cautious regarding dividends and bonus payments to secure their financial standing. In addition, the lower minimum level over which it was necessary to disclose participation in a listed company would be maintained by CONSOB through October. These steps were intended to reduce the financial markets' volatility and increase the transparency of the stock holdings of Italian companies that were listed on the Stock Exchange.

In the UK, several tax and expenditure policies have been undertaken to aid individuals and families during the health crises. To simplify the process for companies to access financing, the government introduced three different loan programs. Both the Coronavirus Large Business Interruption Loans Scheme and the Coronavirus Small Business Interruption Loans Scheme were offered through the British Business Bank. The government also launched the Bounce Back credit program for SMEs. Furthermore, it delayed self-employed people's income tax payments by 6 months and delayed VAT payments for the second quarter of 2020 until the end of the year. Up to the end of October, the government covered 80% of furloughed workers' salaries. Moreover, in September, the government supported 70% of wages and in October, it supported 60% of wages, with employers carrying the remaining 20% of wages. The self-employment program was prolonged for an additional 3 months, but at a lower level of 70% of income. Meanwhile, the Trade Credit Reinsurance plan was active for 9 months and provided government guarantees for trade credit insurance for business-to-business operations up to £10 billion.

In addition, in order to assist companies in boosting innovation and growth through grants and loans, the government set up a £1 billion program. The government contributed £150 million to the Catastrophe Containment and Relief Trust of the IMF and a new £2.2 billion loan to the IMF Poverty Reduction and Growth Trust (PRGT) to assist the global response to COVID-19.

A set of measures announced in September 2020 in the UK, included a 6-month Job Support Scheme (JSS), prolonging the Self Employment Income Support Scheme for the companies who are still operating despite lower demand caused by the coronavirus, expanding the temporary 15% VAT cut for the tourism and hospitality industries to the end of March 2019, enabling VAT payments delayed until the end of March, and self-assessed income tax due on July 20, lengthening the application deadline for loans under the CBILS, CLBILS, and BBLS to the end of November; and raising the maximum maturity of CBILS and BBL loans to 10 years. Moreover, the government has started a new initiative called Job Entry: Targeted Support (JETS) to aid job seekers who have been receiving unemployment insurance for at least 13 weeks. In order to align with the stricter containment measures, some of the policies introduced in the September package were gradually changed. In addition, the JSS has been adjusted for enterprises that remain open. Furthermore, the government would reimburse social contributions and two-thirds of employee salaries, up to a maximum of £2100 per month, for companies that must shut down as a result of the restrictions.

The UK government announced a new set of policies in November in response to the second lockdown, which included delaying the JSS, eliminating the Job Retention Bonus, prolonging the CJRS until the end of March 2021, rising the grant of the SEISS, and extending the deadline for applying for government-guaranteed loans until the end of January 2021. Then, the government declared in December that it will continue both the corporate support program and the furlough plan for one more month, to April 2021.

A day after the UK government implemented the strictest COVID-19 restrictions since last spring, in January 2021, it unveiled a £4.6 billion financial assistance program for struggling UK companies. It revealed an additional £59 billion in March 2021 (nearly 2.6% of GDP). This is divided into additional disease support measures costing £43 billion for the year 2021, in addition to $15.7 billion in new efforts to speed up the restoration process. The furlough plan was extended for 6 months. Other policies included a 3-month extension of the current stamp duty cut to the end of June, a 6-month prolongation of the increase in universal credit benefit payment, and a continuation of the whole VAT cut for the hospitality industry to the end of September 2021. Additional financing was made available in the form of company grants, discounted business rates were maintained through the end of the year, and this was supported by a significant tax relief for companies that attempts to incentivize future investment to be pushed forward to this year and the following. Future tax hikes would primarily take the form of a corporate tax increase of 6% (from 19% to 25%) in 2023 and a lock on income tax limits.

The estimated cost of COVID-19 support measures for FY2020–21 was £280 billion and the government set aside £55 billion for this purpose during FY2021–22. The central bank increased its holdings of UK government bonds and nonfinancial company bonds by £450 billion, reduced the Bank Rate by 65 basis points to 0.1%, and established a new Term Funding Scheme to further encourage lending to the real economy. Other significant actions included deploying the joint HM Treasury-Bank of England COVID-19 Corporate Financing Facility and three government loan guarantee schemes replaced by the Recovery Loan Scheme from April 2021, totaling £352 billion in liquidity and loan guarantees applicable (19.5% of GDP). HM Treasury and the BoE consented to temporarily enlarge the use of the government's debt account at the BoE to offer a short-term source of additional liquidity to the government if necessary. Establishing a Contingent Term Repo Facility to supplement the Bank's current sterling liquidity facilities in collaboration with the central banks of Canada, Japan, the Euro Area, the US, and Switzerland; boosting the availability of liquidity through the established US dollar liquidity swap line arrangements, maintaining banks' Systemic Risk Buffer (SRB) rates at the level set in December 2019 until at least December 2022, and any decision made regarding rates in December 2022 taking effect immediately, lowering the UK countercyclical capital buffer (CCyB) rate from a previous trend toward 2% by December 2020 to 0%, with the expectation that it will stay there for at least a year.

The UK government announced in March 2021 that a new mortgage guarantee program would be available starting in April 2021 for buyers of residences up to £600,000 in value with just a 5% deposit. Additionally, the government announced that the stamp duty land tax (SDLT) exemption would be extended through June 2021. Considering the strengthening in US dollar funding conditions, the central banks have agreed to cease providing dollar liquidity at maturity on April 2021. However, they would still conduct weekly operations with a 7-day maturity. However, the Prudential Regulatory Authority stated in December 2020 that it planned to move back toward the common framework for bank distributions. This decision evidenced a degree of reduction in the uncertainty surrounding COVID-19 at the time and the ability of banks to resist significant losses, as determined by the outcomes of the two stress tests conducted by the Prudential Regulation Committee (PRC) and the FPC. Moreover, by mandating that companies give a 3-month payment hold on loans and credit cards, the Financial Conduct Authority (FCA) introduced a package of tailored temporary remedies to support clients afflicted by the coronavirus. The mortgage moratorium was expanded in November to the end of April, and the FCA also extended the window for requesting a payment delay for consumer credit by 6 months.

In Spain, the contingency fund budget assistance for health services, the claim to unemployment benefits for workers momentarily laid off under the Temporary Employment Adjustment Schemes (ERTE) due to COVID-19, the efforts made by regional governments for social services, education, and support to companies, direct help for company solvency support, and an exceptional gain for self-employed workers affected by economic activity are among the key measures (roughly 7.4% of GDP, or €85 billion). Additional financial resources and increased budgetary flexibility were provided, among other things, to facilitate the expansion of the social benefit for energy supplies, the maintenance of the education system, and other industry and sectoral support initiatives. Some additional measures include tax subsidies for some property owners that lower rents on estates used for activities related to the hotel, restaurant, and tourism sectors, tax payment postponements for small and medium-sized enterprises and self-employed, prolonging of the deadlines for filing tax returns, moratoria of social security contributions for the self-employed and companies in certain industries, flexibility for SMEs and self-employed to determine their income tax and VAT installment payment, momentary rises in the module system's tax reductions for income tax and VAT, and reductions in the contribution for salaried farm laborers, the removal of the late payment penalty for tax obligations for companies receiving funding through the Instituto de Crédito Oficial (ICO) Guarantee Lines, a lowering of the VAT on digital publications from 21% to 4%, greater worker options in accessing pension savings, change of spending caps for specific lines of ministries and subnational governments.

Concerning monetary policy, Spain has included additional measures to those decided at the level of the Euro Area's currency union. Furthermore, the government of Spain has provided up to €100 billion in government guarantees to companies and entrepreneurs, covering both loans and commercial paper issued by medium-sized companies that participate in Spain's Alternative Fixed Income Market (MARF), investments and liquidity provision, established a state rescue fund to aid the strategic companies, and created a capitalization fund for medium-sized companies.

The Spanish government set up guarantees for listed companies, as well as public guarantees for exporters through the Spanish Export Insurance Credit Company, guarantees for loan maturity extensions to farmers using the special 2017 drought credit lines, guarantees to provide financial support on living costs for vulnerable families, extra loan guarantees for SMEs and self-employed individuals through the Compañía Española de Reafianzamiento. Additional funding for the ICO credit lines, assurances for financing operations conducted by the European Investment Bank, support for the European SURE instrument, loans for the industrial sector to enhance digital transformation and modernization, a moratorium on nonmortgage loans and credits, including consumer credits, for the most helpless, are some additional measures.

Lastly, the Bank of Spain would implement a legal system's flexibility to the banks it regulates when it did come to transition periods and the intermediate minimum standards for own financing and eligible debts (MREL) targets, and banks would be permitted to rely on expert knowledge when determining the credit risk of forborne exposures.

In the Netherlands, the third support package, which the government unveiled in August 2020, largely aimed to strengthen, and modify existing expenditure-side policies until June 2021. The government also wanted to encourage employees to relocate to growing industries. Public funding has been committed for training, reskilling, career counseling, and platforms to help with job transition. Additionally, tax incentives were implemented to encourage private investment. The government had budgeted 40.9 billion (or 4.7% of GDP) in assistance for 2021, up from the 27.8 billion (or 3.4% of GDP) in support for expenditures in 2020.

To encourage bank lending, the Dutch central bank has lowered the systemic buffer requirements for the three biggest banks. Additionally, the central bank has acted to temporarily soften regulatory requirements for smaller banking institutions. Furthermore, banks under DNB's direct supervision were permitted to disregard particular central bank exposures when figuring their leverage ratios. Moreover, the Financial Stability Report from May 2021 stated that a ceiling for mortgage loan risk weighting would be implemented in January 2022 after previously being delayed. The biggest Dutch banks provided small and medium-sized companies a 6-month extension on loan repayment. On October 2020, the government made debt restructuring easier for companies with financial issues. The goal of the policy would be to stop bankruptcy.

In Switzerland, the government maintained its efforts to help the economy by expanding initiatives already set up and with a focus on assisting groups and sectors that were struggling with long-lasting negative effects from the crisis, even as more constraints on economic activity were implemented in order to limit the second wave of the pandemic. Federal Council (FC) also extended coverage for the short-term work plan for staff on request and reimbursement for SE income losses to June 2021. In a package made public in November, the FC enhanced credit for the purchase of COVID-19 vaccination, updated occupational benefit policies, and unveiled "Innovation Switzerland," an incentive program designed to support companies in maintaining their inventive strength throughout the pandemic. In an effort to assist viable companies that incurred significant losses as a result of the COVID-19 epidemic, the FC and cantonal governments together announced the approval of the COVID-19 Hardship Assistance Ordinance in November. In December, the FC suggested increasing the program's overall budget from CHF1 billion to CHF2.5 billion and asked the Parliament for more latitude in determining who qualifies for hardship assistance. In December, the FC made additional adjustments to the hardship ordinance, enabling qualifying companies to obtain double subsidies, lowering the amount of income loss needed to meet the criteria for compensation for self-employed individuals, raising aid for the cultural sector, and further loosening the rules regarding the short-term work plan.

In January 2021, due to more stringent restrictions, the Swiss FC increased fiscal support to reduce the effect on the economy. The eligibility requirements and conditions for the program's hardship assistance were modified by the FC as well, and the maximum amount of assistance that a company might receive was also raised. In order to broaden and prolong the short-term work plan's coverage, the FC once more modified its rules. Later, the FC unveiled new federal fiscal support plans worth up to CHF 8.5 billion. Then, the FC announced in February that the hardship assistance program would grow from CHF5 billion to CHF10 billion, with CHF3 billion set aside to assist larger companies that were previously excluded from the program's protection. The FC also provided CHF940 million to make up for self-employed individuals' income losses. The total cost of the program, which also contained several additional policies, was close to CHF6 billion. The FC added extra COVID-related expenditure of CHF1.3 billion to the first supplementary budget that was approved in late March, along with lesser sums set aside to support civil defense and tourism traffic. The government also made amendments to a number of COVID-related regulations, including the hardship ordinance and the policy on lost wages, with the majority of these revisions aiming to strengthen economic support and make the terms of these programs more transparent.

Concerning the monetary and macrofinancial actions in Switzerland, the SNB kept its policy rate at -0.75% through the end of August 2020 and made the decision to stop providing dollar liquidity at the maturities beginning in July 2021 on April 2021. A provisional exemption of central bank deposits from the measurement of banks' leverage ratio was instituted by the Swiss Financial Market Supervisory Authority (FINMA) until January 2021. The capital made available by this waiver, according to FINMA, should have been used to enhance liquidity provision and should have not been dispersed as dividends or in any other way that is specifically tied to 2019. Regarding the exchange rates and balances of payments, to prevent further appreciation of the Swiss franc, the SNB boosted its FX market interventions and purchased assets worth 110 billion CHF in 2020. In Q1 2021, the SNB's interventions decreased and came to CHF 296 million.

In Sweden, the stated and executed fiscal policies for 2020, including capital injections, liquidity support, and guarantees, were assessed by the government to cost SEK 803 billion (16.0% of 2019 GDP, respectively). Furthermore, the government offered significant economic stimulus policies and reforms totaling SEK 105 billion and SEK 85 billion for 2021 and 2022. (2.1% and 1.7% of 2019 GDP, respectively). On November 2020, the government suggested expanding short-term layoffs by 7 months till June 2021 and tax deferrals by 1 year until March 2022. Later, the state credit guarantee plan for loans to companies was suggested to be extended by the government, from December until late June 2021. Moreover, sole traders would continue to get aid based on their turnover starting in April 2021.

With an extension declared in March 2021 to cover May and June of 2021, the Swedish government announced in February that extended turnover-based assistance will also be accessible to sole traders and trading partnerships who have obtained unemployment insurance and have picked parental or sick leave during the period. The government unveiled the 2021 Spring Fiscal Policy Bill in April, which includes additional steps to stop the virus's propagation, reduce the pandemic's effects on the economy, and help Sweden recover from the disaster. The government first proposed in May to cover

July, August, and September 2021 with turnover-based assistance for sole traders and trading partnerships with at least one natural person partner.

Sweden's Riksbank's repo rate would be used as the benchmark for the new lending facility, which would allow monetary policy contracting parties to borrow an infinite amount with a maturity of 3 and 6 months at an interest rate that corresponds to that rate. Other important monetary measures include the decrease of the lending rate for overnight loans by 55 basis points to 0.2% and then to 0.1%, lending of up to SEK 500 billion to companies via banks, rising acquires of securities by up to SEK 700 billion 2021 and 2022, establishing a swap facility between the Riksbank and the US Federal Reserve, allowing banks to borrow up to USD 60 billion against collateral until late September 2021, reducing restrictions on using covered bonds as collateral, and momentarily accepting that all credit institutions regulated by the Swedish FSA can relate to becoming provisional money institutions.

In 2021, Romania demonstrated a strong economic recovery as the first quarter GDP showed a 2.8% quarter over quarter increase. This growth in GDP has been believed to be the fastest growth among the other EU nations. Earlier on December 27, 2020, Romania launched a vaccination program where healthcare workers were the first to get vaccinated. Then in the middle of January 2021, a second stage of the program began where other vulnerable groups got the vaccine. Later in April, the vaccine was made accessible to the general public. As infections increased during the end of March, certain restrictions on opening hours and circulation were placed on areas with high infection rates like gyms, shops, and restaurants. As vaccinations got pushed out and infection rates began started to decline in May, restrictions began to be lightened. Businesses in the entertainment and hospitality industry were able to open back up with limited capacity. As well, the nightly curfew was relaxed, the requirement for wearing facemasks outdoors was removed, and retail businesses were able to resume operating at normal hours. Then in June, restrictions have been further lightened as the number of people allowed to attend outdoor cultural, artistic, sports, and entertainment activities and indoor restaurants have increased, and people are allowed back to playgrounds, gyms, and swimming pools with some caps. Later on July 01, the maximum capacity for restaurants, private events, and indoor and outdoor activities was increased further and the cap for tourism facilities and gyms had been removed.

The Romanian government decided to extend fiscal support measures that assist health care, families, and businesses in 2021. These support measures were seen in the 2021 budget and the government extended the potential rescheduling of tax payments. Lastly, the overall envelope of government guarantees on loans was raised to where it amounted to around 4% of the GDP.

The Romanian government during the first half of 2021 to aid in monetary support, provided 2 billion RON for providing repo transactions that provide liquidity to credit institutions. This amount was significantly less than the 42 billion RON spent on repo transactions in 2020. Whereas 5.4 billion RON in government securities were purchased on the secondary market. Along with this, until March 2021, legislation established by the Government is in place that will ensure banks defer repayments on loans made by households and businesses affected by COVID-19 for a period of up to 9 months. The European Central Bank provided a euro repo line to the Romania central bank for €4.5 billion ($5.1 billion) that would remain in place till March 2022.

In Turkey, a new omnibus regulation that contained additional provisional measures to boost employment in the industries that are most severely affected by the pandemic was enacted by Parliament in late April 2021. Along with the restriction on layoffs, the short-term work allowance system for all industries was also extended through June. In addition, loan postponements for farmers, a grant initiative for small companies and tradespeople, a lending program for SMEs backed by the Credit

Guarantee Fund, and an increment in bonus pensions were all announced in May and June 2021. Moreover, up until the end of July, there were reductions in the withholding tax on TL bank deposits and some VAT rate reductions for particular industries.

Also in Turkey, the maximum term for retail car loans and credit card installment plans for the acquisition of particular products was restricted in December 2020 by the bank regulator. A new Turkish Lira loan instrument for SMEs in the export industry was formed to help trade finance, debt enforcement and bankruptcy processes were momentarily suspended. Additionally, dividend payments by banks and companies in 2020 were also suspended.

The infection rate of COVID-19 began to slow down in Iran in January 2021, but curfews and distance learning was kept in place. At this time, Iran Air had allowed flights to Qatar, Dubai, and Turkey. A month later mass vaccinations began with plans to vaccinate around 60 million Iranians by the end of March 2022. Essential workers, high-risk individuals, and injured war veterans were the first to receive the vaccine. By the middle of June, 5.1 million Iranians had gotten at least one vaccine. At this time the government issued the emergency use of its domestically made vaccine since the vaccines ordered from other nations mostly did not arrive.

Most of the fiscal measures taken by Iran were introduced in 2020 but remained in place in 2021. These measures were for funding toward the health sector, supporting the unemployment insurance fund, and sending cash to vulnerable households. To fund these measures, Sukuk bonds, the National Development Fund, and proceeds from privatization were used.

The Central Bank of Iran, between April and September 2020, lowered reserve requirements for commercial banks with the goal of boosting lending to people and businesses impacted by the pandemic. The Central Bank of Iran in September 2020 began to set aside 1% of the nation's sovereign wealth fund to help the stock market remain stable. All in all, Iran struggled with the pandemic, but the economy has begun to gradually recover due to a resurgence in consumption and improved oil sector conditions.

In Saudi Arabia, the real nonoil GDP had declined by 2.3% in 2020, but during the first quarter of 2021, it grew by 2.9% year-over-year. The bounce back in real nonoil GDP continued during the second quarter of 2021 as the PMI grew during April and May due to the 15-month high easing taking place during February and March. The Saudi authorities announced on June 12, 2021, that the 2021 Hajj season starting in mid-July would be restricted to 60,000 attendants. Vaccination began in the middle of December 2020 and over 17.6 million doses of the vaccines have been given out to individuals. Due to vaccinations, international travel was able to resume on May 17, 2021. As 2021 began, the majority of the fiscal measures had been withdrawn since most of the deferred tax payments were paid off by the end of 2020. For the sectors still feeling the impact of COVID, the wage support program for private sector companies' use of the unemployment insurance fund (SANED) had been extended through July 2021.

The Saudi Central Bank (SAMA) took several monetary measures during the pandemic, but by the end of December 2020, SAMA's Loan Guarantee Program ended. On top of this, extensions to the Deferred Payments Program were prolonged until the end of September 2021 and extensions to the Guaranteed Facility Program were prolonged till March 14, 2022.

The Abu Dhabi government in the United Arab Emirates on December 09, 2020, declared that all economic, touristic, entertainment, and cultural activities would return within 2 weeks. In January 2021, when COVID-19 cases began to increase, the government initiated tighter safety measures and mandated COVID-19 tests for all government employees. As well, the capacity for malls and venues was reduced, international visitors and tourists were required to take a PCR test upon arrival, and activities that lead to large gatherings were limited. By July 01, 2021, 15,362,342 doses of the COVID-19 vaccine had been given to citizens.

The Dubai government on January 6th, 2021, announced additional stimulus to provide fiscal support from January to June 2021 at an amount of AED 315 million. Similar strategies were incorporated by other Emirates nations to promote commerce and businesses and to provide advantages to the sectors negatively impacted the most by the pandemic. The combined value of the two incentive packages for Sharjah equated to AED 993 million ($0.27 billion). Lastly, the government put in place numerous revenue-generating measures to deal with the needs caused by the crisis, to provide relief and support to businesses and their continuity, and to promote recovery.

The Central Bank of the UAE (CBUAE) passed a package of measures for monetary support known as the Targeted Economic Support Scheme (TESS). Monetary support was further needed by the UAE which resulted in the TESS being extended twice, once in November 2020 until the end of June 2021 and then a second time in April 2021 until the end of June 2022. Financing provided by the CBUAE under the TESS for loan deferrals was extended as well.

Israel had been severely impacted by the pandemic and had a declining economic activity output of 6.5% during the first quarter of 2021 following new outbreaks, but as vaccination became more popular and cases of COVID declined, the economy was able to reopen again. On February 07, 2021, most domestic restrictions were lifted, however, strict restrictions over international travel remained due to the rapid global spread of highly contagious variants of COVID. Since the vaccination campaign began in December 2020, around 57.1% of the Israeli population has received two doses of the vaccine.

The Israeli government has created several fiscal measures throughout the pandemic amounting to around NIS 202.3 billion and of this, during the first 5 months of 2021, NIS 35.8 billion were implemented. Along with this, through currency swaps of up to USD 15 billion, the Bank of Israel supplied extra USD liquidity. The Bank of Israel during the course of 2021 planned on purchasing 30 billion USD.

During the lunar new year in 2021, the Chinese government promoted reductions in intercity travel while enforcing stricter testing and quarantine requirements. The economy during the first quarter of 2021 had lower sequential growth, but strong year-one-year growth of 18.3% because of the economic contraction of 6.8% in the first quarter of 2021. China was able to get 40% of its population vaccinated by the end of June 2021 and planned to have 70%–80% vaccinated between the end of 2021 and the beginning of 2022.

Chinese discretionary fiscal measures totaled an estimated RMB 4.9 trillion (which equates to around 4.7% of GDP) and were to be used for epidemic prevention/control, manufacturing of medical equipment, tax relief, waiving social security contributions, distribution of unemployment insurance and extension to migrant workers, and public investments. Of the RMB 4.9 trillion, RMB 4.2 trillion of the measures were implemented in 2020. The support provided by the PBC toward the monetary policy for market stability and the government's actions to prevent the tightening of financial conditions were still in effect post-COVID.

Following COVID-19, the exchange rate has been able to adjust flexibly in China. For the daily trading band's central parity formation, the countercyclical adjustment factor had been phased out and the reserve removed the requirement on FX forward. The raised ceiling on cross-border financing for financial institutions was reduced to normal in December and for enterprises, it was reduced to normal in January 2021. However, in January, the macroprudential adjustment coefficient for overseas lending via domestic enterprises grew by two-thirds and resulted in a higher ceiling. The fresh quota on domestic institutional investors was established while restrictions on foreign institutional investors were lifted. On June 15, a raised percentage from 5 to 7 was put into place for the FX reserve requirement ratio for financial institutions.

Due to the severity of the pandemic in Japan, the Tokyo Olympic Games had been postponed from July 23, 2020 to August 08, 2021. On June 21, 2021, the Olympic Committee decided that there would be a spectator limit of 50% of the capacity with a maximum of 10,000 people at each venue. Furthermore, due to a state of emergency on January 13, 2021, the "Business and Residence Tracks" which limited business exchanges and activities between nations close to Japan, were suspended until cases declined. Around this time, Japan enforced border measures toward preventing new variants from spreading resulting in quarantine precautions enhancing for travelers upon entrance, reentrances, or return to Japan. To enter Japan, the government created a mandate that requires the submission of a negative COVID-19 test result 72 h prior to ones flight and another round of testing to take place upon arrival.

The Japanese government adopted a package on December 08, 2020, worth ¥73.6 trillion (equates to 13.1% of the 2019 GDP) which includes plans to contain COVID-19, promote a positive economic period during and after the pandemic, and secure safety and relief. Along with this, the measures taken by the government incentivize firms to invest in digitalization and green technologies. Following the pandemic, the exchange rate in Japan has been able to flexibly adjust.

The impact of COVID-19 was felt in India's economy as the FY2020/21 GDP has a growth of −7.3%, but growth was returning at 1.6% year-on-year during the first quarter of 2021. As India began manufacturing vaccines, on January 3, 2021, the Covaxin and AstraZeneca vaccines received emergency use authorization (EUA) from India's Central Drugs Standard Control Organization (CDSCO). Following this, on January 11, the Prime Minister announced the initiation of a plan for the largest vaccination campaign in the world beginning on January 16th with the goal of providing 300 million people with vaccination. After a few months, manufacturers of the vaccines were allowed to begin selling 50% of their products on the open market and all individuals over the age of 18 were able to get vaccinations.

The central government of India took multiple measures to provide fiscal support during and following the pandemic in two categories. The first was above-the-line measures (including government spending, expedited spending, and foregone or deferred revenues) which were present mostly during the pandemic. The second was below-the-line measures created to support businesses and provide credit provision to multiple sectors. During April and May 2021, below-the-line measures toward the easement of tax compliance burdens were put in place due to a resurgence of infections. As well, measures were put in place that provided credit support to businesses, poor households and electricity distribution companies and there was large support toward the agricultural sector with the goal of infrastructure development. The central government announced in April that food rations composed of food grains would be given to 800 million people during May and June (at a cost of roughly 260 billion rupees). The central government also accelerated the release of the Disaster Response Fund to state governments during May and prolonged a program that offered interest-free loans to states for capital expenditures through FY2021/22 (costing 150 billion rupees).

The Reserve Bank of India (RBI), on January 08, 2021, announced the gradual resumption of operations under the updated framework for liquidity management, including the variable rate reverse repo auction. Later in February 2021, there was an extension of cash reserve requirement reductions against the loans of micro, small, and medium enterprises (MSME) for banks until December 2021. Following suit, the RBI on May 04, unveiled measures to provide relief toward easing liquidity and financing conditions, including special Long-Term Repo Operations (SLTRO) for small finance banks and on-tap liquidity assistance to COVID-associated healthcare infrastructure and services. The reintroduction of plans for COVID-related stressed retail and MSME loans allowed lenders, until the end of September 2021, to invoke restructuring of loans. Lenders were able to extend moratoriums on repayments or the loan tenors for at most 2 years for all loans changed during the past resolution plan. Additionally, banks have enabled the use of countercyclical provisional buffers for creating particular provisions for nonperforming loans until the end of March 2022.

Following the pandemic, India increased the limit on FPI investment in corporate bonds to 15% of outstanding stock during FY 2020/21. On top of that, the restrictions on Central Government issued securities on nonresident investment were lifted. Along with this, adjustments toward foreign direct investment policy were made where it was required government approval in order for an organization from a country sharing a land border with India to invest.

The National Assembly in South Korea on December 02, 2020, established the 2021 budget which would amount to 482.6 trillion in budgeted revenue and 558 trillion in budgeted expenditures. These budgets varied from the budget plan created in 2020 in which the budgeted revenue was around KRW 23 trillion (1.2% of GDP) lower than projected and the budgeted expenditure was around KRW 11 trillion (0.6% of GDP) higher than projected. After several months, the National Assembly on March 25, 2021, passed a supplemental budget worth KRW 14.9 trillion (0.8% of GDP) with measures toward the implementation of vaccines, relief for small business owners and workers, employment support, assistance to low-income households, and financial aid for small business. A new budget worth 33.0 trillion won was announced on July 01 (1.6% of GDP), which include a COVID-19 relief program and measures on disease control, employment and social safety nets, boosting of local economies, and support to housing and livelihood, financed through tax revenue overperformance and some budget surpluses. The additions to the package would not negatively impact the projected fiscal balance.

The President of South Korea, Moon Jae-in, on March 24, unveiled a KRW 100 trillion (5.3% of GDP) stabilization plan. This plan would increase lending of state-owned and commercial banks to SMEs, small merchants, mid-sized firms, and large companies, establishing a bond market stabilization for purchasing corporate and financial bonds and commercial paper, and financing through public institutions for issuing corporate bond collateralized bond obligation and the purchase of direct bonds. Additionally, this plan would assist short-term money market financing associated with stock finance loans, Bank of Korea (BOK) repo purchases, refinancing support conducted by public financial institutions, and the establishment of a fund for equity market stabilization that would be financed by leading and holding financial companies. A month later, on April 22, further measures worth KRW 25 trillion (1.3% of GDP) were implemented for the creation of vehicles for purchasing corporate bonds and commercial paper, further funds for SME lending, and financial support to exporters and specific industries. The financial support to exporters improved the package announced on April 8th for the easing of financial constraints. President Moon also revealed the establishment of a fund for KRW 40 trillion (2.1% of GDP) to assist seven crucial industries including aviation, shipping, shipbuilding, automobiles, general machinery, electric power, and communications. The capital for this fund would be raised by issuing bonds backed by the government and private contributions. Businesses would gain support through loans, investments, and payment guarantees as long as they maintained employment, limited executive compensation, dividends, and other payouts, and shared profits from business normalization going forward. To maintain financial market stability, measures for BOK lending programs to nonbanks containing corporate bonds as collateral, the expansion of BOK repo operation to nonbanks, temporary bans on stock short-selling in equity markets, a short-term easement on repurchasing shares, and the temporary easement of loan-to-deposit ratios for banks and other financial institutions were put in place.

In Russia vaccination began on January 18, 2021, and had slow progress where, even with some growth, by the end of June only around 12% of the population was fully vaccinated; the goal for 60% of the population being vaccinated by the end of the summer failed.

Key fiscal measures were established by Russia to mitigate the effects of the pandemic in 2021 where businesses in the restaurant, hotel, and entertainment industries were provided subsidized loans for payments for 12 months toward minimum wage employees under conditions of preserved employment. Additionally, zero import duties were implemented for medical pharmaceutical resources and gear and budget grants were established to assist salary payments for firms hiring individuals that lost their jobs in 2020. The measures provided loans to SMEs and impacted industries, provided assistance to airlines, automakers, and airports, and expanded qualifications for subsidized mortgage lending. The total cost of social spending announced on April 2021 was approximately 0.3% of GDP over the 2 years.

During the first half of 2021, the Deposit Insurance Fund reduced its contribution from 0.15% to 0.1%. At the same time, the Central Bank of Russia (CBR) set up measures to relax regulations on liquidity for systemically influential credit institutions and to safeguard retail borrowers who were afflicted by the pandemic. A law enacted by Parliament ensures that SMEs and affected citizens will be able to defer loan payments for up to 6 months. The CBR advised banks to use the same strategy for restructuring retail loans as required by law (fast approval or rejection, restructuring from the application date, no penalties during the consideration period). CBR recommended banks to keep restructuring loans to affected SME and retail borrowers until July 01, 2021. As well, restructured retail loans would not be fully provisioned until July 01, 2021. Several other measures were taken to provide aid to financial markets such as the ensuring of services of nonbank financing institutions, the promotion of remote customer services, and measures in the region of AML/CFT and currency control. On top of this, new credit risk assessment procedures and lower risk weights, applied to subordinated bonds of a large nonfinancial corporation, in mortgage lending have saved around Rub 300 billion (around 0.3% of GDP) of capital in the banking sector.

The Indonesian government in the middle of January 2021 initiated its vaccination program and began vaccinating health-care workers. Around 11% of the population had one vaccination dose (5% were fully vaccinated) as of June 30. Even though Indonesia's GDP during the first quarter of 2021 declined by around 0.7%, economic activity has demonstrated a positive recovery quarter over quarter since the latter half of 2020. Indonesia is still dealing with volatility; however eternal pressures have stayed relatively moderate.

In Indonesia, the corporate income tax rate had been permanently reduced from 25% to 22% in 2021 and then to 20% in 2022. As well, in 2021 the government set up a budget for the national economic recovery program (PEN) at IDR 699.4 trillion. In February 2021, Bank Indonesia (BI) lowered its policy rate by 25 bps. By 2021, only the buyer-of-last-resort arrangement was left in action. Through repo deals and purchasing government bonds owned by deposit insurance agency (LPS), BI has also been financing LPS. As part of its efforts to increase financial deepening, access to financial services, and monetary operations, BI has introduced Sharia-compliant financial instruments and promoted cooperation between the baking sector and FinTech firms. The regulator OJK has instituted new share buyback policies and placed limitations on stock price falls in an effort to reduce stock market volatility. In order to promote loan restructuring, OJK has also loosened bank loan classification and restructuring procedures. Furthermore, they have postponed the implementation of mark-to-market valuation of government and other securities, loosened the requirements for meeting the Liquidity Coverage Ratio and Net Stable Funding Ratio standards, and permitted the use of the Capital Conservation Buffer.

To ensure orderly market conditions, BI has interfered in the spot and domestic nondeliverable foreign exchange markets as well as the domestic government bond market. According to BI, global investors are able to utilize both global and domestic custodian banks to complete investment transactions in Indonesia. As well, the stimulus packages included steps to relax import and export restrictions in an effort to lessen the virus' impact on the global supply chain.

During the first week of February 2021, the Prime Minister of Thailand, Prayuth Chan-Ocha, decided to relax restrictions and allow the reopening of businesses and schools. On April 1st, Thailand reduced its 14-day quarantine to 10 days for travelers, but travelers from nations with COVID variants of concern this 14-day quarantine period would remain in place. Following additional waves of COVID, the government made more restrictions to ensure the safety of individuals and avoid the spread of infections. Finally, on July 01, 2021, the Phuket "sandbox" scheme allowed for totally vaccinated tourists from low-to-medium-risk nations to visit Thailand.

The government in Thailand set up fiscal measures in January 2021 to provide support against the second COVID wave and would provide $7 billion in cash handouts. On top of this, starting in February, all beneficiaries would receive THB 3500 per month for 2 months. The King of Thailand on May 25 authorized an emergency decree that enabled borrowing 55 billion baht by the Ministry of Finance with the goal of mitigating the economic and social impact of the pandemic. On top of this, on June 01, 2021, the government established an economic stimulus package containing cash handouts, copayments, and e-vouchers at a value of 140 billion baht.

The Bank of Thailand (BOT) made available up to THB 500 billion to financial institutions through the end of 2021 for on-lending to SMEs, especially in tourism and related industries, at a rate of 2% annually. The interest on these loans is insured by the government for the first 6 months and is guaranteed for 2 years. Thereafter, the loans can be extended for up to another 8 years but would have a 1.75% per year fee. Between January 01, 2020, to December 31, 2021, the BOT loosened rules pertaining to the classification of borrowers and levels of loan loss provisions in order to promote debt restructuring by financial institutions. The changes enabled borrowers who have felt the impacts of COVID-19 to immediately be classified as normal so long as they could make repayments accordingly with a debt restructuring agreement regardless of if they were already classified as NPL. The Cabinet in the middle of February 2021 authorized a THB 50 billion soft loan program, that would be available till the end of June 2021, to provide loans for up to 3 years with low-interest rates to SMEs associated with the tourism sector and informal workers. The following month, two new measures were unveiled by authorities for the facility of special loans for businesses with a credit guarantee scheme and toward debt rebuilding done by asset warehousing with buy-back options. These measures had the purpose of assisting and transforming viable firms for the postpandemic world.

To deal with household debt, the BOT worked with nine associations in Thailand (the Thai Bankers' Association, Association of International Banks, Government Financial Institutions Association, Thailand Leasing Association, Thai Hire-Purchase Association, Vehicle Title Loan Trade Association, Thai Motorcycle Hire-Purchase Association, Credit Card Club—The Thai Bankers' Association and the Personal Loan Club) to implement the following measures. The first was reductions to minimum credit card and revolving repayments from 10% to 5% in 2020 and 2021 and to 8% in 2022. The second was imposing a 3-month moratorium on personal (installment payments) and auto loans. The third was a temporary ban on for hire-purchase or leasing of motorcycles and automobiles for 3 months on principal and interest or 6 months on principle. The fourth and final was to set up a 3-month temporary ban on principal repayments for housing, SME, and microfinance loans while taking lower interest payments into consideration on a case-to-case basis. The BOT had a Corporate Bond Stabilization Fund (BSF) created to aid in bridge financing of up to THB 400 billion by December 31, 2021, with high-quality firms holding bonds that mature during 2021, but at "penalty" rates higher-than-market. However, as of now, this BSF has not had any takers. In the FX market, the BOT provided some liquidity to prevent disorderly market conditions and allow adjustments to the exchange rate.

At the beginning of March 2021, the Philippines began COVID vaccinations and by June 23, around 6.1% of the population had received at least the first dose of the vaccine. To reach herd immunity by the end of 2021, the Philippine government plans to administer 500,000 doses of the vaccine daily.

The Philippine government established a second stimulus package for fiscal support known as the "Bayanihan II" Act which would provide support to vulnerable households, hard-hit sectors, and capital injections into state-owned banks. The funds from Bayanihan that were not spent had been extended to June 30, 2021. For further fiscal support, on March 26, 2021, the government revised and passed the Corporate Recovery and Tax Incentives for Enterprises (CREATE) Act with a focus on meeting the needs of businesses adversely impacted by the COVID-19 pandemic and increasing the Philippines' capacity to draw in highly desirable investments. This CREATE Act lowered the corporate income tax rate from 30% of net taxable income to 25% for large and nonresident foreign corporations (net taxable income above PHP 5 million). At the same time, the Act reduced this rate for small- to medium-sized corporations to 20%. The corporate income tax rate for foreign corporations will further decrease starting in 2022 where it will decline by one percentage point annually till it reaches 20% by 2027.

The Philippine government on February 2021 passed the Financial Institutions Strategic Transfer (FIST) Act in order to allow financial institutions to facilitate the sale of nonperforming assets, strengthen the institutions' balance sheets, and increase the capacity for lending. Furthermore, the structural policy under Bayanihan II Act allowed private initiatives that are deemed to be of national significance and have a strong potential for economic return or employment may be exempt from certain permits, licenses, or other regulations in order to avoid delays in their execution. These initiatives toward regulatory relief are anticipated to hasten the creation of jobs and high-impact investments.

The Australian government took a more liberal approach in the policy response to the pandemic. Fiscal stimulus has been implemented at the Commonwealth level through FY2025, totaling A$312 billion (1534% of 2020 GDP), in the form of expenditure and revenue measures. By the end of

FY2021 (June 2021), over two-thirds of the stimulus will have run its course, including the well-known JobKeeper wage subsidy program, which distributed expected payments of A\$89 billion (4.5% of 2020 GDP) through the end of March 2021. The stimulus plan includes a health response package worth A\$20 billion (1.0% of GDP), which will be used to ensure access to COVID-19 vaccines, launch a national vaccination program, improve the health system, safeguard those who are most at risk, such as senior citizens, from the COVID-19 outbreak, and give financial support to the States and the Territories.

The government unveiled the FY2022 budget on May 11, 2021, adding A\$48.4 billion (2.5% of GDP) in additional stimulus measures through FY2025. These measures included additional tax breaks for low- and middle-income earners, extending temporary full expensing and loss carry-backs for businesses, and increasing spending on infrastructure investment and training programs. Separately, the new budget increases social spending significantly over FY2022–25, including for programs for the elderly (0.9% of GDP) and people with disabilities (0.7% of GDP), as well as a number of initiatives to support women, including those that support their safety, education, health, and retirement. Additionally, A\$1.6 billion is invested to finance high-priority low-emission technologies. The FY2021 Budget introduced an additional stimulus package on October 06, 2020 (amounting to A\$98.2 billion, or 5% of GDP). It included a brand-new program called JobMaker (A\$73 billion), which included both new policies (such as loss carrybacks and a personal income tax cut) and the extension of policies that had already been in place (the temporary Coronavirus Supplement, other income support measures, full expensing, and infrastructure investment, among others). Separately, the budget demonstrated the government's determination to spend A\$1.9 billion on green technologies to reduce carbon output.

A series of economic and health measures totaling A\$217.1 billion (11% of GDP) until FY2024 were launched by the government in March 2020. The government updated Australia's Economic and Fiscal Outlook on July 23, 2020. The cost estimate for the JobKeeper wage subsidy program was updated in July and is now estimated to be A\$85.7 billion (down from A\$130 billion), with a 6-month extension at a tapering level to the end of March 2021. A new JobTrainer Skills package (a training program for job seekers) was added in the July update. The first round of stimulus measures totaled A\$17.6 billion and was announced on March 12. They included a one-time stimulus payment to welfare recipients, accelerated depreciation deductions, a broadening of the applicable eligibility criteria for instant asset write-offs, cash flow assistance for businesses, and financial support (including tax and fee waivers) to sectors, regions, and communities that were disproportionately affected by the pandemic. The Coronavirus Supplement, a top-up payment to JobSeeker unemployment benefits and welfare users, as well as further economic support for people and businesses, were included in a second rescue package worth A\$66 billion that was unveiled on March 22. To assist Australians in keeping their employment, the historic JobKeeper pay subsidy program (worth A\$130 billion) was unveiled on March 30.

The Reserve Bank of Australia (RBA) has announced a comprehensive package of monetary easing since the start of the epidemic, including policy rate decreases, a yield curve goal, term funding facilities, and the purchase of government bonds. In March 2020, the Overnight Cash Rate objective was lowered to 0.25%, and then again in November 2020, it was lowered to 0.1%. Exchange settlement balances held by commercial banks with the RBA now have a 0% interest rate. Through purchases of government bonds on the secondary market, the RBA also implemented yield targeting on 3-year government bonds, with the target rate set at the nightly funds' rate. To maintain market liquidity during the early stages of the epidemic, the RBA carried out longer-term repos and expanded the list of securities that qualified as eligible collateral for open market operations to include investment-grade securities issued by nonbank firms. Additionally, a swap line has been established with the US Federal Reserve for the provision of up to $60 billion in US currency liquidity. The RBA launched the A$90 billion Term Funding Facility (TFF) in March 2020 to allow banks to access 3-year funding at 25 basis points until September 2020, supporting the issuance of credit, particularly to SMEs. With access extended through June 2021, the facility was subsequently increased to A$200 billion at a rate of 10 basis points. Additionally, the RBA said that it would purchase A$100 billion worth 5–10-year government bonds on the secondary market in November 2020 from the Australian Government as well as the States and Territories. The purchasing program was prolonged to September 2021 and increased to A$200 billion. The RBA also increased its forward guidance by saying that it will not raise the cash rate until real inflation is sustainably back within the target range of 2%–3% and that it does not anticipate doing so until at least 2024.

The RBA left the criteria of the Term Funding Facility, the cash rate objective (0.1%), the 3-year government bond yield target (0.1%), and both unchanged as of June 01, 2021. The RBA reaffirmed that the prerequisites for a cash rate increase are not anticipated to be satisfied until 2024. The Term Funding Facility will not be renewed and shall terminate on June 30, 2021.

Through FY2024–25, the government has announced fiscal measures totaling NZ$62.1 billion (19.3% of GDP). The COVID-19 Response and Recovery Fund is included in the total, of which NZ$5.1 billion has been set aside as a backup in case of a revival. The following fiscal measures have been announced; a permanent increase in social spending to protect vulnerable people (total NZ$2.4 billion or 0.7% of GDP), a wage subsidy to support employers severely impacted by the impact of COVID-19 (NZ$13.9 billion or 4.3% of GDP), a permanent increase in healthcare-related spending, the cost of managed isolation, and the purchase of vaccines, income relief payments to help people who lost their jobs ($0.6 billion, or 0.2% of GDP), revenue measures, such as a temporary tax loss carry-back program and a permanent change in business taxes ($8.6 billion, or 2.7%), infrastructure investment ($3.8 billion, or 1.2%), transportation projects ($0.6 billion, or 0.2% of GDP), support for the aviation sector ($0.6 billion, or 0.2% of GDP), and education (NZ$3.4 billion or 1.1% of GDP), government R&D (NZ$0.2 billion, or 0.1% of GDP), training and Flexi-wage subsidies (NZ$0.6 billion, or 0.2% of GDP). The Comeback Support Payment and Wage Subsidy Scheme are just two of the emergency measures the administration has announced for a potential resurgence. A NZ$1.5 billion debt funding arrangement (convertible to equity) between the government and Air New Zealand has been authorized in order to maintain freight operations, domestic flights, and a small number of foreign flights. To encourage private sector R&D investment, the New Zealand government has launched a NZ$0.2 billion short-term R&D loan program. Until the end of 2023, the New Zealand government will also offer loans to small enterprises with 50 or fewer employees up to NZ$100,000. Lastly, the government declared on March 28, 2020, that all imports of hygiene and medical supplies for the COVID-19 response would be temporarily exempt from tariffs.

The Reserve Bank of New Zealand (RBNZ) held the official cash rate (OCR) at 0.25% and left the Funding for Lending Program (FLP) and the Large-Scale Asset Purchase (LSAP) of up to NZ$100 billion unchanged at its May 2021 Board meeting (FLP).

On March 17, 2020, the OCR was lowered by 75 basis points. The FLP, which began in December 2020, gave banks access to 3-year funding valued at up to NZ$28 billion at a rate of 0.25%, allowing them to decrease borrowing rates for businesses and families. In August 2020, the RBNZ increased the LSAP program's purchasing limit of government bonds and Local Government Funding Agency

(LGFA) bonds in the secondary market from NZ$60 billion for a 12-month period to NZ$100 billion by June 2022. The RBNZ has been supplying liquidity in the foreign exchange swap market since March 2020 and has reestablished a temporary US dollar swap line with the US Federal Reserve worth US$30 billion. The RBNZ announced corporate open market operations (COMO), which will offer up to NZ$500 million per week in open market operations with banks against corporate paper and asset-backed securities for 3 months. The TAF, which was established by the RBNZ, gives banks access to collateralized loans of up to 12 months. Term Lending Facility (TLF), a longer-term funding program for banks at 0.25% for up to 3 years length initially for 6 months starting May 26, 2020, was also announced by the RBNZ. The TLF's facility was extended to February 01, 2021, and the TLF's credit term was increased to 5 years in August 2020. The TLF was later extended once more, this time until July 28, 2021.

With effect from May 01, 2020, the RBNZ lifted the temporary limitations on mortgage loan-to-value ratios (LVR). These limits were reinstated by the RBNZ in March 2021 at prepandemic levels, and the LVR restrictions for investors were further tightened starting in May 2021. A variety of financial initiatives have also been announced to assist homeowners and SMEs. These include deferring principal and interest payments for mortgage holders and SMEs impacted by COVID-19 and the BFGS for a period of 6 months. On March 31, 2021, the favorable regulatory treatment of loans with repayment deferrals came to an end. The government also implemented limitations on evictions from rental properties between March and June 2020 and a 6-month cap on residential rent hikes until September 25, 2020. To October 31, 2021, the government has extended the Business Debt Hibernation Program, which enables companies to put their current debts on hold for a period of 10 months.

The Bank of Papua New Guinea (BPNG) instructed commercial banks to lower their respective Indicative Lending Rates and decreased the Kina Facility Rate (KFR), the country's main policy rate, by 200 basis points from 5% to 3%. Additionally, BPNG decreased the Cash Reserve Requirement from 10% to 7% in order to give commercial banks more liquidity. As part of a plan to improve liquidity for the private sector, BPNG spent K750 million buying government securities in the secondary market. The margin on central bank borrowing was raised by BPNG by 25 basis points to 100 basis points on both sides of KFR in order to promote interbank activity. On a case-by-case basis, all financial institutions agreed to grant customers who have lost their jobs a 3-month reprieve from loan repayments and interest payments. The domestic FX interbank market will receive US dollar liquidity from BPNG. However, during the SoE, it instructed Authorized Foreign Exchange Dealers to provide precedence to medical and pharmaceutical enterprises, as well as retailers and wholesalers of medical products, especially when importing items connected to COVID-19.

The Central Bank of Nigeria (CBN) reduced its monetary policy rate by 100 basis points in May and another 100 basis points in September in response to COVID-19, increasing the liquidity available to nonbank financial institutions, and lowering the market yield on government securities significantly. Additional measures were also implemented, including a 1-year moratorium on CBN intervention facilities and a reduction of interest rates on all applicable CBN interventions from 9% to 5%; the establishment of an N50 billion ($139 million) targeted credit facility; and a liquidity injection of N3.6 trillion (2.4% of GDP) into the banking system, with N100 billion going to support the health sector, N2 trillion going to the manufacturing sector, and N1.5 trillion going to impacted industries.

However, to the northeast, due to decreased travel and tourism, decreased worker remittances, capital outflows, and a slowdown in domestic activities as people were encouraged to stay at home, the epidemic had an adverse effect on the Egyptian economy. Egypt's exports and Suez Canal revenue both declined as a result of the weakening global demand. To lessen the impact of COVID-19 on the economy, the government announced stimulus measures in the USD 6.13 billion package (EGP 100 billion, 1.8% of GDP). A 14% increase has been made to pensions. EGP 50 billion has been designated as part of the EGP 100 billion stimulus package for the tourist industry, which accounts for over 12% of Egypt's GDP.

At the southernmost point of the African continent, the South African Central Bank (SARB) gradually lowered the policy rate, doing so by 100 basis points on March 19, 2020, another 100 basis points on April 14, 2020, 50 basis points on May 21, 2020, and 25 basis points on July 23, 2020, bringing it to 3.5%. The SARB announced measures to ease liquidity conditions on March 20, 2020. These included increasing the number of repo auctions to two in order to provide intraday liquidity support to clearing banks at the policy rate; lowering the upper and lower limits of the standing facility to lend at the repo rate and borrow at 200 basis points below the repo rate; and increasing the size of the main weekly refinancing operations as necessary. The government declared the beginning of a single strategy to allow banks to relieve debt for customers on March 23, 2020. The SARB announced additional measures to address the liquidity pressures seen in the funding markets on March 25, 2020. The primary refinancing instruments' maturities will be increased from 3 to 12 months through the program's acquisition of government securities on the secondary market across the full yield curve. It announced a temporary relaxation of bank capital requirements on March 28, 2020, and cut the liquidity coverage level from 100% to 80%.

Similarly, in the northernmost part of Africa, the Bank of Algeria reduced its main policy rate by 25 basis points to 3.25% on March 15 and reduced the reserve requirement ratio from 10% to 8%. The Bank of Algeria said on April 6 that it was lowering the ratios for banks' solvency, liquidity, and NPLs. Additionally, banks are permitted to postpone payments on some loans without having to make a provision for them. The Bank of Algeria said on April 30 that it was lowering its reserve requirement ratio from 8% to 6%, lowering haircuts on government securities used in refinancing operations, and lowering its main policy rate from 3.25% to 3.00%. On September 14, the Bank of Algeria announced the start of 1-month open market operations and a drop in the reserve requirement ratio from 6% to 3%.

Right beside Algeria, since March 2020, the Moroccan central bank has lowered the policy rate by 75 basis points to 1.5%. Loan payments for small- and medium-sized firms and independent contractors have been delayed until June 30 in order to support entrepreneurs. The Capital Market Authority decided to lower the maximum variation thresholds that apply to financial instruments listed on the Casablanca Stock Exchange in order to lower volatility. More specifically, Bank al-Maghrib chose a three-pronged strategy to increase liquidity provision to the banking sector due to the growing demand for liquidity support in the banking system (both in DRH and in EUR/USD): broaden the range of collateral accepted for repos and credit guarantees to include public and private debt instruments (including mortgages), lengthen and increase central bank refinancing operations to support banking credit to (V)SMEs, and provide FX swaps. Additionally, Bank al-Maghrib decided to reduce reserve requirements from 2% to zero in order to boost liquidity.

In Kenya, the central government initially set aside Ksh40 billion (0.4% of GDP) as part of the FY2019/20 budget for COVID-19-related expenses, including the health sector; social protection; and funds for hastily paying existing debts to maintain businesses' cash flow during the crisis. The maximum term of repurchase agreements was increased from 28 to 91 days on March 24, and the central bank announced flexibility to banks regarding loan classification and provisioning for loans that were performed on March 02, 2020, but was restructured because of the pandemic. The policy rate was reduced by 100 basis points to 7.25%, banks' cash reserve ratio was decreased by 100 basis points to 4.25%, and the maximum term of repurchase agreements was increased. In order to discourage the usage of cash, the central bank has also pushed banks to make loan terms more flexible for borrowers depending on pandemic-related circumstances and supported the waiving or lowering of transaction fees for mobile money.

To the near north, Ethiopian authorities set aside about 30 billion birr (or 800 million) for COVID-19-related expenses in the fiscal year 2020/21, including the purchase of medical equipment, increased pay for health workers, food assistance for quarantines and isolation areas, and the acquisition of hygiene facilities, disinfectants, and personal protection equipment. To aid in debt restructuring and avert bankruptcy, the central bank gave private banks 15 billion birr (0.45% of GDP) in additional liquidity. Additionally, it has given the Commercial Bank of Ethiopia (CBE) a 3-year ETB 16 billion liquidity line and used commercial banks to pump cash into the hospitality and tourism industries.

Likewise, the Ghanaian government spent roughly 2.1% of the GDP in 2020, of which 0.3% went on healthcare. The majority of these funds were used as part of the Coronavirus Alleviation Program to deal with the social and economic repercussions of the pandemic, including support for selected industries (such as the pharmaceutical sector, which supplies COVID-19 drugs and equipment), support for SMEs, financing of guarantees and first-loss instruments, construction or renovation of 100 district and regional hospitals, and issues with a test kit, pharmaceutical, equipment, and bed capacity. On March 18, 2020, the Monetary Policy Committee (MPC) reduced the policy rate by 150 basis points to 14.5%. They also announced a number of steps to lessen the effects of the pandemic shock, such as lowering the primary reserve requirement from 10% to 8%, lowering the capital conservation buffer from 3% to 1.5%, changing the provisioning and classification rules for particular loan categories, and taking actions to make mobile payments easier and less expensive.

Comparably on May 12, the Bank of Tanzania (BoT) lowered the collateral haircut requirements for government securities and lowered the discount rate from 7% to 5%. The BoT Statutory Minimum Reserves requirement is lowered from 7% to 6% as of June 08. The BoT provides banks and other financial institutions regulatory latitude to conduct case-by-case debt restructuring operations. The daily balance limit was increased from US$ 2170 to US$ 4340 and the mobile money providers' daily transaction limit was increased from US$ 1300 to US$ 2170.

In Côte d'Ivoire, the West-African Economic and Monetary Union (WAEMU), a regional central bank (BCEAO), has implemented measures to better satiate banks' need for liquidity and lessen the adverse effects of the pandemic on economic activity. The BCEAO adopted a full allotment approach in April 2020 at a fixed rate of 2.5% (the minimum monetary policy rate), enabling banks to fully satisfy their liquidity needs at a rate that is approximately 25 basis points lower than it was before the crisis. The ceiling and floor of the monetary policy corridor were reduced by 50 basis points by the Monetary Policy Committee in June 2020 to 4% and 2%, respectively.

Chapter 17

Evidence on national and local economies during the COVID-19 crisis aftermath

Chapter outline

Abstract

In this chapter, we focus generally on evidence regarding national and local economies during the COVID-19 crisis aftermath around the world. We also specifically look at employment data and how economic effects are distributed across economies. We supplement the formal data reported in the text, tables, and figures in the book with recent press coverage of rapidly changing current conditions as of the book deadline. Economic problems such as high and variable inflation, domestic and international supply chain disruptions, etc., appear around the globe. As indicated, in this and remaining chapters of Part V, we focus on nations other than the US to avoid excessive repetition of well-known evidence largely covered elsewhere in the book.

Keywords: COVID-19, Aftermath, Real economy, GDP, Unemployment, Local economies

17.1 Evidence of GDP and unemployment outcomes during the aftermath

Canada experienced a sharp decline in real GDP growth in 2020 (down to −5.2%) and a sharp rise in 2021 (up to +4.5%). Conversely, their population increased steadily during this period while their unemployment rate shot up close to 10% in 2020. The Canadian government demonstrated its commitment to aiding its vulnerable populations with several fiscal responses, beginning with a $60.3 billion package (2.7% of GDP) dedicated to supporting increased testing, vaccine development, medical supplies, mitigation efforts, and greater support for Indigenous communities.

Brazil also experienced a steep drop in GDP (down to −3.9%), with a quick recovery in 2021 (up to +4.6%). Their population steadily increased following previous trends, although the unemployment rate grew significantly (close to 2%), up to 13.8% in 2020, and experienced a gradual decline in the following years. The state also experienced a distinctive decrease in public debt as a percentage of GDP in 2020. The authorities announced several fiscal measures totaling 12% of GDP in 2020 to reduce the repercussions of COVID-19, of which the direct impact on the primary deficit was 7.2% of GDP. In a similar trend to Brazil's Mexico experienced a substantial dip in GDP growth (about −8%) in 2020, which has since stabilized and increased by about +4.8%. Mexico navigated an increase in unemployment of almost +1% from 2019 to 2020, preceding a sharp decline as the negative effects

The Economic and Financial Impacts of the COVID-19 Crisis Around the World
https://doi.org/10.1016/B978-0-443-19162-6.00011-6
Copyright © 2024 Elsevier Inc. All rights reserved.

of the pandemic subsided. A total of 0.7% of GDP was spent on above-the-line fiscal measures in 2020, while 1.2% of GDP was spent on below-the-line fiscal measures.

The real sector of Argentina suffered a decrease in real GDP growth of almost 10%, coupled with an extremely high inflation rate. The unemployment rate increased following an upward trend (up to 11.6% in 2020), followed by a steady decline into 2021. According to estimates by law enforcement officials, the announced measures will total about 6.5% of the 2020 GDP, with 4.5% allocated in the budget and 2% off-budget.

The Colombian government faced a historic low for GDP growth (down to −7%, the lowest rate since the 1980s), although their inflation rate continued a downward trend through 2020. Colombia's labor force contracted as the unemployment rate rose to +15.9% in 2020. The National Emergency Mitigation Fund (FOME), which will receive 1.3% of GDP from domestic bond issuance and other budgetary resources in addition to a portion of its funding from regional and stabilization funds, was created after the Colombian government issued an emergency declaration for the state (approximately 1.5% of GDP), however, the Fiscal Rule Consultative Committee approved the government's request to temporarily suspend the fiscal rule in 2020 and 2021, and the government now projects that the overall deficit will be 7.8% of GDP in 2020 and 8.6% of GDP in 2021.

In Chile, real GDP growth experienced a worrying dip in 2020 (−6.1%) coupled with a spike in unemployment to almost +11% in 2020. On March 19, 2020, the Chilean administration released a package of fiscal initiatives worth US$11.75 billion (or roughly 4.7% of GDP), with a focus on boosting company liquidity and employment.

The Peruvian state underwent negative real GDP growth in 2020 of −11% alongside an extreme unemployment rate in 2020 that almost doubled from the previous year (up to 13.9% from 6.6% in 2019). During the national lockdown, the government-sanctioned S/. Three billion (0.5% of GDP) for the health emergency and S/. Seven billion (1.1% of GDP) in direct handouts to assist poor households. In late July, it was reported that needy households would receive an additional cash transfer of around S$6.4 billion (0.9% of GDP). In late October, a new pay subsidy scheme was introduced, covering 35%–55% of the wage bill for businesses that reported a sales decline of at least 30% in April or May 2020 and either recalled furloughed employees or added new positions.

Regarding the state of Guatemala, a decrease in GDP growth was realized in 2020 of almost 6% (down to −1.8% from 4% in 2019). Increasing health-care spending (0.2% of GDP) and supporting various industries with cash transfers (1.2% of GDP), salary subsidies (0.3% of GDP), and funding for SMEs (0.6% of GDP) were the two primary initiatives of the fiscal reaction.

In Ecuador, the government navigated a decline in real GDP growth of almost 8%, down from 0% in 2019. Alongside there was an upward trend in unemployment that existed before the pandemic, rose by 5.3% in 2020.

Real GDP growth in the Dominican Republic displayed a decline of over 10%, down from 5.1% in 2019 to −6.7% in 2020. Conversely, the unemployment rate followed a decreasing trend to 5.8% in 2020 and spiked to 7.4% in 2021. Prior administration's initial economic initiatives cost RD$32 billion (or $576 million USD, or 1/4 of GDP), or 34 of GDP.

German real GDP Growth has strongly decreased due to the pandemic in 2020 (about −5% compared to the previous year). However, it has recovered rapidly in the following years (with an increase of about +6.5% in 2021 compared to 2020). Moreover, even if the unemployment rate increased from

2019 to 2020 following the beginning of the crisis (by about +0.60%), it has fallen back slightly and reached in 2022 a rate close to those that could be seen before the crisis. It is certain that this was also facilitated by the several local governments that presented their own economic assistance programs in addition to the federal government's fiscal measures.

France in 2020 real GDP growth has significantly fallen (by around −10% as compared to the prior year). However, it quickly bounced back in the years that followed with a gain of about 15% in 2021 over 2020. In addition, the unemployment rate has only decreased in recent years and the health crisis has not impacted this factor. This is mostly because of the emergency programs, which received additional funding in the budget for 2021 and further funding in combination with ongoing containment efforts.

Among the most industrialized nations in Europe, Italy has seen a significant decline in real GDP growth in 2020 as a result of the pandemic (approximately −10% from the previous year). However, it recovered quickly in the years that followed (with a gain of roughly +16% in 2021 compared to 2020), and although it fell slightly in 2022, it continued to be higher than precrisis rates. As for the unemployment rate, it has not been affected by the crisis and has remained fairly constant over the years. This especially occurred because the government approved new support packages in March and May 2021 with the intention of extending aid for restoring the economy.

In the UK, the pandemic has considerably slowed down the country's real GDP growth in 2020 (down about 12% from the previous year). However, in the years that followed, it quickly regained (especially with a gain of almost 18% above 2020 in 2021). The UK's unemployment rate dramatically rose once the crisis began (about +0.7% compared to the prior year) and has not really recovered in 2021. However, there was a progression in 2022, with the rate falling by around 0.4% from the previous year, though the government paid 80% of furloughed employees' salaries up until the end of October. In addition, the government has launched a program called Job Entry: Targeted Support (JETS) to help job seekers who have been obtaining unemployment benefits for at least 13 weeks. The government then announced that the furlough plan will be extended as part of the assistance for families to July 2021. Lastly, it is important to know that the HM Treasury and the BoE agreed to temporarily increase the use of the government's debt account at the BoE to provide short-term supply of additional liquidity to the government if necessary and that the government supported the international response to COVID-19 with contributions to the IMF's Catastrophe Containment and Relief Trust and a new loan to the IMF Poverty Reduction and Growth Trust.

The pandemic caused a significant decline in real GDP growth in Spain in 2020 (approximately −13% from the year before). However, the following years saw a swift recovery (with a rise of almost +16% in 2021 over 2020). Additionally, it should be highlighted that while the unemployment rate rose from 2019 to 2020 when the crisis began (reaching a rate of about 15.50% in 2020), it then started to decline in the years that followed, reaching a number even lower than before the crisis in 2022. This can be explained by the Temporary Employment Adjustment Scheme request for workers temporarily laid off as a result of COVID-19, and the efforts of regional governments for social services and education, which are some of the important initiatives undertaken. Indeed, among other things, extra financial resources and budgetary flexibility were made available to support the extension of the social benefit for energy supplies and the upkeep of the educational system. Adjusting the budget ceilings for particular ministry departments and local governments was also another action made.

In the Netherlands, the third assistance package was published by the government in August 2020 and primarily aimed to reinforce and adjust current expenditure-side policies through June 2021.

In 2021, the government budgeted several billion in assistance, an increase from the expenditure support budget for 2020.

Switzerland had a significant decline in real GDP growth in 2020 as a result of the pandemic (approximately −3.5% from the year before). The country's real economy soon bounced back the next year (with a gain of almost 6.75% in 2021 over 2020). Additionally, it should be noted that while the unemployment rate grew from 2019 to 2020 after the crisis began (by roughly 1%), it then began to decline in 2021 and eventually reached a rate even lower than that seen in the years prior to the crisis in 2022. This can also be explained by the fact that due to stricter regulations, the Swiss FC increased budgetary support in January 2021 to minimize the impact on the economy. In addition, the government revised a number of COVID-related policies, such as the hardship ordinance and the lost wages policy, with the majority of these changes intended to increase financial assistance and make the conditions of these programs clearer. Lastly, the FC revealed a three-pillar strategy to guide the change of economic policies once the pandemic situation would improve.

In 2021 and 2022, the Swedish government provided significant economic stimulus programs and reforms of several billion. Moreover, the government proposed extending short-term layoffs by 7 months till June 2021 starting in November 2020. In April, the government released the 2021 Spring Fiscal Policy Bill, which aims for reducing the impact of the pandemic on the economy and assisting Sweden in its recovery from the crisis. Furthermore, beginning in April 2021, sole proprietors would continue to get assistance based on their turnover. Moreover, the Swedish government announced in March 2021 that prolonged turnover-based support would be available to sole proprietors and trading partnerships who had picked parental or sick leave and had obtained unemployment insurance.

In Romania, the pandemic significantly slowed down the country's real GDP growth in 2020 (a decline of about 8% compared to the previous year). However, in the years that followed, it recovered quickly (including a gain of almost 10% in 2021 compared to 2020). Concerning the unemployment rate, it also increased in 2020 (approximately +1%) and decreased slightly in 2021 and again in 2022. However, it is important to recognize that Romania's economy showed evidence of strong recovery. In fact, estimates show that it has shown the fastest GDP growth among the other EU countries. Romania was the first among member countries to rollout vaccines to health-care workers, after initiating a vaccination campaign earlier in December 2020, helping to make the country's strong economic recovery possible.

Meanwhile, in Turkey, the pandemic did not have a negative impact on real GDP growth. On the contrary, there was an important increase between 2020 and 2021 (around +9%), followed by a significant decline in 2022 (although the real GDP growth rate remains higher than the ones before the crisis). In addition, it should be noted that the unemployment rate has begun a gradual decline since 2019. This is partly because, in addition to the ban on layoffs, the short-term work allowance scheme was also extended through June for all industries.

In Saudi Arabia, there was a decline in its real GDP growth resulting from the pandemic in 2020 (by around −5% compared to the previous year). However, Saudi Arabia in the subsequent year was able to recover (with an increase of +8% from 2020 to 2021). The real nonoil GDP declined by 2.3% in 2020, but the real nonoil GDP was able to bounce back and during the first quarter it grew (by around 2.9% year-over-year). The growth in the real nonoil GDP continued during the second quarter of 2021 as the PMI grew between April and May as a result of the 15-month high easing occurring between February and March. Furthermore, around the start of the pandemic, there was an increase in the unemployment rate from 2019 to 2020 (by around +1%). However, the rate of unemployment declined in

2021 (by around −2%) and even further in 2022 (by around −1%) where it is now at a rate better than prior to the pandemic. This was facilitated due to the response by the Saudi authorities to provide support through fiscal measures and wage support programs during the pandemic.

Like Saudi Arabia, the United Arab Emirates experienced a drop in its real GDP growth in 2020 (by around −7.8% compared to 2019), followed by a rebound in the subsequent year (with an increase of +8% from 2020 to 2021) and the real GDP growth rate has continued to grow in 2022.

The pandemic also caused a decline in Israel's real GDP growth rate in 2020 (by around 6% compared to 2019), followed by a recovery (with an increase of around 7% from 2020 to 2021) and Israel's real GDP growth has remained at a rate above where it was prior to the pandemic. Also, around the start of the pandemic, there was an increase in the unemployment rate from 2019 to 2020 (by around +0.50%) in Israel and this increase continued from 2020 to 2021 (by around +0.75%). However, the rate of unemployment declined in 2022 (by around −1.25%) to a rate that is similar to where it was prior to pandemic. During the first quarter of 2021, as more vaccinations were given out and cases of COVID-19 declined, the economy improved.

A similar trend was seen in China, a decrease in its real GDP growth rate due to the pandemic in 2020 (by around −3.5% compared to 2019) and a recovery in the following year (with an increase of around +5.5% from 2020 to 2021). This growth did not last for long as it declined again (by around −4.5% from 2021 to 2022). Furthermore, around the start of the pandemic, there was an increase in the unemployment rate from 2019 to 2020 (by around +0.10%). Then the rate of unemployment declined from 2020 to 2021 (by around −0.35%), but this decline lasted only for a short-time as from 2021 to 2022 the unemployment rate increased again (by around +0.4%).

Japanese real GDP growth rate declined in 2020 (by around −3.7% compared to 2019) and increased in the following year (by around +6.5% from 2020 to 2021) but eventually leveled out with little growth in 2021 when it reached the point (by around 0.15%) higher than it was before the pandemic. Moreover, around the start of the pandemic, there was an increase in the unemployment rate from 2019 to 2020 (by around +0.40%). Then from 2020 to 2021 the unemployment rate remained mostly stagnant and then declined from 2021 to 2022 (by around −0.1%) but was still at a point that was higher than before the pandemic.

Real GDP growth shows a similar trend in India throughout the pandemic, with a decrease in real GDP growth rate in 2020 (by around −11% compared to 2019), an increase in 2021 (by around +16% from 2020 to 2021), and then a slight decline (by around −2% from 2021 to 2022) where it is now at a point above where it was prior to the pandemic. In India, the severity of the pandemic was felt in India's economy as the FY2020/21 GDP has a growth of −7.3%, but growth returned at 1.6% year-on-year during the first quarter of 2021. Additionally, around the start of the pandemic, there was an increase in the unemployment rate from 2019 to 2020 (by around +3%). Then from 2020 to 2022, the unemployment rate declined (by around −2%) to a rate that was similar to where it was prior to the pandemic.

South Korean real GDP growth rate declined due to the pandemic in 2020 (by around −2.75% compared to 2019). However, in the following year, the real GDP growth increased (by around +4.5% from 2020 to 2021) and then the GDP fell (by around −1% from 2021 to 2022) where it is now at a point similar to where it was prior to the pandemic. In addition, around the start of the pandemic, there is a slight increase in the unemployment rate from 2019 to 2020 (by around +0.15%). Then from 2020 to 2021, the unemployment rate dropped (by around −0.25%) and then further fell from 2021 to 2022 (by around −0.5%) to a point that is lower than prior to the pandemic.

In Russia, there was a decline in its real GDP growth rate due to the pandemic in 2020 (by around −4% compared to 2019). However, in the following year, the real GDP growth rebounded and increased (by around +6% from 2020 to 2021), but this rebound did not last as real GDP growth then greatly fell (by around −10%) to a point far lower than it was prior to the pandemic. Also, around the start of the pandemic, there was an increase in the unemployment rate from 2019 to 2020 (by around +1%). Then from 2020 to 2021, the unemployment rate fell (by around −0.8%) and continued to fall from 2021 to 2022 (by around −0.5%) to a point that was similar to prior to the pandemic.

In Indonesia, after a decline in its real GDP growth rate due to the pandemic in 2020 (by around −7% compared to 2019), the real GDP growth rate rebounded and increased in the following year (by around +6% from 2020 to 2021) and the increase continued (by around +1% from 2021 to 2022) where it ended at a point close to where it was prior to the pandemic. Even though Indonesia's GDP during the first quarter of 2021 declined by around 0.7%, economic activity has demonstrated a positive recovery quarter over quarter since the latter half of 2020. Indonesia is still dealing with volatility; however eternal pressures have stayed relatively moderate. Moreover, around the start of the pandemic, there was an increase in the unemployment rate from 2019 to 2020 (by around +2%). Then from 2020 to 2021, the unemployment rate fell (by around −0.5%) and then continued to fall from 2021 to 2022 (by around −0.5%) to a point that was slightly above where it was prior to the pandemic.

Real GDP in The Philippines exhibits a similar trend, with the growth rate declining due to the pandemic in 2020 (by around −15% compared to 2019), rebounding and increasing in the following year (by around +14% from 2020 to 2021), and the increase continuing (by around +1% from 2021 to 2022) where it ended at a point almost the same as it was prior to the pandemic. Furthermore, around the start of the pandemic, there was an increase in the unemployment rate from 2019 to 2020 (by around +5%). Then from 2020 to 2021, the unemployment rate declined (by around −2%) and then continued to decline from 2021 to 2022 (by around −1%) where it ended at a point higher than it was prior to the pandemic.

The Australian government navigated a stark decrease in real GDP growth (−6.7% in 2020). The unemployment rate followed an upward trend that was at 5.4% in 2020 but did not reach its height until 2021 (6.2%). When formulating its response to the pandemic, the Australian government adopted a more liberal stance. Through FY2025, the Commonwealth has implemented fiscal stimulus measures totaling A$312 billion (15.34% of 2020 GDP), which take the shape of expenditure and tax initiatives. Over two-thirds of the stimulus have been used up by the end of FY2021 (June 2021), including the well-known JobKeeper wage subsidy program, which made payments totaling A$89 billion (4.5% of 2020 GDP) through the end of March 2021.

New Zealand experienced negative real GDP growth in 2020 (−2.1%). Their unemployment rate did not experience a significant increase (up to 4.6% in 2020 from 4.1% in 2019) and had since steadily decreased. The government has made financial announcements totaling NZ$62.1 billion through FY2024–25 (19.3% of GDP). Included in the total is the COVID-19 Response and Recovery Fund, of which NZ$5.1 billion has been set aside as a fallback in the event of a revival.

The pandemic had a negative impact on the Egyptian economy due to decreased travel and tourism, worker remittances, capital outflows, and a slowdown in domestic activity as individuals were urged to stay at home. In Egypt, EGP 50 billion of the EGP 100 billion stimulus plan has been allocated for the travel and tourism sector, which generates about 12% of Egypt's GDP and over 4% of GDP in terms of revenues. Egypt's GDP growth decreased during the pandemic, however, not as much as in other nations. The GDP growth decreased from about 6% to about 3% before rising to 6% once again in

2022. Egypt's population was increasing, while the unemployment rate had remained constant at about 8%. In 2020, the government of Ghana spent about 2.1% of the country's GDP, with 0.3% going to health care. Ghana's GDP growth was flat in 2020, spiked in 2021, and then fell again in 2022. Ghana was seeing rapid expansion in terms of its population. 2020 saw a sharp decline in Kenya's GDP growth while the public debt to GDP remained relatively stable. Kenya's GDP growth accelerated in 2021, as did that of many other nations, before slowing down to a more typical rate in 2022. In terms of population, Kenya was expanding quickly. In Nigeria, GDP growth experienced a sharp decline in 2020 and a sharp rise in 2021. Morocco's GDP growth decreased in 2020, falling to about −7%. Morocco saw a significant population increase both during and after the pandemic, as did the majority of African nations. Additionally, throughout the pandemic, unemployment remained constant at about 11%. In South Africa, GDP growth started to decline in 2020 before rising to about 4% in 2021 and 2022. Similar to other African nations, South Africa is experiencing population growth, and its unemployment rate of 35% has remained constant.

17.2 Evidence on employment on the national and local levels during the aftermath

Canada implemented several fiscal policy responses concerning their employment. Households and businesses received about $290 billion (13.2% of GDP) in direct aid, which included wage subsidies, payments to workers without sick leave, and access to employment insurance, an increase from the previous year.

Brazil implemented numerous budgetary measures to help its vulnerable populations of low-income and unemployed people, including raising health spending, providing vulnerable households with short-term income support, giving low-income and unemployed people cash transfers, and supporting jobs (partial compensation for furloughed workers and temporary tax breaks). The government provided credit lines totaling more than 1% of GDP to SMEs and microbusinesses to pay for the investment, working capital, and payroll expenses.

On March 19, 2020, the Chilean government released a package of fiscal initiatives worth US$11.75 billion (or roughly 4.7% of GDP), focusing on boosting company liquidity and employment. The package of measures includes increased health-care spending, improved unemployment benefits, and subsidies, among other financial incentives.

Among the policy actions to safeguard lives and livelihoods totaling $1.2 billion in 2020 were the distribution of food baskets, temporary relaxation of the requirements for unemployment insurance eligibility, exceptional cash transfers to low-income families ($250 million), and increased health spending ($550 million). Additional attempts included postponing payroll contributions, tuition, health insurance, utilities, and housing help, in addition to temporary price caps on staple foods. All of these actions were taken to maintain employment, including the potential for mutually agreed-upon modifications to employment contracts as well as the temporary adoption of shorter workweeks and more flexible work arrangements.

The German government introduced new fiscal measures regarding the actions undertaken related to employment, to help families and young employees. In Italy, the initiatives implemented in relation to employment, compensation for firms and the self-employed, extension of the ban on firing employees, short-term employment programs, and offering assistance to employees were significant initiatives.

In the UK, the income tax payments for self-employed were deferred for 6 months. Additionally, the government covered 70% of wages in September and 60% of wages in October, with employers covering the remaining 20% of wages. Lastly, the UK government declared a new set of policies in November, including the removal of the Job Retention Bonus. In Switzerland, the Federal Council expanded protection for the staff's short-term work plan. The FC revised its occupational benefit policies in a package that was announced in November. Later, in June, the FC augmented a number of aid policies, including simplified procedures for short-term work assistance and criteria for individuals in fixed-term employment relationships, an expansion of the end-of-September dateline for trainees and personnel on call in open-ended work arrangements, and a raising of the ceiling on hardship support for severely impacted firms.

To support employment in Iran, the government set up fiscal measures in 2020 for funding toward the health sector, providing cash to vulnerable households, and aiding the unemployment insurance fund. These fiscal measures remained in place throughout 2021 and were funded by Sukuk bonds, the National Development Funds, and proceeds from privatization. In Saudi Arabia, the Saudi authorities established fiscal measures to deal with the pandemic and the majority of these measures had been withdrawn at the beginning of 2021 as most of the deferred tax payments were paid off by the close of 2020. In the United Arab Emirates, to provide fiscal support, the government in Dubai announced on January 6th, 2021, that additional stimulus would be provided from January to June 2021 (totaling AED 315 million). As well, similar strategies were incorporated by other Emirates nations to promote commerce and businesses and to provide advantages to the sectors hindered the most by the pandemic. These incentive packages for Sharjah have a combined value of AED 993 million ($0.27 billion). In January 2021, with an increase in COVID-19 cases, the government initiated tighter safety measures and mandated COVID-19 tests for all government employees.

In Israel, to provide fiscal support, the Israeli government established multiple fiscal measures throughout the pandemic in which NIS 35.8 billion were implemented during the first 5 months of 2021. The total amount for the fiscal measures amounted to around NIS 202.3 billion.

To provide fiscal support, the Chinese government set up discretionary fiscal measures that totaled around RMB 4.9 trillion (equates to around 4.7% of GDP). These fiscal measures were for epidemic prevention/control, tax relief, manufacturing of medical equipment, waiving social security contributions, distribution of unemployment insurance and extension to migrant workers, and public investments. During 2020, RMB 4.2 trillion of these fiscal measures were implemented.

The Japanese government adopted a package on December 8, 2020, worth ¥73.6 trillion (equates to 13.1% of the 2019 GDP) which includes plans to contain COVID-19, promote a positive economic period during and after the pandemic, and secure safety and relief. Along with this, the measures taken by the government provide incentives for firms investing in digitalization and green technologies for firms.

The central government of India took several measures during and following the pandemic in two categories. The first was above-the-line measures (including government sending, expedited spending, and foregone or deferred revenues) which were present mostly during the pandemic. The second was below-the-line measures which were felt both during and after the pandemic and were created to support businesses and provide credit provision to multiple sectors. During April and May 2021, below-the-line measures toward the easement of tax compliance burdens were put in place due to a resurgence of infections. Also, measures were put in place that provided credit support to businesses, poor households and electricity distribution companies and there was large support toward the agricultural sector with the goal of infrastructure development. The central government announced in April that food rations composed of food grains would be given to 800 million people during May and June (at a cost of roughly 260 billion rupees) and accelerated the release of the Disaster Response Fund to state governments during May. Lastly, to increase the accessibility of vaccines, oxygen and oxygen-related equipment, customs duties, and other taxes on vaccines were waived.

In South Korea, to provide fiscal support, the National Assembly in South Korea on December 2, 2020, established the 2021 budget which would amount to 482.6 trillion in budgeted revenue and 558 trillion in budgeted expenditures. These budgets varied from the budget plan created in 2020 in which the budgeted revenue was around KRW 23 trillion (1.2% of GDP) lower than projected and the budgeted expenditure was around KRW 11 trillion (0.6% of GDP) higher than projected. After several months, the National Assembly on March 25, 2021, passed a supplemental budget worth KRW 14.9 trillion (0.8% of GDP) with measures toward the implementation of vaccines, relief for small business owners and workers, employment support, assistance to low-income households, and financial aid for small business. A new budget was announced by the government on July 1st worth 33.0 trillion won (1.6% of GDP) which would include a COVID-19 relief program, measures on disease control, measures on employment and social safety nets, measures to boost local economies, and support to housing and livelihood. The additions to the budget would be financed through tax revenue overperformance and some budget surpluses but would not negatively impact the projected fiscal balance.

The Russian government established measures to deal with the effects of the pandemic in 2021 where businesses in the restaurant, hotel, and entertainment industries were provided subsidized loans for payments for 12 months toward minimum wage employees under conditions of preserved employment. Along with this, zero import duties were put in place for medical pharmaceutical resources and gear and budget grants were established to assist salary payments for firms hiring individuals that lost their jobs in 2020. As well, the measures provided loans to SMEs and impacted industries, provided assistance to airlines, automakers, and airports, and expanded qualifications for subsidized mortgage lending. The total cost of social spending was announced on April 2021 in the President's State of the Nation Address, and it was approximately 0.3% of GDP over the 2 years.

In Thailand, the government set up measures in January 2021 to provide support against the second COVID wave and would provide $7 billion in handouts of cash. On top of this, starting in February, all beneficiaries would receive THB 3500 per month for a period of 2 months. The King of Thailand on May 25 authorized an emergency decree that enabled borrowing of 55 billion baht by the Ministry of Finance with the goal of mitigating the economic and social impact of the pandemic. On top of this, on June 1, 2021, the government established an economic stimulus package containing cash handouts, copayments, and e-vouchers at a value of 140 billion baht. As well, the Cabinet in the middle of February 2021 authorized a THB 50 billion soft loan program, that would be available till the end of June 2021, to provide loans for up to 3 years with low-interest rates to SMEs associated with the tourism sector and informal workers. The following month, two new measures were unveiled by authorities for the facility of special loans for businesses with a credit guarantee scheme and toward debt rebuilding done by asset warehousing with buy-back options. These measures had the purpose of assisting and transforming viable firms for the postpandemic world.

The Philippine government established a second stimulus package for fiscal support known as the "Bayanihan II" Act which would provide support to vulnerable households, hard-hit sectors, and capital injections into state-owned banks. The funds from Bayanihan that were not spent had been extended to June 30, 2021. For further fiscal support, on March 26, 2021, the government revised and passed the Corporate Recovery and Tax Incentives for Enterprises (CREATE) Act with a focus on meeting the needs of businesses adversely impacted by the COVID-19 pandemic and increasing the Philippines' capacity to draw in highly desirable investments. This CREATE Act lowered the corporate income tax rate from 30% of net taxable income to 25% for large and nonresident foreign corporations (net taxable income above PHP 5 million). At the same time, the Act reduced this rate for small to medium-sized corporations to 20%. The corporate income tax rate for foreign corporations will further decrease starting in 2022 where it will decline by one percentage point annually till it reaches 20% by 2027. Lastly, the revenue lost was estimated to have amounted to 0.7% of the GDP in 2021. Furthermore, the structural policy under Bayanihan II Act allowed private initiatives that are deemed to be of national significance and have a strong potential for economic return or employment may be exempt from certain permits, licenses, or other regulations in order to avoid delays in their execution. These initiatives toward regulatory relief are anticipated to hasten the creation of jobs and high-impact investments.

17.3   Evidence of exposure by industry and other economic vulnerabilities during the aftermath

In Peru, the onset of the pandemic caused exposure to certain sectors that required new regulations to be implemented. New tax deferrals for the Peruvian tourism industry went into effect on May 16, 2021. The Dominican government extended all social assistance programs to run through the end of 2020. The government raised health-care spending, notably through budget reallocations, on pharmaceutical industry support, tests in private labs, rent for two private medical facilities, and medical supplies and equipment. On the revenue side, prolonged payment due dates and some tax advantages offer tax relief. Additionally, while the QEC and FASE I programs concluded at the end of April, the government has already launched a new program that will specifically target the workers in the tourism industry from May through July 2021. The CBDR announced on March 1, 2021, that the RLF would be increased by RD$25 billion, with the additional funds to be earmarked for specific industries such as manufacturing, construction, mortgages for affordable housing, business, and SMEs. Five billion RD has been allotted to each sector. As of June 1, 2021, roughly RD$195.5 billion (or nearly 5.0% of the 2020 GDP) of the RD$215.8 billion (almost 5.0% of the 2020 GDP) made available to financial intermediation entities to provide liquidity to economic agents had been disbursed, financing industries such as trade, manufacturing, exports, agriculture, construction, and tourism.

The Colombian government has implemented conservative policies for the reopening of industries. On April 27, the construction and manufacturing sectors were permitted to resume operations; on May 11, a broader range of industrial and commercial services sectors did the same. Although municipal governments (including Bogota) have been slow to loosen restrictions, some services, including a few retail segments, were permitted to reopen on June 1. Supplemental government budget support for health was also confirmed, including partial payment for COVID-19 tests and vaccines, faster direct contracting for emergency response services, payments to providers for ICU accessibility, and the formation of a National Tracking and Contact Center, a one-time bonus for health workers, and new lines of credit offering liquidity support to the coffee sector, the education sector, the public transportation sector, the technology sector, health and public sector providers, and all tourism-related companies, new credit lines for SME payroll and loan payments, working capital for large corporations, and corporates in the sectors most affected by the pandemic.

In Guatemala, the two main programs of the fiscal reaction were increasing health-care resources (0.2% of GDP) and supporting various industries with cash transfers (1.2% of GDP), salary subsidies (0.3% of GDP), and funding for SMEs (0.6% of GDP). More focused actions were implemented as part of the National Emergency and Economic Recovery Plan, including expediting the process for tax refunds to exporters, delaying income tax payments and Social Security contributions for a quarter, eliminating taxes on medical goods, expanding the availability and scope of energy subsidies, and promoting low-cost housing.

The Italian government, in order to provide urgent assistance to the industries affected by the most recent round of COVID-19 preventative measures, approved a package in October. The UK launched a package of measures in September 2020, including a 6-month Job Support Scheme (JSS), an extension of the Self Employment Income Support Scheme for businesses that are still operating despite lower demand brought on by the health crisis, and an extension of the provisional 15% VAT cut for the tourism and hospitality industries to the end of March 2019. Furthermore, the JSS has been modified for businesses that are still operating. In addition, the government would pay back social contributions and two-thirds of employee salaries for businesses that had to close due to the restrictions, up to a maximum of £2100 each month. The 6-month program ran from November onward. Finally, while the devolved administrations received more funding, firms in England got a greater payment for being required to close. High-alert zones would provide cash for businesses in the hospitality, lodging, and entertainment sectors. Other measures included extending the increase in universal credit benefit payments by 6 months and extending the full VAT reduction for the hospitality sector through the end of September 2021.

In Spain, measures for industry and sectoral assistance have been established. Additional measures include a moratorium on social security contributions for the self-employed and firms in specific industries and tax rebates for particular property owners that cut rents on estates used for activities related to the hotel, restaurant, and tourism sectors. An important reduction in the VAT on digital publications has been made. Public guarantees are provided to exporters by the Spanish Export Insurance Credit Company and guarantees for farmers using the special 2017 drought credit lines to prolong their loan maturities.

While additional restrictions on economic activity were implemented in Switzerland in order to contain the pandemic, the government continued its efforts to assist the economy by extending existing measures and placing a focus on supporting groups and sectors that were experiencing long-lasting negative effects from the pandemic. The FC increased some amounts set aside to bolster civil defense and tourism traffic to the first supplementary budget that was authorized in late March.

In Romania, as the number of infections rose at the end of March, limited access to a certain types of business, such as gyms, stores, and restaurants, was imposed. Restrictions started to soften in May as immunizations were pushed out and infection rates started to drop. Businesses in the hospitality and entertainment sectors were permitted to reopen at a reduced capacity. Additionally, retail establishments were able to reopen at regular hours. Then, in June, the number of individuals allowed to participate in outdoor cultural, artistic, sporting, and entertainment events rose, the capacity of indoor restaurants increased, and people were once again permitted to use playgrounds, gyms, and swimming pools with some restrictions. In July, the quota for tourist sites and gyms had been lifted, and the maximum capacity for food establishments, private events, and both indoor and outdoor activities had been raised further.

The Turkish Parliament approved a new omnibus regulation in late April 2021 that included extra provisional initiatives to increase employment in the sectors most adversely impacted by the pandemic. Additionally, there were reductions in the withholding tax on TL bank deposits up until the end of July, as well as various VAT rate reductions for specific industries.

In Saudi Arabia, the religious movement, the Hajj, would be restricted in 2021 to only 60,000 attendants to prevent further infections. As increased vaccinations were given out to individuals, starting in the middle of December 2020, this allowed for international travel to reopen on May 17, 2021. Additionally, in the sectors facing the impact of the pandemic, the government-authorized wage support program for private sector companies use of the unemployment insurance fund (SANED) would be extended through July 2021. In the United Arab Nations, the Abu Dhabi government on December 9th, 2020, announced that all economic, touristic, entertainment, and cultural activities would return within 2 weeks. The following month in January, with an increase in COVID-19 cases, the government initiated tighter safety measures where the capacity for malls and venues was reduced, international visitors and tourists were required to take a PCR test upon arrival, and activities that led to large gatherings were limited. Lastly, the government put in place several revenue-generating measures to deal with the needs created due to the crisis, to provide relief and support to business and their continuity, and to promote recovery.

On February 7th, 2021, the majority of domestic restrictions had been lifted in Israel, but restrictions remained over international travel due to the rapid spreading of COVID-19 variants. During the first quarter of 2021 in Israel, as a new outbreak began, there was a declining economic activity output of 6.5% and this was resolved as vaccinations became more popular to the point the economy could reopen again.

In China during the lunar new year of 2021, the Chinese government established reductions for intercity travel while enforcing stricter testing and quarantine requirements. During the first quarter of 2021, the economy had lower sequential growth, but strong year-over-year growth of 18.3% due to the economic contraction of 6.8% during the first quarter of 2021. In Japan, due to the severity of the pandemic, the Tokyo Olympic Games had been postponed from 2020 July 23-August 8, 2021. On June 21, 2021, the Olympic Committee decided that there would be a spectator limit of 50% of the capacity with a maximum of 10,000 people at each venue. Around January 2021, Japan enforced border measures toward preventing new variants from spreading resulting in quarantine precautions enhancing for travelers upon entrance, reentrances, or return to Japan. To enter Japan, the government created a mandate that requires the submission of a negative COVID-19 test result 72 h prior to ones fight and another round of testing to take place upon arrival.

President Moon Jae-in of South Korea revealed the establishment of a fund for KRW 40 trillion (2.1% of GDP) to assist seven crucial industries including aviation, shipping, shipbuilding, automobiles, general machinery, electric power, and communications in South Korea. The capital for this fund would be raised by issuing bonds backed by the government and private contributions. Businesses would gain support through loans, investments, and payment guarantees as long as they maintained employment, limited executive compensation, dividends, and other payouts, and shared profits from business normalization going forward. In Indonesia, the government in 2021 established a budget for the national economic recovery program (PEN) at IDR 699.4 trillion. As well, the corporate income tax rate had been permanently reduced from 25% to 22% in 2021 and then to 20% in 2022.

In Thailand, during the first week of February 2021, the Prime Minister of Thailand Prayuth Chan-Ocha decided to relax restrictions and allow the reopening of businesses and schools. On April 1,

Thailand reduced its 14-day quarantine to 10 days for travelers, but for travelers from nations with COVID variants of concern the 14-day quarantine period would remain in place. Following additional waves of COVID, the government imposed more restrictions to ensure the safety of individuals and avoid the spread of infections. Finally, on July 1, 2021, the Phuket "sandbox" scheme allowed for totally vaccinated tourists from low-to-medium risk nations to visit Thailand.

BPNG provides US dollar liquidity to the domestic FX interbank market in Papua New Guinea. However, the SoE urged Authorized Foreign Exchange Dealers to provide priority to medical and pharmaceutical companies, as well as retailers and wholesalers of medical products, particularly when importing materials related to COVID-19. BPNG provided additional foreign currency for these purposes.

In Kenya, the central government initially allocated Ksh40 billion (0.4% of GDP) as part of the FY2019/20 budget for costs associated with COVID-19, including the health sector (enhanced surveillance, laboratory services, isolation units, equipment, supplies, and communication); social protection (cash transfers and food relief); and funds for hastily paying existing debts to maintain businesses' cash flow during the crisis. For COVID-19-related costs in the fiscal year 2020/21, Ethiopian authorities.

Ethiopian authorities set aside about 30 billion birr (or 800 million), including the purchase of medical equipment, increased pay for health workers, food assistance for quarantines and isolation areas, and the acquisition of hygiene facilities, disinfectants, and personal protection equipment.

The majority of these funds were used in Ghana as part of the Coronavirus Alleviation Program to address the social and economic effects of the pandemic, including assistance for specific industries (such as the pharmaceutical sector, which provides COVID-19 drugs and equipment), assistance for SMEs, financing of guarantees and first-loss instruments, construction or renovation of 100 district and regional hospitals, and problems with the test kit, pharmaceutical, and equipment issues.

Chapter 18

Evidence on households during the COVID-19 crisis aftermath

Chapter outline

Abstract

This chapter focuses on the economic outcomes for households around the world outside the US during the COVID-19 crisis aftermath, including evidence on consumer demand and spending; credit cards; and mortgages, auto loans, and student loans. Individual nations have different findings, but problems of inflation and economic slowdowns adversely affecting household incomes and finances are common.

Keywords: COVID-19, Aftermath, Real economy, Households, Household debt and spending

18.1 Evidence on inflation and consumer spending during the aftermath

Canada has exhibited positive growth in median household income, continuing an increasing trend from 2018 to 2022. Conversely, consumer price index experienced a sharp decline in 2020, falling from about 2% in 2019 to less than 1% in 2020. This reduced inflation encouraged further consumer spending during the pandemic. In addition, households and businesses will receive nearly $290 billion (13.2% of GDP) in direct assistance, including salary subsidies, compensation to employees who cannot take time off for illness, and increased access to employment insurance.

The Brazilian median household income declined in 2020 and has since experienced a rise, while consumer price index plateaued from 2018 to 2019 started increasing at the end of 2020 and has continued to grow since. This has inhibited consumer spending due to the consistent rise in prices.

Mexico experienced a decrease in the median household income in 2020, although not a noteworthy reduction (down to about 18,000 in 2020 from about 22,000 in 2019). Inflation has been a major contributing factor to consumer price index. Consumer prices exhibited a growing percentage starting in 2020 and continuing into 2022.

The median household income in Chile decreased as well in 2020, although it quickly rebounded higher than prepandemic rates in 2021. Inflation experienced an upward trend through 2019–20, which

The Economic and Financial Impacts of the COVID-19 Crisis Around the World
https://doi.org/10.1016/B978-0-443-19162-6.00022-0
Copyright © 2024 Elsevier Inc. All rights reserved.

has continued and has significantly spiked from the end of 2021 to 2022. (For reference, the CPI was about 3% in 2020, 4% in 2021, and has spiked to just shy of 12% in 2022.)

In Peru, coupled with an extremely high rate of unemployment, other macroeconomic measures, such as the median household income, experienced worrying downtrends in 2020, down from almost $17,000 in 2019 to just above $14,500 in 2020. Conversely, the inflation rate had a slight decline from 2019 to 2020 but has since skyrocketed up from just shy of 2% in 2020 to approximately 8% in 2022. Aid was authorized by the government during the state of emergency. Three billion (or 0.5% of GDP) was allocated for the health emergency. Direct subsidies totaling $7 billion (1.1% of GDP) were made to help disadvantaged households. It was announced that poor households would receive an additional cash transfer of approximately S$6.4 billion in the late July (0.9% of GDP). In addition, new efforts worth around 0.2% of GDP were announced on May 26, 2021, which included increased health spending, household support, and temporary employment.

The Argentinian government navigated varying real-sector responses to the global pandemic. Regarding their median household income, they saw a decline in income of close to $5000 from 2019 to 2020. The consumer price index actually declined from 2019 to 2020; however, then began an upward trajectory of inflation into 2021 and 2022.

In Dominican Republic, prior administration's initial economic initiatives cost RD$32 billion (or $576 million USD, or 1/4 of GDP), or 34% of GDP, which includes the Quédate en Casa program (RD$17 billion) aimed at assisting the most vulnerable households, including those of unauthorized immigrants. Under this program, 452,817 families will receive extra transfers of RD$2000 (approximately US$36) per month. The number of homes covered by the present Comer es Primero program, which pays RD$5000 (about US$90) per month, has expanded from 0.8 to 1.5 million households.

Germany, following the COVID-19 crisis, has taken revenue compensation initiatives in order to protect its population from suffering a loss of income (of up to 75%). However, the increase of inflation in Germany has strongly increased the consumer prices growth (by about +8%) during the 2 years that followed 2020.

In France, the rise in inflation has significantly accelerated the increase in consumer prices growth during 2021 and 2022 (by around +6%). The typical household income has also changed considerably in the last few years. In Italy, increased family income assistance was among one of the actions taken in the aftermath of the COVID-19 crisis. However, the rise in Italian inflation has considerably increased the rise in consumer prices growth over the 2 years that followed 2020 (by around 7.5%).

Consumer price index has increased significantly in 2021 and again in 2022 (by about +8% compared to 2020) in the UK as well. However, the income of the median household was also higher in the years following 2020. Indeed, to help people and families during the pandemic, a number of tax and expenditure reforms have been implemented.

The pandemic in Spain has significantly impacted inflation, which in turn greatly accelerated the rise in consumer price index in 2021 and 2022 (by nearly +9.5% in 2022 compared to 2020). In addition, the median household income has decreased drastically in 2020. However, commitments have been made to support financially families in need with their living expenses.

In Switzerland, although the median household income has increased since the beginning of the crisis (compared to the years before the pandemic), the consumer prices growth has also raised significantly (about +3% from 2020 to 2022). However, in November 2020, tax deferrals by 1 year until March 2022 have been accepted. In Romania, inflation has pushed consumer price index as well. In 2021 and 2022 as well, the rate has only increased (leading to an increment of about +10.5% compared to 2020). However, the median household income has also risen in the years following the start of the pandemic. Indeed, the Romanian government made the decision to continue providing families with financial assistance in 2021.

Consumer price index increased only slightly in 2021 in Turkey, but then rose sharply in 2022 (with about +53% compared to the previous year). As for the median household income, it has been changing considerably since the beginning of the crisis, undergoing significant ups and downs.

In Saudi Arabia, the increase in inflation following 2019 has resulted in increases in the consumer prices growth (by around +5.5% from 2019 to 2020). Although the consumer prices growth rate has declined since 2020 (by around −1% from 2020 to 2022), it is still nowhere near what it was at prior to the pandemic. In the United Arab Emirates, the consumer prices growth rates were not significantly affected at the start of the pandemic as the rate only slightly declined (by around −0.25% from 2019 to 2020). However, as inflation increased following 2020, the consumer prices growth rate has increased (by around +7% from 2020 to 2022), where it is far above the rates from prior to the pandemic.

The consumer prices growth rates declined in Israel between 2019 and 2020 (by around −1.25%). However, as inflation increased following 2020, the consumer prices growth rate increased (by around +4%), which is at a rate much higher than it was prior to the pandemic.

In China as well, the consumer prices growth rates declined between 2019 and 2020 (by around −0.3%) and then again between 2020 and 2021 (by around −1.75%). However, as inflation increased following 2021, the consumer prices growth rate increased (by around +1.6%), which is a rate close to, but still below where it was prior to the pandemic.

Japan shows a similar trend to China, with consumer prices growth rates declining between 2019 and 2020 (by around −0.5%) and then further declining between 2020 and 2021 (by around −0.25%). Inflation increased following 2021, and the consumer price index rate increased (by around +1.75%), where it is now at a rate more than double what it was prior to the pandemic.

Consumer prices growth rate increased in India between 2019 and 2020 (by around +3.5%) and then declined between 2020 and 2021 (by around −1.5%). As there was a bit of an increase in inflation, the consumer price index rate increased from 2021 to 2022 (by around 1.7%).

In South Korea, the consumer price index rate slightly increased between 2019 and 2020 (by around +0.15%) and then as inflation increased so did the growth rate at a much higher rate between 2020 and 2021 (by around +2%). Furthermore, from 2021 to 2022 the consumer price index rate continued to grow (by around +3%) to a point over double what it was prior to the pandemic.

Consumer price index rate slightly declined in Russia between 2019 and 2020 (by around −1%) and then as inflation increased between 2020 and 2021 so did the growth rate (by around +3.5%). As inflation continued to increase from 2021 to 2022, the growth rate increased as well (by around +8.5%) to a point that is far higher than what it was prior to the pandemic.

In Indonesia, the consumer price index rate declined between 2019 and 2020 (by around −1%) and continued to decline between 2020 and 2021 (by around −0.5%). But as inflation began to increase, the growth rate increased as well from 2021 to 2022 (by around +3%) to a point that was nearly double where it was prior to the pandemic.

In the Philippines, the consumer price index rate increased slightly between 2019 and 2020 (by around +0.2%). From 2020, inflation began to increase along with the growth rate (by around +2%) and this increase continued from 2021 and 2022 (by around +0.5%) to a point that was above where it was prior to the pandemic.

The pandemic caused significant volatility in the real sectors of Australia. Although the real GDP growth and public debt significantly increased, inflation reached a low point (down from about 1.5% in 2019 to less than 1% in 2020), while the median household income increased by about $5000 from 2019 to 2020.

New Zealand has since experienced a gradual increase in inflation, reaching approximately 7% in 2022, up from its range of between 1% and 2% in 2020. Their median household income did not experience much volatility and slightly increased with the onset of the pandemic, and continued that trend into 2021.

All financial institutions in Papua New Guinea have agreed to provide customers who have lost their jobs a 3-month reprieve from loan repayments and interest payments on a case-by-case basis. In Egypt, pensions have increased by 14%. In order to assist entrepreneurs, loan repayments for small and medium-sized businesses and independent contractors in Morocco have been postponed until June 30.

18.2   Evidence on consumer credit cards during the aftermath

In the Dominican Republic, banks were allowed to cover reserve requirements with public and BCRD bonds up to RD$22.3 billion (roughly 12% of GDP), which is equivalent to a 2% reduction in the reserve requirement rate, to release RD$30.13 billion (US$553.7 million; roughly 2% of GDP) to the economy. This money will extend credit to people and businesses at a maximum interest rate of 8.0%. On April 16, 2020, the Monetary Board decreased the criteria for gaining access to these funds, enabling financial intermediaries to lend to any industry, and extending the loan maturity from 1 to 4 years. The BCRD has also provided funding for small company loans and microcredits for people.

The Financial Conduct Authority of the UK launched a set of temporary solutions for customers affected by the coronavirus by requiring firms to set a 3-month payment hold on loans and credit cards. The FCA also extended the period for requesting a payment deferral for consumer credit by 6 months, extending the mortgage moratorium's deadline from the end of November to the end of April.

In Thailand, to deal with household debt, the BOT worked with nine associations in Thailand (the Thai Bankers' Association, Association of International Banks, Government Financial Institutions Association, Thailand Leasing Association, Thai Hire-Purchase Association, Vehicle Title Loan Trade Association, Thai Motorcycle Hire-Purchase Association, Credit Card Club—The Thai Bankers' Association and the Personal Loan Club) to implement the following measures. The first was reductions to minimum credit card and revolving repayments from 10% to 5% in 2020 and 2021 and to 8% in 2022. The second was imposing a 3-month moratorium on personal (installment payments) and auto loans. The third was a temporary ban on for hire purchase or leasing of motorcycles and automobiles for 3 months on principal and interest or 6 months on principle. The fourth and final was to set up a 3-month temporary ban on principal repayments for housing, SME, and microfinance loans, while taking lower interest payments into consideration on a case-to-case basis.

18.3 Evidence on consumer mortgages, auto loans, and student loans during the aftermath

In 2020 and 2021, housing costs in Canada will increase quickly. To ensure homeowners do not borrow more than they can afford to pay back, OSFI implemented a "mortgage stress test." The minimum qualifying rate for uninsured mortgages will be 5.25% as of June 1, 2021, which is equal to the higher mortgage contract rate plus 2%. After that, qualified homeowners sign mortgage contracts at the lender's rate. Under the Insured Mortgage Purchase Program, the government will purchase up to $150 billion of insured mortgage pools through the Canada Mortgage and Housing Corporation (CMHC); $95 billion in credit facilities were announced by the federal government (including $13.8 billion in forgiven loans) to lend, and the Office of Superintendent of Financial Institutions (OSFI) reduced the Domestic Stability Buffer for D-SIBs from 2.25% to 1% of risk-weighted assets.

In Mexico, the government provided employees with mortgages via the Housing Institute with discounted unemployment insurance for 3 months (5.9 billion pesos). In addition, housing developments received increased funding (4 billion pesos). In Chile, the Financial Market Commission has proposed a series of regulations intended to make it simpler for people to get credit for their homes and enterprises. These regulations change how assets received as payment and margins in derivative transactions are considered, give delayed loans additional consideration when formulating provisions, use mortgage guarantees to protect SME loans, and revise the Basel III standards implementation schedule.

The central bank of Peru stated in December 2020 that it would provide long-term interest rate swaps and repos to assist banks in managing the risk of rising rates on long-term loans such as mortgages and business loans. The exchanges will require the central bank to pay a variable rate in return for a fixed rate, with maturities ranging from 3 to 7 years. The maturation of repos takes 1–3 years.

In Dominican Republic, the CBDR announced on November 25, 2020 that mortgage loans could be provided with the money made available by the RLF. On March 1, 2021, the CBDR stated that it would enhance the RLF by RD$25 billion, with the extra money going to specific sectors such as manufacturing, construction, mortgages for affordable housing, business, and SMEs.

Several of the measures implemented in Germany have been extended until the past 2021, given the circumstances. Grants, traineeship subsidies, governmental loan guarantees, and tax loss carryback are some examples of policies with increased access.

The UK government stated in March 2021 that purchasers of properties up to £600,000 in worth will be allowed to apply for a new mortgage guarantee program starting in April 2021 with just a 5% down payment. The government also said that the waiver from the stamp duty and land tax would last until June 2021.

In Spain, more alternatives for workers to access their pension savings have been made available. Furthermore, additional measures include a moratorium on nonmortgage loans and credits, such as consumer credit for the most vulnerable individuals.

India's central government prolonged a program that offered interest-free loans to states for capital expenditures through FY2021/22 (costing 150 billion rupees). In Russia, Parliament enacted a law that ensures that SMEs and affected citizens will be able to defer loan payments for up to 6 months.

In New Zealand, from May 1, 2020, the RBNZ lifted the temporary limitations on mortgage loan-to-value ratios (LVR). These limits were reinstated by the RBNZ in March 2021 at prepandemic levels, and the LVR restrictions for investors were further tightened starting in May 2021. Various financial initiatives have also been announced by the New Zealand government, the RBNZ, and the New Zealand Bankers Association to assist homeowners and SMEs. These include deferring principal and interest payments for mortgage holders and SMEs impacted by COVID-19 and the BFGS for 6 months. On March 31, 2021, the favorable regulatory treatment of loans with repayment deferrals ended.

On March 23, 2020, the South African government announced the start of a single plan that would permit banks to forgive debt for consumers. Due to the growing need for liquidity support in the banking system (both in DRH and in EUR/USD), Bank al-Maghrib in Morocco decided to implement a three-pronged strategy: expand the types of collateral accepted for repos and credit guarantees to include public and private debt instruments (including mortgages), lengthen and expand central bank refinancing operations to support banking credit to (V) SMEs, and offer FX swaps.

Chapter 19

Evidence on nonfinancial firms during the COVID-19 crisis aftermath

Chapter outline

Abstract

We turn attention in this chapter to the economic outcomes for nonfinancial firms in different nations around the world outside the US during the COVID-19 crisis aftermath. We include evidence on firm failures and performance, stockholders, and other stakeholders; and assess risk and dividend policy outcomes. Again, variation across countries, abounds, and significant inflation and economic slowdowns causing harm are frequent.

Keywords: COVID-19, Aftermath, Real economy, Nonfinancial firms, Failure, Stockholders, Dividends

19.1 Evidence on nonfinancial firm failures and performance during the aftermath

The Canadian government dedicated large percentages of funding toward supporting households and firms, including wage subsidies, widely available employment insurance, and more direct aid. In Colombia, measures were taken to support businesses and boost their performance. The government established a payroll subsidy equal to 50% of the minimum wage per worker for firms that saw a 3-month revenue decrease of over 20%. The government budget for 2021 includes steps to boost the economy, such as increased infrastructure spending and extensions of assistance programs for individuals and enterprises. Emergency funds from 2020 that are still available can be used in 2021. For the reopening of industries, the Colombian government has enacted conservative policies. Construction and manufacturing sectors were able to resume operations on April 27, and a more comprehensive range of industrial and business services sectors was able to do the same on May 11. Some services, including a few retail segments, were allowed to resume on June 01 despite municipal governments (including Bogota) taking their time to relax restrictions.

In Peru, many measures were adopted by the government to facilitate the continued growth of businesses in the country and to ease complicated financing issues that impede performance. The government is allowing consumers and businesses flexibility in how they repay their tax arrears and

The Economic and Financial Impacts of the COVID-19 Crisis Around the World
https://doi.org/10.1016/B978-0-443-19162-6.00033-5
Copyright © 2024 Elsevier Inc. All rights reserved.

has granted SMEs a 3-month extension for filing income tax declarations. These tax measures are expected to provide temporary support in the range of 2.0% of GDP. The government also authorized the creation of an S$800 million (or 0.1% of GDP) fund to help qualified SMEs access operational capital and debt refinancing, as well as plans to expand the program to cover around 0.5% of GDP. In addition, it has decreased reserve requirements and, through repo operations, injected liquidity into financial markets (Reactive Peru). According to a notice from the bank regulatory body, financial institutions are permitted to adjust the terms of their loans to individuals and companies affected by the COVID-19 outbreaks without changing the loans' classification. The central bank stated on December 2020 that it would provide long-term interest rate swaps and repos in order to assist banks in managing the risk of rising rates on long-term loans such as mortgages and business loans.

The administration presiding over the Dominican Republic made facilitating business performance a priority during the pandemic. On March 16, 2020, the Monetary Council of the Central Bank of the Dominican Republic (BCRD) loosened its stance on policy and took steps to boost liquidity and aid the economy. On April 16, 2020, the Monetary Board decreased the criteria for getting access to more money, letting financial intermediaries lend to any industry, and increasing the loan length from 1 to 4 years. The BCRD has also provided funding for small company loans and microcredits for people.

In order to sustain the performance of businesses, the German government proceeded to expand the number of public guarantees for firms and nonprofit organizations. The newly created Economic Stabilization Fund (WSF) and the public development bank KfW allocated funds for public equity injection into businesses that were important. Moreover, to help firms in need, the German government expanded already-existing fiscal provisions.

In France, a fiscal package introduced in September 2020 intended to help with the recovery of the French economy was also integrated into the 2021 budget to ensure that firms in France could remain in business. The reconstruction plan strongly emphasizes transforming the economy to be more sustainable, enhancing the competitiveness of French businesses, and promoting social and territorial solidarity. It includes several initiatives, many of which were backed by grants from the EU Recovery Fund.

Grants to SMEs and the self-employed have been deployed in Italy to help firms maintain a certain level of productivity. The government has also raised the waivers for social contributions for the affected businesses. Furthermore, in order to continue helping firms, it also decided to include further support packages. A few of the financing initiatives Italy has implemented are the SME Capital Strengthening Scheme, the Relaunch Fund, the Fund for Start-ups and Innovative SMEs, and the National Tourism Fund. The "Rilancio" regulation provided for a fund for corporate restructuring and targeted historical and strategic firms of importance to the country, as well as businesses that have power over important networks or resources.

In the UK, several measures have been taken to maintain company performance. In order to promote easier access to financing for firms, the government launched three separate loan programs. The British Business Bank provided both the Coronavirus Large Business Interruption Loans Scheme and the Coronavirus Small Business Interruption Loans Scheme. The Bounce Back credit program for SMEs was additionally introduced by the government. VAT payments will be extended until March 2021. An additional 3 months of the self-employment program were added, though at a lesser level of 70% of income. The Trade Credit Reinsurance Plan, which provided government guarantees for trade credit insurance for business-to-business transactions up to £10 billion, was in effect for 9 months during this time. Furthermore, the government established a program to support firms to increase innovation and growth through grants and loans. Other measures announced in September 2020 include the extension of the application deadline for loans under the CBILS, CLBILS, and BBLS to the end of November, and extending the maximum duration of CBILS and BBL loans to 10 years. In addition, self-employed people may be eligible for grants of up to £3750, or 40% of their earnings. Moreover, the UK government introduced a new set of policies in November, extending the CJRS until the end of March 2021, increasing the grant of the SEISS, and extending the deadline for applications for loans with government guarantees until the end of January 2021. Then, in December, the government stated that it would extend the corporate support program through April 2021. Furthermore, the UK government announced a new financial aid program for struggling firms, following the implementation of the toughest COVID-19 restriction in January 2021, and an additional financial injection in March 2021. This is segmented into new initiatives to accelerate the recovery process as well as additional disease support measure expense for the year 2021. In order to encourage the future investment to be brought forward to the following years, additional funding was made available in the form of firm grants, and discounted business rates were maintained till the end of the year. This was backed by a substantial tax deduction for firms. Future tax increases would mostly take the form of a 6-percentage point corporate tax rise in 2023 and a lock on income tax thresholds.

In Spain, support for businesses, direct assistance with firm solvency, and a special benefit for self-employed workers who were negatively impacted by economic activity were some of the important measures taken to maintain the productivity of firms. Additional initiatives included delaying tax payments for small and medium-sized firms and the self-employed, extending the deadlines for filing tax returns, granting flexibility to SMEs and the self-employed in assessing their income tax and VAT installment payments, temporarily increasing the tax reductions available under the module system for income tax and VAT, lowering the contribution required of salaried farm laborers, and eliminating the late payment penalty for corporate tax obligations for firms obtaining financing from the Instituto de Crédito Oficial Guarantee Lines. The Spanish government has also given businesses and entrepreneurs government guarantees covering investments, liquidity, loans, and commercial paper issued by medium-sized firms that participate in Spain's Alternative Fixed Income Market. In addition, a state rescue fund was established to assist strategic companies, and a capitalization fund for medium-sized firms was generated. Through the Compañía Española de Reafianzamiento, additional loan guarantees were provided to SMEs and self-employed workers. Additional initiatives included raising funding for the ICO credit lines, providing security for financing operations carried out by the European Investment Bank, supporting the European SURE instrument, and providing loans to the industrial sector to assist in digital transformation and modernization.

To boost business performance in the Netherlands, the Dutch government intended to promote staff relocation to growing sectors. Public funding has been allocated for job transition platforms, career counseling, reskilling, and training. In addition, tax incentives were introduced to promote private investment.

In Switzerland, several measures have been undertaken. The incentive program "Innovation Switzerland" was presented in a package that was publicly disclosed in November. It was created to assist firms and preserve their capacity for innovation throughout the crisis. Later, the FC introduced billions in new federal fiscal support measures. In May, the FC made adjustments to ensure that, should the crisis persist longer than expected, the necessary policy support would not be suddenly interrupted.

With regard to the measures taken in Sweden to keep companies running, the government proposed prolonging the state credit guarantee scheme for loans to firms in December until the late June 2021.

In order to help firms, the Romanian government chose to maintain fiscal assistance measures in 2021, and delayed potential tax payments rescheduling. The total amount of government loan guarantees was also increased. However, it can be observed that the number of loans, as well as deposits, decreased significantly after the beginning of the pandemic.

In Turkey, in May and June 2021, loan postponements for farmers, a grant program for small businesses and tradespeople, a lending initiative for SMEs supported by the Credit Guarantee Fund, and an increase in bonus pensions were all introduced to limit firm failures.

The Australian government released many policies pertaining to the success of firms, the economy, and health in March 2020, totaling A$217.1 billion (11% of GDP) through FY2024. The initial round of stimulus measures announced on March 12, totaled A$17.6 billion and included a one-time stimulus payment to welfare recipients, accelerated depreciation deductions, an expansion of the applicable eligibility criteria for instant asset write-offs, cash flow assistance for businesses, and financial support (including tax and fee waivers) to industries, geographic areas, and communities that were disproportionately affected by the pandemic. The Coronavirus Supplement, a top-up payment to JobSeeker unemployment benefits and welfare users, as well as further economic support for people and businesses, were included in a second rescue package worth A$66 billion that was unveiled on March 22. The RBA also initiated yield targeting on 3-year government bonds through purchases made in the secondary market, with the target rate set at the overnight fund's rate. The RBA conducted longer-term repos and increased the range of securities that qualified as appropriate collateral for open market operations to include investment-grade securities issued by nonbank entities in order to sustain market liquidity during the early stages of the outbreak.

New Zealand's government implemented several measures in order to maintain positive firm performance. The government has sanctioned a NZ$1.5 billion debt financing agreement (convertible to equity) with Air New Zealand in order to continue freight operations, domestic flights, and a limited number of international flights. The New Zealand government has started a NZ$0.2 billion short-term R&D loan scheme to promote private sector R&D investment. In addition, through the end of 2023, the New Zealand government will lend small businesses with 50 or fewer employees up to NZ$100,000.

19.2 Evidence on nonfinancial firm stockholders and other stakeholders during the aftermath

The Brazilian business confidence index experienced a dramatic low (down to approximately 30% in 2020 from 60% at the beginning of 2020) midway through 2020 and then began a steady increase back up to over 60% at the end of the year.

Argentinian businesses were highly pessimistic about the future performance in 2020. The BCI was negative for almost all of 2020, hitting a low of close to −40%. As the aftereffects of the pandemic eased and the economy began growing again, confidence grew in 2021, hitting a high at approximately 60%. However, the index has recently experienced low levels of trust in 2022, wavering around 10%–15%.

Regarding Chile's real sector growth, there was a great deal of volatility between indices during the pandemic. The Business Confidence Index exhibited lower numbers than usual in 2020, hitting a low at approximately 32%, although this has since rebounded.

Peru's Business Confidence Index indicates a decrease in confidence only for a short period of time in 2020, which quickly grew back to prepandemic levels in the late 2020 and early 2021 (the jump down occurred about midway through 2020, going from a high of a little over 50% to a low of approximately 10%). Mexican firms experienced a decrease in confidence for the future growth midway through 2020, going from approximately 44% to about 35%.

In Japan, on January 13, 2021, the "Business and Residence Tracks" which limited business exchanges and activities between nations close to Japan were suspended until cases declined. In India, adjustments toward foreign direct investment policy were made, where it was required for government approval in order for an organization from a country sharing a land border with India to invest.

In Indonesia, to ensure orderly market conditions, the Bank of Indonesia interfered in the spot and domestic nondeliverable foreign exchange markets as well as the domestic government bond market. According to the BI, global investors are able to utilize both global and domestic custodian banks to complete investment transactions in Indonesia. In addition, Indonesian stimulus packages included steps to relax import and export restrictions in an effort to lessen the virus' impact on the global supply chain.

Australian firms were highly pessimistic about the future growth in 2020, demonstrated by the significantly negative BCI, with a low of about −63% in 2020. In New Zealand, firms have exhibited large pessimism through the BCI since 2019, illustrated by a negative BCI. In 2020, New Zealand's BCI fell further at one point in the year and then rose slightly to reflect past trends of the index. In the early 2021, there were instances of positive confidence, but only for a short time, hitting a high at approximately 10%.

Additional steps were taken in Nigeria, such as a 1-year suspension of CBN intervention facilities, a drop in interest rates from 9% to 5% for all applicable CBN interventions, the creation of a N50 billion ($139 million) targeted credit facility, and a liquidity injection of N3.6 trillion (2.4% of GDP) into the banking system, with N100 billion going to support the health sector and N2 trillion going to the manufacturing sector. Due to the deterioration of the worldwide demand, Egypt's exports and Suez Canal revenues both decreased. In the USD 6.13 billion package, the government announced stimulus measures to mitigate the impact of COVID-19 on the economy (EGP 100 billion, 1.8% of GDP).

19.3 Evidence on other nonfinancial firm risk and financial needs during the aftermath

The Mexican Central Bank implemented many policies postpandemic to enhance liquidity. In addition, the CNBV and the National Insurance and Surety Commission (CNSF) cautioned banks and insurance firms from paying dividends, carrying out share buybacks, or taking other actions linked to shareholder compensation.

The central bank of Peru stated on December 2020 that it would provide long-term interest rate swaps and repos to assist banks in managing the risk of rising rates on long-term loans such as mortgages and business loans. The trades will require the central bank to pay a variable rate in return for a fixed rate, with maturities ranging from 3 to 7 years.

In Ecuador, the government decreased banks' contribution rate to the Liquidity Fund by 3 percentage points of deposits (to 5%) to solve the liquidity crisis in the financial system, releasing around $950 million in liquid assets. While the demand for cash also eventually decreased, this action helped rebalance internal liquidity. In addition, the Ecuadorian government mandated the adjustment of interest rate caps, launched a working capital facility (Reactivate Ecuador) for businesses receiving the World Bank financing, and introduced an unusual voluntary deferral of private loan commitments, which should strengthen the real economy. Still, supposing that the deferrals are kept in place for a long time, they could weaken the financial institutions' balance sheets and pose risks to the financial system, mainly as the economy transitions from the emergency period into the postemergency one.

In Germany, to reduce risks for firms, the requirement for severely indebted or fragile ones to file for insolvency was temporarily postponed, from March 2020 to late April 2021. In Italy, in order to lessen risk, CONSOB agreed to preserve the lower threshold at which it was essential to declare ownership of a listed firm through October 2020.

The Institute for the Diversification and Saving of Energy has delayed payments on some loans made to businesses in Spain. In addition, the government has granted approval to evaluate FDI in strategic sectors, given the Consorcio de Compensación de Seguros permission to act as a reinsurer of credit insurance risks, and made momentary changes to corporate resolution frameworks in a perspective to reduce the amount of financial imbalances.

In the Netherlands, a law was adopted in October 2020 to make debt restructuring simpler for firms with financial problems in order to reduce risk. The policy's objective would be to prevent bankruptcy. Moreover, small and medium-sized firms were given a 6-month extension on loan repayment by the largest Dutch banks.

In an attempt to aid viable businesses that suffered large losses as a result of the pandemic, the Federal Council and cantonal governments in Switzerland jointly declared the ratification of the COVID-19 Hardship Assistance Ordinance in November. In addition, FC extended the due date for SE income loss reimbursement to June 2021. In December, the FC proposed raising the program's total budget and requested more flexibility from the Parliament when assessing who was eligible for hardship support. Updates to the hardship ordinance were made by the FC in December, letting qualified businesses to receive double subsidies, lowering the level of income loss required to qualify for compensation for self-employed people, boosting aid for the cultural sector, and further loosening the rules for the short-term work plan. The FC also upped the maximum amount of support that a firm may get and modified the eligibility criteria and conditions for the program's hardship aid. The FC once more changed its guidelines in order to extend and expand the short-term work plan's coverage. Then, in February, the FC announced that the hardship aid program will expand, with several billion set aside to help larger corporations that were previously unprotected by the program. The FC also contributed several million to make up for the income losses suffered by self-employed people.

In Turkey, to limit the risks and assist with trade financing, the processes of debt repayment and bankruptcy were temporarily put on hold and a new Turkish Lira loan instrument for SMEs in the export sector was created.

The historic JobKeeper pay subsidy program in Australia, worth A$130 billion, was revealed on March 30 to help Australians stay in their jobs. Other measures include setting aside up to A$15 billion for investments in asset-backed securities to help finance small banks and nonbank financial institutions and A$20 billion for loan guarantees between the Commonwealth government and participating banks to meet the short-term cash flow needs of SMEs. The RBA conducted long-term repos and increased the range of securities that qualified as appropriate collateral for open market operations to include investment-grade securities issued by nonbank entities to sustain market liquidity during the early stages of the outbreak. The APRA also postponed issuing new licenses in response to the considerable economic risks. Dividend payment caps were implemented for banks and insurers in April 2020 to boost capital buffers. Later, in July, these limitations were relaxed, and starting in January 2021, they were eliminated.

In New Zealand, the RNBZ and the banks also agreed that no dividends on ordinary shares or redemption of non-CET1 capital instruments would be accrued after April 2020. On March 31, 2021, the RBNZ relaxed the restrictions, allowing banks to pay shareholders up to 50% of their profits as dividends until July 01, 2022, when they intend to be repealed.

Nigeria's business confidence index fell to −66.2 in the middle of 2020, and this downward trend in the index will persist. The business confidence index in Kenya was largely normal and consistently resides in the 50 range with the exception of a brief time in 2020.

The business confidence index in Ghana briefly went negative in 2020, spiked in the middle of 2021, and then fell down to normal levels in 2022. In Morocco, the business confidence index dropped to about −21.4 in 2020 before rising sharply to values above those before to the epidemic in the middle of 2021.

In South Africa, the business confidence index dropped to about 5 in 2020 before rapidly rising to about 44, which is above prepandemic levels. In Egypt, the business confidence index dropped in 2020, but it quickly recovered and returned to normal levels shortly after.

Chapter 20

Evidence on banks during the COVID-19 crisis aftermath

Chapter outline

Abstract

This chapter shifts to banking sector aftermath, focusing primarily outside the US. We provide evidence on lending and relationships; bank profitability; and bank risk. Banks set aside reserves for expected loan losses from anticipated or actual second COVID-19-related recessions, which may harm future lending. The entire set of problems for banks during the aftermath, whatever they turn out to be, will likely pale in comparison to the losses already incurred during 2022 by Decentralized Finance (Defi) firms, such as Digital Technology Financial Firms (DTFFs) and others that invest in new financial instruments, such as NFTs, SPACs, and cryptocurrencies that already failed in many cases, as discussed in earlier chapters.

Keywords: COVID-19, Aftermath, Banks, Lending, Relationships, Bank profitability, Bank risk

20.1 Evidence on bank lending during the aftermath

Canada experienced a sharp decline in loans and deposits due to the pandemic. However, they are recovering gradually. Risk-weighted assets dropped close to 50% in 2020 in terms of asset quality; problem loans increased sharply across the board. The Canadian government ensured the preservation of positive lending relationships through the pandemic. Under the Insured Mortgage Purchase Program, the government will purchase up to $150 billion of insured mortgage pools through the Canada Mortgage and Housing Corporation (CMHC); $95 billion in credit facilities were announced by the federal government (including $13.8 billion in forgiven loans) to lend, and the Office of Superintendent of Financial Institutions (OSFI) reduced the Domestic Stability Buffer for D-SIBs from 2.25% to 1% of risk-weighted assets. Farm Credit Canada will also receive funds from the federal government, increasing its ability to lend growers, agribusinesses, and food processors an additional $5.2 billion. In addition, OSFI announced on June 17, 2021, that as of October 31, 2021, the Domestic Stability Buffer would increase from its existing percentage of 1%–2.5% of all risk-weighted assets. The government also announced the creation of the Standing Term Liquidity Facility, which would allow for the granting of loans to accredited financial institutions in need of immediate liquidity.

The Economic and Financial Impacts of the COVID-19 Crisis Around the World
https://doi.org/10.1016/B978-0-443-19162-6.00019-0
Copyright © 2024 Elsevier Inc. All rights reserved.

The pandemic significantly affected the minimum amount banks were required to hold in Mexico, as seen by the decrease in risk-weighted assets of approximately 5%. Problem loans and their metrics increased as well. Loans significantly decreased from 2019 to 2020 by over 6%. Additionally, deposits decreased by about 3%.

In the Dominican Republic, on August 22, the BCRD announced that the criteria for joining the RLF would be considerably loosened to allow for the refinancing of loans for houses and enterprises of any size.

Guatemala implemented policies to maintain positive liquidity and lending regulations. Banco de Guatemala lowered its policy rate to a historic low of 1.75% in June 2020. A year later, the board reiterated its position to maintain its pace at 1.75. The Monetary Board relaxed lending regulations in April 2020 to allow debt restructuring for debtors who were temporarily experiencing a lack of liquidity. The easing measures were phased down gradually starting in January, and as of May statistics, the banking system is still stable. Banco de Guatemala purchased GTM Treasury Bonds for GTQ 10.6 billion with special permission from Congress (about USD 1.5 billion, 96.8% of the total bond issuance authorized by Congress). Last year, the government used the funds to fund COVID-19 emergency programs.

The Chilean banking sector saw a significant decrease in risk-weighted assets from 2019 to 2020 (approximately 10%). Problem loans increased by almost $2 M in 2020, as well as the asset quality metrics of problem loans/gross customer loans and problem loans/risk-weighted assets. Regarding loans and deposits, there was an approximate decrease in loans of 6% and a decrease in deposits by about 2%.

Peru saw its bank capital metrics stay consistent through the pandemic, except for risk-weighted assets, which dropped significantly from 2019 to 2020 (by about 12%). Asset quality metrics show that problem loans increased by approximately $1 M, and lending was negatively impacted by the pandemic, demonstrated by the decrease in loans by about 6% from 2019 to 2020. Conversely, deposits increased by about 4% from 2019 to 2020.

While there were profitability issues in the banking sector in Brazil due to the pandemic, problem loans did decrease in 2020. Loan loss reserves/gross loans continued an almost constant straight-on trend and then an initial gradual decline beginning toward the end of 2020. Additionally, loans decreased slightly from 2019 to 2020 while deposits/assets continued increasing.

Argentina's banking sector saw an increase in risk-weighted assets in 2020. There were also multiple changes in asset quality due to the pandemic, including a decrease in problem loans, gross customer loans, and problem loans/risk-weighted assets. The loan loss reserves/gross loans percentage also increased from prepandemic levels. Loans decreased by approximately 7% from 2019 to 2020, while deposits increased (around 15% in 2019 to about 33% in 2020). Regulations that limit banks' holdings of central bank paper to free up capital for SME lending, lower reserve requirements for bank lending to households and SMEs, a temporary relaxation of bank provisioning requirements and bank loan classification rules (i.e., an extension of the 60-day nonperforming loan definition), and a moratorium on both bank account closures caused by bounced checks and credit denial to businesses are all steps that have been performed to encourage bank lending.

In Germany, the loan and deposit rates dropped significantly in 2020. However, it can be noted that from 2021 onward, the latter has risen again. Furthermore, it has been mandated for German banks that were subject to national oversight and under ECB guidelines to suspend dividend payments, share repurchases, and bonus payments until December 2020.

Meanwhile in France, while loans have significantly decreased following the health crisis, there has been no impact on deposits (on the contrary, they have increased significantly between 2020 and 2021). In Italy, loans fell significantly as a result of the pandemic, and deposits fell in 2020 as well but increased rapidly and significantly in 2021.

In the UK, the health crisis has had some impact on loans, which have fallen sharply in 2020 and 2021. On the contrary, deposits have increased since the beginning of the pandemic. The UK has implemented various initiatives alongside these trends such as the deployment of the combined HM Treasury-Bank of England COVID-19 Corporate Financing Facility and the three government loan guarantee programs substituted with the Recovery Loan Scheme beginning in April 2021.

The Dutch central bank has reduced the systemic buffer standards for the three largest banks in the Netherlands in order to promote bank lending. In Switzerland, the pandemic has led to a decrease in the number of loans. However, between 2020 and 2021, the number of deposits has risen sharply (approximately +2%).

Sweden's new lending facility would permit monetary policy contracting parties to borrow an unlimited amount with a maturity of 3 and 6 months at an interest rate that is equivalent to the repo rate of Sweden's Riksbank. Reducing the lending rate for overnight loans, lending up to SEK 500 billion to firms via banks, developing a swap facility between the Riksbank and the US Federal Reserve, and permitting banks to borrow up to USD 60 billion against collateral until late September 2021 are all important monetary measures.

In Romania, as a result of the crisis, loans dropped significantly. Deposits have also followed a similar path with a decrease between 2020 and 2021. In Turkey, as a result of the crisis, loans have decreased over the years, while deposits have increased.

Between April and September 2020, the Central Bank of Iran decreased its reserve requirements for commercial banks in order to achieve the goal of boosting lending between people and businesses impacted by the pandemic. As well, in September 2020, the Central Bank of Iran to ensure the stability of the stock market started setting aside 1% of the nation's sovereign wealth fund.

In Saudi Arabia during the pandemic, the Saudi Central Bank (SAMA), took multiple monetary measures, but by the end of December 2020, SAMA's Loan Guarantee Program can to a close. Additionally, extensions were put in place for the Deferred Payments Program till the end of September 2021 and for the Guaranteed Facility Program till March 14, 2022. In the United Arab Emirates, the Central Bank of the UAE (CBUAE) initiated a package of measures for monetary support called the Targeted Economic Support Scheme (TESS). During the pandemic, the UAE needed further monetary support which resulted in the TESS being extended twice, once in November 2020 till the end of June 2021 and then a second time in April 2021 till the end of June 2022. As well, financing provided by the CBUAE under the TESS for loan deferrals was extended until the end of 2021.

The Bank of Israel conducted currency swaps of up to USD 15 billion to supply extra USD liquidity during the pandemic, and during the course of 2021, planned on purchasing 30 billion in USD.

In China, the exchange rate has been able to adjust flexibly following the pandemic. For the daily trading band's central parity formation, the countercyclical adjustment factor had been phased out and the reserve removed the requirement on FX forward. The raised ceiling on cross-border financing for financial institutions was reduced to normal in December and for enterprises, it was reduced to normal in January 2021. However, in January, the macroprudential adjustment coefficient for overseas lending via domestic enterprises grew by two-thirds and resulted in a higher ceiling. A fresh quota on domestic institutional investors was established, while restrictions on foreign institutional investors were lifted. On June 15, a raised percentage from 5 to 7 was put into place for the FX reserve requirement ratio for financial institutions.

The exchange rate was able to adjust flexibly following the pandemic in Japan as well. In India following the initial phase of the pandemic, the Reserve Bank of India (RBI) on January 8, 2021, announced the gradual resumption of operations under the updated framework for liquidity management, including the variable rate reverse repo auction. Later in February 2021, there was an extension of cash reserve requirement reductions against the loans of micro, small, and medium enterprises (MSME) for banks until December 2021. Following suit, the RBI on May 4 unveiled measures to provide relief toward easing liquidity and financing conditions, including special Long-Term Repo Operations (SLTRO) for small finance banks and on-tap liquidity assistance to COVID-associated healthcare infrastructure and services. The reintroduction of plans for COVID-related stressed retail and MSME loans allowed for lenders, until the end of September 2021, to invoke restructuring of loans. Also, lenders were able to extend moratoriums on repayments or the loan tenors for at most 2 years for all loans changed during the past resolution plan. Additionally, banks have enabled the use of countercyclical provisional buffers for creating particular provisions for nonperforming loans until the end of March 2022. Lastly, by late May, the RBI had expanded its timeline set in place for compliance with the payment system requirements and the Emergency Credit Line Guarantee Scheme (ECLGS) until September 30, 2021. On top of that, the restrictions on Central Government issued securities on non-resident investment were lifted.

The President of South Korea, Moon Jae-in, on March 24, unveiled a KRW 100 trillion (5.3% of GDP) stabilization plan. This plan would increase lending of state-owned and commercial banks to SMEs, small merchants, mid-sized firms, and large companies, establishing bond market stabilization for purchasing corporate and financial bonds and commercial paper, and financing through public institutions for issuing corporate bond collateralized bond obligation and the purchase of direct bonds. Additionally, this plan would assist short-term money market financing associated with stock finance loans, Bank of Korea (BOK) repo purchases, refinancing support conducted by public financial institutions, and the establishment of a fund for equity market stabilization that would be financed by leading and holding financial companies. A month later, on April 22, further measures were unveiled worth KRW 25 trillion (1.3% of GDP) for the creation of vehicles for purchasing corporate bonds and commercial paper, further funds for SME lending, and financial support to exporters and specific industries. The financial support to exporters improved the package announced on April 8th for the easing of financial constraints. On top of this, measures for, BOK lending programs to nonbanks containing corporate bonds as collateral, the expansion of BOK repo operation to nonbanks, temporary bans on stock short-selling in equity markets, a short-term easement on repurchasing shares, and the temporary easement of loan-to-deposit ratios for banks and other financial institutions and the domestic currency liquidity coverage ratio for banks were put in place to maintain financial market stability. Furthermore, The BOK made efforts to facilitate funding in foreign exchange by establishing a facility where banks and nonbank financial institutions can engage in repos where they can obtain foreign exchange from the BOK during periods warranted by certain market conditions.

In Russia, during the first half of 2021, the Deposit Insurance Fund reduced its contribution from 0.15% to 0.1%. At the same time, the Central Bank of Russia (CBR) set up measures to relax regulations on liquidity for systemically influential credit institutions and to safeguard retail borrowers who were afflicted by the pandemic. The CBR advised banks to use the same strategy for restructuring retail loans as required by law (fast approval or rejection, restructuring from the application date, no penalties during the consideration period). CBR recommended banks keep restructuring loans to affected SME and retail borrowers until July 1, 2021. Several other measures were taken to provide aid to financial markets such as the ensuring of services of nonbank financing institutions, the promotion of remote customer services, and measures in the region of AML/CFT and currency control.

In February 2021, Bank Indonesia (BI) lowered its policy rate by 25 bps. By 2021, only the buyer-of-last-resort arrangement was left in action. Through repo deals and purchasing government bonds owned by deposit insurance agency (LPS), BI has also been financing LPS. As part of its efforts to increase financial deepening, access to financial services, and monetary operations, BI has introduced Sharia-compliant financial instruments and promoted cooperation between the baking sector and FinTech firms. Furthermore, in order to promote loan restructuring, OJK has also loosened bank loan classification and restructuring procedures. Additionally, the time for publicly traded companies to produce shareholder meetings has been extended by 2 months. They have postponed, for 6 months, the implementation of mark-to-market valuation of government and other securities, loosened the requirements for meeting the Liquidity Coverage Ratio and Net Stable Funding Ratio standards, and permitted the use of the Capital Conservation Buffer.

In Thailand, the Bank of Thailand (BOT) made available up to THB 500 billion to financial institutions through the end of 2021 for on-lending to SMEs, especially in tourism and related industries, at a rate of 2% annually. The interest on these loans is insured by the government for the first 6 months and is guaranteed for 2 years. Thereafter, the loans can be extended for up to another 8 years but would have a 1.75% per year fee. Instead of using these loans, other businesses would utilize existing credit programs for SMEs that would make the most of the funds set aside by the BOT. Between January 1, 2020, and December 31, 2021, the BOT loosened rules pertaining to the classification of borrowers and levels of loan loss provisions in order to promote debt restructuring by financial institutions. The changes enabled borrowers who have felt the impacts of COVID-19 to immediately be classified as normal so long as they could make repayments accordingly with a debt restructuring agreement regardless of if they were already classified as NPL. Also, the BOT had a Corporate Bond Stabilization Fund (BSF) created to aid in bridge financing of up to THB 400 billion by December 31, 2021, with high-quality firms holding bonds that mature during 2021, but at "penalty" rates higher-than-market. However, as of now, this BSF has not had any takers. In the FX market, the BOT provided some liquidity to prevent disorderly market conditions and allow adjustments to the exchange rate.

The Philippine government on February 2021 passed the Financial Institutions Strategic Transfer (FIST) Act in order to allow financial institutions to facilitate the sale of nonperforming assets, to strengthen the institutions' balance sheets, and increase the capacity for lending.

The Australian banking sector saw a decrease in risk-weighted assets of about 1.3%, while problem loans increased by approximately $7 M. Lending decreased, as shown by the decrease in loans of around 1.6%, and deposits increased by about 2%. (All comparisons are between 2019 and 2020.)

In New Zealand, the banking sector saw an almost consistent value of risk-weighted assets from 2018 to 2020, as well as the ratios for bank capital. The asset quality metrics show a significant increase in problem loans from 2019 to 2020 (from approximately 2300 to 3000). In terms of loans and deposits, the ratio of loans to assets decreased from about 82.5% in 2019 to 81% in 2020. Conversely, deposits increased from 2019 to 2020 (by about 3.5%). Term Lending Facility (TLF), a longer-term funding program for banks at 0.25% for up to 3 years, initially for 6 months starting on May 26, 2020, was also announced by the RBNZ. The TLF's facility was extended to February 1, 2021, and the TLF's credit term was increased to 5 years in August 2020. The TLF was extended later, this time until July 28, 2021. Access to the TLF is contingent upon each bank making loans under the Business Finance Guarantee Scheme (BFGS), a $6.25 billion initiative in which the government assumes 80% of the credit risk in exchange for certified suitable collateral. In August 2020, the BFGS was enlarged to provide more medium-sized businesses with access to loans by raising the maximum loan amount from NZ$0.5 million to NZ$5 million and lengthening the maximum duration from 3 to 5 years. In order to encourage interbank activity, BPNG increased the margin on central bank borrowing in Papa New Guinea by 25 basis points to 100 basis points on both sides of KFR.

The number of repo auctions was increased to two in South Africa in order to help clear banks with intraday liquidity at the policy rate. Additionally, the upper and lower limits of the standing facility to lend at the repo rate and borrow at 200 basis points below the repo rate were lowered, and the size of the main weekly refinancing operations was increased as needed. For cooperative financial institutions, the South African Reserve Bank on May 12, 2020, issued a series of prudential priority measures on prudential considerations, supervisory actions, and governance and operational difficulties.

On March 24, Kenya's central bank announced flexibility to banks regarding loan classification and provisioning for loans that were performing on March 2, 2020, but were restructured due to the pandemic. The maximum term of repurchase agreements was also increased from 28 to 91 days in that country. In Kenya, the central bank has also pushed banks to make loan terms more flexible for borrowers based on pandemic-related circumstances and supported the waiving or lowering of transaction fees for mobile money in an effort to discourage the use of cash.

In Ethiopia, the central bank provided private banks with 15 billion birr (0.45% of GDP) in additional liquidity to help with debt restructuring and prevent bankruptcy. Additionally, the daily balance cap was raised from US$2170 to US$4340, and the daily transaction cap for mobile money providers was raised from US$1300 to US$2170.

The BCEAO in Côte d'Ivoire also established a framework that invites banks and microfinance institutions to accommodate requests from solvent customers with COVID-19-related repayment difficulties to postpone for a 3-month renewable period up to the end of 2020 debt service becoming due, without having to classify such postponed claims as nonperformable.

20.2 Evidence on bank profitability during the aftermath

Regarding banking profitability in Canada, the metrics available demonstrate the significant impact the pandemic had on the sector. Due to the ROAA decline, the bank's efficiency in generating profit from its assets declined. Canada saw an almost 20% decline in ROAA in 2020. The pandemic caused a large increase in total assets in Mexico, while the returns on these assets decreased from about 1.90% in 2019 to 1.20% in 2020 (ROAA decrease percentages).

Brazilian banks suffered large negative impacts from the onset of the pandemic. The profitability metrics indicate that profitability took a large hit in 2020, including a sharp decline in ROAA and total assets. The Chilean banking sector also suffered from a significant decrease in profitability due to the pandemic. ROAA decreased by approximately 50% while total assets increased by about $60 M. In

Argentina, the number of assets in the banking sector increased while their returns decreased (shown by the decrease in ROAA from about 2.50% in 2019 to about 2.00% in 2020), indicating a large decline in profitability in the banking sector from 2019 to 2020. Peru's banking sector saw a significant decrease in ROAA as well (from approximately 2.25% in 2019 to 0.50% in 2020) and saw total assets increase by about $20 M.

Meanwhile, the profitability of the banking sector in Germany has not been significantly impacted by the crisis. In fact, in 2020, an increase in total assets compared to the years before the health crisis and a strong increase in the ROAA between 2020 and 2021 (around +0.1%) were observed.

Concerning the profitability of the banking sector in France, it has been strongly impacted in 2020 (around −0.2% compared to the previous year in terms of ROAA). However, it recovered in 2021 with maintenance of total assets compared to 2020 (which had already increased) and a return to precrisis rates in terms of ROAA.

The Italian banking sector profitability suffered significantly in 2020 as well (about −0.32% in terms of ROAA compared to the prior year). Although total assets were maintained in 2020 (which had previously expanded), this measure recovered in 2021 with a return to precrisis rates for ROAA.

The UK banking industry's profitability also suffered significantly in 2020 (by about −0.20% in terms of ROAA compared to 2019). Yet, it immediately bounced back in 2021.

In Spain, in terms of ROAA, the banking industry's profitability suffered a significant setback in 2020 (approximately −0.75% compared to the prior year). However, it quickly rebounded in 2021, returning to precrisis ROAA rates. Additionally, since the start of the pandemic, the total assets have greatly expanded.

The profitability of the Swiss banking sector has been lightly impacted by the crisis, with ROAA falling slightly without reaching concerning levels in 2020 and 2021. In Romania, the profitability of the banking sector fell sharply in 2020 (by about −0.45% in terms of ROAA compared to 2019). Although it rebounded in 2021, the rate remained lower than those observed in the years before the crisis.

In Turkey, the profitability of the banking sector has not been greatly affected by the pandemic, with ROAA hardly changing throughout 2019 through 2021. However, it can be noted that there was a significant decline in total assets in 2021 compared to 2020 (which had a notable increase compared to previous years).

The profitability of Saudi Arabia's banking sector has been impacted by the pandemic as the return on average assets has declined from 2019 to 2020 (by around −0.75%). The following year in 2021, the return on average assets began to recover and is around the same rate as the one prior to the pandemic. In the United Arab Emirates as well, the return on average assets has declined from 2019 to 2020 (by around −0.9%). Later, in 2021, the return on average assets began to increase (by around +0.4%), but it is still not close to where the rates were prior to the pandemic.

In Israel as well, the profitability of the banking sector has been impacted by the pandemic as the return on average assets has declined from 2019 to 2020 (by around −0.2%), with a recovery in the return on average assets in 2021 (by around +0.45%) to rate that is higher than it was prior to the pandemic.

The profitability of China's banking sector measured as the return on average assets declined from 2019 to 2020 as well (by around −0.08%), with a slight recovery in 2021(by around +0.02%), but this is still at a rate much lower than it was prior to the pandemic. In Japan, the return on average assets in the banking sector declined from 2019 to 2020 (by around −0.01%). Then in 2021, the return on average assets has been able to recover (by around +0.03%) to a rate that is a bit above the rate prior to the pandemic.

In India, the profitability of the banking sector has been positively impacted by the pandemic as the return on average assets has been able to increase from 2019 to 2020 (by around +0.4%) and continue to grow from 2020 to 2021 (by around +0.2%). The return on average assets has been able to grow to a point that is double what it was prior to the pandemic.

The return on average assets in South Korea's banking sector has declined from 2019 to 2020 (by around −0.06%) and recovered in 2021 (by around +0.09%) where it is now at a point higher than it was prior to the pandemic.

In Russia, the return on average assets in the banking sector declined from 2019 to 2020 (by around −0.05%), and in Indonesia as well (by around −0.75%). Then in 2021, the return on average assets in Indonesia's banking sector began recovering (by around +0.25%) where it is now at a point below where it was prior to the pandemic.

The profitability of the Philippines' banking sector shows a similar trend during the pandemic, with the return on average assets declining from 2019 to 2020 (by around −0.4%) and recovering in 2021 (by around +0.2%) where it is now at a point slightly below where it was prior to the pandemic.

While total assets in Australia increased, there was a significant decrease in ROAA between 2019 and 2020 by about 20%. Profitability in the banking sector took a large hit due to the pandemic. New Zealand saw total assets increase by about $50 M, coupled with an almost 20% decline in ROAA from 2019 to 2020, significantly impacting the profitability of the banking sector.

Kenyan banks had a decline in profitability in 2020, which was followed by a rebound to average profitability levels in 2021. In contrast to several other African nations, Nigeria's banks maintained a higher level of profitability. There were successive declines in profitability between 2020 and 2021. Additionally, they observed a rise in deposits and a fall in loans.

In 2020 and 2021, bank profitability in Ghana decreased. Additionally, annual declines in bank capital were occurring. Bank profitability in Morocco continued the pattern of declining in 2020 and rising in 2021.

Bank profitability in South Africa continued to deteriorate in line with the prepandemic South African trend; but, since the pandemic was the root cause of this decline, the decline was more pronounced. In Egypt, bank profitability and total assets both experienced significant declines.

20.3 Evidence on bank risk during the aftermath

The Brazilian government dedicated multiple programs to mitigating risk through the pandemic. Credit lines totaling more than 1% of GDP have been provided by the government to SMEs and microbusinesses to pay for the investment, working capital, and payroll expenses. Public banks have increased the range of loan options available to consumers and enterprises, focusing on fostering working capital (credit lines add up to 4.5% of GDP).

In Ecuador, to address the liquidity issue in the financial system, the government reduced the banks' contribution rate to the Liquidity Fund by three percentage points of deposits (to 5%), freeing up about $950 million in liquid assets. In response to the waning demand for cash, this step helped to rebalance internal liquidity. Additionally, they implemented a unique voluntary deferral of private loan commitments and ordered the modification of interest rate restrictions. They also started Reactivate Ecuador, a working capital facility for companies receiving World Bank assistance. The deferral measures will boost the real economy. Still, suppose they are left in place for an extended period. In that case, they may undermine the balance sheets of financial institutions and present risks to the financial system, especially as we transition from the emergency period into the nonemergent one.

All ECB operational and regulatory support provided by the authorities was expanded to German banks under national direction regarding measures taken to reduce bank risks in Germany. The release of the countercyclical capital buffer was postponed by the Financial Stability Council until the end of 2021. France has implemented a few further measures to those decided at the level of the currency union for the Euro Area to reduce monetary risks.

In Italy, in addition to monetary policy at the level of the currency union, significant measures were also implemented in the emergency Cura Italia and Liquidity Decree programs of the Italian government. The existing liquidity support initiatives have been extended till the end of 2021. In addition, only principal payments would be included in loan moratoria. New guaranteed loans would be made available at slightly lowered guaranteed rates after June. The duration of new and ongoing guaranteed loans has also been extended from 6 to 10 years. Lastly, the Bank of Italy has issued a series of measures to support the banks and nonbank intermediaries that are subject to its oversight, in keeping with the objectives of the ECB and EBA. The Bank of Italy has issued a series of measures to support the banks and nonbank intermediaries that are subject to its oversight, in keeping with the objectives of the ECB and EBA. Among these measures are delaying some disclosure requirements, temporarily operating below specific capital and liquidity limits, and postponing on-site inspections. The aim of these actions was to lessen the volatility of the financial markets.

In order to limit the risk of the banking sector in the UK, several measures have been undertaken. Cooperation with the central banks of Canada, Japan, the Euro Area, the US, and Switzerland will be used to establish a Contingent Term Repo Facility to support the Bank's current sterling liquidity facilities; the established US dollar liquidity swap line arrangements will also be leveraged to increase liquidity availability and to retain banks' Systemic Risk Buffer rates at the 2019 level until at least the end of 2022 and reduce the UK Countercyclical Capital Buffer rate from its prior pattern of 2% by December 2020 to 0%, with the expectation that it will remain there for at least a year. However, the central banks have agreed to suspend supplying dollar liquidity at maturity on April 2021 due to strengthening US currency funding circumstances. Yet, they would continue to carry out weekly procedures with a maturity of 7 days. The Prudential Regulatory Authority, on the other hand, announced in December 2020 that it intended to return to the standard framework for bank distributions. In light of the findings of the two stress tests conducted by the Prudential Regulation Committee and the FPC, this decision revealed a degree of decrease in the uncertainty regarding COVID-19 at the time and the capacity of banks to withstand substantial losses. The BoE underlined to the eight major UK banks in February 2021 the importance of early RAF submissions. In this context, it should have been highlighted that the BoE and the PRA had postponed the due dates for these reports scheduled for May 2020 by a year in order to assist banks with their operational needs during the COVID-19 crisis.

Spain has added some extra measures to the monetary policy decisions made at the level of the currency union for the Euro Area. When it came to transition periods and the intermediate minimum standards for own financing and eligible debts targets, the Bank of Spain would apply a legal system's flexibility to the banks it oversees, and banks would be allowed to rely on professional knowledge when assessing the credit risk of forborne exposures.

In order to reduce the risk in the Netherlands, the central bank has periodically lightened regulatory standards for smaller banking institutions. Moreover, while calculating their leverage ratios, banks overseen by DNB were allowed to ignore certain central bank exposures. Furthermore, a ceiling for mortgage loan risk weighting was to be introduced in January 2022 after having been delayed, according to the Financial Stability Report from May 2021.

In Switzerland, the SNB held its policy rate at -0.75% to the end of August 2020 with regard to the monetary measures. The decision to suspend delivering dollar liquidity at maturities starting in July 2021 on April 2021 was decided by the Swiss National Bank. The Swiss Financial Market Supervisory Authority (FINMA) introduced a temporary exemption of central bank deposits from the measurement of banks' leverage ratio until January 2021. According to FINMA, the capital made accessible by this waiver should have been used to increase liquidity provision and should not have been distributed in the form of dividends or in any other manner. To prevent the Swiss franc from strengthening further in terms of exchange rates and balances of payments, the SNB intensified its FX market operations and bought assets in 2020. Yet, the SNB's interventions strongly declined in 2021.

Sweden announced and implemented fiscal measures in order to reduce risks for 2020 including capital injection, liquidity boost, and guarantees, which were evaluated by the government to cost several billion.

For monetary support during the first half of 2021, the Romanian government contributed some billion RON for repo transactions that offer liquidity to financial institutions. This amount was far less than the multiple billion RON that would be spent on repo transactions in 2020. Furthermore, until March 2021, regulations put in place by the government would guarantee banks delay repayment on loans granted to people and firms affected by COVID-19 for a period of up to 9 months. Moreover, the central bank of Romania received a euro repo line from the European Central Bank that would be in effect until March 2022. Lastly, the Romanian government has operated in foreign exchange markets to control excessive volatility and fix the exchange rate in order to guarantee financial stability.

Regarding Turkish monetary operations, the bank regulator in December 2020 reduced the maximum period for retail auto loans and credit card instalment plans for the purchase of certain products. Additionally, 2020 saw a suspension of bank and corporate dividend payments.

In Russia, the Central Bank of Russia recommended banks to keep restructuring loans to affected SME and retail borrowers until July 1, 2021. As well, restructured retail loans would not be fully provisioned until July 1, 2021. The cancelation of risk weight additions for mortgage loans provided prior to April 1, 2020, were measured to boost retail and mortgage lending. On top of this, new credit risk assessment procedures and lower risk weights, applied to subordinated bonds of large nonfinancial corporations, in mortgage lending have saved around Rub 300 bn (around 0.3% of GDP) of capital in the banking sector. Along with this, the CBR eliminated risk buffers for consumer loans issued by August 31, 2019, and reduced risk buffers for unsecured loans put in place since September 1, 2020. The CBR increased its limit on banks' fees established during the lockdown for online retailers. Since the macroprudential anticrisis measures had been proving successful, in spring 2021, the CBR gradually phased these measures out by raising the macroprudential buffers for home loans with a down payment between 15% and 20%. Thus, beginning on July 1, 2021, macroprudential buffers for unsecured consumer loans were restored to their prepandemic level.

In Papua New Guinea, the Kina Facility Rate (KFR), the primary policy rate for the country, was lowered by 200 basis points from 5% to 3% by the Bank of Papua New Guinea (BPNG), which also gave commercial banks instructions to drop their respective indicative lending rates. Additionally, BPNG lowered the Cash Reserve Requirement from 10% to 7% in order to increase the liquidity available to commercial banks.

In response to COVID-19, the Central Bank of Nigeria (CBN) cut its monetary policy rate by 100 basis points in May and another 100 basis points in September. This increased the liquidity available to nonbank financial institutions and significantly decreased the market yield on government securities.

The South African Central Bank (SARB) steadily dropped the policy rate to 3.5% in the southernmost tip of the African continent, doing so by 100 basis points on March 19, 2020, another 100 basis points on April 14, 2020, 50 basis points on May 21, 2020, and 25 basis points on July 23, 2020. On March 28, 2020, they announced a temporary easing of the bank capital requirements in South Africa and reduced the level of liquidity coverage from 100% to 80%.

On March 15, the Bank of Algeria in northern Africa lowered its main policy rate by 25 basis points to 3.25% and lowered the reserve requirement ratio from 10% to 8%. On April 6, the Bank of Algeria announced that it was reducing the ratios for bank liquidity, solvency, and NPLs. Banks are additionally permitted to defer payments on some loans without being required to make a provision for them. In addition to reducing haircuts on government securities used in refinancing operations and cutting its main policy rate from 3.25% to 3.00%, the Bank of Algeria announced on April 30 that it was lowering its reserve requirement ratio from 8% to 6%. The beginning of 1-month open market operations and a reduction in the reserve requirement ratio from 6% to 3% were both announced by the Bank of Algeria on September 14. The Moroccan central bank has reduced the policy rate by 75 basis points, to 1.5%, since March 2020.

Bank al-Maghrib in Morocco decided to lower reserve requirements from 2% to 0% in order to increase liquidity provision and make it simpler for banks to refinance their contributions to credit unions and microcredit organizations. Kenya saw a reduction in the policy rate of 100 basis points to 7.25%, a reduction in the banks' cash reserve ratio of 100 basis points to 4.25%, and an increase in the maximum period of repurchase agreements.

In Ethiopia, commercial banks were employed to inject funds into the hospitality and tourism sectors, giving the Commercial Bank of Ethiopia (CBE) a 3-year ETB 16 billion liquidity line. The Monetary Target Committee (MPC) in Ghana decreased the policy rate by 150 basis points to 14.5% on March 18, 2020. Ghana announced a number of measures to lessen the effects of the pandemic shock, including a reduction in the primary reserve requirement from 10% to 8%, a reduction in the capital conservation buffer from 3% to 1.5%, a change in the provisioning and classification rules for specific loan categories, and steps to make mobile payments more convenient and affordable.

The Bank of Tanzania (BoT) reduced the government securities' collateral haircut requirements on May 12 and slashed the discount rate from 7% to 5%. As of June 8, the BoT Statutory Minimum Reserves requirement has been reduced from 7% to 6%. Additionally, the BoT will grant regulatory flexibility to banks and other financial institutions so they can carry out individual debt restructuring procedures.

The West-African Economic and Monetary Union (WAEMU) regional central bank (BCEAO) in Côte d'Ivoire has put in place measures to more effectively satiate banks' liquidity needs and lessen the negative effects of the pandemic on economic activity. In order to fully satisfy banks' liquidity needs at a rate that is approximately 25 basis points lower than it was prior to the crisis, the BCEAO adopted a full allotment approach in April 2020 at a fixed rate of 2.5% (the minimum monetary policy rate). In June 2020, the Monetary Policy Committee lowered the monetary policy corridor's ceiling and floor by 50 basis points to 4% and 2%, respectively.

Chapter 21

Financial markets during the COVID-19 crisis aftermath

Abstract

Our final chapter on the COVID-19 crisis aftermath evidence focuses on financial markets outside the US. We review evidence on equity, bond, and CDS markets around the world in the aftermath. Economic turmoil has resulted in financial markets for traditional assets in bear market territory with losses of 20% or more in some places. New nontraditional assets such as cryptocurrencies have recorded much greater percentage losses, as have the stocks of some even loosely related high-tech firms.

Keywords: COVID-19, Aftermath, Financial markets, Stock markets, Bond market, Nontraditional assets, Cryptocurrencies

21.1 Evidence on the stock market during the aftermath

The Canadian stock market experienced a sharp decline in the late 2019 and a gradual recovery into 2020, which regained prepandemic levels of growth in the late 2020. It has since grown substantially and reached levels of growth higher than prepandemic levels in the late 2021. The Mexican financial sector and the stock market experienced large deviations from prepandemic prices beginning at the end of 2019. Levels of growth were low in 2020 and have since exceeded prepandemic levels in 2022.

Financial markets in Argentina during the pandemic experienced small stents of growth and decline from 2019 to 2020. However, midway through 2020, a growing trend continued into 2022. The Chilean stock market experienced a significant dip in the late 2019, which rebounded into 2020, and experienced a growing trend that exceeded prepandemic levels in 2022.

The Peruvian financial sector experienced a significant volatility due to the effects of the pandemic. At the end of 2019, the financial market growth reached a new low, although trends shifted to strong positive growth which continued until the end of 2020. The Peruvian financial sector has since experienced volatility and has returned to a lower level of development in 2022. In Brazil, pandemic

The Economic and Financial Impacts of the COVID-19 Crisis Around the World
https://doi.org/10.1016/B978-0-443-19162-6.00018-9
Copyright © 2024 Elsevier Inc. All rights reserved.

significantly affected the stock market, which took a huge hit toward the end of 2019 and did not rise to prepandemic levels until 2021.

As for the Germany Stock Market Index, after its initial fall in spring 2020, it only recovered significantly until 2021. However, from the second half of 2021, the index has only gradually declined to the level it had in the early 2020.

As for the France Stock Market Index, it has been noticeably impacted by the crisis. The index fell very slightly in the first quarter of 2020, but later rose significantly until mid-2021 before starting a gradual decline (however, the value is still much higher than in the early 2020).

The crisis has not had much of an effect on the Italian Stock Market Index either. However, it is important to recognize that several measures were taken with the intention of improving the transparency of the stock holdings of Italian firms that were listed on the Stock Exchange. Thus, the first half of 2020 saw a very little decrease in the stock market index, while the second half saw a strong increase that lasted until the mid-2021 before beginning a slow decline (however, the value is still higher than in the early 2020).

In addition, in the UK, the UK Stock Market Index was not significantly impacted by the crisis. In the first quarter of 2020, it decreased a bit, but from the mid-2020 on, it increased steadily. However, it began to settle while slightly fluctuating starting in the middle of 2021.

The crisis just had a small effect on the Spanish Stock Market Index during spring 2020. However, in the second half of the year, the index experienced a significant surge, which subsequently mainly stabilized (even though there is a slight decline over time). It is important to note that the Spanish government has established guarantees for listed companies.

Regarding the Switzerland Stock Market Index, the pandemic had little impact on it. In general, it only progressively increased from the start of 2020 until the middle of 2021. Yet, it began to consistently decline in the second part of 2021 until 2022.

In Sweden, monetary policy has increased the number of securities purchased in 2021 and 2022 by up to SEK 700 billion. In Romania, the stock market has not been significantly impacted by the crisis. In fact, the Bucharest Stock Exchange Trading Index has only increased gradually since the beginning of 2020. However, it began to decrease around the mid-2021. Indeed, the fact that several billion RON in government securities were invested on the secondary market helps partially to explain this activity.

The pandemic did not significantly impact the stock market in Turkey either. Indeed, the Turkish stock market index has only increased since the beginning of the crisis and has risen sharply since spring 2021, reaching in 2022 a very high rate exceeding the rates seen during the last 5 years.

For the Saudi Arabia Stock Market Index, the pandemic was moderately negatively impacted the market as it declined during the spring of 2020. However, going forward, the market was able to rebound and has increased from 2020 to 2022 to greater than it was prior to the pandemic.

The pandemic exhibited no negative impact on the United Arab Emirates Market Index, as it has been able to steadily increase from the start of 2020 to 2022. The market in the United Arab Emirates in 2022 is at a point that is much higher than it was prior to the start of the pandemic.

Similarly, in Israel, the Israel Stock Market Index, the pandemic did not significantly impact the market as it has had a steady increase from the start of 2020 to 2022. If anything, the market in Israel has benefited as it has reached a rate much higher than it was at the start of the pandemic.

For the China Stock Market Index, the pandemic's the impact on the market was mostly neutral as it did experience growth during 2020 and 2021. However, the market slowly leveled out during 2022 to a point close to where it was prior to the pandemic. Following the pandemic, the support provided by the PBC toward the monetary policy for market stability and the government's actions to prevent tightening on financial conditions was continued to remain in place.

The Japan Stock Market Index was able to grow during the pandemic, experiencing the most growth between 2020 and 2021. However, between 2021 and 2022, there were fluctuations in this growth, but it still remained to be positive overall to where it is still above the rates prior to the pandemic.

Regarding the pandemic's impact on the financial markets in India, the India Stock Market Index was able to grow on a consistent basis from 2020 to 2021. Then following 2021, the growth increased and then experienced fluctuations but remained positive overall through 2022.

The South Korea Stock Market Index was able to grow on a consistent basis from 2020 to 2021. Then following 2021, the growth increased with periods of fluctuations, but overall remained positive through 2022 to a point far higher than what it was prior to the pandemic.

Similarly, in Russia, the Russia Stock Market Index was able to grow on fairly consistent basis from 2020 to 2021, only experiencing a decline during the spring of 2020. This growth lasted until the spring of 2021, where the market rapidly began to fall and has continued to fall until 2022. In 2022, the market is at a point slightly lower than where it was prior to the pandemic.

In Indonesia, the Indonesia Stock Market Index was able to grow in a consistent basis from 2020 to 2021, experiencing a large period of growth during the middle of 2020. Then, in 2022, the growth started to level out and it is now at a point above where the market was prior to the pandemic. The regulator has instituted new share buyback policies (enabling listed businesses to repurchase their shares without a prior shareholder's meeting) and placed limitations on stock price falls in an effort to reduce stock market volatility.

The Philippines Stock Market Index was also able to grow on a fairly consistent basis starting in the middle of 2020 and continuing until the middle of 2021. However, from the middle of 2021 through 2022, the market began to decline, and it is not at a point lower than where it was prior to the pandemic.

The pandemic caused a significant dip in Australia's stock market's growth at the end of 2019. However, the stock market began growing and continued into 2022. The pandemic caused a dip in stock market growth at the beginning of 2020 in New Zealand. However, the market quickly regained an upward trajectory, so much so that it could exceed the growth levels in 2019 significantly.

In Papa New Guinea, the Central Bank of Papa New Guinea spent K750 million purchasing government assets on the secondary market as a part of a strategy to increase liquidity for the private sector. Through the program's purchasing of government assets on the secondary market over the entire yield curve, the principal refinancing instruments' maturities in South Africa will be raised from 3 to 12 months.

In order to reduce volatility, the Capital Market Authority of Morocco decided to lower the maximum variation criteria that are applicable to financial instruments listed on the Casablanca Stock Exchange. In 2019 and 2020, the Kenyan stock market experienced a sharp decline as it lost over half of its value. The Nairobi Securities Exchange Ltd. 20 Index peaked in 2022 at roughly 1700 points after beginning its journey at roughly 3000 points in 2020.

The Nigerian Stock Exchange All Share Index lost nearly half of its value before rising quickly to levels higher than those seen before the pandemic, around 48,880. The Ghana Stock Exchange Composite Index fell in 2020 from 3500 to roughly 1800. Midway through 2021, it would then rise to about 3000.

In Morocco, the Casablanca CFG 25 decreased from around 13,000 to 9000 in 2020. During the pandemic, the index began to rise in both 2021 and 2022. The South Africa Stock Market Index dropped from over 60,000 to slightly under 40,000 points in South Africa. The Egyptian Exchange Index lost approximately half of its value, dropping to about 9000 in 2020, where it stayed for the next 2 years.

21.2 Evidence on the bond market during the aftermath

The Canadian bond market experienced a gradual decline entering 2020, remained low, and gradually increased in 2021 and 2022. The Canadian government made consistent strides toward improving profitability and purchase programs through the announcement of the Provincial Money Market Acquisition Program (PMMP), the Provincial Bond Acquisition Program (PBPP), the Corporate Bond Purchase Program (CBPP), and the purchase of Government of Canada securities in the secondary market. The Bank of Canada announced in its "forward guidance" that it would hold off on raising the policy interest rate until the recovery was well underway and inflation was consistently moving toward its target level.

The pandemic negatively impacted the Mexican bond market. The 10Y Bond Yield reached a low in the late 2021 after a negative trend in growth prepandemic. However, it began an up-trend in the late 2020 that has continued to grow in 2021 and 2022. The central bank also launched a corporate securities repo facility to strengthen the corporate bond market. The central bank has used the US$60 billion swap line with the Federal Reserve to guarantee the proper operation of financial markets. It conducted roll-over auctions with decreasing demand and held two auctions for commercial banks worth a combined $5 billion on two separate occasions. It has been decided to keep the swap facility open until September 30, 2021. To avert surges in short-term interest rates, more liquidity is being made available during trading hours and sterilized after the market closes. To decrease the maturities of government bonds held by private institutions and enhance their liquidity position, the Central Bank actively participated in government bond swaps. Bond swaps to extend maturities were carried out in the late 2020 when market circumstances improved.

The onset of the pandemic did not much affect the 7Y Bond Yield in Argentina. The Argentinian bond market experienced multiple small dips in growth close to May and September 2021 and flattened approximately midway through 2022.

Meanwhile, the Chilean 10Y Bond Yield was significantly affected by the pandemic. Entering 2019, it had experienced a downtrend that slightly rebounded before the onset of the pandemic. Although in 2020, it reached a low, its growth quickly became positive, significantly exceeding 2019 levels in 2021 and 2022.

The pandemic did not have much of an effect on the 10Y Bond Yield in Peru. While growth was low in 2020 and 2021, it began a significant upward trajectory at the beginning of 2021 and continued in 2022. In Brazil, the pandemic did not significantly affect the 10Y either. The bond market declined in 2019, followed by a sharp increase toward the end of 2019, and dropped again, but never too much below the dip in 2019, and has since increased consistently. The onset of the continuous growth began at a low point in 2020.

As for Germany, the crisis did not impact the 10Y Bond Yield. It remained relatively constant from 2020 to the mid-2021, and then increased significantly (approximately +2%). The crisis had no effect on the French 10Y Bond Yield. From 2020 through the middle of 2021, it was largely stable before rising dramatically (by about +3%).

The Italian 10Y Bond Yield was slightly impacted by the crisis represented by a small decline that has remained constant for a certain period. However, it only climbed rather quickly (by roughly +3.5%) beginning in 2021.

The British 10Y Bond Yield was unaffected by the crisis. Since the pandemic, the yield rate has only gone up, and it will be even higher in 2022. This is particularly related to the central bank's decision to raise its holdings of the UK government bonds and nonfinancial firm bonds, lower the bank rate, and launch a new Term Funding Scheme in order to promote lending to the real economy.

The pandemic had no impact on the Spanish 10Y Bond Yield. From 2020 through the middle of 2021, it stayed largely stable before beginning to expand rapidly in autumn 2021 and early 2022. In Switzerland, the crisis has had no impact on the 10Y Bond Yield. Indeed, since the start of the pandemic until the mid-2021, the rate has been quite stable. Yet, in the second half of 2021, a major increase has begun.

In Sweden, monetary policy reduced constraints on using covered bonds as collateral. In Romania, the bond market has been impacted by the pandemic slightly. While in the first half of 2020 the Romania 10Y Bond Yield decreased, it has been increasing gradually and very significantly from fall of 2021, reaching record levels compared to the last 5 years.

The Turkish bond market has been slightly impacted by the crisis. After falling modestly in spring 2020, the 10Y Bond Yield during summer 2020 remained quite constant. However, it rose sharply again in autumn 2020 and then again in spring 2021. Yet, since the end of 2021, the rate has fallen sharply and has reached one of the lowest rates since the beginning of the crisis.

For the 10-year Israel Bond Market, the pandemic did not initially cause for any major fluctuations, but for the 2 years following 2020, the rate has increased to a point higher than it was prior to the pandemic (by around +2.5 since the start of 2020).

In China, the pandemic caused for an increase in the 10Y Bond Yield during the first half of 2020 (by around +0.65). The rate then started to decline and level out until 2022, where it is now at a point similar to where it was before the pandemic. For the 10-year Japan Bond Market as well, the pandemic caused for an increase in the rate during the fall of 2020 (by around +0.16). The rate then had some decline but picked back up toward the middle of 2021 and continued to grow throughout 2022, where it leveled out and stays at a point above where it was prior to the pandemic.

For the 10-year India Bond Market, the pandemic caused for a slight increase in the beginning of 2020 (by around +0.25). The rate steadily grew from 2020 to 2021 and then started to grow quicker from 2021 to 2022, where it is approaching a point near where it was prior to the pandemic. Following the pandemic, India increased the limit on FPI investment on corporate bonds to 15% of outstanding stock during FY 2020/21.

The 10 Bond Yield of in South Korea declined in 2020 (by around −0.25). Following the beginning of 2020, the rate fluctuated until 2021 where it then began to grow. This growth continues throughout 2022 and the rate is at a point almost double, where it was prior to the pandemic.

For the 10-year Russia Bond Market, the pandemic caused for an increase during the fall of 2020 (by around +1), while the remainder of the growth was fairly steady until the middle of 2021. At this point, the rate shot up (by around +5) and then fell back down a bit as it leveled out in 2022 at a point higher than where it was prior to the pandemic.

For the 10-year Indonesia Bond Market, the pandemic also caused a decline in the beginning of 2020 that continued until the middle of 2020 (by around −1). Then, the rate grew from the middle of 2020 to 2021, then declined until the middle of 2021, and then increased again until 2022. As of this writing, the rate is fluctuating at a point similar to where it was prior to the pandemic.

In the Philippines Bond Market, the 10Y Bond Yield increased in the fall of 2020 (by around +1.5), fell slightly during the start of 2021, where it took off and grew through 2022 to around prepandemic levels.

The pandemic caused volatile returns in the Australian 10Y Bond Yield. The Australian bond market saw a downtrend from 2019 into 2020, started to rebound in 2021, and exceeded prepandemic levels in 2022.

New Zealand experienced a significant decline in its 10Y Bond Yield due to the pandemic. The market reached a new low approximately midway through 2020, although shortly after, it began increasing again. Once the aftereffects of the pandemic subsided, the market reached high levels of growth in the late 2021 and 2022.

After the pandemic, Kenya's 10Y Bond Yield grew gradually, reaching a high of about 13.87% by 2022. The pandemic in Nigeria prompted 10Y Bond Yields to fall to about 4%, but this level did not last long as they rose to over 13.3% during the following 2 years.

In 2022, the 3-month Bond Yield for Ghana climbed significantly, rising from 11.5% to about 28.3%. The 10Y Bond Yield in Morocco fell in 2020 and remained at a similar level until 2022, when there was a significant spike. The 10Y Bond Yield in South Africa rose rapidly to about 12.5% in 2020 before sharply dropping to normal levels in the early 2021. Since then, the Bond Yield has started to increase and is now about 10.6%. The 10-year Bond Yield in Egypt remained roughly constant at 14% until 2022, when it increased.

21.3   Evidence on the CDS market during the aftermath

Canada's sovereign CDSs market reached its lowest point in the mid-2019, rose and plateaued in 2020, continued to rise in 2021, and experienced some volatility coming into 2022. The Brazilian sovereign CDSs market experienced considerable growth in 2020 and has since experienced small spikes of growth and declines going into 2021 and 2022.

Sovereign CDSs in Argentina experienced low prices until the late 2019, when prices began increasing. Due to the global pandemic, prices continued to increase in 2020, but later experienced a sudden and significant decline in September 2020. Chilean 5Y Sovereign CDSs experienced significant growth at the beginning of 2020; however, a few months into the year, it began a downtrend and reached a low in September 2020. Although the pandemic impeded continuous growth, levels in 2020 did not fall below prepandemic stagnant growth.

In Peru, sovereign CDSs experienced wavering prices prepandemic that spiked in March 2020. The prices declined and have since remained relatively stable in 2021 and 2022. The Mexican market for sovereign CDSs saw a sudden increase in prices in 2020, although this returned to prepandemic levels in 2021.

Concerning the CDSs Market in Germany, in the spring of 2020, the 5-year CDSs value rose sharply (by about +15) and then returned to the level it had been before the crisis began in the mid-2020. It then remained constant for a certain period and started to rise again around the beginning of 2022. It is important to note that the government continued to increase the number of public guarantees it provided to credit insurers throughout this period.

Regarding the CDSs market in France, the value of 5-year CDSs increased significantly (by around +30) in the first half of 2020 before dropping back to its precrisis level in the second half. After that, 5-year CDS values were mostly steady, until climbing slightly toward the start of 2021 and again in the early 2022.

5-year CDS prices in Italy rose dramatically (by about +150) in the first half of 2020 before reverting to its precrisis level in the second half. Following that, values remained mainly constant for a while before beginning to grow at the beginning of 2022. It is important to understand that insurance firms had to submit their most recent Solvency II ratios on a weekly basis. IVASS (Insurance Supervisory Authority) advised insurance companies to be cautious with dividend and bonus payments in order to protect their financial standing, following EIOPA's guidance.

Concerning the UK CDSs Market, the 5-year CDSs value increased significantly (by roughly +20) in the spring of 2020 and only gradually decreased for a certain period, before experiencing a significant rebound in the middle of 2022.

The value of 5-year CDSs on the Spanish CDSs market rose sharply in the first half of 2020 as well before reverting to its precrisis level in the second. After that, it reached a point of stability and was mostly constant through 2021 before beginning to slowly increase in 2022.

In Sweden, a measure implemented the temporary acceptance that all credit institutions subject to Swedish FSA regulation might relate to become provisional money institutions. In Turkey, the CDSs market was slightly impacted by the crisis. After increasing in spring 2020, the value of 5-year CDSs during the summer stagnated and fell back at the end of the year. However, from spring 2021 onwards, the CDSs value increased again, and in a progressive manner (approximately +500 since the beginning of 2021).

For the CDS Market in Saudi Arabia, the 5-year CDS increased rapidly during the spring of 2020 and slowly fell back down during 2020. The CDS eventually stabilized in 2021, but at rates lower than prior to the pandemic.

The CDS Market in the United Arab Emirates (UAE) follows a similar trend. The 5-year CDS increased rapidly during spring of 2020 and then began to decline during the summer of 2020. The CDS from this point until October 2022 has declined overall to a point lower than it was prior to the pandemic. However, the CDS has experienced several periods of sudden increases such as the one seen in the spring of 2021 or the beginning or 2022. In Israel, the 5-year CDS increased rapidly during the spring of 2020 (by around +30), where it peaked before May. The CDS then declined and started to stabilize in September 2020.

In China, 5-year CDS values increased rapidly during the spring of 2020 (by around +45). The CDS then declined until 2021 and then increased mostly steadily through 2022. For the CDS Market in Japan, the 5-year CDS increased rapidly during the beginning of 2020 as well (by around +30), then declined until end of 2020 where it started to stabilize throughout 2022 and then toward the end of 2022, the CDS increased again.

For the CDS market in India, the 5-year CDS increased rapidly during the spring of 2020 (by around +170). The CDS then declined until it eventually began to level out in September of 2020. For the CDS Market in South Korea, the 5-year CDS increased rapidly during the spring of 2020 (by around +25). Then, the CDS declined until the end of 2020, where it experienced some growth but then declined again at the start of 2021. The decline in the CDS eventually began to level out as it approached the beginning of 2022.

In the Russian CDS market, the 5-year CDS barely grew between 2019 and 2021 and only experienced noticeably growth following 2022, where by October 2022 the CDS grew by over 10k.

For the CDS Market in Indonesia, the 5-year CDS grew rapidly during the beginning of 2020 (by around +150). Then, the CDS declined until 2021, where it began to level out and slowly increased at a steady rate until October 2022. For the CDS Market in the Philippines, the 5-year CDS grew rapidly during the spring of 2020 (by +110). Then, the CDS declined and leveled out as it approached September 2020.

Sovereign CDSs in Australia experienced a severe price spike in 2020. The pandemic significantly affected prices, although prices declined and remained stable from 2021 into 2022. New Zealand saw a significant impact on its sovereign CDS market due to the pandemic as well. Although prices previously were relatively consistent, there was a large and sudden increase in value in 2020. However, this returned to a similar level as prepandemic levels in 2021.

Midway through 2020, sovereign CDS in South Africa grew to slightly over 400, and by the late 2020, had risen back to a level above the prepandemic level. Sovereign CDS in Egypt rose to about 600 in 2020 before dropping to levels above those prior to the outbreak.

Part VI

Lessons learned from the COVID-19 crisis

We now arrive at the last part of our journey together about the lessons learned from the crisis. We offer a single Chapter 22 to learn these lessons, fulfill the goals of the book, and bid our dear readers adieu.

We argue at the start of the book in Part I that researchers and policymakers need compilations of research and data on the economic and financial impacts of the COVID-19 crisis on a global basis. It is also essential for them to have a comprehensive assessment of these findings and a set of specific research and policy strategies for dealing with future economic and financial crises. To be most useful, these strategies must be devised ex ante when the origin and intensity of future crises are unknown. As discussed below, acting early has several advantages.

The first five parts of the book and the chapters they comprise provide the bulk of the research and data compilations required, and the additional data included in this part are described in these other places in the book. To the degree possible, these book parts and chapters also supply assessments of the research and policy implications derived for the specific economic segments studied, or research or policy topics scrutinized. We do our best to complete the assessment job in this Part and Chapter 22, as well as fulfill the other goals of the book of devising ex ante research and policy strategies for dealing with future unknown crises to generate better ex post outcomes.

We here offer an overall assessment of the research and data on the COVID-19 crisis and its consequences and interpret how it may apply to a world that is increasingly challenged in new ways. Using this assessment, we also provide a specific set of research and policy preparations for contending with future economic and financial crises of unknown origin and intensity. We cautiously also go a little further with some rough suggestions for how our *Expect the Unexpected* research and policy preparations may be adapted for other types of future crises. We recognize that these rough suggestions would require expertise beyond our own to evaluate and implement. Nonetheless, we include a surprise specific rough adaptation to another global crisis that readers will recognize, with the hope that we may be of service to assist in the tackling of this worldwide problem.

Chapter 22

"Expect the Unexpected" and prepare for future crises

Chapter outline

Abstract

We wind up the book and complete our mission by drawing conclusions from assessing the research and data compiled on COVID-19 and applying those lessons. We provide our *"Expect the Unexpected"* blueprint strategy of specific research and policy preparations for the future economic and financial crises of unknown origin and intensity. We also provide broad suggestions for adapting the *"Expect the Unexpected"* research and policy preparations to other types of future crises.

Keywords: COVID-19, Research and policy preparations, Future economic and financial crises, Other types of future crises

22.1 Assessments of research and data compiled on COVID-19 and applying these assessments in a challenging new world

The research and data on the economic and financial impacts of the COVID-19 crisis allow researchers and policymakers to make significant headway in understanding the workings of the three main economic segments of society—the real economy, banking sector, and financial markets, all broadly defined. We are also much better able to comprehend the range of economic and financial crises that affect these economic segments. Of most importance, we may now be able to employ the new knowledge to devise comprehensive strategies to combat these crises over the cycle to foster better economic and financial outcomes.

The reasons why the COVID-19 crisis is so informative are clear. Crises generally provide the best lessons in any field. Failures teach more than successes, global crises are failures at massive scale, and COVID-19 is much more massive than most. Among its other unique epistemological advantages, COVID-19 provides the most plausibly exogenous set of economic shocks, which are depicted by the disease bombs on our book's cover. These shocks provide researchers clear advantages in terms of clean econometric identification in quasi-natural experimental settings, one of the highest standards

The Economic and Financial Impacts of the COVID-19 Crisis Around the World
https://doi.org/10.1016/B978-0-443-19162-6.00013-X
Copyright © 2024 Elsevier Inc. All rights reserved.

in drawing inferences from empirical research. Prior global economic and financial crises were caused in large part by harmful behavior in the sectors that were initially most affected, making inference more difficult. As examples, drawing conclusions about the effects of the Crash of 1929 and the Global Financial Crisis (GFC) on financial markets and the banking sector that they harmed, respectively, is problematic. The Crash of 1929 was brought about largely because of actions by financial market participants and the GFC was due in large part to bank behavior, so research inferences about the effects of these crises are significantly compromised.

Several other features of COVID-19 also enhance the research benefits. The government policy reactions were much faster and larger in magnitude than in other crises, allowing for fruitful comparisons among global crises to ascertain the effects of such speed and magnitude. COVID-19 also features the fastest and steepest economic declines in recorded history, as well as the fastest turnaround, and an aftermath that is still creating new economic and financial damages for study. COVID-19 also completes the set of three global crises of the last century—along with the Crash of 1929 and the GFC. COVID-19 is the only one of the three in which real economy damages affected banks and financial markets before the converse occurred, so we can now more clearly see how economic and financial crises differ by the economic segments of origin.

Research and policy conclusions from the crisis suggest that quality economic stewardship demands attention during all phases of economic and financial cycles—boom, crisis, and aftermath—to keep crisis damages in check. We also learn that fast and large policy responses at the beginnings of crises appear to pay great dividends as they help reduce problems quickly. The speed and size of large financial aid packages are admittedly costly in terms of losses due to fraud, waste, excessive subsidies, moral hazard, political connections, etc., all documented in the first five parts of the book. However, these costs are almost surely strongly outweighed by the economic and financial benefits from acting quickly and in large magnitudes. Policy delays and underfunding contributed significantly to the Great Depression over the decade of the 1930s and other unfavorable outcomes following the Crash of 1929. Underwhelming policy responses also contributed to the tens of trillions of the US dollars of lost output and destruction of financial assets during and after the GFC in the US alone. Damages such as these or far worse might have visited us had it not been for the stronger policy responses to the COVID-19 crisis, although this cannot be rigorously proven nor can the savings from avoiding these problems be accurately assessed.

It is also possible to blunt many of the costs of fraud, waste, and other misuses of government aid in the future. This would require the cooperation of researchers and policymakers to create a set of off-the-shelf policies with built-in flexibility before crises. Policymakers can then reasonably and calmly implement and adjust these policies when the frenzied confusion of the new crisis arrives.

The research also suggests that better targeting of government aid may improve outcomes. This includes aiming more of the aid during crises at households or firms that are in greatest need of outside support, rather than supporting those with more financial means or access, designating aid for particularly productive purposes, such as mitigating labor scarring, and limiting awards of funds that discourage unproductive activities, such as exiting the labor force or engaging in speculative investments.

COVID-19 has also made clear how destructive policy can be in the aftermath of crises if stimulus is not curtailed or eliminated quickly when it is no longer productive. As somewhat detailed already in the Introduction to Part I, this destruction is new and different from the unavoidable problems caused by the crises themselves. The injurious aftermath consequences for the real economy, banking sector, and financial markets—such as inflation, insufficient labor supply, and additional recessions—might be largely mitigated or avoided by better policy. The continuing substantial aid to the economy needs to be reduced or eliminated, which admittedly may be difficult to accomplish.

One final set of lessons from the COVID-19 pandemic concerns the benefits and costs of cooperation among policymakers and private sector agents in the three key economic segments we study in this book. On the benefits side, we observe that the favorable economic and financial "surprises" of mitigated damages relative to expectations at the start of COVID-19 discussed in the Introduction to Part I are likely due to the concerted efforts of many factors. The massive policy response that we already belabored plus the prudential policies enacted in the aftermath of the GFC boosted the resilience of the banking sector. This was combined with real economy efforts by technology companies that allowed for remote work, school, and shopping using the internet, pharmaceutical companies that developed vaccines and treatment drugs quickly with government aid, and banks and financial market participants that kept funds flowing with government funding aid, all contributed to the favorable consequences during the crisis. The costs imposed during the aftermath of the COVID-19 crisis conversely show how failure to cooperate and misaligned incentives for all these public- and private-sector agents combined to result in losses for all economic segments.

Before proceeding to offer our specific research and policy suggestion blueprint for contending with future crises, we briefly note that applying these lessons in a cooperative fashion may face significant challenges in the new world order we are observing. We currently witness that policymakers continue to push new stimulus packages well into the problematic aftermath in which the damages from such stimuli are publicly acknowledged. Examples include central banks choosing not to offset expansive fiscal stimulus in the face of risking inflation and focusing on its "temporary" nature. This does not inspire confidence in policymaker willingness to apply COVID-19 lessons. The moves toward deglobalization, dismantling of international supply chains, and uncoupling of economies being pushed in nation after nation may also suggest challenges to the future cooperation. The increased militarization of national resources, the war in Ukraine and similar threats to Taiwan, and the consequent uncertain and shifting international alliances raise similar concerns. Finally, the use of modern technologies for nefarious purposes at large scale—such as social media to spread disinformation and Digital Technology Financial Firms (DTFFs) to mislead and defraud investors—pose challenges as well.

22.2 *"Expect the Unexpected"* specific research and policy preparations for the future unknown economic and financial crises

For our final two sections of this chapter and the book, we return somewhat to our more pictorial style from Chapter 1 and focus on creatively designed tables to offer most of our communications. In our set of specific strategies for dealing with the future economic and financial crises in this section and one other type of crisis in the next section, we emphasize the importance of hand-in-glove cooperation between researchers and policymakers. It is never possible to conceptualize, forge, or implement optimal policy. Nonetheless, policy is almost always better when it is informed by research, and research is almost always better when researchers understand the formulation and implementation of policy.

Our three-phase research and policy strategy for preparing, implementing, and adjusting for economic and financial crises includes two sets of tasks during the boom phase prior to the crisis, and one set each during the crisis and aftermath. As shown in Table 22.1, one set of tasks during the boom involves preparing "Off-the-Shelf" policies in advance for later implementation in the future economic and financial crises that are unknown in origin or intensity at the time these policies are formulated.

TABLE 22.1 Preparations of "Off-the Shelf" policies in advance for implementation in future unknown economic and financial crises.

Cycle Phase	Economic Segment	Preparations Specific to the Segment	Preparations for the Overall Magnitudes of the Policies
Boom	Real Economy	Prepare "Off-the-Shelf" Policies for Household Distress and Hardening	Make advance preparations for the overall magnitudes of fiscal, monetary, and regulatory policy responses.
		Prepare "Off-the-Shelf" Policies for Small Business Distress and Hardening	
		Prepare "Off-the-Shelf" Policies for Other Critical Industry Distress and Hardening	
	Banking Sector	Prepare "Off-the-Shelf" Policies for Bank Distress and Hardening	
	Financial Markets	Prepare "Off-the-Shelf" Policies for Financial Firm Distress and Hardening	

As shown in the table, some of the policies focus on contending with the distress imposed on the economic segments of the society by the crisis and other policies are for hardening the segments to withstand the distress.

Policies for distress include, for example, stimulus payments to households to help those out of work be fed and sheltered and maintain their demands for goods and services to support the rest of the economy. Policies for hardening include boosting deposit insurance and safeguards for pension funds and mutual firms that invest households' savings to keep them resilient. "Off-the-shelf" means that the distribution details, legal requirements, and other specifications, that can be carefully chosen in advance, are the policies taken care of and can be implemented quickly with only minor adjustments when the time comes.

The policies are set up for all three economic segments of the society that all must work for positive economic and financial outcomes during the crisis to come. We divide the real economy segment into three groups for policy attention—households, small businesses, and workers and firms in critical industries that are needed to support the economy. Households and small businesses typically need more external help during crises and everyone depends on critical industries. Aid for large nonfinancial businesses that are generally more capable of managing crisis conditions on their own is not planned in advance, but could be provided on a more ad hoc basis if needed in a severe crisis. Policies also are designed for banks and financial markets that are always critical to the function of the economy. The far right of the table indicates that policies that have broad impacts, such as fiscal, monetary, and regulatory policies are applied with reasonable overall magnitudes to avoid either excessive or deficient economic and financial stimulus overall.

Table 22.2 reveals that the second set of tasks during the boom involves actions to offset current excesses in the different economic segments and overall excesses during the boom itself. As discussed earlier in the book, economic and financial agents in all segments tend to engage in excessive risk-taking of all types during booms that exacerbate cycles and hasten and intensify future crises. Therefore, actions such as stricter enforcement of bank capital standards and securities laws that offset or lean against such excesses in the segments overall lessen the distress in the subsequent crises and ease the future tasks of contending with such distress. As discussed earlier, the effects of excesses

TABLE 22.2 Actions to offset current excesses in advance of future unknown economic and financial crises.

Cycle Phase	Economic Segment	Actions to Offset Excesses Specific to the Segment	Actions to Address the Overall Magnitudes of the Excesses
Boom	Real Economy	Actions to Offset Current Household-Specific Excesses	Engage in fiscal, monetary, and regulatory policy actions that lean against current excesses in real economy, banking sector, and financial markets at levels generally consistent with currently observed such excesses.
		Actions to Offset Current Small Business-Specific Excesses	
		Actions to Offset Current Other Critical Industry-Specific Excesses	
	Banking Sector	Actions to Offset Current Banking-Specific Excesses	
	Financial Markets	Actions to Offset Current Financial Market-Specific Excesses	

TABLE 22.3 Actions to implement and adjust existing "Off-the-Shelf" distress and hardening policies in current economic or financial crisis.

Cycle Phase	Economic Segment	Implement and Adjust Existing Policies Specific to the Segment	Adjust Overall Magnitudes of the Policies
Crisis	Real Economy	Implement and Adjust Existing Policies for Household Distress and Hardening	Adjust overall magnitudes of fiscal, monetary, and regulatory policy responses as needed to be consistent with observed overall needs of the real economy, banking sector, and financial markets.
		Implement and Adjust Existing Policies for Small Business Distress and Hardening	
		Implement and Adjust Existing Policies for Other Critical Industry Distress and Hardening	
	Banking Sector	Implement and Adjust Existing Policies for Bank Distress and Hardening	
	Financial Markets	Implement and Adjust Existing Policies for Financial Firm Distress and Hardening	

during the boom preceding COVID-19 may have had much less effects for financial crises such as the GFC, but the nature of the next crisis is unknown during the boom and may be of any type.

Table 22.3 indicates that the only tasks imposed on policymakers when the crisis arrives are implementing and adjusting the existing policies to fit the specific situation. As noted above, these tasks must be performed in calm fashion without necessity of making too many important decisions in the frenzied confusion of a new crisis.

Similarly, Table 22.4 shows that we suggest only the seemingly simple tasks of reducing or eliminating policy interventions, when possible, during the crisis aftermath. As discussed, COVID-19 made abundantly clear the dangers of continuing stimulus policies when they are no longer needed, but we recognize that such curtailment of stimulus may be easier said than done.

TABLE 22.4 Actions to reduce or eliminate current policy intervention excesses in the aftermath of an economic or financial crisis.

Cycle Phase	Economic Segment	Reduce or Eliminate Address Current Policy Interventions in the Segment	Adjust Overall Magnitudes of the Policy Interventions
Aftermath	Real Economy	Reduce or Eliminate Interventions for Households	Address overall magnitudes of fiscal, monetary, and regulatory policy responses as needed to be consistent with observed overall needs of the real economy, banking sector, and financial markets.
		Reduce or Eliminate Interventions for Small Businesses	
		Reduce or Eliminate Interventions for Critical Industries	
	Banking Sector	Reduce or Eliminate Interventions for Banks	
	Financial Markets	Reduce or Eliminate Interventions for Financial Markets	

22.3 Rough suggestions for adapting *"Expect the Unexpected"* research and policy preparations for other types of future crises

Our blueprint for contending with economic and financial crises might be usefully adapted for other types of crises by those who are trained professionals in the relevant fields. Health experts, weather experts, and military experts use similar types of strategies to plan for and deal with the realities and aftermaths of the crises in which they specialize of pandemics and other health emergencies; hurricanes, tornados, and other weather natural disasters; and wars, occupations, and military standoffs.

Additionally, our strategies might be usefully adapted in some way for what is likely the greatest global challenge for humanity: the climate crisis. We do not purport to be experts in that field, nor are we aware of how strategies for climate change are currently formulated. Any adaptation of our strategies would have to be thoroughly vetted by relevant experts with the appropriate knowledge. Nonetheless, we conclude our book with some cautiously provided rough suggestions for how our *"Expect the Unexpected"* research and policy preparations might be adapted for climate change.

Whether or not our crisis blueprint is taken up by climate change experts, we believe our rather simple adaptation to another type of crisis may demonstrate the value of our strategies. For policy strategies initiated by researchers to be implemented by policymakers, their usefulness must be demonstrated, and such flexibility for use in another type of crisis may help demonstrate that.

Thus, to wind up the book, we direct readers' attention to the tasks for the climate crisis in Tables 22.5–22.7 and Fig. 22.1. These mostly follow in straightforward fashion from those for the economic and financial crises, with the only a few notable exceptions.

One exception is that it is more difficult to determine when the climate boom ends and the crisis begins. We make the tables under somewhat arbitrary assumption that the climate crisis is in the future, but the boom and crisis could be combined if desired to consider that we are already in the climate crisis.

The second notable difference in the first three climate tables is that, for the real economy, we focus on different groups of critical households and firms. The three groups for the climate crisis are

TABLE 22.5 Preparations of "Off-the Shelf" policies in advance for implementation in future climate crisis.

Cycle Phase	Economic Segment	Preparations Specific to the Segment	Preparations for the Overall Magnitudes of the Policies
Boom	Real Economy	Prepare "Off-the-Shelf" Policies for Reducing Carbon Emissions by Households and Firms Critical to Emissions	Make advance preparations for the overall magnitudes of expenditures on carbon emission reductions, carbon consumption, and climate change protections.
		Prepare "Off-the-Shelf" Policies for Reducing Carbon Consumption by Households and Firms Critical to Consumption	
		Prepare "Off-the-Shelf" Policies for Protecting Critical Vulnerable Households and Firms	
	Banking Sector	Prepare "Off-the-Shelf" Policies to Encourage Bank Financing for Climate Change-Critical Households and Firms	
	Financial Markets	Prepare "Off-the-Shelf" Policies to Encourage Financial Market Financing for Climate Change-Critical Households and Firms	

TABLE 22.6 Actions to offset current excesses or deficiencies in advance of future climate crisis.

Cycle Phase	Economic Segment	Actions to Offset Excesses or Deficiencies Specific to the Segment	Actions to Address the Overall Magnitudes of the Excesses and Deficiencies
Boom	Real Economy	Actions to Offset Current Excesses in Carbon Emissions by Households and Firms Critical to Emissions	Coordinate overall magnitudes of expenditures on carbon emission reductions, carbon consumption, and climate change protections.
		Actions to Offset Current Excesses in Carbon Consumption by Households and Firms Critical to Consumption	
		Actions to Offset Current Deficiencies in Protecting Critical Vulnerable Households and Firms	
	Banking Sector	Actions to Facilitate Bank Financing for Climate Change-Critical Households and Firms	
	Financial Markets	Actions to Facilitate Financial Market Financing for Climate Change-Critical Households and Firms	

TABLE 22.7 Actions to implement and adjust existing "Off-the-Shelf" distress and hardening policies in current climate crisis.

Cycle Phase	Economic Segment	Implement and Adjust Existing Policies Specific to the Segment	Adjust Overall Magnitudes of the Policies
Crisis	Real Economy	Implement and Adjust Existing Policies for Reducing Carbon Emissions by Households and Firms Critical to Emissions	Adjust overall magnitudes of policy responses as needed to be consistent with observed overall needs of the critical households, firms, banks, and financial markets.
		Implement and Adjust Existing Policies for Reducing Carbon Consumption by Households and Firms Critical to Consumption	
		Implement and Adjust Existing Policies for Protecting Critical Vulnerable Households and Firms	
	Banking Sector	Implement and Adjust Policies to Facilitate Bank Financing for Climate Change-Critical Households and Firms	
	Financial Markets	Implement and Adjust Policies to Facilitate Financial Market Financing for Climate Change-Critical Households and Firms	

FIG. 22.1 Actions in the aftermath of a climate change crisis—be thankful for the blue and green outcome on the left or try to survive as best as possible the brown and yellow outcome on the right!

households and firms that are critical to reducing carbon emissions (e.g., energy industry), those that are critical to reducing carbon consumption (e.g., those driving gas guzzling cars and airlines), and those most vulnerable to climate change (e.g., those on coast lines that may need reinforcements or relocation funds).

The third key difference from the economic and financial crises blueprint lies in the final climate change strategies for the aftermath shown in Fig. 22.1. When the aftermath arrives, we throw the blueprint out of the window if we can find one and either be thankful for the blue and green outcome on the left or try to survive as best as possible the brown and yellow outcome on the right!

Thanks so much to the readers for taking this journey with us! *Adieu!*

Appendix

FIG. A1. Key performance indicators (KPIs) and COVID-19 health statistics around the world.

We present key performance indicators (KPIs) and COVID-19 health statistics for 39 major countries around the world, including the top 16 nations in GDP rank as of 2022. We include indicators for all three key economic segments—the real economy, banking sector, and financial markets. These data stretch from 2018 onward, generally to 2022 for the real economy, to 2021 for the banking sector, and as available for financial markets. Real economy statistics include real GDP growth, unemployment rate, public debt to GDP and GDP per capita ratios, inflation rate, and indicators of whether government income and debt relief support were extensive, limited, or none. Banking sector statistics cover various capital ratios, asset quality measures, profitability, and loan, deposit, and efficiency ratios. Financial market indicators include stock and bond market indices and CDS spreads when available. The COVID-19 statistics are cumulative as of December 2022 for virus cases, deaths, and vaccination rates of at least one dose administered for the population of each country.

Figures are based on raw data from John Hopkins University Coronavirus Center, International Monetary Fund (IMF), Bureau van Dijk (BvD) BankFocus, Our World in Data, Google Finance, Trading Economics, and Wikipedia.

Panel A1: Key Performance Indicators for US (GDP Rank: 1st)
US COVID-19 Stats: 99,892,513 Total Cases (30,319.3 Cases/100K Pop); 1,087,410 Total Deaths (330.1 Deaths/100K Pop); 81.3% Vaccinated.

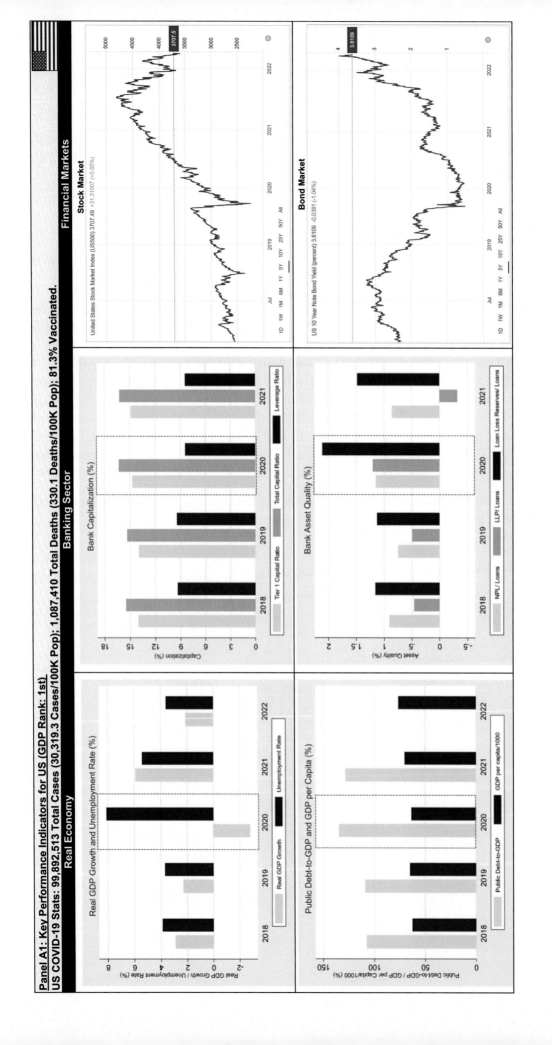

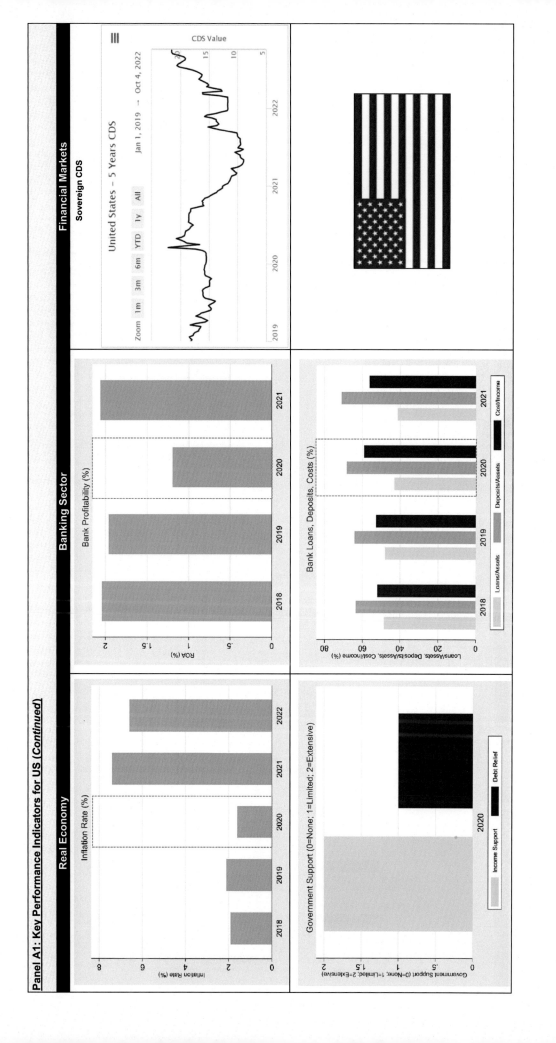

Panel A1: Key Performance Indicators for US (Continued)

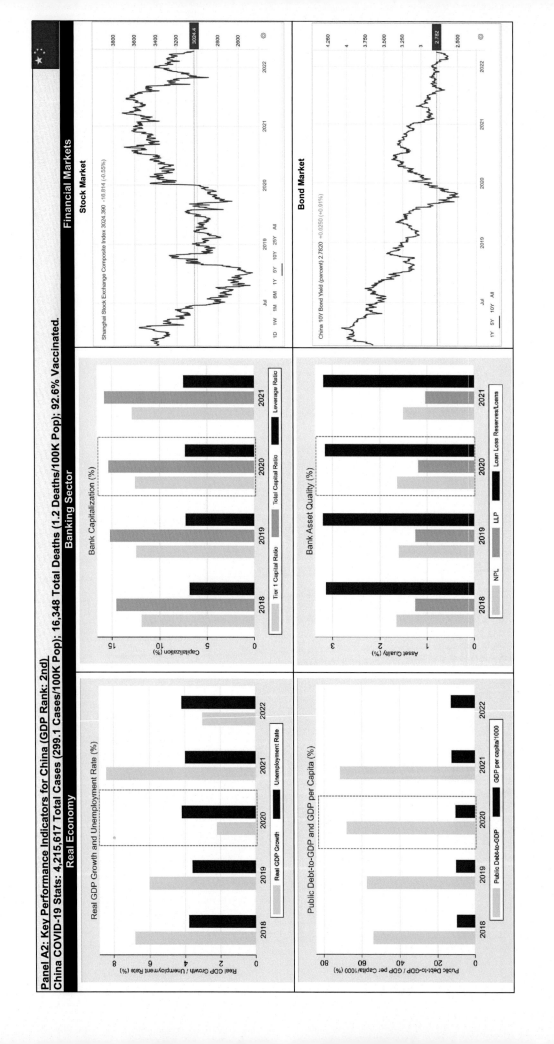

Panel A2: Key Performance Indicators for China (GDP Rank: 2nd)
China COVID-19 Stats: 4,215,617 Total Cases (299.1 Cases/100K Pop); 16,348 Total Deaths (1.2 Deaths/100K Pop); 92.6% Vaccinated.

Panel A2: Key Performance Indicators for China (*Continued*)

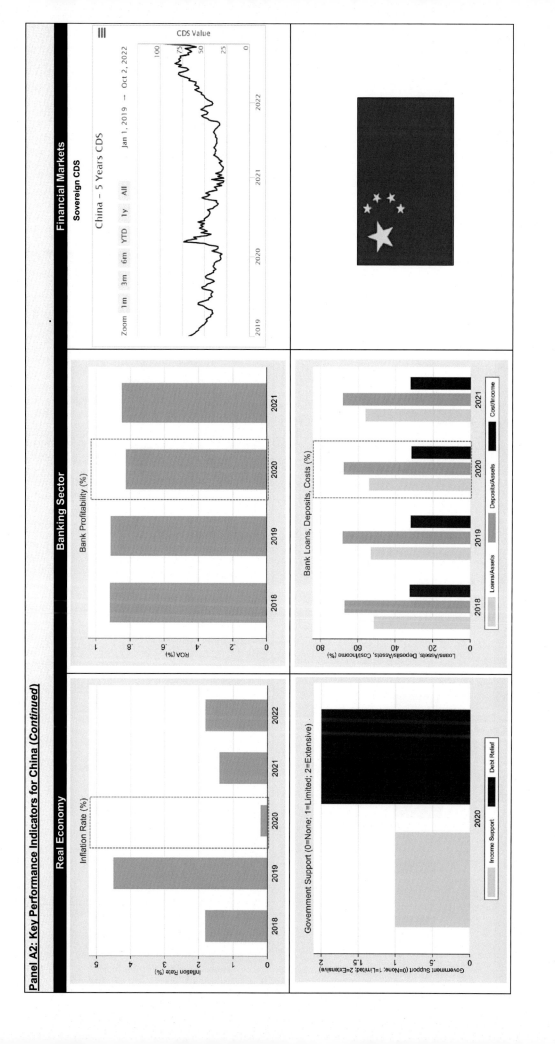

Panel A3: Key Performance Indicators for Japan (GDP Rank: 3rd)

Japan COVID-19 Stats: 27,138,615 Total Cases (21,455.6 Cases/100K Pop); 53,327 Total Deaths (42.2 Deaths/100K Pop); 82.6% Vaccinated.

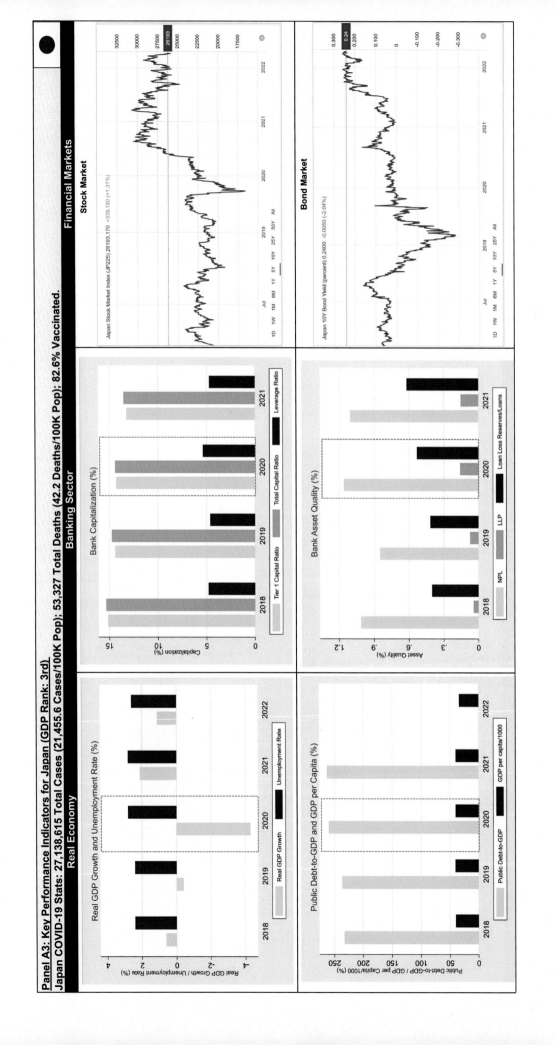

Panel A3: Key Performance Indicators for Japan (*Continued*)

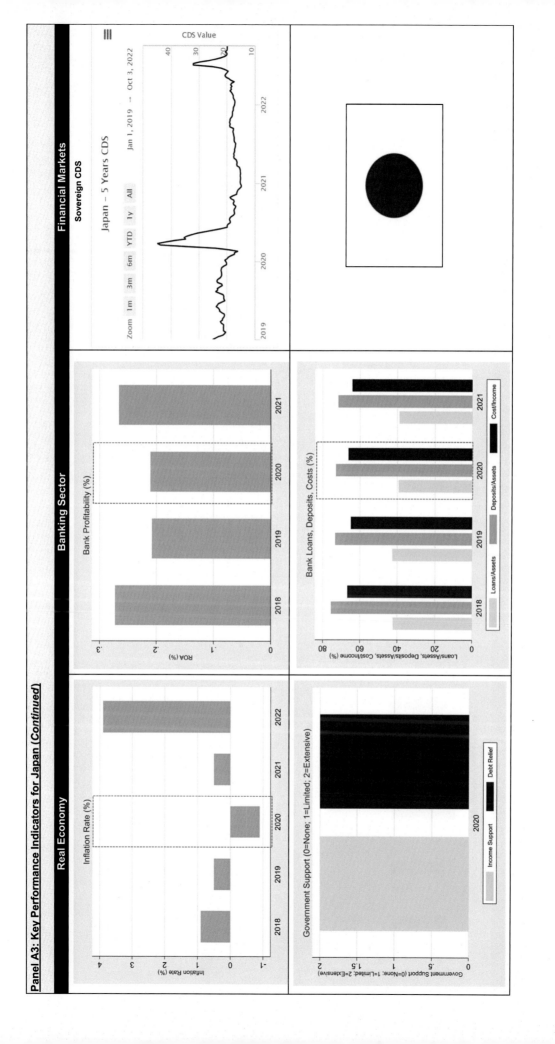

Panel A4: Key Performance Indicators for Germany (GDP Rank: 4th)
Germany COVID-19 Stats: 36,980,883 Total Cases (44,471.7 Cases/100K Pop);159,884 Total Deaths (192.3 Deaths/100K Pop); 78.0% Vaccinated.

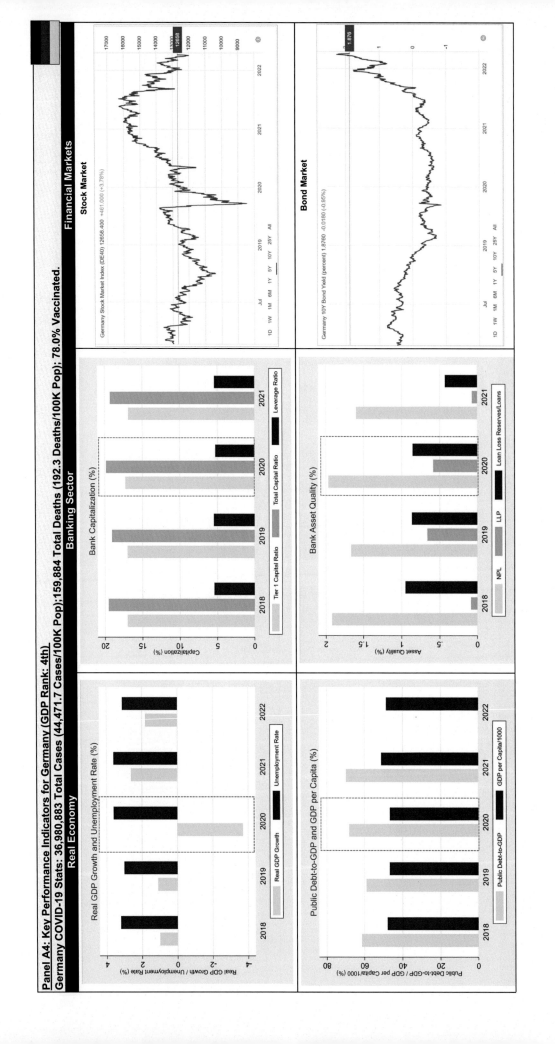

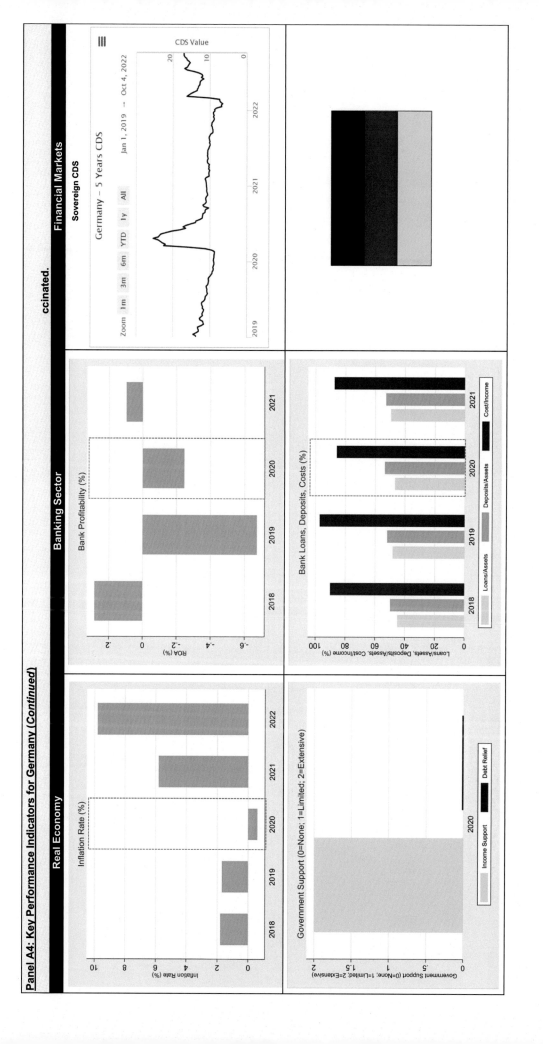

Panel A4: Key Performance Indicators for Germany (*Continued*)

ccinated.

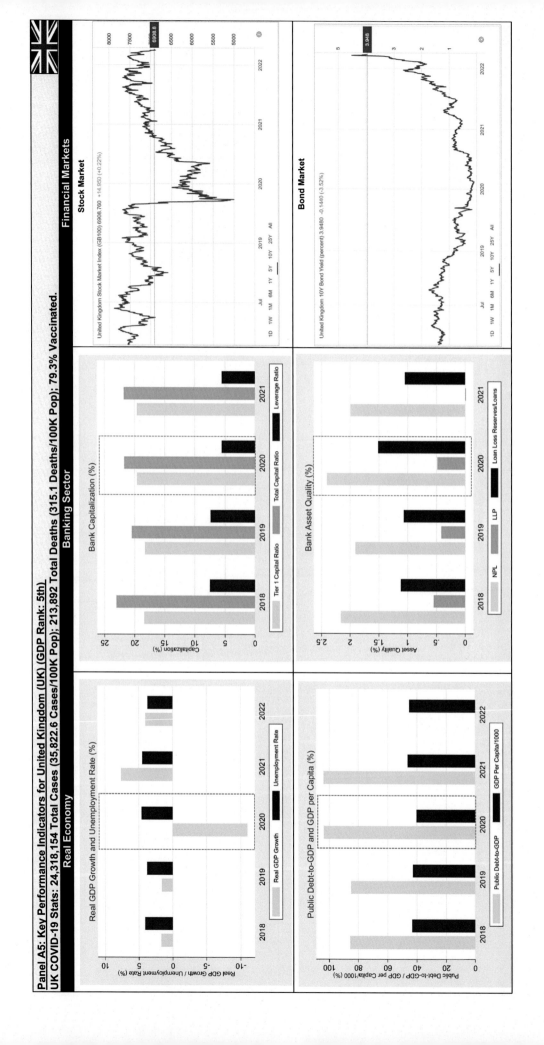

Panel A5: Key Performance Indicators for United Kingdom (UK) (GDP Rank: 5th)
UK COVID-19 Stats: 24,318,154 Total Cases (35,822.6 Cases/100K Pop); 213,892 Total Deaths (315.1 Deaths/100K Pop); 79.3% Vaccinated.

Panel A5: Key Performance Indicators for United Kingdom (UK) (Continued)

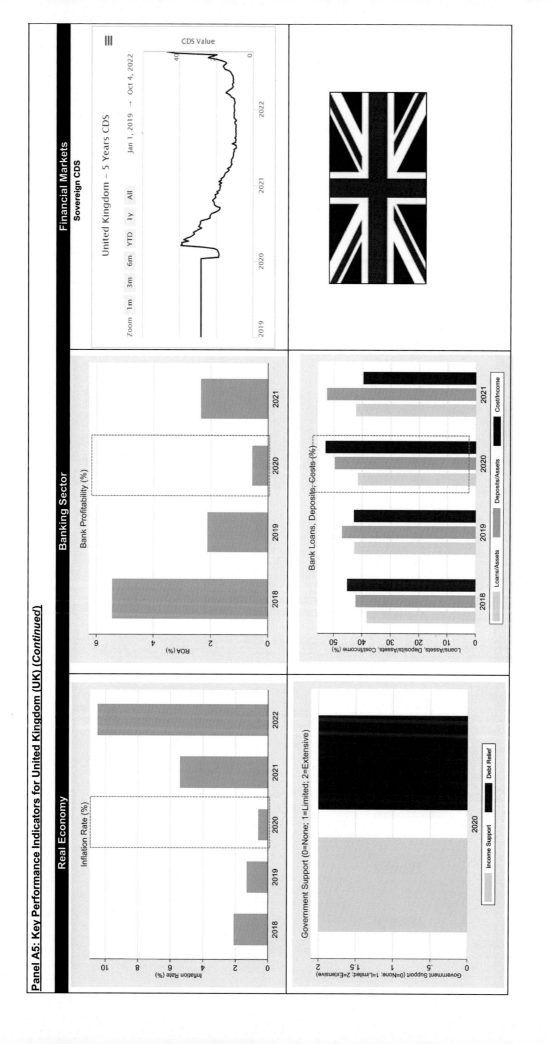

Panel A6: Key Performance Indicators for India (GDP Rank: 6th)
India COVID-19 Stats: 44,677,310 Total Cases (3,237.1 Cases/100K Pop); 530,674 Total Deaths (38.5 Deaths/100K Pop); 74.4 % Vaccinated.

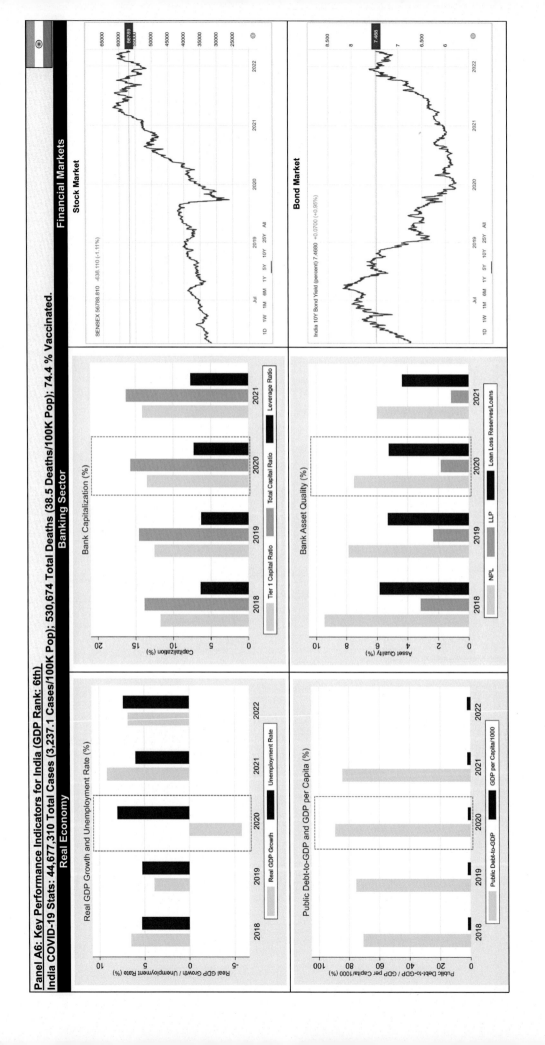

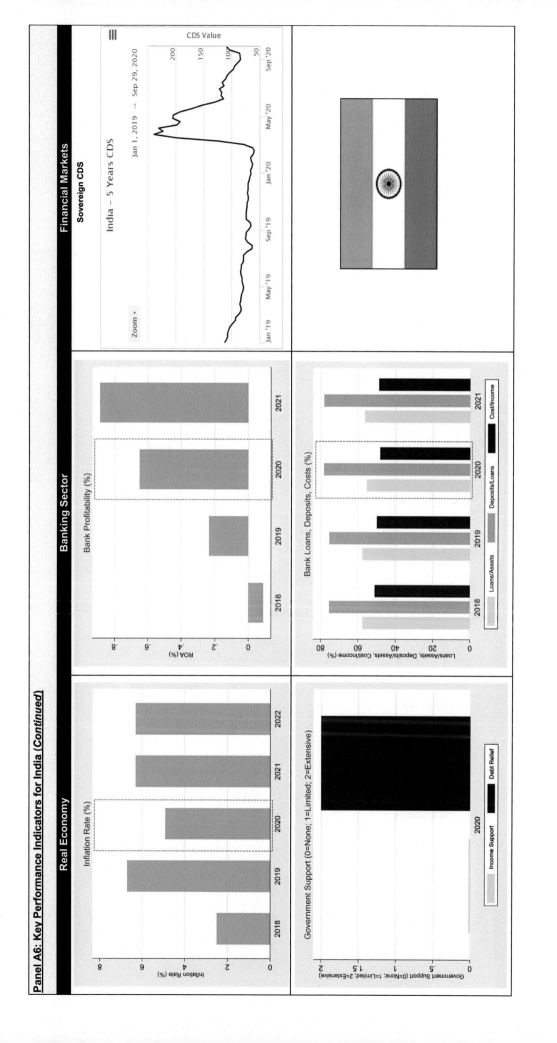

Panel A6: Key Performance Indicators for India (*Continued*)

Panel A7: Key Performance Indicators for France (GDP Rank: 7th)

France COVID-19 Stats: 39,004,649 Total Cases (59,778.1 Cases/100K Pop); 161,400 Total Deaths (247.4 Deaths/100K Pop); 83.7% Vaccinated.

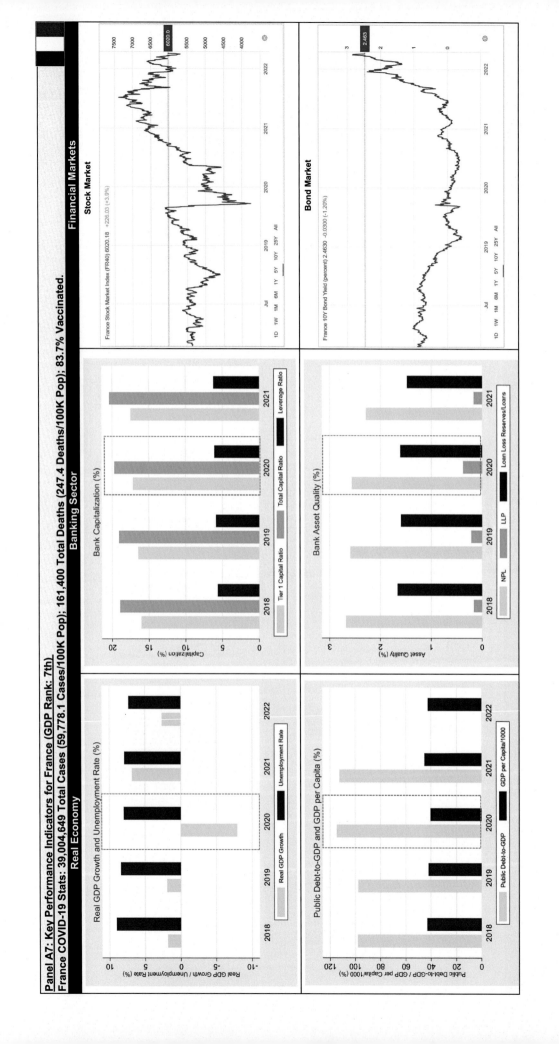

Panel A7: Key Performance Indicators for France (*Continued*)

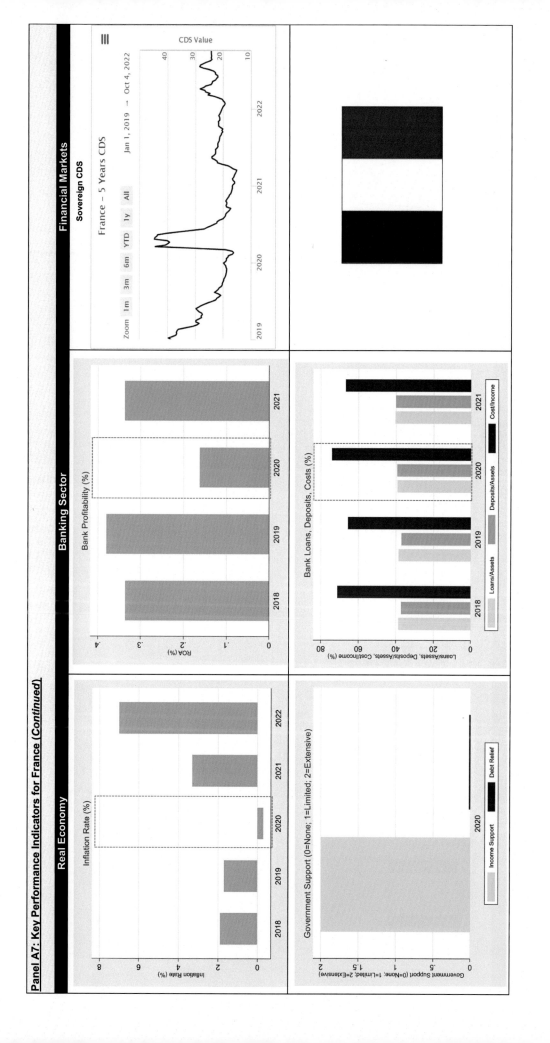

Panel A8: Key Performance Indicators for Italy (GDP Rank: 8th)

Italy COVID-19 Stats: 24,884,034 Total Cases (41,156.8 Cases/100K Pop); 183,138 Total Deaths (302.9 Deaths/100K Pop); 84.1% Vaccinated.

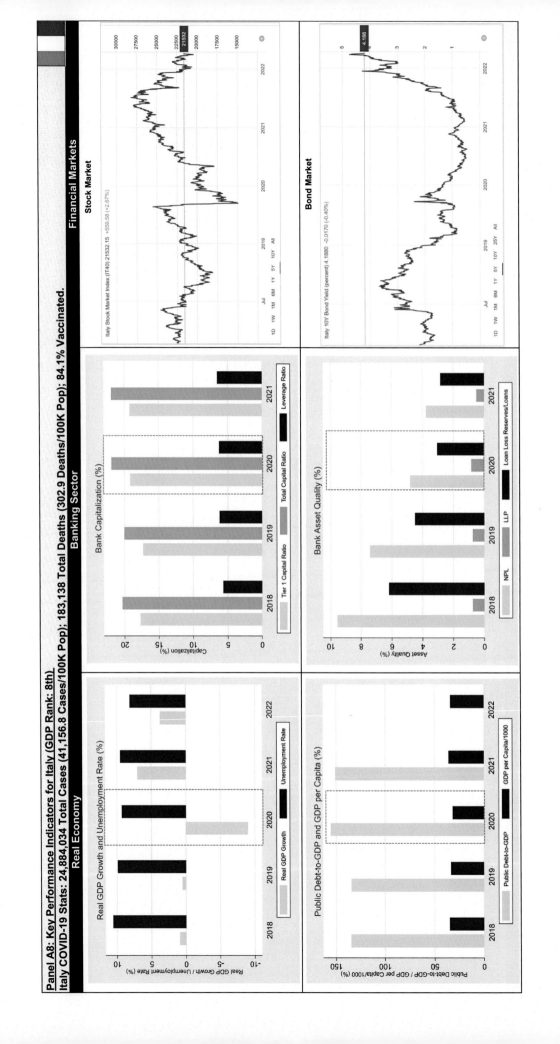

Panel A8: Key Performance Indicators for Italy (*Continued*)

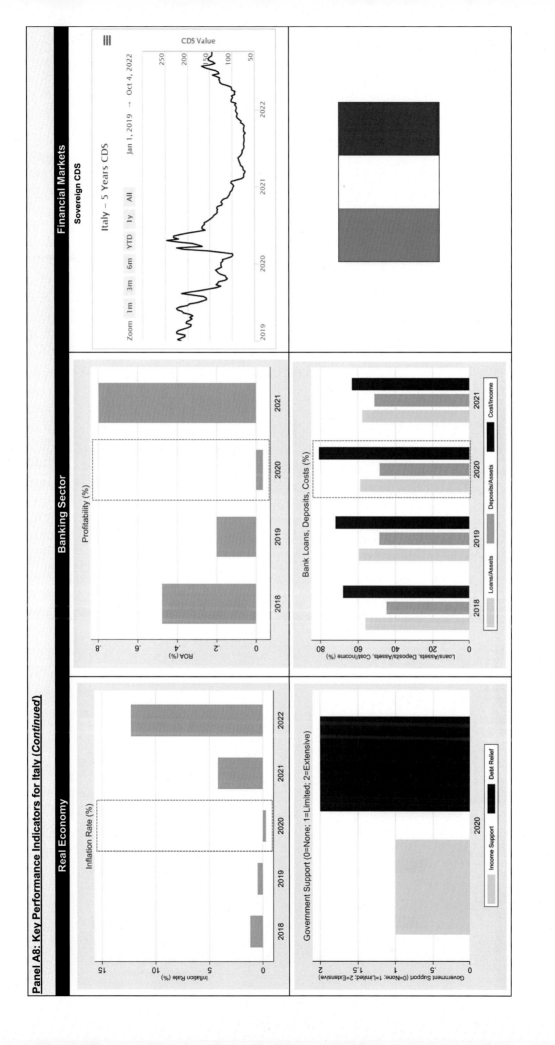

Panel A9: Key Performance Indicators for Canada (GDP Rank: 9th)

Canada COVID-19 Stats: 4,477,829 Total Cases (11,707.7 Cases/100K Pop); 48,807 Total Deaths 127.6 Deaths/100K Pop); 90.3% Vaccinated.

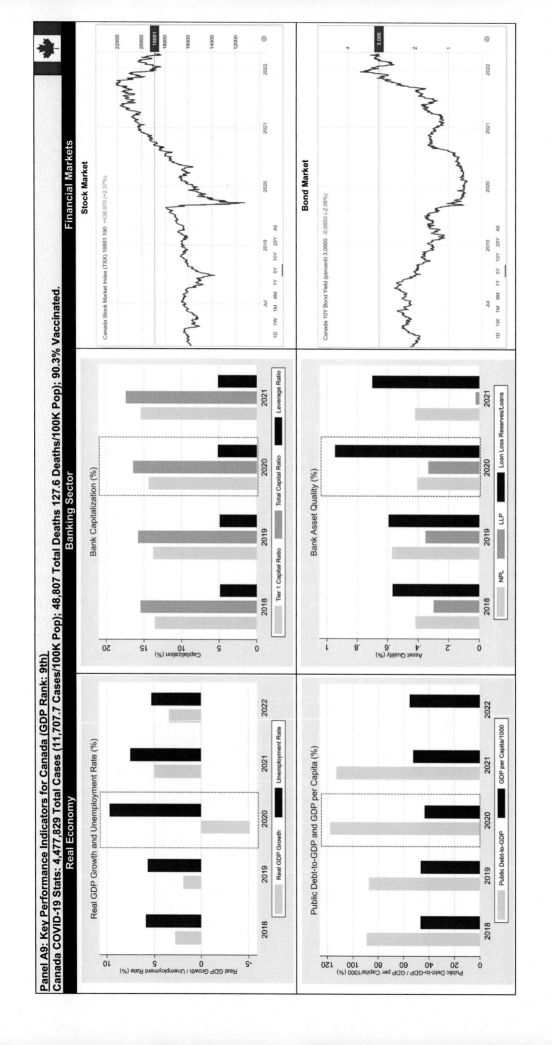

Panel A9: Key Performance Indicators for Canada (*Continued*)

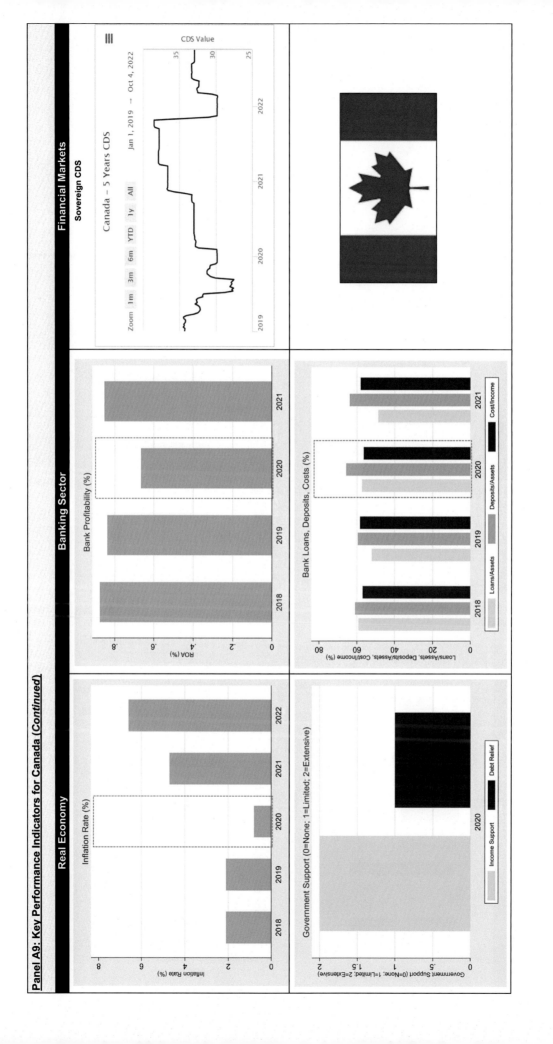

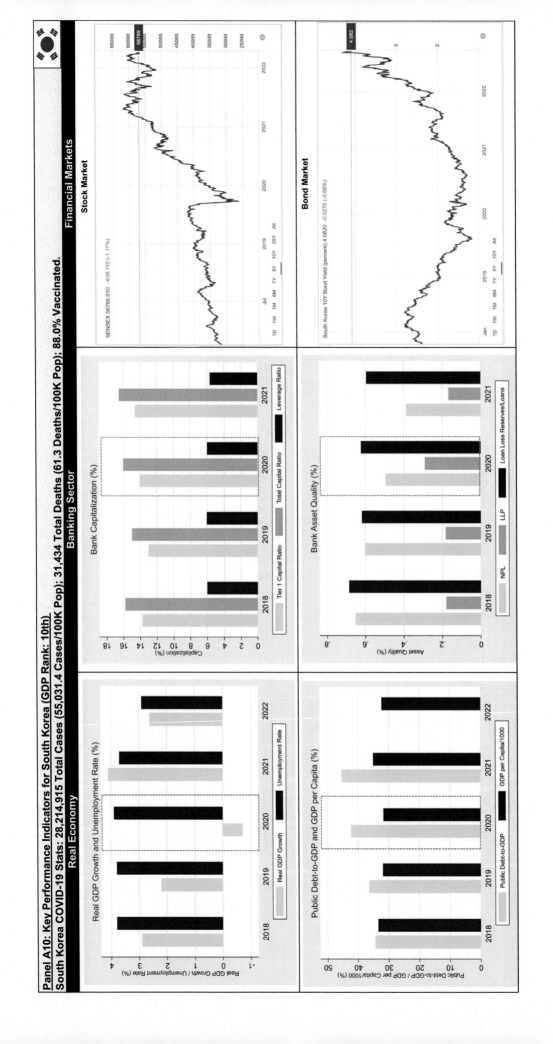

Panel A10: Key Performance Indicators for South Korea (GDP Rank: 10th)
South Korea COVID-19 Stats: 28,214,915 Total Cases (55,031.4 Cases/100K Pop); 31,434 Total Deaths (61.3 Deaths/100K Pop); 88.0% Vaccinated.

Financial Markets

Stock Market

Bond Market

Banking Sector

Bank Capitalization (%)

Bank Asset Quality (%)

Real Economy

Real GDP Growth and Unemployment Rate (%)

Public Debt-to-GDP and GDP per Capita (%)

Panel A10: Key Performance Indicators for South Korea (*Continued*)

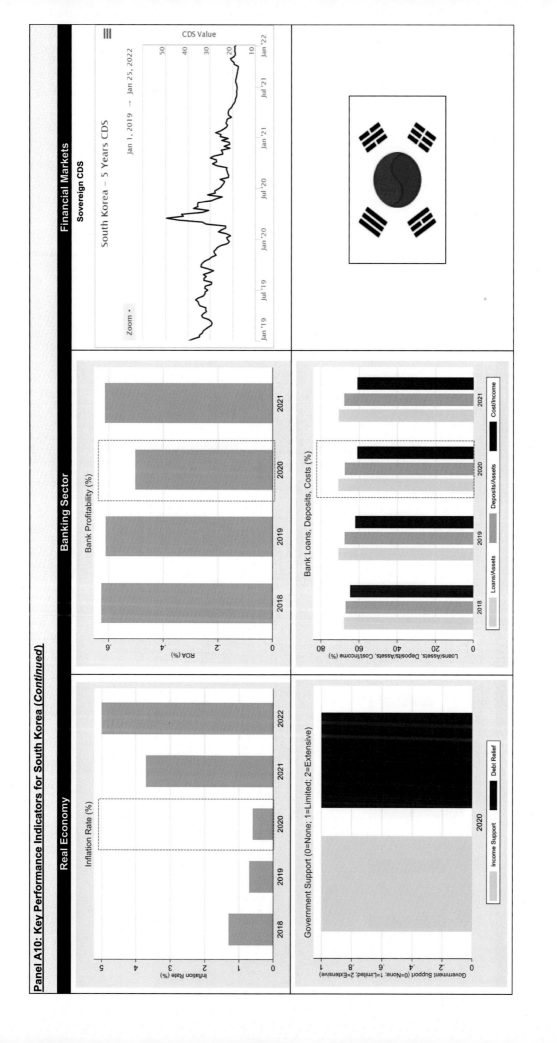

Panel A11: Key Performance Indicators for Russia (GDP Rank: 11th)

Russia COVID-19 Stats: 21,408,756 Total Cases (14,669.9 Cases/100K Pop); 385,083 Total Deaths (263.9 Deaths/100K Pop); 60.0% Vaccinated.

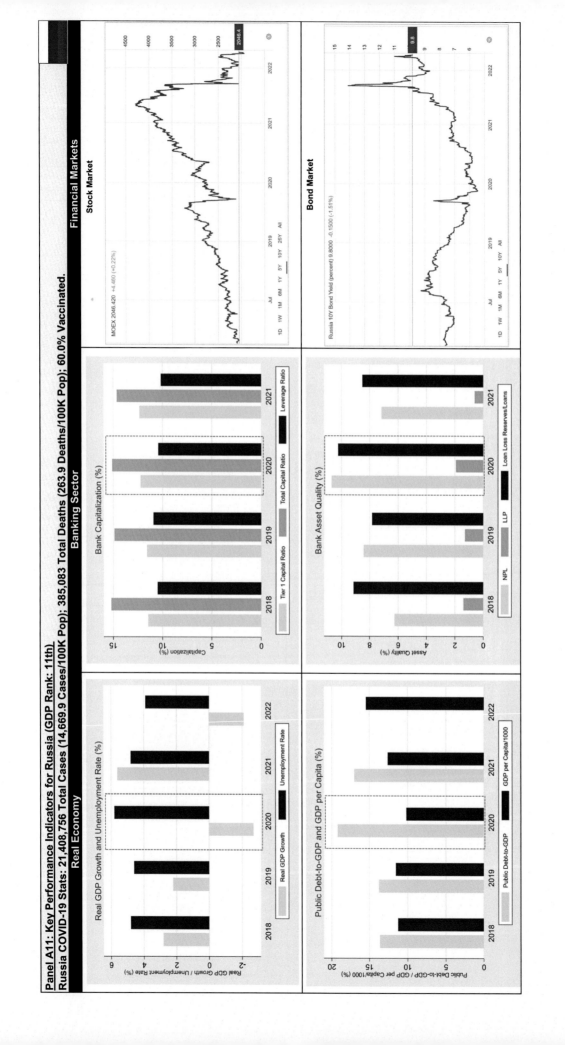

Real Economy

Banking Sector

Financial Markets

Stock Market

Bond Market

Panel A11: Key Performance Indicators for Russia (*Continued*)

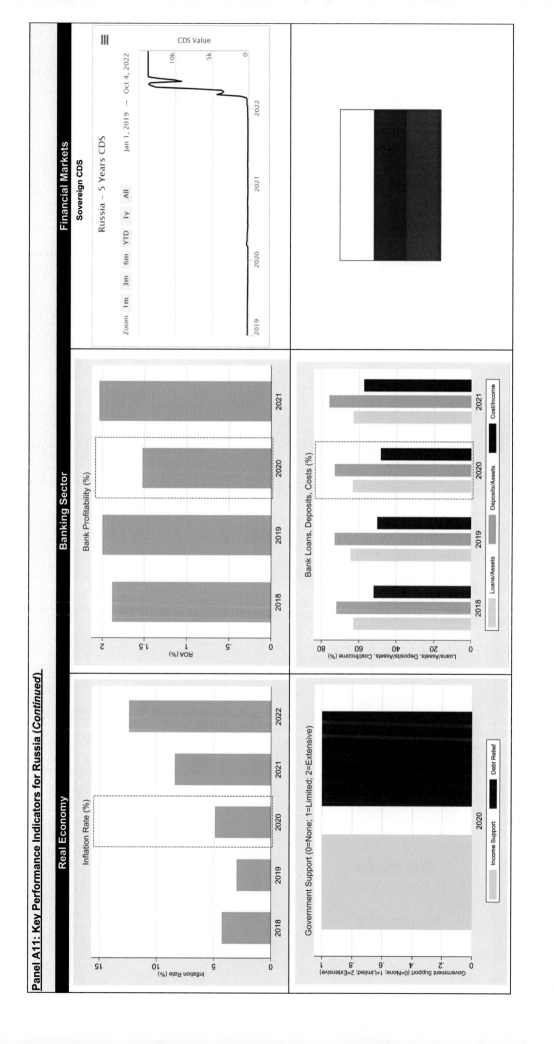

Panel A12: Key Performance Indicators for Brazil (GDP Rank: 12th)

Brazil COVID-19 Stats: 35,869,526 Total Cases (16,875.2 Cases/100K Pop); 691,810 Total Deaths (325.5 Deaths/100K Pop); 88.7% Vaccinated.

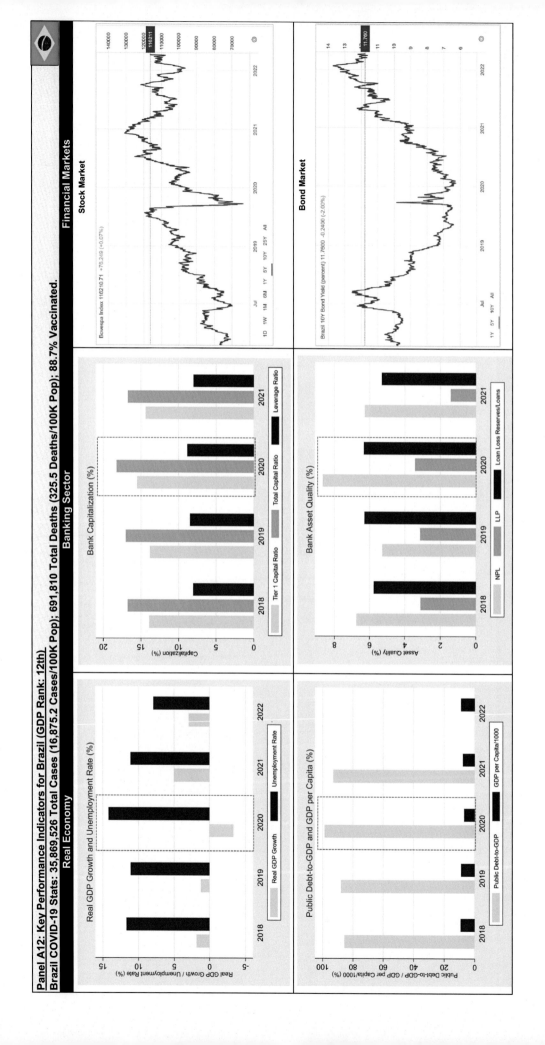

Panel A12: Key Performance Indicators for Brazil (*Continued*)

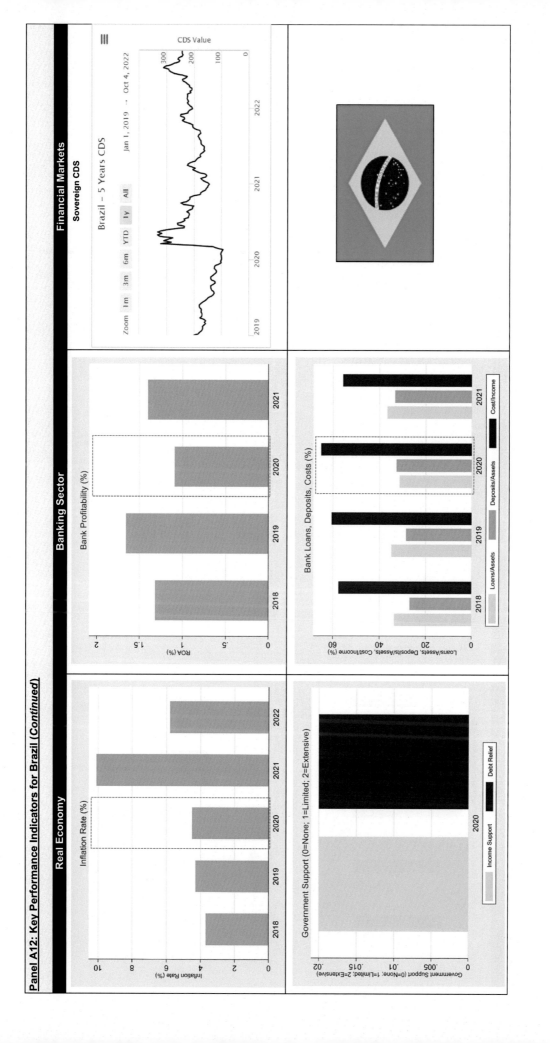

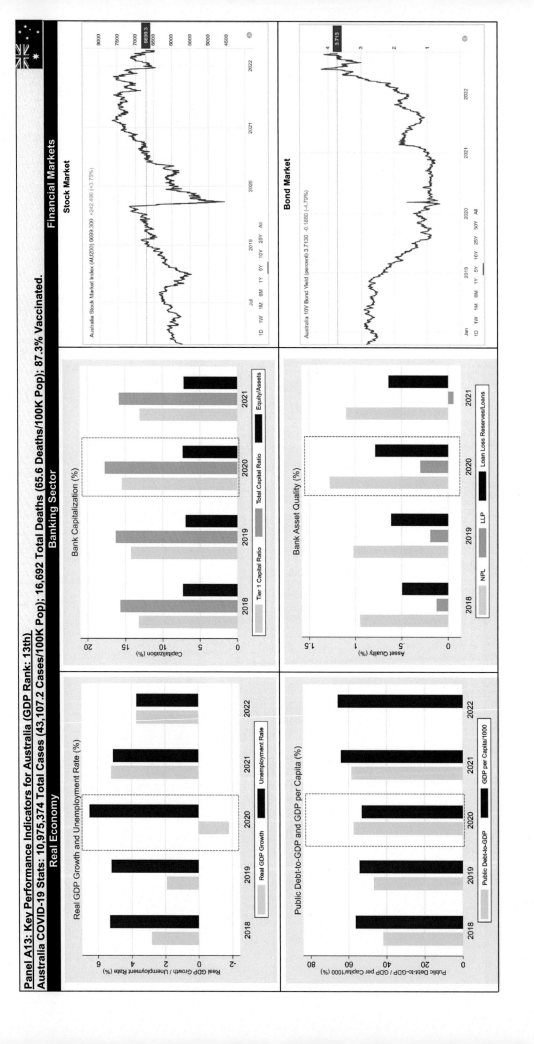

Panel A13: Key Performance Indicators for Australia (GDP Rank: 13th)
Australia COVID-19 Stats: 10,975,374 Total Cases (43,107.2 Cases/100K Pop); 16,692 Total Deaths (65.6 Deaths/100K Pop); 87.3% Vaccinated.

Panel A13: Key Performance Indicators for Australia (Continued)

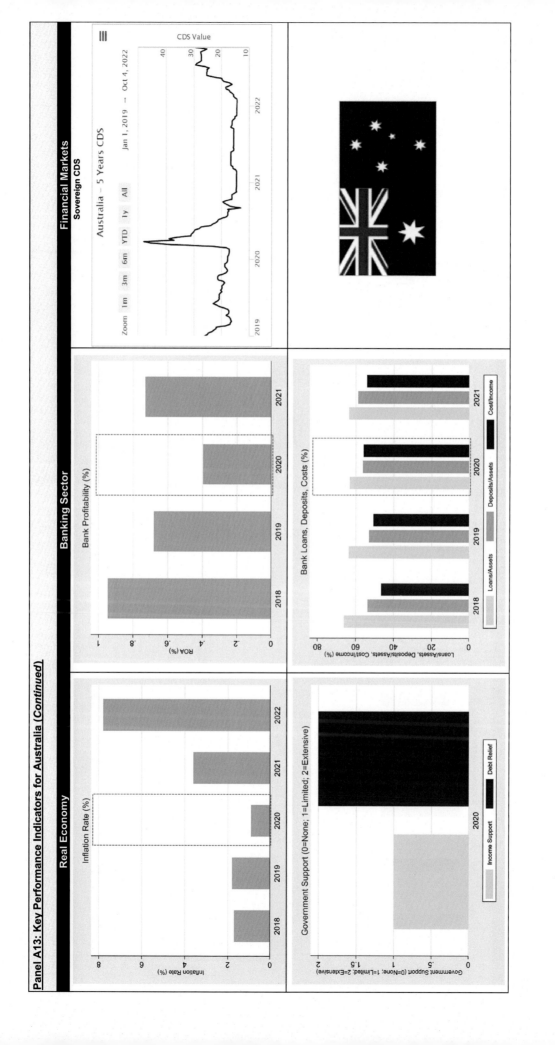

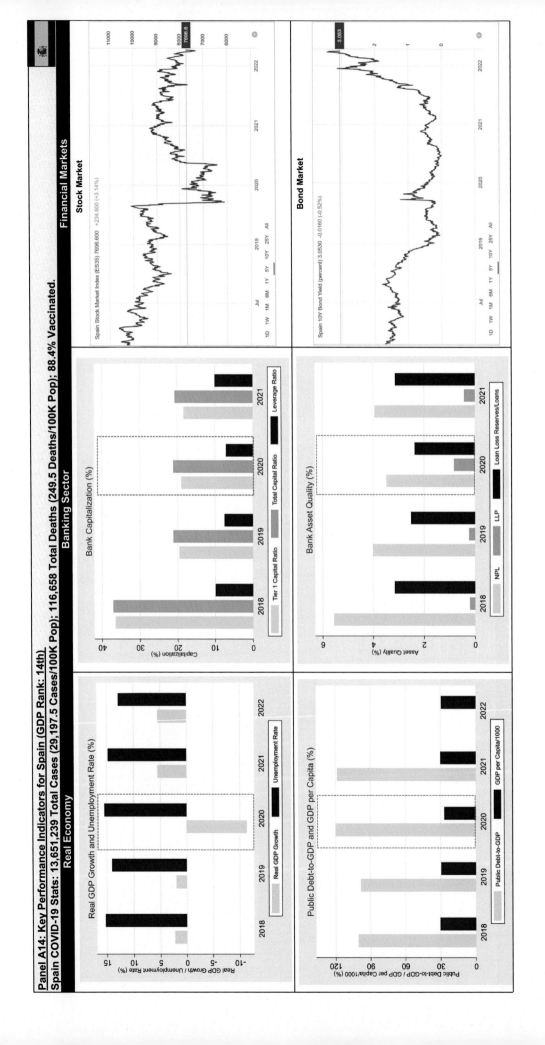

Panel A14: Key Performance Indicators for Spain (GDP Rank: 14th)
Spain COVID-19 Stats: 13,651,239 Total Cases (29,197.5 Cases/100K Pop); 116,658 Total Deaths (249.5 Deaths/100K Pop); 88.4% Vaccinated.

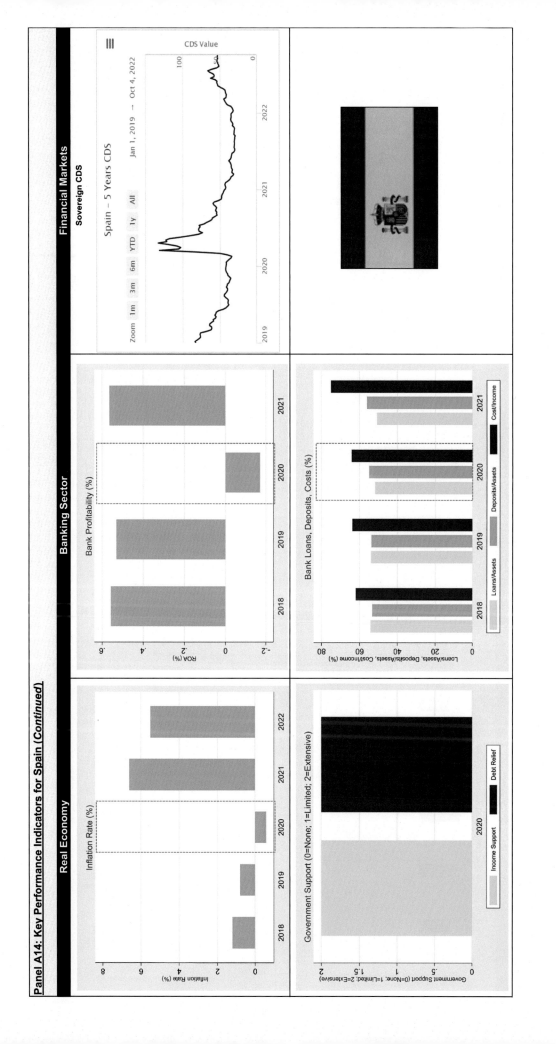

Panel A14: Key Performance Indicators for Spain (Continued)

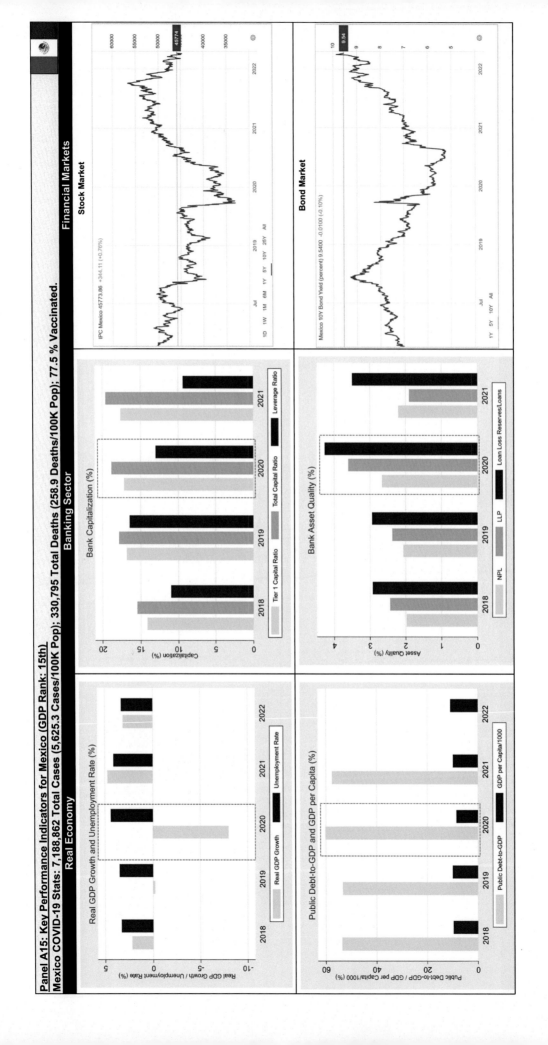

Panel A15: Key Performance Indicators for Mexico (GDP Rank: 15th)
Mexico COVID-19 Stats: 7,188,862 Total Cases (5,625.3 Cases/100K Pop); 330,795 Total Deaths (258.9 Deaths/100K Pop); 77.5 % Vaccinated.

Real Economy

Banking Sector

Financial Markets

Real GDP Growth and Unemployment Rate (%)

Public Debt-to-GDP and GDP per Capita (%)

Bank Capitalization (%)

Bank Asset Quality (%)

Stock Market

Bond Market

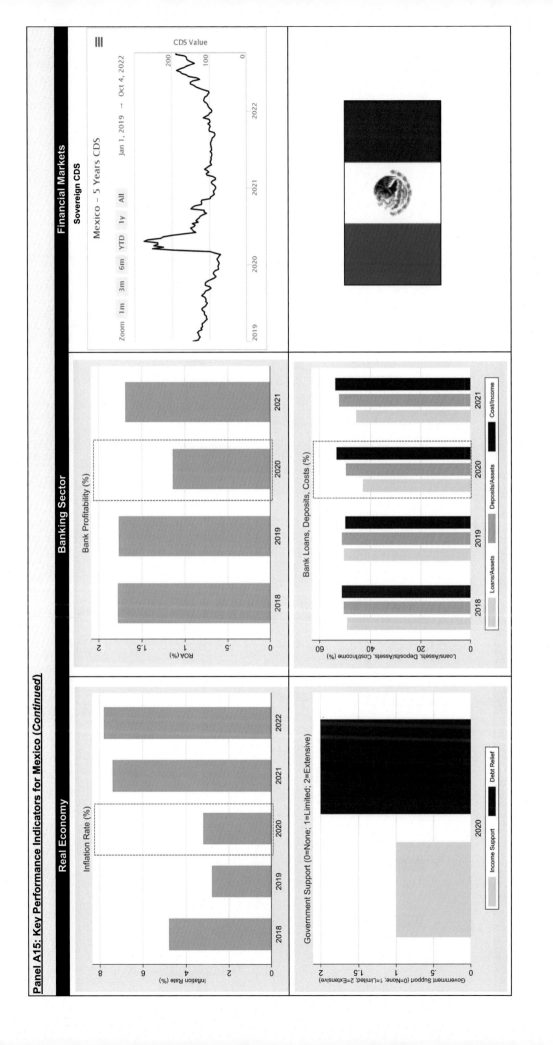

Panel A15: Key Performance Indicators for Mexico (Continued)

Panel A16: Key Performance Indicators for Indonesia (GDP Rank: 16th)

Indonesia COVID-19 Stats: 6,709,597 Total Cases (2,453.0 Cases/100K Pop); 160,398 Total Deaths (58.6 Deaths/100K Pop); 74.4 % Vaccinated.

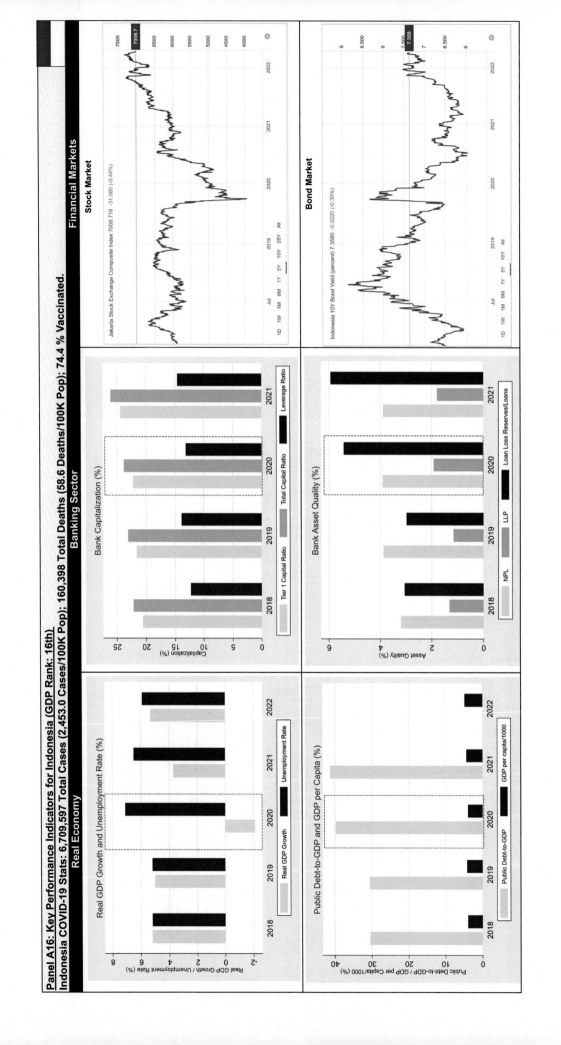

Panel A16: Key Performance Indicators for Indonesia (*Continued*)

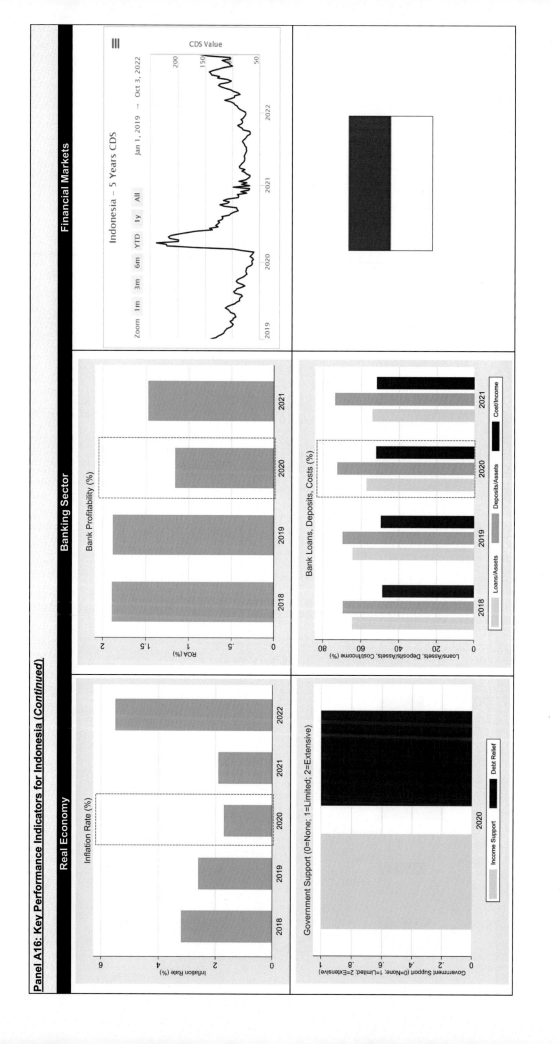

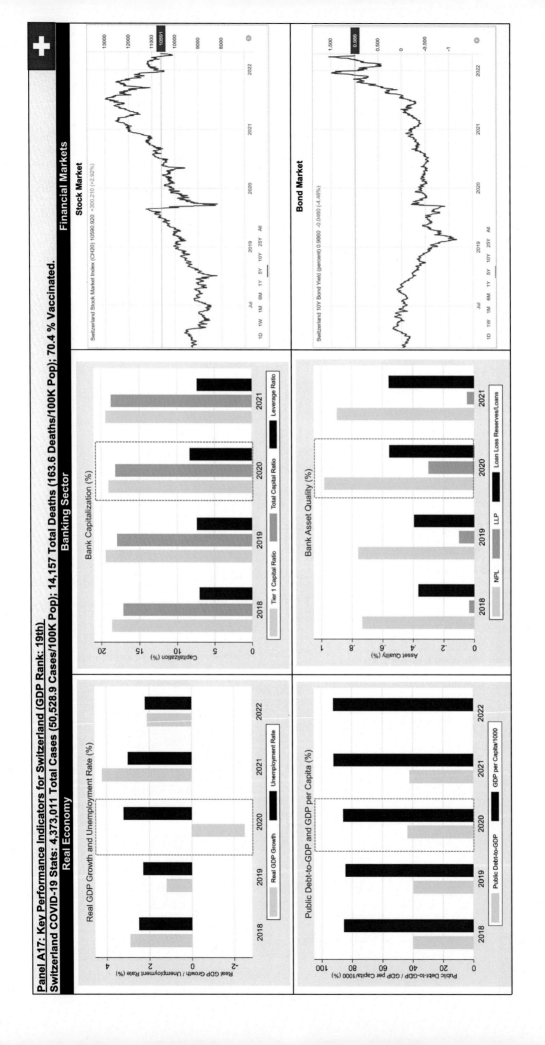

Panel A17: Key Performance Indicators for Switzerland (GDP Rank: 19th)
Switzerland COVID-19 Stats: 4,373,011 Total Cases (50,528.9 Cases/100K Pop); 14,157 Total Deaths (163.6 Deaths/100K Pop); 70.4 % Vaccinated.

Real Economy **Banking Sector** **Financial Markets**

Stock Market

Switzerland Stock Market Index (CH20) 10590.920 +300.210 (+2.92%)

Bond Market

Switzerland 10Y Bond Yield (percent) 0.9860 -0.0460 (-4.46%)

Bank Capitalization (%)

Bank Asset Quality (%)

Real GDP Growth and Unemployment Rate (%)

Public Debt-to-GDP and GDP per Capita (%)

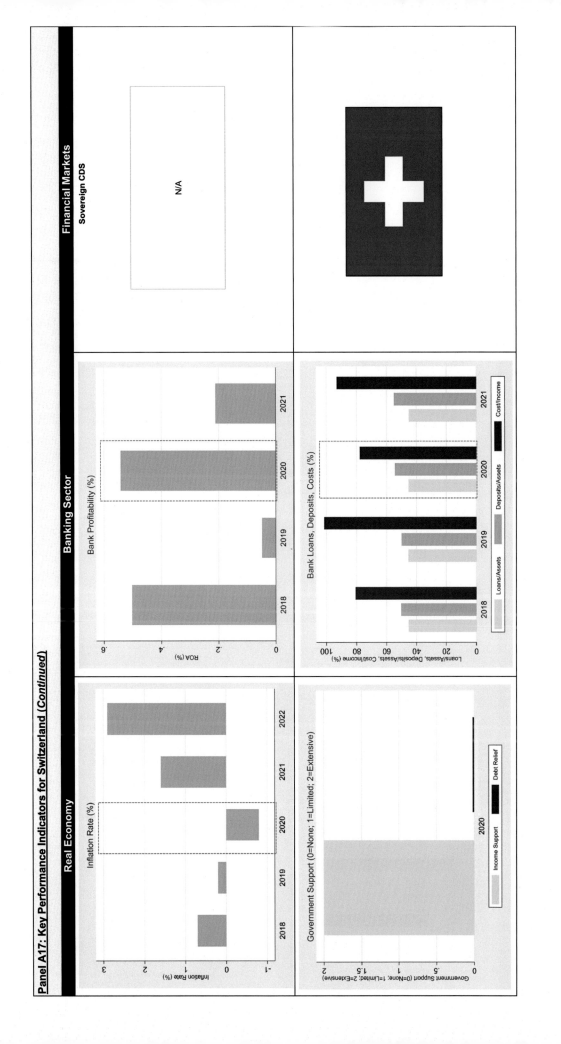

Panel A17: Key Performance Indicators for Switzerland (*Continued*)

Panel A18: Key Performance Indicators for Turkey (GDP Rank: 20th)
Turkey COVID-19 Stats: 16,919,638 Total Cases (20,062.2 Cases/100K Pop); 101,203 Total Deaths (120.0 Deaths/100K Pop); 68.7 % Vaccinated.

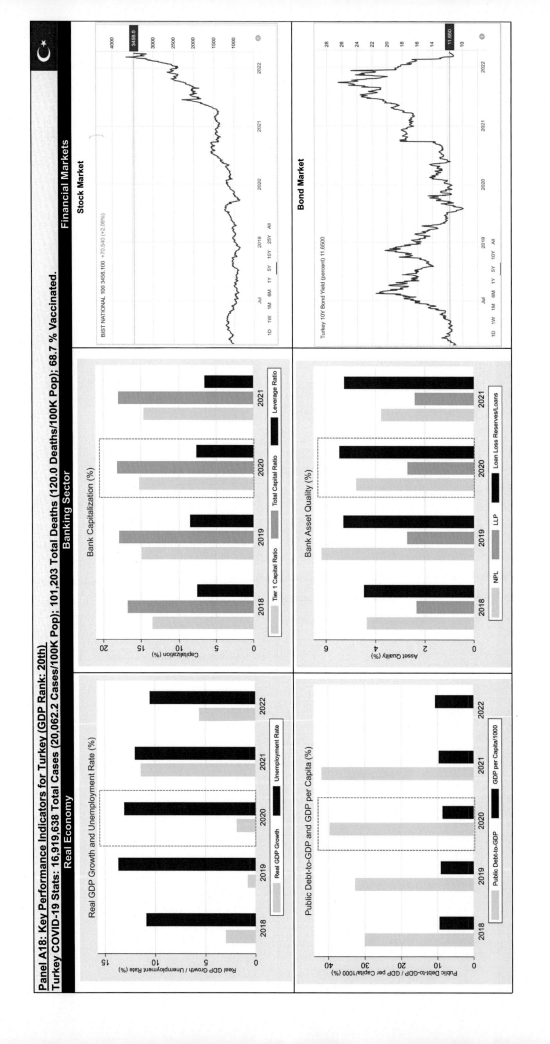

Panel A18: Key Performance Indicators for Turkey (Continued)

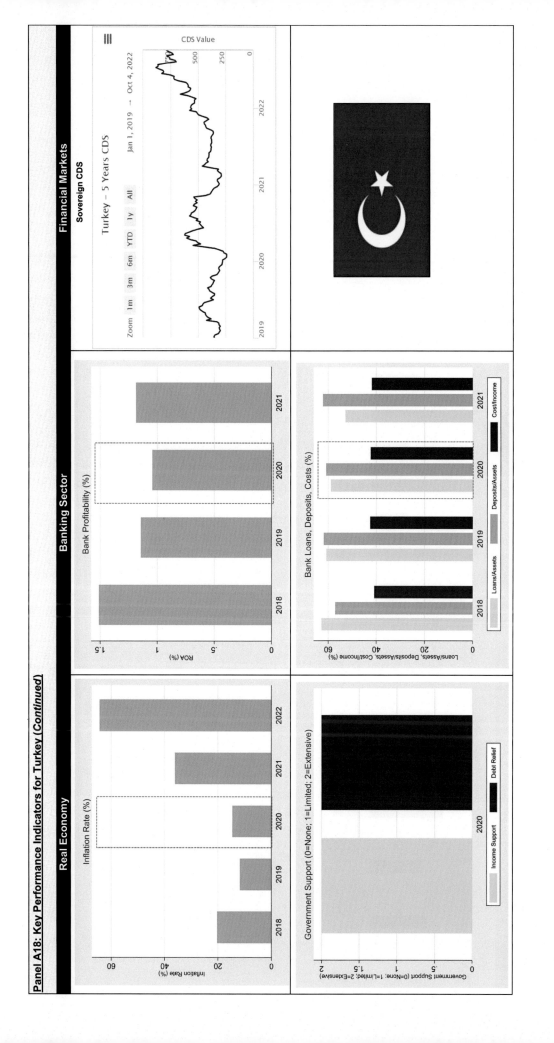

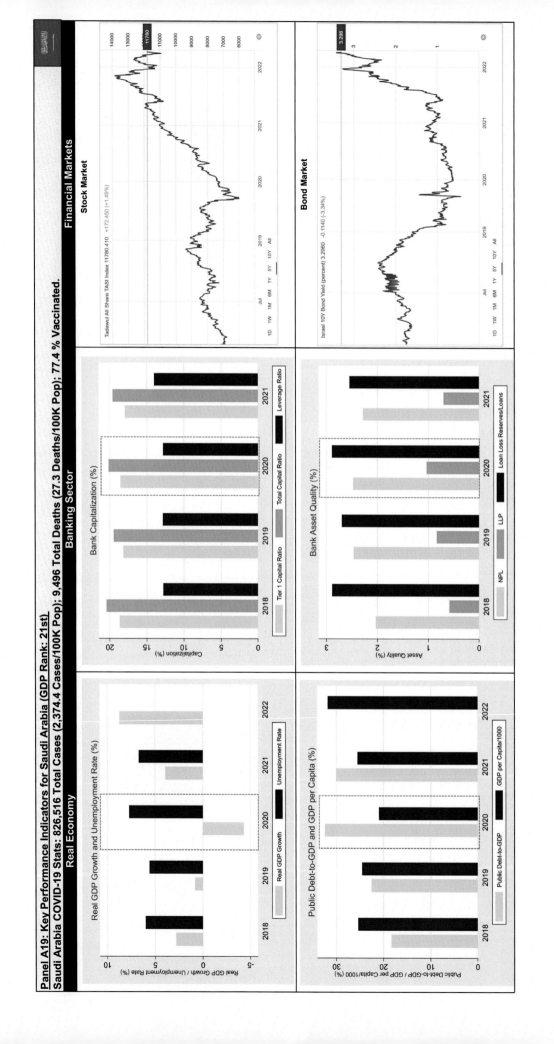

Panel A19: Key Performance Indicators for Saudi Arabia (GDP Rank: 21st)
Saudi Arabia COVID-19 Stats: 826,516 Total Cases (2,374.4 Cases/100K Pop); 9,496 Total Deaths (27.3 Deaths/100K Pop); 77.4 % Vaccinated.

Panel A19: Key Performance Indicators for Saudi Arabia (*Continued*)

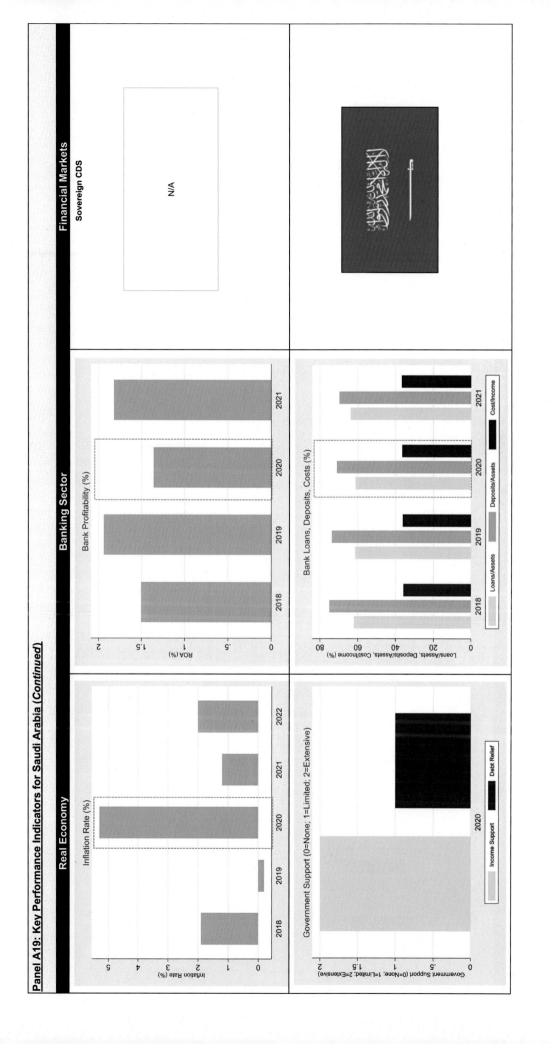

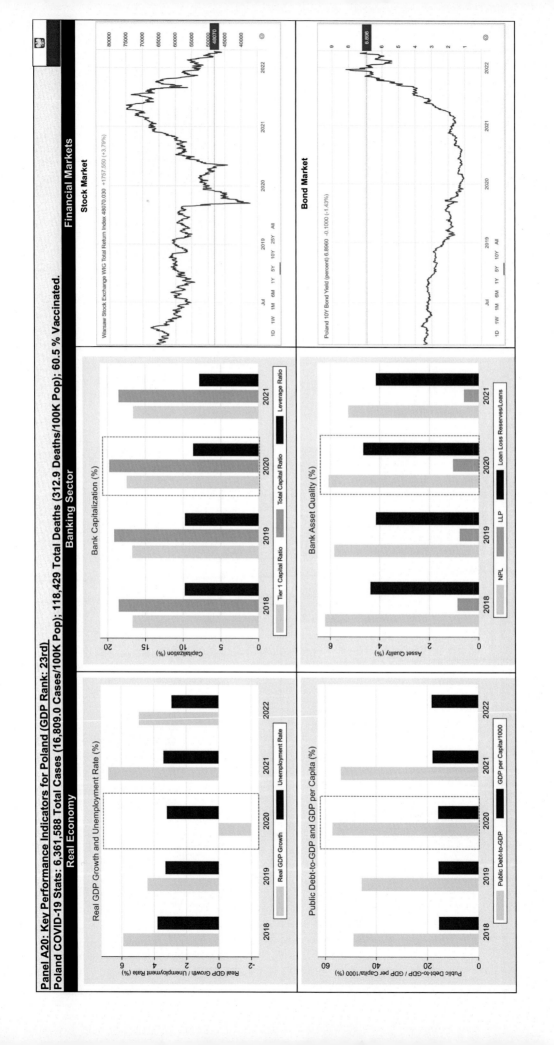

Panel A20: Key Performance Indicators for Poland (GDP Rank: 23rd)
Poland COVID-19 Stats: 6,361,588 Total Cases (16,809.0 Cases/100K Pop); 118,429 Total Deaths (312.9 Deaths/100K Pop); 60.5 % Vaccinated.

Real Economy

Real GDP Growth and Unemployment Rate (%)

Real GDP Growth / Unemployment Rate (%)

Real GDP Growth — Unemployment Rate

2018 2019 2020 2021 2022

Public Debt-to-GDP and GDP per Capita (%)

Public Debt-to-GDP / GDP per Capita/1000 (%)

Public Debt-to-GDP — GDP per Capita/1000

2018 2019 2020 2021 2022

Banking Sector

Bank Capitalization (%)

Capitalization (%)

Tier 1 Capital Ratio — Total Capital Ratio — Leverage Ratio

2018 2019 2020 2021

Bank Asset Quality (%)

Asset Quality (%)

NPL — LLP — Loan Loss Reserves/Loans

2018 2019 2020 2021

Financial Markets

Stock Market

Warsaw Stock Exchange WIG Total Return Index 48070.030 +1757.550 (+3.79%)

1D 1W 1M 6M 1Y 5Y 10Y 25Y All

Jul   2019   2020   2021   2022

80000
75000
70000
65000
60000
55000
50000
48070
45000
40000

Bond Market

Poland 10Y Bond Yield (percent) 6.8960 -0.1000 (-1.43%)

1D 1W 1M 6M 1Y 5Y 10Y All

Jul   2019   2020   2021   2022

9
8
6.896
6
5
4
3
2
1

Panel A20: Key Performance Indicators for Poland (Continued)

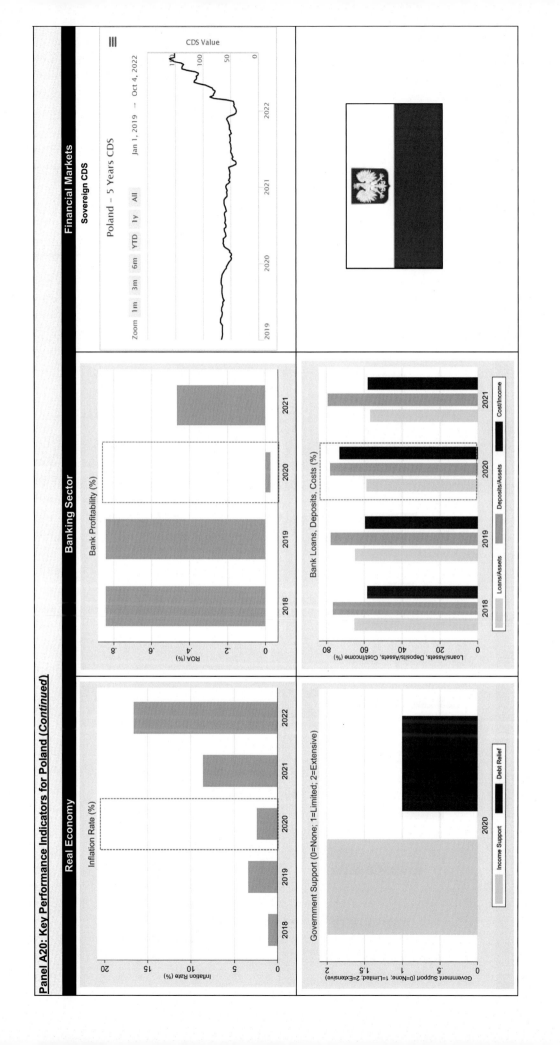

Panel A21: Key Performance Indicators for Nigeria (GDP Rank: 28th)
Nigeria COVID-19 Stats: 266,381 Total Cases (129.2 Cases/100K Pop); 3,155 Total Deaths (1.5 Deaths/100K Pop); 31.0 % Vaccinated.

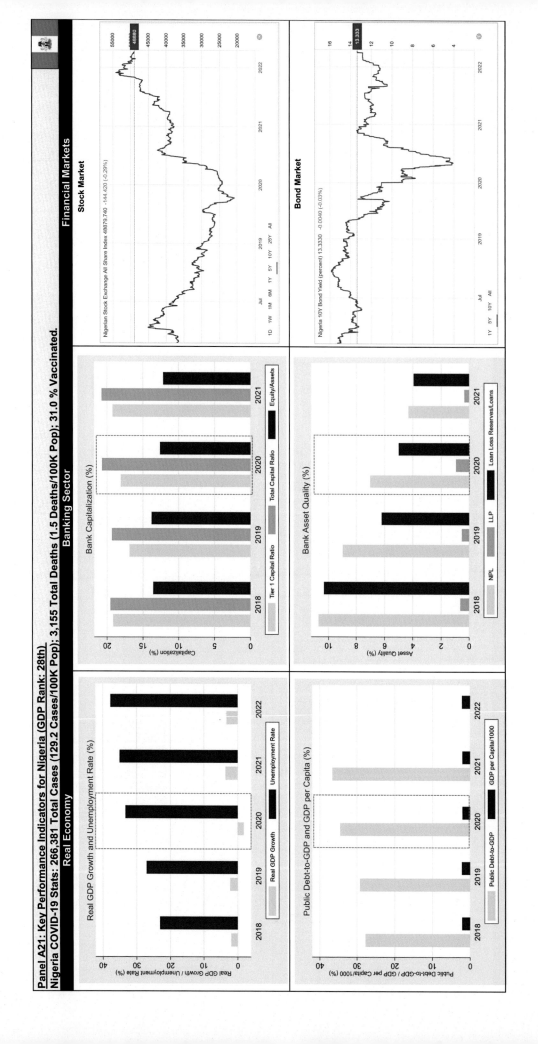

Panel A21: Key Performance Indicators for Nigeria (*Continued*)

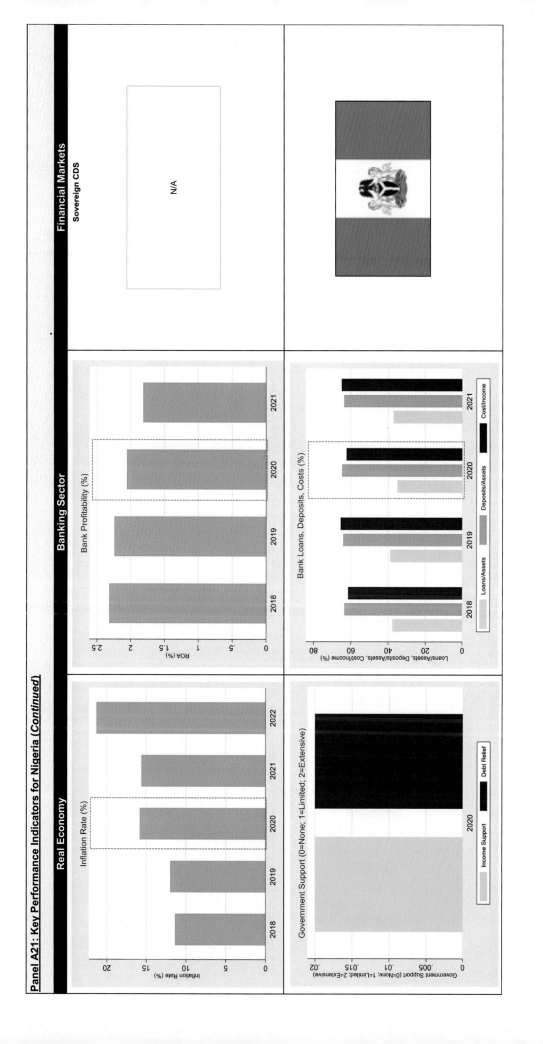

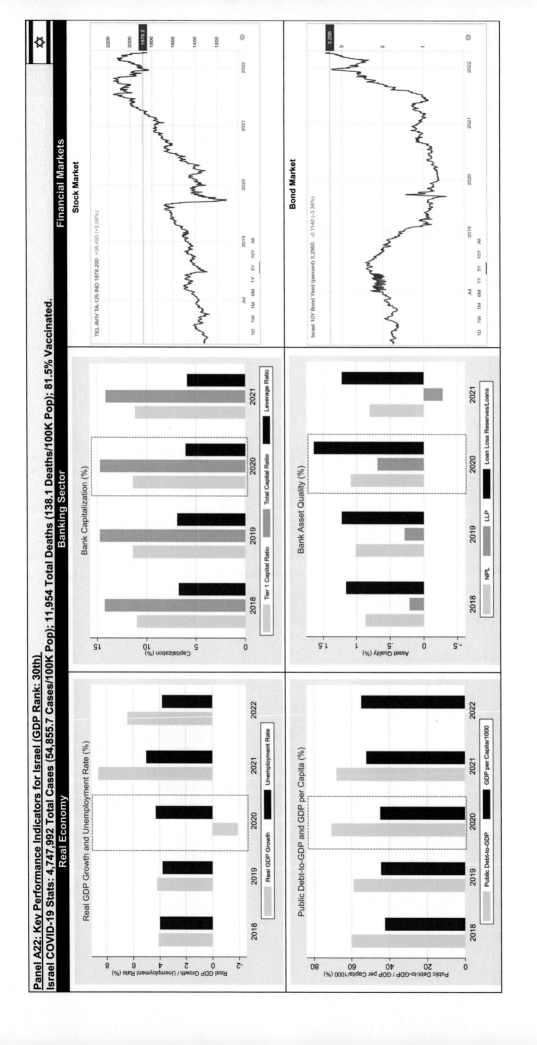

Panel A22: Key Performance Indicators for Israel (GDP Rank: 30th)

Israel COVID-19 Stats: 4,747,992 Total Cases (54,855.7 Cases/100K Pop); 11,954 Total Deaths (138.1 Deaths/100K Pop); 81.5% Vaccinated.

Panel A22: Key Performance Indicators for Israel (*Continued*)

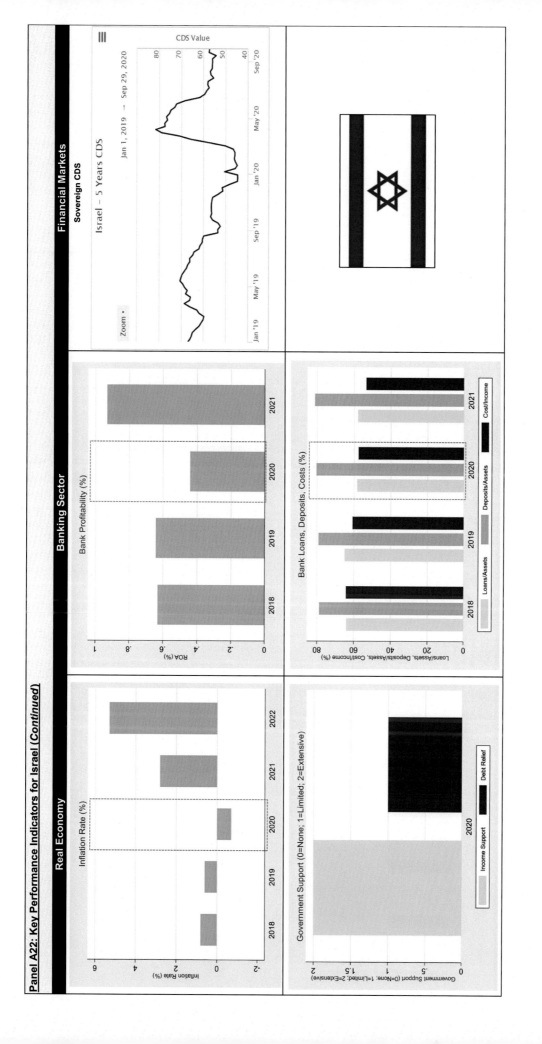

Panel A23: Key Performance Indicators for Argentina (GDP Rank: 31st)
Argentina COVID-19 Stats: 9,766,975 Total Cases (21,610.5 Cases/100K Pop); 130,041 Total Deaths (287.7 Deaths/100K Pop); 91.6 % Vaccinated.

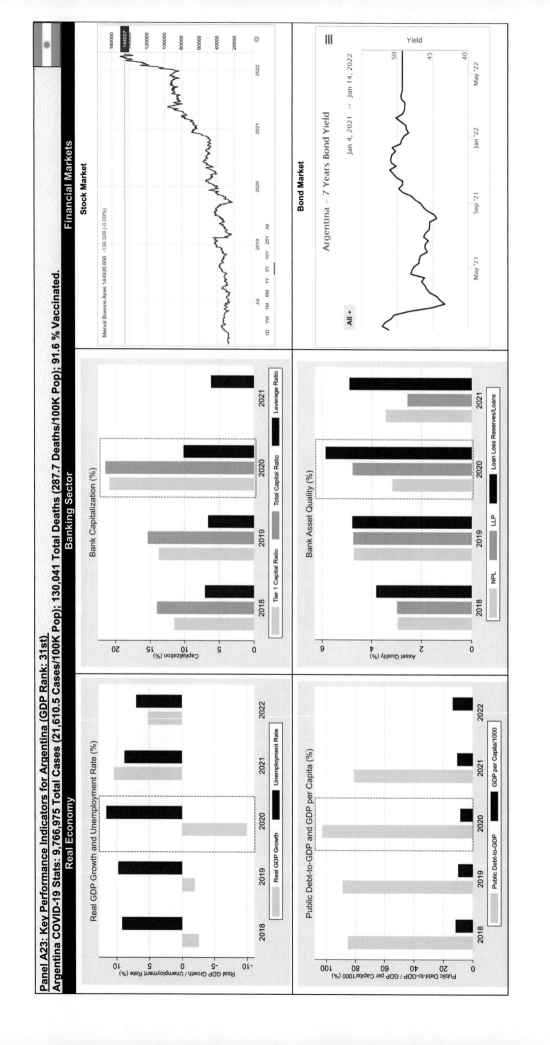

Panel A23: Key Performance Indicators for Argentina (Continued)

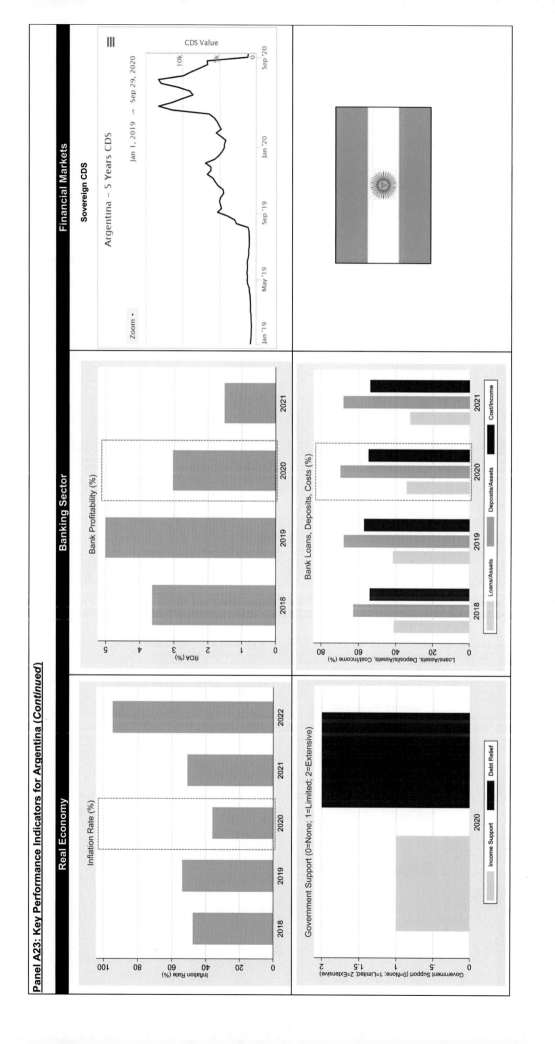

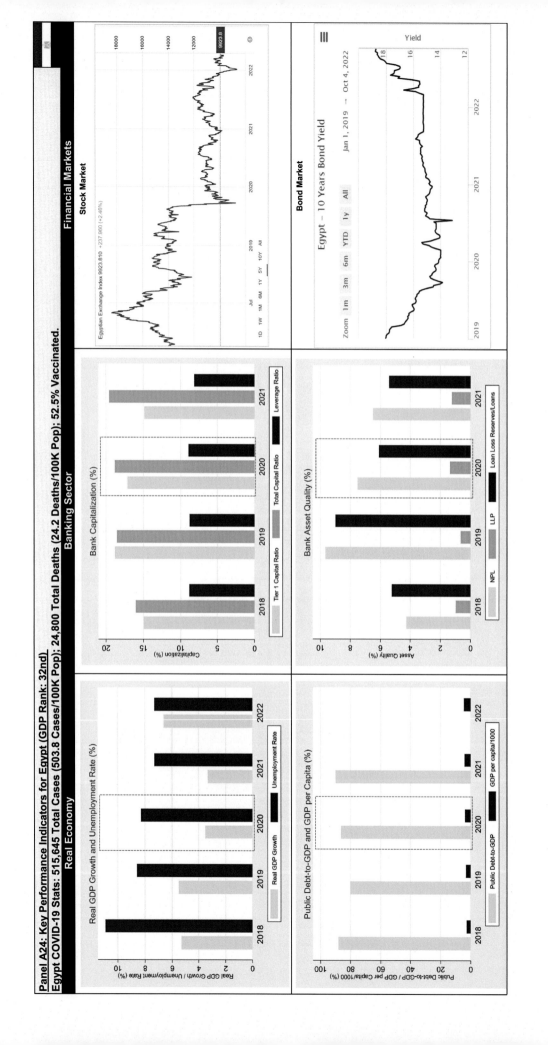

Panel A24: Key Performance Indicators for Egypt (Continued)

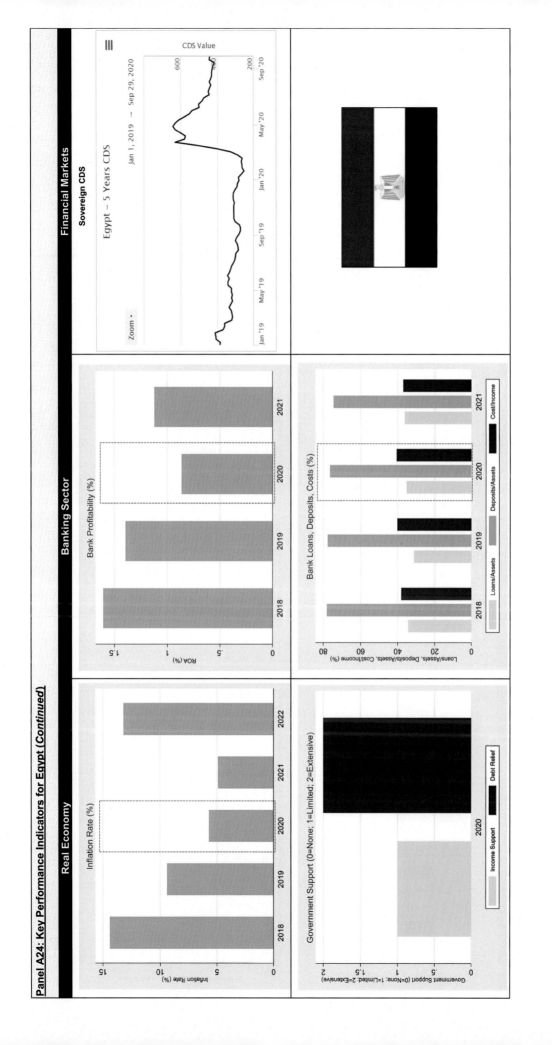

Panel A25: Key Performance Indicators for Philippines (GDP Rank: 34th)
Philippines COVID-19 Stats: 4,056,239 Total Cases (3,701.9 Cases/100K Pop); 65,064 Total Deaths (59.4 Deaths/100K Pop); 71.4% Vaccinated.

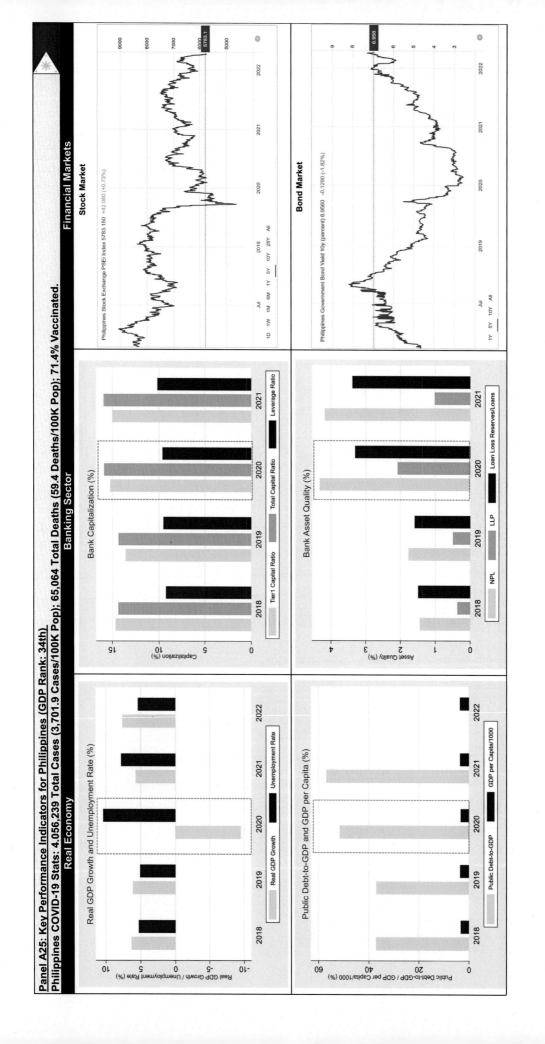

Panel A25: Key Performance Indicators for Philippines (Continued)

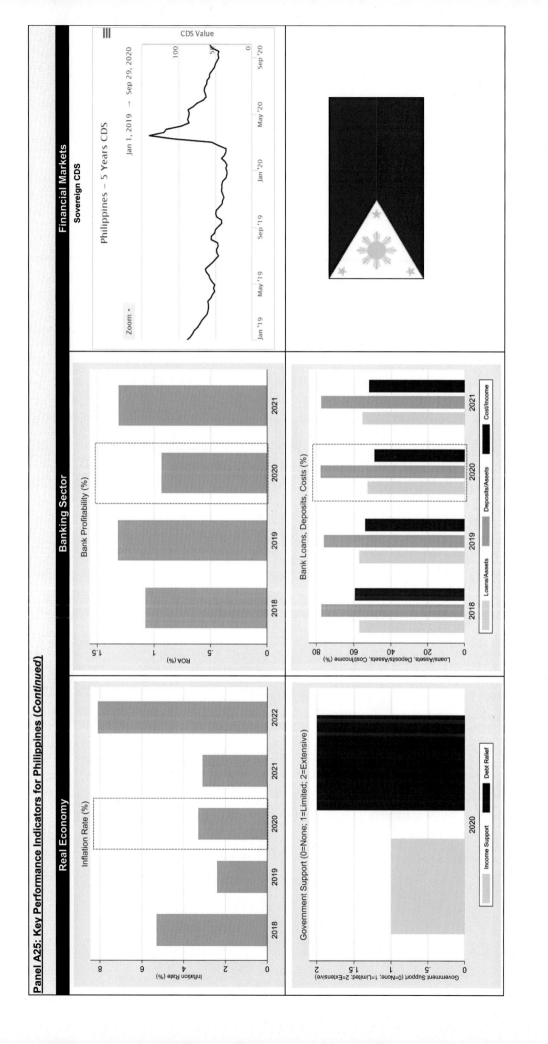

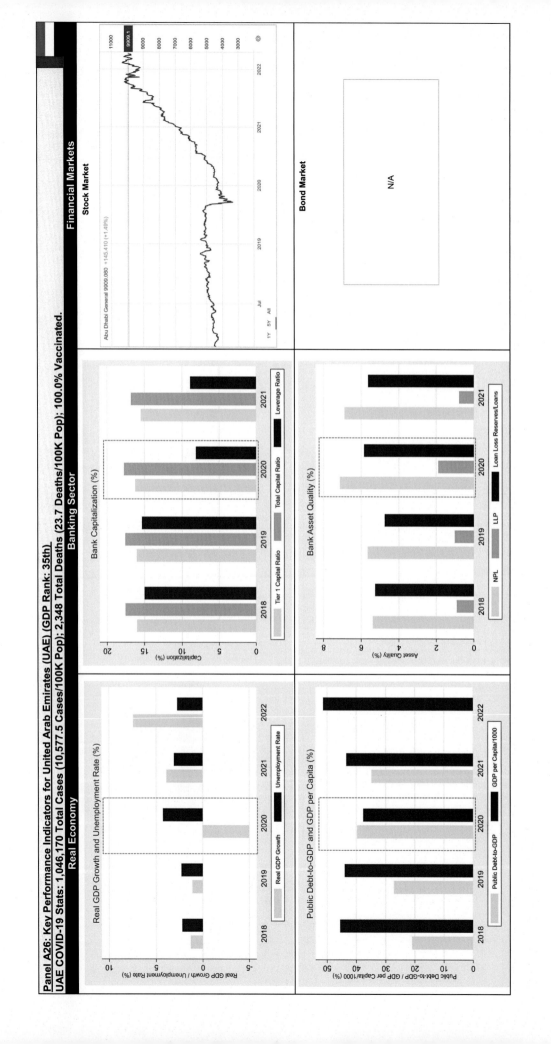

Panel A26: Key Performance Indicators for United Arab Emirates (UAE) (GDP Rank: 35th)
UAE COVID-19 Stats: 1,046,170 Total Cases (10,577.5 Cases/100K Pop); 2,348 Total Deaths (23.7 Deaths/100K Pop); 100.0% Vaccinated.

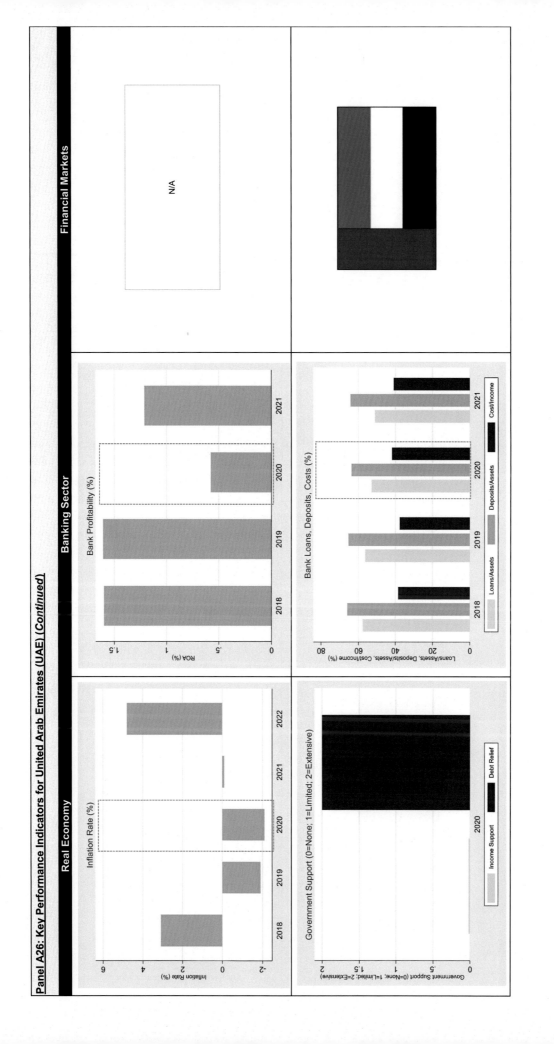

Panel A26: Key Performance Indicators for United Arab Emirates (UAE) (Continued)

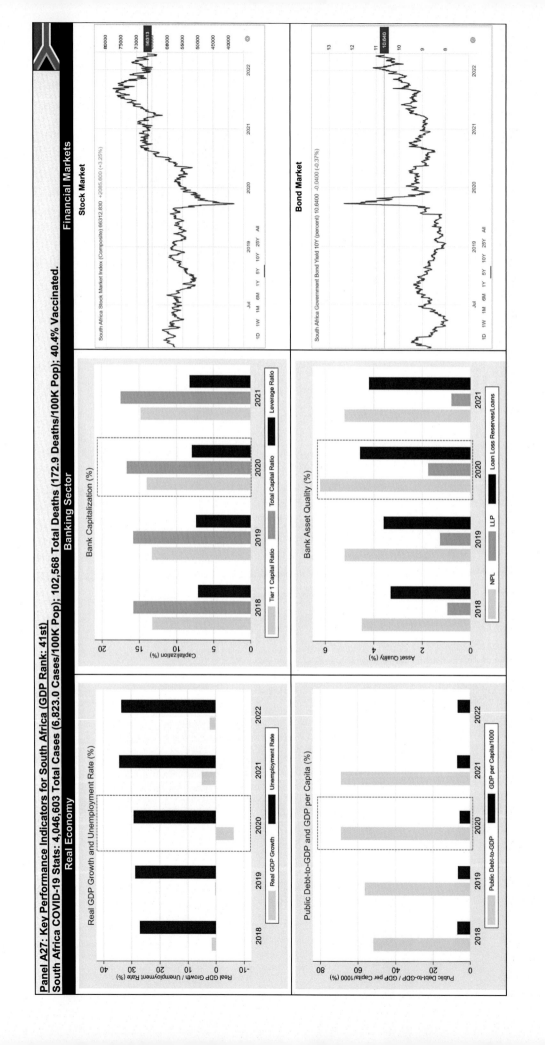

Panel A27: Key Performance Indicators for South Africa (GDP Rank: 41st)
South Africa COVID-19 Stats: 4,046,603 Total Cases (6,823.0 Cases/100K Pop); 102,568 Total Deaths (172.9 Deaths/100K Pop); 40.4% Vaccinated.

Real Economy

Financial Markets

Banking Sector

Panel A27: Key Performance Indicators for South Africa (*Continued*)

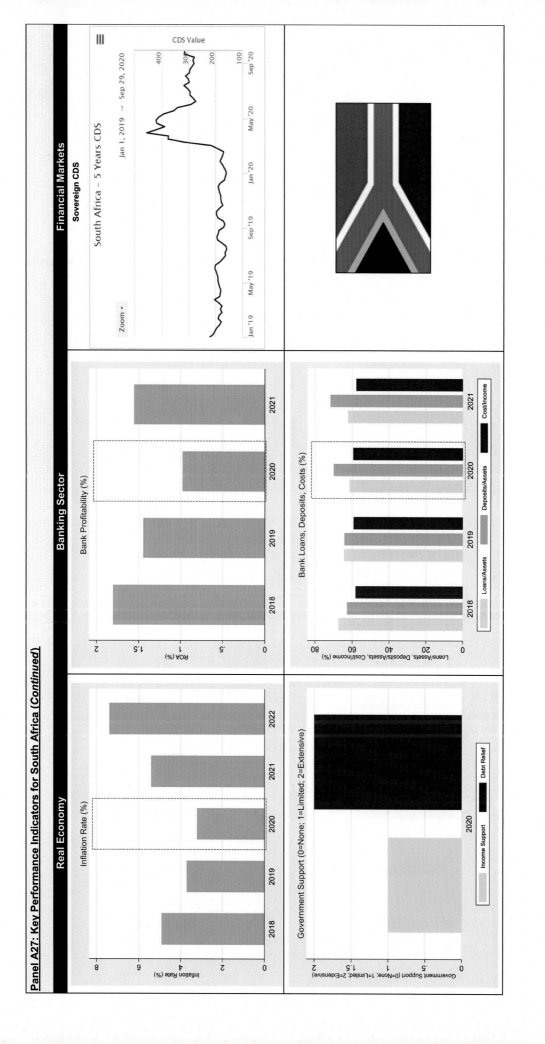

Panel A28: Key Performance Indicators for Finland (GDP Rank: 44th)

Finland COVID-19 Stats: 1,428,446 Total Cases (25,781.0 Cases/100K Pop); 7,783 Total Deaths (140.5 Deaths/100K Pop); 82.0% Vaccinated.

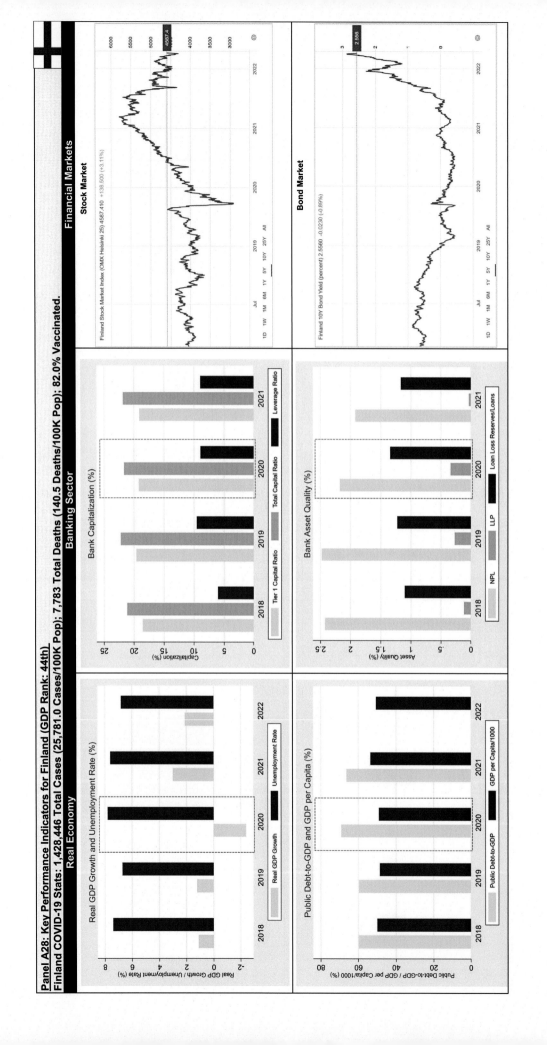

Panel A28: Key Performance Indicators for Finland (Continued)

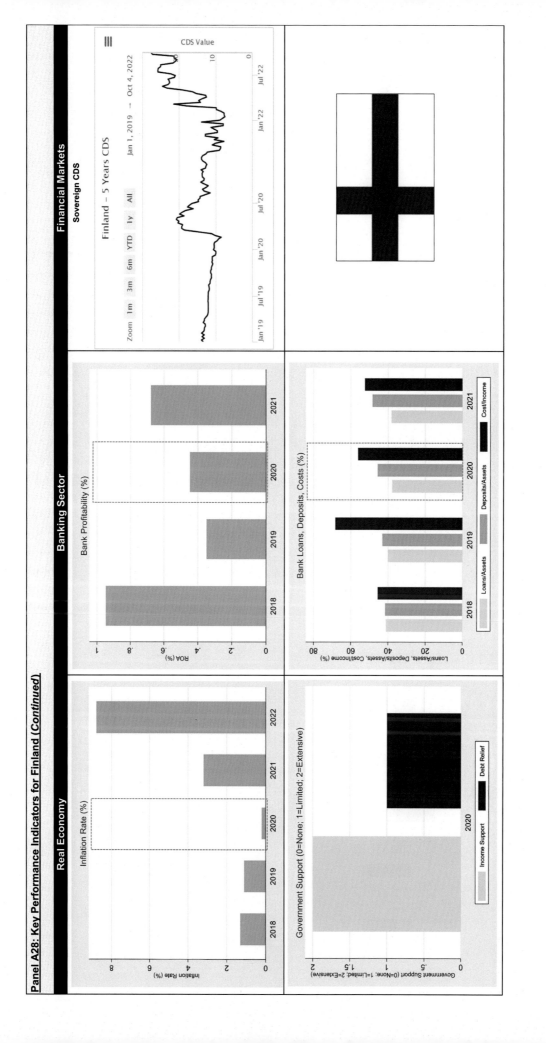

Real Economy

Banking Sector

Financial Markets

Panel A29: Key Performance Indicators for Chile (GDP Rank: 46th)

Chile COVID-19 Stats: 4,983,092 Total Cases (26,067.4 Cases/100K Pop); 62,875 Total Deaths (328.9 Deaths/100K Pop); 94.6% Vaccinated.

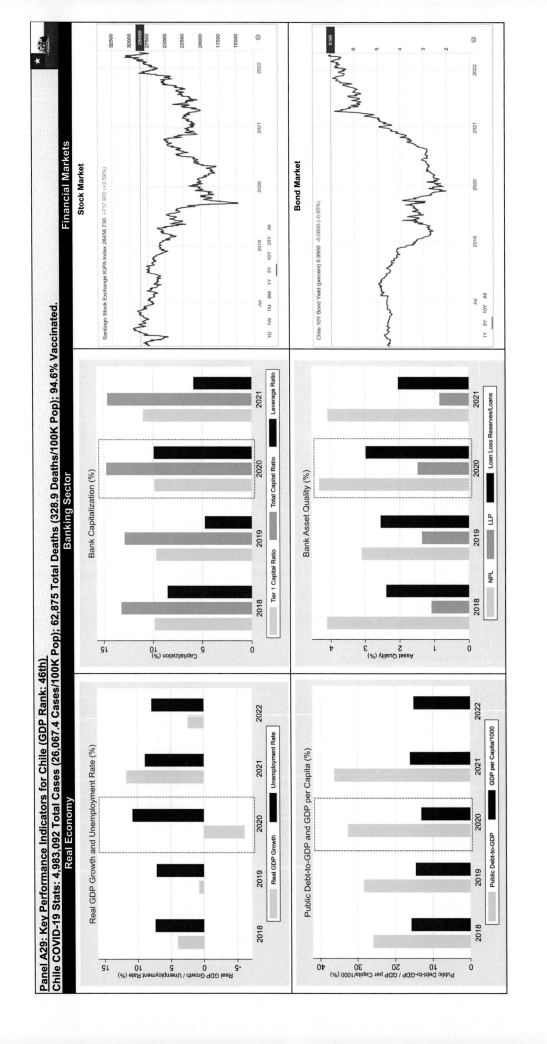

Panel A29: Key Performance Indicators for Chile (Continued)

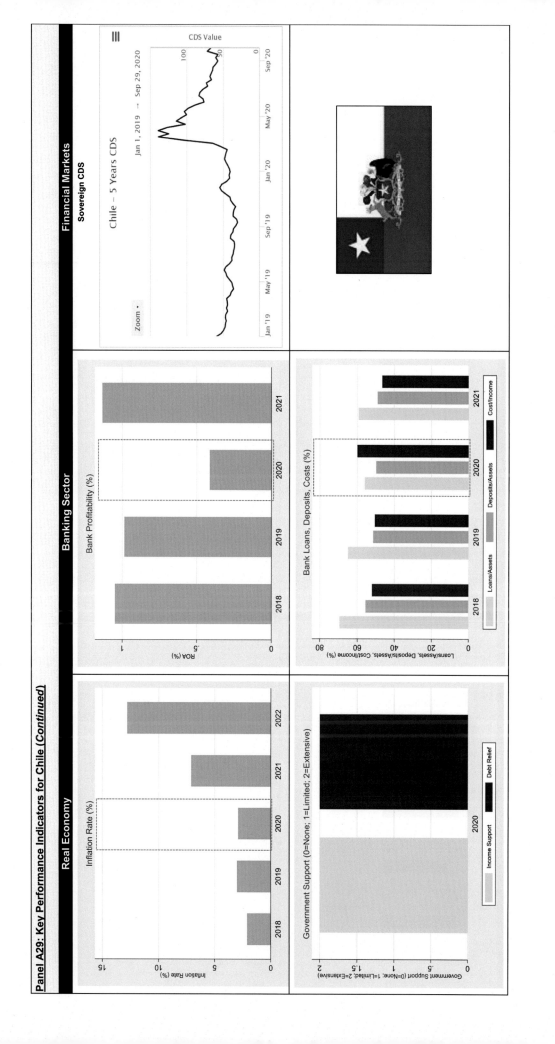

Real Economy

Inflation Rate (%)

Inflation Rate (%)

2018 · 2019 · 2020 · 2021 · 2022

Government Support (0=None; 1=Limited; 2=Extensive)

Government Support (0=None; 1=Limited; 2=Extensive)

2020

Income Support · Debt Relief

Banking Sector

Bank Profitability (%)

ROA (%)

2018 · 2019 · 2020 · 2021

Bank Loans, Deposits, Costs (%)

Loans/Assets, Deposits/Assets, Cost/Income (%)

2018 · 2019 · 2020 · 2021

Loans/Assets · Deposits/Assets · Cost/Income

Financial Markets

Sovereign CDS

Chile – 5 Years CDS

CDS Value

Zoom ▾

Jan 1, 2019 → Sep 29, 2020

Jan '19 · May '19 · Sep '19 · Jan '20 · May '20 · Sep '20

Panel A30: Key Performance Indicators for Romania (GDP Rank: 47th)
Romania COVID-19 Stats: 3,301,662 Total Cases (17,162.7 Cases/100K Pop); 67,310 Total Deaths (349.9 Deaths/100K Pop); 42.5% Vaccinated.

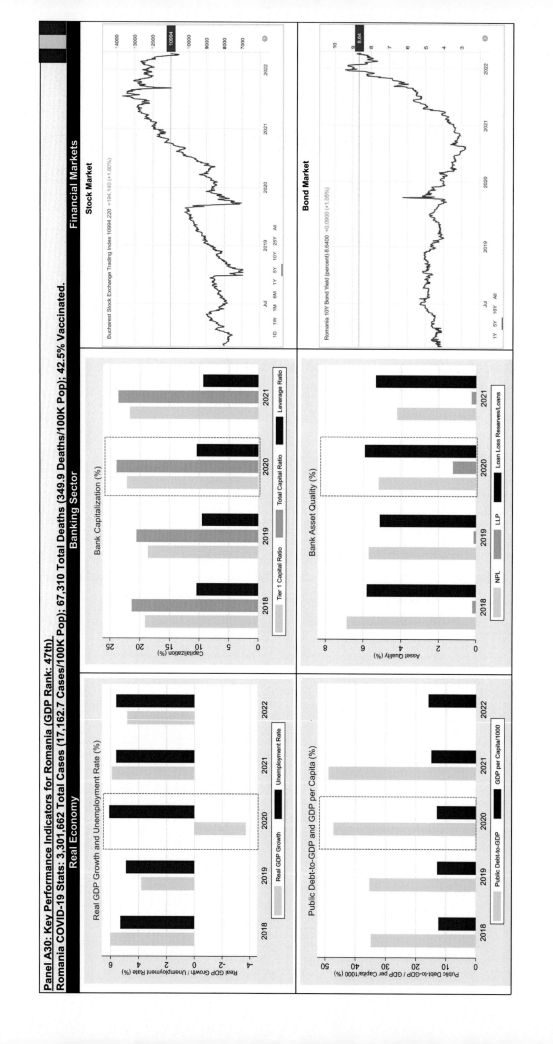

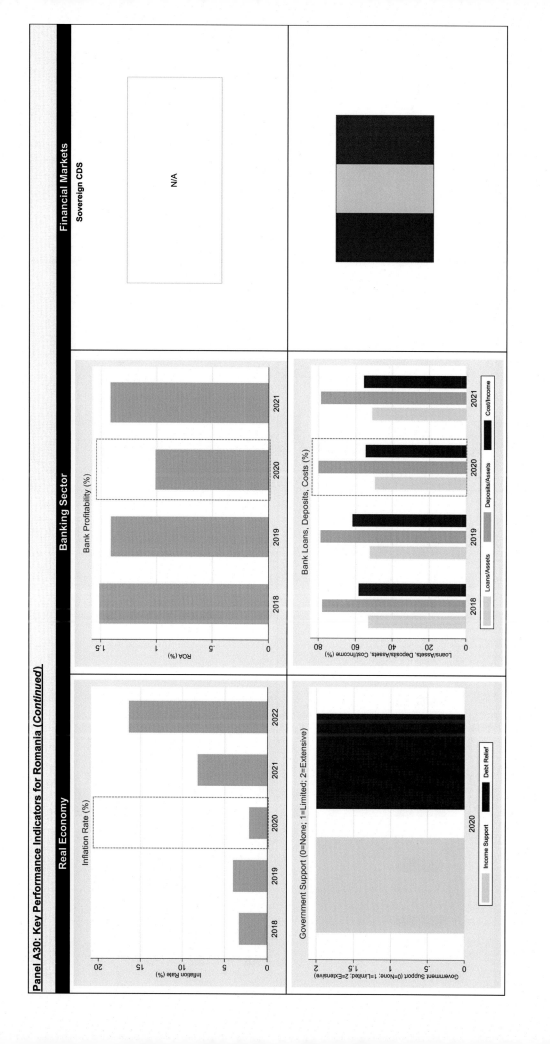

Panel A30: Key Performance Indicators for Romania (*Continued*)

Panel A31: Key Performance Indicators for Portugal (GDP Rank: 49th)

Portugal COVID-19 Stats: 5,551,364 Total Cases (54,442.0 Cases/100K Pop); 25,643 Total Deaths (251.5 Deaths/100K Pop); 95.8% Vaccinated.

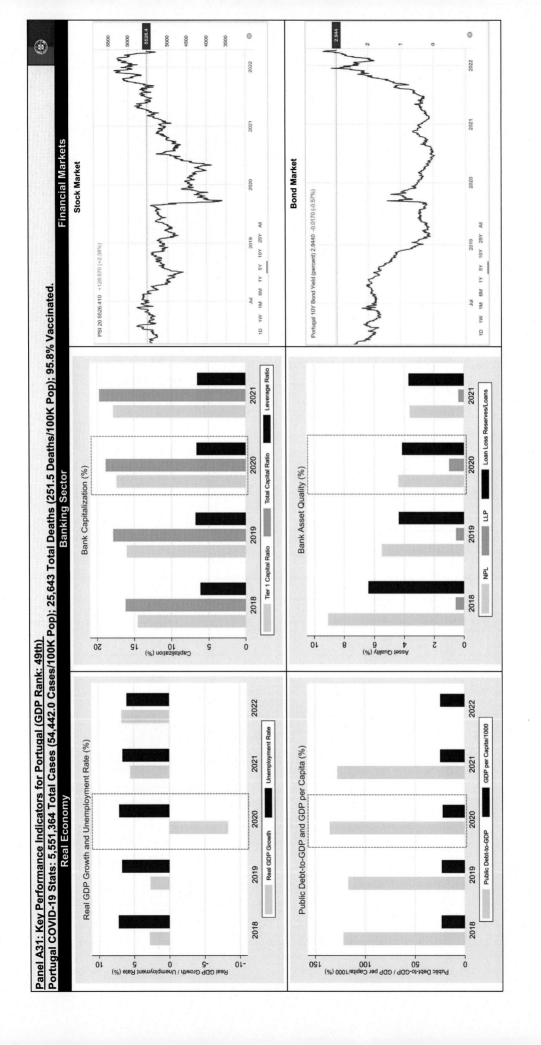

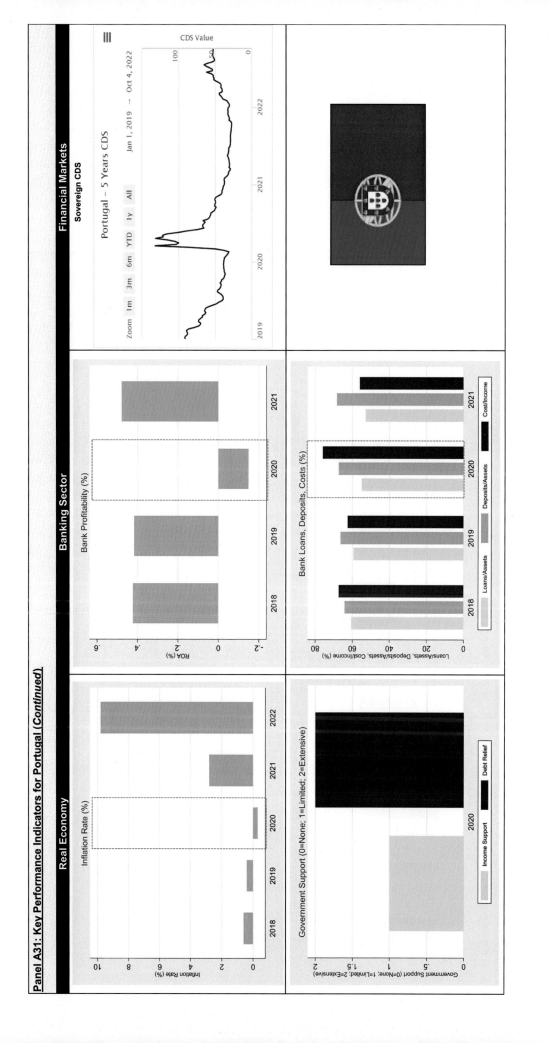

Panel A31: Key Performance Indicators for Portugal (*Continued*)

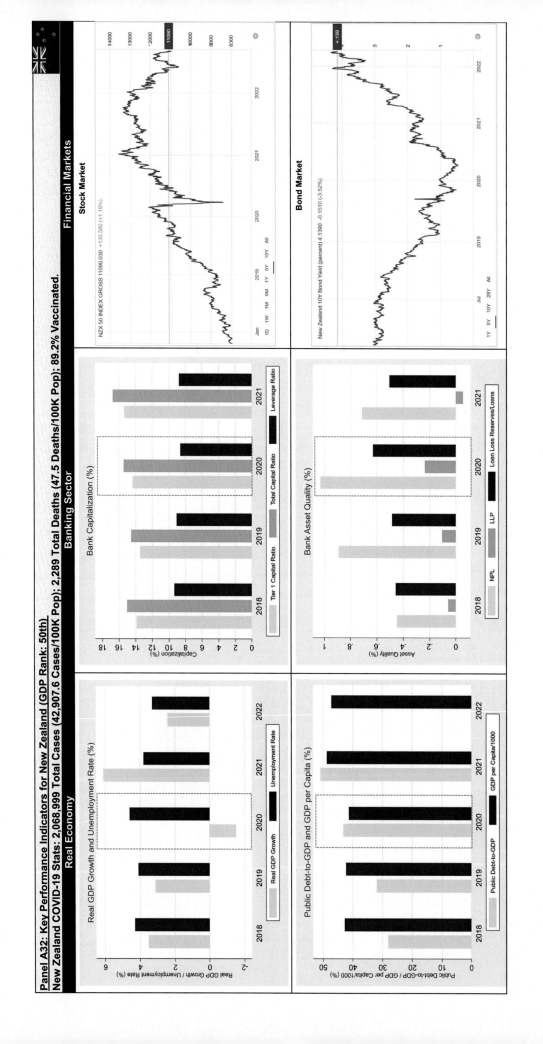

Panel A32: Key Performance Indicators for New Zealand (Continued)

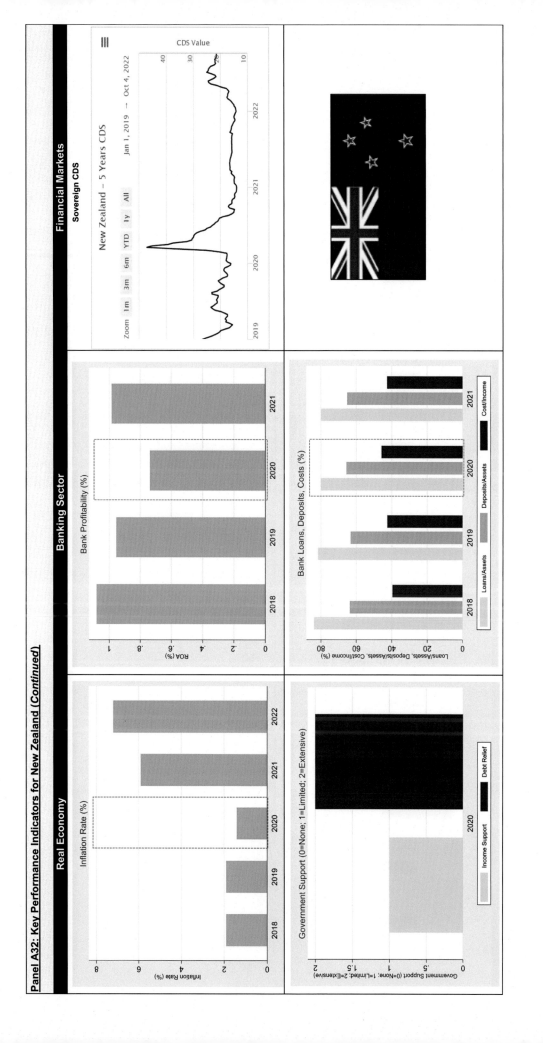

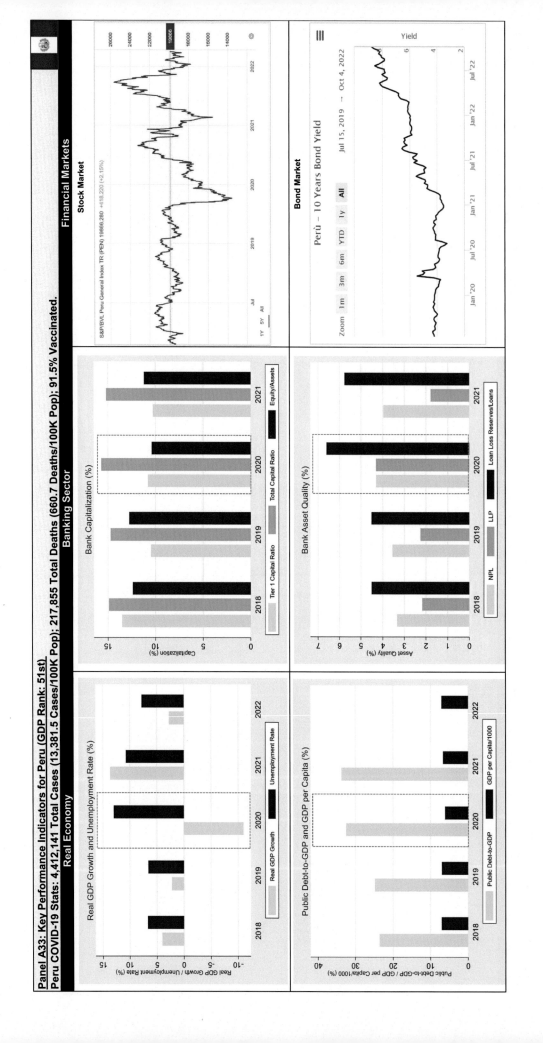

Panel A33: Key Performance Indicators for Peru (GDP Rank: 51st)
Peru COVID-19 Stats: 4,412,141 Total Cases (13,381.5 Cases/100K Pop); 217,855 Total Deaths (660.7 Deaths/100K Pop); 91.5% Vaccinated.

Panel A33: Key Performance Indicators for Peru (Continued).

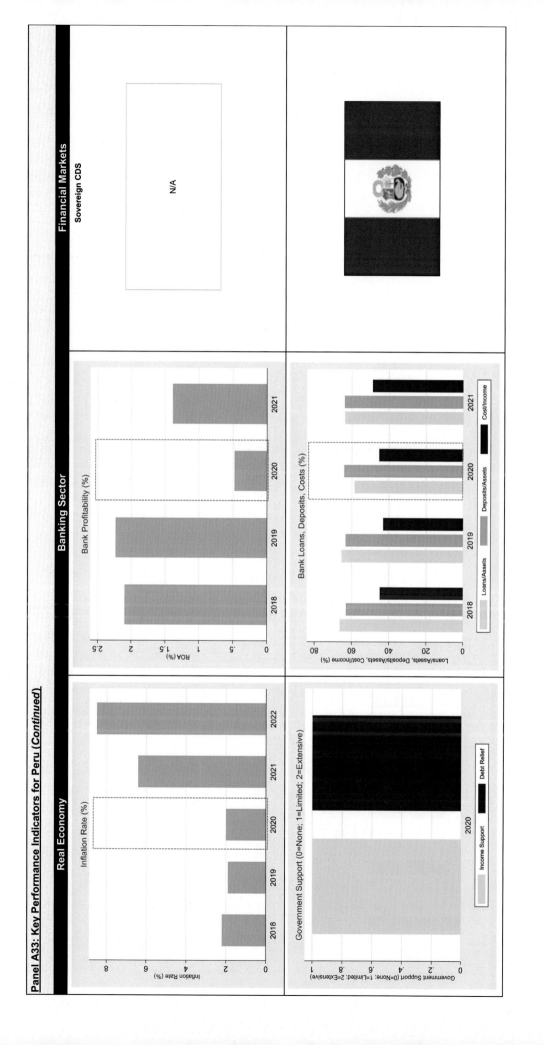

Real Economy

Inflation Rate (%)

Government Support (0=None; 1=Limited; 2=Extensive)

Banking Sector

Bank Profitability (%)

Bank Loans, Deposits, Costs (%)

Financial Markets

Sovereign CDS

N/A

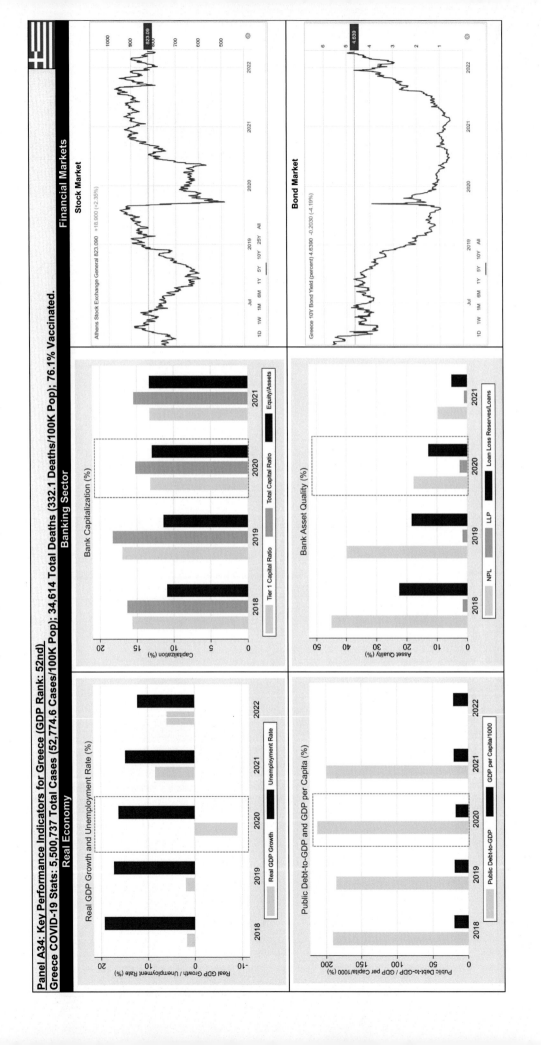

Panel A34: Key Performance Indicators for Greece (GDP Rank: 52nd)
Greece COVID-19 Stats: 5,500,737 Total Cases (52,774.6 Cases/100K Pop); 34,614 Total Deaths (332.1 Deaths/100K Pop); 76.1% Vaccinated.

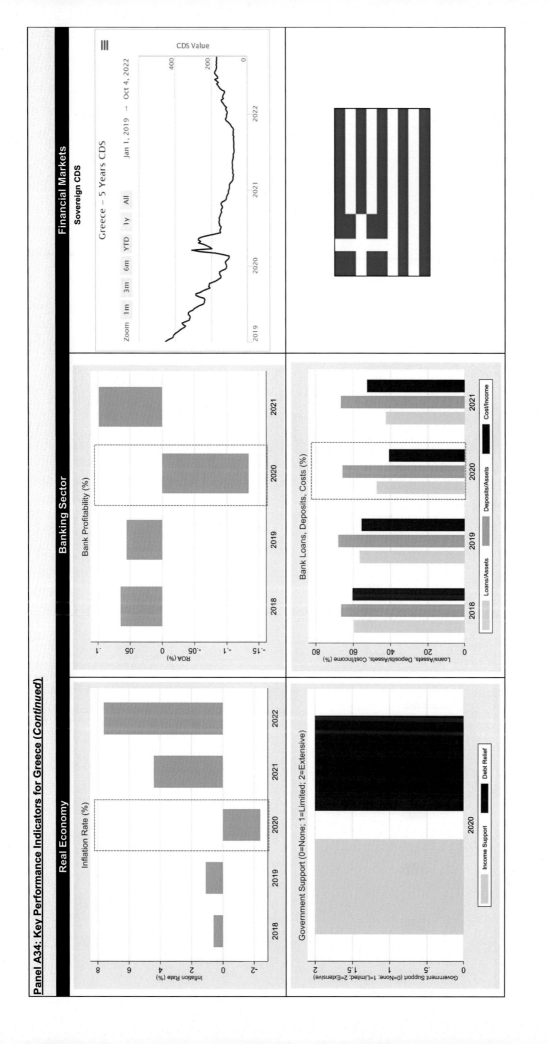

Panel A34: Key Performance Indicators for Greece (*Continued*)

Panel A35: Key Performance Indicators for Ukraine (GDP Rank: 56th)

Ukraine COVID-19 Stats: 5,657,698 Total Cases (12,936.9 Cases/100K Pop); 118,613 Total Deaths (271.2 Deaths/100K Pop); 36.1% Vaccinated.

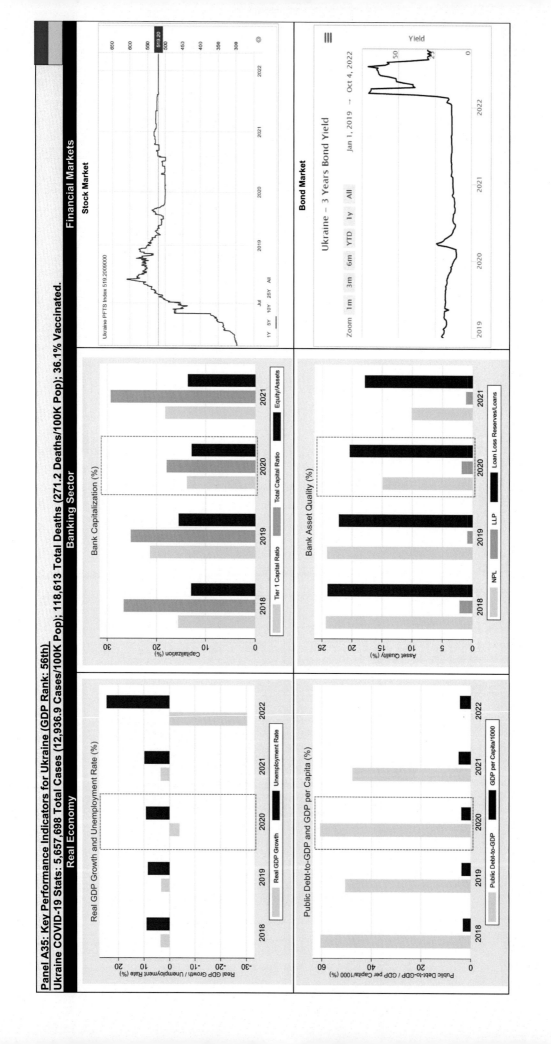

Panel A35: Key Performance Indicators for Ukraine (Continued)

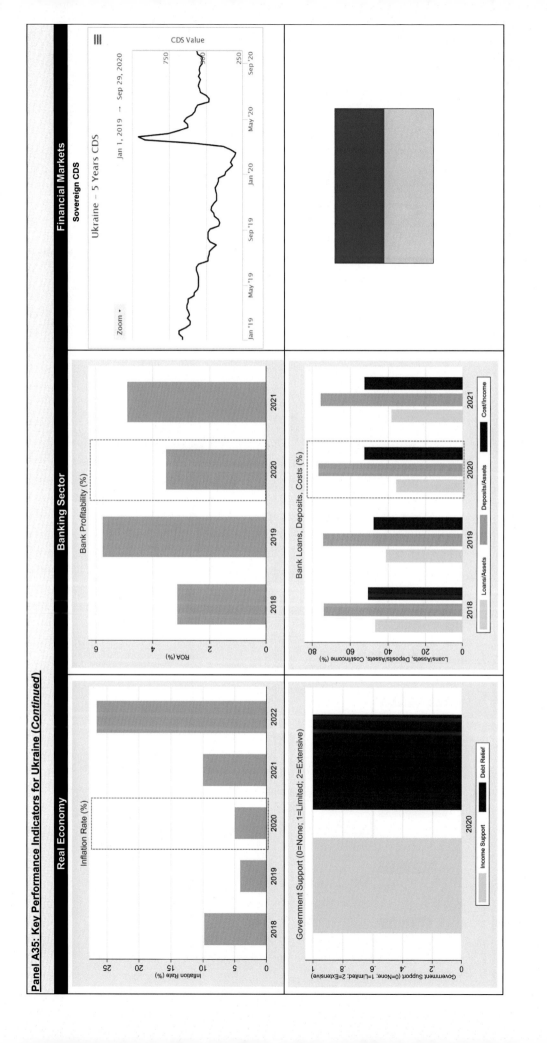

| Real Economy | Banking Sector | Financial Markets |

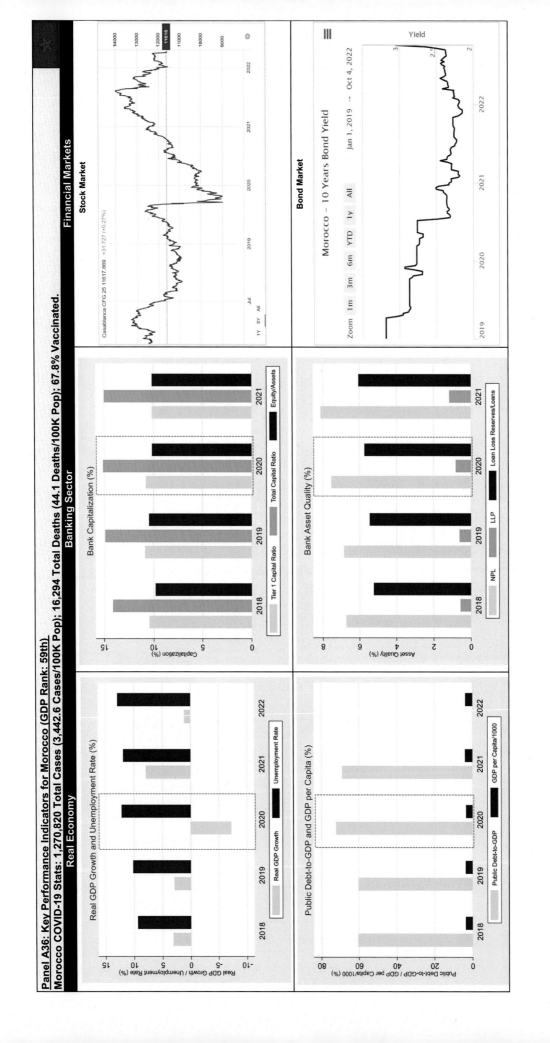

Panel A36: Key Performance Indicators for Morocco (GDP Rank: 59th)
Morocco COVID-19 Stats: 1,270,820 Total Cases (3,442.6 Cases/100K Pop); 16,294 Total Deaths (44.1 Deaths/100K Pop); 67.8% Vaccinated.

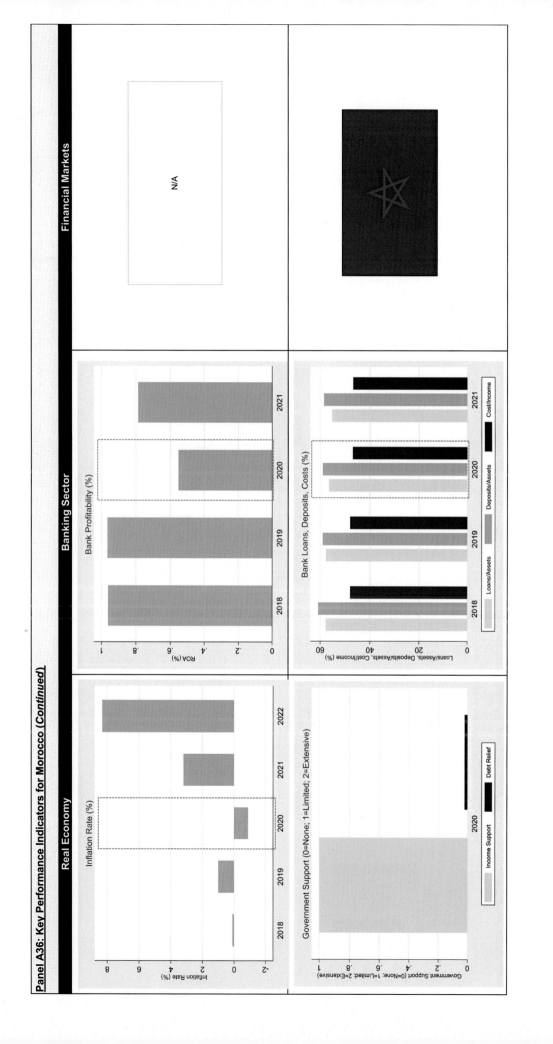

Panel A36: Key Performance Indicators for Morocco (*Continued*)

Panel A37: Key Performance Indicators for Kenya (GDP Rank: 63rd)

Kenya COVID-19 Stats: 342,336 Total Cases (636.8 Cases/100K Pop); 5,688 Total Deaths (10.6 Deaths/100K Pop); 26.3% Vaccinated.

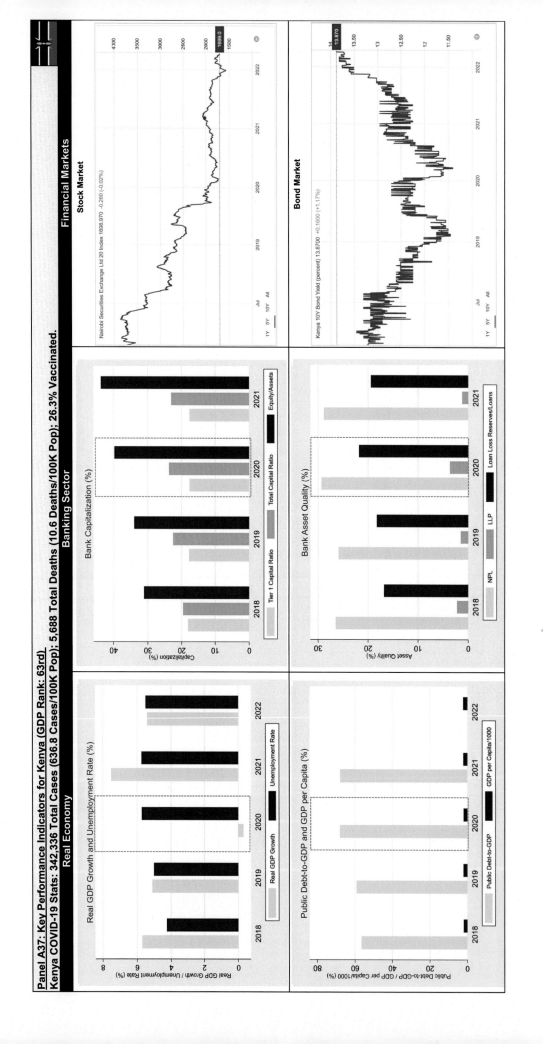

Panel A37: Key Performance Indicators for Kenya (*Continued*)

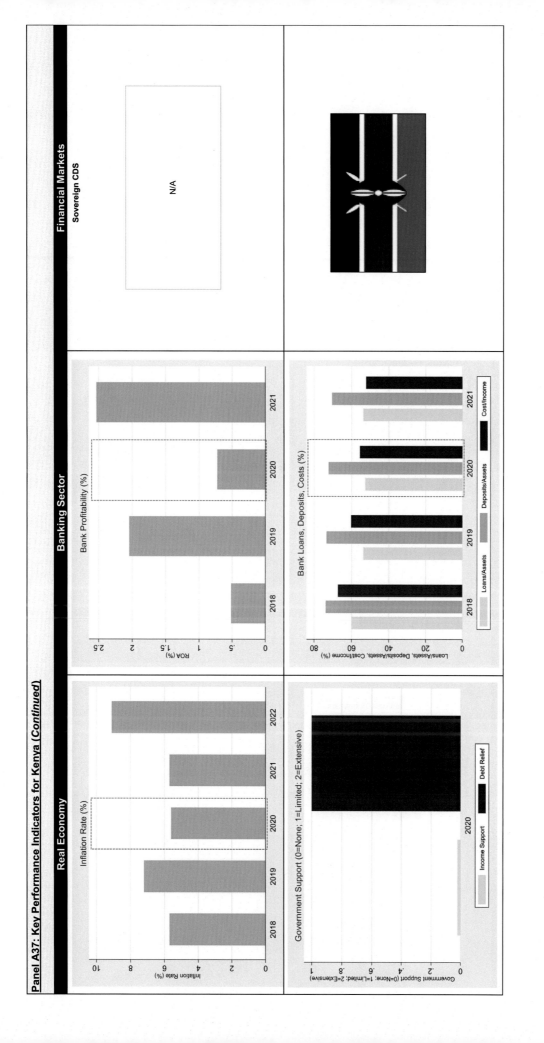

Real Economy

Banking Sector

Financial Markets

Sovereign CDS

N/A

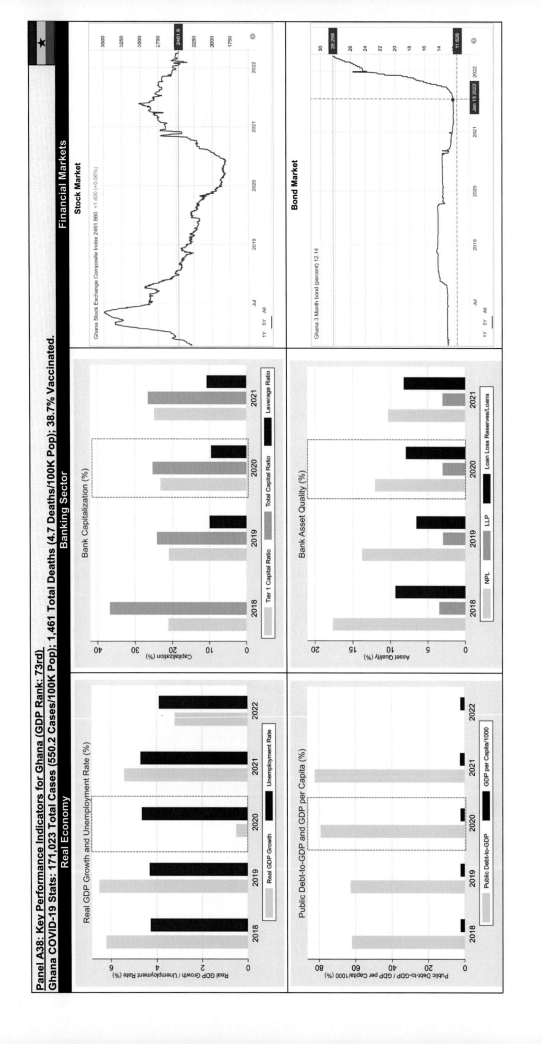

Panel A38: Key Performance Indicators for Ghana (GDP Rank: 73rd)
Ghana COVID-19 Stats: 171,023 Total Cases (550.2 Cases/100K Pop); 1,461 Total Deaths (4.7 Deaths/100K Pop); 38.7% Vaccinated.

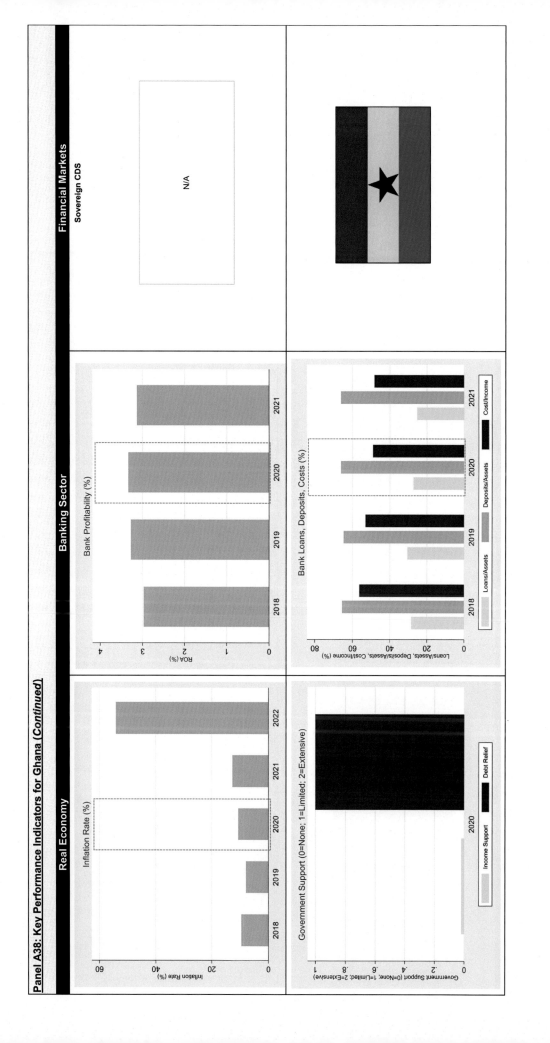

Panel A38: Key Performance Indicators for Ghana (*Continued*)

Real Economy

Inflation Rate (%)

Inflation Rate (%)

2018 2019 2020 2021 2022

Government Support (0=None; 1=Limited; 2=Extensive)

Government Support (0=None; 1=Limited; 2=Extensive)

2020

Income Support   Debt Relief

Banking Sector

Bank Profitability (%)

ROA (%)

2018 2019 2020 2021

Bank Loans, Deposits, Costs (%)

Loans/Assets, Deposits/Assets, Cost/Income (%)

2018 2019 2020 2021

Loans/Assets   Deposits/Assets   Cost/Income

Financial Markets

Sovereign CDS

N/A

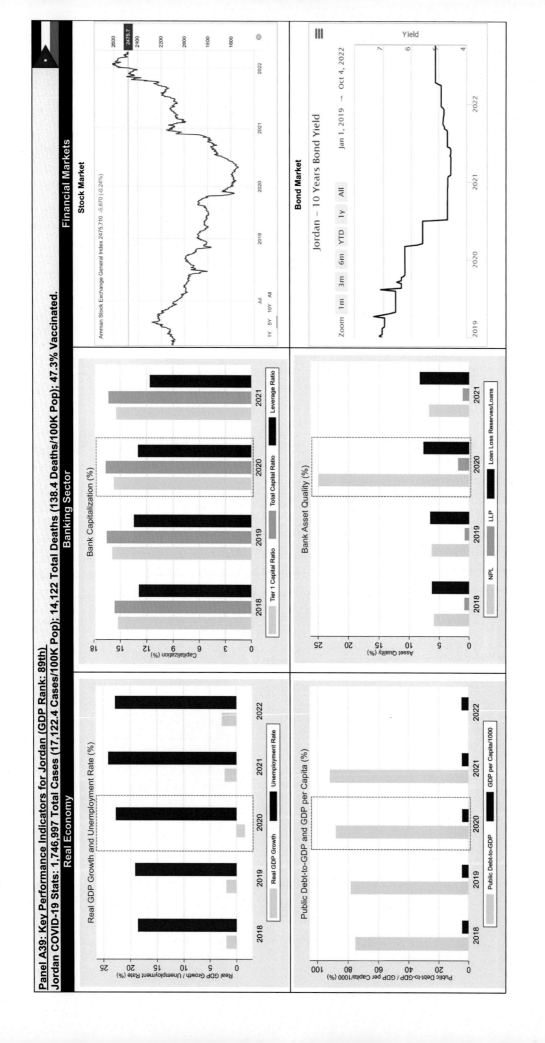

Panel A39: Key Performance Indicators for Jordan (GDP Rank: 89th)
Jordan COVID-19 Stats: 1,746,997 Total Cases (17,122.4 Cases/100K Pop); 14,122 Total Deaths (138.4 Deaths/100K Pop); 47.3% Vaccinated.

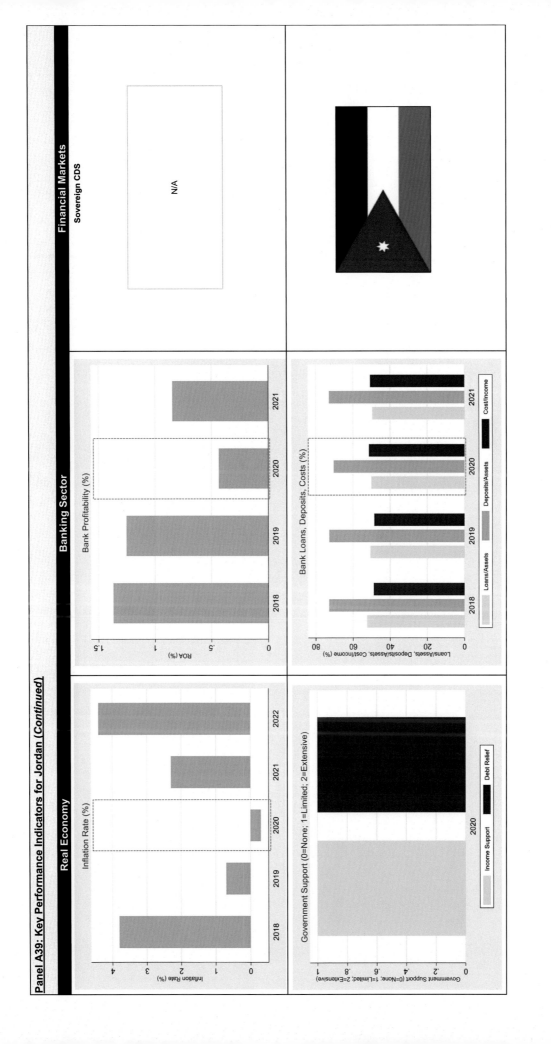

Panel A39: Key Performance Indicators for Jordan (*Continued*)

FIG. A2. Real economy and banking sector key performance indicators (KPIs) compared for select groups of five countries each.

We present real economy and banking sector key performance indicators (KPIs) for 2020 and 2021 compared for seven sets of selected groups of five countries each.

Figures are based on raw data from International Monetary Fund (IMF), Our World in Data, and Bureau van Dijk (BvD) BankFocus.

Panel A: Comparisons of Key Performance Indicators across Countries Set I
Panel A1: Comparisons across 5 countries (Australia, Canada, New Zealand, UK, US), Real Economy

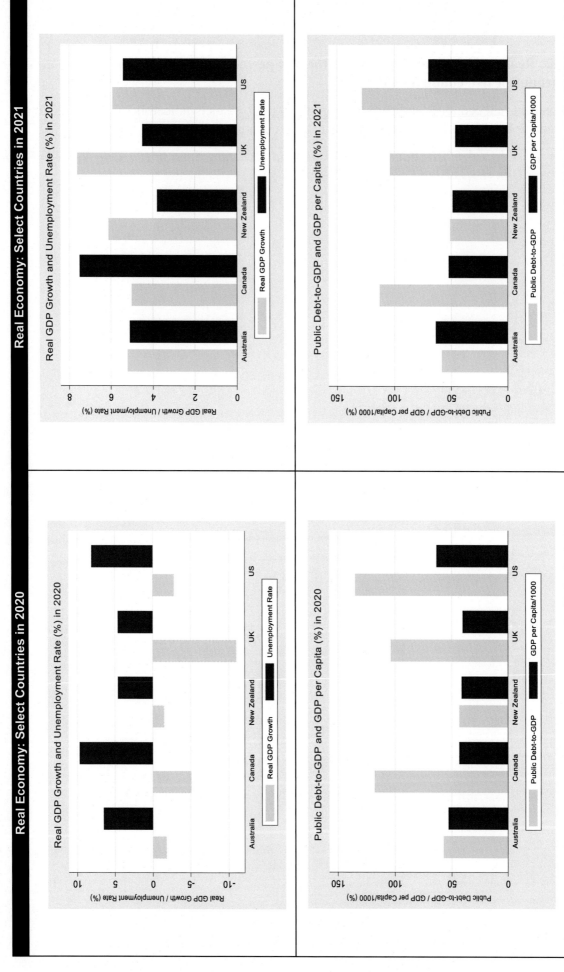

Panel A1: Comparisons across 5 countries (*Continued*)

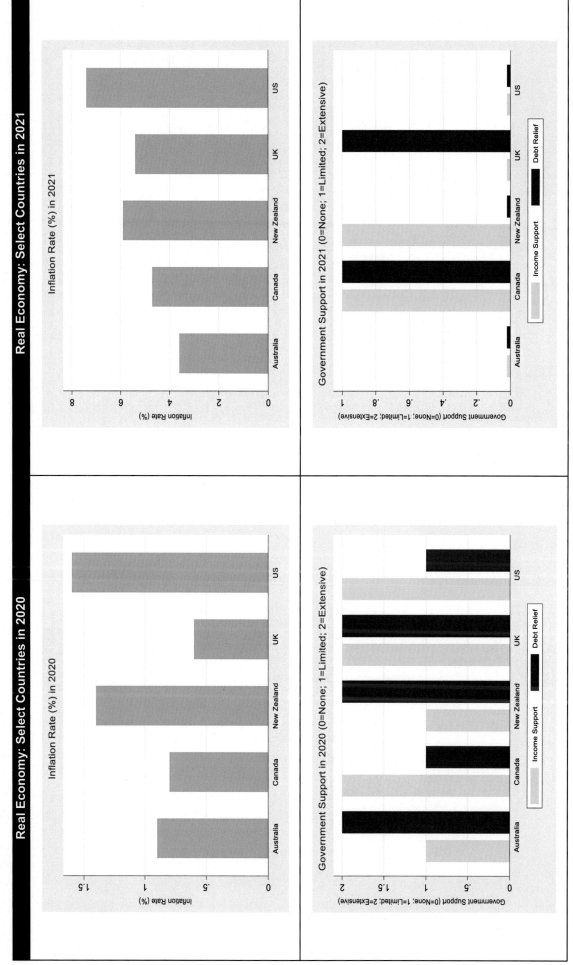

Panel A2: Comparisons across 5 countries (Australia, Canada, New Zealand, UK, US), Banking Sector

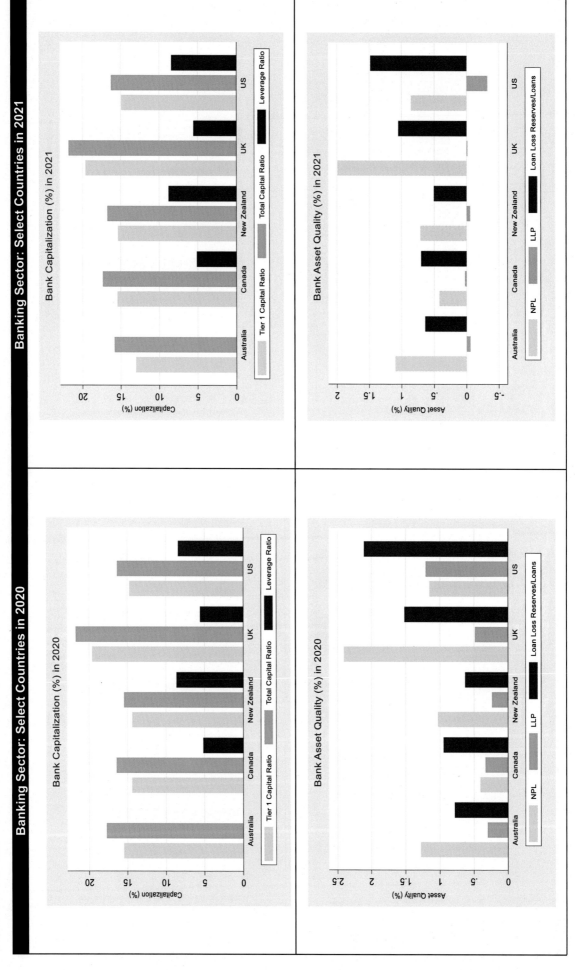

Panel A2: Comparisons across 5 countries (*Continued*)

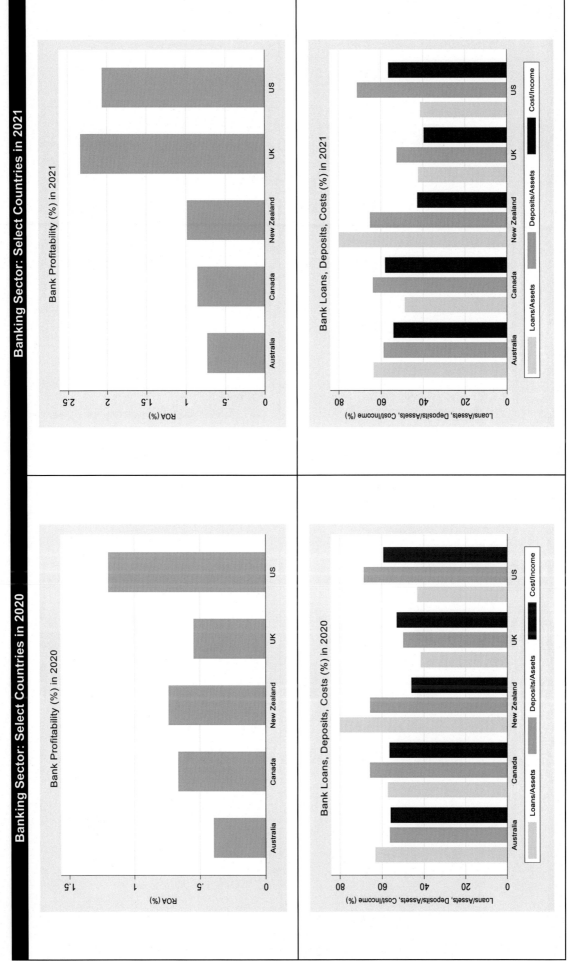

Panel B: Comparisons of Key Performance Indicators across Countries Set II
Panel B1: Comparisons across 5 countries (Finland, France, Germany, Italy, Spain), Real Economy

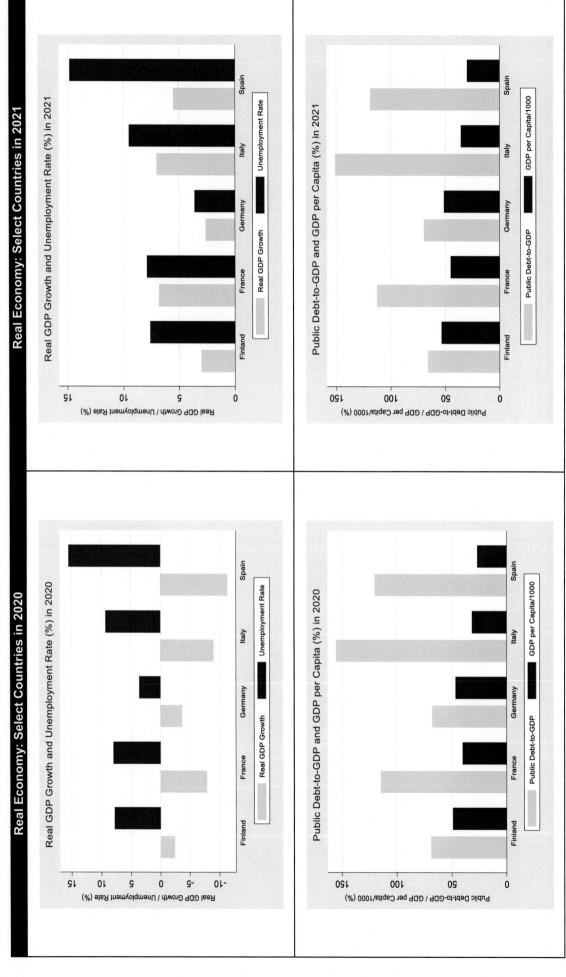

Panel B1: Comparisons across 5 countries (*Continued*)

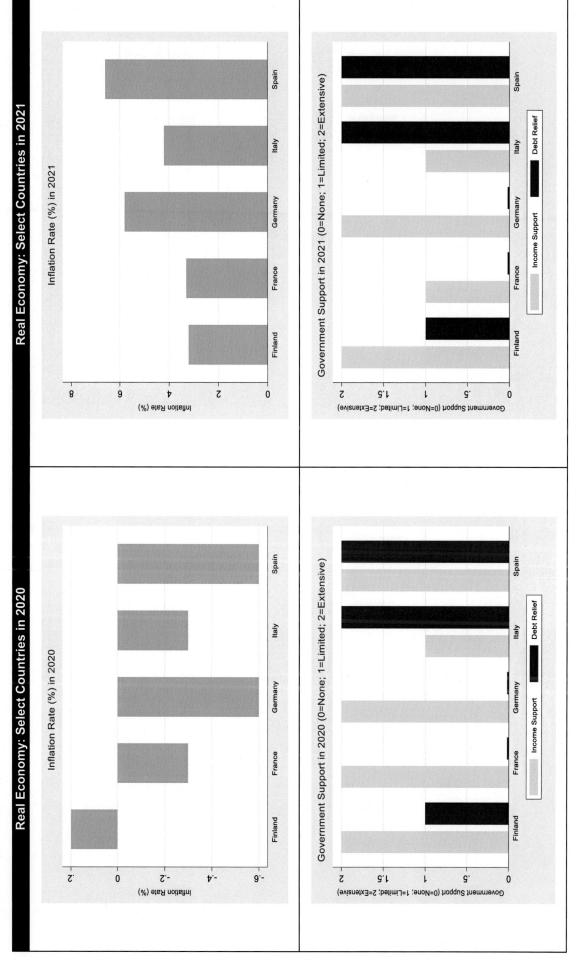

Panel B2: Comparisons across 5 countries (Finland, France, Germany, Italy, Spain), Banking Sector

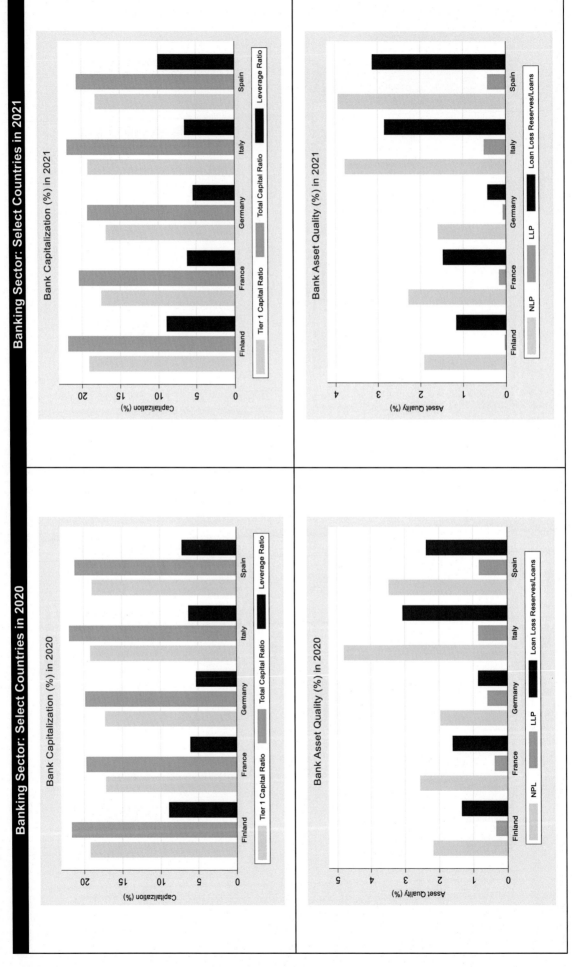

Panel B2: Comparisons across 5 countries (*Continued*)

Banking Sector: Select Countries in 2020

Banking Sector: Select Countries in 2021

Panel C: Comparisons of Key Performance Indicators across Countries Set III
Panel C1: Comparisons across 5 countries (Greece, Poland, Romania, Turkey, Ukraine), Real Economy

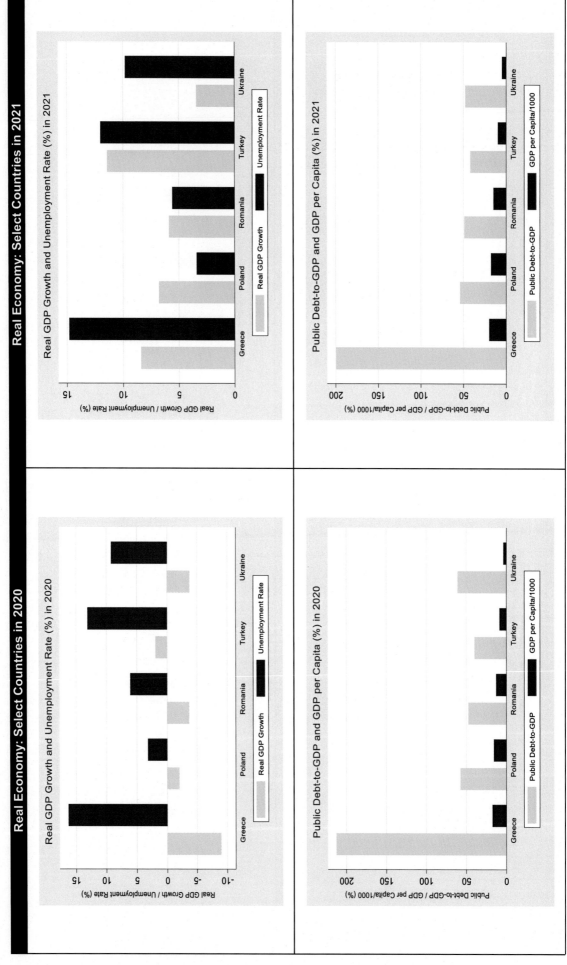

Panel C1: Comparisons across 5 countries (*Continued*)

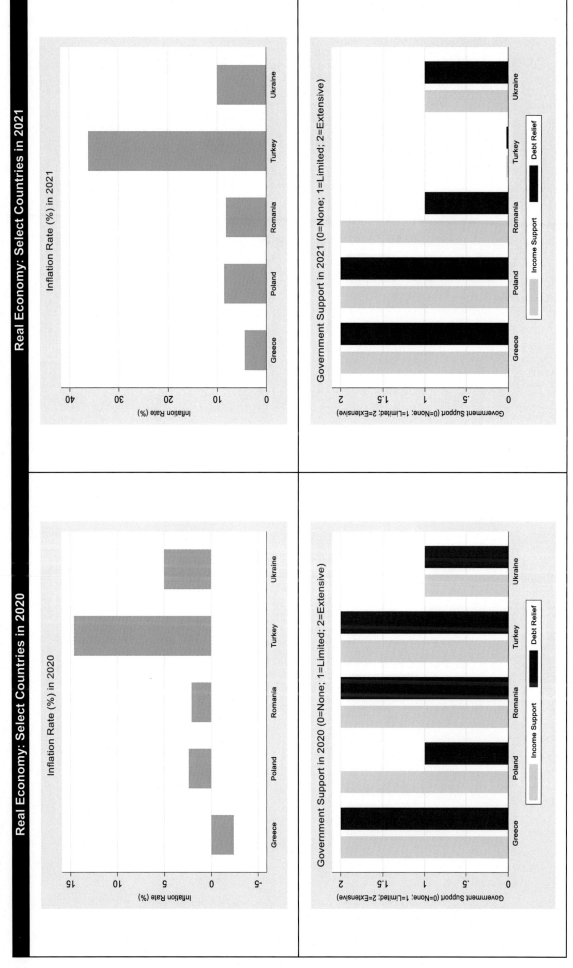

Panel C2: Comparisons across 5 countries (Greece, Poland, Romania, Turkey, Ukraine), Banking Sector

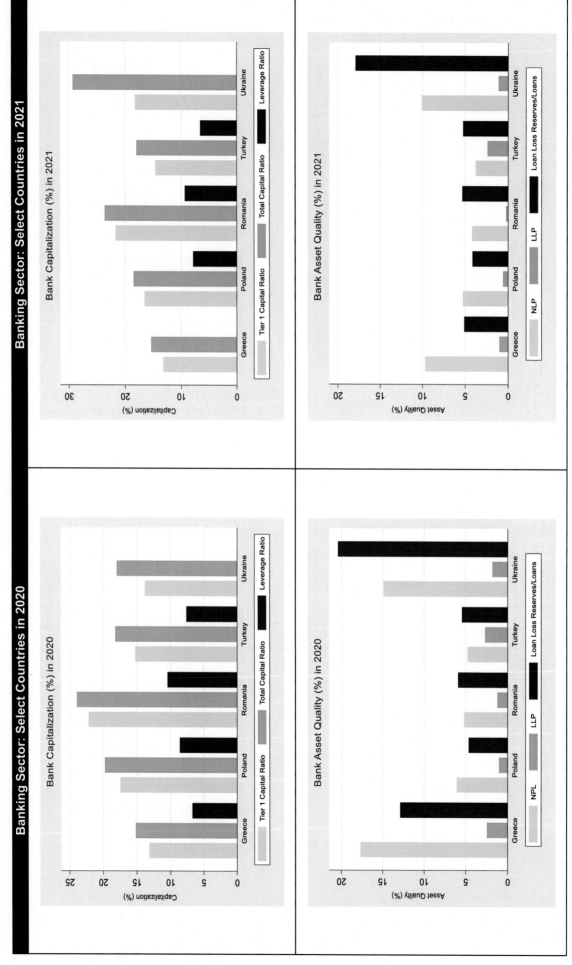

Panel C2: Comparisons across 5 countries (*Continued*)

Banking Sector: Select Countries in 2021

Bank Profitability (%) in 2021

Bank Loans, Deposits, Costs (%) in 2021

Banking Sector: Select Countries in 2020

Bank Profitability (%) in 2020

Bank Loans, Deposits, Costs (%) in 2020

Panel D: Comparisons of Key Performance Indicators across Countries Set IV
Panel D1: Comparisons across 5 countries (Argentina, Brazil, Chile, Mexico, Peru), Real Economy

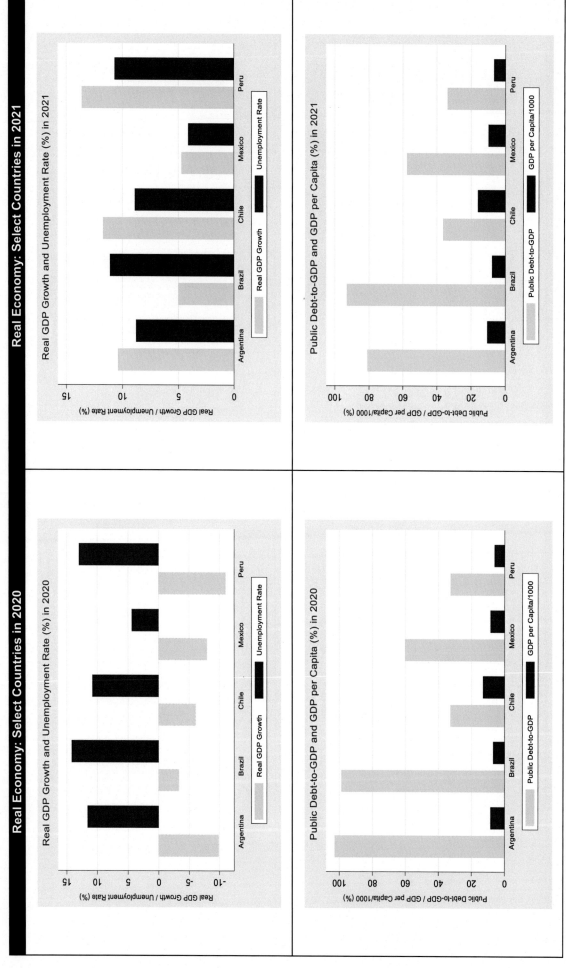

Panel D1: Comparisons across 5 countries (*Continued*)

Real Economy: Select Countries in 2020

Real Economy: Select Countries in 2021

Panel D2: Comparisons across 5 countries (Argentina, Brazil, Chile, Mexico, Peru), Banking Sector

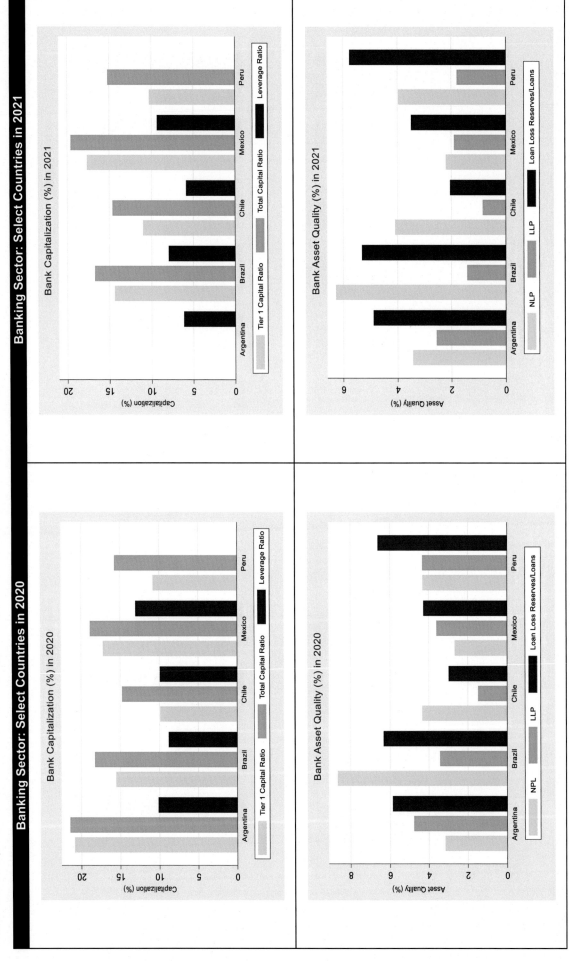

Panel D2: Comparisons across 5 countries (*Continued*)

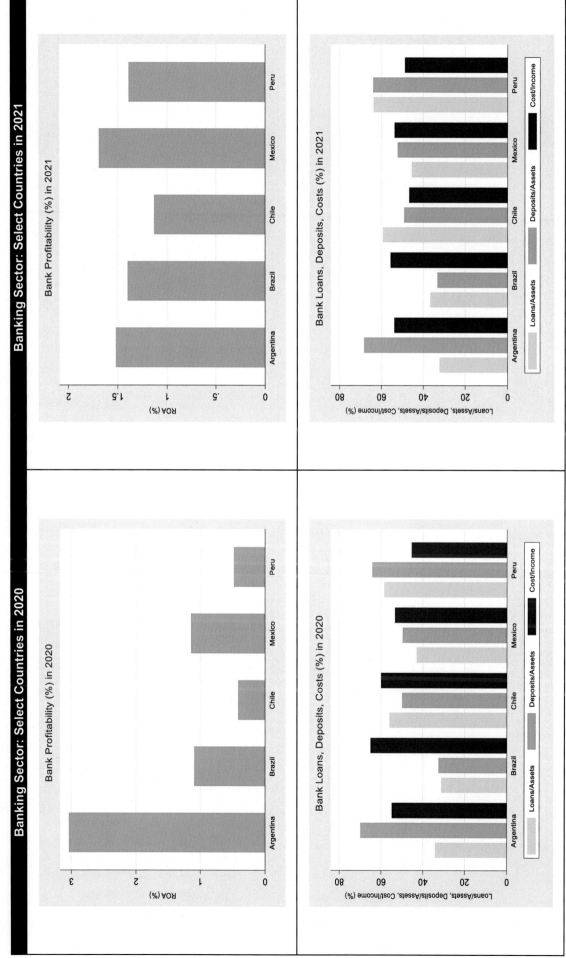

Panel E: Comparisons of Key Performance Indicators across Countries Set V
Panel E1: Comparisons across 5 countries (Egypt, Israel, Jordan, Saudi Arabia, UAE), Real Economy

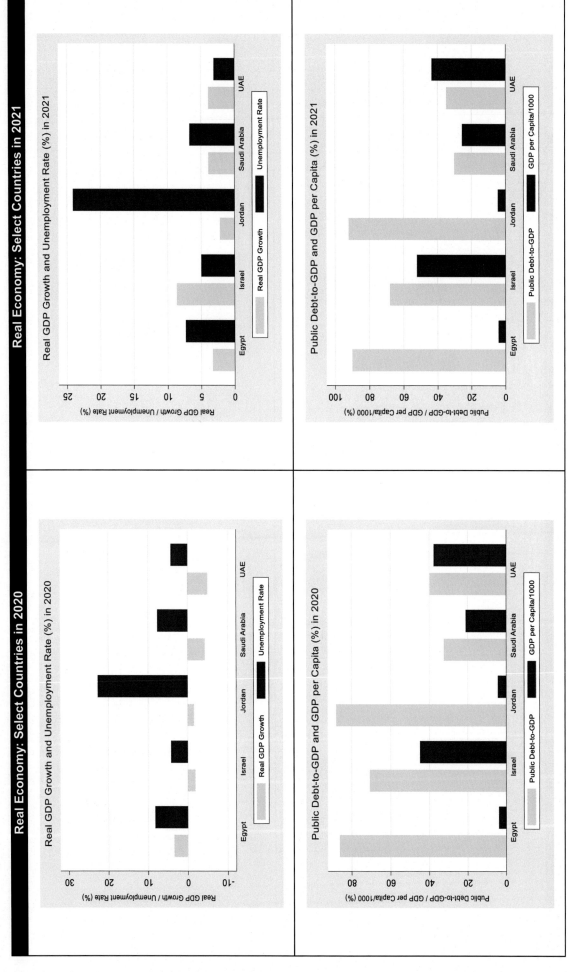

Panel E1: Comparisons across 5 countries (*Continued*)

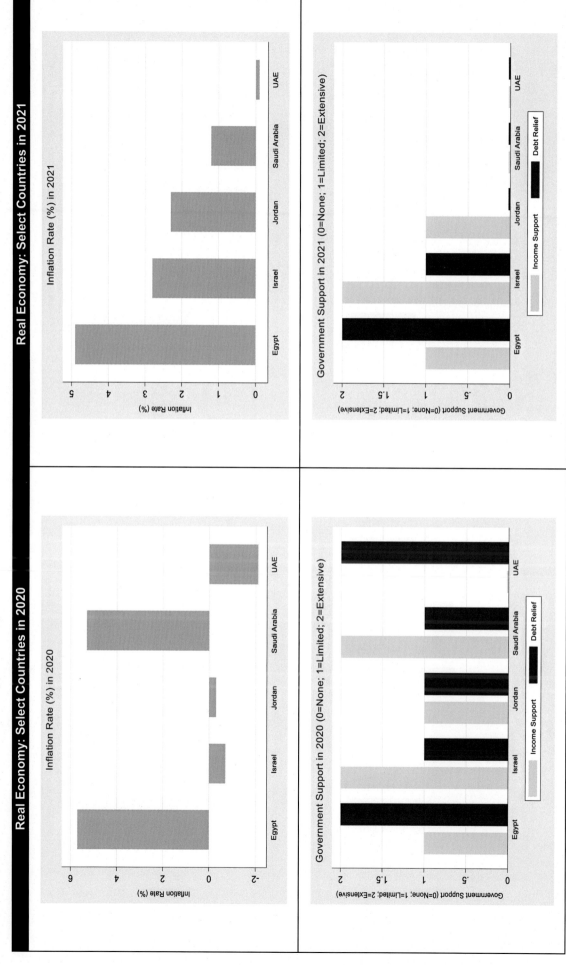

Panel E2: Comparisons across 5 countries (Egypt, Israel, Jordan, Saudi Arabia, UAE), Banking Sector

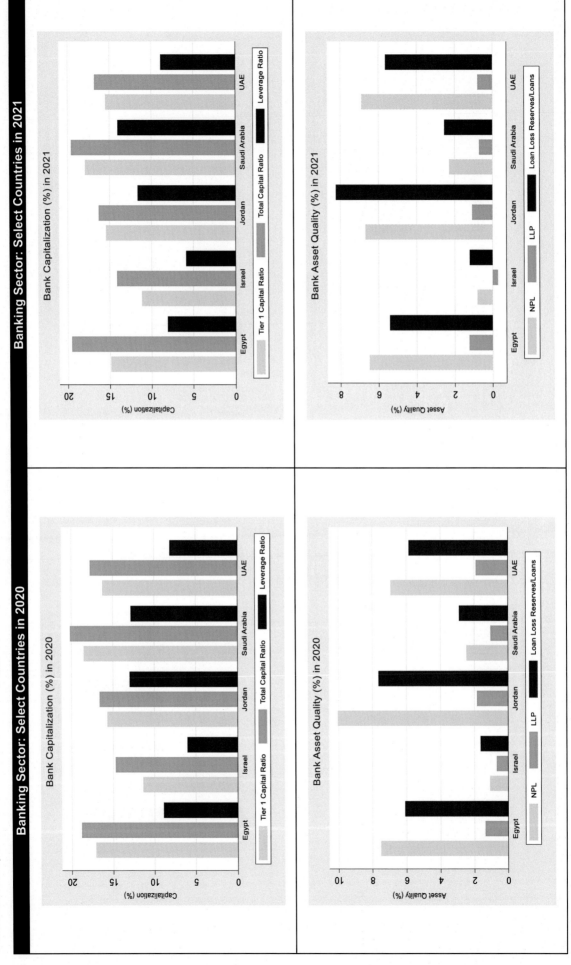

Panel E2: Comparisons across 5 countries (*Continued*)

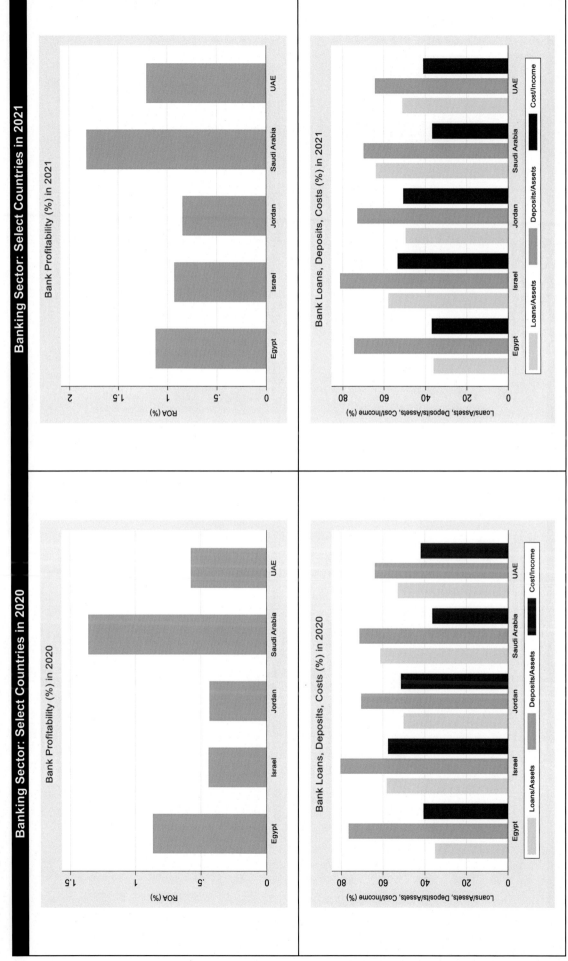

Panel F: Comparisons of Key Performance Indicators across Countries Set VI
Panel F1: Comparisons across 5 countries (Ghana, Kenya, Morocco, Nigeria, South Africa), Real Economy

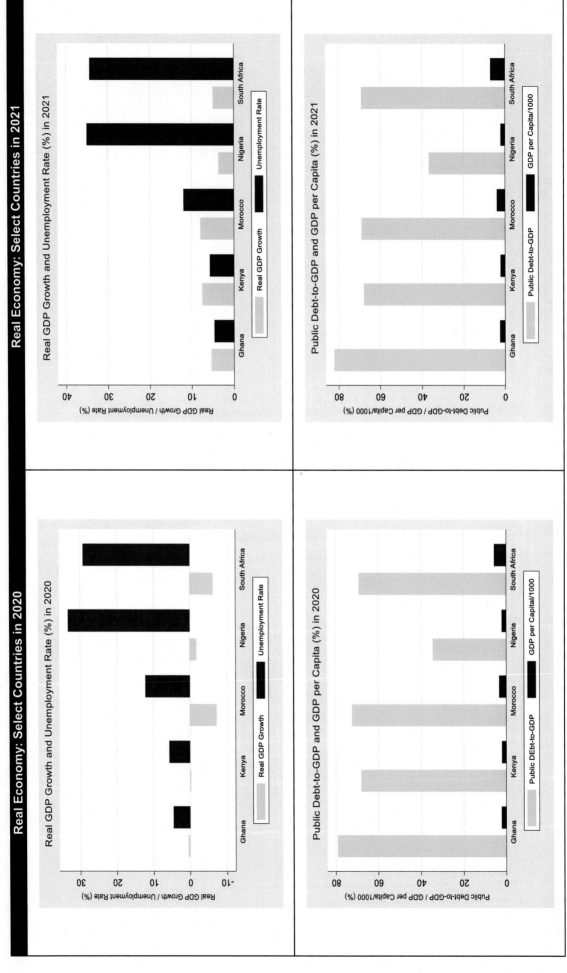

Panel F1: Comparisons across 5 countries (*Continued*)

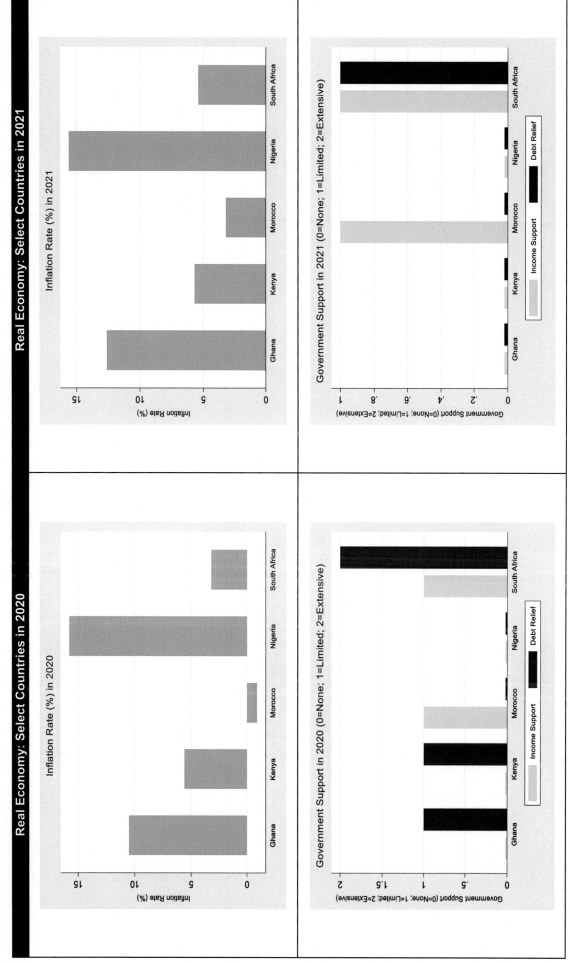

Panel F2: Comparisons across 5 countries (Ghana, Kenya, Morocco, Nigeria, South Africa), Banking Sector

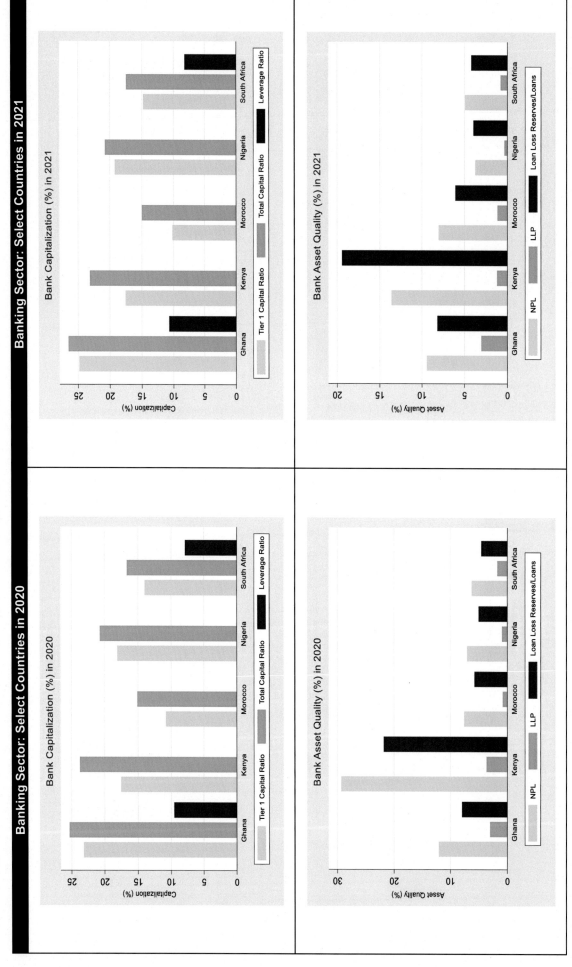

Panel F2: Comparisons across 5 countries (*Continued*)

Banking Sector: Select Countries in 2020

Bank Profitability (%) in 2020

Banking Sector: Select Countries in 2021

Bank Profitability (%) in 2021

Bank Loans, Deposits, Costs (%) in 2020

Bank Loans, Deposits, Costs (%) in 2021

Panel G: Comparisons of Key Performance Indicators across Countries Set VII
Panel G1: Comparisons across 5 countries (China, India, Japan, South Korea, Philippines), Real Economy

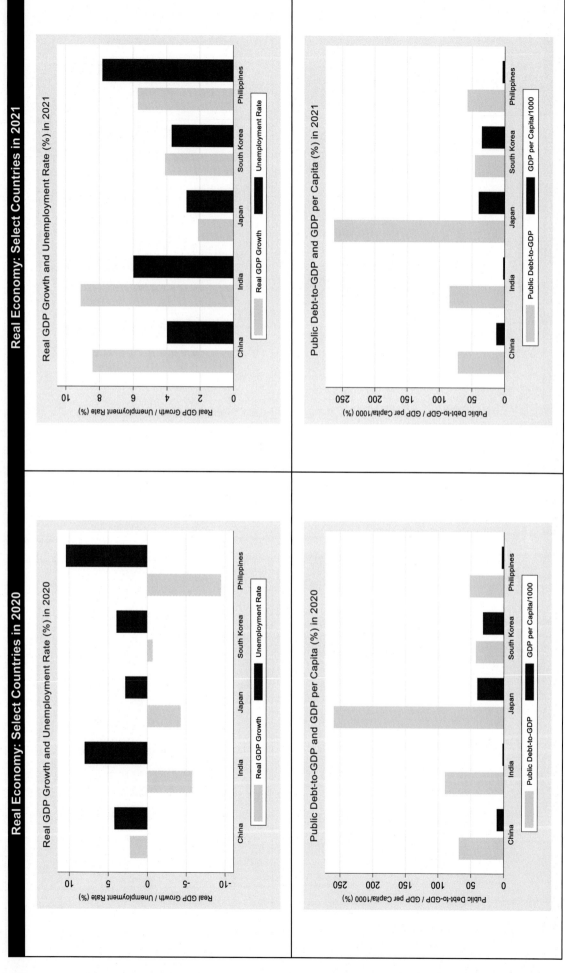

Panel G1: Comparisons across 5 countries (*Continued*)

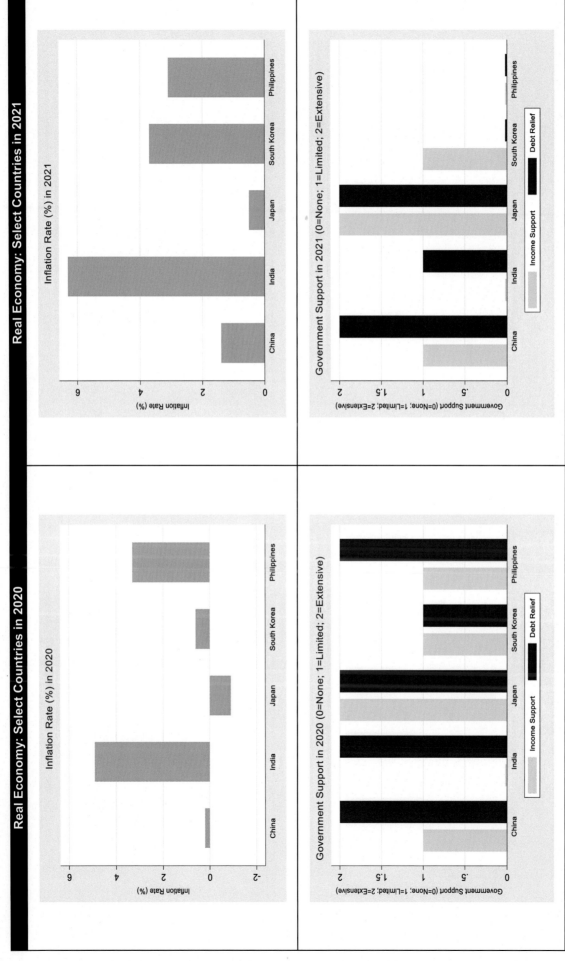

Panel G2: Comparisons across 5 countries (China, India, Japan, South Korea, Philippines), Banking Sector

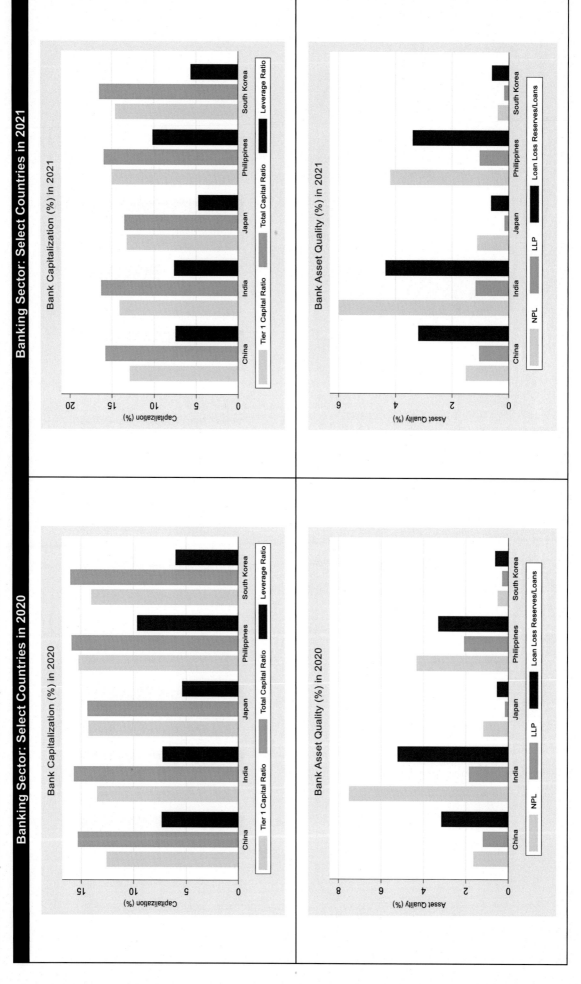

Panel G2: Comparisons across 5 countries (*Continued*)

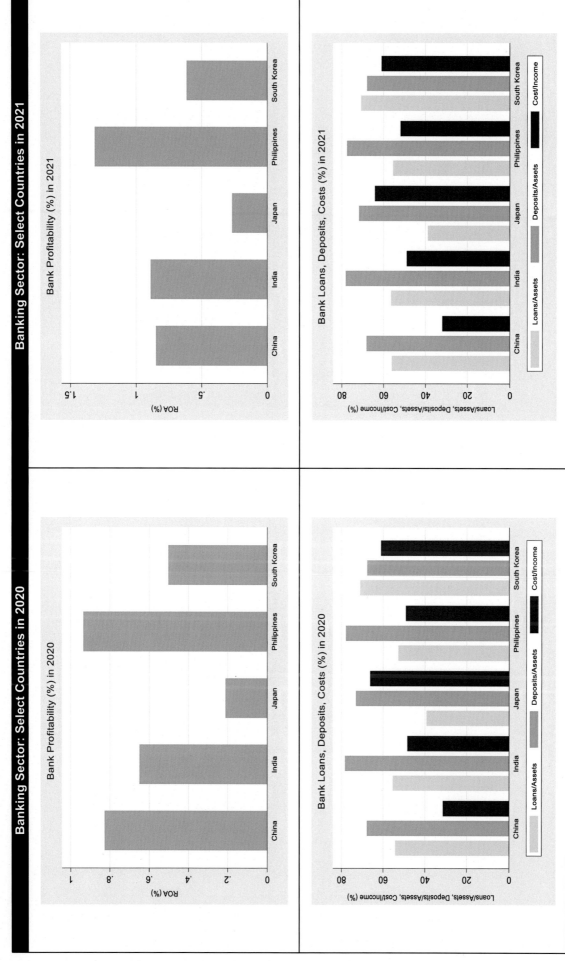

Author Index

Note: Page numbers followed by *np* indicate footnotes.

Subject Index

Note: Page numbers followed by *f* indicate figures and *t* indicate tables.